The Holocaust and World War II Almanac

The Holocaust and World War II Almanac

Volume 3

PEGGY SAARI
AARON MAURICE SAARI
Editors

KATHLEEN J. EDGAR
ELLICE ENGDAHL
Coordinating Editors

GALE GROUP

Detroit
New York
San Francisco
London
Boston
Woodbridge, CT

Edited by Peggy Saari and Aaron Maurice Saari

Staff

Kathleen J. Edgar, *Senior Coordinating Editor*
Ellice Engdahl, *Coordinating Editor*

Julie Carnagie, Elizabeth Des Chenes, Elizabeth Manar, Christine Slovey, *Contributing Editors*
Barbara C. Bigelow, Susan E. Edgar, George Feldman, Kelly King Howes, Lorie Jenkins McElroy, Mary Kay Rosteck, Linda Schmittroth, Christine Tomassini, *Contributing Writers*
Debra M. Kirby, *Managing Editor*
Thomas Romig, *Program Director*

Rita Wimberley, *Senior Buyer*
Dorothy Maki, *Manufacturing Manager*
Evi Seoud, *Assistant Manager, Composition Purchasing and Electronic Prepress*
Mary Beth Trimper, *Manager, Composition and Electronic Prepress*

Debra J. Freitas, *Permissions Associate*
Cynthia Baldwin, *Art Director*
Barbara J. Yarrow, *Manager, Imaging and Multimedia Content*

Marco Di Vita, Graphix Group, *Typesetting*
Laura Exner, XNR Productions, Inc., *Cartographer*
Katherine Clymer, *Indexer*

Library of Congress Cataloging-in-Publication Data

The Holocaust and World War II Almanac / editors, Peggy Saari, Aaron Maurice Saari; coordinating editors, Kathleen J. Edgar, Ellice Engdahl
    p. cm.
    Includes bibliographical references and index.
    ISBN 0-7876-5018-8 (set: hardcover)—ISBN 0-7876-5019-6 (v.1)—ISBN 0-7876-5020-X (v.2)—ISBN 0-7876-5063-3 (v.3)
    1. Holocaust, Jewish (1939-1945). 2. World War, 1939-1945. 3. Holocaust, Jewish (1939-1945)—Biography. 4. World War, 1939-1945—Biography. I. Saari, Peggy. II. Saari, Aaron Maurice.

    D804.17.H65 2000
    940.53'18—dc21
                                                                    00-046647

Table of Contents

Advisory Board

The editors would like to thank the following members of *The Holocaust and World War II Almanac* advisory board for their invaluable assistance.

Armando Delicato majored in history as an undergraduate at the University of Detroit and earned a Masters of Arts in twentieth-century European history at Wayne State University. After teaching history at public schools and at community colleges in Michigan, he earned a degree in library science and is currently a media specialist at North Farmington High School in Michigan.

William J. Munday is a U.S. Navy veteran who has worked or volunteered at various museums and historical sites throughout the country. A military historian, he has studied the subject for more than thirty years. He is a member of several historical and veterans societies, including the Company of Military Historians and the Great Lakes Living History Society. In his spare time, he gives talks and historical demonstrations to students and the public.

Kathy Gillespie Tomajko is Head of Reference Services at the Library and Information Center at Georgia Institute of Technology in Atlanta, Georgia. She was formerly Information Consultant for the School of History, Technology and Society at Georgia Institute of Technology. She is an active member of professional associations, including the American Library Association and Special Libraries Association, and is a past member of publisher advisory committees for the *Internet Reference Services Quarterly* journal, and for the Information Access Company (IAC).

Lynn Whitehouse is Librarian IV at the San Diego Central Library. She supervises the History/Information and Interlibrary Loan sections and is responsible for much of the cultural programming.

Reader's Guide

Between 1939 and 1945, World War II was fought among all the major powers of the world. By the end of the war, more than fifty countries had become involved in the conflict. The scope and brutality of the war greatly impacted the world—more people died during the conflict than in any previous war, and the war changed the political, social, and economic climates of the entire world. *The Holocaust and World War II Almanac* provides a comprehensive range of historical information as well as current studies on World War II and the Holocaust. The three-volume set includes extensive information about the European and Pacific theaters of war as well as the Holocaust. The work also provides biographical profiles of more than 100 men and women who played key or lesser-known roles in the war, whether as civilians or soldiers. Interspersed throughout volumes 1 and 2 are primary sources, which give the reader access to the writings or words of the actual participants in the war or the Holocaust. The primary source documents, complete with introduction and aftermath sections, can be found at the end of the chapter in which that topic is mainly discussed. Each primary source contains enough information for the reader to understand what was happening around the time of the event or topic being described in the source. Information about such events or topics is often restated in the primary source section so that the reader does not have to refer to previous material in the chapter or volume.

Volume 1 begins by exploring the events after World War I (1914–1918) and how certain actions led to the rise of Nazism in Germany, Fascism in Italy, militarism in Japan, and isolationism in the United States. The volume shows how conditions after World War I ultimately led to the Holocaust and World War II. It also details how some world leaders attempted to provoke war while others tried to avoid it; how relationships formed among the Allied countries and among the Axis powers; how Jews, Roma (Gypsies), political prisoners, and others were persecuted by the Nazis and stripped of their rights; how the Nazis were able to conquer so many European countries in a relatively short amount of time; how the war in the Pacific began; how Jews were rounded up for resettlement and sent to ghettos, then labor camps and ultimately death camps; and how the Allies joined forces to thwart the expansion of the German and Japanese empires, which had caused much death among the civilian populations in conquered countries.

Volume 2 continues the story of the war and the Holocaust. The work discusses the Allied invasion of France; life on the home front; spies, secrets, and codes; major turning points in the war, including further fighting in France and the Pacific; the defeat of Nazi Germany and the liberation of the death camps; the use of two atomic bombs and the surrender of Japan; the plight of displaced persons; the Nuremberg Trials; recovery after the war; and memorials for the dead. The volume contains four appendices: A) Jewish Victims of the Holocaust—explains that the number of reported Holocaust victims is different in various sources and discusses some of the reasons why the numbers can never be more precise. B) Nuremberg War Crime Trials—provides detailed information on many of the Nuremberg Trials and includes a chart indicating defendants' names, sentences, and the outcomes. C) Japanese War Crimes— The Tokyo Trials—describes the nature of the trials, the tribunal convened to hear the cases, and the defendants brought to stand trial and why. D) World War II and Holocaust Film Overview—presents a brief look at many of the films devoted to the World War II era, including those produced during the conflict and those being released in recent years, plus many issued in between.

Volume 3 offers the life stories of more than 100 individuals who played a role in World War II and the Holocaust. The biographees were selected in order to present a diversity of wartime experiences, from Axis and Allied leaders to death camp survivors to women on the home front. The subjects include political and military leaders, enlisted men and women, and civilians, including journalists, musicians, and diarists. The volume includes readily recognizable figures, such as U.S. President Franklin D. Roosevelt, British Prime Minister Winston Churchill, Japanese Premier Hideki Tōjō, Soviet leader Joseph Stalin, and Nazi führer Adolf Hitler. The work also features Holocaust survivors, including Renée Roth-Hano, Elie Wiesel, and Simon Wiesenthal; military leaders such as American General Dwight D. Eisenhower, German Army General Erwin Rommel, British Field Marshal Bernard Montgomery, and American Women's Army Corps Director Oveta Culp Hobby; Holocaust victims such as Jewish teenager Anne Frank and Polish photographer Mendel Grossman; journalists/artists, including Edward R. Murrow, Ernie Pyle, Margaret Bourke-White, and Bill Mauldin; Holocaust rescuers such as Miep Gies, Chiune (Sempo) Sugihara, Corrie ten Boom, and Raoul Wallenberg; and Nazi officials Adolf Eichmann, Heinrich Himmler, and others. Also profiled are lesser known people, including American pacifist Jeannette Rankin, Austrian conscientious objector Franz Jaggerstatter, and Hungarian resistance fighter Hannah Senesh (Szenes). In order to include a diversity of experiences, the editors have provided several composite biographies as well on groups of people such as the Comfort Women, Rosie the Riveter, the Navajo Code Talkers, and the Tuskegee Airmen.

Each volume begins with a research and activities section, glossary, and a timeline of events and noteworthy achievements by some of the people profiled in this set. The *Holocaust and World War II Almanac* contains some 800 images, including black-and-white photographs, maps, and illustrations. Due to the nature of this work, some of the photos depict the dead or wounded as well as acts of brutality. Please view them at your own discretion. Chapters and biographies contain sidebars of related information—some focusing on people associated with the war, others taking a closer look at pivotal events. Individual bibliographies appear after each primary source entry and after all biographies. Comprehensive bibliographies appear at the back of each volume as well, followed by a cumulative index for all three volumes.

On occasion, readers might note differences in figures reported in primary sources and the text. This occurs because scholars continue to study the Holocaust and World War II era, seeking to uncover more information about that period. Historians continue to attempt to calculate precisely the total number of losses, in terms of people, resources, and property. As such, the most recent estimates were unknown when the primary sources were written years ago. As noted in Appendix A: Jewish Victims of the Holocaust, historians are unable give an exact figure because of the nature of the war and the way the "Final Solution" was conducted. Records simply do not exist for each individual who was believed to have been killed. The same logic applies to those fighting in Resistance movements and the armed services, as well as those civilians killed while defending their homelands. Plus, not all countries used the same methods for tracking those who died. In some areas, people were buried in mass graves without identification; many of those murdered at death camps were cremated, leaving no trace of their existence. In addition, estimated losses vary significantly between authoritative sources. In this work, the editors have tried to present the most commonly accepted ranges.

Acknowledgements

The editors wish to extend their gratitude to Nancy A. Edgar and Jennifer Keirans for their invaluable assistance during the compilation of this project. Thanks are also extended to the Reader's Advisor team for its support, including Beverly Baer, Dana Ferguson, Nancy Franklin, Robert Franzino, Prindle LaBarge, Charlie Montney, and

Kathy Meek. Special thanks to the Imaging department, including Dean Dauphinais, Senior Editor; Robyn V. Young, Project Manager; Kelly A. Quin, Editor; Leitha Etheridge-Sims, Mary K. Grimes, and David G. Oblender, Image Catalogers; Pam A. Reed, Imaging Coordinator; Randy Bassett, Imaging Supervisor; Robert Duncan, Senior Imaging Specialist; Dan Newell, Imaging Specialist; and Christine O'Bryan, Graphic Specialist. Additional thanks are extended to Larry Baker and Barbara McNeil.

Comments and Suggestions

The Holocaust and World War II Almanac staff welcomes your comments and suggestions for other topics in history to consider for future projects. Please write: Editors, *The Holocaust and World War II Almanac,* Gale Group, 27500 Drake Rd., Farmington Hills, MI 48331-3535; call toll-free: 1-800-347-4253; or send email via http://www.gale group.com.

Timeline

1871 Germany is unified under the domination of the state of Prussia, and the German empire is ruled by a kaiser.

1899 Houston Stewart Chamberlain publishes *The Foundations of the Nineteenth Century*, a book that uses racial theory to explain European history.

1903 Russian anti-Semites circulate *The Protocols of the Elders of Zion*, a forgery that describes the master plan of an alleged Jewish conspiracy to dominate the world.

1914 World War I begins in Europe. At that time, it is known as the Great War.

1916 Jeannette Rankin becomes the first woman elected to the U.S. Congress; she immediately causes controversy by voting against her country's entry into World War I. About 50 other Congressmen vote against war as well, but the focus is on Rankin, the only female member of Congress.

1917 The czar is overthrown in Russia and a Communist government ascends to power after the Bolshevik Revolution. The Russian empire is eventually renamed the Union of Soviet Socialist Republics (USSR), commonly known as the Soviet Union.

1918 The German army is defeated by the Allies in World War I and revolution breaks out in Germany. The kaiser is overthrown and a republic is proclaimed on November 9. The new government agrees to an armistice, ending the war, on November 11.

1919 During the month of June, Adolf Hitler joins the small German Workers' party in Munich. The party soon changes its name to the National Socialist German Workers' party (NSDAP), more commonly known as the Nazi party.

On June 23, Germany signs the Treaty of Versailles. The treaty removes some territory from German control, severely limits the size of the nation's armed forces, and requires Germany to pay reparations and accept guilt for causing World War I. Extreme nationalist groups in Germany blame socialists, communists, and Jews for Germany's defeat.

Communist revolutions in various parts of Germany are put down with much bloodshed.

1920 The League of Nations is formed.

1922 Benito Mussolini and his Fascist party march on Rome. Mussolini is named premier of Italy and eventually establishes a dictatorship that becomes a model for Hitler's Third Reich.

1923 Hyperinflation hits Germany; German currency becomes worthless, causing severe economic distress.

During the year, Alfred Rosenberg reissues an official Nazi party version of *The Protocols of the Elders of Zion*.

In November Adolf Hitler leads a failed attempt to overthrow the German government. Police end the rebellion, called the Munich Beer-Hall Putsch, by arresting Hitler and the other leaders of the party. Sixteen Nazis are killed and others wounded.

1924 At his trial for treason and armed rebellion as a result of the Beer-Hall Putsch, Adolf Hitler gains the attention of extreme nationalists. While serving only eight months of a five-year prison sentence, Hitler dictates his book *Mein Kampf* ("My Struggle"), which outlines his racial beliefs about the superiority of the German people and the inferiority of Jews.

1926 Germany joins the League of Nations.

Anti-Semitic Catholic priest Charles Coughlin broadcasts his first radio sermon in the United States.

Hirohito becomes emperor of Japan, calling his reign "Showa" (meaning "enlightened peace").

1927 Chiang Kai-Shek establishes the Kuomintang (Nationalist) government in Nanking (Nanjing), China.

1928 The Nazi party receives about 800,000 votes—2.6 percent of the total—in national elections.

1929 The Great Depression begins; it will not end until 1939. The worldwide economic depression hits Germany especially hard.

1930 The Nazi party receives almost 6.5 million votes in national elections and becomes the second-largest party in the Reichstag, or German parliament. As part of highly organized campaign tactics, storm troopers (members of the Sturmabteilung or SA) attack opponents, break up meetings, and intimidate Jews and political dissidents.

1931 Vidkun Quisling is one of the cofounders of the Nordic Folk Awakening movement in Norway, which advocates many of the same ideas and principles as Germany's Nazi party.

The Japanese army seizes Manchuria in a short war with China, establishing Manchuria as the "independent" country of Manchukuo, actually controlled by the Japanese.

American journalist Dorothy Thompson interviews Adolf Hitler, a rising German politician, for *Cosmopolitan* magazine.

1932 Although Adolf Hitler receives 11 million votes in July in the first round of elections for German president, and more than 13 million votes (almost 37 percent) in the second round, Paul von Hindenburg, aged military hero of World War I, is reelected president. The SA is briefly banned because of its use of increased violence during the campaign.

1933 Adolf Hitler becomes chancellor of Germany on January 30. Although much of the government at the time is composed of oldline conservatives who believe they can use the Nazis, within a few months Hitler and the Nazi party have taken control of the country.

The Reichstag building is set ablaze on February 27, and Hitler receives emergency powers from President Paul von Hindenburg. Freedoms of speech and of the press are restricted. Acting as police, storm troopers arrest 10,000 opponents of the Nazis, especially Communists.

On March 4, 1933, Franklin D. Roosevelt begins the first of four terms as president of the United States.

Joseph Goebbels is appointed Hitler's minister of enlightenment and propaganda.

Dachau, the first permanent concentration camp, is opened in a suburb of Munich in March. Communists are among the first 10,000 opponents of the Nazis who are arrested and sent to the new camps.

The new Reichstag meets without Communist members, who have been arrested or are in hiding. The Nazis and their allies win support from the Catholic parties and pass the Enabling Act, giving Adolf Hitler dictatorial powers.

In April Nazis organize a national boycott of Jewish-owned businesses. Inge Deutschkron, a young Jewish girl living Berlin, witnesses the boycott. The first anti-Jewish laws are also passed, removing almost all Jews from government jobs, including teaching positions. Further laws follow, and by the end of the year, 53,000 Jews leave Germany.

German labor unions are abolished and replaced by the German Labor Front, run by the Nazis. The Social Democratic party (the largest party before the Nazi rise to power) is outlawed; all other parties follow.

Homosexual researcher Magnus Hirschfeld's Institute for Sexual Science in Berlin is destroyed by the Nazis.

The Nazis conduct public book burnings of works written by Jews and anti-Nazis and impose censorship throughout Germany.

1934 Adolf Hitler orders the murder of SA leader Ernst Röhm and his supporters in what has become known as the Night of the Long Knives, June 30.

Upon the death of German President Paul von Hindenburg, Adolf Hitler combines the offices of chancellor and president, becoming führer, or leader, of the Third Reich, with absolute power. All army officers and soldiers swear allegiance to Hitler.

Adolf Hitler orders American journalist Dorothy Thompson out of Germany, giving her twenty-four hours to leave the country.

Harry S Truman is elected to the U.S. Senate and begins to build a reputation as an effective leader.

1935 On March 16, Germany announces the reintroduction of the military draft and a major expansion of its army, violating the Treaty of Versailles.

German film director Leni Riefenstahl's *Triumph des Willens* (*Triumph of the Will*) premieres. The documentary of a 1934 Nazi party rally at Nuremberg later gains fame as a blatant propaganda film.

Germany passes the Nuremberg Laws, drafted by Wilhelm Frick, which define Jews in racial terms, strip them of German citizenship, and ban marriages and sexual relationships between Jews and non-Jews.

Italy invades Ethiopia on October 3. On May 5, 1936, Ethiopia surrenders.

1936 On March 7, the German army enters the Rhineland, an area of western Germany that had been demilitarized by the Treaty of Versailles.

During the month of March, participation in the Hitler Youth organization becomes mandatory. All ten-year-old boys are required to register at government offices for membership.

The Spanish Civil War begins in July.

Adolf Hitler and the Nazis temporarily ease anti-Jewish actions as the Olympic Games open in Berlin, Germany.

Germany and Italy enter into agreements that develop into a political and military alliance called the Rome-Berlin Axis.

Germany and Japan sign the Anti-Comintern Treaty.

1937 In the first example of aerial bombing against a civilian population, the German air force bombs Guernica, Spain, on April 26, aiding Francisco Franco's fascist troops during the Spanish Civil War.

Neville Chamberlain becomes British prime minister.

Buchenwald concentration camp is established, July 16, 1937.

During the month of July, Japan invades China, capturing Peking (Beijing), Shanghai, Canton, and other major cities. In Nanking (Nanjing), invading Japanese troops rape, torture, and murder tens of thousands of Chinese civilians. This event became known as the "Rape of Nanking."

Karl Koch becomes commandant of the Buchenwald concentration camp, and his wife, Ilse, receives the nickname "the Beast of Buchenwald" as she begins to terrorize prisoners.

1938 Austrians vote in favor of *Anschluss,* an agreement that makes their country part of Nazi Germany. The German army moves into Austria, and crowds cheer Hitler as he enters Vienna. Anti-Semitic laws rapidly go into effect.

Jewish psychotherapist Bruno Bettelheim is arrested by the Nazis and placed in the Dachau concentration camp.

An international conference is held in Évian, France, to discuss the plight of Jewish refugees in Europe. No solutions are found to resolve the crisis.

Europe is at the brink of war as Adolf Hitler makes territorial demands on Czechoslovakia. At a conference in Munich in September, leaders of France and Great Britain agree to grant Germany a section of Czechoslovakia with a large German-speaking population. British Prime Minister Neville Chamberlain signs the Munich Pact with Adolf Hitler, who will soon break his promise not to invade Czechoslovakia.

In Paris, Herschel Grynszpan, a young Jew, shoots and kills Ernst vom Rath, a German embassy official. Grynszpan's actions spark *Kristallnacht* ("Crystal Night" or the "Night of Broken Glass")—a series of organized Nazi attacks throughout Germany in which Jews are beaten, synagogues are burned, Jewish homes and businesses are destroyed, and 30,000 Jewish men are arrested and sent to concentration camps. *New York Times* reporter Otto D. Tolischus alerts the world to Nazi aggression in his account of *Kristallnacht.*

Italian dictator Benito Mussolini adopts the anti-Jewish laws of Adolf Hitler.

First nuclear fission of uranium is produced.

1939 Eugenio Pacelli becomes Pope Pius XII.

Hitler violates the Munich agreement by taking over the remainder of Czechoslovakia by March, and implements anti-Semitic measures there.

The Spanish Civil War ends on March 31.

In accordance with the principles of the Jehovah's Witnesses, young Elisabeth Kusserow refuses to salute the Nazi flag in spring 1939 and is sent to reform school for six years.

Several hundred Jews attempt to emigrate from Germany on board the steamship *St. Louis* in May, but are forced to return to Europe.

During the course of the year, Wilhelmine Haferkamp and other fertile German women receive the Mother's Cross, a medal honoring their Aryan child-bearing accomplishments.

German-born physicist Albert Einstein, at the urging of colleague Leo Szilard, writes a letter to U.S. President Franklin D. Roosevelt, urging American development of an atomic bomb.

On August 23, Germany and the Soviet Union sign the Nazi-Soviet Pact. The two countries promise not to attack each other and secretly agree to divide Poland after it is conquered by Germany.

U.S. General George C. Marshall is sworn in as chief of staff, the highest office in the U.S. Army.

World War II officially begins when Germany invades Poland on September 1; two days later, Great Britain and France declare war on Germany. Poland surrenders to Germany on September 27.

The Nazi euthanasia program begins. In time, 70,000 mentally and physically disabled Germans, including children, are murdered by Nazi doctors and their staffs.

On September 21, Reinhard Heydrich, second in command of the SS, issues a directive to Nazi task forces ordering the "resettlement" of Jewish Poles to urban centers (specifically ghettos) near railroad lines.

In October Adolf Hitler appoints Hans Frank governor-general of certain sections of Poland that later become the "resettlement" areas for Jews and others the Nazis deem unfit for Reich citizenship.

Great Britain begins evacuating children from London to rural towns during the month of November in order to protect them from potential German air raids.

On November 23, Jews in German-occupied Poland are ordered to wear the yellow Star of David on their clothing at all times.

1940 The Lódz ghetto is created in Poland in February, and sealed in April. Jewish photographer Mendel Grossman begins to capture pictures of life there.

On April 10, Germany invades Norway and Denmark. Denmark soon surrenders, but fighting continues in Norway, where Norwegian troops are aided by British and French forces. The Norwegian government flees to Great Britain.

Heinrich Himmler, head of the SS, orders the building of a concentration camp at Auschwitz in occupied Poland.

Winston Churchill becomes prime minister of Great Britain on May 10.

Germany invades the Netherlands, Belgium, Luxembourg, and France on May 10. Luxembourg capitulates shortly after the invasion, the Netherlands surrenders on May 14, and Belgium gives in on May 28.

Italy declares war on France and Great Britain, and invades France on June 10.

French troops evacuate Paris on June 13 and German forces take the city the next day. France signs an armistice with Germany on June 22 and German troops occupy northern France, while a government friendly to Germany (Vichy France) maintains some independence in the south.

Anti-Jewish measures soon begin in western European countries controlled by Germany.

The Germans begin bombing Great Britain in a long air campaign known as the Battle of Britain. American radio journalist Edward R. Murrow broadcasts dramatic reports about the Nazi air raids over London. Defeated by the fighter pilots of the British Royal Air Force (RAF), however, Hitler eventually abandons plans to invade Great Britain.

Field Marshal Philippe Pétain is appointed head of the German-controlled Vichy government in France. He is later convicted of collaborating with the Nazis.

Japanese diplomat Chiune Sugihara, head of the Japanese embassy in Kaunas, Lithuania, disobeys orders and issues transit visas to thousands of refugees.

Italy invades Egypt on September 14.

Germany, Japan, and Italy sign a military alliance called the Tripartite Pact. Within six months, Hungary, Romania, Slovakia, and Bulgaria also join the alliance.

Benjamin O. Davis, Sr., becomes the first African American general in the U.S. Army.

Italy invades Greece.

The Warsaw ghetto in Poland is sealed and nearly 450,000 Jews, including Janina David and her family, are confined within its walls. Chaim A. Kaplan records his observations of the sealing of the ghetto in his diary, later published as *Scroll of Agony*.

American journalist Ernie Pyle arrives in London to report on the war in England.

1941 Germany sends General Erwin Rommel to North Africa in February so that his Afrika Korps can help Italy with its invasion of the area. The seesaw battle for territory will continue until May 1943, when the Germans surrender to the Allies, ending the war in Africa.

A ghetto in Kraków is decreed, established, and sealed, between March 3 and March 20.

The U.S. Congress passes the Lend-Lease Act, signed by President Franklin D. Roosevelt, on March 11. It provides war aid to Great Britain, and later to the Soviet Union and other countries.

The Nazi government orders Franziska Schwarz, a deaf German woman, to appear at a health center for sterilization on March 21. The first attempt (in 1935) had failed.

As German forces attack Yugoslavia, Josip Broz Tito calls for unified resistance to German occupation and begins to organize the Partisans.

On April 13, Japan and the Soviet Union sign a treaty promising that neither will attack the other.

Rudolf Hess makes a flight to Great Britain with the hope of persuading the British to side with Germany in World War II.

Oveta Culp Hobby is named director of the new Women's Auxiliary Army Corps (WAAC), which will eventually be made part of the U.S. Army and renamed the Women's Army Corps (WAC).

The HMS *Hood* is sunk by the German battleship *Bismarck* on May 24. Only three of the 1,400 members of the *Hood* crew survive.

On May 27, the British Royal Navy tracks down the German battleship *Bismarck*. After repeated attacks, the *Bismarck* is sunk, and more than 2,000 German sailors on board die.

American pilot Jackie Cochran flies a Hudson V bomber plane from Canada to Great Britain, becoming the first woman to fly a military aircraft over the Atlantic Ocean.

On June 22, Germany invades the Soviet Union in an offensive called Operation Barbarossa and quickly takes control of much of the country. Special murder squads known as Einsatzgruppen follow the German army into the Soviet Union to eliminate Jews, political dissidents, and others.

In July the United States bans trade with Japan.

Hermann Göring, second to Hitler in Nazi hierarchy, gives Reinhard Heydrich the authority "to carry out all necessary preparations ... for a total solution of the Jewish question" throughout Nazi-controlled Europe.

After pressure from the Japanese government, the Vichy French government allows Japan to establish bases in the southern part of French Indochina (Vietnam).

British Prime Minister Winston Churchill and U.S. President Franklin D. Roosevelt meet aboard a warship off the coast of the British colony of Newfoundland (now a province of Canada) in August and issue the Atlantic Charter, in which they agree to promote peace and democracy around the world.

Rudolf Höss, commandant of the Auschwitz concentration camp, oversees the first experiments using poisonous gas for the mass extermination of humans. The first victims of gassing are 600 Soviet prisoners of war and 250 Poles.

Kiev, the capital of the Ukraine, falls to the German army on September 19. More than 33,000 Jews are murdered at Babi Yar outside Kiev on September 29 and 30.

During October, construction begins on Birkenau (Auschwitz II) in Poland.

On October 17, Hideki Tōjō becomes premier of Japan.

Avraham Tory, a Lithuanian Jew, survives an October 28 Nazi-ordered action that removes nearly 10,000 people, about half of whom are children, from the Kovno ghetto.

In Poland, the construction of an extermination camp at Belzec begins on November 1.

Gonda Redlich arrives at the ghetto in Theresienstadt, Czechoslovakia, a Nazi "model Jewish settlement," during December.

Japan bombs the U.S. naval base at Pearl Harbor, Hawaii, on December 7. The United States and Great Britain declare war on Japan the next day. Japan's allies, Germany and Italy, declare war on the United States on December 11, and the United States declares war on them in return.

Jeannette Rankin becomes the only member of the U.S. Congress to vote against American involvement in World War II.

The death camp at Chelmno, in the western part of Poland, begins operation. Jews are gassed in sealed vans.

British troops in Hong Kong surrender to the Japanese on December 25.

1942 Rationing begins in the United States. In January, rationing of rubber is announced, sugar is rationed in May, and by the end of the year, gasoline is also being rationed.

Manila, capital of the Philippines, surrenders to the Japanese on January 2.

Despite having a transit visa, Jewish psychotherapist Viktor E. Frankl remains in Vienna with his parents, who are unable to procure visas, and is sent to a concentration camp in early 1942. Before the war ends, he is transferred to other camps.

Reinhard Heydrich calls the Wannsee Conference, where the "Final Solution," a plan to eliminate all European Jews, is transmitted to various branches of the German government.

In the month of February, the U.S. Marine Corps inducts twenty-nine Navajos to begin training as "Code Talkers"; the men will use the Navajo language to provide secure communications during battles in the Pacific.

Hollywood movie director Frank Capra arrives in Washington, D.C., on February 15, to begin work on *Why We Fight,* a series of documentary films designed to educate soldiers about the causes of World War II and the reasons for American involvement.

Executive Order 9066, signed by U.S. President Franklin D. Roosevelt, directs all Japanese Americans living on the West Coast of the United States into internment camps.

Slovakian Jews become the first Jews from outside Poland to be transported to Auschwitz.

American forces surrender to the Japanese at Bataan on April 9.

American aviator James "Jimmy" Doolittle leads a U.S. Army Air Corps bombing raid on Tokyo and other Japanese cities that is credited with turning the tide of American wartime morale.

During May, some 1,000 British bombers destroy Cologne, Germany's third-largest city.

On May 6, American and Filipino troops on the island of Corregidor in Manila Bay surrender to the Japanese.

On May 7, Allied naval forces ordered to the area by Chester W. Nimitz, commander in chief of the Pacific Fleet, defeat the Japanese fleet in the Battle of the Coral Sea in the Pacific. It is the first great aircraft carrier conflict.

African American sailor Dorie Miller receives the Navy Cross on May 27 for his heroic performance during the Pearl Harbor bombing.

Reinhard Heydrich dies of his wounds on June 4, as a result of an earlier assassination attempt by Czech resistance fighters in Prague.

The U.S. Navy defeats the Japanese fleet at the Battle of Midway, June 4–7, in one of the most decisive naval engagements in history. Rear Admiral Raymond A. Spruance is given tactical responsibilities during the battle.

In June, General Dwight D. Eisenhower takes command of all U.S. forces in Europe.

Erwin Rommel becomes the youngest German officer to be named a field marshal, the highest rank in the German military, in June.

Anne Frank and her family move into a secret annex constructed in the top stories of her father's office building in Amsterdam.

Etty Hillesum secures a job as a typist for the Jewish Council in Amsterdam, the Netherlands, during the month of July, and assists new arrivals at the Westerbork transit camp, where Dutch Jews are held before deportation to death camps in Poland.

During July, British bombers attack Germany's second largest city, Hamburg, on four straight nights, causing a firestorm that kills 30,000 civilians.

The Treblinka death camp begins receiving Jews from Warsaw. It is the last of the three camps, along with Belzec and Sobibór, created to exterminate Polish Jews. The Nazis call this plan "Operation Reinhard," in honor of the assassinated Heydrich.

Judenrat official Adam Czerniaków commits suicide on July 23 after the Nazis order him to hand over 9,000 Jews from the Warsaw ghetto for deportation.

Jewish orphanage director Janusz Korczak and 200 orphans under his care are deported from the Warsaw ghetto in Poland to the Treblinka concentration camp, where they all die in the gas chambers.

On August 7, American troops land on the mid-Pacific island of Guadalcanal in the Solomon Islands in the first American offensive operation of the war in the Pacific.

Edith Stein, a Jew who converted to Catholicism and became a nun, is killed at the Auschwitz concentration camp.

On August 24, Benjamin O. Davis, Jr., officially takes command of the Tuskegee Airmen, trained at the Tuskegee Institute in Alabama, the first African American pilots to enter the U.S. Army Corps.

During the month of September, Brigadier General Leslie Groves, an American civil engineer, is named head of the Manhattan Engineering District (later called the Manhattan Project), which was formed by the U.S. government to develop nuclear weapons.

In September and October, Polish Jews Shimson and Tova Draenger join other Jewish youths in forming the Jewish Fighting Organization to work against the Nazis.

On September 13, Germany begins its attack on the Soviet city of Stalingrad.

Hirsch Grunstein and his brother go into hiding in Belgium to escape the Nazis. The boys stay with a couple that volunteers to give them shelter.

Popular orchestra leader Glenn Miller enlists in the U.S. Army on October 7 with the goal of starting the Glenn Miller Army Air Force Band, which eventually performs for troops in war zones in Europe.

In October 1942 Odette Marie Celine Hallowes, a mother and wife, parachutes into France as a spy for Great Britain; she is later confined to a concentration camp and tortured by the Nazis.

In the Battle of El Alamein in Egypt, Field Marshal Bernard Montgomery leads the British Eighth Army in an important strategic victory against Italian troops and Field Marshal Erwin Rommel's German Afrika Korps.

On November 8 the Allies launch Operation Torch, an invasion of German-occupied North Africa that ends with the Germans being chased from the region. U.S. General George S. Patton takes command of the First Armored Corps (a tank division) and leads it to victory.

Physicist Enrico Fermi achieves the first self-sustaining nuclear fission chain reaction in his laboratory at Columbia University in New York City.

Wladyslaw Bartoszewski, a Catholic Polish resister, helps form a Jewish relief committee called Zegota.

1943 Allied leaders meet at Casablanca, Morocco, in January, and Cairo, Egypt, in November of the same year, to discuss the progress of the war.

German Jewish rabbi Leo Baeck is arrested and sent to the Theresienstadt concentration camp in Czechoslovakia, where he remains until after the camp is liberated by the Soviets at the end of World War II.

On February 2, the Germans surrender to Russian troops at Stalingrad, a major turning point in the war.

Hans and Sophie Scholl are arrested on a Munich university campus for distributing pamphlets for the White Rose resistance group.

Prelude to War, the first film in the *Why We Fight* film series directed by Frank Capra, wins the Oscar for best documentary.

Small groups of Jews in the Warsaw ghetto begin attacking German troops on April 19. They continue fighting for almost one month until the Germans have killed almost all of the Jewish resisters and completely destroyed the ghetto. Jewish resistance leader Mordecai Anielewicz is one of those killed during the Warsaw Ghetto Uprising, on May 8.

U.S. General George S. Patton commands American troops in Sicily, a large island south of the Italian mainland. In July American forces, along with British and Canadian troops, begin the Allied invasion that will continue on the Italian mainland.

Italian dictator Benito Mussolini is removed from office by the Fascist Grand Council on July 25 and tries to establish a separate government in northern Italy, with the help of Adolf Hitler.

During August, Jackie Cochran becomes the director of the Women's Airforce Service Pilots (WASPs).

Austrian farmer Franz Jaggerstatter is executed for refusing to serve in Hitler's army.

The Allies invade the Italian mainland on September 3; the new Italian government surrenders to the Allies on September 8. German troops in Italy continue fighting.

German attempts to deport Danish Jews are defeated when most of the entire Jewish population of Denmark is safely transported to Sweden.

British spy Noor Inayat Khan is captured and tortured by the Nazis in occupied France.

In December U.S. General Dwight D. Eisenhower is put in command of the planned Operation Overlord.

1944 During the course of 1944, Women's Airforce Service Pilots member Ann B. Carl becomes the first woman to test-pilot a jet plane when she conducts an evaluation flight of the turbojet-powered Bell YP-59A.

The Allies land at Anzio, Italy, on January 22.

After abandoning his university studies in order to fight racism, young Italian Jew Primo Levi is sent to Auschwitz in February, having been arrested two months earlier.

Dutch resistance worker Corrie ten Boom, along with several of her family members, is arrested by the Gestapo for hiding Jews in her Amsterdam home. She and her sister are later sent to the Vught concentration camp.

Hannah Senesh (also transliterated as Szenes), a Jew living in Palestine, parachutes behind enemy lines in Yugoslavia as part of a British-sponsored rescue mission to reach Jews and other resisters.

The Germans occupy Hungary on March 19, 1944, and begin large-scale deportations of Hungarian Jews; by July, more than 400,000 Jews have been sent to Auschwitz.

The United States Army enters Rome, the capital of Italy, on June 4.

On June 6, now known as D-Day, Allied forces land in Normandy in northern France during the largest sea invasion in history, called Operation Overlord. After heavy fighting, the Allies break out of Normandy and sweep eastward across France. By the end of August, France is liberated.

The United States passes the "GI Bill" on June 22, making a college education available to almost all veterans of the U.S. armed services.

On the third anniversary of the German invasion of the Soviet Union, June 22, the Soviets launch a massive offensive called Operation Bagration along an 800-mile front in White Russia (Belarus). The Soviets inflict immense losses on the German army and drive them back almost 400 miles within one month.

Young Swedish businessman Raoul Wallenberg arrives in Budapest, Hungary, to help save the surviving Jews trapped in the city.

On July 20, a small group of German army officers, eager to end the war, unsuccessfully attempts to assassinate Adolf Hitler. Many of the conspirators, along with their families, are tortured and executed.

The Soviet army enters Lublin in eastern Poland in late July and liberates the nearby Majdanek death camp. The Soviets confiscate numerous Nazi documents before they can be destroyed.

On August 4, after living undetected for twenty-five months, Anne Frank, her family, and the four others hiding in the secret annex are reported to the Nazis. The annex dwellers are all sent to the Auschwitz concentration camp.

Paris is liberated by Free French and American forces on August 23.

On September 15, U.S. Marines land on Peleliu island, one of the Palau Islands in the western Pacific Ocean.

During the course of October 1944, industrialist Oskar Schindler is granted permission by the Nazis to establish a munitions factory in Czechoslovakia. This allows Schindler to spare Jewish prisoners from death by employing them there.

Concentration camp prisoner Róza Robota participates in the inmates' revolt at Auschwitz, which leads to the destruction of one of the crematoria.

German army commander Erwin Rommel is suspected of being involved in the July 20 failed attempt to assassinate Adolf Hitler and is forced to commit suicide on October 14.

U.S. General Douglas MacArthur returns to liberate the Philippines from Japanese control, just as he had promised three years earlier he would.

The largest naval battle in history, the Battle of Leyte Gulf in the Philippines (October 23–26), ends in almost total destruction of the Japanese fleet.

On October 26, SS chief Heinrich Himmler orders the destruction of the concentration camps and their inmates.

The 761st Battalion, an African American tank unit, arrives in France to take part in the Allied drive toward Germany.

Franklin D. Roosevelt is elected to a fourth term as president of the United States.

The Germans launch a major counteroffensive on December 16 against the Americans in the Ardennes Forest region of Belgium and France. The conflict becomes known as the Battle of the Bulge. After some initial success, the Germans are defeated.

1945 On January 12, the Soviets launch an offensive along the entire Polish front, entering Warsaw on January 17 and Lódz two days later. By February 1, they are within 100 miles of the German capital of Berlin.

As Soviet troops approach, the Nazis begin the evacuation of the Auschwitz death camp on January 18, forcing about 66,000 surviving prisoners on a death march. Soviet troops reach the camp on January 27.

On January 31, U.S. Army Private Eddie Slovik becomes the only American soldier executed for desertion during World War II; in fact, he becomes the only U.S. soldier executed for desertion since 1864.

In February, Allied leaders British Prime Minister Winston Churchill, U.S. President Franklin D. Roosevelt, and Soviet dictator Joseph Stalin meet in Yalta in the Soviet Union to discuss strategies for ending the war and to plan future forms of government for Germany and other parts of Europe. They also schedule the first United Nations conference.

On February 14, Allied raids on Dresden result in firestorms as the city is crammed with German refugees from the fighting farther east.

American marines land on Iwo Jima in the Pacific on February 19.

On March 7, American troops cross the Rhine River in Germany, the last natural obstacle between the Allied forces and Berlin.

American troops land on Okinawa on April 1, beginning the largest land battle of the Pacific war. Japanese forces are defeated by June.

Pastor Christian Reger is freed from Dachau on April 2 after spending five years at the camp for defying the state-sponsored religion known as the German Faith Movement.

On April 4, Kim Malthe-Bruun, a Danish resister, writes a letter to his mother from prison, informing her that he is to be executed by the Nazis.

German Protestant minister Dietrich Bonhoeffer is executed on April 9 for his participation in the plot to assassinate Adolf Hitler.

U.S. General George S. Patton and his Third Army liberate the Buchenwald concentration camp in Germany on April 11, 1945. American photographer Margaret Bourke-White accompanies U.S. forces when they liberate the camp, and her photographs document the deplorable conditions found there. American reporter Edward R. Murrow broadcasts his impressions of the Buchenwald concentration camp a few days after its liberation.

U.S. President Franklin D. Roosevelt dies of a cerebral hemorrhage in Warm Springs, Georgia, on April 12; Vice President Harry S Truman takes the oath of office and becomes president.

British troops liberate the Bergen-Belsen concentration camp. French prisoner Fania Fénelon is among those freed.

While reporting on the Allied invasion of Okinawa, Ernie Pyle is killed by a Japanese sniper on the island of Ie Shima on April 18.

American cartoonist Bill Mauldin wins the Pulitzer Prize during 1945 for his Willie and

Joe cartoons, which realistically portray the experiences of average U.S. infantrymen through the eyes of two scruffy GIs.

On April 20, Soviet troops reach Berlin, Germany.

Swedish diplomat Folke Bernadotte negotiates a deal with Nazi official Heinrich Himmler that allows 10,000 women to be released from the Ravensbrück concentration camp.

On April 28, former Italian dictator Benito Mussolini is captured by resistance fighters and executed. His body is put on public display.

American troops liberate the Dachau concentration camp.

Eva Braun marries Adolf Hitler in his Berlin bunker on April 29.

With the advancement of Soviet troops into Berlin, Adolf Hitler and Eva Braun commit suicide in Hitler's underground bunker on April 30.

On May 8, V-E Day, the new German government officially surrenders unconditionally to the Allies.

Nazi leader Hermann Göring is arrested by American troops during May 1945; a year later, he commits suicide after being condemned to death for war crimes.

Heinrich Himmler, the senior Nazi official responsible for overseeing the mass murder of 6 million European Jews, is captured by the Allies on May 21. Two days later, he commits suicide.

J. Robert Oppenheimer, leader of a group of scientists working to develop an atomic bomb, oversees a successful bomb test on July 16 at the Alamogordo Bombing Range (the Trinity test site) in the New Mexican desert.

The Potsdam Conference begins on July 16. U.S. President Harry S Truman, British Prime Minister Winston Churchill, and Soviet leader Joseph Stalin confirm occupation of Germany by four Allied powers (France, Great Britain, the Soviet Union, and the United States) and issue an ultimatum to Japan demanding unconditional surrender.

The USS *Indianapolis* is sunk by Japanese forces on July 19; search and rescue efforts are delayed and many of the surviving crewmen are consumed by sharks.

On August 6, the United States releases an atomic bomb on Hiroshima, Japan. Some 70,000 people are killed initially during the blast.

The Soviet Union declares war on Japan on August 8; a large Soviet force invades Manchuria the following day.

The United States drops an atomic bomb on Nagasaki, Japan, on August 9.

On August 15, the Allies accept the unconditional surrender of Japan. Japanese leaders sign formal surrender papers aboard the USS *Missouri* in Tokyo Bay on September 2, V-J Day.

U.S. President Harry S Truman and other world leaders sign a charter establishing the United Nations as an international peace-keeping organization.

War crimes trials begin in Nuremberg, Germany, in November. Justice Robert H. Jackson of the U.S. Supreme Court gives the opening address for the United States before the International Military Tribunal at Nuremberg.

1946 The first session of the United Nations General Assembly opens in London, England.

On January 19, the International Military Tribunal for the Far East (IMTFE) is convened to begin prosecution of Japanese war crimes.

Hermann Göring, one of the highest Nazi officials to be accused and convicted of war crimes, testifies in his own defense during the Nuremberg Trials.

U.S. Brigadier General Telford Taylor becomes chief counsel for the remaining Nuremberg Trials after Justice Robert H. Jackson of the U.S. Supreme Court resigns.

1947 During the course of the year, Holocaust survivor Simon Wiesenthal forms the Jewish Historical Documentation Center in Austria to track down Nazi war criminals.

U.S. Secretary of State George C. Marshall proposes the European Recovery Act, or the Marshall Plan, an outline for helping European countries recover from the effects of the war.

India gains its independence from Great Britain.

1948 On May 14, the state of Israel is established.

The Soviets block all overland traffic between Berlin and the Allied-controlled zones of Germany between June 1948 and May 1949. Allies airlift food and fuel to West Berlin during those eleven months in more than 275,000 flights.

U.S. President Harry S Truman issues Executive Order 9981, which calls for the integration of the U.S. armed forces.

On December 23 Japanese Premier Hideki Tōjō is executed for war crimes.

1949 American radio personality Mildred Gillars ("Axis Sally") stands trial for treason in January.

On April 4, the North Atlantic Treaty Organization (NATO) is founded.

The Soviets establish East Germany as a Communist state called the German Democratic Republic (East Germany); France, Great Britain, and the United States combine their power zones into a democratic state called the Federal Republic of Germany (West Germany).

Defeated by the Communists, Chinese leader Chiang Kai-Shek flees his homeland with others loyal to his Nationalist party, taking refuge on the island of Formosa (now Taiwan) on December 10.

1952 Israel and Germany agree on restitution for damages done to Jews by the Nazis.

American General Dwight D. Eisenhower is elected president of the United States.

1953 During 1953, George C. Marshall of the United States wins the Nobel Peace Prize for his efforts to assist Europe's recovery from World War II, becoming the first member of the military to receive the prize.

On August 28, the Israeli parliament passes the Yad Vashem Law, which establishes the Martyrs' and Heroes' Remembrance Authority to commemorate the 6 million Jews killed in the Holocaust, the communities and institutions destroyed, the soldiers and resistance members who fought the Nazis, the dignity of the Jews attacked, and those who risked their lives in order to aid Jews.

1955 The Soviet Union declares an end to war with Germany.

1957 After emigrating to the United States, Gerda Weissmann Klein writes a memoir called *All but My Life.*

1958 Elie Wiesel revises and abridges a previous work, and the result is published in France as *La Nuit,* an autobiographical novel detailing Wiesel's experiences during the Holocaust. The work is published in English in 1960 as *Night.*

1959 German industrialist Alfried Krupp is made to pay reparations to former concentration camp inmates who were forced to work in Krupp's munitions factories.

1960 In May Adolf Eichmann is arrested in Argentina by the Israeli Security Service.

During 1960, former journalist William L. Shirer publishes *The Rise and Fall of the Third Reich: A History of Nazi Germany.*

1961 Jewish journalist Hannah Arendt covers the trial of Adolf Eichmann, a notorious Nazi criminal who escaped to Argentina after the war. Born in Germany, Arendt had fled her homeland during the rise of Nazism. Ultimately, Arendt writes *Eichmann in Jerusalem: A Report on the Banality of Evil.* The views she expresses about the character of Eichmann create considerable controversy.

Communists build the Berlin Wall in order to stop East Germans from fleeing to West Germany.

1962 Former Nazi official Adolf Eichmann is executed after being found guilty of war crimes for his part in the murder of hundreds of thousands of Jews.

1967 Franz Stangl, former commandant of the Sobibór death camp who oversaw the gassing of more than 100,000 people in his first two months there, is taken to Germany to stand trial for war crimes.

1970 After serving twenty years in prison, former Nazi Albert Speer publishes his autobiography, *Inside the Third Reich.*

1971 Beate and Serge Klarsfeld discover former SS officer Klaus Barbie in La Paz, Bolivia. Barbie is not extradited until 1983.

1976 Japanese American activist Michiko Weglyn publishes *Years of Infamy: The Untold Story of America's Concentration Camps,* which exposes the suffering of more than 100,000 Japanese Americans imprisoned in U.S. internment camps during World War II.

1979 A U.S. television miniseries called *Holocaust* is broadcast; it is later credited with breaking the silence about the Holocaust in Germany.

1983 Donald Carroll publishes "Escape from Vichy," an article about American writer Varian Fry, who helped rescue between 1,500 and 4,000 Jews in German-occupied France.

The judgment against Fred Korematsu, who tried in 1944 to claim that internment of Japanese Americans was unconstitutional, is overturned on October 4.

1985 Human remains found in Brazil are confirmed to be those of Nazi doctor Josef Mengele, who performed inhumane medical experiments on prisoners at Auschwitz.

1987 On July 4, former SS officer Klaus Barbie is found guilty of crimes against humanity and is sentenced to life in prison.

1988 The U.S. Congress formally apologizes to Japanese Americans for interning them in camps during World War II. Survivors are offered a one-time payment of $20,000.

1989 The Berlin Wall is destroyed on November 9. The Brandenburg Gate connecting East and West Germany opens on December 22.

1990 Gypsy Holocaust survivor and artist Karl Stojka opens an exhibit titled *The Story of Karl Stojka: A Childhood in Birkenau,* which displays more than 100 paintings depicting his life in a concentration camp.

East Germany and West Germany are reunited on October 3, 1990.

1992 Holocaust survivor Isabella (Katz) Leitner publishes *Isabella: From Auschwitz to Freedom* and *The Big Lie,* both of which describe her experiences during the Holocaust.

1993 The United States Holocaust Memorial Museum in Washington, D.C., is dedicated on April 27.

The Israeli Supreme Court overturns the death sentence of alleged former Nazi John Demjanjuk and acquits him.

1997 Riva Shefer, a seventy-five-year-old Latvian Jew who survived a Nazi labor camp, becomes the first recipient of money from a $200 million Swiss fund established to aid Holocaust survivors.

1998 Fred Korematsu is awarded the Presidential Medal of Freedom, the highest civilian honor in the United States, in January 1998.

The Vatican issues a document stating that Pope Pius XII, leader of the Catholic church during the Holocaust, did all he could to save Jews. Many historians disagree.

Maurice Papon, a former official of the French Vichy government, is sentenced to ten years in prison for helping the Germans illegally arrest and deport French Jews.

In July, German automaker Volkswagen agrees to pay reparations to slave laborers who worked in its factories during the war.

On October 11, Edith Stein becomes the first Jewish person in modern times to be declared a saint by the Roman Catholic church.

1999 Dinko Sakic, the last known living commandant of a World War II concentration camp, is tried for war crimes.

2000 During the year 2000, Germany sets aside $5 billion to provide compensation to slave laborers forced to work for the Nazis during World War II. The money is contributed equally by the German government and German industry

Pope John Paul II makes a historic visit to Israel in March and tours the Israeli Holocaust memorial Yad Vashem.

On August 9, Simon Wiesenthal is awarded the U.S. Presidential Medal of Freedom.

Glossary

Abwehr The intelligence service of the German armed forces' high command.

Afrika Korps Highly effective German troops who fought under General Erwin Rommel in the North African desert.

air raid An attack by aircraft on a target on the ground, often forcing people to take cover in air raid shelters.

Aktion (plural, *Aktionen*) Raid against Jews, often in ghettos, primarily to gather victims for extermination.

Allies Countries that fought against the Axis powers (Germany, Italy, and Japan) during World War II. The makeup of the Allies changed over the course of the war; the first major Allied countries were Great Britain and France. Germany defeated France in 1940, but some Free French forces continued to fight with the Allies until the end of the war. The Soviet Union and the United States joined the Allies in 1941.

Anschluss The annexation of Austria by Nazi Germany on March 13, 1938.

Anti-Comintern Pact Agreement signed in Berlin on November 25, 1936, by Germany and Japan. They were joined in 1937 by Italy, and later by Bulgaria, Hungary, Romania, Spain, and other states. The signers agreed to fight the Commu-

nist International organization (Comintern), that is, the Soviet Union.

anti-Semitism The hatred of or discrimination toward Jews.

appeasement The policy adopted by some European leaders, notably British Prime Minister Neville Chamberlain, toward Adolf Hitler prior to World War II. These leaders attempted to appease Hitler with political and economic concessions.

Ardennes Large forested area in southeastern Belgium; site of the 1944–1945 campaign known as the Battle of the Bulge.

Arrow Cross party A Fascist party in Hungary.

Aryan The name, used by the Nazis and others, of the "race" of people speaking languages thought to be derived from Sanskrit. Aryans were viewed by the Nazis as a superior race.

Aryanization The confiscation of Jewish businesses by the German authorities.

Atlantic Charter Agreement signed in 1941 by U.S. President Franklin D. Roosevelt and British Prime Minister Winston Churchill in which the two countries stated their commitment to worldwide peace and democracy.

Axis Coalition formed by Germany, Italy, and Japan to fight against the Allies during World

War II; during the course of the war, Hungary, Romania, Croatia, Slovakia, Finland, and Bulgaria also joined the Axis.

Beer Hall Putsch A failed attempt by Adolf Hitler and the Nazis to overthrow the Bavarian government on November 9, 1923. Also known as the Hitler Putsch or the Munich Putsch.

blackout Mandatory measure requiring citizens to turn off all lights in homes, businesses, and other facilities, as well as cars and other vehicles; the practice was intended to discourage enemy air raids as pilots would be unable to locate targets in the darkness.

blackshirts Fascists in Italy under the dictatorship of Benito Mussolini.

blitzkrieg "Lightning war"; the military strategy of sending troops in land vehicles to make quick, surprise strikes against the enemy while airplanes provide support from the air. This worked effectively for German troops in Poland and France.

brownshirts See **Sturmabteilung.**

Bund Jewish socialist, non-Zionist resistance group, active mainly in Poland between World War I and World War II.

Bund Deutscher Mädel (BDM) "German Girls' League"; the Nazi organization for girls; the female equivalent of the Hitlerjugend (Hitler Youth).

cavalry Originally referred to horse-mounted troops; in more recent times, refers to troops using armored vehicles, such as tanks.

Code Talkers A group of Native Americans who used the Navajo language as an effective American code in the Pacific theater during World War II.

collaboration Cooperation between citizens of a country and its occupiers.

commissar A Communist party official or Soviet government official.

communism An ideology and/or political philosophy that advocates the abolition of private property, and in which the state controls the means of production.

concentration camp *Konzentrationslager;* a place where people are held against their will without regard to the accepted forms of arrest and detention. During World War II, the Nazis used concentration camps to hold Jews, Roma (Gypsies), political dissidents, religious figures, homosexuals, and others they considered enemies of the state.

conscientious objector One who refuses to fight in a war for moral, religious, or philosophical reasons.

crematorium (plural, crematoria) An oven designed to incinerate human corpses.

D-Day Usually refers to June 6, 1944, the day Allied forces launched Operation Overlord, an invasion of German-occupied France on the beaches of Normandy; also a military term designating the date and time of an attack.

death marches Forced marches of concentration camp inmates (usually Jews) during the German retreat near the end of World War II; also refers to forced marches of Allied prisoners of war (POWs) in the Pacific (i.e., the Bataan Death March).

deportation Banishment; being sent out of a country.

displaced persons (DPs) Persons forced out of their countries of origin during war. After World War II, DPs had a difficult time finding refuge.

draft System by which a country requires a certain segment of its population to perform a term of military service; also called military conscription or selective service.

Einsatzgruppen "Special action groups"; mobile units of the Schutzstaffel (SS) and Sicherheitsdienst (SD), the military wing of the Nazi party, that followed the German army into Poland in September 1939, and into the Soviet Union in June 1941. Their official duties included the elimination of political opponents and the seizure of state documents. In the Soviet Union, in particular, they carried out mass murders, primarily of the Jewish population.

Endlösung See "Final Solution."

euthanasia Generally refers to mercy killing; the Nazis used the term to refer to the murder of those they deemed unfit to live, including the mentally or physically challenged.

Executive Order 9066 Order issued by U.S. President Franklin D. Roosevelt on February 19, 1942, directing all Japanese Americans on the West Coast to be sent to internment camps.

fascism Political system in which power rests not with citizens but with the central government, which is often run by the military and/or a dictator.

"Final Solution" In full, "Endlösung der Judenfrage in Europa," or "final solution of the Jewish problem in Europe"; Nazi code name for the physical extermination of all European Jews.

Free French Movement headed from outside France by General Charles de Gaulle that tried to organize and encourage French people to resist the German occupation.

Freikorps "Free Corps"; volunteer units consisting mostly of former members in the German army; much of the Sturmabteilung (SA), or storm troopers, was made up of Free Corps members.

führer "Leader"; Adolf Hitler's title as the head of Nazi Germany.

gas chamber A room in which people are killed by means of poisonous gas.

Geheime Staatspolizei (Gestapo) Secret state police in Nazi Germany.

Generalgouvernement General Government; the Germans' name for the administrative unit comprising those parts of occupied Poland that were not incorporated into the Reich. It included five districts: Galicia, Kraków, Lublin, Radom, and Warsaw.

gentiles Non-Jews, especially Christian non-Jews.

Gestapo See Geheime Staatspolizei.

ghettos Crowded, walled sections of cities where Jews were forced to live in substandard conditions; conditions often led to disease and/or starvation.

GI An abbreviation of "government issue"; a term for members of the U.S. armed forces.

Gyspies See Roma.

Hitlerjugend "Hitler Youth"; organization founded in 1922 that trained German boys to idolize and obey German leader Adolf Hitler, to follow Hitler's policies precisely, and to become Nazi soldiers.

Holocaust Period between 1933 and 1945 when Nazi Germany engaged in the systematic persecution and elimination of Jews and other people deemed inferior by the Nazis, such as citizens of eastern Europe and the Soviet Union, Roma (Gypsies), homosexuals, and Jehovah's Witnesses. Also called sho'ah in Hebrew.

Home Army Secret military resistance organization in Poland.

internment camps Guarded facilities usually used to hold citizens of an enemy country during wartime.

island hopping Allied strategy in the Pacific for taking islands one after another, skipping those that were deemed of little military value.

isolationism A country's policy of remaining out of other countries' affairs. Isolationism was a strong force in American politics before World War I (1914–1918) and continued to be an important factor until Japan attacked the United States in December 1941.

Judenrat (plural, *Judenräte*) "Jewish Council"; a committee of Jewish leaders formed in ghettos under German orders.

Junker A landed Prussian noble; Junkers controlled the German military until the end of World War I (1914–1918).

Kapo Probably from the Italian word *capo*, or "chief"; supervisor of inmate laborers in a concentration camp.

Kristallnacht "Night of the Broken Glass"; organized pogrom against Jews in Germany and Austria on November 9–10, 1938.

Lebensraum "Room to live"; Nazi idea that the German people, or Aryan race, needed expanded living space to survive and increase in size.

Lend-Lease Program U.S. legislation passed in 1941 (prior to the United States entering the war) that allowed the United States to send supplies needed for the war effort to countries fighting Germany, such as Great Britain and the Soviet Union. Payment was to be made after the war.

liquidation The Nazi process of destroying ghettos by sending prisoners to death camps and burning the buildings.

Luftwaffe German air force.

Maginot Line Defensive fortifications built to protect France's eastern border.

Manhattan Project Project funded by the U.S. government that secretly gathered scientists at facilities in New York City; Chicago, Illinois; Los Alamos, New Mexico; and other locations to work on the development of an atomic bomb.

Mein Kampf "*My Struggle*"; Adolf Hitler's book expounding his ideology, published in two volumes (July 1925 and December 1926).

Munich Pact Agreement signed by the leaders of France, Great Britain, Nazi Germany, and Italy in September 1938, allowing the Nazis to take over the Sudetenland, an area between Austria and Germany. The accord became famous as a symbol of the British and French policy of appeasement of Germany.

Nacht und Nebel "Night and Fog"; code name for rounding up suspected members of the anti-Nazi resistance in occupied western Europe; people were said to disappear in the "night and fog."

Nazi Abbreviated name for the Nationalsozialistische Deutsche Arbeiterpartei, or the National Socialist German Workers' party, the political organization led by Adolf Hitler, who became dictator of Germany. The Nazis controlled Germany from 1933 to 1945, promoting racist and anti-Semitic ideas and enforcing total obedience to Hitler and the party.

Nazi-Soviet Pact Mutual non-aggression treaty signed by Nazi Germany and the Communist Soviet Union in 1939, despite Adolf Hitler's hatred of communism; allowed Hitler to avoid a two-front war in Poland. Also called the Molotov-Ribbentrop Pact.

Night of the Long Knives *Nacht der langen Messer*; Nazi purge of the Sturmabteilung (SA), or storm troopers, June 30–July 1, 1934.

Nuremberg Laws Laws issued in 1935 to further the exclusion of Jews from German life. The first removed Jews' citizenship; the second defined Jews racially and prohibited them from engaging in marital and other relations with Germans. The laws were proclaimed at the annual Nazi party rally in Nuremberg on September 15, 1935, and were expanded on November 14, 1935.

Nuremberg Trial Trial of twenty-two major Nazi figures in Nuremberg in 1945 and 1946 by the International Military Tribunal. Other World War II war crimes trials are also sometimes referred to as the Nuremberg Trials.

occupation Control of a country by a foreign military power.

Operation Overlord Code name for the Normandy invasion, a massive Allied attack on German-occupied France. Also called D-Day.

Operation Reinhard Nazi plan to eliminate European Jews; named in honor of Reinhard Heydrich, chief architect of the "Final Solution."

Operation Torch British and American invasion of North Africa in November 1942.

pacifism A belief opposing war and violence as problem-solving techniques; sometimes is expressed as passivism or a refusal to bear arms.

Palestine Region in the Middle East captured by the British from the Ottoman Turks. In exchange for Jewish help capturing the region, the British promised the establishment of a Jewish national homeland in Palestine.

partisans Guerilla fighters.

Pearl Harbor Inlet on the southern coast of the island of Oahu, Hawaii, and the site of the Japanese attack on a U.S. naval base on December 7, 1941. The attack prompted the United States to enter World War II officially.

pogrom An organized massacre of or violence against a specific group of people, often Jews.

Potsdam Declaration Statement released by British Prime Minister Winston Churchill, U.S. President Harry S Truman, and Soviet leader Joseph Stalin on July 26, 1945, demanding the unconditional surrender of Japan.

prisoner of war (POW) Person captured during a war, especially by enemy forces during combat.

Prussia The largest state in the German empire from 1871 to 1918.

radar Technology using radio waves to detect objects or topographical features. Initial development of radar began in 1935; it allowed combatants in World War II to detect incoming planes. Later, the technology advanced so that radar devices could be fitted into planes, allowing pilots to locate potential bombing targets more easily.

RAF See Royal Air Force.

ration To make something available in fixed amounts; to limit access to scarce goods; the allotted amount of something.

Red Army An abbreviation for Rabochya Krest-yanskaya Krasnaya Armiya, or "Workers' and Peasants' Red Army," the official name of the Soviet army until June 1945, when it was changed to Soviet Army.

Reich "Empire"; Adolf Hitler's regime as dictator of Germany was called the Third Reich. The First Reich was the Holy Roman Empire; the second was proclaimed by Otto von Bismarck.

Reichstag German parliament.

reparations Compensation required from a defeated nation for damage or injury during war.

resettlement The Nazi term for forcing Jews into ghettos and concentration camps.

resistance An organized movement in a conquered country designed to attack and subvert occupying troops and, often, native collaborators.

"Righteous among the Nations" Title given by Yad Vashem (Holocaust memorial and museum) to non-Jews who risked their lives to save Jews in Nazi-occupied Europe.

Roma (Gypsies) Dark-haired and dark-skinned, nomadic people who are believed to have originated in India.

"Rosie the Riveter" A nickname for more than 6 million women who entered the American workforce as factory workers during World War II, filling job vacancies left by men heading off to war.

Royal Air Force (RAF) The British aerial armed force.

SA See Sturmabteilung.

Schutzstaffel (SS) "Security squad"; unit that provided Adolf Hitler's personal bodyguards and concentration camp guards.

SD See Sicherheitsdienst.

segregation The forced separation of races. During World War II, African Americans and whites in the United States were segregated in many public places, including schools, and the military.

Selektion (plural, *Selektionen*) "Selection"; the process of selecting, from among Jewish deportees arriving at a Nazi camp, those who were to be used for forced labor and those who were to be killed immediately. The term also refers to the selecting, in ghettos, of Jews to be deported.

sho'ah The Hebrew term for "holocaust"; the mass destruction of Jews by the Nazis.

Sicherheitsdienst (SD) "Security police"; special unit that served as the intelligence service of the Schutzstaffel (SS).

Sonderkommando "Special squad"; SS or Einsatzgruppen detachment. Also refers to the Jewish units in extermination camps who removed the bodies of those gassed for cremation or burial.

SS See Schutzstaffel.

Star of David Jewish religious symbol; the Nazis forced Jews to wear a badge shaped like the Star of David for identification purposes.

Sturmabteilung (SA) "Storm troopers" (also known as Braunhemd, or brownshirts); members of a special armed and uniformed branch of the Nazi party.

swastika Ancient symbol originating in South Asia; appropriated by the Nazis as their emblem.

synagogue Jewish house of worship.

theater From a military standpoint, an area of operations during a war. The two main areas of operations during World War II were the European and Pacific theaters.

Third Reich The official name of the regime that Adolf Hitler headed as führer of Germany; means Third Empire. See also Reich.

Treaty of Versailles Restrictive agreement that Germany was forced to sign in 1919 after World War I (1914–1918). Germany was required to claim responsibility for the war and pay damages to other countries.

Tripartite Pact Agreement that established a military alliance between Germany, Italy, and Japan in 1940. Also known as the Axis or Three-Power Pact.

Tuskegee Airmen Group of African Americans who became the first black Army Air Corps pilots.

U-boat A contraction of *Unterseeboot*; a German submarine.

V-E Day Victory in Europe Day, the day on which German forces officially surrendered, May 8, 1945.

Vichy Regime set up in France in 1940, after the Germans invaded the country. Headed by Field Marshal Philippe Pétain, it was actually under German control. Its name comes from the French town where it was headquartered.

V-J Day Victory over Japan Day, the day on which Japanese forces officially surrendered, September 2, 1945.

Volksdeutsche "Ethnic Germans"; Germans living outside Germany.

WAC See Women's Army Corps.

Waffen-SS Military unit of the Schutzstaffel (SS), the Nazi security squad.

Wannsee Conference Meeting called by Reinhard Heydrich in 1941 to inform the German government of the "Final Solution," a plan to eliminate European Jews.

war crimes Violations of the laws or customs of war; the basis for trials held by the Allies after World War II.

Wartheland (Warthegau) Western Polish district annexed to the Reich after September 1939.

WASPs See Women's Airforce Service Pilots.

Weimar Republic Democratic German government in existence from 1919 to 1933, imposed upon Germany at the end of World War I (1914–1918).

Women's Airforce Service Pilots (WASPs) Organization that recruited and trained women pilots to perform non-combat flying duties.

Women's Army Corps (WAC) Organization that allowed American women to serve a variety of non-combat roles.

World War I A conflict that raged throughout Europe from 1914 to 1918. Austria-Hungary, Germany, Turkey, and Bulgaria fought against Serbia, Russia, France, Great Britain, Japan, Italy, and, later, the United States, along with twenty-one other nations.

Yad Vashem Holocaust memorial in Jerusalem.

Yiddish Language spoken by eastern European Jews.

Zionism Movement that advocated the formation of a Jewish nation in Palestine.

Zydowsk Organizacja Bojowa (ZOB) Military wing of the Jewish underground in the Warsaw ghetto.

Zyklon B Hydrogen cyanide; the brand name of a pesticide used by the Nazis in their euthanasia program and later, especially in the gas chambers of Auschwitz.

Research Ideas

The following research ideas are intended to offer suggestions for complementing social studies and history curricula, to trigger additional ideas for enhancing learning, and to suggest cross-disciplinary projects for library and classroom use.

Ration Recipes

Look in cookbooks published during the 1940s or women's magazines published during World War II and note how recipes account for rationing. What kinds of ingredient substitutions do they specify? Make one of the recipes and invite others to rate the flavor, or adapt a recipe from a modern cookbook to account for rationing.

Personal History

Interview a veteran of World War II or someone who lived during the war. Create a list of questions before the interview. Perhaps ask the interviewee where he or she was during the war, how the war changed his or her life, and what was his or her impression of the war's importance both at the time and in retrospect.

Design a Holocaust Memorial

Create a sketch or a paper model for a historic marker, public display, or building commemorating a person, place, or event in Holocaust history. Explain how and why you made your design choices, and why you felt your chosen person, place, or event was worthy of commemoration.

Atom Bomb Debate

Study the decision to drop atom bombs on Hiroshima and Nagasaki. Taking into consideration only what was known at the time about the bombs, form two teams, one in favor of dropping the bomb and the other against, and debate the issues. Then repeat the debate, taking into consideration what is currently known about the effects of atomic bombs. Discuss how the first and second debates differed.

Turning Points

On a large map of the world, use pushpins to mark the sites of battles that were important turning points during the war. For each site, create a note card explaining who fought there, who won, and why that battle was significant.

Modern Opinions from Historical Figures

Form a group of four to six people and choose a current event in world politics as the basis for a panel discussion. One person will serve as moderator for the discussion; the remaining group members should each choose a prominent individual involved in World War II. After researching both the issue and the prominent individuals, students will present the positions they think their selected historical figures would have taken on the subject.

War-Inspired Artwork

Choose a creative work related to World War II; this can be anything from a piece of architecture (like the memorial to the USS *Arizona* in Pearl Harbor, Hawaii) to a painting, song, or poem inspired by the war (such as Randall Jarrell's poem "The Death of the Ball Turret Gunner"). Explain the work's relationship to the war: is it about a battle, or an individual's experience of the war? What emotions does the piece evoke: bravery, fear, loneliness, anger?

Create a Board Game Based on Nazi Confiscation of Jewish Property

Trace the history of a painting that was taken from its original owner and ended up in a foreign museum by making a Monopoly-type game.

War Journal

Imagine that you were alive during World War II. You can choose to have lived in any country involved. Write a journal of your activities over the course of one week.

Propaganda

Rent a video of a movie created during World War II that is about the war. Some examples of films available on videocassette include Frank Capra's *Why We Fight* documentary series, *Casablanca*, and *Mrs. Miniver*. Write an essay discussing whether the film has a particular political message and what that message is.

Battlefield Tour

Create an itinerary for a World War II battlefield tour. You could choose to focus the tour on sites in the Pacific, sites throughout Europe or North Africa, or on one specific country. List the sites you'll be visiting on the tour, giving the name of the battles fought, codenames for the operations (if any), key events of the battles, the commanders involved, the victors, and why the battles were important.

D-Day Newspaper Article

Write an article about the June 6, 1944, invasion of France from the viewpoint of either an American or a German war correspondent.

Rescuers

Research individuals who saved or helped save Jewish lives during the Holocaust. Be sure to include less well-known people as well as more famous figures. Write their names and a brief description of the rescue(s) they made on slips of paper that can be pinned to a map in the appropriate places.

Trials

Imagine that you were a guard at a Nazi concentration camp. After the war, you are tried at Nuremberg for war crimes. Explain the reasons for your actions. Or, imagine that you are one of the prosecutors at the Nuremberg trials. Explain the types of questions you would ask and what criteria you would use to determine guilt or innocence.

Mordecai Anielewicz

As Nazi leader Adolf Hitler put plans into place to eliminate the European Jewish population through systematic genocide, his first step was to establish ghettos, which were small, quarantined areas that soon became riddled with disease and poverty. Mordecai Anielewicz (pronounced More-da-keye On-yell-a-wits) was one of the young Polish-Jewish men and women who put themselves at risk by supplying the Warsaw ghetto in Poland with food, medical supplies, and weapons for defense. In 1943 Anielewicz participated in the Warsaw Ghetto Uprising, the most famous of the Jewish attempts to resist Nazi rule.

Escape and Return to Warsaw

Mordecai Anielewicz was born into a poverty-stricken family in the slums of Warsaw, Poland, circa 1919. While growing up, Mordecai and other Jewish children were subjected to beatings by other, non-Jewish youth. As a result, Anielewicz learned how to defend himself at a very early age. After completing high school, he became one of the leaders of a Zionist group that sought to establish a Jewish homeland in Palestine, which is now Israel.

World War II officially began in 1939 with Hitler's attack and conquest of Poland. The Nazis overtook Warsaw, the capital of Poland, through an aggressive aerial attack. They continued to

Born c. 1919
    Warsaw, Poland
Died May 8, 1943
    Warsaw ghetto, Poland

Jewish anti-Nazi resistance leader; led uprisings in the Warsaw ghetto

"I have lived to see Jewish resistance in the ghetto in all its greatness and glory."

(Reproduced by permission of Bildarchiv Preussischer Kulturbesitz)

Mordecai Anielewicz (right) and a group of young Zionists. (Leah Hammerstein Silverstein/USHMM Photo Archives)

bomb railroads and destroy small villages and towns. The people living in these areas were left homeless, wandering their once peaceful streets. Anielewicz and some of his friends set out from Warsaw for southern Poland to establish an escape route for Polish Jews who wanted to flee to Palestine. However, the Soviet army occupied the southern part of Poland, and Anielewicz was captured and imprisoned. Upon his release, he went to the former Polish city of Vilna, which by then had been absorbed into Lithuania, where a large number of Jewish youths from Warsaw were seeking refuge. Anielewicz organized the return of a group of young people to Warsaw to set up underground political and educational activities. He and his fiancée, Mira Furhrer, felt it was their duty to return to Poland and dedicate themselves to help-

ing their fellow Jews. They volunteered to become part of the teaching efforts in Warsaw.

Jews Restricted to Ghettos

In October 1940, the Nazis issued an edict requiring all Jews in Warsaw to live together in an old section of the city that came to be known as the Warsaw ghetto. The ghetto was enclosed by nine-foot-high brick walls topped with barbed wire to deter anyone with thoughts of escape. The walls were constantly patrolled by armed guards charged with simple orders: shoot to kill. All the Jews in Warsaw and nearby areas—more than 400,000 people in all—had to leave most of their belongings behind and move into the ghetto with only those things they could carry. Most people brought pots and pans, blankets, clothing, and other supplies they could manage. Similar Jewish ghettos were being established elsewhere in Poland.

Once he had relocated to the Warsaw ghetto, Anielewicz taught classes, organized political activities, and attended secret meetings with other Nazi resistance group members. He was involved with an early effort headed by Pinya Kartin, a former soldier. The group surmised that, being vastly outnumbered, the best possible approach for Warsaw's Jews was one of tactical resistance. By bombing military buildings and disrupting essential transportation, the Jewish group would be able to dismantle the Nazis' ever-tightening grip. Anielewicz worked on an underground newspaper so that important information could be shared among members of the resistance movement. The paper encouraged people of the ghettos to take up arms in opposition to Nazi rule with such pleas as: "Jewish workers! Jewish Youth! Gather your forces and pool them for battle. Stand united shoulder to shoulder." Soon after, Kartin was identified as a spy and was shot to death by the Nazis. His followers immediately disbanded, lacking leadership and fearing the tyranny of the Nazi regime.

Resistance Efforts as Leader

Anielewicz continued to urge Jews of the Warsaw ghetto to join together in resistance groups and refuse to surrender to the will of the Nazis. In 1940 he became the head of *Zydowska Organizacja Bojowa* (ZOB), or Jewish Fighting Organization. The other main resistance group was called the Jewish Military Union. The two groups, consisting mainly of teenagers and people in their twenties, soon began working together. Some of the young women, especially those with fair skin and light-colored eyes, became messengers. It was their job to bring information, goods, and money to and from the ghetto. Without the typical dark coloring characteristic of many Jews, these female messengers were able to travel more easily through the city without arousing suspicion.

During 1940 and 1941, Anielewicz put his efforts into strengthening the defenses of the people who lived in the ghetto. He sought help from a group of Polish citizens who remained loyal to the former Polish government, which was in exile in London, England. Unfortunately, these efforts failed. In 1942, the Nazis commanded large groups of people to leave the Warsaw ghetto and go to a nearby concentration camp called Treblinka. The Nazis classified them as enemies of the state and mandated that they be quarantined from the rest of society. Most were subjected to hard labor until they died, while others were put to death. When Anielewicz discovered what was happening at Treblinka, he knew it was time for the members of the resistance groups to arm themselves.

As of 1943, only about one-sixth of the Jews originally sent to live in the Warsaw ghetto remained there. By then, most of the ghetto inhabitants believed that death was their ultimate fate under Nazi rule, and they vowed to resist at all costs. The ZOB and Jewish Military Union organized members of the underground to protect various sections of the ghetto. In order to obtain weapons for the job, the resistance groups collected money and dealt with various smugglers and Nazi deserters. Money, sometimes contributed by American and European supporters to purchase food, was used to buy arms instead. In order to maintain security, Jewish resistance leaders ordered that many of the Nazi spies and thieves who preyed on the Jews should be killed.

The Jews Fight Back

On January 18, 1943, members of the Nazi SS surrounded three sections of the Warsaw ghetto and ordered the Jews to come out. The resisters answered the commands with gunfire and grenades. The surprised Nazis began to storm the buildings with the intent of killing the Jews. As they entered, the Nazis were met with Jews swinging clubs and throwing chairs. At other entrances, the Nazis only found empty rooms. The highly organized resistance fighters had already escaped via underground passages. Several Nazis were killed, and the SS retreated.

The next day, the Germans returned and, though they were able to capture 6,000 people, the soldiers left in fear for their lives. After four days of confrontation, the Nazis stopped the deportation of the Jews. The people in the ghetto believed that their armed resistance had caused the Germans to back down. For three months the ghetto was relatively quiet, and Anielewicz and the ZOB continued their defense preparations. Responding to the strong showing of Jewish resistance, Heinrich Himmler, head of the SS, came to investigate. He decided that the ghetto was becoming dangerous and unmanageable for the Germans—and that it had to be destroyed.

The Conflict Resumes

On April 19, 1943, German tanks rolled into the Warsaw ghetto. The Nazis chose to attack on the first day of Passover—the Jewish holiday commemorating the Jews' escape from Egypt during Biblical times. By attacking on a holiday, the Nazis hoped to catch the Jews off guard. However, the Jews had prepared as best they could for the possible return of the Nazis. They bravely defended themselves, although they had very few weapons. Writer Seymour Rossel described the arms used by the resistance fighters to fend off more than 2,000 fully armed Germans. "They had three machine guns, about eight rifles, some hand grenades, some Molotov cocktails (bottles filled with gasoline-soaked rags that would be ignited and thrown) and perhaps three hundred pistols and revolvers."

During the first conflicts, led by Anielewicz, the Jews pushed back the Germans. The Germans later returned with more soldiers, and the fighting grew even more intense. Jews were driven from their dwellings and many escaped in underground passageways. Jürgen Stroop, the Nazi SS general in charge, used planes, tanks, and artillery to attack the ghetto. Soldiers with dynamite and flame throwers went from house to house looking for Jews. Even very young Germans, part of the Hitler Youth group, were instructed to kill any Jew on sight.

Stroop, who reported his progress to Nazi headquarters in Berlin each day, was shocked that the Jews would rather be burned alive than surrender. In one of his reports he said: "With their bones broken, they still tried to crawl across the street into buildings which had not yet been set on fire…. Despite the danger of being burned alive, the Jews … often preferred to return into the flames rather than risk being caught by us." Women used both hands to fire heavy pistols at the Nazis. Some people, waiting to be searched, pulled hand grenades out of their clothing, burning up both their captors and themselves.

After two weeks the Nazis were still unable to stop the fighting of the ghetto inhabitants. In a letter to a member of the resistance, Anielewicz wrote: "I have no words to describe to you the conditions in which the Jews are living. Only a few chosen ones will hold out; all the rest will perish sooner or later. The die is cast…. The main thing is: My life's dream has come true; I have lived to see Jewish resistance in the ghetto in all its greatness and glory."

On May 8, the Germans were able to take over the bunker on Mila Street that served as Jewish headquarters. Many of the resistance leaders took their own lives that day so that they would not be subjected to Nazi brutality. Anielewicz was killed in the fighting. In June the conflict came to an end. The Nazis burned the entire ghetto down to the ground. At Himmler's order, the ghetto's historic Tlomacka synagogue was blown up. Himmler was reported as saying, "The Jewish quarter of Warsaw is no more."

Mordecai Anielewicz is memorialized by a monument in Israel at the site of the Kibbutz Yad Mordecai. A collective farming community, the kibbutz is named in his honor.

SOURCES

Books

Adler, David A., *Child of the Warsaw Ghetto,* Holiday House (New York), 1995.

Gilbert, Martin, *The Holocaust: A History of the Jews of Europe During the Second World War,* Holt Rinehart and Winston (New York), 1986.

Haas, Gerda, *Tracking the Holocaust,* Runestone Press (Minneapolis), 1995.

Korczak, Janusz, *Ghetto Diary,* Holocaust Library (New York), 1978.

Mark, Ber, *Uprising in the Warsaw Ghetto,* translated from Yiddish by Gershon Freidlin, Schocken Books (New York), 1975.

Marrin, Albert, *Hitler,* Puffin Books (New York), 1993.

Rogasky, Barbara, *Smoke and Ashes: The Story of the Holocaust,* Holiday House (New York), 1988.

Skipper, G. C., *World at War: The Invasion of Poland,* Children's Press (Chicago), 1983.

Zeinert, Karen, *The Warsaw Ghetto Uprising,* Millbrook Press (Brookfield, CT), 1993.

Leo Baeck

Leo Baeck (pronounced Bek) grew up in an era in which anti-Semitism was kept secret. With the defeat of Germany in World War I in 1918, he witnessed the widespread growth of anti-Jewish feelings and the eventual persecution and murder of millions of his fellow Jews. Throughout the ordeal, he realized the necessity for keeping one's religious faith and putting it into action.

Born May 23, 1873
    Lissa, Germany
Died November 2, 1956
    London, England

World-renowned rabbi; a leader of the German Jews in World War II; concentration camp survivor

"We Jews know that the commandment of God is to live."

Life in Germany

According to Baeck's family history, his ancestors settled in Moravia, part of today's Czech Republic. Many of Baeck's ancestors were rabbis, including his father, Samuel. By the time Baeck was born in 1873, the family had moved to Germany. He was one of eleven children who lived a comfortable German-Jewish middle-class life. They lived in a town that was a peaceful, pleasant center of Jewish learning.

Baeck excelled in high school, graduating at the top of his class. As a young man he studied to become a rabbi, first in Breslau, Germany, and later in Berlin. This stage of his life was difficult for Baeck as he had very little money for food and had to borrow the books necessary to complete his coursework. Nevertheless, he received excellent religious training as well as German non-religious teaching. He earned his Ph.D. in philosophy in

(Library of Congress)

1895 and was ordained a rabbi in May 1897, at the age of twenty-four.

Baeck first served as a rabbi to a congregation near Breslau, Germany, where he stayed for ten years. During that time he met and married Natalie Hamburger, a shy and kind woman who gave birth to their daughter, Ruth, and offered him the stability of family life. Baeck was popular with both adults and students, whom he frequently invited to his house for lively discussions. When people had disputes, they came to Baeck to mediate. During these years, he began his lifelong practice of having dialogues with Gentiles (non-Jews). His education at German universities gave him the ability to present his ideas effectively in non-Jewish circles. In 1905 Baeck issued his first book, *The Essence of Judaism.* In the work, he emphasized that it was the responsibility of the Jew to do God's will on Earth. He contended that Judaism had not died with the coming of Christianity, but that it was very much alive and thriving—the Christian religion was derived from the Jewish religion.

Moves to Düsseldorf and Berlin

In 1907 Baeck was invited to become a rabbi in the prosperous German city of Düsseldorf. There he initiated dialogue sessions with students. He also began to talk about the importance of education for women. As a result of his open-minded, interfaith discussions, he was well known throughout the city. In 1912, after five years in Düsseldorf, Baeck became a rabbi to Berlin's Jewish community. During the next thirty years, he was assigned to various synagogues throughout the city. He became an expert on the Jewish sources of Christianity, especially the Jewish origins of the New Testament.

After World War I began in Europe in 1914, Baeck volunteered to serve as a "chaplain" for the Jewish troops who were fighting for Germany. The forty-one-year-old rabbi brought food to wounded soldiers in field hospitals, wrote letters to their families, and offered services for the dead.

The Rise of Anti-Semitism

Following Germany's defeat in World War I, both soldiers and private citizens felt a sense of betrayal. Some looked for a scapegoat to explain why Germany had lost the war. Over time, they began to blame the loss on the Jews, even though many Jews had fought bravely alongside their German countrymen. Military and business leaders united in denouncing the Jews, whom they accused of causing the German defeat. These accusations were unfounded, yet when coupled with the history of anti-Semitism that began many centuries earlier, they provided dangerous fuel for a growing fire.

Shortly before the end of World War I, Baeck had returned to Berlin to resume his duties as a rabbi. Throughout the 1920s, the city's Jews often chose the tall, dignified rabbi to be their spokesman before the Christian majority. His lectures were known for their excellence, clarity, and spiritual insight. Baeck served as president of the German B'nai Brith organization, which raised money for scholarships, hospitals, and other charitable Jewish institutions. By the late 1920s, Baeck was one of the most prominent Jews in Berlin.

The Rise of Hitler

In 1929, just as Germany was beginning to experience economic recovery, the world was hit with a global depression. Unemployment rose dramatically in Germany and the people began to listen to the hate-filled speeches of Nazi party leader Adolf Hitler. The new leader led his Nazi party with fiery diatribes, preaching that the Jews were responsible for the country's difficult economic conditions.

In 1933 Hitler assumed power in Germany, and the Nazis stepped up their anti-Jewish activities. Hitler made laws forbidding Jews to work as lawyers or as members of the civil service. As anti-Semitism grew, the Jews established an organization—the Representative Council of Jews in Germany—headed by Baeck, which supervised educational and charitable programs and provided aid to Jewish people wishing to leave the country. Between 1934 and 1935, the Nazis enacted the Reich Citizenship Laws that stripped Jews of their citizenship and banned marriages between Jews and non-Jews. The laws also permitted the Gestapo to arrest, then imprison Jews in concentration camps without cause, placing them there with others Hitler deemed to be "enemies of the state." Jews were also forbidden to use public beaches, telephones, hospitals, colleges, barbershops, and dining or sleeping cars on trains.

In response to a declaration by Hitler that German children should be taught "the necessity of blood purity," Baeck wrote a special sermon. In that sermon he said "the lies uttered against [the

Jews], the false charges made against [their] faith and its defenders are hateful. Let us trample these falsehoods beneath our feet...." As a result of the sermon, the Nazis imprisoned Baeck. However, because a British reporter threatened to tell the world about the arrest of this prominent man, Baeck was released.

As conditions for the Jews in Germany worsened, Baeck used his influence to obtain as many visas as possible to enable German Jews to leave for other countries. Although he could easily have left Germany himself, Baeck chose to stay and help his fellow Jews. He urged his wife, Natalie, and his daughter, Ruth, to leave, but they refused. In October 1937 Natalie became ill and died from a stroke. After his wife's death, Baeck began to devote all of his time and energy to helping the Jews of Germany survive the Third Reich.

Baeck Helps Protect and Rescue Children

On November 7, 1938, the political climate in Germany became even more difficult for Jews, including Baeck. On that day, Herschel Grynszpan, a 17-year-old Jew, shot and mortally wounded low-level Nazi official Ernst vom Rath in Paris, France. Grynszpan gunned down vom Rath in retaliation for the deportation of his parents and siblings from Germany to Poland, where they had no place to live. They had been forced to leave with only a suitcase apiece and very little money. The Nazis used the incident as an excuse to initiate various pogroms against German-Jews two days later. Jewish shops were targeted on *Kristallnacht* ("Crystal Night" or "Night of Broken Glass"), which occurred on November 9 and 10. The Nazis vandalized Jewish shops and burned synagogues, and tons of broken glass filled the streets. Although reports vary, the United States Holocaust Memorial Museum lists the damage done by the Nazis as follows. "In two days, over 1,000 synagogues were burned, 7,000 Jewish businesses were trashed and looted, dozens of Jewish people were killed, and Jewish cemeteries, hospitals, schools, and homes were looted while police and fire brigades stood by.... The morning after the pogroms 30,000 German Jewish men were arrested for the 'crime' of being Jewish and sent to concentration camps, where hundreds of them perished." Baeck traveled throughout the city on *Kristallnacht* helping Jewish children escape the violence.

By 1939 two-thirds of Germany's Jews had fled the country. That year, the Nazis attacked Poland, and in a short time they conquered Denmark, Norway, Holland, and Belgium. Baeck arranged for a trainload of Jewish children to be rescued from Berlin and sent to safety in London, England. When asked how long he would be staying in Germany, Baeck replied: "Until the last Jew is saved."

As the brutality of World War II increased, Baeck insisted that his daughter and her family leave the country for England. His organization for the welfare of Jews was taken over by the Nazis, who were interested in making money on the sale of the life-saving visas for which people were willing to spend large sums of money. Baeck decided to remain with the group, despite the Nazi presence, because he felt he could do more for the Jews from the inside than from the outside.

By 1940 Hitler had intensified his efforts to rid Europe of the Jews, whom he referred to as "vermin." Jews were forbidden to drive cars, walk on city streets, go to the movies, buy new clothing, or own radios or any other appliances. Each was required to wear a yellow Star of David (a Jewish symbol) on the outside of his or her clothing for identification. Baeck's was the only seminary for Jewish youth that was allowed to stay open. However, in September 1941, the Gestapo barged into the seminary and declared that it would now serve as a center for the deportation of Jews.

In mid-1941 Hitler began to implement a secret plan that was called the "Final Solution." These were the code words used by the Nazis to refer to the complete elimination of all European Jews. All of Europe's Jews were to be rounded up and sent to concentration camps. There the men, women, and children would be killed. At first some were shot or placed in the backs of trucks and asphyxiated. However, the Nazis deemed these methods as too costly and ineffective, so they developed a new method. They then placed Jews in rooms that looked like showers. Instead of water, the spigots released poisonous gas, murdering those in the room through suffocation.

Although the horrors that took place at Auschwitz (one of the largest and deadliest of the concentration camps) and other camps were not yet known to Baeck, he was aware of many other cruel acts. Adults and children were starving in the Jewish ghettos. Ghettos, such as that in Warsaw, Poland, were crowded, walled sections of cities where Jews were forced to live in inferior conditions and apart from non-Jews. Every day thousands of Jews began to disappear as they were sent from the ghettos to Nazi labor camps, where the

The Story of a Dignified Death

Before Leo Baeck was a prisoner at Theresienstadt, another Jewish man, Jacob Edelstein, served as head of the camp's Council of Elders. The council was comprised of a group of Jewish leaders who managed Jewish affairs as best they could within the camp. In 1938 the Nazis accused Edelstein and three other men of giving false daily reports. Edelstein was sent to Birkenau, a death camp, in Poland. A year after Edelstein's death in June 1944, Yossl Rosensaft recalled the day that Edelstein was taken away. Rosensaft's report appears in the book *The Holocaust: A History of the Jews of Europe During the Second World War* by Martin Gilbert.

Rosensaft recalled: "Jacob was in the same barracks as I was—number thirteen—on that Monday morning. It was about 9 a.m. and he was saying his morning prayers, wrapped in his prayer shawl. Suddenly the door burst open and [a Nazi lieutenant] strutted in, accompanied by three SS men. He called out Jacob's name. Jacob did not move. [The lieutenant] screamed: 'I am waiting for you, hurry up.'" Rosensaft added: "Jacob turned round very slowly, faced [him] and said quietly: 'Of the last moments on this earth, allotted to me by the Almighty, I am the master, not you.' Whereupon he turned back to face the wall and finished his prayers. He then folded his prayer shawl unhurriedly, handed it to one of the inmates, and said to the lieutenant, 'I am now ready.'" Rosensaft concluded: "[The lieutenant] stood there without uttering a word, and marched out when Edelstein was ready. Edelstein followed him and three [Nazi soldiers] made up the rear. We have never seen Jacob Edelstein again."

majority of the inmates were actually worked to death or gassed. At first Baeck intended to meet with every Berlin Jew whose name appeared on lists to be sent away. When that became impossible, he took to meeting people in streets and alleys, carrying messages from them to their loved ones.

Arrest and Imprisonment at Theresienstadt

On January 27, 1943, the Nazis arrested Baeck and sent him to Theresienstadt (Ter-rays-en-shtott) concentration camp in Czechoslovakia. This camp was the least harsh of all the camps. It housed Jews who were World War I veterans, artists, spouses of non-Jews, and other prominent citizens. Theresienstadt, with its bakeries, medical rooms, and shops, was in stark contrast to the other camps, in which people lived under deplorable conditions. The Nazis used Theresienstadt as a model to deceive foreign representatives into believing that Jews were being treated humanely in all the camps. Baeck was pho-tographed to add credibility to Hitler's claims. The houses and barracks at Theresienstadt, originally built as a military installation to house 10,000 people, now held six times that number. Adults and children were forced to sleep in wooden bunks stacked five high. Dysentery and diarrhea contributed to the filth and foul smells.

Life in the Camp

Baeck was assigned to collect garbage. He and his partner were strapped to a heavy wagon and canvassed the camp carrying away rat-infested trash. During his rounds Baeck met and comforted people. He was fond of saying "[t]he soul and the hour meet each other. What is given to us, we have to do." At the camp, Baeck organized prisoners to nurse victims of a typhus epidemic. He also found time to write portions of a book for later publication. Like other prisoners, Baeck's days were numbered. It was only because of mistaken identity that Baeck stayed alive in the camp. Nazi official Adolf Eichmann had ordered that Baeck be killed. However, Eichmann saw the name of another rabbi named Beck on the death rolls and assumed that Baeck was dead, even making an announcement to that effect.

In mid-1943 Baeck learned the truth of the mass murders that were commonplace at Auschwitz and other camps. After much soul-searching, he chose not to share the information with other prisoners at Thereseinstadt. He believed that such news would devastate the morale of the prisoners, and he realized that hope must be kept alive. By 1944 information coming from Germany became very difficult to obtain and the fate of Baeck was unknown. In early 1945 it became obvious that the Allies were winning the war. Some Nazis hoped that the Allies would show them mercy if they freed Jews in concentration camps. In February 1945 Baeck's daughter, Ruth, received a letter from a freed Dutch Jew. He told Ruth that Baeck had been told he could leave too, but he preferred to stay and be of help.

On April 30, 1945, knowing that the war was over for Germany, Hitler committed suicide in order to escape falling into the hands of approaching Soviet troops. At Hitler's request his body and that of his new wife, Eva Braun, were burned. The Nazis' rule came to an end with their surrender to the Allies on May 8, 1945.

Life After Liberation

One week after the suicide of Hitler, Theresienstadt was liberated by the Allies. The Soviets, with representatives of the Red Cross relief organization, brought food and medical supplies to the camp. Trainloads of emaciated people, sick with various diseases, arrived from other camps for treatment at Theresienstadt. Baeck nursed the sick, in some cases cleaning maggots from their infected wounds. He also wrote letters for former prisoners, informing their loved ones that they had survived. Shortly after the Nazis' surrender, a U.S. Army major was dispatched to Theresienstadt to transport Baeck, who had become known as "the pope of the German Jews," to England to join his family. The esteemed rabbi refused to leave for two months until all Jews in the camp had someplace to go.

In early July 1945, Baeck, slightly stooped over and 50 pounds lighter than before his imprisonment, was reunited with his daughter, son-in-law, granddaughter, and three sisters in London. Throughout his seventies Baeck lived in London and continued his work. He was elected president of the British Council for the Protection of the Rights and Interests of the Jews from Germany. In 1947 he visited the United States, met President Harry S Truman at the White House, and gave talks to various liberal Jewish groups. He was also the first famous German Jew to return to Germany after the war. He helped families in trouble and shared funds he had received from his book royalties.

In 1948 Baeck was offered a six-month visiting professorship at Hebrew Union College in Cincinnati, Ohio. Instead, he kept this post for several years, traveling to Great Britain where he became a British citizen. Baeck found time to complete his second book, *This People Israel: The Meaning of Jewish Existence*. In 1956 he was hospitalized in London with intestinal cancer. In his conversations with others, he refused to dwell on his illness; he insisted on talking with his family about their plans for the future.

Death and Memorialization

Leo Baeck died on November 2, 1956. Eulogies were given for him around the world. In his honor, the new German government in Berlin issued a postage stamp featuring Baeck's image. His books were translated into many languages. Leo Baeck Institutes were opened in London, New York, and Israel, to offer extensive collections on German-Jewish history and scholarship. Schools and colleges were named after him. When asked before his death if he could forgive the Germans, Baeck replied, "I forgive the Germans? It is for the Germans to forgive themselves."

SOURCES

Books

Baeck, Leo, *This People Israel: The Meaning of Jewish Existence*, translated by Albert H. Friedlander, Holt, Rinehart and Winston (New York), 1965.

Baker, Leonard, *Days of Sorrow and Pain: Leo Baeck and the Berlin Jews*, Macmillan (New York), 1978.

Boehm, Eric H., *We Survived*, Yale University Press (New Haven, CT), 1949.

Friedlander, Albert H., *Leo Baeck: Teacher of Theresienstadt*, Overlook Press (Woodstock, NY), 1991.

Gilbert, Martin, *The Holocaust: A History of the Jews of Europe During the Second World War*, Holt, Rinehart and Winston (New York), 1985.

Neimark, Anne E., *One Man's Valor: Leo Baeck and the Holocaust,* E.P. Dutton (New York), 1986.

Stadtler, Bea, *The Holocaust: A History of Courage and Resistance,* edited by Morrisen David Beal, Behrman House (West Orange, NJ), 1994.

Periodicals

Gruenewald, Max, "Leo Baeck: Witness and Judge," *Judaism,* Autumn 1957.

Other

United States Holocaust Memorial Museum, http://www.ushmm.org (September 2000).

Nikolaus (Klaus) Barbie

An SS officer, Klaus Barbie was sent to France after Germany conquered the country during World War II. He ordered the arrest and sometimes the imprisonment of thousands of French Jews. He is remembered for his active involvement in the brutal torture of prisoners, which earned him a reputation as "The Butcher of Lyon." Initially, he escaped prosecution for war crimes. However, long after the war ended, he was discovered hiding in South America. He was returned to France, tried, and convicted on 341 counts of crimes against humanity, including murder, extermination, enslavement, deportation, and other acts committed against a non-military population.

Born October 25, 1913
    Bad Godesberg, Germany
Died September 25, 1991
    St. Joseph Prison, France

Soldier; head of German secret police in Lyon, France; known as "The Butcher of Lyon"

"The Jews? That was not my affair. [Others] were in charge of that."

Troubled Childhood in Germany

Nikolaus Barbie, later nicknamed Klaus, was born in 1913, the first of two sons born to Nikolaus Barbie and Anna Hees. Both his parents were Catholics and schoolteachers descended from farming families. The couple married when Klaus was three months old. Barbie's father was badly wounded in World War I (1914–18) when the future SS officer was just an infant. Although he did not die from the wounds until 1933, Barbie's father was in so much pain that he took to drinking heavily for relief. When he was drunk, he was often physically abusive to his sons. Some histori-

(Reproduced by permission of Archive Photos, Inc.)

ans assert that the young Barbie developed a life-long hatred for the French because his father had been wounded in the war against them and other Allied countries.

Until he was eleven years old, Barbie attended the same school where his father taught. From 1923 to 1925, he attended boarding school and found he enjoyed the independence of that experience. For recreation he favored swimming and fencing. In 1925 his family moved to the city of Trier, where Barbie attended secondary school. He was disappointed at having to rejoin his family in their troubled home. His teachers described him as an intelligent boy who avoided conflict. He considered the priesthood at a young age, but as he matured, this ambition eventually died. In 1933 both his father and his brother died, leaving no money for Barbie to attend college. He did not pass his school exams until 1934, when he was twenty years old. Seeing that his options were limited, Barbie volunteered for a work camp run by the Nazi party. Führer Adolf Hitler had just assumed power in Germany.

Hitler's political platform was constructed partly on his extreme contempt for Jews. He blamed the Jews for causing Germany's defeat in World War I. He also considered them to be a "poisonous" race that did not deserve to live. His ultimate goal was to eliminate all the Jews in Europe. Many Nazi party members agreed with Hitler's feelings toward the Jews and were willing to carry out the Jews' destruction. Barbie soon became one of Hitler's elite.

Begins SS Career

In 1935, not yet twenty-two years old, Barbie joined the Schutzstaffel, or Security Squad, more commonly called the SS. The unit was originally formed to act as bodyguards for Hitler. In a book about Barbie, a German newspaperman was quoted by author Ladislas de Hoyos: "All the SS men have this in common: cold eyes like those of fish, reflecting a complete absence of inner life, a complete lack of sentiments." Barbie became a dedicated follower of Hitler. He was an ambitious man whose ultimate goal was to be a member of the Sicherheitsdienst or Security Police, commonly called the SD. The SD served as the intelligence service of the SS. Barbie began a slow but steady rise through the SS ranks. He attended espionage school set up by the Nazis and became an enthusiastic persecutor of Jews in Berlin, Germany's capital city.

Sometime in the late 1930s, Barbie became engaged to Regine Willms, a loyal Nazi Party member who was employed in a Nazi Women's Association nursery school. She was an accomplished cook who liked painting and music. The couple had to pass complicated medical tests devised by SS Chief Heinrich Himmler to make sure they were "racially pure," meaning they had no Jewish blood. After a thorough investigation of his background, Barbie passed the tests; it was noted that he had been born the "perfect SS baby." In April 1940 Regine promised to attend the Nazi School for Mothers, in which she would learn to raise children obedient to the Nazis. That month, the couple was finally allowed to marry, eight months after World War II began in Europe.

Barbie Goes to War

Almost immediately after his wedding ceremony, Barbie was called to active military duty and sent to Amsterdam, Holland. There his primary task was to round up and torment Jews as well as keep an eye on Jewish and Christian groups to make sure no resistance to Nazi party policies surfaced. Witnesses in Amsterdam later remembered Barbie for his coldness and cruelty. He soon fell out of favor with his supervisor, who complained of Barbie's fondness for wine and women. He was sent to fight in the Soviet Union (now Russia) and then transferred to France in mid-1942. It was in France that his reported brutality reached its peak.

Because of his training in espionage, Barbie was assigned to hunt down leaders of the French resistance—French patriots who worked secretly to weaken Germany's army in France. Barbie was especially interested in Jean Moulin, who was known to be the right-hand man of French resistance leader Charles de Gaulle. Because French resistance efforts centered around the city of Lyon, Barbie headed there to capture Moulin.

Barbie in Lyon

While ordinary citizens in Lyon were living on rationed food, SS officers lived like kings. Barbie and other Nazis took over a large hotel and began their activities of arresting, interrogating, beating, and torturing suspected resistance leaders and Jews. Finally, so many people had been arrested that the SS had to move into larger quarters, where an underground network of cellars and thick-walled rooms muffled the screams of SS victims.

When Barbie could not convince his prisoners to talk, he kidnapped their family members and threatened to kill them. He was said to be fond of kicking and hitting his victims. Sometimes, he let his dogs attack them.

Magnus Linklater and his coauthors offer this portrait of Barbie: "[He] considered himself a civilized German: he played the piano, though badly, and enjoyed long … discussions about German history and the consequences of the war. He prided himself on his knowledge of France and the French language, and he felt at home in the city of Lyon. He particularly enjoyed his daily walks … with his Alsatian, Wolf…. Without [his wife], who was for most of the war in [the German city of] Trier, he behaved much like any other unattached officer, eating out in expensive restaurants, getting drunk, and frequenting the nightclubs."

In February 1943, under Barbie's command, a raid was carried out against the offices of a local Jewish organization. Eighty-four people were seized and sent to a concentration camp, where the Nazis confined people they regarded as "enemies of the state." Only two of the eighty-four survived. One of the most severe crimes Barbie was charged with committing occurred in April 1944; Barbie later denied responsibility for the act. It involved a raid carried out on a Jewish children's home in the town of Izieu, in which forty-three children, age three to fourteen years, and ten Jewish workers were rounded up and sent to concentration camps. All of the children and nine of the ten workers died in the camps.

Captures Famed Resistance Leader

Barbie clinched his reputation as "The Butcher of Lyon" with his torture and murder of Jean Moulin, who was the highest-ranking member of the French resistance ever captured by the Nazis. Moulin was known throughout France as a hero for his bravery in defying the Germans. Barbie, who admired Moulin's courage, considered this capture to be a great personal challenge. In 1943, with the assistance of some French men who betrayed their own countryman, Barbie captured Moulin and personally interviewed him.

Despite beatings and torture, Moulin refused to reveal the names of his comrades. Barbie had hoped that his handling of Moulin would ensure a promotion. However, Barbie got carried away in his interrogation of Moulin. On the way to Berlin

Resistance in France

French leader Charles de Gaulle (1890–1970) headed the Free French resistance during World War II. Such resistance groups struggled to free their countries from occupying Nazi troops. When France surrendered to Germany in June of 1940, de Gaulle refused to accept the surrender and fled to London, England. There, he led a group of Free French forces and eventually was accepted by the Allies as the leader of the "Fighting French." He also delivered radio addresses in which he kept alive the spirit of his countrymen, proclaiming that "France has lost a battle, but she has not lost the war." When the Allies entered Paris—France's capital city—in triumph in August 1944, de Gaulle marched with them.

De Gaulle served briefly as president of France after the Nazis were driven out. He convinced the French Parliament to adopt the practice of bringing a person to trial charged with "crimes against humanity." Such crimes included murder, extermination, enslavement, deportation, and other pitiless acts committed against the non-military population of a country. Previously such acts committed during wartime had not been recognized as crimes. Because of de Gaulle's work, France was finally able to try, convict, and imprison Klaus Barbie for his crimes against humanity.

for further questioning, Moulin died. Barbie later claimed Moulin had killed himself by hurling his head against a wall with intense force.

Barbie's superiors disapproved of the outcome of the Moulin interrogation. Nevertheless, Barbie received a medal and was recommended for promotion for his work in eliminating many enemy groups of the Nazis. But Barbie, himself, was unhappy with his handling of the Moulin affair, and

Barbie during his trial for war crimes in France. (Reproduced by permission of © Hulton Getty/Liaison Agency)

he became moody and unpredictable. He often flew into rages, and his conduct toward prisoners was extremely brutal. He began traveling to the countryside on surprise raids, rounding up prisoners for questioning. On their way to carry out such a raid in August 1944, Barbie and his men were ambushed, and he suffered several gunshot wounds. He was taken back to Germany and hospitalized.

While Barbie was recuperating, Paris was liberated from the Germans on August 25, 1944. Allied soldiers entered the French capital in a victory that was celebrated around the world. While Barbie was recovering in the hospital, Germany suffered several more defeats in battle and finally surrendered in May 1945. The war in Europe was over, although the war in the Pacific continued for several more months. Barbie was released from the hospital shortly after the Germans surrendered, and he was soon rounded up by victorious U.S. troops. In the chaos that surrounded the end of the war, however, Barbie convinced the Americans that he was a displaced person of French nationality. He was given a bicycle, and he pedaled away.

Postwar Activities

A warrant was issued for Barbie's arrest, yet he was able to hide himself from the Allies until 1947. By then, the remaining Allies (France, Great Britain, and the United States) were at odds with

the Soviet Union and its communist social and economic system. For democratic and capitalistic societies, the communistic aim for a classless society was considered a worse threat to world peace than the recently defeated Germans. The Allies decided they were willing to overlook the crimes of some of the former Nazi leaders to take advantage of their knowledge and skills against the new threat of the Soviet Union. Barbie, still in Germany, was hired as a spy for the United States. Soon he had recruited many of his former Nazi comrades and was running a vast spy ring on the U.S. payroll.

However, in 1949 Barbie's continued presence in Europe became known to the French, who demanded that he be turned over to them for trial for war crimes. U.S. officials, wishing to conceal the extent of Barbie's secret work for them, arranged for Barbie to escape to South America. He was given false identity papers under the name of Klaus Altmann, which he chose himself. In the city of Trier, Barbie had known a man named Altmann—a Jew who later died in the gas chamber at Auschwitz. In March 1951, the new "Altmann family"—Klaus, Regine, their nine-year-old daughter Ute Marie, and four-year-old son Jorge—set sail on an Italian ship for Buenos Aires, Argentina. From Argentina the family soon moved to Bolivia, where Barbie supported himself as an auto mechanic, having been given a quick training course by the American Counter Intelligence Corps (CIC).

Barbie in South America

Barbie was not satisfied working as a mechanic. South America was a continent at war, and Barbie knew the process well. It was not long before he was involved in theft, fraud, forgery, drug running, arms selling, spying, and politics. He was able to live in luxury once again. He was befriended by Bolivia's president and carried out espionage work for him. Barbie also obliged his new friend by showing his soldiers how to torture prisoners. All the while he was living openly, dining out in restaurants, and hobnobbing with fellow German exiles. Finally, in 1971, suspicions were aroused about this German who held Bolivian citizenship. Barbie was reported to Nazi-hunter Simon Wiesenthal. Beate Klarsfeld, another Nazi hunter, actually made the case by identifying "Klaus Altmann" as the notorious "Butcher of Lyon." It was twelve years before Barbie was brought to justice. In 1983, with a new government in place in Bolivia, Barbie was expelled and sent to France. He was sixty-nine years old and in poor health. He kept insisting that what he had done was only his duty.

Back in France

Barbie's return to France for trial caused a sensation. The French were still trying to come to terms with the fact that the Nazis had been aided by thousands of French collaborators, men and women alike. The collaborators had turned their own friends, families, and neighbors over to Nazis. The ailing Barbie was confined to jail for four years before his case came to trial. Showing no signs of remorse, Barbie claimed to have no knowledge of what had happened to the Jews he had rounded up and deported. Witnesses testified that Barbie did know that many were being put to death. A telegram he sent announcing the murder of the children of Izieu was also used as evidence against him. On July 4, 1987, Klaus Barbie was found guilty of crimes against humanity and was sentenced to life in prison. In 1990 he sought to be released from prison because he had cancer of the blood; his request was refused. He died in prison in 1991.

Some have asked whether any point was served in bringing this old, sick man—who said he was only following orders—back to France to stand trial. Many people, including his victims, viewed his trial and subsequent imprisonment as simple justice finally served.

SOURCES

Books

Beattie, John, *The Life and Career of Klaus Barbie: An Eyewitness Record,* Methuen (London), 1984.

Bower, Tom, *Klaus Barbie, the "Butcher of Lyons,"* Pantheon Books (New York), 1984.

Chevrillon, Claire, *Code Name Christiane Clouet: A Woman in the French Resistance,* translated by Jane Kielty Stott, Texas A & M University (College Station, TX), 1995.

Dabringhaus, Erhard, *Klaus Barbie: The Shocking Story of How the U.S. Used This Nazi War Criminal as an Intelligence Agent,* Acropolis Books (Washington, DC), 1984.

de Hoyos, Ladislas, *Klaus Barbie: The Untold Story,* translated from the French by Nicholas Courtin, McGraw-Hill (New York), 1984.

Klarsfeld, Serge, *The Childen of Izieu: A Human Tragedy* translated by Kenneth Jacobson, H. Abrams (New York), 1985.

Linklater, Magnus, Isabel Hilton, and Neal Ascherson, et al, *The Nazi Legacy: Klaus Barbie and the International Fascist Connection,* Holt, Rinehart and Winston (New York), 1984.

Paris, Erna, *Unhealed Wounds: France and the Klaus Barbie Affair,* Methuen (New York), 1985.

Murphy, Brendan, *The Butcher of Lyon: The Story of Infamous Nazi Klaus Barbie,* Empire Books (New York), 1983.

Wilson, Robert, *The Confessions of Klaus Barbie, the Butcher of Lyon* edited by James Osborne, Arsenal Editions (Vancouver, British Columbia, Canada), 1984.

Periodicals

Dowell, William, "A Verdict on the Butcher: After a Final Scuffle with History, Barbie Is Convicted," *Time,* July 13, 1987, p. 40.

Folke Bernadotte

Born January 2, 1895
Stockholm, Sweden
Died September 17, 1948
Jerusalem, Israel

Member of Swedish royal family;
diplomat; negotiated the exchange or
release of an estimated 30,000 prisoners
during World War II

*"The object is to save human life and to try
to [lessen] human suffering and any
means to this end is legitimate."*

(National Archives/USHMM PhotoArchives)

One of the most unlikely and unsung heroes of the Holocaust was Count Folke Bernadotte. His early life gave little indication of the dedication and courage he would later display. As a member of the Swedish royal family and the husband of a woman who was heir to millions of dollars, Bernadotte could have devoted himself to trivial pursuits. Instead, he worked on behalf of war victims; his desire to help others carried on after the war was over. It would be his postwar work that ultimately led to his assassination.

A Modest Upbringing

Bernadotte was born in 1895 in Stockholm, Sweden, one of five children of Prince Oscar and Ebba (Munck) Bernadotte. His father, the son of King Oscar and Queen Sophia, caused a stir when he gave up his claim to the throne to marry the woman he loved, a commoner. Bernadotte's father was a religious man who avoided the trappings of palace life and worked to help Sweden's poor people. About his childhood, Bernadotte once wrote: "My upbringing was strict. I remember that my father often said a child should learn to obey before it reached two years of age. My parents very much insisted on honesty, obedience and punctuality. Already when we were small our thoughts were directed towards trying to help others."

Ralph Hewins, a longtime friend and Bernadotte's biographer, wrote that life in the Bernadotte household was so dull that "the Bernadotte children's friends rather dreaded an invitation" to their home. A lot of time was devoted to attending church services, gathering for family prayers, and studying. Despite the hours spent on his studies, however, Bernadotte was described as a boy "of limited cleverness," not especially bright but enthusiastic and willing, handsome, and unselfish.

His parents took him to England for the summer when he was nine years old. While there he quickly learned to speak English, a skill that proved valuable in his future career. Later he mastered German and French. In the fall after his return from England, Bernadotte was sent to a school where he attended classes with members of Sweden's upper middle class. He excelled at athletics and was a popular student. He enjoyed history and religion classes. Once, when asked his ambition, he declared: "I shall be a Papa." Overall he was an "ordinary small boy" who did not display any particular qualities that one might expect in a future world figure. When he graduated at age eighteen, wrote Hewins, he was "an outdoors boy and not at all 'bookish.'" He was somewhat shy and reserved.

Seeks His Destiny

After graduation, Bernadotte was unsure which career path to follow. In fact, he was well into adulthood before his career came together in a way that would prove satisfying to him. He entered the Royal Swedish Military Academy, where he performed well and graduated tenth in his class in 1915. He became an accomplished horseman, but began to wonder if a military career was right for him. A hemophiliac, Bernadotte could easily bleed to death even if he received only a minor wound in battle. The fact that he had problems giving orders also complicated matters. According to Hewins: "His main trouble was a tendency to see every order from the men's as well as the officers' side."

At age thirty-three, while Bernadotte vacationed in France, he met his bride-to-be, the American heiress Estelle Manville. Estelle's father, Hiram Manville, had made millions in the manufacture of asbestos products. Although Estelle's mother was delighted that her daughter desired marriage to a man with a royal title, her father wished to know more about him. According to author Ted Swarz, Hiram Manville was dismayed to find that "his daughter's beloved had spent his entire adult life in the Swedish Royal Life Guards Dragoons, riding horses and preparing for battles everyone knew would never occur [because Sweden observed a policy of neutrality in European conflicts]. Despite a history that implied great honor, the Royal Life Guards Dragoons was by Bernadotte's time essentially a gentleman's club … a way to claim a career without ever doing meaningful work."

After a lavish wedding in 1928 that cost $250,000, Hiram Manville arranged for his new son-in-law to work for six months as a clerk in a New York bank. Since Bernadotte would one day inherit the Manville millions, Hiram Manville wanted him to learn money management. Bernadotte willingly and enthusiastically accepted the job, but he simply could not master it. The Bernadottes, who by then were expecting their first child, decided to move to Sweden.

Becomes Diplomat

Between 1929 and 1936, the Bernadottes had four sons. Both parents were devoted to their family and were devastated by the tragic and unexpected deaths of two of the young boys. Bernadotte resigned from the Swedish Army and began to devote time to the Swedish Boy Scouts. In 1939 he was made head of the Swedish Scout Union of the Boy Scout Association.

Meanwhile, in 1933, Bernadotte was asked to travel to Chicago, Illinois, to represent Sweden at a huge festival being organized by Americans of Swedish ancestry who resided there. While in the United States, Bernadotte also visited several cities with large Swedish populations. His tour was a great success, and the newspapers were full of stories about his charming personality. Over the next several years, he tried several business ventures and failed, but when asked to perform roles requiring diplomacy, he showed exceptional skill. Meanwhile, Europe was gearing up for war, but Bernadotte was largely unaware of it.

War in Europe

World War II began in Europe in 1939 when the Nazis invaded Poland. Bernadotte was once again in the United States, this time working on the Swedish Exhibit at the New York World's Fair. At this time, the Soviet Union—long an enemy of Sweden—launched a surprise attack against neighboring Finland. Bernadotte was torn. "[I]t was my

The Red Cross and the Holocaust

An international organization devoted to relieving human suffering, the Red Cross takes its name from its flag (a red cross on a white background), which is patterned after the flag of Switzerland (a white cross on a red background), where the Red Cross was founded in 1863.

A major relief agency today, the Red Cross has volunteers and staff members at branches in more than 135 countries who carry out tasks according to each country's needs. The Red Cross has prevented untold misery throughout the world during times of war, peace, and natural disasters. During World War II, members of the International Committee of the Red Cross, including Count Folke Bernadotte, worked as go-betweens for the protection of prisoners and victims of war. Despite the activities of Bernadotte and others,

however, the International Committee finally acknowledged that the organization had not done enough to help the victims of the Holocaust, who included approximately 6 million Jews.

In 1997 the International Committee of the Red Cross admitted "moral failure" because it had been too silent. A spokesperson for the committee, which is based in Geneva, Switzerland, indicated that the organization could and should have done more.

The Red Cross had an opportunity to save Jewish lives as early as 1940. Yet the opportunity was missed when the International Committee concluded (on the basis of a German report) that tales of the mass murder of Polish-Jewish prisoners of war were unfounded. The Red Cross was also responsible for providing travel papers to Nazi criminals such as Josef Mengele, who was responsible for hundreds of thousands of deaths at Auschwitz. Mengele escaped to South America after the war.

---

duty as a soldier to be home in Sweden in case my country should become drawn into war," Bernadotte recalled. On the other hand, he still had to run the Swedish Exhibit. He received a telegram from Swedish leaders asking him to remain in the United States to enlist a group of Scandinavian-American volunteers to help Finland.

The U.S. government was unwilling to permit Bernadotte to train an army to serve in another country. Before Bernadotte's plans progressed far, Finland made peace with the Soviet Union. However, Sweden was now faced with a different problem—Germany. The Germans swept into Norway and Denmark; Sweden was almost entirely surrounded by Germans. Sweden hoped to remain uninvolved in the conflict, but its leaders initially felt inclined to offer some assistance. Sweden had a long-standing history of good relations with Germany. As the war dragged on, and news spread of German mistreatment of Scandinavian prisoners, Jews, and others, Sweden's attitude changed. Stories circulated

of prisoners confined in concentration camps, where they were forced to labor long hours under crowded, unsanitary conditions, with little food.

Bernadotte's War Work

Bernadotte's life and career entered a new phase after the war began. He was placed in charge of a group that cared for airplane pilots and other military personnel seeking refuge in neutral Sweden—regardless of what side they represented. He arranged for medical treatment, food, clothing, and even entertainment. According to Hewins, between 1940 and 1945, Bernadotte's organization showed 40,000 movies to 6 million military moviegoers and arranged theatrical performances for 2 million servicemen and women. He proved to be such an organizational genius that his wartime responsibilities increased.

In 1943 Bernadotte was named vice-chairman of the Swedish Red Cross, becoming president in

Bernadotte negotiated on behalf of the Swedish Red Cross. (Yad Vashem Photo Archives/USHMM Photo Archives)

1946. By then the extent of German brutality—and the Nazis' ambition to control Europe—were becoming widely known. If Sweden was overtaken by the Germans, Red Cross assistance would be vital. Bernadotte also saw a role for the Red Cross assisting war victims in neighboring countries.

One of Bernadotte's initial accomplishments as a representative of the Red Cross was to oversee the first successful exchange of prisoners between Germany and Great Britain. Some had endured as many as four years of imprisonment by the Germans. More than 5,000 British invalids and others landed on Britain's shores in an emotional homecoming witnessed by thousands. "I never had a task which interested me more than this," wrote Bernadotte.

In 1945, with Germany under constant siege by Allied bombers, Bernadotte went to Berlin, Germany's capital. He persuaded Nazi official Heinrich Himmler to release more than 7,000 Scandinavians being held in concentration camps. Among them were more than 400 Danish Jews. Shortly afterward, Bernadotte arranged for the release of 10,000 women, including 2,000 Jews, being held in the Ravensbrück concentration camp. They were taken to Sweden. At Bernadotte's request their rescue was not publicized for fear

that the news would endanger other rescue efforts if Hitler learned of it. According to biographer Hewins: "Bernadotte and the Swedish Red Cross [never got] deserved credit for the magnitude of their achievement at Ravensbrück. One only had to stare at the ... living corpses as they were carried on to the Swedish hospital trains to realize the hell on earth from which Bernadotte ... had saved them at the last flickering moment between life and death."

Bernadotte has been credited with helping to save approximately 32,200 concentration camp victims and prisoners of war, at risk to his own life. Hewins wrote: "Among the saved were people from thirty different nations—including one Chinese—and blessed was the name of Bernadotte the whole world round."

A Death in Jerusalem

Having earned a worldwide reputation, Bernadotte continued his efforts on behalf of peace after the war. In 1948 the United Nations, newly formed to help resolve international disputes, chose Bernadotte to go to the then-new Jewish nation of Israel and help mediate a dispute between Israel and its neighboring Arab countries. While traveling in a car flying the United Nations flag in Israel, Bernadotte was assassinated by members of a Jewish terrorist organization. He was fifty-three years old. Bernadotte's assassins were never brought to justice, so their motives remain undisclosed. Some historians speculate that the assassins believed that Bernadotte was urging Israel to accept unfair compromises.

Bernadotte's body was returned to Stockholm, Sweden. At the funeral, his casket was carried by forty-eight Boy Scouts; the procession included 2,500 more Boy Scouts. Floral tributes came from around the world, many from people he had rescued from concentration camps. A hero in his own time, Bernadotte made contributions that are often forgotten today.

SOURCES

Books

Hewins, Ralph, *Count Folke Bernadotte: His Life and Work,* Hutchinson (New York), 1950.

Marton, Kati, *A Death in Jerusalem,* Arcade (New York), 1996.

Schwarz, Ted, *Walking with the Damned: The Shocking Murder of the Man Who Freed 30,000 Prisoners from the Nazis,* Paragon House (New York), 1992.

Bruno Bettelheim

Bruno Bettelheim survived nearly a year in Nazi concentration camps where he was confined with other people regarded as "enemies of the state" by the Nazis. Following his ordeal, he relocated to the United States and became a world-famous authority on the treatment of emotionally disturbed children. His death provoked a storm of controversy about his beliefs and practices that makes it difficult to untangle the truth about the man and his teachings.

Childhood in Vienna

Bettelheim was raised in a non-religious Jewish family in Vienna, Austria, at the beginning of the twentieth century. His father, Anton Bettelheim, was a lumber merchant who came from a wealthy family. His mother was Pauline Seidler, who had wed Anton in an arranged marriage. In addition to Bettelheim, the couple had a daughter, Margarethe, who was four years older than their son. The siblings shared a longstanding rivalry. Although he was cared for by nannies and maids on occasion, young Bettelheim also spent a lot of time with his mother, who enjoyed telling him fairy tales. Bettelheim later recalled that his parents were kind and gentle with him, and he appreciated having the emotional support of his family.

Bettelheim was a short, sensitive boy who liked to daydream. As a child, he suffered from a number

Born August 28, 1903
 Vienna, Austria
Died March 13, 1990
 Silver Spring, Maryland, United States

Psychotherapist; author; concentration camp survivor; head of Orthogenic School in Chicago, Illinois

"*Being one of the very few who were saved when millions like oneself perished [entails] a special obligation to justify one's luck and very existence.*"

(Reproduced by permission of AP/Wide World Photos)

of illnesses, including measles, mumps, scarlet fever, diphtheria, and intestinal disorders. A good student, he did not excel at sports, in part because the lenses of his glasses were improperly made. Bettelheim was four when his father was diagnosed with an incurable disease. The challenges the family encountered due to this illness intensified after his father had a stroke nine years later. Bettelheim himself suffered from depression throughout his life.

Bettelheim entered high school in 1914. Along with friends, he joined a group that spent much of its time hiking and picnicking in nearby forests and discussing the future. He graduated near the top of his class and decided to further his education by pursuing a college degree in philosophy.

Forced to Leave College

During his first years at Vienna University, Bettelheim became interested in psychoanalysis—a system of examining a person's emotional state that was pioneered by Sigmund Freud. Bettelheim also studied Latin, German literature, music, philosophy, and dramatic readings. At the same time, he enrolled in an international trade school to learn accounting and business management. His grades at both schools were excellent.

In 1926 Bettelheim's father experienced a slow, painful death. For the final two years of Anton's life, Bettelheim and his mother were his primary caregivers. Upon his father's death, Bettelheim was forced to stop his studies at the university and take over the family lumber business.

First Marriage

Bettelheim fell in love with Gina Alstadt, who also suffered from depression. In 1920s Vienna, many young people were optimistic about a future they believed would see the development of a society built upon the equality of individuals. However, unlike his friends, Bettelheim viewed what lay ahead for the world with a sense of dread. Bettelheim married Alstadt on March 30, 1930, and they moved into an apartment in Vienna. Although the couple shared similar interests, the marriage was often troubled.

Bettelheim's lumber business prospered, and he expanded it to include furniture manufacturing. In the late 1920s, Gina Bettelheim and a friend opened a kindergarten to serve the children of the many Americans who had come to Vienna to study psychoanalysis. Around 1932 they opened a summer camp for children with behavioral problems. Eventually, a young patient named Patsy Crane moved in with the Bettelheims. Her mother, Agnes, believed the couple could help Patsy with her emotional problems. She was unaware of the strain already evident in the Bettelheim marriage. In 1936 Bettelheim met a young Swiss woman named Trude Weinfeld, who listened carefully to his ideas, even encouraging him to return to the university to earn a Ph.D. He grew increasingly fond of her. That same year, Gina Bettelheim met a successful young dentist and gradually fell in love with him.

Arrested By Nazis

In the spring of 1937, Bettelheim returned to Vienna University to study philosophy and psychology, while continuing his work as a lumber merchant. Bettelheim received his Ph.D. in February 1938. While Bettelheim was pursuing his studies, Adolf Hitler and the Nazi party were preparing for war. They had come to power in Germany on a platform that included hatred toward Jews. In March of 1938, Hitler, facing no armed opposition, took over Austria in an event known as the *Anschluss*. With the anti-Semitic Nazis in Austria, the Bettelheims feared for their safety. Gina fled to the United States with little Patsy. Bettelheim remained in Vienna because he felt he could not abandon his mother and sister. Soon full-scale persecution of the Jews began. Jewish people were seized by the police and attacked, and their shops were looted. Bettelheim's car was confiscated by the Nazis. He tried unsuccessfully to obtain a visa to go to the United States.

In May 1938 Bettelheim was twice arrested and released by the Nazis. In June, along with thousands of other so-called "enemies of the state," he was arrested a third time and deported to the Dachau concentration camp in Germany. Transported by train to the camps, the Jews were struck, punched, and kicked by the Nazis. Suffering from a head wound, Bettelheim was taken to a clinic by a sympathetic guard and allowed to stay for a week to recover.

Upon Bettelheim's release from the clinic, his hair was cut short, and he was placed in a crowded, wooden barrack. The inmates worked long hours digging gravel pits and building roads, while being verbally abused by the guards. Prisoners were mercilessly whipped and hung up on trees by their shoulders for small infractions of the rules. Dreadful though it was, conditions at Dachau were not as bad as at some of the other camps. Although the food was crude and bad tasting, it was enough to sustain a person's health. Occasionally, sporting matches and concerts were put on by the prisoners. They could also receive small amounts of money sent by friends or family outside the camp.

Back in Vienna, Bettelheim's company was closed on July 7, 1938, but was reopened one week later with a new Nazi owner. Such business takeovers occurred all over Austria at the time. Bettelheim received a paltry sum in exchange for his prosperous business. With the support of Agnes Crane (Patsy's mother), the U.S. government approved a visa application on Bettelheim's behalf, which was to be issued immediately upon his release from Dachau.

Deportation to Buchenwald

In September 1938 Bettelheim and other prisoners were taken on a cramped train to the Buchenwald concentration camp. With filthy trenches for toilets, the camp was much worse than the one at Dachau, and even more violent. Bettelheim wrote that he was assigned a job indoors mending stockings, where he stayed relatively safe and warm. His version of his experiences at the camp cannot be verified, however, because he failed to name fellow prisoners in his writings who could later be interviewed.

In fact, any attempt to write a complete and accurate biography about Bettelheim is made more challenging by the fact that he sometimes embellished the truth. Some co-workers from his past have even referred to him as a liar. Most accounts support the notion that he liked to describe events in the form of stories, and often the tales were exaggerated in order to make them more interesting or to make him look better.

Release and Relocation

In 1939 the contagious disease typhus, caused by unsanitary conditions, had become a major problem in the concentration camps. To decrease the incidence of typhus, Hitler reduced the number of prisoners at Buchenwald by ordering the release of some—including Bettelheim. He was warned that if he did not leave Germany within one week, he would be re-arrested. Bettelheim

Bettelheim's Thoughts on Concentration Camps

Throughout his lifetime Bettelheim gave a great deal of time and thought to life in the concentration camps. Writer Nina Sutton explained the three stages Bettelheim experienced when internalizing the reality of his situation. First, there was a positive stage in which he strove to derive lessons from his experience. Second, there was a stage in which he acknowledged the guilt he felt in being a survivor. He described this as "the morally unacceptable feeling of happiness" that wells up when one discovers it is not he who will die, but the next man. Finally, there was the stage of despair caused by the world's silence in the face of the Nazis' persecution.

traveled to Antwerp, Belgium, where he boarded the S.S. *Gerolsein* for the United States.

After arriving in the United States, Bettelheim moved to Chicago, Illinois, where he became a research assistant at the University of Chicago. After a short visit, both he and his wife concluded that their marriage was at an end. Within the year his mother, his sister, and Trude Weinfeld joined Bettelheim in the United States. In May 1941 Bettelheim was divorced from Gina and married Trude Weinfeld. Later, Gina also remarried.

The Beginning of Fame

Bettelheim obtained a teaching job at Rockford College, ninety miles from Chicago, to which he commuted for several years. Trude gave birth to the couple's first child, Ruth, in 1942. They later had another daughter, Naomi, and a son, Eric. In 1943 Bettelheim wrote a famous article titled "Individual and Mass Behavior in Extreme Situations" that won him acclaim in academic circles. The article used his experiences in concentration camps to examine how human beings adapt to stress.

Bettelheim giving a speech on emotionally disturbed children. (Library of Congress)

In 1944 Bettelheim became both assistant professor of psychology at the University of Chicago and head of its Sonia Shankman Orthogenic School. The latter was a residential treatment center for emotionally disturbed children age six to fourteen. Bettelheim specialized in the treatment of autistic children. Such children have withdrawn from everyday life and fail to respond normally to outside stimulation. Bettelheim once said that his dedication to the school resulted from his experience in the concentration camps, and his anger at the prospect that lives should be wasted "whether trapped behind metal or emotional barbed wire." He became an associate professor at the university in 1947 and was appointed a full professor in 1952.

The staff he headed at the Orthogenic School was said to idealize and, sometimes, fear him. Largely composed of young women, the staff seemed to have blind trust in Bettelheim's authority and what they saw as his genius. Many have reported that Bettelheim was very understanding, but at times could be cruel and bullying.

A Prolific Writer

During his lifetime Bettelheim wrote nearly twenty books. Some of the best-known are *Love Is Not Enough, The Children of the Dream, The Uses of* *Enchantment, The Informed Heart,* and *A Good Enough Parent.* He became widely respected as one of the foremost authorities on the treatment of autistic children. Bettelheim believed that a major cause of a child's autism was having a "deficient" mother and that the best treatment was the removal of the child from the family. He wrote extensively about the relationship between social health and family life, as well as countless articles that were published in popular magazines.

Critics of Bettelheim

Bettelheim's ideas were opposed by people who contend that some mothers of autistic children have raised a number of perfectly normal kids. Some suggest that autism may have a genetic component. Bettelheim developed a reputation for sometimes treating the parents of his young patients in a disrespectful manner. Biographers note that he was said to view the parents of autistic children as the source of the problem and himself as the children's defender.

Richard Pollak, whose younger brother spent years in treatment with Bettelheim, wrote a critical book about him in 1997 called *The Creation of Dr. B.* According to Pollak, Bettelheim's power to terrorize those under him and his talent for telling stories contributed to his international success. Pollak contended that Bettelheim made false claims about his training in Vienna, which made him appear to be a legitimate expert in psychoanalysis, when in fact he was not.

According to critic Lev Raphael: "Bettelheim also falsified the success rate of patients at his Orthogenic School in Chicago ... [where he treated] children ... who weren't severely disturbed, while making exaggerated claims of their illness." Writer Christopher Lehmann-Haupt observed that "despite [Bettelheim's] insistence that hitting the children was strictly forbidden, he evidently smacked and punched his charges, sexually abused several of the girls, and relied in general on threats to intimidate his staff."

In Bettelheim's defense, writer Nina Sutton pointed out that in dealing with disturbed children, Bettelheim's aim was to "get them gradually to understand ... that even the most miserable of lives ... is valuable as soon as one succeeds in giving it meaning. This is what ... being cured meant for him: finally to acknowledge the value of one's own life." And, said Sutton, "He saved my life" is the statement that occurred most often in the testimonies of the former students and counselors she spoke to about Bettelheim.

Old Age and Death

Bettelheim retired from the Orthogenic School in the early 1970s, continued writing books about his experiences at the school, and taught occasional classes. He took several trips to Europe and to Israel. He and his wife moved to California in 1973. His connection to the Orthogenic School was cut off when he had a disagreement with the new director in the early 1980s. In May 1986 the University of Chicago held a conference honoring him and his work. Bettelheim became seriously depressed after the death of his wife from cancer in 1984. This, coupled with his own ailments, proved to be too much for him. He committed suicide in 1990 at his home in Silver Spring, Maryland. Years after his death, the controversy about the man and his methods still continues.

SOURCES

Books

Bettelheim, Bruno, *The Informed Heart: Autonomy in a Mass Age,* Free Press (Glencoe, IL), 1960.

Bettelheim, Bruno, *Love Is Not Enough: The Treatment of Emotionally Disturbed Children,* Free Press (Glencoe, IL), 1950.

Bettelheim, Bruno, *Surviving and Other Essays,* Vintage Books (New York), 1980.

Feig, Konnilyn G., *Hitler's Death Camps: The Sanity of Madness,* Holmes & Meier (New York), 1979.

Pollak, Richard, *The Creation of Dr. B: A Biography of Bruno Bettelheim,* Simon & Schuster (New York), 1996.

Sutton, Nina, *Bettelheim: A Life and a Legacy,* Basic Books (New York), 1996.

Periodicals

Bandler, Michael J., "The Good Enough Parent's Parent," *Parents',* November 1987, p. 189.

Bettelheim, Bruno, "Individual and Mass Behavior in Extreme Situations," *Journal of Abnormal and Social Psychology,* October 1943, pp. 417–452.

Dietrich Bonhoeffer

Born February 4, 1906
Breslau, Germany
Died April 9, 1945
Flossenbürg concentration camp

German Protestant minister and writer;
participated in an assassination plot
against Hitler

*"In the long run, human relationships are
the most important thing in life."*

(Reproduced by permission of Archive Photos, Inc.)

A powerful religious leader who courageously acted according to his conscience, Dietrich Bonhoeffer became
famous after his death. Once he recognized the evils of the government headed by Adolf
Hitler and the Nazi party, Bonhoeffer dedicated
himself to the struggle to overthrow the Nazi government. Throughout World War II, he engaged in
several unsuccessful attempts to assassinate Hitler.

Childhood and Youth

Dietrich Bonhoeffer was the son of prominent
German parents; his German lineage can be traced
back to the fifteenth century. His father was a
respected professor, and his mother was a homemaker who influenced her children to become vir-
tuous and idealistic. Bonhoeffer and his twin sister,
Sabine, were born in 1906—the sixth and seventh
of eight children. The family lived in a spacious and
comfortable house in Breslau, Germany, with two
servants and a nanny for the children. Summers
were spent at a house in the Harz Mountains where
the children played among the hills and forests.

When Bonhoeffer was six years old, his family
moved to Berlin, Germany, and his father began
teaching at Berlin University. Bonhoeffer began to
attend school at age seven, and by the age of ten he
had begun to read classic German literature. In his
teens, he played music with friends, organized par-

ties, and wrote plays. He considered becoming a professional musician but thought the late-night schedule of travel and performing would not suit him. His brother Walter was killed in 1918 during World War I. This incident made Bonhoeffer think a great deal about the meaning of death, and he and his sister had long discussions about it.

At age fourteen, Bonhoeffer considered becoming a Protestant minister. His sister Sabine later wrote that he had an "open and considerate nature." She said that Bonhoeffer had "the gift of perfect assurance of manners; he listened attentively and attached great value to dealing politely with other people and keeping a certain distance … from respect of the other's personality on which he did not want to [intrude]."

Embraces the Ministry

Bonhoeffer's family experienced many food shortages, as did many Germans after World War I. The aftermath of the war wreaked havoc on the German economy. By 1923 inflation had become so serious that people had to carry bags full of paper money to purchase a loaf of bread. That year, Bonhoeffer began his religious studies at the University of Tubingen. He was then a powerful-looking young man, over six feet tall, with blond hair and intense blue eyes. Writer Mary Bosanquet described Bonhoeffer as a man with great energy, a quick mind, and robust health. He was also a very sensitive person.

In the 1920s in Germany, it was customary for students to attend more than one university to gain experience. Excelling at his studies, Bonhoeffer was able to attend several schools with great success. He completed his studies and earned the equivalent of a doctoral degree from Berlin University in 1927 at age twenty-one. He studied German liberal theology, and later became attracted to the teachings of famed German religious scholar Karl Barth. Bonhoeffer spent 1928 serving a small congregation in Barcelona, Spain. In 1930, he traveled to the United States where he studied at the Union Theological Seminary in New York as an exchange student.

Bonhoeffer was appointed as lecturer at Berlin University and was made chaplain at the Technical College in Berlin in 1930. His income at the university depended entirely upon his ability to attract students to attend his classes voluntarily. He was ordained a minister in November 1931. According to Mary Bosanquet: "A remarkable feature of Bonhoeffer's life at every stage was the amount that he contrived to pack into his days…. He contrived to live the broad and rich life which humanists admire with what was little more than the overflow from his deeper spiritual energies."

The Rise of Nazism

While Bonhoeffer pursued the ministry, Adolf Hitler and his Nazis were rising to power in Germany. The country's defeat in World War I paved the way for the Third Reich to emerge. Since Germany's defeat in the war, unemployment in the country was very high, inflation soared, and the economy was in great turmoil. The streets were filled with the angry, hungry, and poor, and bloody street battles were a common occurrence. German citizens were looking for a way out of their dire situation. Dozens of new political parties arose at that time, all promising solutions to Germany's many problems. The Nazi party was one of the groups guaranteeing that it could bring change. Nazi leader Adolf Hitler was a hypnotic speaker who talked of returning Germany to economic stability and prosperity. He blamed the Jews not only for the German loss in World War I, but also for the economic strife plaguing Germany. Hitler demanded that Germany be allowed to return to a position of strength in the world. He preached the superiority of the Aryan race. For many of those who qualified as Aryans, Hitler's message was one they were eager to hear.

When a punishing, world-wide depression began in the late 1920s, Hitler took advantage of the desperation felt by many people. He used clever tactics and charismatic speaking skills to convince people to get behind the Nazi Party. Hitler became dictator of Germany after the 1933 election through a series of carefully calculated tactics. His grand scheme for building a mighty German empire required that the Nazis take control of every aspect in peoples' lives. One way he planned to accomplish this was to use the German Protestant church. He wanted to enlist people in his cause in such a way that they would believe the church was behind him. Thus began the "Faith Movement" in Germany.

Bonhoeffer Rejects Nazism

Bonhoeffer was concerned about the growth of Hitler's "Faith Movement." It held that every nation should develop its own form of the Christ-

Bonhoeffer (fourth from the left) and the leaders of the Confessing Church. (Reproduced by permission of Bildarchiv Preussischer Kulturbesitz)

ian faith, rooted in the "soil of the country and the blood of its people." Leaders of the pro-Nazi faith movement in Germany believed that God wanted the German people to unite under a powerful leader, namely Adolf Hitler. They said people should devote their energies toward the common good of the nation, and to keep the Aryan race free from so-called "tainted alien" blood.

Bonhoeffer opposed such teachings. He denounced the theory that membership in a church can ever be based on race. In a sermon rejecting these ideas, Bonhoeffer said: "God shall rule over you, and you shall have no other Lord." As a result of his opposition to Nazi church policies, Bonhoeffer was sent to London, England, from 1933 through 1935, where he served as a chaplain. He later returned to Germany, where he became a member of the anti-Nazi Confessing Church. He then went to Pomerania in Germany to lead a new seminary for like-minded young men.

Bonhoeffer's seminary was suppressed by the Nazis in 1937. They objected to the seminary's refusal to support their policies of violence and racial oppression. In fact, the Nazis rejected every aspect of traditional Christianity, partly because it interfered with the German people giving complete allegiance to Hitler, whom the Nazis revered in god-like fashion. Bonhoeffer continued teaching anyway. However, his stance caused him to lose the right to teach at a university, speak in public, and publish his opinions.

Recruitment for Espionage

German Admiral Wilhelm Canaris, leader of the Nazis' intelligence service, was secretly opposed to Hitler's policies and plotted with others to oust Hitler from power. The admiral requested that Bonhoeffer visit clerics he knew in other countries. Although the official purpose was for Bonhoeffer to gather information for the Nazis, Canaris actually wanted him to have secret conversations with religious leaders to enlist their help in overthrowing Hitler and the Nazis. Bonhoeffer made trips to Sweden and Switzerland to try to accomplish these aims.

In 1942 he brought plans to the British Bishop George Bell, known as the patron of the oppressed Christians and Jews in Germany. The plans concerned possible terms of peace that would be enacted if the group was successful in overthrowing the Nazis and Hitler. Bonhoeffer was later asked how he, as a Christian and religious scholar, could take part in the resistance against Hitler. Bonhoeffer replied that if he, as a minister, witnessed a drunk driver speeding down the highway, his main responsibility would not be to bury the victims of the drunken driver or comfort the family. Rather, his chief duty was to wrench the steering wheel out of the hands of the driver.

Arrest and Imprisonment

Bonhoeffer was arrested in 1943 and sent to prison where he awaited trial. His arrest warrant charged him with "destruction of fighting power." In addition to a history of preaching against the Nazis' anti-Semitic policies, he was jailed for his role in assisting Jews to escape from Germany. Various members of his family were also involved in these efforts. They were also imprisoned and eventually executed. Shortly before being sent to jail, Bonhoeffer had became engaged to Maria von Wedemeyer. His fiancée's mother publicly announced their engagement on the day of his arrest. Bonhoeffer and von Wedemeyer communicated by letter and occasionally saw one another during his two-year imprisonment. Bonhoeffer underwent months of interrogation about his trips throughout Europe, his professional duties as a pastor, and his loyalty to the Third Reich. For a while, Bonhoeffer was able to provide clever answers and avoid incriminating himself and others about many matters. However, he was eventually condemned to death when his role in the anti-Nazi plot was uncovered.

Character and Convictions

Bonhoeffer spent time at several prisons and prison camps, including Buchenwald, Regensburg, and Flossenbürg. He was always able to establish good relationships with many of the guards. Fellow prisoner Fabian Von Schlanbrendorff wrote that Bonhoeffer treated everyone with kindness and politeness, which often meant he won over the guards who were often cruel to other prisoners. While in prison Bonhoeffer wrote many letters to various friends and family members discussing his experiences in confinement and his thoughts

Admiral Wilhelm Canaris was one of the men who plotted to assassinate Hitler in 1944. (Reproduced by permission of © Hulton Getty/Liaison Agency)

about various religious and political matters. These writings were later published and read worldwide; they serve as an inspiration to other ministers. The English edition is called *Letters and Papers from Prison*.

British Captain Payne Best, who was captured on the borders of Holland in 1940, was confined in the same prison as Bonhoeffer. He wrote to Sabine in 1951 about the final days of Bonhoeffer's life. "[Dietrich]," he observed, "was different; just quite calm and normal, seemingly perfectly at his ease … his soul really shone in the dark desperation of our prison." Bonhoeffer had much time to consider the great questions in life while he was imprisoned. Concerning his detention behind bars, Bonhoeffer once wrote: "If I were to end my life here, in these conditions, that would have a meaning that I think I could understand."

Execution and Legacy

On April 9, 1945, Bonhoeffer was executed by hanging along with others who had participated in efforts to assassinate Hitler. A prison doctor described what happened: "On the morning of the day … between five and six o'clock, the prisoners … were led out of their cells and the verdicts read

Memorials to a French Hero

During the Nazis' systematic persecution and murder of millions of Jews and other innocent people, few Jews were rescued in Nazi-occupied Europe. This occurred due to anti-Jewish sentiment, indifference, and fear on the part of those who might have rescued them. However, among those who did take the risk to help the Jews were some Christian members of the clergy, like Father Jacques de Jesus.

Born in France in 1900, Father Jacques, named Lucien Bunuel at birth, joined a Roman Catholic religious order. During World War II, Father Jacques was head of a boys' school in Avon, France. He turned the school into a covert refuge for Jews and for young men who wanted to avoid becoming forced laborers for the Nazis.

In January 1943 Father Jacques enrolled three Jewish boys in the school under false names to protect them from the Nazis. He also hid a fourth Jewish boy, claiming the boy was the school custodian. In addition, he found shelter for that boy's father with a local family. He rescued a prominent Jewish scientist by appointing him to the school's faculty.

When the Gestapo discovered Father Jacques's actions, they arrested him, his mother and sister, the three students he had sheltered, and the scientist. All those captured were sent to concentration camps; only Father Jacques survived the experience. Father Jacques was imprisoned in several Nazi concentration camps before being liberated by American troops in May 1945. His liberators found him as a sickly man, weighing a mere seventy-five pounds. Father Jacques died a few weeks later.

In 1985 Father Jacques was memorialized at Yad Vashem, the Martyrs' and Heroes' Remembrance Authority in Jerusalem, Israel. His story was recounted in a 1987 French film directed by Louis Malle. The film, *Au Revoir les Enfants,* was Malle's tribute to his former headmaster.

---

to them. Through the half-open door of a room in one of the huts I saw Pastor Bonhoeffer, still in prison clothes, kneeling in fervent prayer to the Lord his God. The devotion and evident conviction of being heard [by God] that I saw in the prayer of this intensely captivating man, moved me to the depths." Just three weeks after Bonhoeffer's death, Hitler committed suicide, knowing that the war was lost. One week later, Germany surrendered to the Allies. The war in Europe came to an end, although the war in the Pacific continued for several more months. The victims of the Nazis were freed.

Letters and Papers from Prison, Bonhoeffer's most widely read work, was first published in German in 1951 and later published in English. The book examined the problems that faced Christians in the twentieth century. Bonhoeffer's other books were *The Cost of Discipleship,* written in 1937 and published in English in 1947, and *The Community of Saints,* which was written in 1929 and published in English in 1963. Throughout his life, Bonhoeffer was an ethical individual who was passionately opposed to violence. However, when he believed that there was no other recourse to stopping the evil of the Nazis, he was prepared to do what needed to be done to stop it. This young religious scholar, who showed so much promise, became famous after his death and continues to inspire succeeding generations.

SOURCES

Books

Bethge, Eberhard, *Dietrich Bonhoeffer,* Harper and Row (New York), 1977.

Bonhoeffer, Dietrich, *Letters and Papers from Prison,* translated from German by Reginald Fuller and revised by Franke Clarke and others, SCM Press (London), 1967.

Bosanquet, Mary, *The Life and Death of Dietrich Bonhoeffer,* Harper & Row (New York), 1969.

Goddard, Donald, *The Last Days of Dietrich Bonhoeffer,* Harper & Row (New York), 1976.

Leibholz, Sabine, *The Bonhoeffers,* Sidgwick and Jackson (London), 1971.

Robertson, Edwin Hanton, *The Shame and the Sacrifice: The Life and Martyrdom of Dietrich Bonhoeffer,* Macmillan (New York), 1988.

Wind, Renate, *Dietrich Bonhoeffer: A Spoke in the Wheel,* translated by John Bowden, Eerdmans (Grand Rapids, MI), 1992.

Zimmerman, Wolf-Dieter, and Ronald Gregor Smith, *I Knew Dietrich Bonhoeffer,* translated by Käthe Gregor Smith, Harper & Row (New York), 1967.

Martin Bormann

Born June 17, 1900
Halberstadt, Germany
Died May 2, 1945?
Berlin, Germany

German Nazi Party secretary; last
right-hand man of German
dictator Adolf Hitler

*"[Hitler] towers over us like Mount Everest
… [he is] the greatest human being we
know of … his poise in the face of fantastic
difficulties is marvelous; and so indeed is
everything else about him.…"*

Martin Bormann's contemporaries described him as an unlikable man, completely without moral sense. He was one of the major planners of the "Final Solution"—the Nazi plan calling for the total elimination of all European Jews. By the end of World War II in 1945, Bormann had become second only to Nazi leader Adolf Hitler in the power he wielded. As Hitler's aide, Bormann worked in secret, so the extent of his power was virtually unknown outside the Nazi inner circle. Hitler trusted him completely, but Bormann was feared and hated by most others who knew him. Bormann's disappearance after the war remains the biggest unsolved mystery in the brutal reign of the Nazis.

Youthful Pursuits

Bormann was born in 1900 in Halberstadt, an old and picturesque town in Germany. His father, Theodor, had played the trumpet in a military band before retiring from the army and taking a job as a postal clerk. Theodor died when Bormann was only four years old. Soon after, his mother married a bank director, and Bormann was brought up in a comfortable, middle-class home. World War I began in Europe in 1914, when Bormann was only fourteen. In June 1918, as soon as he was old enough, Bormann interrupted his studies at an agricultural trade school to join the army.

That was the end of his formal education. The war ended later the same year without Bormann seeing any combat, and he left the army in 1920.

Bormann took a position as the manager of a large farm. Like many other ex-soldiers, he was unhappy with conditions in Germany after the war. The German economy was in shambles and unemployment was exceedingly high. The Treaty of Versailles that ended the war imposed many unpopular conditions on Germany. One of the conditions called for the German army to be disbanded. Many Germans felt humiliated and looked for a scapegoat. Some blamed their problems on the Jews. Sharing in this frustration, Bormann joined an anti-Jewish organization. He also joined a group, run by a man named Rossbach, that promoted the overthrow of the German government and the reestablishment of Germany as a great power. Bormann became the treasurer of the Rossbach organization. By this time Bormann was twenty-three years old. He had brown eyes and brown hair and stood about five-feet seven-inches tall. According to writer James McGovern, Bormann was endowed with "a powerful build and a short thick neck from which derived his nickname, 'The Bull.'" Known as a hard worker, he was also good with figures. Bormann was soon able to demonstrate his utter ruthlessness when it came to protecting his position.

Ready to Kill

In 1923 another member of the Rossbach organization made the mistake of "borrowing" some money from the organization's treasury. The thief was already under suspicion as a spy. Bormann, Rudolf Hess, and a few other men took the hapless burglar to a forest, beat him, cut his throat, fired two bullets into his head, and buried him. Bormann was sentenced to a year in prison for the crime. Although his precise role in the murder was never fully determined, Bormann was suspected of being the instigator of the crime and the man who provided the car. This detached involvement became his typical mode of operation; he was always manipulating behind the scenes.

While Bormann sat in prison, Hitler was building the Nazi Party into a major political force. The head Nazi attracted large crowds that listened with enthusiasm to his hate-filled, anti-Semitic speeches. He shouted accusations against the Jews, blaming them for the loss of World War I and charging them with holding Germany back from becoming a world power. His followers sometimes attacked and humiliated innocent Jews in the streets.

Bormann joined the Nazi Party after his release from prison. He quickly rose through the ranks. In 1933 he again teamed with Rudolf Hess, who became deputy führer. Bormann worked as chief of the cabinet in Hess's office and proved himself to be very efficient. Some considered him to be a model secretary. He never sought glory or titles. Although he has since been described as coarse, brutal, and lacking in culture, Bormann appeared to have an unassuming nature. This demeanor masked Bormann's slow and gradual rise in Hitler's esteem. At first, this went unnoticed by other Nazi Party officials.

Becomes Hitler's Loyal Comrade

Bormann's dedication to the Nazi Party and its ideologies also marked his personal life. In 1929 Bormann married Gerda Buch, the daughter of a high-ranking Nazi official of Aryan blood. Gerda was noted for her hatred of religion in any form. The couple eventually had ten children; the first was named Adolf in honor of the führer. Gerda raised her children to believe that Jews were evil. Nazi officers like Bormann were also encouraged to impregnate German girls of Aryan blood to populate the new empire that Hitler dreamed of creating. Some girls were willing to do this to help Hitler's cause. Gerda supported Bormann's activities in this regard.

As the Nazi Party worked toward its goal of building a powerful nation without Jews throughout the 1930s, violence against German Jews escalated. Thousands were imprisoned for no reason other than their Jewish heritage. Laws were passed denying German Jews all legal rights. Vast numbers of Jews fled the country, only to be turned away by the anti-Jewish governments of Germany's neighbors. Meanwhile, Hitler had built up the German army, in violation of the Treaty of Versailles. By 1939 Hitler felt that Germany was ready for another war. He stated that all of the Jews in Europe would be eliminated as the result of a second world war. In September 1939 Hitler moved German troops into Poland, and thus began World War II.

In 1941 Bormann's boss, Rudolf Hess, made a mysterious flight to England and was taken prisoner. Bormann seized the opportunity and assumed the newly vacated position of his boss. Some have speculated that Bormann encouraged

Strong Opinions about Bormann Held by His Fellow Nazis

All of the high-ranking Nazis who surrounded Hitler had strong, negative opinions about Bormann. One of them called the deputy the most sinister man in Hitler's inner circle, next to Heinrich Himmler. Another alleged that Bormann was an "arch-scoundrel" and added that the word "hate" was "far too weak" to describe his feelings. At the Nuremberg trials after the war, Nazi official Hermann Göring was asked if he knew Bormann's whereabouts. Göring replied: "If I had my say about it, I hope he is frying in hell."

At one time or another these men complained to Hitler about Bormann. On one occasion Hitler replied: "I know that Bormann is brutal. But there is sense in everything he does and I can absolutely rely on my orders being carried out by Bormann immediately and in spite of all obstacles." Nazi architect Albert Speer said: "Even among so many ruthless men, Bormann stood out by his brutality and coarseness." Speer noted that if Hitler had voiced only a few critical words about Bormann, "all Bormann's enemies would have been at his throat." But Hitler never said those words.

Hess to make the flight so he could have his job. In his new role, Bormann put Hitler's daily affairs in order and explained matters to him in a clear and concise way. The führer began to appreciate and depend on Bormann more and more. As the war continued, Hitler's behavior became more and more peculiar. It was Bormann who calmed Hitler and kept him from knowing the truth about how the war was being lost. According to some historians, Bormann actually became more powerful than the führer himself.

Bormann's duties were many and varied. He became Hitler's gatekeeper, controlling who was allowed to see Hitler and admitting them only after they informed him of the nature of their business. He filled jobs with people of his own choosing. He controlled Hitler's finances and even oversaw the construction of Hitler's vacation home in the mountains. His rival, Nazi official Albert Speer, described how Bormann accomplished this task with the crudeness that was typical of him. Speer was a gifted architect in charge of designing new buildings for Hitler's future German empire. He called Bormann "this brutal contractor [who] ravaged the natural beauty of the place, forcibly buying up old farms, tearing down buildings, turning the forest paths into paved promenades and creating a complex of concrete buildings."

Bormann's Policies

Although Bormann did not kill people himself during the war, he was aware of the murders taking place, and he approved of them. As Hitler's chief assistant, he played an important role in ordering the building of concentration camps throughout Europe. In these camps the Nazis confined, and later murdered, millions of people they deemed to be "enemies of the state." Bormann was also a supporter of the policy of euthanasia—the mercy killing program set up by doctor Karl Brandt. In addition, he was especially known for his hatred and persecution of Christian churches and for the extremely harsh measures he proposed for the treatment of Jews and the conquered peoples of Europe. Bormann opposed Christian churches because he believed they stood in the way of the Nazis assuming total control over people's lives. He wanted to break the influence of churches once and for all. As for the Jews, Bormann decreed in 1942 that "the permanent elimination of the Jews from the territories of Greater Germany ... [must be] carried out ... by the use of ruthless force in the special [concentration] camps."

Attends Hitler's Suicide

By 1945 Hitler could no longer deny that Germany had lost the war. He believed that he must commit suicide in order to escape capture. Bormann was with him right up until the end. Shortly before the suicide, Bormann witnessed the wedding ceremony of Hitler and Eva Braun even though Braun detested him. Bormann expressed the desire to commit suicide along with Hitler, but the führer ordered him to consider the interests of Germany before his own. Hitler instructed Bormann to live on and carry out the Nazi vision of a great German empire. Bormann was the first person to enter the room after Hitler and Braun committed suicide on April 30, 1945. He was one of six people who tended to the disposal of the couple's bodies in a garden, where they were set on fire with gasoline. As the bodies of Hitler and Braun burned, Bormann left the premises and disappeared into oblivion.

While the war was still raging, three of the Allies (Great Britain, the Soviet Union, and the United States) had issued a warning to Nazi leaders. They warned those responsible for the torture and murder of millions of innocent people that they would search every inch of the earth to bring the perpetrators to justice. Although many were caught and sentenced to hang following their trials at Nuremberg, Bormann eluded capture. His fate remained a mystery for many years. Since Bormann could not be found, authorities were unsure if he was dead or alive. Thus, the Nuremberg court tried him *in absentia*. He was found guilty and sentenced to death.

The Biggest Unsolved Nazi Mystery

Bormann was the subject of an intensive search by British and American agents who were anxious to bring him to trial for his war crimes. Rumors surrounding his whereabouts persisted for decades. Some historians speculate that he made his way to Italy, where his wife lay gravely ill. From there, Bormann traveled to South America. Another theory is that Bormann tried to escape from the invading Soviet army. He was riding in a tank that was hit by Soviet anti-tank shells and was killed. Regardless of Bormann's fate, his wife died in 1946. By the terms of her will, all of the anti-Christian couple's children were to be raised as Catholics. The reasons for her request are unknown. However, some people suggest that the Catholic church did her a favor and this was her way of repaying the debt.

Bormann was a primary target of famed Nazi-hunter Simon Wiesenthal. At a 1967 news conference, Wiesenthal asserted that Bormann was alive and living comfortably in South America. The Nazi hunter noted that Bormann had many friends and sufficient funds at his disposal. Another account of Bormann's whereabouts surfaced in 1972 when a series of reports was published in European and American newspapers. The account was written by Hungarian-born, American writer

During Hitler's rise to power, few suspected that he would ultimately end his life in suicide. (Reproduced by permission of AP/Wide World Photos)

Ladislas Farago. Farago, a former secret service agent, claimed he had discovered Bormann alive, but ailing, in South America. The story caused a sensation because Bormann was still at the top of the most-wanted list of condemned Nazi criminals. Farago claimed that 50,000 Nazi criminals had found their way to South America and lived there openly. The writer further contended that South American leaders were not sheltering Bormann simply out of kindness. He said that Nazi leaders had been stashing away gold and other valuables stolen from Jews and others as early as 1943. According to Farago, Bormann used the treasure to finance a new life in South America.

Shortly after Farago made his claim, a skeleton was unearthed in a railroad yard in Berlin, Germany. The German government declared that the body was that of Bormann. The cause of death was declared to be suicide, and the official death date was given as May 2, 1945, two days after the death of Bormann's idol, Adolf Hitler. Farago dismissed the report by the German government. He claimed that neither the Germans nor anyone else was interested in bringing Bormann to justice. "How convenient," he said. "The Germans have a big file on Bormann, and they've always looked for him where they were sure he wasn't."

Nazi-Era Gold in Swiss Banks

A controversy that had been quietly simmering for half a century erupted in worldwide news headlines in the 1990s—the matter of Nazi-era gold still being held in Swiss bank accounts. Swiss banks have long been known for their strict refusal to release any information about money held in secret bank accounts.

Switzerland declared a policy of neutrality in World War II. As Nazi persecution of Jews elsewhere in Europe grew worse in the 1940s, and the Nazis began to confiscate Jewish property, many Jews sent their money to be deposited in secret accounts in Switzerland. Many of those Jews, however, died in Nazi concentration camps. The heirs of those victims are seeking the release of money held in the secret bank accounts. Jewish organizations seeking the gold on behalf of the heirs estimate it could be worth between $3 billion and $7 billion.

The controversy over the victims' gold has focused attention on Jewish valuables said to have been stashed in Swiss banks by high-ranking Nazis. Included in the treasures are gold bars—the gold was melted down from items taken from the Jews when they were sent to Nazi death camps. The gold bars were made from fillings and crowns extracted from the victims' teeth as well as jewelry. The gold was to be used to finance the escape of Nazi officials if Germany lost the war. Martin Bormann would have had the authority to withdraw the funds from the Swiss banks.

SOURCES

Books

Fest, Joachim C., *The Face of the Third Reich: Portraits of the Nazi Leadership,* translated from the German by Michael Bullock, Da Capo Press (New York), 1999.

Kilzer, Louis, *Hitler's Traitor: Martin Bormann and the Defeat of the Reich,* Presidio Press (Novato, CA), 2000.

Manning, Paul, *Martin Bormann: Nazi in Exile,* Stuart (Secaucus, NJ), 1981.

McGovern, James, *Martin Bormann,* Morrow (New York), 1968.

Speer, Albert, *Inside the Third Reich: Memoirs by Albert Speer,* translated from the German by Richard and Clara Winston, Bonanza Books, distributed by Crown Publishers (New York), 1982.

Vincent, Isabel, *Hitler's Silent Partners: Swiss Banks, Nazi Gold, and the Pursuit of Justice,* W. Morrow (New York), 1997.

Whiting, Charles, *The Hunt for Martin Bormann,* L. Cooper (London), 1996.

Periodicals

Fennel, Tom, "Naming Names: Swiss Banks Issue a Long-sought List of Nazi-era Accounts," *Macleans,* August 4, 1997, p. 30.

Hirsh, Michael, "Nazi Gold: The Untold Story," *Time,* November 4, 1996, pp. 47-48.

Nelan, Bruce W., "The Goods of Evil," *Time,* October 28, 1996, pp. 54–55.

Trevor-Roper, Hugh, "Martin Bormann Was Last Seen Definitely in a Tank in Berlin on May 2, 1945. Does He Live?," *The New York Times Magazine,* January 14, 1973, pp. 12+.

Warren, Howard, "Writer in Detroit Tells of Nazi's Open Life in Brazil," *Biography News,* January/February 1975, p. 29.

Wilson, Victor, "Author Claims Nazi War Criminal Is Still Alive," *Biography News,* January/February 1975, p. 29.

Margaret Bourke-White

During World War II, many journalists became famous for reporting on the conflict in Europe, but none was more well-known than photojournalist Margaret Bourke-White. Throughout her life, Bourke-White was a pioneer in the field of photography and led the way for women to enter the professional world. She was a prize-winning photographer and journalist, and her photographs for *Life* magazine brought the war into millions of American homes, while her courage on the battlefront became legendary. An adventurous lady who loved to fly, Bourke-White was the first accredited woman war correspondent during World War II and the first woman to accompany a bombing mission. When the Nazi death camps were liberated by American troops, Bourke-White captured the images in a series of powerful photographs.

Fascination with Photography

Born in New York City on June 14, 1904, Margaret White was the daughter of Joseph and Minnie Elizabeth (Bourke) White. (Bourke-White added her mother's name to her own after her first marriage ended.) Bourke-White's parents encouraged her independence and believed in female equality, telling her that fear was her only enemy. She has been described as self-confident, occasionally arrogant, and indifferent to opinion and criti-

Born June 14, 1904
    New York, New York, United States
Died August 27, 1971
    Darien, Connecticut, United States

Photojournalist

"Nothing attracts me like a closed door. I cannot let my camera rest till I have pried it open, and I wanted to be first."

(Library of Congress)

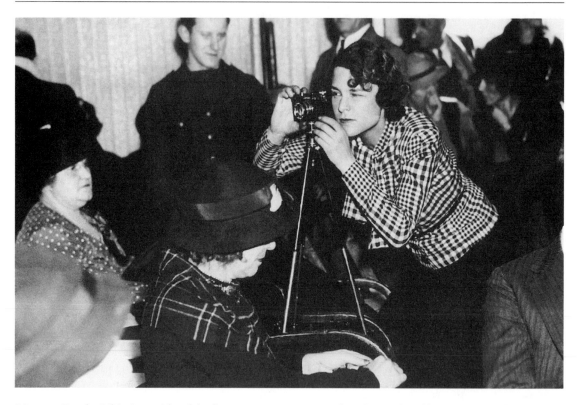

Margaret Bourke-White is considered the first woman war correspondent. (Reproduced by permission of AP/Wide World Photos)

cism. Growing up in New Jersey, she was taught by her father the ethic of work and was introduced to the magic and power of machines. Thus she came naturally to her love of industrial photography and all its potential and power. Initially, though, Bourke-White wanted to become a scientist and enrolled in 1921 at Columbia University. Due to concerns with money, however, she changed schools. She was introduced to photography at the University of Michigan (where she attended school from 1923 to 1925) by Clarence T. White, one of the nation's most influential teachers of photography. Also in 1923, when she was just one day short of being twenty years of age, Bourke-White married another photographer named Everett Chapman. They divorced in 1925. She later transferred to Cornell University, where she began to reveal her photographic talents.

After she graduated with her bachelor's degree in 1927, Bourke-White left Cornell and went to Cleveland, Ohio, where she was determined to be a "good photographer," she said, and to tell the truth about Cleveland. She saw Cleveland mainly near Terminal Tower, photographing that landmark so much and so well that it launched her career as a photographer. After graduation she opened a stu-

dio in Cleveland, where she found the industrial landscape "a photographic paradise." Initially specializing in architectural photography, her prints of the Otis Steel factory came to the attention of *Time* magazine publisher Henry Luce, who was planning a new publication devoted to the glamour of business. In 1929 Luce invited her to come to New York City to work on the forthcoming magazine *Fortune.* She accepted Luce's offer and became the first staff photographer for the magazine, which made its debut in February 1930, with her photographs in the lead article. It was later said that her photographs made *Fortune* successful. Her subjects included the Swift meat packing company, shoemaking, watches, glass, paper mills, orchids, and banks. With access to the right people, Bourke-White's career soon began a meteoric rise.

In 1931 the Soviet government invited Bourke-White to come to Russia. Armed with many cameras and a great supply of film, she made the journey and photographed everything that she could. It was the first of three trips she made to the Soviet Union. Excited by the drama of the machine, her trips gave her the chance to be the first photographer to seriously document the USSR's rapid industrial development. In her autobiography, *Por-*

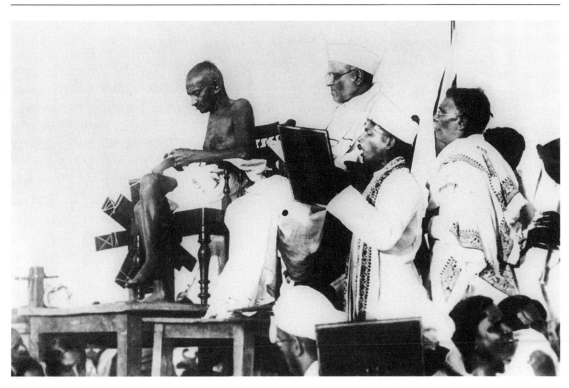

Indian leader Mohandas K. Gandhi, who preached nonviolence, was assassinated. The last journalist to see him before his death was Margaret Bourke-White. (Library of Congress)

trait of Myself, she voiced her credo about art and photography this way: "I believe any important art coming of this industrial age will draw inspiration from industry because industry [is] alive, vital. Art must have flesh and blood. Industrial subjects [are] close to heart of life today. Photography [is] suitable [to] portray industry because [it is] an honest kind of medium. Beauty of industry lies in its truth and simplicity." She published her work in the book *Eyes on Russia* in 1931. In 1934 Hollywood released film versions of two of her travelogues—*Eyes on Russia* and *Red Republic*—and, later in the year, *Our Daily Bread.* Bourke-White was not satisfied with these works and she never made any more movies.

Bourke-White began working out of a New York City studio in the new Chrysler Building, and handled lucrative advertising accounts. In 1934, in the midst of the Depression, she earned over $35,000. But a *Fortune* assignment to cover the drought in the Plains states opened her eyes to human suffering and steered her away from advertising work. She began to view photography less as a purely artistic medium and increasingly as a powerful tool for informing the public. By the mid-thirties, Bourke-White's politics had begun to lean to the left, though she claimed to be politically indifferent. It was in 1936 that Bourke-White

began her long and famous association with *Life* magazine, which popularized the photo-essay, entering her position two months before publication began. Her picture of the Fort Peck dam in Montana adorned the cover of *Life*'s first issue, November 11, 1936. On one of her next assignments she flew to the Arctic circle.

In 1936 she collaborated with Erskine Caldwell, author of *Tobacco Road*, on a photo-essay revealing social conditions in the South. The result of their efforts became her best-known book, the social document *You Have Seen Their Faces*, published in 1937. While covering the Louisville flood in 1937, Bourke-White composed her most famous single photograph, contrasting a line of black people waiting for emergency relief with an untroubled white family in its car pictured on a billboard with a caption celebrating the American way of life. In early 1940 Bourke-White worked briefly for the new pictorial newspaper *PM,* but by October she had returned to *Life* as a freelance photographer. She and Caldwell had married in 1939 and they traveled across the United States and produced the book *Say Is This the U.S.A.?* They also decided to begin working on a book similar to *You Have Seen Their Faces* focusing on the events occurring in Europe. By this time,

Robert Capa Records D-Day Invasion

Considered one of the great war photographers, Robert Capa was born Endre Friedmann in 1913 in Budapest, which was then part of the Austro-Hungarian Empire. The son of middle-class Jewish parents, he grew up under the dictatorship of Regent Miklós Horthy but accepted the ideas of the artist Lajos Kassák, who spearheaded the avant-garde movement in Hungary. Kassák's anti-fascist, pro-labor, pacifist beliefs influenced Capa for the rest of his life. At age eighteen Capa was arrested by the secret police for his political activities. He was released through the intervention of his father but was banished from Hungary. Moving to Berlin, Germany, in 1931, he worked as a darkroom assistant at Dephot (Deutscher Photodienst), the leading photojournalism enterprise in Germany. This agency was distinguished by its use of new small cameras and fast film that allowed photographers to capture fleeting gestures and to take pictures even in poor light. Capa soon mastered the technology and was occasionally sent out on small photographic assignments. In his first major break, he was sent to Copenhagen, Denmark, to photograph Bolshevik leader Leon Trotsky.

When Adolf Hitler rose to power in Germany, Capa moved to Paris, France. There he met Gerda Pohorylles, who called herself Gerda Taro, and fell in love. She wrote the text for his stories and acted as his agent. Taro found she could charge much more for a photo taken by a "rich American" photographer named Robert Capa than she could for the work of a poor Hungarian named Endre Friedmann. Thus, the internationally known Robert Capa was born. Capa and Taro were sent to Spain to cover the Spanish Civil War, where Capa took the picture that made him famous: a dying Loyalist soldier falling from the impact of a bullet. In July 1937 Taro was killed by a tank that sideswiped the car she had clambered onto in the retreat from Brunete. She was twenty-six. Capa later dedicated his book *Death in the Making* (1937) to Taro.

From 1941 to 1945 Capa photographed World War II in Europe as correspondent for *Collier's* and *Life* magazines. On D-Day, June 6, 1944, he landed in the second wave of Allied forces on Omaha Beach. The soldiers were pinned down by unexpectedly heavy fire and scrambled for shelter. Crouching with them, Capa snapped pictures of the incoming troops. He sent the film to a photo lab in London, England, where the lab assistant tried to process the film as quickly as possible by turning up the heat in the print dryer. The emulsion melted on the negatives and the surviving eleven photos are slightly out of focus because of the melting. Nevertheless, the blurring adds to their effectiveness by conveying the confusion and danger of the moment.

After the war, Capa became what he always claimed he wanted to be—an unemployed war correspondent. He worked on a variety of projects, including a book about Russia with text by American author John Steinbeck. He briefly returned to war photography to cover the Israeli war of independence (1948-1949). In 1948 he cofounded the Magnum Photo Agency with Henri Cartier-Bresson, David ("Chim") Seymour, William Vandivert, and George Rodger. Though he was often short of cash himself, he was generous in his support of others.

While on an assignment in Japan, Capa was asked to fill in for a photographer covering the French Indochina War. He was killed when he stepped on a land mine on May 25, 1954, at Thai-Binh.

Bourke-White was considered by many the fore-most photojournalist in America.

Wartime Photographs

In the spring of 1941, again loaded down with photography equipment and supplies, Bourke-White traveled with Caldwell to the Soviet Union. They were the only foreign journalists in the Soviet Union when the Germans invaded Russia. By the next year, she and Caldwell had begun to drift apart and the two divorced in 1942. During World War II, Bourke-White served as an accredited war correspondent affiliated with both *Life* and the U.S. Army Air Corps. She survived a torpedo attack and the sinking of the ship she was taking to North Africa and she accompanied the bombing missions which destroyed the German airfield of El Aouina near Tunis. She later covered the Italian campaign (recorded in the 1944 book *They Called It "Purple Heart Valley": A Combat Chronicle of the War in Italy*) where she earned respect for her daring to get pictures in dangerous situations by disregarding enemy fire. She photographed the Allied advance into Germany, and in the spring of 1945, she was with General George Patton as his troops opened the gates of the concentration camp at Buchenwald. Her pictures showed the world the state of the prisoners still there, documenting what had happened to them and those who had not survived the camps. Photographs taken at the Erla work camp, just hours after an SS massacre of over 300 inmates, further demonstrated the brutality of the German army and the horror of the camps. She said about the war that it was not worth fighting if it did not lead to a better world and felt that the younger generations in Europe must be convinced that if they worked with the Allies this could happen.

Life After World War II

After World War II, Bourke-White issued another series of photographs in *Dear Fatherland, Rest Quietly* in 1946. That same year she spent five months in South Africa, where she recorded the cruelty of apartheid. Her pictures conveyed to Americans what was happening all over the world and in their own country. She was often regarded as a role model. She was given honorary degrees by universities, and Canada named a lake after her. In 1947 *Real Fact Comics* devoted an issue to her life. Despite her fame, in the early 1950s Bourke-White fell victim to Senator Joseph McCarthy and McCarthyism because of her interest in the Soviet Union. Yet she still was able to work, unlike some of McCarthy's targets. She had always shown unbounded energy and drive in her obsession with her work and the freedom to do it, but in 1951, Bourke-White began to show symptoms of Parkinson's disease. Her strong and reliable body was becoming undependable, but she refused to give in to the disease. She traveled to Korea to focus on war again in 1952, but rather than taking pictures of the war itself, she focused on the effects that it had on a Korean family. Due to the disease, this was her last major assignment, but in 1955, she forced Luce to give her an assignment on the first rocket trip to the moon for *Life*. Luce said of Bourke-White that she was not someone who would accept the word "no" if she wanted to do something. In *Portrait of Myself*, she wrote: "Nothing attracts me like a closed door. I cannot let my camera rest till I have pried it open, and I wanted to be first." For Bourke-White, work meant a great deal.

In her lifetime, she took photos of thirty-four countries and the Arctic and photographed many world leaders, capturing the images of such notable men and women as U.S. President Franklin Roosevelt and his wife, Eleanor Roosevelt, British Prime Minister Winston Churchill, Soviet leader Joseph Stalin, Ethiopian Emperor Haile Selassie, and Indian spiritual leader Mohandas K. Gandhi. For her work, Bourke-White was awarded First Prize by the Cleveland Museum of Art in 1928, the American Woman of Achievement Award in 1951, and received numerous other recognitions. She wrote a dozen books, and, in 1936, was named one of America's top ten living American women. A television dramatization of her life was broadcast in 1960 and she published her autobiography, including her struggle with Parkinson's, in 1963. Bourke-White lived with Parkinson's for twenty years and died on August 27, 1971.

SOURCES

Books

Bourke-White, Margaret, *Portrait of Myself,* Simon & Schuster (New York), 1963.

Bourke-White, Margaret, *They Called It "Purple Heart Valley": A Combat Chronicle of the War in Italy,* Simon and Schuster (New York), 1944.

Callahan, Sean, *Margaret Bourke-White: Photographer,* Little, Brown (Boston), 1998.

Contemporary Heroes and Heroines, Vol. 1, Gale Research (Detroit), 1990.

Encyclopedia of World Biography, second edition, Gale Research (Detroit), 1998.

Goldberg, Vicki, *Margaret Bourke-White: A Biography,* Addison-Wesley (Reading, MA), 1987.

Hood, Robert, *Twelve at War: Great Photographers Under Fire,* Putnam (New York), 1967.

Rubin, Susan Goldman, *Margaret Bourke-White: Her Pictures Were Her Life,* Abrams (New York), 1999.

Silverman, Jonathan, *For the World to See: The Life of Margaret Bourke-White,* preface by Alfred Eisenstaedt, Viking (New York), 1983.

Karl Brandt

Karl Brandt was an intelligent man and a gifted surgeon according to historians. Yet he agreed to head the Nazis' euthanasia program, which killed at least 200,000 innocent people. Ultimately, Brandt's program allowed German doctors to kill anyone they deemed unworthy of life. Doctors began by killing any child considered by them to be "defective." The program was later expanded to include "defective" adults and Jews. The Nazis used the term "defective" to refer to anyone with a physical or mental handicap. With Brandt at the helm, the mercy-killing initiative led to murderous experiments on living human beings. After World War II, Brandt was sentenced to hang for his crimes. Almost to the very moment that the hangman's noose tightened around his neck, he insisted that his actions were justified in a time of war and what he had done was right.

Born January 8, 1904
    Mulhouse, Alsace, Germany
Died June 2, 1948
    Landsberg Prison, Lech, Germany

Surgeon; Hitler's personal doctor; head of Nazi euthanasia program that killed at least 200,000

"Death can mean deliverance. Death is life—just as much as birth. It was never meant to be murder."

Educated in Germany

The son of a German policeman, Brandt was born in 1904 in Alsace, a picturesque, fertile region of Europe that France and Germany had fought over for centuries. At the time of Brandt's birth, Alsace belonged to Germany, but when World War I ended in 1918, Germany was forced to surrender the region to France. As a result, a bitter Brandt, who considered himself German, felt that he had

(Main Commission for the Investigation of Nazi War Crimes/USHMM Photo Archives)

to leave Alsace to remain a German citizen. In 1928 Brandt received his license to practice medicine and took a position at a clinic in Bochum, Germany. In his twenties, he acquired a reputation among doctors as a talented surgeon with a gift for treating head and spinal injuries. He was described by his contemporaries as tall, elegant, proud, intelligent, decent, idealistic, sincere, and ethical. He was also ambitious but easily influenced by people with stronger personalities.

Ironically, Brandt's early role model was fellow Alsace citizen Albert Schweitzer, a humanitarian, missionary, and winner of the Nobel Prize for peace. Brandt had hoped to become a doctor and join Schweitzer at his mission in a French-controlled part of Africa. He was frustrated to learn that he would have to become a French citizen and serve in the French army before he could qualify as an assistant to Schweitzer. Brandt fervently believed that it was a great injustice for his homeland to be in the hands of the French; therefore it was unthinkable that he should join the French army. In 1932 Brandt joined the Nazi Party—then a growing political force that promised its supporters that Germany would once again rise to greatness after its humiliating defeat during World War I. They promised to take back Alsace from the French, a cause dear to Brandt's heart. Sometime in the 1930s, Brandt married a German swimming champion named Anni and fathered a child.

Launches Career as Nazi Doctor

Brandt came to the attention of Nazi Party leader Adolf Hitler in 1933 when he was called to treat Hitler's niece and a companion for injuries sustained during an auto accident. Brandt made a good impression on Hitler and was invited to become one of his personal physicians. Hitler, a man with an unfaltering will, became Brandt's new role model. Brandt rose rapidly in Hitler's esteem and in the Nazi Party. As early as 1935, Hitler had made no secret of his steadfast intention to eliminate the "incurably ill" one day. He considered them unproductive and full of "bad genes." He deemed that there was no place for them in his planned new "master race" of pure white, non-Jewish people who would one day rule the world. Hitler also knew he could not begin a large-scale program of killing the handicapped unless German citizens were distracted by a large-scale war. Otherwise, such actions would surely draw heated protest from private citizens. However, a faction existed that did not want to wait for an "official" euthanasia program to be implemented. They asked Hitler for help. By 1938 Hitler began receiving letters from some family members of mentally handicapped children. They requested the "mercy death" of their loved ones.

Hitler was especially interested in a letter from a man whose child had been born blind, without a leg and part of an arm. Hitler told Brandt to examine the child and, if the father's description was correct, to kill her. Brandt obeyed, and Hitler was pleased. He gave Brandt permission to treat similar cases in the same fashion, and Brandt was happy to oblige. After World War II began when Hitler invaded Poland in 1939, the Nazis immediately implemented their official euthanasia program. Hitler declared that in a time of war and hardship, it was not practical for the state to spend money to care for handicapped children in institutions. Naturally, his loyal friend Brandt came to mind as the logical choice to head up the official euthanasia operation. The operation was staffed with loyal Nazi-sympathizing doctors willing to end the lives of their young patients.

The Killing of Children Begins

Brandt and Reichsleiter Philip Bouhler quickly established the Reich Committee for the Scientific Registration of Serious Hereditarily and Congenitally Based Illnesses. The Reich Committee drew up a list of medical conditions that would qualify for mercy killing. The conditions included impairments such as: "idiocy" (which included a large majority of mental handicaps, especially when they are associated with blindness and deafness); malformations of all kinds; and paralysis. All medical personnel who were present at the birth of an impaired baby were required to report the infant to the Reich Committee. Furthermore, the committee was also notified about any institutionalized children under the age of three who exhibited any of the listed conditions.

A medical panel set up by Brandt then examined the reports and made the decision whether the child would live or die. A plus sign indicated a "garbage child," who would be killed; a minus sign meant the child would be allowed to live. As the program evolved, the age limit of the qualifying children increased, and the criteria for euthanasia expanded. Soon Jewish children were added to the list just because of their ancestry. Five thousand

ADOLF HITLER

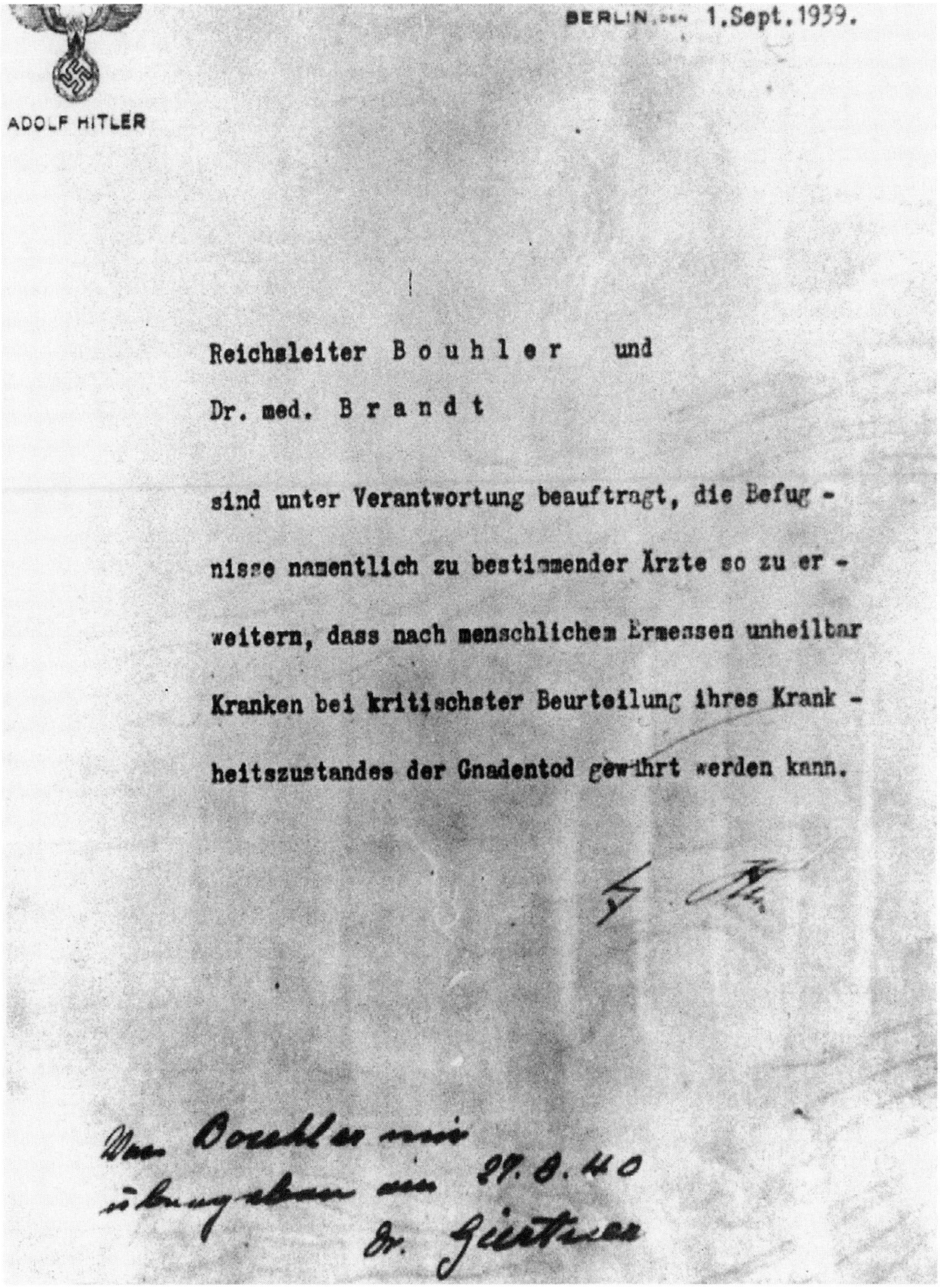

BERLIN, DEN 1.Sept.1939.

Reichsleiter Bouhler und

Dr. med. Brandt

sind unter Verantwortung beauftragt, die Befug - nisse namentlich zu bestimmender Ärzte so zu er - weitern, dass nach menschlichem Ermessen unheilbar Kranken bei kritischster Beurteilung ihres Krank - heitszustandes der Gnadentod gewährt werden kann.

Von Bouhler mir übergeben am 27.8.40 Dr. Gürtner

A reproduction of the letter signed by Adolf Hitler authorizing Brandt to implement Operation T-4. (Stadtarchiv Nuerenbuerg/USHMM Photo Archives)

children were killed by doctors who, upon medical licensing, had taken an oath to "do no harm."

The early methods of extermination were varied; the children were killed with overdoses of drugs, by injections of poisonous chemicals, or by starvation in institutions dedicated to that task. Later, gas chambers were introduced. The gas chambers were sealed rooms, sometimes masked as showers, that were filled with poisonous gas in order to kill the people locked inside en masse. Soon the program, which came to be known as Operation T-4, was expanded to include mentally or physically ill adults. Those people who were considered "lives unworthy of living" or "useless eaters" were rounded up by male nurses, who were members of Hitler's secret police. Wearing white uniforms with tall black boots and carrying stethoscopes, they escorted their victims by bus to special centers, where the victims were shot to death. Later, gas was used, because some of the secret police were upset at having to shoot their victims. The Nazis also thought that the use of bullets was too costly. Gassings were considered more cost effective.

Wins Public Over

Although Brandt had little to do with carrying out the actual killings, he was the top medical authority in charge of the secret program. Wanting to test the support of the public sector, Brandt decided to gauge public opinion of the euthanasia program through the use of a movie and a poll. The movie *I Accuse* was released in 1941. Its plot involved a doctor whose wife was incurably ill. She begged her husband to give her a deadly injection to relieve her pain and suffering. The film's message indicated that mercy killing was acceptable because the patient wanted to die. The film also suggested that in cases where the patient was mentally ill, the state should intervene and carry out the killing. The Nazis were already doing this secretly. The SD, the intelligence agency of the Nazi Party, then prepared a report saying the film had been "favorably received and discussed" by the public. The report told Hitler that his hold over the German people was so great that the public accepted the program of mercy killing carried out by Brandt. Calling themselves scientists, Brandt and the other Nazi doctors said their actions were in the interests of science.

Operation T-4 Halted

Such a program could not remain secret for long. Some religious leaders and family members

of adult victims began to protest. Oddly, no such protest had been registered about the killing of children. Heinrich Himmler, head of the SS, finally recommended to Hitler that the program be stopped. He complained that it was stirring up unrest at a time when Germans needed to concentrate on winning the war. In August 1941, Hitler told Brandt to end the practice of killing mental patients. But the order was given too late—the murder of such patients was beyond Brandt's control. A period known as "wild euthanasia" followed, when doctors all over Germany carried out the killings on a large scale. In some places, the murders even continued after the war was over. The victorious Allies insisted the practice be halted. It is estimated that 200,000 innocent people were murdered in the Nazis' "mercy-killing" program.

In 1942 Hitler placed Brandt in charge of all German medical facilities. In this new role, he was present at meetings where Nazi doctors discussed the horrible experiments they were conducting on human beings in concentration camps. Brandt was also present at a demonstration where victims were killed by carbon monoxide gas and morphine injections to see how the two methods of killing compared.

Falls Out of Favor with Hitler

Brandt remained in Hitler's good graces until two weeks before Hitler committed suicide. By then it was obvious that Germany was crumbling. Berlin, the capital city, was being bombarded. Many high Nazi officials had taken their families to places where they could surrender to the advancing Allied troops rather than be killed by bombs. When Hitler learned that Brandt had placed his family in the path of the Allies, he was furious. Hitler's mental stability had greatly diminished. Some historians attribute Hitler's increasing irrationality to stress, the effects of syphilis, or other factors. He accused Brandt of sending secret documents to the Allies by way of his wife, Anni. He ordered that Brandt be killed, but Himmler intercepted the order, saving the doctor's life. Brandt, however, did not escape the Allies. The case of the *United States* v. *Karl Brandt et al* came to trial in Nuremberg, Germany, on December 9, 1946, and continued until August 20, 1947. Twenty-three doctors and scientists were charged with war crimes and crimes against humanity. The graphic details of human experiments were revealed at the trial. Such tests had

The Nazis' Crimes Defined

The trials of the Nazi leaders by four of the Allied powers (the United States, Great Britain, the Soviet Union, and France) were unique events in human history. The several trials were collectively known as the Nuremberg Trials after the city of Nuremberg, Germany, where they were held. They marked the first time in history that a group of victorious powers had established an international court in which they could try their defeated enemies on charges of violations of criminal laws. The Nuremberg Tribunal, as the group of powers was known, made it clear that a nation's conduct must be governed by laws *even during wartime.*

The Tribunal defined war crimes and crimes against humanity this way:

"War Crimes: namely, violations of the laws or customs of war. Such violations shall include, but not be limited to, murder, ill-treatment or deportation [forced removal from one's city or country] to slave labor or for any other purpose of civilian population of or in occupied territory, murder or ill-treatment of prisoners of war or persons on the seas, killing of hostages, plunder of public or private property, wanton [excessive] destruction of cities, towns or villages, or devastation not justified by military necessity";

"Crimes Against Humanity: namely, murder, extermination [total destruction], enslavement, deportation, and other inhumane acts committed against any civilian population, before or during the war, or persecutions on political, racial or religious grounds in execution of or in connection with any crime within the jurisdiction of the Tribunal, whether or not in violation of the domestic law of the country where perpetrated."

U.S. Brigadier General Telford Taylor made the opening statement at the Doctors Trial, which was the case that involved Karl Brandt. He described the charges against the doctors and scientists:

"The defendants in this case are charged with murders, tortures, and other atrocities committed in the name of medical science. The victims of these crimes are numbered in the hundreds of thousands. A handful only are still alive; a few of the survivors will appear in this courtroom. But most of these miserable victims were slaughtered outright or died in the course of the tortures to which they were subjected.... The victims of these crimes are numbered among the anonymous millions who met death at the hands of the Nazis and whose fate is a hideous blot on the page of modern history."

---

involved infecting patients with diseases, immersing people in icy water, forcing them to drink seawater, and exposing them to the effects of mustard gas.

Brandt was asked whether he thought an order to conduct experiments on human beings was reasonable when the patient would probably die as a result. He replied that under the Nazi form of government, "any personal code of ethics must give way to the total character of the war." As for his involvement in Operation T-4, Brandt "made no apology for the program, and declared it to be justified—justified out of pity for the victim and out of a desire to free the family and loved ones from a lifetime of needless sacrifice," according to writer Robert Jay Lifton.

The court was unimpressed with the doctors' statements. Sixteen of the men, including Brandt, were found guilty. Of the sixteen, seven, including Brandt, were sentenced to hang. He was executed on June 2, 1948. Some of the Nazi doctors contended that no laws banned human experimentation. The Nuremberg court responded with a statement called the Nuremberg Code, which defined when medical experiments on human beings were justified. The first point made in the statement was this: "The voluntary consent of the human subject is absolutely essential."

Sources

Books

Conot, Robert E., *Justice at Nuremberg,* Harper & Row (New York), 1983.

Gallagher, Hugh Gregory, *By Trust Betrayed: Patients, Physicians, and the License to Kill in the Third Reich,* Holt (New York), 1990.

Lifton, Robert Jay, *The Nazi Doctors: Medical Killing and the Psychology of Genocide,* Basic Books (New York), 1986.

Lifton, Robert Jay, and Amy Hackett, "Nazi Physicians," *Encyclopedia of the Holocaust,* Macmillan (New York), 1990.

Speer, Albert, *Inside the Third Reich: Memoirs by Albert Speer,* translated from the German by Richard and Clara Winston, Bonanza Books, distributed by Crown Publishers (New York), 1982.

Wilhelm, Hans-Heinrich, "Euthanasia Program," *Encyclopedia of the Holocaust,* Macmillan (New York), 1990.

Eva Braun

By most accounts, Eva Braun was an ordinary woman whose only distinction was her connection to Adolf Hitler. She was uninterested in politics and had little to say about Hitler's work. Her devotion to him was complete and unfaltering.

Early Life in Munich

Braun was born in Munich, Germany, on February 6, 1912. She was the second of three daughters born to Freidrich (Fritz) and Franciska Dronburger Braun. Her father was a schoolteacher, which placed the family in the German middle class. Braun attended a convent school founded in the eighteenth century by English nuns. She was a lively and athletic girl who had little aptitude or interest in her studies and barely managed to earn a diploma. Her teachers thought her frivolous. In 1929, at the age of seventeen, she left the convent and took a job as a bookkeeper and assistant to photographer Heinrich Hoffmann, who was Hitler's personal photographer. Thus, fate threw her in the path of the man who would soon become dictator of Germany.

The First Suicide

At the time Braun met Hitler through her work, he was involved in a stormy relationship with Angela (Geli) Raubel, the daughter of his half

Born February 6, 1912
  Munich, Germany
Died April 30, 1945
  Berlin, Germany

Mistress, then wife for one day, of dictator Adolf Hitler

"A Germany without Adolf Hitler would not be fit to live in."

(Reproduced by permission of AP/Wide World Photos)

Braun posing for a photo. (USHMM Photo Archives)

sister. Hitler was then thirty-nine years old, and Raubel was twenty. For a time, Raubel enjoyed her connection to the man who was becoming famous throughout Germany. But soon she began to resent his control over her and yearned to go out with younger people. Finally, after an intense quarrel with Hitler, Raubel committed suicide in 1931. Hitler was shattered by her death. Some people say his deep reaction to her suicide is an indication that she was the only woman he ever really loved. Others believe Hitler murdered her. He became withdrawn and depressed, turning the room where she died into a shrine. He then turned to Braun, also a much younger woman, for consolation. According to author Robert Payne, Hitler was attracted to the fair-haired, blue-eyed woman because she resembled Raubel, but was quieter and less moody. Payne wrote: "Her difficult task was to be his mistress while remaining invisible, and she succeeded so well that very few people outside Hitler's immediate circle knew of her existence."

Braun Becomes Hitler's Secret Mistress

In the early 1930s, Braun became Hitler's mistress, and he gave her a suite of rooms in his home. However, because he was unwilling to have their relationship become public knowledge, the couple pretended, even in front of Hitler's staff of servants, to be only friends. When important guests came to visit, Braun was told to stay in her room. Although she wanted to meet these visitors, she accepted Hitler's orders because she simply had no choice. Braun kept a diary, and after World War II, twenty-two pages of it were found. They cover a brief period in 1935, when she was 23 years old. In the pages, she complains of Hitler's casual treatment of her, of her growing feelings of loneliness, and her fear of becoming an "old maid." It is obvious from her diary pages that she had little to occupy her thoughts except Hitler, who was often away. Realizing the futility of her reality, Braun, on at least two occasions, attempted suicide. Rather than giving Braun expensive gifts, Hitler occasionally embarrassed Braun by handing her envelopes full of money in public. She extended her wealth when Hitler gave her and photographer Hoffmann the exclusive rights to his photographs.

The War Years

After World War II began in 1939 when Hitler invaded Poland, the Nazi leader stayed closer to home. He and Braun now had more time to spend together, and the couple grew closer. Braun gained confidence in knowing that she no longer had to contend with rivalry from Hitler's other female admirers. The wives of Hitler's aides did not like Braun and tried to avoid her, but she did develop a friendship with Albert Speer, Hitler's architect and one of the most important members of his government. In his book *Inside the Third Reich,* which he wrote after the war, Speer offered a portrait of Braun. He described her as a simple woman who "dressed quietly and wore the inexpensive jewelry that Hitler gave her…. She was sports-loving, a good skier with plenty of endurance with whom my wife and I frequently undertook mountain tours [Hitler did not like snow]…." Speer also wrote that she was "pleasant and fresh-faced rather than beautiful and [she] had a modest air." She put up with Hitler's hurtful remarks such as "[a] highly intelligent man should take a primitive and stupid woman. Imagine if on top of everything else I had a woman who interfered with my work!"

Braun apparently suited Hitler well. She must have been a good listener, because Hitler has been described as a man who monopolized conversations. She occupied herself with swimming, skiing, mountain climbing, playing with her two black

Scotch terriers, and watching movies. She was a kindhearted woman who occasionally pleaded with Hitler to spare Jewish acquaintances of hers. When Hitler became enraged with his aide Rudolf Hess and cut off relations with him, Braun secretly saw that Hess's wife received a small allowance.

The Last Suicide

By 1945 it was obvious that Germany was losing the war. The walls of Berlin would soon echo the footfalls of the Allied troops. As Berlin was being bombed, Hitler ordered Braun to stay in Munich for her own safety. After only two weeks, she returned unexpectedly to Berlin, telling her friends her place was at Hitler's side no matter what happened. Braun was well aware of Hitler's impending doom, and the route he would probably take to remedy his defeat. She found Hitler a sick and broken man who believed that everyone but Braun had betrayed him. He had decided to kill himself, and Braun agreed to join him in the act. In return, Hitler granted Braun's wish that he make her his wife. Hitler then dictated his will, which said: "Since I did not feel that I could accept the responsibility of marriage during the years of struggle, I have decided now, before the end of my earthly career, to take as my wife the girl who, after many years of loyal friendship, came of her own free will to this city, already almost besieged, in order to share my fate. At her own request she goes to her death with me as my wife.... My wife and I choose to die in order to escape the shame of overthrow.... It is our wish that our bodies be burned immediately."

Hitler then joined Braun, who was dressed in a long black silk gown. According to the marriage laws existing in Germany on April 29, 1945, Hitler and Braun swore that they were both of pure Aryan descent and that they suffered from no hereditary diseases that would prevent them from marrying. They exchanged rings that, according to author Robert Payne, "had probably been torn off the fingers of dead Jews in one of the concentration camps." With the ceremony concluded, the couple hosted a champagne wedding breakfast attended by eight guests. The next day Braun, Hitler, and his two secretaries discussed methods of committing suicide. Braun proposed to take poison because, according to one of the secretaries, "she wanted to be a beautiful corpse." Hitler readied his poison capsules.

One version of the story is that he tested a poison capsule on his pet dog to be sure it worked; the

Eva Braun's Diary

Below is an excerpt from Eva Braun's diary, dated February 18, 1935.

"Yesterday he [Hitler] came quite unexpectedly, and we had a delightful evening. The nicest thing is that he is thinking of taking me from the [photographer's studio where she worked] and—but I had better not get excited about it yet—he may give me a little house. I simply mustn't let myself think about it. It would be marvelous. I wouldn't have to open the door to our 'beloved customers,' and go on being a shop girl. Dear God, grant that this may really happen not in some far-off time, but soon....

"I am so infinitely happy that he loves me so much, and I pray that it will always be like this. It won't be my fault if he stops loving me."

dog died. Later, at about 3:30 in the afternoon of April 30, 1945, Hitler and Braun were found dead in their suite. Braun had taken poison. Whether Hitler died from a pistol shot or from poison remains a mystery. The bodies were carried to the garden and burned, as shells from the approaching Soviet army exploded all around. The bodies were then buried in shallow graves, where they were discovered by the Soviets four days later.

SOURCES

Books

Braun, Eva, *The Private Life of Adolf Hitler: The Intimate Notes and Diary of Eva Braun*, edited by Paul Tabori, Aldus Publications (London), 1949.

Gun, Nerin E., *Eva Braun: Hitler's Mistress*, Meredith Press (New York), 1968.

Infield, Glenn B., *Eva and Adolf*, Grosset and Dunlap (New York), 1974.

Langer, Walter, *The Mind of Adolf Hitler*, New American Library (New York), 1985.

Payne, Robert, *The Life and Death of Adolf Hitler,* Praeger (New York), 1973.

Sereny, Gitta, *Albert Speer: His Battle with Truth,* Knopf (New York), 1995.

Shirer, William, *The Rise and Fall of the Third Reich,* Simon & Schuster (New York), 1960.

Speer, Albert, *Inside the Third Reich,* translated from the German by Richard and Clara Winston, Macmillan (New York), 1970.

Toland, John, *Adolf Hitler,* Doubleday (New York), 1976.

Frank Capra

Frank Capra was a well respected and critically acclaimed filmmaker who focused his art on portraying honest, hardworking people who triumphed over seemingly unbeatable obstacles as well as powerful and deceitful opponents. Capra's background as a film director made him an ideal candidate to create a series of inspirational documentary films aimed at helping American troops understand why the United States was fighting World War II.

Optimism a Capra Trademark

Born in Bisaquino, Sicily, in 1897, Capra moved to the United States with his family at the age of six. Settling in East Los Angeles, California, where his father worked picking oranges, Capra contributed to the family income by selling newspapers and playing the banjo in local bars. One of seven children, he also earned money so he could attend the California Institute of Technology, where he earned a degree in engineering in 1918. Capra later wrote in his autobiography: "My goal was to leap across the tracks—to rise above the muck and meanness of peasant poverty. I wanted freedom from established caste systems, and … freedom could only be won by success." He enlisted in the U.S. Army in 1918 during World War I. After serving in the war, Capra could not find work as an engineer, so he began drifting around

Born May 18, 1897
 Bisaquino, Sicily
Died September 3, 1991
 La Quinta, California, United States

American film director

"My goal was to leap across the tracks—to rise above the muck and meanness of peasant poverty. I wanted freedom from established caste systems, and … freedom could only be won by success."

(Reproduced by permission of AP/Wide World Photos)

the West, supporting himself by playing poker and selling books.

In 1922 Capra was living in San Francisco when he met some filmmakers who had formed a small production company. Although he did not know anything about making movies, Capra convinced them to let him direct a film. Capra received seventy-five dollars for his work on *Fultah Fisher's Boarding House*, an adaptation of a poem by English poet Rudyard Kipling. Enjoying his experience as a director, Capra became interested in the film industry. He was hired as an apprentice at a film laboratory, where he worked in exchange for food and lodging.

Soon he was employed by Hollywood director Bob Eddy as a propman and editor. Then followed a six-month stint as a joke writer for a studio run by Hal Roach. Capra was fired because the studio did not believe his jokes were funny. Capra began a new writing job with director Mack Sennett, who assigned him to work with Harry Langdon, a comic actor who was popular in silent movies. When Langdon moved over to the First National studio in 1926, he took Capra with him as his director. At First National, Capra co-wrote and co-directed Langdon's hit movie *Tramp Tramp Tramp* (1926) and directed two subsequent successes, *The Strong Man* (1926) and *Long Pants* (1927).

Capra was fired by Harry Langdon over a dispute about who deserved the most credit for the team's success. Capra returned to working with Mack Sennett. The turning point in Capra's career came in 1928 when he was hired as a director for Columbia Pictures. The studio gave him complete freedom to make the type of films he envisioned. He was also paired with screenwriter Robert Riskin, who had formerly worked as a journalist and playwright. With Riskin's help, Capra released a long series of highly successful films during the 1930s and early 1940s.

The typical Capra film was a comedic fable featuring an idealistic central character—an unlikely hero who overcomes tremendous odds and triumphs in the face of cynicism and materialism. Although the films touched on darker themes, invariably the endings conveyed a mood of rosy optimism. Praised for his skill in handling actors, staging complex scenes, and recreating authentically American dialogue onscreen, Capra received best director Oscars for *It Happened One Night* (1934), *Mr. Deeds Goes to Town* (1936), and *You Can't Take It With You* (1938). Another acclaimed film, *Mr. Smith Goes to Washington* (1939), starred Jimmy Stewart as an idealistic freshman senator who finds himself immersed in political corruption. In Capra's films, his outlook was essentially optimistic, and the world he created in his films was one in which the good and pure of heart won out over evil and corruption. Presented with a mixture of sentiment and screwball comedy, later known as "Capracorn," these themes were well received by audiences who had been demoralized by the Great Depression.

Recruited for Propaganda Films

One of Capra's highest-ranking fans was General George Marshall, the U.S. Army chief of staff. Shortly after the United States entered World War II in December 1941, Marshall saw the need for propaganda films that would educate soldiers regarding the role of the United States in the conflict. Preferring a producer who knew how to make entertaining films, he immediately thought of Capra. For his part, Capra was eager to contribute to the country's war effort, and he especially wanted to counter the mood of pessimism and despair that saturated the American public. He was given the rank of major in the Signal Corps, the branch of the military that handled training films. Upon his arrival in Washington, D.C., on February 15, 1942, he was faced with an internal power struggle with other officers in the Signal Corps, who felt Capra was ill equipped to educate soldiers.

The conflict was resolved by June through the creation of a special unit, the 834th Signal Services Photographic Detachment, which included eight officers and thirty-five enlisted men under Capra's command. Capra had a small budget and realized he would have to rely on existing footage. Capra began using newsreels, Allied and enemy propaganda, combat films, and even entertainment films. By 1943 his staff had grown to 150. The total cost of Capra's films came to only $400,000, which was less than 1 percent of the $50 million the War Department spent on films during the war.

Technically, Capra was not the director of these films because very little new footage was shot. He referred to himself as an "executive producer" in order to receive credit for shaping the films through expert editing and content selection, which was based on guidance from the army and subject to approval by Marshall, the secretary of war, and other high-level officials. Homesick for his wife, two sons, and daughter, Capra moved his family to the Washington, D.C., area while he

Hollywood Goes to War

Other members of the Hollywood entertainment community also contributed to the war effort. Although many actors, directors, and writers stayed at home, they used their celebrity status either by selling war bonds or appearing at fund-raising events. Some stars went overseas to entertain the troops, or served in the Hollywood or Stage Door Canteens, two of the entertainment clubs set up for soldiers on leave. Photographs, called "pin-ups," of female actors and singers like Betty Grable, Jane Russell, and Marlene Dietrich decorated the bunks of countless soldiers, reminding them of the world they had left behind.

Some actors refused to participate in the conflict due to conscientious objections, while others created a soldierly, macho image on the screen. One of the most popular stars was John Wayne, who appeared in many war movies but was exempted from military service because he was too old, married, and a father.

Some celebrities served in the military. When the war broke out, Jimmy Stewart was a successful, young actor who had appeared to critical acclaim in *Mr. Smith Goes to Washington,* among other films. He enlisted in the Air Corps and became a pilot. First assigned to do a radio show to amuse the troops, Stewart petitioned to be transferred to combat detail. In July 1943 he was promoted to the rank of captain and sent to England to join the 445th Bombing Group, which was flying bombing raids all over Europe. He flew twenty missions and won a number of medals, including a Distinguished Flying Cross.

Movie idol Clark Gable had recently lost his wife, Carole Lombard, in a plane crash when he joined the army. Some of his admirers wondered if he was so grief stricken that he hoped to be killed in the war. After attending officers' training school in Miami Beach, Florida, Gable was recruited by General H. H. "Hap" Arnold to make a film about aerial gunners. He joined the 351st Heavy Bombardment Group, planning to make a movie showing the unit's day-to-day operations. In April 1943, the group was assigned to an air base in England, and Gable began flying combat missions, earning the respect of the men who flew with him. He returned to the United States in December, only to learn that the gunner film had been canceled.

War hero Audie Murphy took a different path to fame. A Texas farm boy who enlisted in the army in 1942 when he was eighteen, Murphy went on to become the most decorated American soldier of the war. Among Murphy's thirty–seven medals and other decorations was the Medal of Honor, which he earned for his single-handed fight against a German infantry company in January 1945. He was said to have killed 241 Germans. After the war, Murphy was recruited to become an actor. He appeared in forty-five films, including *The Red Badge of Courage* (1951) and *To Hell and Back* (1955), which was based on his own life story. He died in a plane crash in 1971.

recruited a group of skilled screenwriters from Hollywood to work as consultants in compiling an effective script, which would be narrated by actor Walter Huston. Some of these writers were later dismissed due to fears that they might slip a pro-Communist message into the films. Some artists and other Americans had turned to communism during the Great Depression thinking it would help the nation's problems. But the government had come to believe that communism threatened the American political system and lifestyle.

Looking for ideas to inspire him, Capra visited New York's Museum of Modern Art (MOMA)

Frank Capra helped produce propaganda films during the war, including the *Why We Fight* series. (Reproduced by permission of the Kobal Collection)

with Russian-born director Anatole Litvak, who had directed films in Germany from 1927 to 1933 and who would work closely with Capra on his war films. Watching all of the Nazi propaganda films in MOMA's collection, they were particularly impressed by the director Leni Riefenstahl, who produced *Triumph des Willens* (*Triumph of the Will*). This film of the Nazis' 1934 Nuremberg Party Congress presented the event as a grandiose spectacle with music that powerfully underscored all the marching soldiers, speeches, and waving flags. As quoted in Joseph McBride's biography of the director, Capra emerged with a feeling of dread: "It scared the hell out of me. My first reaction was that we were dead, we couldn't win the war.... I sat there and I was a very unhappy man. How can I possibly top *this*?"

Capra formulated a method that would utilize excerpts from *Triumph of the Will* to motivate American soldiers. In preparing the first film of the *Why We Fight* series, which would be titled *Prelude to War,* Capra explained the events leading up to the war in Europe with footage from German

propaganda films and newsreels. The narration was simply but strongly worded, describing the war as "a common man's life-and-death struggle against those who would put him back into slavery. We lose it—and we lose everything. Our homes, the jobs we go back to, the books we read, the very food we eat, the hopes we have for our kids, the kids themselves—they won't be ours anymore. That's what's at stake. It's us or them. The chips are down."

Prelude to War *Is a Success*

Realizing that approximately thirty-seven percent of U.S. troops had less than a high school education, Capra needed to simplify complex issues. Consequently, the *Why We Fight* series did not provide extensive historical analysis of the causes of the war. It also featured stereotypical (and insulting) references to the enemy, such as portraying the Germans as discipline-craving robots and the Japanese as "blood-crazed" people. The film troubled some critics. When questioned on the

Jimmy Stewart (second from right) and Donna Reed (third from right) in a scene from Capra's *It's a Wonderful Life*. (Reproduced by permission of the Kobal Collection.)

issue while speaking to an Ohio film association in 1979, Capra is quoted in McBride's book as defending his intention, which was not to produce "hate films" but that some hate did creep into the dialogue. "At the time there was a need for these films.... I'm glad and I'm proud that I was able to satisfy that need, but now I don't like to see these films because of the memories they bring back."

In July 1942 Capra moved his unit to Hollywood, both to be close to movie industry resources and to avoid the political scene in Washington. In August he was promoted to the rank of lieutenant colonel; *Prelude to War* was shown to the troops in

October. General Marshall and President Franklin D. Roosevelt wanted the public to see the film, so it began a commercial run. In March 1943, *Prelude to War* was one of four war films to receive an Oscar for best documentary. The award was given to the army and accepted by Capra.

Despite the acclaim the *Why We Fight* films received upon release, there is some question as to whether they accomplished their intended goal. A postwar study conducted by the military, based on surveys of soldiers taken during the war, showed that the films did increase the knowledge of events leading up to the war, but seemed to have little or

Films in Capra's *Why We Fight* Series

Prelude to War (1942)
The Nazis Strike (1943)
Divide and Conquer (1943)
The Battle of Britain (1943)
The Battle of Russia (1944)
The Battle of China (1944)
War Comes to America (1945)

no effect on the troops' motivation to fight. In some cases, the films even diminished motivation by presenting the enemy as stronger than previously suspected.

In addition to the *Why We Fight* series, the 834th made ten other propaganda films (including such titles as *The Negro Soldier, Your Job in Germany,* and *Know Your Enemy—Japan*). They also produced fifty issues of the *Army-Navy Screen Magazine* and forty-six installments of the weekly *Staff Film Report,* which collected classified battle film and other footage to be shown to the president, Joint Chiefs of Staff, and other high-level commanders. In August 1943 Capra turned over the command of the 834th to Litvak and became commanding officer of the Signal Corps' Special Coverage Section, charged with the duty of supervising combat photography. Capra received the Distinguished Service Medal on June 14, 1945.

After the war, Capra joined fellow directors George Stevens and William Wyler to form a new production company, Liberty Films. The company produced only one film, *It's a Wonderful Life* (1946), starring Jimmy Stewart as a discouraged man who is allowed to see what the world would have been like if he had never been born. Although Capra felt this was his best film, it was not popular with the audiences of the period. *It's a Wonderful Life* is the Capra film best known to contemporary audiences, however, because it is run numerous times on television each Christmas season.

By 1950 Capra's most creative years were behind him. His last film was *Pocketful of Miracles* (1961), a remake of *Lady for a Day* (1931). After Capra died in 1991, he was succeeded in the film industry by his son, Frank Capra Jr., a film producer, and his grandson, Frank Capra III, a director.

SOURCES

Books

Bohn, Thomas, *An Historical and Descriptive Analysis of the 'Why We Fight' Series,* Ayer (New York), 1977.

Capra, Frank, *The Name above the Title: An Autobiography,* Macmillan (New York), 1971.

Carney, Raymond, *American Vision: The Films of Frank Capra,* Cambridge University Press (Cambridge, England), 1986.

Glatzer, Richard, and John Raeburn, *Frank Capra: The Man and His Films,* University of Michigan Press (Ann Arbor, MI), 1974.

McBride, Joseph, *Frank Capra: The Catastrophe of Success,* Simon & Schuster (New York), 1992.

Poague, Leland, *The Cinema of Frank Capra: An Approach to Film Comedy,* A. S. Barnes (Cranbury, NJ), 1974.

Scherle, Victor and William Levy, *The Films of Frank Capra,* Carol Publishing Group (Secaucus, NJ), 1977.

Periodicals

Arnold, Gary, "Though More than 60 Years Old, Films of Frank Capra Stay Fresh," *Insight on the News,* February 9, 1998, p. 38.

Ann B. Carl

In 1942 Ann B. Carl was one of 25,000 women who applied for training as pilots in the Women's Flying Training Detachment, which was being organized as a civilian arm of the Army Air Corps by aviator Jacqueline Cochran. Like its counterpart, the Women's Auxiliary Ferrying Service (WAFS), the group was hiring women pilots for domestic military flying so that male pilots could be available for combat overseas. Carl was among the 1,070 Women's Airforce Service Pilots (WASPs) who graduated from the training program in Houston, Texas. During a tour of duty at Wright Field (now Wright Patterson Air Force Base) in Dayton, Ohio, she worked as a test pilot, flying most of the military aircraft being used in World War II. The highlight of Carl's career, however, was an evaluation flight of the turbojet-powered Bell YP-59A, during which she became the first woman to test-pilot a jet plane. This milestone was to remain unchallenged for ten years.

Born August 1918
   Augusta, Georgia, United States

WASP and test pilot

"To have our war service terminated before the war's end made us feel incomplete, that we had not been 'in at the finish.'"

Trip to Pre-War Europe

Ann Baumgartner Carl was born in 1918 in Augusta, Georgia, where her mother was living while Carl's father was stationed in France during World War I (1914–1918). After the war the family moved to Plainfield, New Jersey, which was located within commuting distance of her father's job at a law firm in New York City. Her mother, an artist, was active in the cultural community. When Carl

Cornelia Fort Dies On Active Duty

Women's Auxiliary Ferrying Service (WAFS) pilot Cornelia Fort (1919–1943) was the first American woman to die on active military duty. While growing up in Davidson County, Tennessee, she would have seemed an unlikely candidate for such a distinction. The oldest daughter of a wealthy doctor, she lived on a large estate and attended elite private schools. In 1937, at age nineteen, she was presented to society at a debutante ball, the first step in preparing her to become the wife of a Southern gentleman. Fort decided to take another direction in life, however, when her father died three years later: She signed up for flying lessons and immediately became enthralled with airplanes. By 1941 she was the first female flight instructor in Nashville, and later that year she took a job as an instructor with the newly formed Civilian Pilots Training Program at Fort Collins, Colorado.

In the fall of 1941, she transferred to Honolulu, Hawaii, where she taught flying to defense workers, soldiers, and sailors. On December 7, 1941, Fort became an eyewitness to history. That Sunday morning she and one of her students were readying for take-off in a plane at John Rodgers Airport in Honolulu. The student, who was completing his solo training, was in the pilot's seat. Just as they were ascending, Fort saw a military plane flying in low over the runway from the sea. Realizing it was headed directly toward her own plane, she seized the controls just in time to avoid a collision. As the incoming aircraft continued flying in the direction of the U.S. military base at Pearl Harbor, about a quarter of a mile away, she noticed that it was a Japanese war plane. Then she also saw clouds of smoke in the distance. Later she learned about the Japanese attack on Pearl Harbor, the event that forced American entry into World War II.

In January 1942, while Fort was still in Hawaii, she was invited by aviator Jacqueline Cochran to join other American women pilots who would be flying with the Royal Air Force Air Transport Auxiliary in Great Britain. Although Fort could not accept the offer because of commitments in Hawaii, she had another chance in the fall. This time she was asked to be one of several women fliers who were starting the Women's Auxiliary Ferrying Service, or WAFS, which was part of the Ferrying Division of the Air Transport Command. Hired to fly planes from factories to military air bases, the women would free male pilots for combat training. Fort was told she had to report to New Castle Army Air Base in Delaware within twenty-four hours, and she leaped at the opportunity to take part in the war effort.

As she embarked on the new adventure, she often flew with primitive equipment—untested planes with open cockpits, no radios, and no navigation instruments—a situation made doubly difficult in bad weather. After she delivered a plane to its destination, she had to find other transportation back to the base; thus a trip across the country might take several days. In March 1943 Fort was one of several male and female pilots assigned to take BT-13 aircraft to Love Field in Dallas, Texas. During the flight the landing gear on another plane clipped Fort's airplane, causing it to crash to the ground; Fort was killed in the crash. She was the first of thirty-eight American women pilots who died while flying military planes during World War II. They received no recognition for their services, however, because they were classified as civilians by the army. In 1945 an airpark named in Fort's honor was built near her childhood home in Tennessee.

For more information on Cornelia Fort, see the PBS web site at *The American Experience: Fly Girls*, http://www.pbs.org/wgbh/amex/flygirls.

was fourteen, the Baumgartners moved to Bernardsville, New Jersey. While growing up she attended private schools and was influenced by her mother's interest in art and her father's background in engineering. She was especially close to her brother, Tom, who was four years younger. After graduating from Walnut Hill School at Natwick, Massachusetts, in 1935, she entered Smith College in Northampton, Massachusetts, majoring in pre-medical studies. When she graduated four years later, however, she was uncertain about pursuing a career in science. Her parents decided to give her a trip to Europe on an Italian freighter both as a graduation gift and as a chance to find direction in life. Carl had planned to travel with a friend, but the young woman changed her mind at the last minute because Nazi Germany was preparing for war in Europe. Carl went alone, and the experience gave her a sobering perspective on the world.

In her autobiography, *A WASP Among Eagles* (1999), Carl describes her experiences in pre-war Europe at ports she visited during the trip aboard the freighter *Saturnia*. Carl writes: "….I began to notice the rift between … Germans who were Nazis and the other passengers. The Nazis spoke confidently in loud voices, played loud music, drank, and sang loud songs, while the Europeans glanced at them with hatred and half-closed eyes…. When the ship stopped at Venice, and I sat drinking coffee in St. Mark's Square, I saw what amounted to a marching column, circling the square, singing and clapping loudly. 'Nazis,' I heard in disgust around me. Later I came to recognize, and fear, that marching song in other European towns."

Carl ended her journey in England, where she was joined by her mother. They were visiting relatives on September 1, 1939, the day Nazi Germany invaded Poland and started World War II.

Upon returning to the United States, Carl abandoned her plans to go to medical school. Instead, she devoted her time to the war effort and looked for work. She took a few jobs before settling into a position as a medical researcher in Newark, New Jersey, and moving to Greenwich Village in New York. Now that she was earning a salary, she decided to act on her dream of becoming a pilot, so on weekends she went back to New Jersey to take flying lessons. Soon she realized she wanted to fly airplanes full time. She stayed in New York a while longer, however, leaving the research job to work as an editor and writer. After receiving her pilot's license, she flew submarine-spotting missions along the Atlantic coast for the national Civil Air Patrol. In 1942 she read about the Women's Flying Training Detachment and, thrilled at the prospect of joining the war effort, she immediately submitted an application to the program. After an interview with Cochran, Carl was told to report to the training center at Houston Municipal Airport on January 3, 1943, as a member of the Class of 43-W-3.

From WASP to Pioneering Test Pilot

At Houston, Carl expected to find an official military facility with barracks, mess hall, and infirmary; instead she arrived at a rundown terminal surrounded by stray buildings at the end of a single runway. The "mess hall" was a local restaurant, and the "barracks" were nearby motels. Having financed the trip to Houston themselves, trainees had supplied their own uniforms—white shirt, khaki trousers, and overseas caps—but the air corps had given them over-sized surplus flying coveralls. As civil service employees they would earn $150 a month and were expected to pay for their own meals. The training aircraft promised by the air force were not yet ready, so the women had been issued Piper Cubs, Taylorcrafts, and Aeroncas. Although the planes were decrepit and the flight instructors surly, Carl underwent rigorous training: She took ground courses and studied navigation, meteorology, engine operation, and Morse code. When the new planes finally arrived, she learned to operate a PT-19 and a BT-13.

Just as she was preparing to qualify for solo flying, however, she was quarantined with a case of the measles. During her convalescence, she considered dropping out of the program and enrolling in medical school. By the time she was released from quarantine, the training center had been relocated to Avenger Field at Sweetwater, Texas, which provided actual military-base facilities. The improved environment raised Carl's spirits, giving her a new sense of commitment to her goal, but she had fallen behind the W-3 class because of her illness. Now a member of class 5, she trained on a twin-engine Cessna C-78 and the North American AT-6; in order to catch up with her classmates she also had to do extensive night flying. On September 11, 1943, she graduated from the WASP program. (In July 1943 the Women's Flying Training Detachment had merged with the WAFS. Headed by Cochran, the group was called the Women's Airforce Service Pilots, or WASP.)

Female aviators put their flying skills to work as they did their part to help the Allies win the war. (Photograph by Hugh Morgan/USAF Museum; reproduced by permission)

For her first assignment Carl was sent with a fellow graduate, Betty Greene, to join a WASP contingent of the tow-target squadron of the artillery base at Camp Davis, North Carolina. Carl and Greene were replacing two women who had died in unexplained accidents at the base, which had a history of problems that Cochran was trying to keep secret. At the outset the women encountered hostility and harassment from pilots in the men's squadron, who did not believe women were capable of flying airplanes. Nevertheless, Carl gained experience with a variety of planes such as the A-24, the Douglas Dauntless dive-bomber, the Lockheed B-34, and the Curtiss A-25 dive-bomber. Her job was to test artillery and radar tracking, experiment with robot drone planes, and tow practice targets. In February 1944, Carl and Greene were temporarily transferred to Wright Field. They were involved in the testing of clothing and oxygen masks in the B-17 bomber and in single-engine aircraft at different temperatures and altitudes. After undergoing experiments in oxygen deprivation, Carl and Green helped select the WASP flight uniform, which was adapted from medium-sized air corps men's clothing. One of Carl's tasks was also to help perfect a women's relief tube, a device used for urination during flight.

Challenged by the job of a test pilot, Carl requested a permanent transfer to Wright Field. In March 1944 she was assigned to the Fighter Flight Test Branch (FTT), where she became the only female test pilot of military combat planes. Although she was still a WASP, she had no further contact with her unit. At FTT, Carl tested fighter planes for performance in stalls, spins, dives, glides, forced landings, and other situations. She was also involved in tests of a tail warning device and a gunsight on the P-51 and with experiments on a high-altitude camera for a P-38. While temporarily assigned to the Bomber Flight Test (BFT), she participated in performance and cross-country tests on the B-25 bomber and the Martin B-6. She also conducted propeller and engine tests on the B-17 Flying Fortress, and landing gear tests on the B-24 four-engine Liberator bomber. At BFT, Carl was part of the team that conducted one of the first midair-refueling tests, and she flew the B-29 Superfortress on long-range flights to determine its capacity to carry heavy bombs. After returning to FTT, Carl was involved in the earliest altitude compression tests on the RP–47E, the first plane equipped with a pressurized cockpit. The highlight of Carl's career, however, was her evaluation flight of the Bell YP-59A.

The FTT team had eagerly awaited the arrival of the experimental plane from the air corps testing field at Muroc Dry Lake in California. The air corps had set the goal of quickly producing a jet-propelled fighter that could be used in combat against German and Japanese aircraft. Development of the Bell YP-59A had thus far been kept secret, so the FTT follow-up evaluation was crucial to the future of the project. Once the plane had taxied onto the runway, the team members took turns going up on thirty-minute test flights. After the male team members had flown the plane, Carl climbed aboard to conduct her own evaluation. In *WASP Among Eagles* she writes: "I was alone with the jet. Weighed down with responsibility. I advanced the power and the engines whined, black smoke trailing. Visibility with the tricycle gear was good, and taxiing could be controlled just with the rudder. Cleared for take-off, I pushed the engines into a high scream and started down the runway. As advertised, it took a while to get airborne. Settled into the climb, suddenly the jet noise stopped." Carl began to wonder, "Had the engines quit already? No, we (the plane and I) were still climbing. Then I realized the jet noise was now behind me. I looked out at the elliptical wings and the narrow nose ahead of me. As we slid along silently it was strange to realize I was the only jet up there, perhaps the only jet over the United States that day."

As Carl touched down on the airstrip in an "uneventful" landing, she reflected on the significance of her experience. "I admit," she writes, "I did wonder idly whether a local reporter might be there to check on the first woman to fly a jet, but, of course, the project was still very much a secret, and others from FTT had flown it that day as well, the men, that is. Actually, this 'first' was to remain unchallenged for ten years." Although the Bell YP-59A was never put into service, it did prove the feasibility of jet propulsion; fifty of the planes were built for demonstration purposes.

The WASPs were disbanded in December 1944 and Carl was required to turn in her equipment. She remained for a brief time at Wright Field, participating in the conceptualization of the XP-82, which became the fastest propeller-driven fighter by the end of World War II. In the conclusion of *WASP Among Eagles,* Carl reflects on the cancellation of the WASP program: "To have our war service terminated before the war's end made us feel incomplete, that we had not been 'in at the finish.' After honing our skills and dedicating ourselves to the war effort, we were now surplus. And 38

In the town of Sweetwater, Texas, on the grounds of Avenger Field where the Women Airforce Service Pilots (WASPs) trained, a sole aviator stands in honor of the contributions made by women pilots during World War II. (Reproduced by permission of Susan E. Edgar)

WASPs had given their lives." She derived a greater sense of achievement from her work as a test pilot. Earlier in the book Carl notes that she had been transformed from a carefree young woman to a mature and disciplined flyer. Yet, she writes, "There was something else—something bigger than my own accomplishments. It had to do with being a part, a small part, with my colleagues at Wright Field, in winning the war against the evil forces of Nazism."

In 1945 she married Bill Carl, an air force major she met while working on the design of the XP-82; the couple had two children. Ann Carl later returned to flying as an instructor and pilot in private industry. She was also a regular columnist on science and the environment for such publications as *Newsday* and the *Bulletin of the Atomic Scientists.* In 1977 the Carls set out on a two-year, round-the-world sailing trip, with the former WASP as navigator. This experience was the subject of her book *The Small World of Long-Distance Sailors* (1985). During the fiftieth-anniversary celebration of jet flight in 1992, Carl was invited to give a lecture at the National Air and Space Museum in Washington, DC.

Sources

Books

Carl, Ann B., *A WASP Among Eagles: A Woman Test Pilot in World War II*, Smithsonian Institution Press (Washington, DC), 1999.

Other

The American Experience: Fly Girls, http://www.pbs.org (August 27, 2000).

WASP WWII Home Page, http://www.wasp-wwii.org/ (May 5, 2000).

Neville Chamberlain

Neville Chamberlain's tenure as prime minister of Great Britain is often associated with his failure to fend off war with dictators Benito Mussolini of Italy and Adolf Hitler of Germany. For many years his policy of appeasement was criticized and condemned, but a new faction of historians has defended his actions as a stalling tactic that allowed England time to arm itself for the later conflict. Although Chamberlain was called weak and inefficient by those who did not approve of his policies, others claim he was a man of integrity who devoted his life to public service.

Born March 18, 1869
　　Birmingham, England
Died November 9, 1940
　　Hampshire, England

Prime Minister of Great Britain from 1937 to 1940

"How horrible, fantastic, incredible it is that we should be digging trenches and trying on gas-masks here because of a quarrel in a far-away country between people of whom we know nothing."

Rises in British Government

The Chamberlain family had been shoemakers in the eighteenth century, and over the next 100 years they steadily ascended the social and economic ladder as businessmen of the upper middle class. Joseph Chamberlain, Neville's father, abandoned business in favor of politics, becoming a radical advocate of social welfare as a member of England's Liberal Party. Neville's mother, Florence Kenrick, who was his father's second wife, died in childbirth when Neville was six years old. After Florence's death, Joseph Chamberlain spent less time at home. Neville reportedly found comfort in his large troupe of younger siblings and cousins. He went away to school at Rugby where, despite

(USHMM Photo Archives)

academic success, he was supposedly unhappy because of his poor relationship with the school's headmaster and separation from his family.

Chamberlain left Rugby in 1886 and attended Mason College in Birmingham to study science and engineering design. In 1890, while working in an accounting firm, his father suddenly announced that the family was going to start a business growing and processing sisal (a fibrous plant used in rope-making and other products) in the Bahamas. Neville and his brother Austen were placed in charge of the operation and moved to the Bahamas to search for a suitable piece of land. Upon settling on Andros Island, twenty miles from Nassau, they established the Andros Fibre Company. Austen soon returned to England and Neville became the company's managing director. He worked long days of hard labor, clearing the land and assembling buildings. Although the plantation seemed promising at first, it eventually failed and Chamberlain returned to England. Chamberlain soon went into business in Birmingham, buying a company called Hoskins and Son that manufactured berths for ships. He involved himself in local politics, although he was not as passionate or liberal as his father about social issues. He was elected to the Birmingham city council in 1911.

By the time Chamberlain was in his early forties he was still unmarried, and his friends and relatives were beginning to think he might live the remainder of his life as a bachelor. In 1911, however, he married Anne Cole, with whom he later had a daughter and a son. Chamberlain served as lord mayor of Birmingham from 1915 to 1916. His career in national politics began during World War I (1914–18) when he became director of National Service, overseeing the drafting of soldiers into the armed forces. He was elected to the House of Commons in 1918 as a member of the Conservative Party. Chamberlain rose rapidly into the upper levels of government, serving as minister of health from 1923 to 1929 (and again in 1931) and as chancellor of the exchequer from 1923 to 1924 and 1931 to 1937. He gained a reputation as a skilled, orderly administrator with the ability to push through needed reforms.

Misjudges Hitler's Goals in Europe

In the late 1930s, Germany and Italy were taking aggressive actions against other countries and threatening world peace. This was the dominant concern when Chamberlain was elected prime minister in 1937, and his first act was to establish avoidance of war as his top priority, contending that appeasement of Hitler and Mussolini was of the best policy for Great Britain. Chamberlain's position has received criticism over the years, but at the time many other leaders supported it. Foreign Minister Anthony Eden, however, strongly disagreed and warned Chamberlain about the dangers of negotiating with dictators. He felt that Great Britain needed to take a firm stand against Hitler and Mussolini. Though Chamberlain had supported sanctions against Italy after its conquest of the East African country of Ethiopia, he eventually established a treaty with Mussolini that accepted Italy's acquisition of this country, with the condition that Italy would stay uninvolved in the Spanish Civil War (1936–1939).

Meanwhile, Germany was eager to reclaim some territory in Czechoslovakia, which it had lost in World War I, and where many Germans still lived. Hitler demanded that any area of Czechoslovakia that had more than 50 percent Sudeten Germans would have to be ceded to Germany, but he claimed he did not want war and would not try to gain any more of Czechoslovakia once these areas were under German control. Chamberlain told the British Parliament that the issue was unworthy of military conflict, but when meetings with the leaders of Czechoslovakia, France, Germany, and Italy broke down, he seemed resigned to war despite his reservations. According to *Historic World Leaders,* Chamberlain "broadcast to the nation: 'How horrible, fantastic, incredible it is that we should be digging trenches and trying on gas-masks here because of a quarrel in a far-away country between people of whom we know nothing.'" Yet, after meeting with Hitler once again, Chamberlain and the leaders from France and Czechoslovakia decided that it was in their best interest to avoid another war with Germany and, along with Mussolini, they signed the Munich Pact on September 30, 1938. In this agreement Germany promised to occupy only specified Czech territories and to leave the rest of the country unoccupied.

Chamberlain made a triumphant return to London and was photographed waving the signed agreement in his hand, proclaiming that he had secured "peace in our time." He was praised as a superb diplomat by the press, public, and other statesmen, but the glory was short-lived. On March 14, 1939, Germany violated the conditions of the Munich Pact and invaded all of Czechoslovakia. Great Britain then formed an alliance with

Poland and agreed to take action if Germany tried to occupy Poland. On September 1, 1939, German troops moved into Poland, and Chamberlain had no choice but to respond to the aggression. Two days later Great Britain declared war on Germany. Chamberlain's failed efforts at peace led to discontent within his own party and the refusal of the opposition, the Labour Party, to work with him. Many critics felt he had completely misjudged Hitler. After occupying Poland, the Nazi leader began to implement his plans to conquer all of western Europe. Great Britain's inability to intercept the German invasion of Norway and Denmark was the final blow, and Chamberlain resigned in May 1940. Winston Churchill became the new prime minister.

Chamberlain stayed on in the government, serving as lord president of the council, but by the end of the summer he had become ill with cancer. He resigned from his post in October and died a month later. He was buried at Westminster Abbey in London. In his village church in the town of Hampshire, a memorial reads "Neville Chamberlain. Prime Minister of Great Britain 1937–1940. Write me as one that loves his fellow-men."

SOURCES

Books

Charmley, John, *Chamberlain and the Lost Peace,* I. R. Dee (Chicago), 1990.

Dilks, David, *Neville Chamberlain,* Cambridge University Press (Cambridge), 1984.

Historic World Leaders, Gale Research (Detroit), 1994.

Macleod, Iain, *Neville Chamberlain,* Atheneum (New York), 1962.

Periodicals

Bartlett, J. W., "Munich Agreement Is Signed: September 30th, 1938," *History Today,* September, 1998, p. 40.

Other

Arthur Neville Chamberlain—Britain in World War II, http://www.britaininworldwar2.future.easyspace.com/commanders/chamberlain.html (May 5, 2000).

Beattie, A. J., *Neville Chamberlain,* http://www.grolier.com/wwii/wwii_chamber.html (May 5, 2000).

Chiang Kai-Shek

Born October 31, 1887
Zhejiang, China
Died April 5, 1975
Taipei, Taiwan

Chinese general and leader of the
Kuomintang Party

*"Promises must be kept and action must
be resolute."*

(Reproduced by permission of Archive Photos, Inc.)

As a young man Chiang Kai-Shek fought under the revolutionary leader Sun Yat-Sen, who in 1912 successfully ended the reign of the Manchus, a minority ethnic group that had controlled the government of China for three hundred years. After Sun's death, Chiang attained substantial power as head of the military of the Kuomintang, or Nationalist Party, and battled against Japanese invaders as well as warlords, rival politicians, and the Communist Party within his own country. During World War II, Chiang and his wife tried to influence public opinion in the United States to raise money for China's war against Japan. Although they were successful for a while, Chiang was unable to stop the tide of change that swept over China when Communists led by Mao Zedong took power.

Finds Home in Military

Chiang's father, Chiang Su-an, was a village leader and manager of a government-owned salt company. When he died, his nine-year-old son was left to the care of his mother, Wang Tsai-yu, and paternal grandfather, who sent him to work for some relatives who owned a shop. It is speculated that Chiang was mistreated and unhappy, but it is known that he ran away and joined the army. There he found a new home and remained devoted to the military for the rest of his life. When he was eighteen, he passed the entrance examination for the Baoding Military Academy. Prior to this acceptance, at the age of fourteen, Chiang had entered a traditional arranged marriage to a young woman named Mao Fumei; their son, Chiang Ching-kuo, was born before Chiang entered the academy. The couple eventually divorced.

In 1907 Chiang went to Tokyo to attend the Japanese Army Military State College. Like many other Chinese students living in Japan, he became involved in the revolutionary movement, led by Sun Yat-Sen, that aimed to overthrow China's Manchu government. Chiang returned to China in 1911 to participate in fighting near the city of Shanghai. The Manchus were defeated, a republican government was formed, and Sun became the first president. When Sun resigned a year later, General Yuan Shikai was named president. Disappointed in Yuan's repressive rule, Sun withdrew to Japan. After taking part in an unsuccessful counter-revolution to remove Yuan from power, Chiang and other members of Sun's *T'ung-meng Hui* (Revolutionary Alliance; later the Kuomintang party) also fled to Japan. Chiang returned to Shanghai in 1915, spending a few years involved in questionable business practices and organized crime as part of a secret organization called the "Green Gang."

The death of President Yuan Shikai in 1916 led to disorder in China as power was divided among approximately 200 warlords. In 1918 Sun Yat-Sen formed another government ruled by the Kuomintang. The capital was established at Guangzhou, located in southern China, and Chiang became Sun's military adviser. Meanwhile, most of the warlords supported a rival government that had been established at Beijing in the northern part of the country. While establishing the government, Sun had relied on supplies and advice from the Soviet Union, which produced strong ties to the ruling Soviet Communist Party. Chiang was sent to Moscow in 1923 to study the Soviet military and political systems, an experience that soured him toward the communist form of government. He returned to China in 1924 to become director of the Whampoa Military Academy, where he was to train young men to be loyal, capable soldiers.

Leading the Kuomintang to Power

When Sun died in 1925, China remained a divided country. Taking charge of the Kuomintang, which still controlled only two southern regions, Chiang set out to unify China forcibly. In a military campaign called the Northern Expedition, he moved his army into northern China and captured the city of Hankou. They defeated numerous warlord armies, which were then absorbed into the Nationalist army. In March 1927 the Kuomintang established a new central government at Nanjing (also called Nanking). Chiang's distrust of communism led him to purge all Communist sympathizers from the Kuomintang, executing many of them. Despite his efforts to oust the communist way of thinking, however, the movement continued to grow in China.

On December 1, 1927, Chiang wed the polished and charming Soong Mei-Ling, the younger sister of Sun Yat-Sen's wife. They were married only after Chiang made assurances to her devoutly Christian family that he had divorced his second wife, Chen Chieh-ju, whom he had married after divorcing his first wife in 1921. His third wife, known as Madame Chiang, had been educated in the United States and would prove an effective spokesperson for her husband when he later sought aid from the West. Although a majority of the Chinese followed Buddhism, Chiang was baptized into the Christian faith on October 23, 1930, since Madame Chiang was a Christian.

From 1927 to 1931, Chiang ruled the Kuomintang government while trouble brewed among rebellious warlords, devious political leaders, and the Communists. In 1931 Japan occupied Manchuria, a region in northeast China, but Chiang decided not to try to regain the region. He felt it was necessary first to attack China's growing Communist Party. Chiang retired from public life when public opinion turned against him for not resisting the Japanese invasion of Manchuria. Within a year he was called back to lead the government; it had become clear that no one else could do a better job of bringing the hostile groups together, despite Chiang's inability to control the Communists, who had gained control of some regions of China.

Fighting the Japanese

The Japanese remained a threat throughout the early 1930s, leading some Chinese to call for the Kuomintang and the Communists to put aside their differences in order to fight their common enemy. In 1936 a former military officer named Chang Hsueh-Liang kidnapped Chiang in an attempt to persuade him to cooperate with the

Madame Chiang Kai-Shek

In the 1920s Chiang Kai-Shek began courting Soong Mei-Ling, a woman from a noted Shanghai family, and in 1927 they were married. She was the daughter of Soong Yao-ju, or Charles Jones Soong, who had gone to college in the United States and returned to serve as a Methodist missionary before becoming a businessman. Madame Chiang Kai-Shek's brother, T.V. Soong, attended Harvard and held several important positions in the Kuomintang government. Her two sisters worked for the party as well and also gained power through their marriages to other important political figures. Like her father and siblings, Madame Chiang reached young adulthood in the United States. Her sister Soong E-Ling was the first Chinese woman to earn a degree from an American college, graduating from Wesleyan in 1909, as did sister Soong Ching-Ling in 1913. Madame Chiang was at Wesleyan her freshman year, but transferred to Wellesley College in Massachusetts to be in closer proximity to her brother at Harvard; she graduated in 1917. All three sisters returned to China after their graduations and became involved with the Kuomintang through Sun Yat-Sen, who was a friend of the Soong family.

Soong E-Ling worked for Sun and in 1914 married H. H. Kung, who became a finance minister. Soong Ching-Ling married Sun one year later, but she was widowed in 1925.

Described as intelligent and charming, Madame Chiang found several ways to help her husband in his quest to keep China free from both foreign aggression and communist influence. In the years just before World War II she attempted to aid China's orphans and homeless people, find work for poor women, and promote children's education, but her efforts did little to ease the great suffering of her people. Madame Chiang played her most important role during the war, when she served as her husband's voice in pleading for help from the rest of the world. When General Claire L. Chennault arrived with his Flying Tigers, a small but effective group of American fighter pilots who battled the Japanese in China and Burma, Madame Chiang helped him communicate with her husband and was made honorary commander of the group.

The high point of Madame Chiang's wartime career was her visit to the United States from November 1942 to May 1943. She spoke to crowds at rallies and addressed Congress, describing how the war had affected her country and asking for help in the form of money and supplies. Her picture even appeared on the cover of *Time* magazine. After the Communists took over China in

Communists in resisting Japanese aggression. When he was released, Chiang claimed he had made no agreements; nevertheless, his Kuomintang Party and the Communist Party soon formed a "United Front" against the Japanese. War broke out in July 1937 when Chinese and Japanese forces clashed at the Marco Polo Bridge near Beijing. By the fall of 1938 the Japanese had conquered all of eastern China, controlling most of the fertile farmland in the country and thus forcing the starvation of millions of Chinese peasants. As World War II raged in Europe during 1941, Allied countries joined China's fight against Japan,

which was expanding its empire throughout the eastern Pacific region. Chiang had been serving as commander in chief of China's army, and now the Allies put him in command of the entire Chinese theater of war. Chiang and his wife traveled to the United States to request help with their war effort through the Lend-Lease Program, which allowed Allied nations to borrow money and weapons with the promise of paying for them after the war. Although Chiang was portrayed by both Chinese and American propaganda as a courageous leader struggling against a brutal enemy, some American leaders felt that precious war supplies and funds

Eleanor Roosevelt, wife of U.S. President Franklin Roosevelt, meets with Madame Chiang Kai-Shek. (Reproduced by permission of AP/Wide World Photos)

1949, Madame Chiang fled with her husband to Taiwan, where he served as president until his death in 1975. Madame Chiang left Taiwan after his death and since then she has spent most of her time living quietly in New York City. She celebrated her 103rd birthday in March 2000.

For more information on the Soong sisters, see Barbara A. Brannon's article "China's Soong Sisters at Wesleyan," *Wesleyan Magazine,* (Fall 1997) or the online version at http://www.wesleyancollege.edu/campus/history/soong.html.

were being wasted on China. General Joseph W. Stilwell, the leading military adviser on China, claimed that the Chinese leaders were incompetent and corrupt, criticizing Chiang for his refusal to modernize his army and his lack of aggressive action against the Japanese. Stilwell suggested that Chiang wanted to conserve his troops for a future struggle with the Communist Party and was more concerned with retaining his own power than helping the Chinese people.

President Franklin D. Roosevelt hoped that Chiang could lead China to greatness. In Novem-

ber 1943 Chiang represented his country at the Cairo Conference, a meeting of world leaders where the Allies mapped out their plans for the war in Asia. By 1944 the Japanese had conquered a majority of Chinese territory while the Kuomintang government and military grew increasingly weaker. The Communists continued to work behind Japanese lines in northern China in attempts to strengthen their own troops and win over more Chinese. The war in Asia ended in August 1945 when the United States dropped atom bombs on Hiroshima and Nagasaki and forced Japan to surrender.

General Joseph Warren Stilwell

Joseph W. Stilwell was born in Florida in 1883. He graduated from West Point in 1904, and served as an intelligence officer during World War I (1914–1918), attaining the rank of colonel. During the 1920s and 1930s, he served in China, becoming proficient in Chinese culture and language. In February 1942 he was promoted to lieutenant-general, was appointed to the position of commander of the U.S. military in the China-Burma-India theater, and was named Chiang Kai-Shek's Allied chief of staff. He was assigned the tasks of improving the fighting efficiency of China's armed forces and of directing the flow of U.S. aid to the Chinese. This proved to be a highly complex political and diplomatic assignment, one to which his brusque personality may not have been well-suited. He was often at odds with Chiang Kai-Shek.

Stilwell was known as "Vinegar Joe" due to his cantankerous manner and scathing condemnation of pretentiousness and incompetence. In 1942, when asked about his "glorious retreat" with a group of defeated soldiers across the mountains from Burma to India, he snapped, "There's no such thing as a glorious retreat. All retreats are as ignominious as hell. I claim we got a hell of a licking."

Stilwell's Chinese forces succeeded in recapturing Myitkyina, in northern Burma, from the Japanese in summer 1944. This victory won him promotion to four-star general. In spite of this success, Stilwell's ongoing clash with Chiang Kai-Shek led to his recall in 1944. He commanded the Tenth U.S. Army on Okinawa until he died of cancer in 1946, five months before he was due to retire.

Lt. Gen. Joseph W. Stilwell (Library of Congress)

For a year after the war, U.S. Chief of Staff General George Marshall attempted to persuade Chiang to form a coalition government with the Communist Party. These efforts did not succeed and the Communists began a full-scale civil war against the Kuomintang. The Nationalist government had been severely weakened by many years of fighting against Japan. The Chinese people suffered from famine, inflation, crime, high taxes, and forced conscription into the army. Many were attracted to the communist message of equality among social classes and the sharing of resources and power. Communist fighters made steady gains against Chiang's forces; by the end of 1948 the Communists controlled most of northern China.

Chiang appealed desperately to the United States for help, but the American government did not want to get involved in the civil war. On December 10, 1949, Chiang fled to Taiwan (formerly called Formosa), an island located approximately one hundred miles off the eastern coast of China. He

Chiang Kai-Shek in China in 1949, shortly before his retreat to Taiwan. (Reproduced by permission of AP/Wide World Photos.)

made a brief return to China and tried to reorganize his exhausted soldiers, but finally brought them back with him to Taiwan. Over the next two decades, Chiang vowed that he would return to China and vanquish the Communists, but never did. When communist North Korea invaded South Korea in 1950, the United States began to worry about the spread of communism through Asia. Taiwan was not communist and was seen as worth strengthening, so Taiwan received more U.S. aid.

Chiang continued to portray himself as a fighter against tyranny, yet he ruled Taiwan as a dictator. Taiwan's economy prospered, but the country became increasingly isolated as mainland China's relations with other countries, especially the United States, improved. In 1971 the United Nations voted to recognize the People's Republic of China as the true China, and the delegates from Taiwan were expelled. Chiang, who had been elected president in every election since his arrival in Taiwan, died on April 5, 1975. His son from his first marriage became the ruler of Taiwan and served until 1988.

SOURCES

Books

Chang, Chun-ming, *Chiang Kai-Shek, His Life and Times,* St. John's University (New York), 1981.

Crozier, Brian, *The Man Who Lost China: The First Full Biography of Chiang Kai-Shek,* Scribner (New York), 1976.

Curtis, Richard, *Chiang Kai-Shek,* Hawthorn Books (New York), 1969.

Dolan, Sean, *Chiang Kai-Shek,* Chelsea House (New York), 1988.

Loh, P.P.Y., *The Early Chiang Kai-shek,* Columbia University E. Asian Institute Occasional Papers, Books on Demand (New York), 1971.

Winston Churchill

One of the most influential British leaders in history, Winston Churchill became a figure of monumental importance during World War II as he led his country through some of its darkest days. Churchill's career was long and rich, though turbulent, featuring numerous achievements and setbacks. Frequently his fellow politicians scorned him, yet he also joined the ranks of the great political heroes. Though Churchill established a welfare system in Great Britain, prepared the British navy for World War I (1914-1918), and earned a Nobel Prize for literature, he is most remembered for his role in World War II. His powerful speeches, his two-fingered "V for Victory" wave, and his tenacious refusal to give into tyranny inspired hope and courage in people around the world.

Born November 30, 1874
    Oxfordshire, England
Died January 24, 1965
    London, England

British statesman; prime minister; soldier; writer

"I have nothing to offer but blood, toil, tears and sweat."

Begins Political Career

Churchill was the son of an English aristocrat, Lord Randolph Churchill, and a descendant of John Churchill, the First Duke of Marlborough, who led a great military victory against the French in 1702. His mother was Jennie Jerome, an American from New York City whose own mother was one-quarter Iroquois. Although Randolph Churchill had once been a respected political figure, his career eventually collapsed and he died a despondent man at forty-six. Some observers have speculated that the younger Churchill was determined to succeed where his father had failed, or perhaps he wanted to prove his worth to his father, who considered him unintelligent and lazy. Churchill's early years do not reflect the achievements of his later life. He entered Harrow, but was denied admittance to the upper form because he refused to study Greek and Latin, preferring to read and write in English. Churchill was finally admitted to the Royal Military College at Sandhurst after his third attempt.

After leaving Sandhurst, Churchill joined the British army as a cavalry officer. In 1895 he took a break from his military duties to travel to Cuba, where he served as a correspondent for the *Daily Graphic* newspaper, reporting on the clash between Spanish colonizers and guerrilla soldiers fighting for independence. Rejoining his army regiment, Churchill was sent to India, which was then a British colony. In 1897 he served with the Indian army on the Malakand expedition that put down a rebellion in the northwestern part of the country; he subsequently wrote a book on this experience entitled *The Story of the Malakand Field Force* (1898).

The following year Churchill went to the Sudan in northern Africa, serving as both an army officer and a reporter in the Battle of Omdurman, the British army's last cavalry charge. Again, Churchill recorded his adventures in a book, *The River War* (2 vols., 1899). In 1899 Churchill traveled to South Africa to report for the London *Morning Post* on the war between English colonizers and the Boers (Dutch settlers who had arrived in South Africa several centuries earlier). While engaged in fighting near the town of Ladysmith, Churchill was captured by a Boer officer named Louis Botha, who many years later would become South Africa's prime minister and Churchill's good friend. Churchill made a daring escape from a prison camp and returned to the front, an experience he chronicled in *London to Ladysmith via Pretoria* (1900). This book made Churchill world famous.

Churchill's political career began when he was only twenty-six years old. On January 23, 1901, he was elected a member of Parliament for Oldham, located in the Lancashire region. At the time he belonged to the Conservative Party, but by 1904 he had joined the Liberals and become undersecretary of state for the colonies. Churchill also wrote a biography of his father, which was published in 1906. Two years later he married Clementine Hozier, with whom he had four children. Churchill's

political career continued to thrive. From 1908 to 1910 he served as president of the Board of Trade, then from 1910 to 1911 as home secretary. In this position he oversaw early legislation setting up a welfare system. He helped create innovative labor exchanges, introducing benefits for workers such as old-age pension acts.

Builds Up British Military

In 1911 Churchill was named First Lord of the Admiralty, which put him at the head of Britain's navy. Concerned about Germany's rapid buildup of naval power and convinced that peace could be maintained only by preparing for war, Churchill resolved to improve the British navy's equipment. He began converting outdated coal-burning ships to modernized fuel-burning ships while establishing a naval air service. These improvements later proved invaluable, but during the early years of World War I (1914—1918) Churchill planned aggressive military campaigns, and lost his job in 1915 after the failure of one of the attacks in Gallipoli. He was demoted to a minor position and took up painting in his spare time, a hobby he pursued for the rest of his life. He soon quit his new job and volunteered for service in the army in 1916. He was stationed on the western front as commander of the 6th Royal Scots Fusiliers. This appointment did not last long, as Prime Minister Lloyd George soon called on Churchill to rejoin the government.

As secretary of state for war and air, and later for air and colonies, Churchill spent the first few years after World War I working to reform the army and develop Great Britain's air power, even becoming a pilot himself. He was outspoken in his opposition to the Bolshevik revolution in Russia, which lead the Communists to power, and participated in the establishment of the Irish Free State. When Churchill failed to be elected to Parliament in 1922, he turned his attention to writing. He returned briefly to government service when he became chancellor of the exchequer for a short, unhappy stint, but resumed private life by the beginning of the 1930s. This was a difficult decade for Churchill, who warily watched Germany rebuild its power under the dictatorial policies of Nazi leader Adolf Hitler. Strongly opposed to the appeasement of Germany, a policy pursued by British Prime Minister Neville Chamberlain, Churchill warned the House of Commons about the potential dangers of Nazi power in Europe.

Winston Churchill inspecting bombing damage inflicted by the German Luftwaffe in the Battersea area of London. (Reproduced by permission of the Granger Collection, New York)

War Changes Churchill's Fortunes

When Great Britain declared war on Germany in 1939, Churchill was again named First Lord of the Admiralty. As Chamberlain's government was quickly losing favor, many leaders began to heed Churchill's earlier advice. After the Germans overran Poland, northwestern Europe, and France, they began aerial assaults of Great Britain in preparation for a ground attack. Under these threatening circumstances, Churchill was elected to lead the country as prime minister on May 10, 1940. He immediately declared his determination to keep Great Britain safe and to free the rest of the world from Nazi tyranny. The book of Churchill's speeches, *Blood, Toil, Tears and Sweat: The Speeches of Winston Churchill,* is named for the fiery speech he gave to the House of Commons on May 13, when he proclaimed, "....I would say to the House, as I said to those who have joined the Government: 'I have nothing to offer but blood, toil, tears and sweat.' We have before us an ordeal of the most grievous kind. We have before us many, many long months of struggle and of suffering. You ask, what is our policy? I will say: It is to wage war, by sea, land and air, with all our might.... You ask, what is our aim? I can answer in one word: Victory—victory at all costs, victory in spite of all terror, victory, however long and hard the road may be, for without victory, there is no survival...."

Churchill planned war strategy from cabinet war rooms, surrounded by his aides and advisers and seated in front of a huge map of the world. He spoke often before Parliament and gave radio addresses in which he urged the British people to stand firm. He also traveled around the world trying to gain support for the war effort and visiting battlefronts. He made two trips to the United States, where he addressed Congress in December 1941 and May 1942 and met with U.S. President Franklin D. Roosevelt. Churchill considered his ties with Roosevelt crucial to Great Britain's success and, despite the initial reluctance of the United States to enter the war, Churchill and Roosevelt worked out the Lend-Lease Program. This agreement allowed Great Britain to borrow weapons, destroyers, and personnel from the United States. Then the Japanese attack on Pearl Harbor on December 7, 1941—which resulted in the United States declaring war on Japan—fulfilled Churchill's hopes of a closer alliance.

The Allied effort was further strengthened when the Soviet Union (now Russia) entered the war against Germany. Although the Soviet Union was a communist country and Churchill was opposed to communism, the prime minister recognized the value of such a powerful military presence being on the same side as Great Britain and the United States. With the "Grand Alliance" in place against Germany, Italy and Japan (the Axis powers), the first joint British-U.S. campaigns were the Operation Torch landings in North Africa and the invasion of Italy and Sicily, forcing a two-front war. As a result, Nazi forces were spread too thin to attack England. The Americans were also eager to try to regain France and the rest of northwestern Europe, but it was too risky to try this strategy until the British and U.S. armies were better prepared. The time came in June 1944, D-Day, when Allied forces landed on the beaches of Normandy in France. Churchill was so enthusiastic about the campaign that he wanted to land with the troops, and only a special order from King George VI prevented him from taking part in the operation. D-Day was the beginning of the end of the war in Europe: hundreds of thousands of Allied troops moved into France and swept eastward, pushing the Germans over their pre-World War II borders and finally reaching the Nazi capital of Berlin. The Germans surrendered to the Allies in May 1945 as the Allies continued to fight the Japanese in the Pacific region.

Voted Out of Office

During the last year of the war, Churchill played a less prominent role. His strong relationship with Roosevelt began to weaken as a result of their difference of opinion about Joseph Stalin. Churchill felt that the United States and Great Britain should be suspicious of Stalin, while Roosevelt advocated cooperation with the Soviet leader. The war underwent a dramatic shift as the Soviets drove the Germans back onto the eastern front and the Americans concentrated on defeating the Japanese. When the war was over, Churchill participated in the victory celebrations with a great sense of trepidation about the future. Although he was voted out of office in the election of 1945, his removal was not considered a sign of disrespect; instead, it was an indication that he was considered a prime minister for war and the nation wanted someone else to lead them through reconstruction. Churchill then turned to his favorite pursuits: writing another book, *The Second World War,* which was published in six volumes between 1948 and 1953; painting (he exhibited his works at the

Royal Academy of Art); and public speaking. He continued to warn against the spread of communism, urging all English-speaking people to band together to defeat it. In a famous speech he delivered at Westminster College in Fulton, Missouri, he used the words "Iron Curtain" to describe the secrecy surrounding the government of the Soviet Union. The term would be used for years to come by anti-communists.

In 1951, at the age of seventy-seven, Churchill once again became prime minister of Great Britain. Two years later, a few weeks before the coronation of Queen Elizabeth II, he was named a Knight of the Garter. That year he also received the Nobel Prize for literature in recognition of his accomplishments in the fields of history, biography, politics, and memoirs. Churchill resigned as prime minister in 1955, although he continued to hold his seat in the House of Commons until 1964. He received the unusual distinction of being made an honorary American citizen in 1963.

Churchill died in January 1965. His impressive state funeral service at St. Paul's Cathedral in London reflected his stature as a hero to the people of Great Britain and the rest of the world. He was admired for his ability to inspire greatness in people who heard his words, such as those recorded in *Blood, Toil, Tears and Sweat* as part of a speech he delivered at Harrow in 1951: "Never give in, never give in, never, never, never, never—in nothing, great or small, large or petty—never give in except to convictions of honor and good sense."

SOURCES

Books

Bradley, John, *Churchill,* Gloucester Press (New York), 1990.

Charmley, John, *Churchill, The End of Glory: A Political Biography,* Harcourt Brace (San Diego, CA), 1993.

Churchill, Winston, *Blood, Toil, Tears and Sweat: The Speeches of Winston Churchill,* edited with an introduction by David Cannadine, Houghton Mifflin (Boston), 1990.

Driemen, J. E., *Winston Churchill: An Unbreakable Spirit,* Dillon Press (Minneapolis, MN), 1990.

Lace, William W., *Winston Churchill,* Lucent Books (San Diego, CA), 1995.

Manchester, William, *The Last Lion: Winston Spencer Churchill,* Little, Brown (Boston), 1988.

Robbins, Keith, *Churchill,* Longman (London), 1992.

Rodgers, Judith, *Winston Churchill,* Chelsea House (New York), 1986.

Severance, John B., *Winston Churchill: Soldier, Statesman, Artist,* Clarion Books (New York), 1996.

Periodicals

Keegan, John, *Time,* April 13, 1998, p. 114.

Other

"Winston Churchill" in Grolier's *World War II Commemoration,* http://www.grolier.com/wwii/wwii_churchill.html (May 5, 2000).

Winston Churchill Archive Center, http://www.chu.cam.ac.uk/archives/cac/home.htm (May 5, 2000).

Jacqueline Cochran

Born c. 1906
Muskogee, Florida, United States
Died August 9, 1980
Indio, California, United States

American pilot

"I could never have so little that I hadn't had less. It took away my fear."

(Reproduced by permission of Archive Photos, Inc.)

Jacqueline Cochran was an experienced, respected, and fearless pilot with numerous flying records already on her resume when the United States entered World War II in December of 1941. In the wake of the Japanese attack on Pearl Harbor, Cochran saw a way American women could assist the war effort beyond the home front. She suggested that the U.S. government establish an organization of female aviators to perform various noncombat duties, an experiment that was already working well in Great Britain. The result of Cochran's request was the Women's Airforce Service Pilots (WASPs), of which she became director in August 1943. Although the program was canceled in 1944, leaving its members with no veterans benefits and little recognition, Cochran and other female pilots had demonstrated women's eagerness to serve their country as well as their abilities in the air.

Motivated by Difficult Childhood

Cochran celebrated her birthday on May 11 and estimated her birth year as 1906, yet she never knew the identities of her parents. When she was a teenager, she chose her last name from a phone book. Raised by foster parents in northern Florida, Cochran spent her early years traveling as the family found employment in various sawmills. They were extremely poor, and Cochran often slept on the floor, went without shoes, and wore clothing

Jacqueline Cochran in 1937 waving from the cockpit of her plane after setting the speed record for flying from New York to Miami. (Reproduced by permission of AP/Wide World Photos)

made from discarded flour sacks. As recounted in *Women Aviators* by Lisa Yount, Cochran later wrote that this rough background gave her "a kind of cocky confidence … I could never have so little that I hadn't had less. It took away my fear." Cochran began working at a cotton mill in Columbus, Georgia, when she was only eight years old, earning enough money to purchase two pairs of shoes. At age ten she was supervising fifteen other child laborers at the mill, telling them she was destined for a life of wealth and adventure. A strike forced Cochran out of her job, but she soon began working as an assistant in a beauty salon in Columbus.

During her teenage years Cochran found work at other beauty salons in different cities. After she bought herself a Model T Ford in Montgomery, Alabama, she was able to relocate with greater efficiency. By 1929 she was in New York City, working at a popular salon called Antoine's, where she met wealthy clients who often invited her to parties. At one such party she was introduced to an older man named Floyd Odlum. The two became instant friends, and Cochran later learned that Odlum was a multimillionaire. When she told him she would like to become a traveling cosmetics salesperson, he joked that she would need wings for such a job.

This casual comment inspired Cochran to sign up for flying lessons and, in the summer of 1932, she arranged to spend part of her vacation at the Roosevelt Flying School on Long Island. Odlum bet her the cost of the lessons that she would not get a pilot's license in six weeks, a wager Cochran won by earning the license in only three weeks. "A beauty operator ceased to exist and an aviator was born," said Cochran, as noted in Yount's book.

Pursues Career as Test Pilot

Cochran continued taking lessons, even working as an unpaid flight attendant on an airline in exchange for time at the controls of the plane. By the end of 1933 she had acquired enough skill and flying hours to earn a commercial pilot's license. Yet she was still interested in the cosmetics business. Backed by money from Odlum, she started the Jacqueline Cochran Cosmetics Company, which marketed her own hair dyes as well as moisturizing lotions and other products. The company remained in business for the next fifty years, even though Cochran sold her interest in 1964. On May 11, 1936, Cochran married Odlum, who remained a devoted and supportive husband until his death in 1976. The couple purchased a ranch near the

"Yankee Doodle Pilots"

Sung to the tune of "Yankee Doodle Dandy"

We are Yankee Doodle Pilots
Yankee Doodle do or die.
Real live nieces of our Uncle Sam
Born with a yearning to Fly.
Keep in step to all our classes
March to Flight Line with our pals.
Yankee Doodle came to Texas
Just to fly the "PT's"
We are those Yankee Doodle Gals.

town of Indio in the southern California desert, where they spent most of their time.

Cochran began to enter aviation races in 1934 and soon started setting records; within a few years she was ranked among such top women pilots as Amelia Earhart, Anne Morrow Lindbergh, and Edna Whyte. In 1937, the year Earhart disappeared while flying over the Pacific Ocean, Cochran set three speed records, including one for flying from New York to Miami. In 1938 she won the Harmon Trophy, an award given annually by the International League of Aviators to the top woman pilot. Cochran's principal goal, however, was to work as a test pilot. According to Yount, Cochran wrote that she always wanted "to go faster or farther through the atmosphere or higher into it than anyone else and to bring back some new information about plane, engine, fuel, instruments, air, or pilot that would be helpful in the conquest of the atmosphere."

Remaining informed about advances in aviation research and technology, she learned about a young surgeon named Randolph Lovelace in 1937. Lovelace had developed a special oxygen tank and mask for pilots who flew at high altitudes. The device alleviated such problems as nosebleeds and loss of consciousness when pilots flew above 20,000 feet over the earth. Cochran believed Lovelace's invention could prove even more valuable if the United States should have to go to war against Germany, which was stirring up trouble in Europe. She convinced a committee to award

Lovelace the Collier Trophy, which honored people who made major contributions to aviation.

Cochran possessed not only a competitive spirit but also an interest in testing new airplanes. One of her favorite yearly events was the Bendix cross-country air race, in which pilots flew from Los Angeles, California, to Cleveland, Ohio. Having entered the race in 1935 only to withdraw after a treacherous takeoff, she decided to try again in 1938. She made her second attempt in a new military pursuit plane, the P-35, a fast but unreliable aircraft. During the flight Cochran avoided a major catastrophe when she corrected a gas tank malfunction and proceeded to win the race. After picking up her trophy in Cleveland, she immediately took off again and flew to New York City, setting a new women's record for west-to-east transcontinental flight in a propeller-driven plane.

War Presents Need for Female Aviators

In 1939 World War II began as the Nazis invaded Poland. Great Britain and France declared war on Germany in return. Through a special Lend-Lease program, the United States sent supplies, equipment, and airplanes to England. On June 17, 1941, Cochran aided the war effort by flying a Hudson V-bomber from Canada to Great Britain. Since the United States was officially neutral, the flight had to take off from Canada. She became the first woman to fly a military plane over the Atlantic Ocean. Despite Cochran's experience, however, the U.S. government insisted that a male pilot fly with her to perform the takeoff and landing. In addition to publicizing Great Britain's need for airplanes and pilots, Cochran felt that the historic flight demonstrated that women were capable of noncombat military flying. If women could perform duties other than those related to combat, she reasoned, they would free more male pilots for battle.

Cochran's idea had already become policy in Great Britain, where the establishment of the Air Transport Authority (ATA) put women pilots in the cockpit to fly planes from manufacturers to airports located near fighting units. Cochran believed the United States should implement a similar project, so she recruited twenty-five American women to serve in the British program and took them to England for training. These women performed well and some stayed in England for the rest of the war. Another American pilot, Nancy Harkness Love (1914–1976), succeeded in convincing the U.S. government to establish the

Women's Auxiliary Ferrying Squadron (WAFS). Comprised of experienced women pilots, the group was responsible for transporting aircraft to Canada for shipment to England.

Instrumental in Starting WASPs

Cochran was given another opportunity to increase women's involvement in the war effort when her friend General H.H. "Hap" Arnold suggested she set up a program to train more women to fly military aircraft. Some 25,000 women applied to Cochran's program. She accepted 1,830 women, and 1,074 completed the difficult twenty-three-week training—the same success rate for men who joined the Army Air Corps. When the first class of trainees graduated in the spring of 1943, Cochran told them they were being given the best opportunity ever presented to female aviators.

The WAFS and Cochran's group merged in August 1943 and were named the Women's Airforce Service Pilots (WASPs). Cochran was assigned to direct the organization, with Love managing her own group under Cochran's command. The WASPs learned how to fly almost every plane used by the air force, including the gigantic B-29 Superfortresses and the Mustang and Thunderbolt fighter planes. They ferried airplanes between airports; transported cargo, weapons, and troops; and tested new airplanes for safety. They towed targets for anti-aircraft gunnery practice and made low-altitude flights so that radar and searchlight operators could practice spotting the targets. By the end of the war, the WASPs had flown 60,000 hours and 60 million miles, delivering 12,650 planes and performing just as well as male pilots (but with fewer hours lost due to illness or accidents).

Cochran and other women aviators were disappointed and angered when the U.S. Congress terminated the WASPs in December 1944. Since the organization had never been made an official part of the military, the women were not eligible for the veterans' benefits granted to male members of the armed forces. Such benefits included continuing pay and medical care. Three decades later, WASP veterans became angry when the air force announced that it would soon start to train its "first women military pilots." They started a campaign to publicize their accomplishments and gain recognition as the first women U.S. military pilots. On September 20, 1977, Congress voted to allow WASPs or their families to receive benefits.

Nancy Harkness Love directed the Women's Auxiliary Ferrying Squadron (WAFS), which combined with the Women's Airforce Service Pilots (WASPs) under the direction of Jackie Cochran. (Reproduced by permission of AP/Wide World Photos)

Cochran received the Distinguished Service Medal, the second-highest honor an American civilian can receive, for her contributions during World War II. After her war service, she returned to testing new airplanes. In 1947 test pilot Chuck Yeager, a close friend of Cochran, became the first person to fly faster than the speed of sound. To break the sound barrier, the plane must fly so fast that the sound waves carrying the noise it makes cannot keep up with the plane. Cochran longed to join him in testing military jets, but only active air force

German Aviator Hanna Reitsch

While Jacqueline Cochran was proving what women could achieve in the service of the Allies, Hanna Reitsch was performing a similar feat in Germany. Born in 1912 in Hirschberg, Germany (now part of Poland), Reitsch became a stunt pilot known for her skill and daring. A devoted follower of Nazi dictator Adolf Hitler, Reitsch was chosen in 1937 to test military aircraft for the Luftwaffe (the German air force).

After being seriously injured in a plane crash, she was hospitalized for months and was apprehensive about flying. Finally she recovered her health, conquered her fear, and continued flying. In 1944 Reitsch participated in an experiment to test whether the new V-1 buzz bomb could be carried in a manned aircraft that would then become a suicide weapon. The plan was for the pilot to sacrifice his life by intentionally crashing the plane with the bomb onboard. The experiment was banned after two pilots crashed while trying to land, but Reitsch defied the ban and made a successful flight. She later remarked that the two other pilots were not skilled in landing fast planes.

Reitsch made a dramatic visit to Hitler when, in April 1945, he had been forced to hide in an underground bunker while the Soviet Union's Red Army kept up a steady attack on Berlin. Assigned to carry General Ritter von Greim to see Hitler, she landed her plane on a shell-battered Berlin street; she flew out safely several days later through Russian anti-aircraft fire. Reitsch was the first woman—and only civilian—to earn Germany's highest military honor, the Iron Cross. She was eventually captured by the Allies and held for fifteen months before being released without trial. She resumed her flying career, winning many glider championships and establishing a gliding school in the West African country of Ghana in 1962. She died in 1979.

German aviator Hannah Reitsch tested planes to help the Axis powers. (Reproduced by permission of AP/Wide World Photos)

members were allowed to participate. Women had not been allowed to achieve that status yet.

First Woman Pilot to Break Sound Barrier

Cochran found a way to break the sound barrier with her husband's help. He owned the company that made the F-86 Sabre, one of the air force's newest jets, and used his connections to make Cochran a pilot for Air Canada. Cochran was then permitted to borrow a Sabre from the Canadian Air Force, which also owned some of the F-86 planes. She brought it back to the United States to test it. In May 1953 Cochran made an

Created by Walt Disney, the character of "Fifinella" became the symbol of the Women's Airforce Service Pilots (WASPs). This statue honoring the contributions of the WASPs resides in the town of Sweetwater, Texas, where many of the pilots trained. (Reproduced by permission of Kathleen J. Edgar)

historic flight. With Yeager following in a chase plane and ready to assist if she got into trouble, she took the Sabre up to 45,000 feet and went into a nosedive that soon put her at a speed of 500 to 600 miles per hour. Suddenly the noise of the plane died, proving that Cochran had reached Mach 1, the speed of sound. Yeager confirmed her record-breaking flight. Cochran said that becoming the first woman to break the sound barrier was the most thrilling event of her life. She made twelve more flights in the Sabre, breaking three men's records and flying faster than the speed of sound three times. She went on to set even more records, including sixty-nine inter-city and straight line distance records in 1962 alone. She also became the first woman to fly jets over the Atlantic Ocean.

During the 1960s, the National Aeronautics and Space Administration (NASA) was developing a manned space program. Cochran wanted to become an astronaut. According to Young, Cochran said: "I'd have given my right eye to be an astronaut." Instead she helped other women undergo tests to show that they, too, could qualify for space travel. A heart attack in 1971 put an end to Cochran's flying career. When she died in August 1980, she had set about 250 speed, altitude, and distance records (more than any other male or female pilot); earned the Distinguished Flying Cross and Order of Merit from the U.S. government; received the Harmon Trophy fifteen times; and been named "Pilot of the Decade" for 1940-49 by the Harmon trophy committee. She also served as the only woman president of the Federation

Aeronautique Internationale, becoming the only female to receive the organization's gold medal. In 1971 Cochran became the first living woman to enter the Aviation Hall of Fame, and she was featured as part of the U.S. Postal Service's Great Aviators stamp series, issued in 1996.

SOURCES

Books

Bennett, Wayne, *Four Women of Courage,* Garrard (Champaign, IL), 1975.

Cochran, Jacqueline, and Maryann Bucknum Brinley, *Jackie Cochran: An Autobiography,* Bantam Books (New York), 1987.

Cochran, Jacqueline, and Floyd Odlum, *The Stars at Noon,* Arno Press (New York), 1980.

Fisher, Marquita O., *Jacqueline Cochran: First Lady of Flight,* Garrard (Champaign, IL), 1973.

Mondey, David, *Women of the Air,* Silver Burdett (Morristown, NJ), 1981.

Schraff, Anne E., *American Heroes of Exploration and Flight,* Enslow Publishers (Springfield, NJ), 1996.

Smith, Elizabeth Simpson, *Coming Out Right: The Story of Jacqueline Cochran, the First Woman Aviator to Break the Sound Barrier,* Walker (New York), 1991.

Yount, Lisa, *Women Aviators,* Facts on File (New York), 1995.

Other

The American Experience: Fly Girls, http://www.pbs.org/wgbh/pages/amex/flygirls/filmmore/reference/bibliography.html (August 2000).

WASP on the Web, http://www.wasp-wwii.org/wasp/home.htm (August 2000). "WASPs: Women's Airforce Service Pilots," *Air Force News,* http://www.af.mil/news/ (August 2000).

"WASPs: Women's Airforce Service Pilots," *Air Force News,* http://www.af.mil/news/ (August 2000).

The Comfort Women

During World War II, Japanese troops forced foreign women, mainly Koreans, into service as prostitutes. These women became euphemistically known as *ianfu,* or "comfort women." The word "women" is an exaggeration because many of the females involved were in their teens. The comfort women were set up in brothels called *ianjo,* or comfort houses, against their will. Some were held as long as nine years. The shame and humiliation of being bound into this lifestyle caused many comfort women to remain quiet about their experiences. In the late 1980s and early 1990s, women finally started to come forward and share their stories, and some began to seek reparations and apologies from the Japanese government. At first Japan claimed that private entrepreneurs had financed the brothels and that such establishments were not officially sanctioned. Later, documents revealed and Japanese officials admitted that the comfort houses were organized by the government itself. The Japanese government put together a private foundation to pay reparations to former comfort women, but many have refused the payments, saying that the compensation is irrelevant if it does not come from the government itself.

The Japanese in Korea

Japan and Korea have had a long, combative history. In the late nineteenth century, Japan

Between 100,000 and 200,000 "comfort women" were forcibly impressed into service as prostitutes for Japanese troops during World War II

"I have lived my whole life trembling because of this suffering. Even now that my hair has turned white, when I remember my past, my whole body shakes, my skin blushes red and my nerves are on fire."

—KIM YUN SHIM

During the war, members of the Japanese military forced Korean, Chinese, and other women into prostitution. Here, former Korean comfort women begin a hunger strike as they demand compensation from the Japanese government. (Reproduced by permission of AP/Wide World Photos)

gained dominance in Korea through the Treaty of Shimonoseki (1895) after the Sino-Japanese War and the Treaty of Portsmouth (1905) after the Russo-Japanese War. In 1905 Korea became a Japanese protectorate, and on August 22, 1910, Japan annexed Korea. Japan adopted an aggressive plan to diffuse Japanese culture throughout Korea. Korean language and literature were dropped from school curricula in favor of Japanese, and Koreans were conscripted into work and military service in Korea and abroad on behalf of Japan. Japan bought much Korean farmland at cheap prices, and forced farmers who still owned their land to provide food for export, while not being allowed to keep any of it for themselves. Indigenous Korean religion was forbidden, and Koreans had to worship at Japanese Shinto shrines instead.

These authoritarian measures became even more noticeable when Japan entered World War II. Resources were needed to keep the Japanese war effort running, and the Japanese government, accustomed to controlling Korea for more than

thirty years, saw Korea as a logical place from which to extract these resources. More Koreans were conscripted into forced labor in Japan, and by 1945 are estimated to have made up 32 percent of the work force there. In Korea itself, 2.6 million Koreans were forced into service working for the Japanese. Estimates as to the numbers of comfort women enslaved by Japan vary greatly, but most range between 100,000 and 200,000. Since Japan was already conscripting Korean citizens into forced labor, leaders saw Korea as a logical place to find comfort women, and by most accounts a majority of the comfort women were Korean. A contributing factor was the practice, common at the time in Korea, of sending children, especially girls, to work as nannies or maids in exchange for a cash payment. The Japanese took advantage of this system, already in place, and purchased some of the women they used in the comfort houses from their parents or guardians. Poverty also led some children to leave home voluntarily and seek work in more urban areas. Separated from their parents, these children were vulnerable to conscription by Japanese troops.

Kim Pok Sun

In 1944 Kim Pok Sun was an eighteen-year-old woman living with her uncle in a small Korean village. Having heard rumors of women being kidnapped and forced to become comfort women, Kim's uncle encouraged her to stay out of sight in the house. Violating his orders one day, Kim was outside when she was accosted by a Korean man in military dress accompanied by two Japanese military policemen. The Korean man asked her uncle to let Kim come work in Japan for one year, and when her uncle refused, the Japanese military policemen dragged Kim away to a waiting car. She was taken to Seoul, and then traveled to Pusan, Osaka, and Saigon before arriving at her final destination, a comfort house in Rangoon, Burma. There she was imprisoned in a three by five foot room and forced to receive up to twenty soldiers per day. The troops had strict hours for visiting: Soldiers were welcome from nine in the morning to three in the afternoon, petty officers came from three in the afternoon until seven in the evening, and only officers were allowed to spend nights there.

When Allied bomb raids increased in intensity, the camp was moved. Rather than going along with the soldiers, Kim and a friend managed to escape through the jungle to India. When the bombing raids ceased, they headed back to Rangoon to find transport home; Kim's friend drowned along the way. Kim finally returned to her home village, but was never able to find her family. According to Ustinia Dolgopol, Kim "said that it was a miracle that she had survived as many of the women in the comfort station died because of the conditions there."

Japanese Government Institutes Comfort Houses

In the late 1930s Japan was fighting a war of invasion in China. During this action, Japanese troops committed numerous atrocities, including rape, that captured international attention. Officials from other countries denounced the vicious methods used by Japanese soldiers in cities such as Shanghai and Nanking. In order to save face in the international community and to prevent revenge by Chinese troops and civilians, the Japanese government decided to establish the comfort houses. Ustinia Dolgopol explains in the February 1995 issue of *Human Rights Quarterly*: "An entry in the official log of the Ninth Brigade referred to a circular, dated 27 June 1938, which was issued by Naosaburo Okabe, Chief of Staff of the North China Expeditionary Troops. The circular stated that the number of rapes committed by Japanese soldiers was threatening security in northern China, and that the Chinese were taking revenge. In Okabe's view it was necessary to set up 'comfort houses' as soon as possible." It is possible that comfort houses existed as early as 1932, but it was in the late 1930s when they became prevalent. The nationality of the first comfort women remains a topic of debate. Some of them were undoubtedly Chinese, but by the end of the war, a majority of them were probably Korean. Other nationalities represented include Filipino, Dutch, Indonesian, Malaysian, and Taiwanese.

The Japanese government was heavily involved in the establishment of the comfort houses. Some of them were even managed by the government, while others were managed by individuals under the supervision of the government. The Japanese military established formal regulations to cover the day-to-day operation of the houses, and issued licenses. The Japanese navy was also involved in providing facilities for comfort women arriving from various locations, and Japanese military police sometimes abducted women from their families to stock the comfort houses. By the 1940s, comfort women were so common that they were referred to as the "Special Service Personnel Group."

Topics covered in the comfort house regulations were the fees to be charged (which varied

Did the Allies Know about the Comfort Women?

For many years after the war, the plight of the comfort women was virtually unknown. The women, suffering from guilt and shame, were reluctant to come forward about their experiences, and the Japanese government maintained that while centers of prostitution were common near military encampments, they were in no way government-sponsored. Some authors have theorized that the Allies knew about the problem at the conclusion of the war but refused to take action. Won-loy Chan was an American combat intelligence officer responsible for interviewing some of the comfort women when the Allies took control of Burma. In an article in *Human Rights Quarterly*, Ustinia Dolgopol writes that "it is clear from [Chan's] description that he believed most of the women had come to Burma against their will. It was not his impression that they were what the military then referred to as 'camp followers' [prostitutes who set up shop near military encampments]." Even with Chan's research and

opinions available to them, many of the Allies chose to look at the activities of the comfort women as voluntary despite the evidence to the contrary. British military officers, for example, referred to the comfort women as "camp followers," implying a voluntary aspect to their activities.

Dolgopol suggests that colonialism and racism were two contributing factors in the silence of the Allies, and further submits that the Allied reluctance to bring the problem to light resulted in an objectification of the women involved and a compounding of their pain. In her recommendations for providing compensation to former comfort women and their families, Dolgopol suggests "it would be appropriate if the countries making up the Allied Forces, in particular the United Kingdom, the United States, and the Netherlands, contributed….these countries knew of the atrocities perpetrated against the comfort women yet did nothing to prosecute those responsible nor to insure that the world viewed these acts as the heinous crimes that they were. This has contributed to the ongoing suffering of the women. Silence can be a form of aiding and abetting."

according to the rank of the soldier or officer in question), medical examinations for the women, and what hours the facility should be open. The manager of the comfort house would keep track of how many times each particular soldier visited a comfort house, and would prevent too many visits to the same woman in order to prevent bonds from forming. Medical examinations, according to Schiro Ichikawa, a former comfort house keeper, were not to ensure the health of the women but instead to ensure the health of the soldiers who visited them. The freedom of the women was strictly curtailed. Most were not allowed to move about, and hours for taking walks even in designated areas were controlled. Some women were not allowed to talk. Former soldier Yoshiro Suzuki estimated that some of the comfort women were forced to receive up to thirty soldiers per day.

The Aftermath

When the Allied troops entered Asia, they found Korean women in Burma, Manchuria, Borneo, Papua New Guinea, and the Philippines. The women were often interviewed and their responses noted in Allied reports. The U.S. Office of War Information, Psychological Warfare Team created one report about a camp in Burma. According to Ustinia Dolgopol in *Human Rights Quarterly*, twenty women "were told that they were being enlisted to give 'comfort' to the Japanese soldiers, but the nature of what was expected of them was not detailed in any meaningful way. The girls were left with the impression that they would be rolling bandages, visiting wounded and ill soldiers in hospitals, and generally assisting with the cooking, cleaning, and other chores around the camps.

The Recreation and Amusement Association

When the Allies occupied Japan after the end of World War II, Japanese officials made plans to receive these foreigners in their country. One way this was done was through the establishment of the *Tokushu Ian Shisetsu Kyōkai,* or Recreation and Amusement Association (RAA). The RAA set up a system of comfort houses, stocked with Japanese women, designed to cater to the Allied soldiers. According to John W. Dower in *Embracing Defeat: Japan in the Wake of World War II,* "…it was taken for granted that the foreigners would demand sexual gratification. The question was simply: who would provide it?" The RAA was designed as a sort of buffer zone between rapacious Westerners and the majority of Japanese women. A few thousand female Japanese volunteers offered to serve as this buffer.

At the inaugural ceremony of the RAA, Dower writes, the following words were read: "…we have been assigned the difficult task of comforting the occupation army…. And so we unite and go for-ward to where our beliefs lead us, and through the sacrifice of several thousands of [women] build a breakwater to hold back the raging waves and defend and nurture the purity of our race…. We are not compromising our integrity or selling our souls…. We say it loudly: we are but offering ourselves for the defense of the national polity."

The women in the RAA facilities have been estimated to have associated with between 15 and 60 soldiers per day. The service was popular among American GIs and was very inexpensive (a night with a comfort woman cost about the same as one or two packs of cigarettes). In January 1946, alarmed by the rise of venereal disease among their soldiers, occupation forces abolished "public" prostitution. Prostitution simply moved underground, however, and remained a viable industry throughout the 1940s.

Money was offered by the recruiters to either the girls or their families. They were promised a new and more prosperous life in Singapore."

After the war, comfort women attempted to make their way back to their homes. Some were reportedly shot by Japanese soldiers so they would be unable to divulge their mistreatment to Allied troops. Others committed suicide rather than face the shame of returning home. Most Asian cultures at the time placed the highest significance on chastity. The women who had been abused at the hands of the Japanese soldiers felt ashamed and disgraced. Many of the women were suffering from venereal disease—some sought treatment in their home countries, and others did not because they felt they had dishonored their families and countries.

Comfort Women Seek Justice

The only country to include the enslavement of the comfort women in war crimes trials was the Netherlands. In both trials, held in Batavia (now Java), the women in question were European. In general, the Allies refused to prosecute Japan for war crimes that affected its own nationals, including colonial peoples. This effectively precluded any trials for crimes against the comfort women (also precluded were any other crimes committed by the ruling Japanese in Korea).

In the late 1980s, academics and activists began to draw attention to the comfort system. In 1990 a Filipino former comfort woman came forward and made her story public, and later Korean women did the same, notably Kim Hak Soon in 1991. The Japanese government denied any involvement in the establishment of comfort houses. When a group of Korean women brought a lawsuit against the Japanese government seeking compensation for their World War II enslavement as comfort women, documents began to come to light that implicated the government's involvement. The Japanese government then changed its position, as reflected in

---

this statement from Chief Cabinet Secretary Koichi Kato, cited in a *Contemporary Review* article by Robert Lamont-Brown: "We have found documents to prove that the government was involved in the so-called comfort women. But so far we have found no document to show that those women were recruited by force." The South Korean government expressed the belief that Japan was purposely masking the truth.

In January 1992 the Japanese prime minister issued this statement: "I take this opportunity to once again express my most heartfelt apologies for the unbearable pain and suffering brought upon you by my country in the past. Especially with the matter of comfort women coming to light, I am filled with pain and remorse" (cited in "Women's Voices, Women's Pain" by Ustinia Dolgopol). One Korean women's group, Never Again: Justice for Military Comfort Women, began a twelve-woman sit-in outside the Japanese embassy in Seoul that would last for more than six years. The first written apology from Japan to the comfort women came in August 1996, when Prime Minister Ryutaro Hashimoto was recorded by Yvonne Chang of the *Washington Post* as writing: "...I thus extend anew my most sincere apologies and remorse to all the women who underwent immeasurable and painful experiences and suffered incurable physical and psychological wounds as comfort women. I believe that our country, painfully aware of its moral responsibility, with feelings of apology and remorse, should face up squarely to its past history and accurately convey it to future generations."

Despite this admission and apology, the Japanese government still refused to offer compensation to former comfort women, saying any war-related compensation to the Korean people was settled by the Japan-South Korea Treaty in 1965. In July 1995 Japan did set up a private fund, the Asian Women's Fund, to make payments to former comfort women. The fund did not raise as much money as the government had hoped, however (though it had, by April 1998, distributed about $760,000), and also suffered from denunciation by some of the former comfort women, who say private funds are not appropriate compensation for what they suffered—the money should instead come from the government itself. In 1996 a United Nations special investigator into violence against women, Radhika Coomaraswamy, concurred with this view, saying the Japanese government should apologize and issue reparations. According to the *Washington*

Post, Coomaraswamy called the Asian Women's Fund "an insufficient step in the right direction."

In 1998 the South Korean government attempted to bypass Japan, and passed legislation which allowed the South Korean government to provide $25,300 each to 152 South Korean former comfort women. The plan originally involved the South Korean government seeking compensation in turn for the funds they paid out from the Japanese government, but that part of the plan was eventually dropped. Comfort women and their representatives welcomed the announcement, but urged Seoul to demand the Japanese government provide compensation and punish guilty parties. A week later, a Japanese court made an historic ruling granting compensation to three South Korean former comfort women. While the payments, at $2,300 each, were generally regarded by advocates of the comfort women as far too low, the unprecedented nature of the verdict was seen as an encouraging event. According to the *San Francisco Chronicle* of April 28, 1998, in his ruling, Yamaguchi District Judge Hideaki Chikashita "said the government should have compensated the sex slaves for their suffering. Their right to compensation was guaranteed under the constitution and was acknowledged when the government admitted the army's actions..."

Despite the positive nature of Chikashita's ruling, the comfort women have still had an uphill battle trying to achieve compensation and apologies. Some Japanese officials continue to maintain that the comfort women were volunteers. Forty-six Filipino former comfort women had their class action lawsuit rejected by a Japanese court in November 1998.

SOURCES

Books

Dower, John W., *Embracing Defeat: Japan in the Wake of World War II*, W.W. Norton & Company (New York), 1999.

Hicks, George, *The Comfort Women: Japan's Brutal Regime of Enforced Prostitution in the Second World War*, W.W. Norton & Co. (New York), 1995.

Periodicals

Chang, Yvonne, "Japanese Leader Writes Apology to Comfort Women," *Washington Post*, August 15, 1996, p. A34.

Coday, Dennis J., "'I Cannot Die without an Apology'; Korean Women Forced into Sexual Slavery Await Words That Will Ease Torment," *National Catholic Reporter,* October 23, 1998, p. 14+.

Dolgopol, Ustinia, "Women's Voices, Women's Pain," *Human Rights Quarterly,* February 1995, p. 127–154.

"Japan Must Pay Ex-Sex Slaves, U.N. Aide Says," *Washington Post,* February 7, 1996, p. A15.

Kristof, Nicholas D., "Japanese Project for 'Comfort Women' Off to a Slow Start," *San Francisco Chronicle,* May 13, 1996, p. A10.

Lamont-Brown, Robert, "No Compensation for the Comfort Women," *Contemporary Review,* February 1993, p. 80+.

"Ruling in 'Comfort Women' Case / Japan Must Compensate 3 Korean World War II Sex Slaves," *San Francisco Chronicle,* April 28, 1998, p. A8.

"South Korea OKs Aid for Sex Slaves / Japan Won't Help 'Comfort Women,'" *San Francisco Chronicle,* April 22, 1998, p. A8.

Charles E. Coughlin

Born October 25, 1891
Hamilton, Ontario, Canada
Died October 27, 1979
Bloomfield Hills, Michigan, United
States

Roman Catholic priest; radio personality;
anti-Semitic figure who strongly opposed
U.S. involvement in World War II

*"America must hold herself free from
foreign entanglements."*

Father Charles E. Coughlin rose from being the unknown pastor of a small-town church to being one of the most well-known radio voices in America. He offered hope to millions of Americans who were suffering during the Great Depression (1929–1939), a period when the economy was at a standstill and unemployment was high. As the anti-Semitic Adolf Hitler was coming into power in Germany, Coughlin began to spout anti-Jewish notions, and he became the most loved and most hated American of his time.

Early Life

Charles Edward Coughlin was the first-born child of Thomas and Amelia Mahoney Coughlin, who were both devout Catholics of Irish descent. Coughlin's father was an American citizen who worked as a laborer on Great Lakes steamboats until he was forced to seek lighter work because of poor health. He settled in Hamilton, a small town in Ontario, Canada, and first took a job in maintenance at the Catholic church there. Later he became a supervisor at a bakery. Coughlin's mother came from a family of Canadian farmers but later moved to Hamilton and worked as a seamstress. She married Thomas in 1890 and gave birth to Charles about a year later. Amelia was a strong-willed woman; one of her deepest wishes was that her son would become a priest. When her second and last child was born in 1892 and died in infancy, Amelia devoted herself to raising her only child to fulfill the role she envisioned for him. At age twelve, Coughlin was sent to Toronto, Canada, to begin his studies in preparation for the priesthood.

Coughlin excelled in school, developing a reputation as a star rugby player and public speaker. While studying to become a priest, he was exposed to new ideas that were sweeping through the Catholic church. In the early 1900s, the church began to concern itself with justice for the working classes, who were often poorly treated by business owners. This was becoming an important issue in the United States, where hundreds of thousands of European Catholic immigrants were flooding the country looking for work in the new factories opening there. Coughlin developed a lifelong commitment to the poor and a belief that the leaders of industry should give workers a fair share of the country's wealth.

Becomes Pastor in Michigan

In 1916 Coughlin was ordained a Catholic priest. For seven years he taught English, Greek, and history, coached the football team, and enjoyed great popularity with the students at a small college near Windsor, Ontario, just across the river from Detroit, Michigan. Not contented with his duties as a teacher, he also volunteered to give speeches to whatever groups would extend an invitation. His reputation as an electrifying speaker grew, and he came to the attention of church leaders in Detroit. In 1926 Coughlin was chosen to oversee a new parish in Royal Oak, a suburb of Detroit.

At the time Coughlin arrived in Detroit, the city had emerged from the boom days of high employment during World War I (1914–18) and was in the middle of a severe depression. In Detroit, many small businesses had failed and unemployment was high. There was a growing movement against labor unions, which some people considered un-American. Detroit's economy was dependent on the automobile industry, but no one could afford to buy a car due to the economic downturn of the nation. As the demand for automobiles declined, more and more Detroiters lost their jobs. Coughlin believed that America's capitalistic system, in which large companies controlled the production of goods, was responsible for the Great Depression that rocked the whole country beginning in 1929.

In the late 1920s, Detroit was experiencing a housing shortage as well as racial and ethnic tensions. The Ku Klux Klan, a secret society that had begun terrorizing blacks after the Civil War (1861–65), was experiencing a resurgence in northern cities. This time the Klan directed its hatred not only against blacks but also against Jews and Catholics. One of the Klan's scare tactics was to burn crosses on the lawns of churches or people's homes.

Claims to Fight the Ku Klux Klan

Royal Oak, the location of Coughlin's new church, was then a small, rural area whose residents were surprised and not entirely happy to see some of Detroit's excess population headed their way. Whether Ku Klux Klan activity occurred near the Royal Oak church (as Coughlin claimed) is, however, debatable. According to a story circulated by Coughlin, he came up against the Klan only two weeks after the completion of his small, wooden church, named the Shrine of the Little Flower in honor of Catholic Saint Thérése. Coughlin claimed that the Klan set fire to a cross on the church lawn to indicate its displeasure with the Catholic presence there. Coughlin vowed not to give in to fear. Instead, he would build a huge church on the site, with "a cross so high … that neither man nor beast can burn it down," wrote author Alan Brinkley.

A Hollywood movie about the priest's life, filmed in the 1930s, showed a dramatic scene in which Coughlin was awakened from sleep and told to come immediately to his new church. There he was confronted with a great fiery cross burning fiercely next to his small church. The actor portraying Coughlin cried out that he would "construct a church that will stand as a monument in defiance of hatred!" The story has been repeated by Coughlin biographers. Writer Donald Warren asserted that the story was a complete fabrication, invented by Coughlin to make himself appear heroic and a fighter against prejudice.

Begins Radio Broadcasts

At first his following was too small for Coughlin to obtain his dream of building a huge church. In an effort to fight anti-Catholic prejudice and to attract followers for his church, Coughlin took to the airwaves. At the time, commercial radio was only six years old, but was already a major form of entertainment; about two-thirds of American homes had

Coughlin delivering one of his electrifying radio addresses. (Reproduced by permission of AP/Wide World Photos)

at least one radio. Coughlin delivered his first radio sermon on October 17, 1926, and received five favorable letters in response. It was not long, however, before he began receiving thousands of letters from throughout Michigan and nearby states. Many listeners sent small donations that were added to the contributions of those who crowded the church to hear him speak on Sundays. By 1928 construction had begun on the huge tower that would be the centerpiece of Coughlin's magnificent new church. It still stands at a major intersection in Royal Oak. So many Catholics moved into Royal Oak that they became a dominant force there.

Coughlin's commanding presence, combined with his engaging voice and sermons, continued to attract radio listeners, whose numbers eventually reached as high as forty million. The total U.S. population in 1930 was 123 million. In the early broadcasts, he focused on religious and moral issues, but after the stock-market crash of 1929 ushered in the Great Depression, he began to speak about current

topics and their moral implications. In 1930 he was contracted by the Columbia Broadcasting System (CBS) radio network, which was linked to 16 stations in the Northeast. His talks became increasingly political. When questions were raised about whether a radio priest should be involved in politics, CBS dropped his contract. As a result, Coughlin established an independent network of stations to carry his broadcasts. Throughout Coughlin's radio career, his primary audience consisted of Roman Catholics living in eastern industrial cities. However, he also attracted a significant audience of Protestants in the Midwest who appreciated his views on political subjects. By 1932 his office was receiving as many as 80,000 letters a week and his parish was thriving. He built a modern radio office for his broadcasts.

Coughlin and President Roosevelt

The radio priest became sharply critical of U.S. President Herbert Hoover's inability or unwillingness to deal with the Depression. In the 1932 election, he spoke out in favor of Franklin D. Roosevelt for president, using the slogan "Roosevelt or Ruin." Coughlin believed he was responsible for Roosevelt's victory and assumed he would be an important adviser to the new president. He endorsed Roosevelt's early ideas, and the president did consult with Coughlin from time to time. However, Roosevelt rarely followed the priest's advice. By 1934 however, Coughlin had begun to criticize Roosevelt's programs and even occasionally the president himself, but he did not openly break with Roosevelt until January 25, 1935. The break occurred after a radio sermon in which Coughlin accused Roosevelt of "selling out the American people to the international bankers." He was referring to the Jews, who were being blamed by many people for the economic problems of the Depression. Coughlin began using the new slogan "Roosevelt and Ruin."

Also in 1934 Coughlin organized the National Union for Social Justice to assemble his millions of followers into an effective force for political change. The purpose of the organization, according to Coughlin, was "[t]o learn social justice; to organize against sit-down legislatures and Congressmen [lazy lawmakers]; to battle ... anti-Christianity wherever and whenever it is possible; to cure democracy before it withers and perishes; to protect our Supreme Court; to oppose the evils of modern capitalism without joining in the radical labor organizers and to secure an honest dollar and an honest living for all Americans." The organization grew quickly, and although Coughlin claimed to have millions of members, more careful estimates suggest that about one million people belonged to the group at its peak.

Anti-Semitic Rantings

In 1938 Coughlin stunned the U.S. public when he suddenly began to voice anti-Semitic sentiments in his radio addresses. This was the same year that Adolf Hitler and his Nazi Party began implementing anti-Jewish regulations in Germany. Although Coughlin never openly admitted to being an anti-Semite, he spoke in code words, blaming Jews for the Great Depression and other problems. In his newspaper *Social Justice,* he published a false story about a Jewish conspiracy to seize control of the world. He lashed out against evil "international bankers," blaming them for the country's problems. He played to age-old stereotypes that some people

Epilogue

After the world became aware of the horrors of the Holocaust, efforts were made to bridge the gap that existed between Christians and Jews. One such effort is described in Donald Warren's *Radio Priest: Charles Coughlin, the Father of Hate Radio.* The "lone man" described below is representative of the mistrust and even hatred that some people still feel toward the Jews.

"In May 1992, a special effort was made in Detroit's Catholic and Jewish communities to exorcize (set free from) the ghost of Charles Coughlin. The event was a joint fund-raising reception held at the Shrine of the Little Flower.... The occurrence was newsworthy enough to receive an item in *The New York Times.* The article quoted the pastor of Coughlin's [former] church: 'I would change history if I could.' In his remarks on the special occasion, the Catholic official included an apology [to Jews] in the name of the [Catholic] church: 'We need to find forgiveness in our lives whenever possible.'"

Not everyone, however, was ready to disagree with Coughlin.

"Across the street from the Shrine, it was reported that 'a lone man stood ... holding a sign that read: Father Coughlin was on target concerning the Jewish Communist Conspiracy.'"

believed about Jews. One of the stereotypes is that the Jews were secretly trying to take control of the world's money supply. Although some others were more forceful in their charges against Jews, Coughlin had a huge audience.

Coughlin was a strong believer in the isolationist movement of the 1920s and 1930s, which opposed American intervention in European wars. This belief struck accord with a large percentage of Americans, who favored a domestic policy of political introversion. Coughlin was an admirer of Italian dictator Benito Mussolini, and spoke out in favor of Adolf Hitler. Coughlin called Hitler's persecution of the Jews a response against Communism. He claimed the Jews were responsible for the Russian Revolution that established the Communist Party in Russia, and he asserted that they were trying to do the same thing in Germany. Coughlin's influence was so great that as World War II began in Europe with Hitler's attack on Poland in 1939, violent fights broke out on the streets of New York between Coughlin's supporters and his enemies. Coughlin's critics pleaded with him to try to control his followers. These same critics denounced him in newspapers, comparing his viewpoints to Hitler's. They also called Coughlin "an enemy of democracy," "a fascist," and "a Nazi."

Coughlin's radio broadcasts ended in 1940 because he could no longer buy radio air time. He continued to work quietly at the Shrine of the Little Flower. He reportedly made a small fortune investing in the stock market, and he lived a comfortable life in a wealthy suburb of Detroit. He announced his retirement in 1966, possibly forced out by his superior who had received complaints that Coughlin was a racist from parents and students at the Shrine of the Little Flower School. In an interview a few years later, Coughlin remarked to writer Sheldon Marcus: "If I had to do it all over again, I would do it the same way."

Coughlin died of heart failure on October 27, 1979, two days after his eighty-eighth birthday. A writer for the *Detroit Free Press,* which had often been critical of him, wrote: "God is a giver and a forgiver, so why should we hold anything against one of our brothers? We remember not so much what Father Coughlin said, but what he believed. In his priesthood he had a deep loyalty to the Church he served. He never set himself above it. His joy was to be a faithful priest."

Sources

Books

Alexander, Charles, "Coughlin," *McGraw-Hill Encyclopedia of World Biography,* McGraw-Hill (New York), 1973.

Brinkley, Alan, *Voices of Protest: Huey Long, Father Coughlin, and the Great Depression,* Alfred A. Knopf (New York), 1982.

Carpenter, Ronald H., *Father Charles E. Coughlin: Surrogate Spokesman for the Disaffected,* Greenwood Press (Westport, CT), 1998.

Glatzer, Nahum Norbert, "Anti-Semitism," *Encarta,* Microsoft (Redmond, Washington), 1994.

Marcus, Sheldon, *Father Coughlin: The Tumultuous Life of the Priest of the Little Flower,* Little, Brown (Boston), 1973.

Tull, Charles J., *Father Coughlin and the New Deal,* Syracuse University Press (Syracuse, NY), 1965.

Warren, Donald I., *Radio Priest: Charles Coughlin, the Father of Hate Radio,* Free Press (New York), 1996.

Adam Czerniaków

Adam Czerniaków served nearly three years as the leader of the half-million Jews who were forcibly confined in a ghetto in Poland's capital city of Warsaw during World War II. He has been praised by many as a decent, honorable, and dignified man who represented his people with courage during a tumultuous period in world history. Contrarily, he has been condemned by others as a man who contributed to the deaths of millions of European Jews by cooperating with the Nazis.

Early Days in Warsaw

Czerniaków was born in 1880 in Warsaw, which was a center of political, social, and cultural life for Poland's Jews. Although not much is known about Czerniaków's childhood, historians do know that he came from a middle class family. In a diary entry dated July 8, 1940, he noted that he had a troubled childhood. He wrote that his self-control and calm were "the product of my difficult childhood and the conditions of my parents' home. That is where I learned to suffer." His family members were assimilationist Jews, which means they were members of a minority that blended in with the culture of the Polish majority. As a young man he rejected his family's assimilation and began to study the Jewish religion. He studied chemistry at Warsaw Polytechnic, a school that

Born November 30, 1880
    Warsaw, Poland
Died July 23, 1942
    Warsaw ghetto, Poland

Civil engineer; teacher; writer; head of Warsaw Jewish Council; diarist; committed suicide rather than send Jewish children to death camps

"We do our daily work and weeping will not help us."

A *Judenrat* official (possibly Czerniaków) at work in his office in the Warsaw ghetto. (National Museum of American Jewish History/USHMM Photo Archives)

specialized in industrial arts and applied sciences. He then went on to study industrial engineering in Dresden, Germany. Afterward he returned to Warsaw. He soon married a teacher named Felicia. They had one son, Jan.

After graduation, his career was varied. He taught in Jewish vocational schools, worked for the government, went into business for himself, and wrote educational and technical articles and even some poetry. His special interest was the work of Jewish craftsmen. Jews in Poland, like Jews worldwide, had long been discriminated against in certain professions. Subsequently they tended to be heavily concentrated in certain careers, such as law, medicine, and skilled crafts like tailoring and leather working. Half of all craftsmen in Poland were Jewish; in Warsaw this figure approached 80 percent. Czerniaków was active in protecting the interests of Jewish craftsmen, who faced constant efforts by Gentiles to deprive them of their livelihoods. He became interested in public life and served as a representative of Jewish craftsmen on various government bodies.

War in Poland

Discrimination against European Jews gradually turned into widespread hatred. The flames of that hatred were fanned by Austrian-born Adolf Hitler, who was living in Germany. Hitler blamed Jews for Germany's humiliating defeat in World War I (1914–18). When Hitler and his Nazi party rose to power in 1933, they began to persecute German Jews, forcing many to leave the country and confining others in concentration camps reserved for people regarded as "enemies of the state." Hitler wanted to create a new German empire filled with "pure" Germans and devoid of all Jews. In September 1939 Hitler began to fulfill his dream when Germany invaded Poland, starting World War II. In Warsaw, the Polish Jew who was chairman of the Jewish Community Council fled the city; the mayor asked Czerniaków to take over. Although Czerniaków had a visa that would allow him to leave for Palestine (now the Jewish state of Israel) and save himself, the fifty-nine-year-old agreed to stay and assume the position of chairman, which had become a dangerous job.

When the German army marched into Warsaw, officers ordered Czerniaków to establish a Jewish Council to replace the earlier group. It would be called a *Judenrat.* The new Jewish Council would consist of 24 prominent Jews with Czerniaków as chairman. Czerniaków did as he was ordered. He also placed a bottle of lethal poison tablets in his desk drawer. He told the council members that if the Germans ever ordered them to do anything against their consciences, the poison tablets were available to all of them. He also began to keep a diary, in which he recorded his impressions and experiences every day until his suicide.

Czerniaków's first task as chairman of the *Judenrat* was to take a census of Jews and formulate a plan for their eventual placement in ghettos. In the early days of Poland's occupation by the Nazis, the party's plan for mass extermination of European Jews was unknown to most. The Nazis pretended they only wanted to keep peace among Polish Jews and use Jewish labor to assist in the war effort. Czerniaków hoped to secure the safety of Poland's Jews by making the Nazis see that skilled Jewish craftsmen were indispensable to the war effort.

Coordinates Life in the Ghetto

Persecution of Jews living in Warsaw soon began. Their stores and homes were looted; their businesses were taken over; and fines were levied against them for breaking new Nazi rules. Food was in short supply because the Germans were diverting most of it to the army. Before long famine and malnutrition were common. In the spring of 1940, Czerniaków received the order to build a walled ghetto for the confinement of Warsaw's Jews. All Jews between the ages of sixteen and sixty were ordered to bring several bricks to use in building what was to become their own prison. By October 1940, the job was done.

For nearly two years, Czerniaków was in almost daily contact with Nazi authorities regarding the affairs of the Warsaw ghetto, although he tried to run the ghetto with as little Nazi involvement as possible. He was required to submit reports to Nazi authorities. In his reports, he complained bitterly about the terrible conditions in the ghetto, where people were sick and starving. Life in such cramped quarters contributed to a dramatic increase in disease. Through Czerniaków's efforts, thousands of poor Jews were declared exempt from taxes on bread. Nevertheless, between January 1941 and July 1942, nearly 61,000 people died in the ghetto, mostly from starvation and diseases related to malnutrition.

Czerniaków also convinced the Nazis to permit him to provide Jewish labor in an orderly fashion. He wanted to avoid situations in which Jews were forcefully grabbed off the streets to be used for unpaid labor. On several occasions he was arrested

From Czerniaków's Diary

Czerniaków sometimes complained about the Jews in the ghetto, who expected him to secure favors for them from the Nazis. In this diary passage, he described his thoughts while sitting in the Nazi waiting room:

"I sit in a stuffy room resembling a jail. The Jews are constantly grumbling. They don't want to pay for the community [the services he set up to deal with health care, welfare, food distribution, sanitation, and police matters], but demand intervention [with the Nazis] on private affairs or catastrophes. And if the intervention does not succeed or goes on too long, there is no end to their dissatisfaction, as if the matter depended on me. And frequently these are very loud complaints." (July 1940)

By July 1941, though, the extreme suffering imposed on the Jews by the Nazis had taken its toll, muting their complaints. Czerniaków wrote:

"The Jewish masses are quiet and balanced in the face of the intense suffering. In general, the Jews only shout when things are going well for them."

and imprisoned for his harsh comments, but Czerniaków would not soften his complaints to suit the Nazis. Under Czerniaków's direction, the *Judenrat* dealt with health care, welfare, food distribution, sanitation, and police matters. Eventually, 6,000 Jews were working for the city. Like his good friend Janusz Korczak, who operated an orphanage, Czerniaków was especially concerned with children. He succeeded in setting up secret schools for children and covert classes in mechanics and chemistry for adults. Czerniaków's leadership was often challenged. Other, wealthier Jews in positions of power did not like him badgering them for charity on behalf of the less fortunate. Citizens were sometimes unhappy when they asked him to go to the Nazis to get them special favors, and he proved unsuccessful. These favors might include the release of relatives who were in prison for "crimes" such as leaving the ghetto or failing to wear the armbands that identified them as Jews.

Throughout these years, Czerniaków often complained in his diary of feeling ill with headaches and "liver pain"; he suffered from frequent dizziness and nosebleeds. Yet he continued to work seven days a week. According to Josef Kermisz, writing in the introduction to *The Warsaw Diary of Adam Czerniaków: Prelude to Doom*, "Only in work, he believed, lay salvation; he could not believe that the Germans would deprive themselves of the Jews' usefulness and destroy them" due to some "lunatic theory" that the entire Jewish race had to be eliminated.

The Order for Deportation

In the summer of 1942, rumors began to circulate through the ghetto of an impending mass deportation of Warsaw's Jews to the death camps. Nazi authorities assured Czerniaków that this was not true. Still the rumors persisted and ghetto residents grew terrified. Czerniaków tried to encourage them to take heart, saying that there must be a misunderstanding. On July 20, 1942, Czerniaków was once again told that there was no truth to the rumors, that they were "utter nonsense." The next day, several members of the *Judenrat* were arrested and Czerniaków's wife was taken hostage. On July 22 a representative of the Gestapo came to Czerniaków's office. That same day Czerniaków wrote in his diary: "We were told that all the Jews irrespective of sex and age, with certain exceptions, will be deported to the East [it was common knowledge that this meant to the death camps]. By 4 p.m. today a [group] of 6,000 people must be provided." On the afternoon of July 23, Czerniaków wrote: "It is 3 o'clock. So far 4,000 are ready to go. The orders are that there must be 9,000 by 4 o'clock." This was his last diary entry.

According to author Kazimierz Iranek-Osmecki: "He was faced with a tremendous decision. He returned home and wrote these words to his wife [who was still being held hostage]: 'They want me to kill the children of my people with my own hands. There is nothing left for me but to die.'" He asked her

forgiveness for leaving her. He then consumed one of the poison tablets hidden in his desk and died.

The Aftermath

Czerniaków's wife was one of the few mourners at his hastily arranged funeral; his friend Janusz Korczak delivered the eulogy. Korczak praised him for completing "the important task of protecting the dignity of the Jews." People in the Warsaw ghetto regarded Czerniaków's suicide in different ways. Some felt that he had failed them by not clearly warning them of German intentions. Because they were not warned, 300,000 Jews were deported without a chance to defend themselves. Others saw Czerniaków as a hero, who took no salary and defended his people at great risk to his own safety.

Czerniaków was able to describe his plight in his diary. Although a few people knew the diary existed, its location remained a mystery until 1959. A survivor of the Warsaw ghetto bought it from a source she would not reveal and sent it to Yad Vashem, the Martyrs' and Heroes' Remembrance Authority in Jerusalem. With the help of several experts, it was painstakingly translated from the Polish and published in English in 1979. The diary, which is more than 1,000 pages long, has been called by Raul Hilberg, a Holocaust expert and writer, "the most important Jewish record of that time."

SOURCES

Books

Hilberg, Raul, Stanislaw Staron, and Josef Kermisz, eds., *The Warsaw Diary of Adam Czerniaków: Prelude to Doom*, Stein and Day, 1979.

Iranek-Osmecki, Kazimierz, *He Who Saves One Life*, Crown Publishers (New York), 1971.

Lewin, Abraham, *A Cup of Tears: A Diary of the Warsaw Ghetto*, edited by Antony Polonsky, Basil Blackwell (New York), 1988.

Lifton, Betty Jean, *The King of Children: A Biography of Janusz Korczak*, Farrar, Straus and Giroux (New York), 1997.

Tushnet, Leonard, *The Pavement of Hell*, St. Martin's Press (New York), 1972.

Benjamin O. Davis, Jr.

O vercoming obstacles in order to achieve high goals was a longstanding tradition in the family of Benjamin O. Davis, Jr. His father, Benjamin O. Davis, Sr. was the first African American general in the U.S. Army. While his father served as an adviser on race relations during World War II, Davis, Jr. led the Tuskegee Airmen to acclaim as they demonstrated the abilities of black servicemen. Only the fourth African American to attend the U.S. Military Academy at West Point, New York, Davis, Jr. encountered harsh treatment at the academy and was told that he could never become a military pilot. He not only achieved this aspiration, but he also trained hundreds of other black pilots at Tuskegee Army Air Field in Alabama who went on to combat duty in Europe. Under Davis, Jr.'s command, the Tuskegee Airmen became a highly skilled, disciplined unit that, among other accomplishments, never lost any of the bombers it escorted. Davis, Jr. became the first African American air force officer to achieve the rank of general.

Born December 12, 1912
    Washington, D.C., United States

U.S. Air Force general

"[The 332nd Squadron patrol assignment was] a betrayal of everything we had been working for and an intentional insult to me and my men."

A Tradition of Pride and Determination

Benjamin O. Davis, Jr. was born in Washington, D.C., at the home of his grandparents, Louis and Henrietta Davis. His mother, Elnora, died in 1916 and his father soon left Washington to serve with the U.S. Army in the Philippines. Surrounded by aunts,

(U.S. Air Force)

uncles, and cousins, Davis, Jr. and his two sisters, Olive and Elnora, were part of a large, supportive family. In 1919 Benjamin Davis, Sr. married Sadie Overton, a family friend. Assigned to teach military science and tactics at Tuskegee Institute, a school for African Americans, Davis, Sr. moved his family to Alabama. Whenever they left the Tuskegee grounds, however, the Davises experienced the racial prejudice that dominated the South at that time. Jim Crow segregation laws required separate schools, restaurants, movie theaters, rest rooms, and even drinking fountains for black and white people. Although they were forced to endure this inequality, Davis, Sr. refused to show any fear of the Ku Klux Klan. When Klansmen rode past Tuskegee one night, he stood under his front porch light in his white dress uniform with his family seated behind him.

Davis, Jr. first saw a troop of stunt pilots called barnstormers at Bolling Air Field while visiting his uncle in Washington, D.C. The thirteen-year-old youth was awestruck, and when his father later paid for him to ride with a barnstormer, he decided he wanted to be a pilot. The Davis family moved to Cleveland, Ohio, when Davis, Sr. was assigned as an instructor to a black National Guard unit. In 1929 Davis, Jr. graduated at the top of his high school class, then entered Case Western Reserve University in Cleveland. Still determined to be a pilot, he was discontented as a student. Yet no training programs were available for blacks because many people believed they did not have the ability to fly airplanes.

Davis's father suggested that he apply to West Point, despite the fact that no other African American had attended the academy in the twentieth century. (There had been three black graduates in the nineteenth century.) All applicants had to be appointed by an official of the U.S. government, such as the president or a member of Congress, so Davis received an appointment from the only black member of the House of Representatives, Oscar DePriest of Illinois. Davis failed the West Point entrance exam in 1931, but he studied hard and easily passed it the following year. When Davis arrived at West Point, he was informed that white cadets would not be asked to share a room with him. He also learned that he would be given the "silent treatment"—that is, he would be spoken to only about matters of duty—a practice reserved for those who had broken the school's honor code. Davis was to spend the next four years shunned by his fellow cadets, eating his meals in silence and studying and attending activities alone.

Nevertheless, Davis was determined to succeed in spite of the discrimination, and he grew accustomed to life at West Point, settling into a routine of academic study, military training, and drills. As graduation approached, he expressed an interest in applying to the Army Air Corps; at that time, the air force was still part of the army. General William Connor, the West Point superintendent, discouraged him, claiming the Army Air Corps would never train black pilots and white troops would never serve under black officers. Davis did not abandon his goal. In 1936 he graduated from West Point, ranking thirty-fifth in a class of 276. Shortly after graduation he married Agatha Scott, a Connecticut schoolteacher he met at a New Year's Eve dance in New York City two years earlier. The couple held their wedding service in the West Point chapel. Now a second lieutenant, Davis was assigned to the army base at Fort Benning, Georgia, where he and Agatha experienced a different reality than other new arrivals. White officers and their families avoided the Davises. While at Fort Benning, Davis worked with Company F, a black unit commanded by white officers. In the segregated army, African American soldiers were trained for service jobs such as maintaining equipment and grounds, and cleaning stables.

Commands First Black Aerial Squadrons

In 1937 Davis attended the U.S. Army Infantry School, studying war tactics and military history. Like his father, he was assigned as a teacher of military science and tactics at Tuskegee Institute. Having been promoted to the rank of captain, Davis knew he deserved a position with more responsibility. Although he considered quitting, jobs were hard to find and he decided to stay in the army. In 1940 Davis's prospects improved when President Franklin D. Roosevelt responded to pressure from the African American community, which had been instrumental in his election to office, and appointed Davis, Sr. a brigadier general. Given command of the 9th and 10th Cavalries at Fort Riley, Kansas, Davis, Sr. requested that Davis, Jr. be his aide. By 1939 the United States was moving closer to involvement in World War II. As the U.S. government began preparing its armed forces for war, pressure applied by civil rights groups resulted in the formation of a black flying unit called the 99th Pursuit Squadron (also known as the Tuskegee Airmen).

In 1941 Davis received orders to report to Tuskegee Army Air Field for training as the com-

The 761st Tank Battalion

While African American aviators were flying fighter planes on Allied missions over Italy, black soldiers in the 761st Tank Battalion were participating in ground combat in France.

Although widespread racism and discrimination had prevented African Americans from ascending the ranks of the U.S. Army, Lieutenant Lesley James McNair, commanding general of army ground forces, decided to give them more opportunities. McNair is credited with founding the 761st Tank Battalion after he visited the unit at its training camp in Louisiana. When they arrived for duty in France on October 31, 1944, they were welcomed by McNair and General George S. Patton.

As part of the U.S. Army's 26th Division, the 761st Battalion entered battle on November 8, 1944, at Athaniville, France. For the next 183 days they were engaged in constant battle, advancing through six European countries, killing 6,266 enemy soldiers, and capturing 15,818. Among the battalion members noted for their bravery was Staff Sergeant Ruben Rivers of Tecumseh, Oklahoma. Severely wounded in the leg when his tank ran over two landmines, Rivers refused to leave the battlefield and stayed for three more days of combat, though he had a bone protruding from his wound. During a later exchange of gunfire with German troops, Rivers was killed when his tank was hit by an armor-piercing shell. Veterans of the 761st are still pursuing a Medal of Honor for Rivers. On January 24, 1978, the combat record of the 761st Battalion was recognized with a Presidential Unit Citation.

---

mander of the 99th. Since army policy prohibited the training of black and white pilots together, the facility had been created specifically for African Americans; white instructors were assigned to separate housing and other facilities. The nearly 1,000 black pilots were enraged, but Davis told them to focus on their own duties. After completing classroom studies, the Tuskegee Airmen began flight training in bulky BT-13 airplanes. On December 7, 1941, the Japanese bombed the American naval base at Pearl Harbor, Hawaii, and the United States entered World War II. The airmen officially "earned their wings" on March 7, 1942, becoming the first African Americans to enter the U.S. Army Air Corps.

One year later the Tuskegee Airmen finally received combat orders. The squadron was sent to North Africa, where Allied troops had been fighting the German army in Algeria, Morocco, and Tunisia. The Germans had surrendered prior to the arrival of the 99th, but the imminent Allied invasion of Italy provided the Tuskegee Airman with another opportunity for battle. Their first combat mission, a successful attack on Pantelleria Island off the coast of Tunisia, took place on June 2, 1943. The squadron performed strafing missions and escorted the heavy Allied bombers, protecting them from enemy aircraft. During the later invasion of Sicily, the 99th Pursuit Squadron shielded troops landing on the beaches and chased enemy planes away from navy ships. Lieutenant Charles B. Hall became the first member of the 99th to shoot down an enemy plane. Soon the Tuskegee Airmen were flying up to twelve missions per day, bombing air fields, railroad yards, bridges, and factories.

On September 3, Davis was called back to the United States to command the new 332nd Fighter Group, three squadrons of African American pilots who were training for duty. Davis soon learned that the 99th Pursuit Squadron had been criticized by Colonel William Momyer, who had submitted an official report stating that they were poorly disciplined, unable to work together as a team, and tended to panic under fire. The report also implied that black people were unqualified to serve as fighter pilots due to poor reflexes. Momyer suggested that the 332nd therefore be assigned to noncombat

Benjamin O. Davis, Jr. receives the Distinguished Flying Cross medal, which was pinned onto his uniform by his father. (U.S. Army)

duty and that plans to train more black pilots be canceled. Davis was furious, knowing that the report was not based on his squadron's actual performance record but instead on racism. When he met with a committee from the War Department, he avoided allegations of racism, simply providing the committee proof of the squadron's accomplishments in the Italian campaign. The government conducted an independent study of the black pilots' performance, which revealed no difference between their group and any other combat unit. When the 332nd arrived in Italy in January 1944, they learned that the 99th had played a key role in the Allied victory at Anzio, a seacoast town in Italy, where the unit had shot down twelve enemy planes. News of the 99th's accomplishments soon reached newspapers in the United States.

Davis was disappointed when the 332nd Squadron's first assignment was coast patrol rather than combat. In his autobiography he wrote that this was "a betrayal of everything we had been working for and an intentional insult to me and my men." Nevertheless, Davis behaved as if the squadron were performing an important role, and within three months the 332nd was escorting bombers. Davis was promoted to colonel and the squadron moved to a new base at Ramitelli on the east coast of Italy. From there, the unit accom-

plished a successful mission to Munich, Germany, where thirty-nine pilots managed to hold off 100 German fighter planes and shot down one in five enemy planes. Nicknamed the "Red Tails" because of the distinctive red paint on their planes, the Tuskegee Airmen gained a reputation for staying with bombers over the target—the most dangerous part of a bombing mission—and for safely escorting the bombers back to base. Davis had personally led the mission to Munich and in honor of his performance he received the Distinguished Flying Cross, which was pinned onto his uniform by his father. The Tuskegee Airmen had proven the capability of African American servicemen; the unit was awarded more than 100 Distinguished Flying Crosses and three Distinguished Unit Citations.

First Black Base Commander

The Germans surrendered in May 1945, ending the war in Europe. Davis was assigned to command the 477th Bombardment Group, which was preparing to fight the Japanese, but the Japanese surrendered in August. The following March, Davis moved the 477th to Lockbourne Air Base near Columbus, Ohio, which became the first black air base not controlled by white officers. An inspection report later praised Davis for creating an environment in which white troops and white civilian employees worked under African American officers without incident. In September 1947 the U.S. Air Force became a separate branch of the armed forces. An even greater change occurred the following year when President Harry S Truman signed Executive Order 9981, which called for integration of the armed forces. All-black units were to be abolished and black troops fully integrated with white troops. Many felt that the achievements of the Tuskegee Airmen had contributed to Truman's decision.

In 1949 Davis became the first black officer to attend the Air War College. Throughout the 1950s and 1960s he commanded pilots both at U.S. bases and overseas. He worked at the Pentagon as head of the Fighter Branch, commanded pilots fighting in the Korean war, and served in Korea, Japan, Taiwan, and Germany. During the Vietnam war, Davis commanded the 13th Air Force based in the Philippines. At the outset of that conflict, 50,000 African Americans were serving in all capacities of the armed forces; there were twelve black army generals, three black air force generals, and one black admiral. African Americans earned twenty of the 277 Medals of Honor awarded during the war. Davis retired in 1971, having achieved the rank of three-star major general and having served thirty-three years in the military. He became director of public safety for the city of Cleveland, then worked for U.S. Secretary of Transportation John Volpe to help alleviate the problem of "skyjacking," a frequent occurrence at the time. New security systems suggested by Davis resolved the problem in nine months. In 1989 he witnessed the elevation of an African American to the most important post in the military when General Colin Powell became the Chairman of the Joint Chiefs of Staff. On December 9, 1998, Davis himself was promoted to four-star general by President William J. Clinton.

Tuskegee Airmen's Record

111 enemy aircraft shot down

150 enemy aircraft destroyed on the ground

1 German navy ship destroyed (an unusual feat for an air squadron)

40 other enemy boats and barges destroyed

200 escort missions completed without ever losing a bomber (the only fighter group to do so)

SOURCES

Books

Applegate, Katherine, *The Story of Two Generals, Benjamin O. Davis, Jr. and Colin L. Powell,* Dell (New York), 1992.

Davis, Benjamin O., *Benjamin O. Davis, Jr.: An Autobiography,* Smith's Press (Washington, D.C.), 1991.

Reef, Catherine, *Benjamin Davis, Jr.,* Twenty-First Century Books (Frederick, MD), 1992.

Other

Gropman, Alan L., "Benjamin Davis, American," *Air Force,* http://www.aviation.history.com/airmen/davis.htm (May 5, 2000).

Benjamin O. Davis, Sr.

Born May 28, 1877
Washington, D.C., United States
Died November 26, 1970
Chicago, Illinois, United States

First African American general
in the U.S. Army

*"[If] the United States cannot evolve some
kind of platform so that various groups
can get along in harmony, they cannot
make a world peace."*

For most of Benjamin O. Davis's military career, which spanned more than fifty years, the United States armed forces were segregated. Although African Americans had played a role in every American military conflict since the Revolutionary War, it was thought that black and white soldiers should not fight alongside one another. Black soldiers were therefore relegated to duties like cleaning and cooking meals, receiving little opportunity for advancement. In spite of institutionalized discrimination, however, Davis slowly ascended through the ranks to become a U.S. army general. During World War II he advised military leaders on methods of integrating the forces while working to resolve racial conflicts. His efforts helped to begin the process of complete integration of the United States military.

A Hard-Working Family

Benjamin O. Davis was born to Louis and Henrietta Davis, respected members of the African American community in Washington, D.C. Louis, a government messenger, and Henrietta, a nurse, taught their children the importance of education. Benjamin attended the integrated Lucretia Mott Elementary School, which prevented him from encountering racial discrimination until later in life. Davis was interested in history, especially the roles of African American cavalry soldiers and black soldiers during the American Civil War (1861–1865). Although his parents urged him to become a government worker or a minister, Davis aimed for a career in the military. While in high school he joined the Cadet Corps, a group that practiced military drills, and learned about weapons tactics. Although he took some courses at Howard University during his last year of high school, Davis decided to pursue a military career rather than attend college.

In 1898 war erupted in Cuba when revolutionary soldiers fought for independence from Spain. When the United States entered the Spanish-American War on the side of the Cuban revolutionaries, the conflict attracted many young American men of all races to the military. Davis joined a volunteer company and was given the temporary rank of lieutenant, spending his first months as a soldier in various training camps. He encountered racism for the first time when he was stationed in Fort Thomas, Kentucky, and Chickamauga Park, Georgia, where he was shocked at the segregation of African Americans. After the end of the Spanish-American War, Davis enlisted in the army as a private in the 9th Cavalry. His dedication to the military, combined with his ability to write well, take dictation, and type, made him popular with superior officers and helped him to advance through the lower ranks. He was stationed at Samar, an island in the Philippines, where he became a sergeant major, the highest rank available to an enlisted man.

Davis wanted to become an officer, a process that involved special examinations to gauge his knowledge of military history and other subjects. Davis's black colleagues told him that even if he passed the exams, other obstacles would impede his progress. He took the exams and passed, however, becoming a second lieutenant in the 10th Cavalry. In 1902 Davis married Elnora Dickerson, who accompanied him to his new post at Fort Washakie, Wyoming. They were the only African Americans on the base. In 1905 Davis was assigned to teach military history at Wilberforce University, an all-black religious school in Ohio. He was frustrated with the assignment because he felt his skills and training would better serve the army elsewhere. In addition, he was not a particularly religious person, and he felt his military background set him apart from other staff and students. He occasionally argued with Wilberforce's president over what he considered a lack of discipline at the school. He was eventually released from Wilberforce when he was

named military attaché to Liberia, a West African country that had been settled in the nineteenth century by former American slaves. Davis moved his wife and five-year-old daughter, Olive, to Monrovia, the capital of Liberia, where he spent the next two years reporting back to the U.S. government on Liberia's military activities. Finding the Liberian army to be poorly trained and inefficient, he devised reorganization plans. Davis volunteered to stay in Liberia as a military adviser, but U.S. law required that he complete his term of service and return home in 1911.

Davis then served a tour of duty along Arizona's border with Mexico. In 1915 he was promoted to captain, but he was rewarded with reassignment to Wilberforce University. In 1916 Elnora died while giving birth to their third child, a daughter also named Elnora. A son, Benjamin O. Davis, Jr. had been born in 1912. For the next few years Davis relied on his parents and his in-laws for help in raising the children. During World War I (1914–1918) he served as commanding officer of a supply troop in the Philippines. In 1919 Davis married Sadie Overton, who had been a teacher at Wilberforce.

In 1920 his tour in the Philippines was interrupted when a high-ranking officer, who disapproved of black officers interacting with white officers and soldiers, demanded that Davis be replaced. He was assigned to teach at the Tuskegee Institute, an all-black school in Tuskegee, Alabama. Although he enjoyed this position, Davis felt that it was not equivalent to his rank, especially after he was made a lieutenant colonel. Living in the South again, he encountered more racism. He once protested a Ku Klux Klan rally by standing on his front porch in his white dress uniform with his family seated behind him. In 1924 Davis became an instructor to the Ohio National Guard based in Cleveland, yet after he was promoted to colonel in 1929, the army reassigned him to Tuskegee Institute. This outraged the African American community, who publicly denounced the military for improper utilization of an army officer with years of experience.

African American leaders had long been urging the U.S. government to assign black officers to command black soldiers. In 1938 this hope was fulfilled when Davis was made commander of the 369th Cavalry New York National Guard, known as the Harlem Regiment. Davis was simultaneously involved in the Gold Star Mothers' Pilgrimage program, which gave the mothers of slain servicemen the opportunity to visit World War I battlefields

Pearl Harbor Hero: Dorie Miller

The heroic actions of black sailor Dorie Miller during the bombing of the U.S. naval base at Pearl Harbor, Hawaii, demonstrated the wasted abilities of African American military personnel. Strict segregation policies limited the opportunities of black soldiers and sailors, so Miller was serving as a U.S. Navy mess attendant aboard the *West Virginia*. On the morning of December 7, 1941, the *West Virginia* was anchored in the bay at Pearl Harbor when Japanese fighter planes began bombarding the American fleet. Miller had been gathering laundry below decks, but he ran up onto the main deck when he heard the attack. Initially assigned to carry wounded men to safety, he later took over an anti-aircraft machine gun after the operator was killed. Before the battle was over Miller had shot down at least one Japanese plane. Although he had not been trained in the use of the gun, he later confessed that he had learned by watching others operate the weapon.

News of Miller's feat soon reached the African American community. He was celebrated as a symbol of black patriotism and pride, and his admirers asked President Roosevelt to admit him to the Naval Academy. Though he did not enter the Naval Academy, Miller was decorated for his bravery on May 27, 1942, when he received the Navy Cross from Admiral Chester Nimitz, who noted that this was the first time the medal had been given to an African American. Miller continued to serve in the navy until he was killed on November 24, 1943, in the South Pacific when his ship, the *Liscome Bay*, was attacked and sunk by a Japanese submarine.

Dorie Miller. (Reproduced by permission of the Schomburg Center)

and gravesites where their sons had fought and were buried. Davis and his wife accompanied several groups of African American mothers on tours to Europe. By 1940 President Franklin D. Roosevelt was experiencing pressure to eradicate discrimination against blacks in the armed forces. The African American community, which had played an important role in Roosevelt's election victory in 1936, pointed to restrictions on the number of black enlistees; the navy policy of accepting blacks only for mess duty; and the routine denial of promotions for black soldiers. Roosevelt overrode a military law limiting promotions to those age fifty-eight or younger, making the now sixty-three-year-old Davis a brigadier general. Davis was given command of the Fourth Cavalry Brigade at Fort Riley, Kansas. Although he retired from the army in 1941, he was called back to military duty when the United States entered World War II later that year.

Leaves Retirement to Aid War Effort

After the United States entered the war, Davis was assigned to work in Washington, D.C., helping

Brigadier General Benjamin O. Davis, Sr. in England in 1942. Davis came out of retirement to help with the war effort during World War II. (Reproduced by permission of AP/Wide World Photos)

the army's inspector general coordinate the induction of approximately 100,000 African American soldiers into the army. His job involved inspecting black units around the country and helping to solve racial problems that were cropping up as black soldiers intermingled with white soldiers and with the segregated communities near military bases. He helped to produce a film called *The Negro Soldier* which was designed to educate white soldiers about their black counterparts.

Many racial conflicts were caused by the segregation of the U.S. Army, which required black and white soldiers to have meals, attend movies, and have their hair cut at separate facilities on the same base. Other problems developed when white officers used derogatory and belittling terms while speaking to their black recruits and when white townspeople harassed the black soldiers. A number of civil rights leaders were urging a quick end to segregation, but Davis advocated a policy of patience. As World War II progressed and U.S. troops spread out around the world to fight the Axis powers, more racial conflicts erupted overseas. Some white officers and soldiers from the

United States resented the fact that British soldiers interacted socially with blacks.

In 1944 Davis toured the European war zone in an effort to ease this racial tension, asserting that "[if] the people of the U.S. cannot evolve some kind of platform so that various groups can get along in harmony, they cannot make a world peace." Davis also made several strong recommendations to General Dwight D. Eisenhower, commander of U.S. troops in Europe. Pointing to the severe shortage of infantrymen, especially in the wake of the Battle of the Bulge, Davis claimed the situation could be alleviated by allowing African American soldiers to volunteer for the normally all-white combat replacement program. Davis's plan called for black soldiers to be assigned to any units that needed them, instead of exclusively black units. Not ready to implement such a change, Eisenhower modified Davis's idea by allowing black platoons to be fitted into white companies.

Discrimination and segregation in the armed forces existed throughout World War II, but the experiences and contributions of both black and white soldiers, and the input of Davis and other advisers, exposed the injustice within the American military. Six days after Davis's July 20, 1948, retirement from the army, which was marked by a special ceremony in the White House Rose Garden, President Truman issued Executive Order 9981 stating that the military could not discriminate against anyone on the basis of race, religion, or ethnic origin. Davis lived for another twenty years after his retirement. In 1951 he returned to Liberia to represent the United States at Liberia's centennial celebration. He made many other public appearances until 1960, when his health began to decline. Davis died of leukemia on November 26, 1970, at Great Lakes Naval Hospital in Illinois.

SOURCES

Books

Astor, Gerald, *The Right to Fight: A History of African Americans in the Military*, Presidio Press (Novato, CA), 1998.

Fletcher, Marvin E, *America's First Black General: Benjamin O. Davis, Sr., 1880–1970*, University Press of Kansas (Lawrence, KS), 1989.

Greene, Robert Ewell, *Black Defenders of America, 1775–1973*, Johnson Publishing Company (Chicago), 1974.

Other

"New Roles: Gen. Benjamin O. Davis," *National Archives and Record Administration: A People at War*, http://www.nara.gov/exhall/people/new roles.html (May 5, 2000).

Charles
de Gaulle

After the invasion of France by Adolf Hitler and the Nazis in 1940, many French people worked to free their country from the Nazis. Charles de Gaulle, who headed the resistance movement from outside France, proved himself a bold and courageous leader. He became the head of the first postwar government established in France and helped to form a new national identity. De Gaulle's personal ambitions and his desire for a strong, independent France were intrinsically entwined, as exemplified in his comment "Je suis la France" (I am France).

Born November 22, 1890
   Lille, France
Died November 9, 1970
   Colombey-les-Deux-Eglises, France

French general; political leader; president of the Fifth Republic

"Je suis la France [I am France]."

Patriotic Devotion to Country

Charles de Gaulle was born in Lille, a town located in northern France near the border of Belgium. His father was a teacher and headmaster of a Jesuit school. As a child, de Gaulle displayed a good memory and an interest in history. He liked to pretend he was a soldier and thought about serving his country when he became an adult. After graduating from preparatory school, de Gaulle spent a year in the army and then entered the Saint-Cyr military academy. When he graduated in 1912, he enlisted in the 33rd Infantry Regiment. He immediately impressed his commanding officer, Colonel Philippe Pétain, who promoted him from sublieutenant to lieutenant. During World War I (1914–1918), de Gaulle fought in Belgium and was

(Reproduced by permission of AP/Wide World Photos)

wounded twice (1914 and 1915) before taking part in the Battle of Verdun, where he was again injured. Captured by the Germans at Verdun, he spent thirty-two months as a prisoner of war and made five escape attempts.

After the war, Poland and Russia entered into a border dispute. Poland was fighting Russia's Bolshevik army, which had formed after Vladimir Lenin's Bolshevik Party took control of Russia during its 1917 revolution. During the conflict, de Gaulle joined a Polish cavalry unit to gain military experience and further his career. While on leave he married a girl named Yvonne, the daughter of a Paris biscuit manufacturer. When Poland and the newly formed Soviet Union reached a peace agreement, de Gaulle returned to France and lectured on military history at his alma mater, Saint-Cyr. He also attended the Ecole Superieure de Guerre (Higher Military School), where he established himself as a brilliant but arrogant student who did not accept criticism well. His instructors were ready to give him a failing grade when Pétain, now a field marshal, made sure de Gaulle received the high grade that would allow him to earn a promotion. While rising through the ranks of the army, de Gaulle published a number of articles and books on military subjects. In *The Army of the Future* (1934), he recommended the French army be reformed through the use of mechanized, mobile warfare such as armored tanks. Few of his superiors, most of whom advocated the traditional system of fixed fortifications for defense, were ready to listen to his ideas.

Within a few years, however, French military leaders learned the painful lesson that mechanized warfare had became a necessity in the modern world. In the fall of 1939, Germany invaded Poland, prompting France and Great Britain to declare war on Germany. Thus, World War II had begun. Further military conflict erupted on May 10, 1940, when the Germans attacked France. The German army, which had made the change to mechanized, mobile warfare, easily rolled its tanks over fixed fortifications in France. On the same day, Germany also invaded Holland, Belgium, and Luxembourg to extend its European empire. Prior to the invasion, de Gaulle had been assigned to a tank unit in Alsace, France. On May 11 he led an unprepared armored division against the Germans. Nevertheless, his forces performed well in several battles and he was promoted to the rank of brigadier general. On June 5 de Gaulle was called to Paris, where French premier Paul Reynaud named him undersecretary of state for national defense.

A Call to Resistance

Since prospects for a French victory looked bleak, many French leaders wanted to make peace with Germany. De Gaulle was among the few who thought France should keep fighting, even if the government had to relocate to a safe area in North Africa, where France controlled the colonies of Morocco, Algeria, Tunisia, and Equatorial West Africa. On June 16 the government of France was overthrown by the Nazis, who established a new French government, headed by Pétain, de Gaulle's old patron. Pétain's government agreed to move to the southern city of Vichy. Known as the Vichy government, it agreed to cooperate with the Nazis, who controlled northern France, including the city of Paris. Meanwhile, de Gaulle had flown to London aboard a British aircraft, making a favorable impression on British Prime Minister Winston Churchill. The prime minister allowed de Gaulle to use the British Broadcasting Corporation (BBC), the national radio network, to make a four-minute "Call to Honor," in which he urged all French people to resist the Nazis. "Believe me!" de Gaulle said, according to his biographers. "Nothing is lost for France! The same methods which have defeated us may one day bring us victory."

The relative obscurity of de Gaulle prevented his message from having an immediate impact. He gradually began gathering support among his fellow refugees. He called his movement the Provisional French National Committee, more popularly known as the Free French movement. With the help of the British Navy, de Gaulle's forces gained enough strength to attack the pro-Vichy forces at Dakar, French West Africa (now Senegal). Although de Gaulle and his followers lost this battle, they continued to gain popular support. By November 1940, they had approximately 35,000 troops and twenty warships. De Gaulle moved his headquarters to Brazzaville in French Equatorial Africa (now Congo). His biographers note that de Gaulle declared that since no true French government then existed, "it is necessary that a new authority should assume the task of directing the French effort in the war. Events impose this sacred duty upon me. I shall not fail to carry it out." In the spring of 1941 the British and Free French overpowered Vichy forces in Syria and Lebanon, leading to a minor power struggle over the fate of the captured Vichy troops. De Gaulle convinced the British to allow him to try to persuade the soldiers to join

As leader of the Free French movement, Charles de Gaulle urged the French people to continue resisting the Nazis. (Reproduced by permission of AP/Wide World Photos)

the Free French, resulting in an estimated 6,000 of the 25,000 Vichy soldiers becoming part of the movement. In June the Free French won their first victory against the Germans at Bir Hakeim, Libya.

An Increase in de Gaulle's Power

De Gaulle's relationship with the British was not always smooth. However, his dealings with the United States were often stormy. The United States had maintained ties with the Vichy government, which was still the official government of France. U.S. President Franklin D. Roosevelt distrusted de Gaulle, fearing the Frenchman was a potential dictator. When the United States and Britain launched their invasion of North Africa, called Operation Torch, they did not invite the Free French forces to participate. De Gaulle was angered with this decision and was further enraged when the Allies made an agreement that allowed a Vichy commander, Admiral François Darlan, to administer all French colonies in North Africa except Allied-occupied Morocco and Algeria. After Darlan's assassination in December 1942, de Gaulle negotiated a power-sharing arrangement with General Henri Giraud, who had strong links to the Vichy government, and established the French Committee of National Liberation. De Gaulle soon edged out Giraud, who faded into obscurity.

By 1944 de Gaulle was well recognized as the leader of the Resistance (also called the France Combatante or Fighting French) both inside and outside of France. In Nazi-occupied France, the

Women in the French Resistance

The Nazi occupation of France led to the formation of the French Resistance. While Charles de Gaulle led the Free French movement outside France, many secret resistance groups worked inside the country. They carried out a variety of activities, from attacks on German officials by fighting groups called the Maquis, to sabotage, spying, and distribution of propaganda. In the decades following World War II, French Resistance efforts were well known, yet the important role played by French women in the movement was not revealed until many years later. As increasing numbers of men were called away to fight, the contributions of women became crucial to the survival of France. Within the resistance movement, women found a measure of equality with men that had not existed in their prewar world.

The tasks performed by French Resistance women were many and varied. During the first few years of the German occupation, women resisted openly through protests and demonstrations against food shortages. They also called for the return of prisoners of war (POWs) and for the right to send packages to POWs. As the occupation continued, women took on more dangerous and secret responsibilities that could lead to arrest, torture, imprisonment, or even death if they were caught. Some women assisted the Resistance in traditional ways by performing office work or attending to people injured in clashes with the Germans.

Women also opened their homes to Jews; Allied pilots whose planes had crashed in France; and fellow resistance fighters. Farm women hid weapons and city women stashed documents in their apartments. Prior to the war, fathers had been in charge of families; now that men were on the battlefront, mothers assumed the responsibility. A number of French women worked for the Resistance in untraditional ways, especially those who served as "liaison agents." They traveled around the country at great risk to their own safety, carrying messages and money, looking for secure hiding spots for weapons and fighters, and seeking safe sites for parachute drops. Some women also participated as Maquis fighters, though this was not common. Women proved their flexibility and adaptability, displaying innovation and initiative in their war resistance work. After the war, they admitted that the experience showed them that they were capable of moving past traditional women's roles.

Gestapo responded by imprisoning members of de Gaulle's family who were still in the country. When the Allies were planning the massive Normandy Invasion (D-Day)—landing thousands of troops on beaches in Northern France—de Gaulle and his forces were not included. On June 14, 1944, eight days after the initial Allied invasion, de Gaulle landed his troops on the French coast. On August 25 he made a triumphant return to Paris, where he received a tumultuous welcome. By September de Gaulle announced the formation of a temporary government with himself as president. He immediately began working on economic reforms, and in October both the United States and Britain officially recognized de Gaulle's government.

The Fifth Republic

Over the next few months French leaders began refining their newly reorganized government, which they called the Fourth Republic, to feature a strong legislative body and a weaker president. De Gaulle opposed the plan, believing the president should have more power. Since he did not want to be a powerless president, he resigned on January 10, 1946, and returned to his country home at Colombey. He began writing his war memoirs but remained active in politics. In the late 1940s, disgusted with the efforts of the Fourth Republic, de Gaulle formed an organization called the Rally of the French People, which advocated a

Women Who Served in the French Resistance

Berty Albrecht: Before the war, she was a pacifist who fought for working women's rights. With Henri Frenay, she helped found Combat, one of the most active resistance movements. Albrecht decided to publish a secret newsletter, which was widely read. She was captured and tortured three times by the Germans; it is thought that she later committed suicide.

Celia Bertin: A literature student, she was recruited into the resistance because she spoke English and could assist in hiding Allied pilots. While in hiding herself, she wrote a novel. She published numerous books after the war.

Jeanne Bohec: After relocating to London when the Germans arrived in France, she used her knowledge of chemistry and her experience working in an arms factory to help the Free French. Bohec parachuted into France's Brittany region and taught young men how to use weapons.

Sister Edwige Dumas: She helped care for the wounded of both sides after the Allies bombed the city of Calais, and she sheltered resistance fighters wanted by the Germans.

Genevieve de Gaulle-Anthonioz: The niece of General de Gaulle, she followed family tradition by becoming a member of the Resistance. She worked with a youth movement called Defense de la France but was captured by the Germans and sent to the Ravensbrück concentration camp.

Marie-Louise Le Duc: Known as "Madame X" to the British, she helped those who wanted to escape from France, especially Allied airmen. She assisted with secret, nighttime pickups by British boats. Arrested three times, she always managed to escape.

Suzanne Vallon: An ophthalmologist, she fled to London but was sent on active duty to North Africa. Later, she accompanied Allied troops in their invasion of France.

Denise Vernay: She served as a liaison agent in Lyon, which was an unfamiliar city to her. The position required her to memorize messages and addresses and to have few contacts with others. Vernay was caught by the Gestapo and deported.

---

strong chief executive and expressed its ideas through rallies. The group was popular for a short time but eventually collapsed, and de Gaulle officially dissolved it in the early 1950s. Several circumstances brought de Gaulle back to the forefront in France. During the mid-1950s, a dull economy and political squabbling weakened the Fourth Republic. At the same time an independence movement gained momentum in Algeria, which was still a French colony.

Members of the French National Assembly, fearing a possible coup, called on de Gaulle in 1958 to return to his leadership role. Considered the only figure strong enough to lead the nation at such a dangerous time, he became president and head of a new government called the Fifth Republic. De Gaulle soon resolved the Algerian crisis by granting independence to the country. Over the next decade he strengthened France's position in the world, constantly asserting its independence from the United States, Britain, and the Soviet Union. He established ties with West Germany and diplomatic relations with the People's Republic of China, and took steps to promote economic growth and modernization of industry.

By the late 1960s the French economy was strong, but other problems began erupting. In 1968 French students revolted against the country's traditional political and educational systems. Their demands for reforms and a voice in decision-making erupted into fighting in the streets of Paris. De Gaulle was re-elected despite a huge workers' strike that threatened the survival of his government, partially because he convinced voters that communists would take over France if he did not win. In 1969 he proposed a number of reforms that would allow students and workers more involvement in government. When a referendum on these reforms was defeated, de Gaulle resigned the presidency.

De Gaulle again retired to Colombey and continued working on his memoirs, which he completed just before his death on November 9, 1970. At de Gaulle's request, no public ceremony was held.

SOURCES

Books

Aglion, Raoul, *Roosevelt and De Gaulle: Allies in Conflict, a Personal Memoir,* Free Press (New York), 1988.

Cook, Don, *Charles de Gaulle,* Putnam (New York), 1983.

De Gaulle, Charles, *The Complete War Memoirs of Charles de Gaulle,* translated by Richard Howard and Jonathan Griffin, Carroll and Graf (New York), 1998.

Lacouture, Jean, *De Gaulle: The Rebel, 1890–1944,* translated by Patrick O'Brian, Collins Harvill (London), 1990.

Weinberg, Gerhard L., *A World at Arms,* Cambridge University Press (Cambridge, England), 1994.

Williams, Charles, *The Last Great Frenchman: A Life of Charles de Gaulle,* John Wiley and Sons (New York), 1993.

John Demjanjuk

Cases of mistaken identity are more commonly found in fictional accounts of trials than in the real world. But possible mistaken identity was the reason John Demjanjuk's (Dem-yahn-yook) death sentence was overturned by the Israeli Supreme Court in 1993. Demjanjuk had been put on trial for his alleged cruel treatment of Jewish prisoners during World War II. Once the decision was overturned in Israel, it seemed Demjanjuk was exonerated from all charges, but he was later accused of other crimes by the U.S. government. The story of Demjanjuk's life, including his trial as a mass murderer, reads like fiction.

A Poverty-Stricken Childhood

Ivan Demjanjuk (he changed his first name to John when he became a U.S. citizen) was born on April 3, 1920, in a small village in the Ukraine, which was part of the former Soviet Union. Both of his parents were disabled. His father lost several fingers in World War I (1914–18), and his mother lost the use of one of her legs. Young Demjanjuk attended school off and on for nine years, but only completed four grades. It was said that he missed so much school because his father had to use the family's one pair of men's shoes when jobs became available. A famine killed seven to ten million Ukrainians between 1932 and 1933, and starvation

Born April 3, 1920
Dub Makarenzi, Ukraine

Factory worker; farmer; soldier who was tried and acquitted of being the notorious "Ivan the Terrible," a mass murderer of Jews at Treblinka death camp; later charged with other crimes

"… never in my life was I in Treblinka … please do not put the noose around my neck for the deeds of others."

(Reproduced by permission of AP/Wide World Photos)

greatly affected Demjanjuk's village as well. In order to survive the family ate dogs and rats, as well as their pet cat and bird. About these times he once said that there were dead bodies everywhere, but no one moved or buried them. To find some relief, the senior Demjanjuk sold the family's home for the equivalent of eight loaves of bread and they moved to a farm near Moscow, Russia. When the situation there proved no better, the family returned to the village in the Ukraine.

Joins Army

As the Nazis rose to power in Germany during the 1930s under the leadership of Adolf Hitler, they started World War II in 1939 by invading Poland. When they followed with an attack on the Soviet Union, they were met by fierce resistance. The Nazis rounded up Jews, homosexuals, and other people they considered "undesirables," or "enemies of the state," and sent them to forced labor camps where eventually many were killed. Meanwhile, Demjanjuk found a job driving a tractor. He received his draft notice from the Soviet army in 1940, but was not accepted until the following year because he lacked underwear, an army requirement. After completing his military training in 1941, Demjanjuk was sent to fight against the German army. He was injured by fragments from an exploding shell and still bears the scar. In early 1942, Demjanjuk and his unit were taken prisoner by the Germans. The events of Demjanjuk's life from then until the war's end in 1945 remain controversial.

Named a War Criminal

When World War II ended, Demjanjuk found his way to a German camp for displaced persons. There he met Vera Kowlowa, who would later become his wife. The couple spent several years at displaced-person camps throughout Germany. In 1950 their daughter, Lydia, was born at one of them. The following year, Demjanjuk applied to relocate to the United States. Demjanjuk claims that because of his intense fear of deportation to the Soviet Union, where he might have been killed for working for the Germans after his capture, he lied on immigration documents and presented himself as a Polish citizen. Demjanjuk's application to immigrate to the United States was granted. In 1952, his family of three arrived in Indiana, where Demjanjuk found work on a farm. Through the help of friends, they later resettled in Cleveland, Ohio, where Demjanjuk secured work as an engine mechanic, and Vera was

employed at a factory. They remained in these jobs for the rest of their working lives. The couple had two more children, a son, John Jr., and a daughter, Irene. The Demjanjuks first bought a house in Parma, Ohio, and in 1973 moved to the Cleveland suburb of Seven Hills.

During the 1970s, a pro-Soviet journalist in New York accused Demjanjuk of having been a guard at the Sobibór death camp and at a German concentration camp in the town of Flossenbürg. At that point, there was no mention that Demjanjuk had worked at the Treblinka death camp in Poland—that accusation evolved later. In response to a request, the U.S. Immigration and Naturalization Service (INS) sent Demjanjuk's immigration photo and information about him to the Israeli police, who were still looking for war criminals. It was then that the investigation of Demjanjuk may have taken a wrong turn. The Israeli police placed advertisements in the newspaper. They requested that survivors of Sobibór and Treblinka death camps report to Israeli police headquarters regarding an investigation against the Ukrainian Ivan Demjanjuk. As a result, survivors may have arrived at the police station believing that they were supposed to identify Demjanjuk.

In addition, the police showed these potential witnesses a number of pictures, asking them to point out if any of them was the notoriously cruel prison guard "Ivan the Terrible" of Treblinka. Among the smaller and fuzzier pictures was an exceptionally large and clear photo of Demjanjuk. According to writer Frederic Dannen, the way this picture was presented was "suggestive," in the language of police work—witnesses were inclined to pay more attention to this large, clear picture and to think it was more important. While no Sobibór camp survivors pointed out Demjanjuk's picture, five Treblinka camp survivors identified Demjanjuk as "Ivan the Terrible." Israeli authorities sent the results of their investigation to the INS, mentioning that they must have been mistaken about Demjanjuk. Apparently he worked at Treblinka, they said, not Sobibór. In 1981 Demjanjuk underwent a trial in Ohio to determine if his U.S. citizenship should be revoked because he had lied on his application. As a result of this trial, it was determined that he would lose his U.S. citizenship.

Stands Trial

In October 1983 the Israeli police issued a warrant for the arrest of John Demjanjuk. He was extradited by the U.S. government, flown to Israel in February 1986, and held at Ayalon Prison for one year, awaiting his trial. Three Israeli judges were appointed to decide the case that charged him with serving as a death camp guard. He was also charged with (1) crimes against the Jewish people; (2) crimes against humanity (which included murder, extermination, enslavement, deportation, and other cruel acts committed against any civilian population); (3) war crimes; (4) crimes against persecuted individuals; and (5) murder. The Israeli trial of Demjanjuk began on September 6, 1986. The survivors of Treblinka, who had identified Demjanjuk as "Ivan the Terrible" in the 1970s, testified to the same at the trial. Through his trial the whole world learned about the atrocities that had taken place at the Treblinka death camp, where in one year alone, 850,000 people had been murdered.

Based on the testimony of survivors, a picture of a typical day at Treblinka emerged. A train would arrive with about one-hundred Jews packed closely together in each car. The Jews would have arrived there after one- to three-day journeys with no food or water, and a few buckets to use for toilet facilities. After leaving the train, men and women were separated and ordered to remove their clothing. Female prisoners had their heads shaved. The naked prisoners were then herded by whips down a narrow path and forced into gas chambers; the doors were bolted behind them. Crying out in terror, they were gassed to death with carbon monoxide fumes generated by a powerful engine. After thirty minutes their bodies were removed and thrown into a burial pit. In the early days of the camp, the pits were covered with chloride to dissolve the bodies, but the Germans later developed other means of disposing of the corpses—they were burned in special ovens called crematoria. Some of the only Jews to survive the camp were those kept to perform work for the Nazis. These included clothing sorters, barbers, people who pried the gold out of victims' teeth, and corpse carriers.

The Nazis recruited about 100 Soviet army soldiers from prisoner-of-war (POW) camps to help the camp guards. One of the Soviets who operated the gas chambers was the man known as "Ivan the Terrible." During Demjanjuk's trial, witnesses described how "Ivan the Terrible" frequently greeted those about to be gassed with beatings, or cut off their ears or noses with the sword he carried. He also was reported to have broken prisoners' arms and legs with a steel pipe. Often appearing drunk, he struck and berated those who worked for him, insisting that they abuse the prisoners, too. One ex-prisoner remarked: "What pleasure he took in his tasks."

Prosecutors Name Demjanjuk "Ivan the Terrible"

The job of the prosecutors who argued their case before the Israeli court was to show that Demjanjuk was indeed "Ivan the Terrible" of Treblinka. They claimed that in 1942 the captured Demjanjuk volunteered to work for the Nazis at the POW camp where he was being held. They said he was taken to the Nazi training camp for Soviet collaborators at Trawniki, Poland. There he was trained to guard Nazi death camp victims, and was given a uniform, a rifle, and an identification card bearing his photograph. Prosecutors said that Demjanjuk once had a tattoo, later removed, that had identified him as working for the SS, the security squad that acted as Hitler's personal bodyguards and guards at the various camps. They said that from September 1942 until August 1943, Demjanjuk served as a guard at Treblinka, where prisoners named him "Ivan the Terrible."

The Israeli prosecutors based their argument in part on an identification card that featured his picture and was said to be from the Trawniki training camp. The card correctly listed his date of birth, his father's first name, and his blond hair color. It also mentioned that he had a scar. One problem with the identification card was that the picture on it had staple holes, indicating that it might have been removed from some other document. In addition, Demjanjuk's height, nearly six feet, was listed as five-feet-nine. Demjanjuk's lawyers said that the card was forged by Soviet officials (enemies of the Ukrainians) who wanted to injure the reputation of the Ukrainian community in the United States by incriminating Demjanjuk.

During the trial, weeks were spent examining the card in great detail, although the card has never been proven to be an actual training camp identification card. The biggest problem with the card is that it shows that Demjanjuk was sent to a work camp near Chelmno, Poland, and later, in 1943, to the Polish death camp at Sobibór—not Treblinka, where "Ivan the Terrible" performed his harsh deeds.

Demjanjuk's Testimony

The identification of Demjanjuk by concentration camp survivors, whose last contact with "Ivan

Demjanjuk examines a document presented as evidence during his trial in Israel. (Reproduced by permission of AP/Wide World Photos)

the Terrible" had been four decades earlier, was also a problem. Certainly Demjanjuk and the "Ivan the Terrible" described by the survivors shared a strong resemblance. According to witnesses, they had round faces, ears that stuck out, slanted eyes, and thin lips. The survivors who came forward to identify Demjanjuk in court, however, had been exposed to his testimony in America and were aware of his supposed identity and the accusations against him. Demjanjuk's case was so widely covered by Israeli news reports that witnesses believed Demjanjuk must be "Ivan the Terrible." At the completion of the prosecution's case, Demjanjuk's lawyer, John Gill, placed him on the stand to testify in his own defense. Demjanjuk recalled his experiences and refuted charges in testimony that lasted for about one week.

According to Demjanjuk, after his capture by the Germans in 1942, he was eventually taken to a Nazi prisoner-of-war camp in Chelmno, Poland. He claims he stayed there for eighteen months until the spring of 1944. Demjanjuk has described the camp as having terrible conditions, with people dying in

great numbers from disease and starvation. According to his story, he dug peat at the camp, and was then sent to another camp in Austria where he was tattooed to show his blood type. He stated that after the war the tattoo was removed; there is a scar on his arm where the tattoo would have been. Demjanjuk said that in 1945 he was permitted to join the Russian Liberation Army, a military unit that was funded by the Nazis and opposed Soviet leader Joseph Stalin. Later that year he surrendered to the Allies.

Sentenced to Death

In February 1988, three Israeli judges began their private discussions to decide Demjanjuk's fate. Two months later they declared him guilty of being "Ivan the Terrible" and sentenced him to death by hanging. According to Israeli law, all death sentences automatically come under review by the Supreme Court of Israel. Five judges from among the twelve who make up the Israeli Supreme Court were chosen to hear Demjanjuk's appeal in August 1993. Meanwhile, Demjanjuk had spent the previous six years in solitary confinement in an Israeli jail. Sometime in 1991, the written statements of thirty-two former guards and five forced laborers at Treblinka death camp (most of whom were executed by the Soviets as Nazi collaborators) had come into the possession of the Israeli court. The statements all said that "Ivan the Terrible" was a man named Ivan Marchenko. Marchenko, a Ukrainian like Demjanjuk, was last seen in 1944 in Yugoslavia (and there is no evidence of when and if he died).

Some U.S. officials believed that Ivan Marchenko and Ivan Demjanjuk were the same person. One reason was because Demjanjuk had listed "Marchenko" as his mother's maiden name on his application for a U.S. visa. Demjanjuk later said that he had forgotten his mother's maiden name and just used the name of Marchenko, which is common in the Ukraine, to fill in the blank.

Demjanjuk Acquitted

The Israeli Supreme Court ruled in 1993 that the case against John Demjanjuk had not been proved beyond a reasonable doubt. The judgment has been referred to by some as "careful and courageous" because Israel is a Jewish state and the atrocities committed against Jews in the Nazi death camps have particular meaning in Israel. Apparently the written statements taken from the Soviet soldiers played an important role in their decision. "We don't know how these statements came into the world and who gave birth to them," the court wrote. "But ... when they came before us, doubt began to gnaw away at our judicial conscience; perhaps the appellant [Demjanjuk] was not Ivan the Terrible." After the Supreme Court had presented its verdict, Chief Judge Meir Shamgar said: "The matter is closed, but not complete. The complete truth [cannot be known by] the human judge." Also in 1993, the U.S. Court of Appeals determined that the Office of Special Investigations (OSI), which participated in finding evidence about Nazi war criminals, had withheld evidence that might have shown that Demjanjuk was not Marchenko and issued a statement that the OSI had "acted with reckless disregard for the truth" when it stripped Demjanjuk of his citizenship and extradited him to Israel.

Demjanjuk's Life after His Acquittal

Evidence seemed to support the idea that John Demjanjuk was probably a guard at the Sobibór death camp (not Treblinka). Some people feel that Demjanjuk should have been tried in Israel for the offenses he may have committed at Sobibór, but Israel had never tried such a low-level Nazi collaborator and did not pursue the matter. Following his acquittal by the Israeli Supreme Court, John Demjanjuk returned home to Cleveland, Ohio. Demjanjuk issued a news release in 1996 on the third anniversary of his liberation from Ayalon prison. He extended his thanks and greetings to all the people who had supported him over the more than twenty years he was under investigation by the Israeli government. In February 1998, he regained his U.S. citizenship.

Demjanjuk Under Investigation Again

Though Demjanjuk was reported to be readjusting to life within the Ukrainian community in the United States after his press release in 1996, and despite the fact that the U.S. government had reinstated his citizenship in 1998, on May 15, 1999 the U.S. Department of Justice filed new denaturalization papers to revoke Demjanjuk's citizenship. The charges against Demjanjuk as "Ivan the Terrible" had been dropped and were not a part of the new attempt at denaturalization; this time the U.S. government based the denaturalization procedures on new evidence showing that Demjanjuk was a guard at three other Nazi camps (of which he had been formerly implicated) and the charge that he had lied on immigration documents stating he was a guard at none of the camps. The United States accused him again of being a guard trained by the Trawniki unit of the Nazi SS in Poland, though where he served after that was changed. The allegations state that rather than serving at Treblinka, he served at Sobibór (where he was believed to be originally, before the "Ivan the Terrible" accusations surfaced), the extermination camp where approximately 200,000 Polish Jews perished, Majdanek in Poland where 200,000 to 360,000 were killed, and Flossenbürg, a slave labor camp where an estimated 30,000 died. Demjanjuk denied all charges, continuing to state that he was a captive of the Nazis, was forced to labor in a Nazi prison camp, and was never a Nazi guard at any of the death camps. He sued the U.S. government in March 2000, for 5 million dollars, claiming "mental torture." The U.S. government is adamant that he was a guard at the death camps and was involved in Nazi attempts to annihilate the Jews.

SOURCES

Books

Teicholz, Tom, *The Trial of Ivan the Terrible: State of Israel vs. John Demjanjuk,* St. Martin's Press (New York), 1990.

Wagenmaan, W. A., *Identifying Ivan: A Case Study in Legal Psychology,* Harvard University Press (Cambridge, MA), 1988.

Periodicals

"Alleged Death Camp Guard Sues US for Pounds 3m," *Birmingham Post* (England), March 15, 2000, pp. 10.

Beyer, L., "Ivan the Not-So-Terrible," *Time,* August 2, 1993, p. 42.

Dannen, Frederic, "How Terrible Is Ivan?," *Vanity Fair,* June 1992, p. 133.

Kozinski, A., "Sanhedrin II," *New Republic,* September 13, 1993, pp. 16–18.

Seibert, S., "Maybe He Wasn't the Nazis' Ivan the Terrible—But What Was He?" *Newsweek,* August 9, 1993, p. 49.

Sereny, Gitta, "The Two Faces of Ivan of Treblinka," *The Sunday Times,* March 20, 1988, pp. 20–38.

Other

Justice Department Refiles Denaturalization Case Against Nazi Death Camp Guard John Demjanjuk, http://www.usdoj.gov/opa/pr/1999/May/195crm.htm (September 18, 2000).

James Harold Doolittle

General James Harold "Jimmy" Doolittle was one of the best-known American heroes of World War II. When the United States entered the war, he supervised the conversion of automobile factories into airplane manufacturers. Prior to this time, his work with the Shell Oil Company led to the production of a high-octane gasoline for airplanes, which gave the United States an edge over Germany. A daring aviator, planner, and commander, Doolittle made a major contribution to the war effort in 1942 by leading a U.S. Army Air Corps bombing raid on Tokyo that was credited with turning the tide in American wartime morale. He received the Congressional Medal of Honor for this mission. After the raid he was sent to England to supervise air campaigns on North Africa and Germany; at the close of the war he served under General Douglas MacArthur. With the assistance of author Carroll V. Glines, Doolittle told the story of his life in *I Could Never Be So Lucky Again: The Memoirs of General James H. "Jimmy" Doolittle*.

Born December, 14, 1896
    Alameda, California, United States
Died September 27, 1993
    Pebble Beach, California, United States

American aviator

"Well, if we all get to Chungking, I'll throw the biggest Goddam party you ever saw."

A Life Destined for Aviation

Doolittle was born on December 14, 1896, in Alameda, California. His father was a carpenter who, dreaming of striking it rich, took his family to Nome, Alaska, to prospect for gold. They eventually returned to California, settling in the Los Angeles

(Library of Congress)

area. Delicate as a child and small in stature, Doolittle nevertheless developed a love of adventure and a scrappy disposition, taking up motorbike riding and boxing as he grew older. As an adolescent, Doolittle began expressing an interest in flight after he witnessed important events in early aviation history. In 1910, when he was thirteen, he attended an air show. The experience of watching plane theatrics was new to many people as aviation was still in its infancy. Doolittle saw pilot Glenn Curtiss reach 55 miles per hour, breaking the world speed record. He marveled as Louis Paulhan soared to an altitude of 4,165 feet, setting the world altitude record. Two years later Doolittle was at work on his own glider, which he made from wood and fabric. Although he crashed the glider on his first flight attempt, he remained undaunted and repaired the craft, which crashed yet again.

In 1916 Doolittle enrolled at the University of California at Berkeley to study mining engineering. In 1917 he withdrew to enlist in the aviation section of the U.S. Army. (The Air Force would not come into existence until 1947.) He trained as a pilot, hoping to see air combat in World War I (1914–1918). He so impressed his flight instructors that they made him one of their own—he began training others to fly in the United States. During his first year of enlistment, Doolittle married his high school sweetheart, Josephine Daniels. After World War I, he remained in the U.S. Army Air Corps while continuing his education. He was among the first men to receive a doctorate in aeronautics from the Massachusetts Institute of Technology. While he was in the army, he assisted in the testing of new planes, continuously seeking to expand human accomplishments in flight.

In 1922 Doolitte became a public figure when he was the first man to fly non-stop across the continental United States. He piloted his plane from Florida to California in what was then a remarkable speed: twenty-one hours and nineteen minutes. He also was the first to make a flight and landing that relied solely on instruments—a revolutionary contribution to aviation. Doolittle learned how to fly seaplanes, winning the prestigious Schneider Trophy race, and spent time stunt flying and wing walking.

Doolittle became the first aviator to complete an outside loop successfully. On the road to his triumphs, the pilot crashed several times but was fortunate to come out of these disasters virtually unscathed. He is considered by some to have contributed more to modern aviation than pilot Charles A. Lindbergh, whose fame is based on making the first solo nonstop transatlantic flight. Doolittle was also the first North American to fly across the Andes. He also participated in the development and use of instruments such as the Sperry artificial horizon. Such tests did much to increase the safety of flying, enabling flights to take place in varying weather conditions.

Though Doolittle loved his work with the Army, the Shell Oil Company offered to triple his salary. He resigned his commission to join the oil giant in 1930. Remaining in the U.S. Army Reserves to assist in the development of planes, Doolittle pushed Shell to produce high-octane airplane fuels that greatly improved the performance of American airplane engines. His new job required him to compete in air races and aviation exhibitions in the United States and Europe. During these events, Doolittle set a speed record of 296 miles per hour in the Gee Bee, a high-powered but unstable plane that was rarely flown successfully.

Service in World War II

In 1940, with the United States on the verge of entering World War II, Doolittle returned to active duty with the Army Air Corps. His first assignment was assisting factories in preparing for military production, primarily the manufacture of airplanes. On December 7, 1941, Japanese pilots bombed U.S. military facilities at Pearl Harbor in Hawaii. The United States declared war on Japan in return, and thus began America's official entry into World War II. Doolittle was assigned to the Army Air Force headquarters in Washington, D.C., where, at the request of U.S. President Franklin D. Roosevelt, the U.S. military was planning a retaliatory strike on the Japanese. The plan was to transport B-25 bombers on an aircraft carrier, traveling as close to Japan as possible (about 400 miles from Japanese shores). The pilots would then take off from the deck of the *Hornet* and perform the bombing mission. According to the plan, they would then land in Allied-friendly China for refueling. The bombing mission was crucial to the war effort because the Japanese believed that U.S. planes could not reach Japan—the distance was too great.

Doolittle was eager to lead the mission on Tokyo. A *Los Angeles Times* writer recounted Doolittle's tale of how he secured the job. "I asked Gen. [Henry Harley] Arnold if I might personally lead the mission.... He said, 'No, I want you here on my

Henry Harley Arnold, Force Behind the U.S. Air Force

Henry Harley ("Hap") Arnold was one of America's first military aviators. He became chief of staff of the Army Air Corps during World War II and was instrumental in the creation of the U.S. Air Force. Arnold was born on June 25, 1886, in Gladwyne, Pennsylvania. He graduated from the U.S. Military Academy in 1907 and joined the infantry. Early in 1911 he went to Dayton, Ohio, to take flying lessons from Orville and Wilbur Wright and later that year earned the twenty-ninth pilot's license issued in the United States. In 1916 he joined the Aviation Section of the Army Signal Corps and during World War I (1914–1918) served as commander of the 7th Aero Squadron in Panama.

Between the wars, he was a vigorous advocate of air power and an active supporter of former U.S. Army Brigadier General William ("Billy") Mitchell, who was promoting the creation of an independent air force. The army, however, retained control of the Army Air Corps, as the air division of the army was then called, and in 1938 Arnold became chief of the corps. He believed that air power would be the decisive weapon in the next war and thought that the airplane, especially the heavy bomber, should not be shackled to the army. He encouraged development of the "flying fortress," a bomber able to defend itself from enemy fighters and to drop bombs with pinpoint accuracy on industrial targets. Arnold maintained that strategic bombing for selective destruction of key industries would force an enemy into an early surrender, even without physical occupation of the country.

Arnold's efforts were not entirely successful, but in March 1942 the corps became the Army Air Forces and he became the chief of staff. Although technically his organization remained subordinate to the army, it was actually independent, a fact underscored by Arnold's place as an equal on the Combined Chiefs of Staff (the agency composed of American and British heads of service) and his promotion to five-star general. Arnold also shaped the development of the world's most powerful air force. His favorite maxim was: "A second-best air force is like a second-best hand in poker—it's no good at all." His ideas led to the creation of the world's most powerful airforce.

Arnold retired in 1946; a year later, owing largely to his efforts, the U.S. Air Force became an independent service. In his final report he warned that within thirty years the United States would need 3,000-mile-an-hour robot atom bombs, launched from space ships "operating outside the earth's atmosphere." He believed that air power had made mass armies and navies obsolete. He died of a heart attack on January 15, 1950.

staff.' He apparently saw the disappointment on my face because the[n] he said, 'Well, if Biff Harmon [Arnold's chief aide] has no objection, I have no objection.' So I saluted and ran as fast as I could to Harmon's office." Arnold apparently intended to call Harmon and tell him to deny Doolittle's request but, as the pilot told the *Los Angeles Times*, "I got to Harmon's office before the call and he said 'I have no objection if Gen. Arnold has no objection.'"

The Tokyo mission, at first considered impossible by many U.S. military planners, turned out to be more difficult than Doolittle had anticipated. Under Doolittle's leadership, the pilots were trained for the mission while traveling on the *Hornet,* which was commanded by Admiral Raymond A. Spruance. Doolittle warned the crew about maintaining their silence about the mission. In his book *Thirty Seconds over Tokyo,* Captain Ted W. Lawson recounted Doolittle's speech about secrecy. "The reason I want you to keep this thing secret is because if you start talking about it and the news or rumors get around, it'll endanger the lives of many others." He added: "Your lives aren't the only

Spencer Tracy starred in *Thirty Seconds over Tokyo*, which told the story of "Doolittle's Raiders." (Library of Congress)

ones at stake in this thing. There are a lot of people working on this mission. One slip could kill the whole thing."

On the *Hornet,* the crew practiced taking off from the deck in their B-25 bombers. The ship observed radio silence so it would not be detected as it headed toward Japan. "Our bombing problem was complicated," wrote Lawson. "We were told we would drop three 500-pound bombs where they would do the most military damage, yet drop them in the shortest space of time and on as much of a straight line as possible." The mission was further complicated when the *Hornet* was detected by a Japanese patrol boat before the American ship reached the designated take-off point—400 miles off the coast of Japan. Instead, they were about 800 miles away. Although the navy knocked the Japanese boat out of commission, the U.S. pilots did not know if their position had been reported to other Japanese craft. Regardless, they found themselves far from their target, filled with concern about having enough fuel to complete the bombing run.

Shortly after detection, Doolittle ordered his men to commence with the mission immediately. Since the bombers now had an insufficient amount of fuel to arrive at their intended landing strips in

unoccupied China, most of the crew members, including Doolittle himself, were forced to bail out after dropping their bombs on Tokyo, Yokohama, and other cities in Japan. On April 18, 1942, the sixteen American planes did catch the Japanese by surprise. However, after bailing out, some of the men had to find their way through enemy-occupied territory. Eight men were captured and some were rescued by the Chinese who helped the pilots escape from enemy territory. Seven of the pilots were injured; one died in the raid; and two were missing in action. Captain Ted W. Lawson was severely injured in the raid and had to have his leg amputated under primitive medical conditions. Most of the planes were destroyed. Doolittle feared that he would be court-martialed for losing so much expensive equipment. Instead, he was given a rare double promotion to brigadier general and given the Congressional Medal of Honor. The bombers became known as "Doolittle's Raiders."

Although the bombs inflicted minimal damage, they did succeed in demoralizing the Japanese and significantly raising American morale. In *Thirty Seconds over Tokyo,* Lawson recounts the observations of Ramon Muniz Lavalle who was in Tokyo during the raid. Lavalle worked with the Argentine Embassy. Lawson notes that "[Lavalle] was surprised to hear an air-raid alarm in Tokyo that day because he himself was beginning to share the Japanese belief and official boast that their cities could never be bombed." In fact, the Japanese had not built any air raid shelters. During the war, Lavalle told Lawson "[t]hat raid by Doolittle was one of the greatest psychological tricks ever used." Lavalle added: "The results of the Doolittle raid are still evident in Japan. They are stamped into the daily living habits of the Japanese people. Where before they imagined themselves safe from aerial aggression, they now search the skies each morning and each night."

Doolittle was sent to Europe to command Dwight Eisenhower's air units during the planned invasion of North Africa, after which Doolittle was promoted to major general. He had been coolly received by Eisenhower, but gradually won his commander's confidence. Doolittle stayed with Eisenhower throughout the remainder of World War II in Europe, first as commander of the Twelfth Air Force in North Africa (1942–1943), then with the Northwest African Strategic Air Forces. He also commanded the Fifteenth Air Force during the Mediterranean campaigns of 1943, and, finally, from January 1944, commanded the Eighth Air Force based in England.

In his early commands, Doolittle, who often flew missions himself, had been obliged to develop effective air forces, but the Eighth had already been built into a successful unit by its previous commander, Lieutenant General Ira Eaker. Nevertheless, Doolittle profited from the advent of more and better planes, particularly the P-51 fighter, which allowed his forces to achieve air superiority over the heart of Germany itself. A firm believer in strategic bombing, Doolittle commanded the Eighth Air Force during its greatest successes: the first American bombing of Berlin, the sustained bombing campaigns against Germany's oil industry and various manufacturing and rail facilities, and finally the virtual destruction of the Luftwaffe, the German air force.

After the war Doolittle returned to reserve status in the military and rejoined Shell Oil as vice president and director. He continued to be involved with the military, serving on several advisory committees. He helped develop the U.S. Air Force as a separate military division from the army and was part of the National Advisory Committee for Aeronautics, which later became the National Aeronautics and Space Administration (NASA). In 1959 Doolittle retired from these activities; he was promoted to full general in the reserves by President Ronald Reagan in 1985. He received the Presidential Medal of Freedom from U.S. President George Bush in 1989. In 1991, with co-author Glines, he chronicled his life in *I Could Never Be So Lucky Again*. Two years later he died after suffering a stroke at his son's home in Pebble Beach, California. Doolittle was given a burial service with full military honors and laid to rest in Arlington National Cemetery in Arlington, Virginia.

Sources

Books

Boyne, Walter J., *Silver Wings: A History of the United States Air Force*, foreword by James H.

Doolittle, introductory note by Lee Ewing, Simon & Schuster (New York), 1993.

Doolittle, James, and Carroll V. Glines, *I Could Never Be So Lucky Again: The Memoirs of General James H. "Jimmy" Doolittle*, Bantam Books (New York), 1991.

Gabreski, Francis, *Gabby: A Fighter Pilot's Life*, Schiffer Publications (Atglen, PA), 1998.

Getz, C. W., editor, *The Wild Blue Yonder: Songs of the Air Force*, Redwood Press (Burlingame, CA), 1981.

Glines, Carroll V., *The Doolittle Raid: America's Daring First Strike Against Japan*, Orion Books (New York), 1988.

Glines, Carroll V., *Jimmy Doolittle: Daredevil Aviator and Scientist*, Macmillan (New York), 1972.

Glines, Carroll V., *Jimmy Doolittle: Master of the Calculated Risk*, Van Nostrand Reinhold (New York), 1980.

Lawson, Captain Ted W., *Thirty Seconds over Tokyo*, Random House (New York), 1943.

Reynolds, Quentin, *The Amazing Mr. Doolittle: A Biography of Lieutenant General James H. Doolittle*, Arno Press (New York), 1972.

Schultz, Duane P., *The Doolittle Raid*, St. Martin's Press (New York), 1988.

Thomas, Lowell, and Edward Jablonski, *Doolittle: A Biography*, Da Capo Press (New York), 1982.

Toliver, Raymond F., and Trevor J. Constable, *Fighter General: The Life of Adolf Galland*, foreword by James H. Doolittle, Schiffer Publications (Atglen, PA), 1999.

Other

Los Angeles Times, September 28, 1993; and October 14, 1993.

Shimson and Tova Draenger

Shimson Draenger
Born 1917
Kraków, Poland
Died 1943?
Somewhere in Poland

Writer; editor; Polish-Jewish
resistance leader

Tova Draenger
Born 1917
Kraków, Poland
Died 1943?
Somewhere in Poland

Writer; Polish-Jewish resistance worker;
wrote a memoir of young Jewish resisters

*"I swear by … the memory and honor of
dying Polish Jewry, that I will fight with
all the weapons available to me until the
last moment of my life.…"*

—TOVA DRAENGER

Shimson and Tova Draenger, a young Jewish couple living in Kraków, Poland, before and during World War II, repeatedly put their lives at risk opposing the rule of the Nazi party that had taken over their country. They realized the value of the printed word, using the journals and newspapers they published to encourage the rebellion of their fellow Jews. More than fifty years after the war, their tale of courageous and persistent resistance remains an inspiration.

Shimson Becomes Underground Leader

Shimson Draenger, often called Simek, was born in Kraków, Poland, in 1917. When he was thirteen, Shimson joined Akiba, a Jewish youth organization. Its members met on Friday evenings to celebrate the beginning of the Jewish Sabbath through songs and poetry. Eventually Shimson became a leader of the group. He earned a college degree in liberal arts and became the editor of Akiba's weekly newspaper as well as its journal, *The Sayings of Akiba*. During the 1930s, the Nazis experienced a tremendous surge of power in Germany through the use of force and the hypnotic and persuasive speaking skills of their leader, Adolf Hitler. Adamant in their anti-Semitism, the Nazis continually persecuted the Draengers as their power grew. When World War II began with the Nazi invasion and subsequent occupation of Poland in 1939, Great Britain rallied to Poland's defense. Shimson's journal took a hard stance and spoke out against the Nazis. On September 22, 1939, shortly after the Nazis occupied the city of Kraków, Poland, they arrested Shimson for the anti-Nazi material he was publishing. His wife, Tova, was arrested along with him. He was taken to a prison camp in the nearby country of Czechoslovakia, but released in December of that year.

Shimson, described as being a tough and somewhat humorless young man, soon brought his followers back together. Masking their activities under the pretense of carrying out educational work, Shimson began building a branch of Akiba in Warsaw, Poland. Determined to continue resistance activities against the Nazis, he continued to publish his journal as well as his weekly newspaper. From December 1941 through August 1942, Shimson was in charge of a farm set up by the Akiba Youth Organization in the Polish town of Kopaliny. Along with other young people in charge, Shimson managed to convince local residents that the members of the group were Gentiles. The farm served as a cover for Akiba's training of Jewish resistance workers. A colleague of the Draengers stated that the young people were never quite certain how they should proceed in their resistance efforts. There were continual discussions about what the goals of the organization should be and what they could expect their efforts to accomplish realistically.

While working at the farm, Shimson and Tova Draenger took care of their five-year-old nephew, Witek, who became a kind of mascot for the group. As local suspicion continued to attract the attention of the Nazis, the farm was abandoned in August 1942. Shimson and his colleagues moved Akiba's operations to the Kraków ghetto. Shimson and his followers went voluntarily to the ghetto, feeling that there they could be of more help to Kraków's Jews. In the ghetto, Akiba's resistance work found a sharper focus.

Urges Rebellion

The Nazi political platform was built on the contention that Jews were members of a separate, evil race that plotted against German society. During the middle part of World War II, it became clear that the Nazis intended to murder all the Jews of Europe, in an effort they referred to as the "Final Solution." This policy was in stark contrast to their earlier, less violent practice of deporting Jews from Europe for what they called "resettlement" else-

where. The Nazis built hundreds of concentration camps throughout Germany and Eastern Europe, with the intention of clearing out the ghettos in the cities and sending their inhabitants to the camps. The camps were to house the people that Nazi legislation termed "enemies of the state." Once they were relocated, prisoners would be forced to work long hours with very little food. When they were unable to work, they would be killed. Many would be transported in by train and sent directly to the gas chambers—sealed rooms disguised as showers which were filled with poisonous gas in order to kill the prisoners locked inside.

Knowing that the truth of their intentions would incite riots and internal rebellion, the Nazis lied to the Jews of the ghettos, promising them that they were to be resettled in labor camps with good conditions. When Shimson learned about what the Nazis' true intentions were, he declared that the Jews must make all possible efforts to disrupt the Nazi order. In September and October 1942, along with other groups of young Jews, Akiba formed the Jewish Fighting Organization to work against the Nazis' aims. Shimson wrote: "We ought to go from town to town and explain to the people that there are no resettlements; that there is only death! They must have no illusions. They must flee…. They must not try to escape singly but do so in one great mass, so as to flood the trains, roads, the entire countryside…. It is true that [the Nazis'] round-ups would become gigantic massacres, but this is of no importance to us, while to them this would be an open rebellion. For every rebellion undermines the power and upsets their order." Indeed, the information the Nazis wished to conceal had the response they feared. According to a Polish man who knew Shimson well, the cause became his only concern, above personal emotion, and even his marriage.

Arrested

By 1942 Jews were not permitted to leave or enter the Kraków ghetto without special permits checked by German guards. The Jewish Fighting Organization operated an office that forged permits allowing its members free access in and out of the ghetto. They also sold the permits to obtain firearms. Shimson was so skilled at creating the forgeries that German officials often thought his forged signatures were their own signatures. Seeing that direct retaliation, done in a covert manner, was the only way to disrupt the Nazi killing machine, the group decided to act. During late 1942 and early 1943, the Jewish Fighting Organization conducted a series of raids against the Nazis and sabotaged tracks at the railroad station in Kraków. Several German hangouts were attacked by the group, with the most severe damage being done to a popular restaurant, where seven Nazi officers were killed and seven were wounded.

In the same period, Shimson and Tova began producing an underground journal called *The Fighting Pioneer.* The ten-page publication, written in Polish, urged the readers to never give up their struggles against the Nazis. Beginning in September 1942, Shimson's group also published *The Voice of the Democrat,* which was distributed in the streets of Kraków. Shimson was captured by the Nazis in January 1943 and taken to Poland's Montelupich prison. Upon learning that Shimson had been arrested, Tova surrendered to the Nazis and was also sent to Montelupich. Most of Shimson's fellow resistance leaders had already been captured and killed. Conditions in the prison were terrible, with inmates forced to submit to such brutalities as having their heads immersed in buckets of human waste. Always interested in the power of ideas, and hoping to bring inspiration to his fellow prisoners, Shimson established study groups focusing on the Torah and other topics while imprisoned.

Shimson escaped from prison in April 1943, and he and Tova, who had also escaped from prison, were reunited. They hid in a forest and again engaged in resistance activities with other Jews. Shimson resumed his writing and publishing. He encouraged the Jews in the forest to continue their fight and urged those still living in the ghettos to get out at all costs. He also appealed to the people of Poland to keep silent regarding the hiding places of Jews. Shimson was recaptured by the Nazis on November 8, 1943; historians believe he was executed.

Tova Co-founds Resistance Movement

Tova Draenger, who married Shimson Draenger in 1938, was born Gusta Davidson in Kraków, Poland, in 1917. She has been described as attractive, intelligent, charming, and eager to express her feelings. Along with Shimson, she worked on a weekly newspaper for young people and also cofounded and participated in an underground resistance movement in Kraków. Like her husband, she was arrested on September 22, 1939, for being part of the Jewish resistance. Released from prison camp in December 1939, she and

Shimson reorganized the Akiba movement in the cities of Warsaw and Kraków.

Tova Surrenders to the Nazis

In 1941 and 1942, Tova was part of the resistance group that her husband operated on a farm. Co-conspirator Jozef Wulf described her main activities there as helping new members learn to hide from the Nazis and fight against them, performing technical work, and participating in meetings to discuss ideas for the group's actions. In 1942 and 1943, Tova was involved in planning the anti-Nazi raids conducted by the Jewish Fighting Organization. Tova and Shimson had already agreed that if one were captured, the other would surrender. When she learned that Shimson had been arrested on January 18, 1943, Tova surrendered to the Nazis. Reuben Ainsztein referred to Tova's behavior as noble and generous, although he also called it "a romantic gesture typical of the Akiba group, who never ceased to be romantic amateurs in their underground work." However, Ainsztein commended Tova for refusing to reveal any information despite repeated beatings and torture. He told how the Nazis brought her in contact with her husband expecting that she would then break down in tears and tell them what she knew. Instead, she said, "Yes, we have organized Jewish fighting groups and we promise you that if we succeed in escaping from your hands, we shall organize even stronger … groups."

Tova Writes Memoirs

While a prisoner in Montelupich prison, Tova helped to organize a series of activities for the prisoners to help keep up their spirits. These included intellectual discussions, Torah reading, singing, and writing and reciting poetry. At Montelupich, Tova also produced a diary, later published as *Justyna's Narrative,* about the successful raids her group had led against the Nazis. Fearing that these stories would die along with the group's young heroes, Tova wanted to preserve them for future generations. She was concerned that what she wrote might be found by guards, so Tova used fictional names for the characters; the name she chose for herself was Justyna. She wrote her thoughts on pieces of toilet paper. With the help of cellmates, several copies of the diary were produced and hidden on the prison grounds.

In the introduction to the 1996 publication of *Justyna's Narrative,* Eli Pfefferkorn and David H.

Excerpts from *Justyna's Narrative*

The 1996 edition of Tova Draenger's memoir, called *Justyna's Narrative*, recounts the history of the Akiba Movement from April 1941 to March 1943. Tova described the diary as "the true story of the last and most daring revolt of the young fighters." In one passage, the character Justyna, who represents Tova, talks about the difference between the attitudes held by young and elderly Jewish people in the face of Nazi torture and extermination, stating that "[i]n general, the older folks lacked the fighting spirit needed to resist the enemy."

She then asks rhetorically, "But why should that come as a surprise.... " She answers her own question: "Anyone who has not lived through three years of degradation, humiliation and baiting, who has not clung desperately to a life hanging by a thread in the midst of a [raging] storm, will not be able to understand the despair of these people. Only someone who has had the luxury of an unruffled existence could condemn them for having resigned themselves to their fate."

Justyna understands and empathizes with their attitude, stating: "If you could just see into the murkiness of their bruised, despairing souls and live a single hour in that black hopelessness, knowing that all struggle is meaningless and to no avail, knowing that there is nothing at the end of the tunnel but the ugly letters that spell out 'death,' then you would know what they felt, and you would say to yourself, as they said, 'Let come what may'—and wait for it to happen." Yet in marked contrast to this attitude Justyna says: "It was different with the young. They clutched at life, and refused to accept their fate passively. Their powerful desire to live drove them to active resistance, which was not without its ironies, since it was this irresistible lust for life that drove them to engage an overwhelmingly superior enemy, thereby exposing themselves to certain death.... The force demanding their survival was the very force pushing them to their deaths."

Hirsch describe Tova's efforts: "In [Tova's] relatively spacious cell ... a handful of women huddled together in a circle, and in the center of the circle sat [Tova], inscribing tiny letters on scraps of paper. When her fingers became numb from exertion, another woman would take over the writing while she dictated. Every single note was checked by [Tova] before being stashed away....'This is history and it must be accurate,' she insisted." Fortunately, 15 of the book's 20 chapters have survived.

On April 29, 1943, Tova and other women prisoners were lined up two-by-two on a forced march outside Montelupich prison. Tova and another woman attacked the nearest guards when they saw a chance. The other prisoners followed, while several women ran away. Most of the women were killed by machine gun fire, but Tova managed to escape. She rejoined Shimson, who had also escaped. They hid in a forest, where they continued their publishing and other underground activities.

Surrender and Probable Murder

After Shimson was arrested a second time on November 8, 1943, Tova again surrendered to the Nazis. Her fate following the surrender is unknown; it is believed that she was executed. The disappearance of the Draengers brought an end to the Jewish Fighting Organization of Kraków.

Sources

Books

Ainsztein, Reuben, *Jewish Resistance in Nazi-occupied Europe*, Barnes & Noble (New York), 1975.

Draenger, Gusta Davidson, *Justyna's Narrative,*
    edited with an introduction by Eli Pfefferkorn
    and David H. Hirsch, translated by Roslyn
    Hirsch and David H. Hirsch, University of
    Massachusetts (Amherst, MA), 1996.

(Otto) Adolf Eichmann

An SS officer, Adolf Eichmann participated in the murder of millions of people in eighteen countries before he escaped to South America at the end of World War II. Eichmann was kidnapped by Israeli secret agents in 1960 and transported to Israel, where he stood trial for crimes against humanity and the Jewish people. He was found guilty and hanged. He was charged with the following crimes: murder, extermination, enslavement, deportation, and other acts committed against the civilian population of a country. Defending his actions, Eichmann claimed his status as a junior official gave him no authority to issue orders, and that as a good soldier he was simply following orders.

Childhood in Germany and Austria

Born Otto Adolf Eichmann in Solingen, Germany, in 1906, he was the first of five children born to Karl Adolf and Maria Schefferling Eichmann. He went by his middle name, Adolf. His father was an accountant—a stern and devoutly religious man who ran an orderly household. The stringent upbringing had a lasting effect on young Eichmann, who developed a distaste for religion. Eichmann was about ten years old when his mother died. His father remarried shortly thereafter and moved the family to Linz, a picturesque town in Austria. Eichmann was a solitary boy and a poor student who dropped out of high school at the age

Born March 16, 1906
 Solingen, Germany
Died May 31, 1962
 Ramle, near Tel Aviv, Israel

Lieutenant colonel in the SS; planned and directed the rail system that transported millions to death camps; helped develop the gas chamber

"It was a job I had. It wasn't anything I'd planned, nor anything I'd have chosen."

(Library of Congress)

of sixteen to begin an apprenticeship in his father's electrical construction company. An odd footnote to history is that he went to the same high school that Adolf Hitler attended nearly twenty years earlier; Hitler was also a dropout. Easily bored, Eichmann was unable to finish the apprenticeship program. He spent the early 1920s doing odd jobs and drifting from place to place. In one of his many temporary professions, Eichmann was working as a traveling salesperson when he first heard Hitler speak. In 1932 the unfocused nature of his life gave way to the regimented activities of the Nazi party.

Moves Up in Nazi Party

The Nazi party grew out of a small, anti-Jewish group that began in 1918. Hitler became its leader in 1921, and built the party's membership to a great enough number that by the 1933 elections, he was able to take control of Germany. The party had more than two dozen objectives, mainly revolving around systematic repression of the Jews, who were considered "enemies of the state." The Nazi party passed legislation declaring the following: Jews could not be citizens; Jews were to be treated as foreigners; Jews were prohibited from publishing and from holding public office; and Jews were to be expelled from Germany under certain conditions.

When Eichmann was fired from his job as a traveling salesperson in 1934, he made his way to Germany and joined the SS—the military branch of the Nazi party. Although the training was brutal, he excelled. Eichmann discovered within himself a capacity for enduring great pain and a love for precision and order. Not long after, he volunteered to work in the SD, the German Security Office, and moved to Berlin, the capital of Germany. According to author Hannah Arendt, Eichmann's new boss in the SD told him to read two books about Zionism, which may have been among the few serious books he ever read. Zionism—the belief that the Jewish people should have their own nation—was an opinion that Eichmann immediately adopted. For the rest of his life, he would claim that he always favored sending European Jews away to their own nation rather than exterminating them.

When Eichmann next acquired a little knowledge of Hebrew and Yiddish, he became the SD's "expert" on Jews. He visited Palestine, parts of which later became the modern state of Israel, homeland to the Jews, to learn about the Jewish community already established there. He was named director of the "Jewish Emigration Office," an organization that kept track of Jews. Thus began his career as a mastermind behind the Nazis' "Final Solution"—the systematic plan to kill all the Jews of Europe. Between 1937 and 1941, Eichmann was promoted four times. He was often complimented by his superiors for his thorough knowledge of the party's "enemies"—the Jews. He became so powerful that he was assigned his own four-story building to carry out his work. During this period, the Nazis were in the first stage of their solution to the "Jewish question." Jews were not yet being exterminated but were being forced by Eichmann and the Nazis to leave Europe. One of the tactics he used to persuade Jews to emigrate was to have the Gestapo terrorize them. The situation worsened for the Jews, who were informed that anyone fleeing the country would be stripped of his or her property and possessions. As increasing numbers of people escaped Nazi Germany, it became difficult to find countries willing to accept them. Consequently, millions of Jews were left behind in Germany.

Wartime Activities

As Eichmann became increasingly adept at moving large numbers of people, he grew more confident in his own abilities. His power within the party already established, Eichmann married Veronika (Vera) Lieble and had two children. His role as a family man was thwarted by a long string of affairs. He discovered a fondness for gourmet food, fine wines, and luxury cars. Eichmann felt that he was actually helping the Jews by sending them to a place where they would have "soil of their own."

Eichmann's duties were expanded as a result of the Wannsee Conference held on January 20, 1942. There he and other top Nazi officials laid down the details for the "Final Solution." Eichmann later claimed that he had objected to extermination of the Jews, preferring to force them out of Europe. However, since his superiors had adopted the policy, Eichmann believed it was his duty to carry out the plan with efficiency. He oversaw a vast and complicated operation that involved organizing transportation, providing supplies and equipment to German soldiers, and rounding up victims for the concentration camps. At first he had special SS units follow directly behind Hitler's army as it marched through Europe. In each country conquered by the

Nazis, Jews would be rounded up. Some would be lined up in front of trenches and told to kneel. According to Israeli secret service agent Peter Malkin, as soldiers moved along the line, they "fired point-blank into the backs of their heads and, in a move they had practiced, sent each victim pitching forward with a sharp thrust of a boot."

Eichmann saw problems with this method of murdering Jews. First, bullets were scarce and expensive. Second, as the practice continued, some German soldiers felt sympathy for the victims. Eichmann claimed he could understand those feelings because he too was sickened by the sight of blood. Wanting to carry out his orders, but make it easier on the German soldiers doing the trench work, Eichmann began to investigate new killing methods. After discarding several possibilities, he ordered the building of new concentration camps containing large gas chambers, disguised as showers. Here, large numbers of people could be exterminated in a short period of time. The plan was to create the gas chambers, which were sealed rooms, and fill them with poisonous gas in order to kill the people locked inside. The plan proved to be a much more efficient system of genocide than the previous method. When a new type of gas, called Zyklon B, became available, Eichmann's gas chambers became even more efficient. Much later, as part of their training in chemical warfare, German soldiers were required to stand in gas chambers. They called the chambers "Eichmann Hobby Shops."

Eichmann continued the killing even when it became obvious that Germany was losing the war. He later described the situation to Malkin, one of the Israeli agents who captured Eichmann in South America. "Near the end, [Heinrich] Himmler himself wanted me to stop. He thought we could save our skins. But I pressed on. If a man has an assignment to perform, he does not stop until it is done." A witness at the war crimes trials in Nuremberg, held immediately after the war, testified that he heard Eichmann say: "I will leap into my grave laughing, because the feeling I have five million human beings on my conscience is for me a source of extraordinary satisfaction."

Keeps a Low Profile

For his part in the horrors of the Holocaust, Eichmann became a legend among Jews. Knowing that there was a chance Germany might lose the war and he would someday be held accountable for his actions, he deliberately aimed to keep a low profile.

Eichmann at his 1961 trial in Israel. (Reproduced by permission of Hulton Getty/Tony Stone Images)

Michael A. Musmanno, a judge who later appeared as a witness at Eichmann's trial, wrote that he asked an Eichmann associate why the SS officer's military rank was so low, considering the fact he wielded so much power. The reply was that Eichmann preferred this arrangement. He felt that if he had a high rank, he would be more conspicuous and more people would be aware of his activities. Musmanno explained: "Eichmann could operate like a weasel on a chicken farm … and then cunningly disappear before the victims could defend themselves." Even some high-ranking Nazi officers did not know the extent of his power. Whenever Nazi officers posed for photographs, Eichmann arranged to be standing in the last row, with his face hidden by another person. Therefore, few knew what he looked like. When he was captured by the Americans in 1946, he passed himself off as a clerk of no importance and eventually escaped.

Escape and Capture

In 1950 Eichmann made his way to Argentina; his wife and two sons followed in 1952. Under the name Richard Klement, he took a job on the assembly line of the Argentine branch of a German automobile company in Buenos Aires. A conscientious employee, he soon had worked his way up to a man-

Hannah Arendt (1906-1975) Covers Eichmann Trial

Hannah Arendt, the only child of a Jewish engineer, was born in Hannover, Germany, in 1906. She earned a Ph.D. in political theory at the University of Heidelberg (Germany) in 1928. Five years later she fled to France to escape the Nazis and, in 1941, with the assistance of Varian Fry, she fled to the United States. There she became a citizen and taught at several universities, becoming the first woman ever to be named a full professor at Princeton University in New Jersey. When her first book, *Origins of Totalitarianism,* was published in 1951, she established a reputation as a major political thinker.

In 1961 she was asked by *New Yorker* magazine to cover the Adolf Eichmann trial. She wrote a series of magazine articles about the trial, and out of them grew the book *Eichmann in Jerusalem: A Report on the Banality of Evil.* The views she expressed about the character of Eichmann created a considerable controversy.

Arendt believed that Eichmann was a very ordinary man who was not motivated by hatred of the Jews. She believed that he was simply carrying out orders, as he himself claimed ("he left no doubt that he would have killed his own father if he had received an order to that effect"). Many other people believed that Eichmann was an evil man, fully responsible for the actions he performed. Justice Michael A. Musmanno called him "this colossal figure of evil." Israeli agent Peter Malkin, who captured Eichmann in Argentina called him "a monster." Still, he said: "[H]e was not an obviously cruel or thoughtless man. Were he living among us today and, say, running a shoe factory, he would probably be regarded with quiet respect, a steady husband and father, producing excellent shoes at a fair price, a pride to his community." In other words, a "predictable, commonplace" man. Whatever one's point of view, though, writer Leni Yahil concluded: "What cannot be doubted is that Eichmann served the Nazi program for exterminating the Jewish people with zeal and efficiency."

---

agement position. Eventually the Eichmanns had a third son. Eichmann developed friendships among the community of former Nazis in Argentina, all of whom knew who he really was. He even gave an anonymous interview to a Dutch Nazi journalist, in which he stated: "I have to conclude in my own defense that I was neither a murderer nor a mass murderer.... I carried out with a clear conscience and faithful heart the duty imposed upon me." Although it seemed that most of the world had forgotten about him, there were some who could not get Eichmann out of their thoughts. Simon Wiesenthal, a dedicated Nazi-hunter, made the capture of Eichmann a top priority. Evidence collected by Wiesenthal helped bring Eichmann to justice.

Finally, in a daring, carefully plotted, top-secret mission, Israeli secret agents kidnapped Eichmann near his home in 1960. In his account of the cap-

ture, *Eichmann in My Hands,* Malkin spoke of standing guard over Eichmann in the bedroom of the house where he was held captive and interrogated before being taken to Israel. Malkin, who had lost relatives because of his captive's actions, described Eichmann talking about his love for children. He recalled how Eichmann's sense of military discipline reached absurd proportions during his captivity—he would not eat or use the toilet unless ordered to do so. And while he was detained, he continued to insist that what he did was right because he was following orders.

Eichmann's kidnapping caused a worldwide uproar. Argentina charged Israel with violating its rights by abducting Eichmann out of that country. Critics all over the world condemned Israel, flinging accusations of "illegal practices and violence." The kidnapping was only the beginning of the outrage, though. It continued as more than 100 witnesses came forward at trial to present the full details of the Holocaust.

The Trial of Eichmann

Eichmann was accused by an Israeli court of crimes against humanity and against the Jewish people. He was also accused of membership in hostile organizations—the SS, SD, and Gestapo. Eichmann's answer to every charge presented against him was "not guilty." A witness at the trial described Eichmann's demeanor: "I study him as he sits in a bullet-proof glass enclosure, so he may be safe from any possible act of vengeance attempted by some grief-crazed survivor of the crimes attributed to him.… His beady, snakelike eyes sink into a startling skull, over which the yellowish parchment of his skin crinkles and almost crackles.… His thin lips curl, twitch, and bunch at either side of a mouth which any fox could call its own.…"

The witness continued: "Throughout the trial Eichmann remained as rigid and aloof as a slab of stone. Even when a man in the balcony hurled insults at him he did not react. He could not be bothered with people who came to look at him and ask themselves why this man, with the protruding ears, could not have heard the cries of screaming mankind and heeded its plea to cease the mad slaughter."

Eichmann was found guilty on all counts and sentenced to death. He was executed by hanging on May 31, 1962. His last words to the court were: "I had to obey the rules of war and my flag. I am ready."

SOURCES

Books

Arendt, Hannah, *Eichmann in Jerusalem: A Report on the Banality of Evil,* Penguin (New York), 1977.

Clarke, Comer, *Eichmann: The Man and His Crimes,* Ballantine (New York), 1960.

Harel, Israel, *The House on Garibaldi Street: The First Full Account of the Capture of Adolf Eichmann, Told by the Former Head of Israel's Secret Service,* Viking (New York), 1975.

Hausner, Gideon, *Justice in Jerusalem,* Schocken Books (New York), 1968.

Malkin, Peter, and Harry Stein, *Eichmann in My Hands,* Warner Books (New York), 1990.

Musmanno, Michael A., Justice, "Witness Against Eichmann," in *The Verdicts Were Just: Eight Famous Lawyers Present Their Most Memorable Cases,* edited by Albert Alverbach, Lawyers Co-Operative Publishing (New York), 1966.

Pearlman, Moshe, *The Capture and Trial of Adolf Eichmann,* Simon and Schuster (New York), 1963.

Reynolds, Quentin, Ephraim Katz, and Zwy Aldouby, *Minister of Death: The Adolf Eichmann Story,* Viking Press (New York), 1960.

Sachs, Ruth, *Adolf Eichmann: Engineer of Death,* Rosen (New York), 2000.

Yahil, Leni, "Eichmann, Adolf," in *Encyclopedia of the Holocaust,* Israel Gutman, editor in chief, Macmillan (New York), 1990.

Zentner, Christian, and Friedemann Bedürftig, editors, *The Encyclopedia of the Third Reich,* Da Capo Press (New York), 1991.

Albert Einstein

Born March 14, 1879
Ulm, Germany
Died April 18, 1955
Princeton, New Jersey, United States

Scientist; antiwar activist;
human rights activist

*"One cannot help but be in awe when [one]
contemplates the mysteries of eternity, of
life, of the marvelous structures of reality.
It is enough if one tries merely to
comprehend a little of this mystery each
day. Never lose a holy curiosity."*

(Library of Congress)

One of the greatest theoretical physicists in history, Albert Einstein revolutionized scientific thought with his theory of relativity and discoveries that form the basis of quantum physics. A man of contrasts, Einstein was considered a scientific genius who deliberately distanced himself from others (including his own family) in order to carry out his ground-breaking research in an atmosphere of solitude. Yet he also generously contributed his time and energy to humanitarian causes, enduring harsh criticism and even risking death as he took a stand on some of the major issues of his day. Scholars see an irony in the fact that the work of such a great humanitarian provided the theoretical basis for the atomic bomb, one of the most destructive man-made forces in the world. Yet, Einstein was unyielding in his commitment to the right of every human being to freedom, justice, and opportunity. "The most important human endeavor is the striving for morality in our actions," he once wrote. "Our inner balance and even our very existence depend on it. Only morality in our actions can give beauty and dignity to life."

Aptitude at His Own Pace

Albert Einstein was born on March 14, 1879, in Ulm, Germany, the son of Pauline (Koch) and Hermann Einstein, owner of a company that manufactured and sold electrical equipment. No one in the family was particularly gifted in science or math, and for some time it appeared that young Einstein would not have aptitude or skills in any area; he was unable to talk until the age of three and for a number of years afterward still had trouble speaking fluently. In elementary school his performance was dismal at best, leading some people (including his parents) to suspect that he was mentally challenged. From the time he was a small child, however, Einstein showed a preference to educate himself. In his early teens he taught himself advanced mathematics and science, then followed this pattern of independent study throughout his life. Graduating from the Swiss Federal Polytechnic School in Zurich in 1900 with a degree in physics, Einstein worked at a series of temporary jobs before acquiring a permanent position in 1902 as a technical expert with the Swiss Patent Office. For the next seven years he evaluated invention proposals by day, conducted his own research in the evenings, and studied for a doctorate at the University of Zurich when he had time. In 1903 he married Mileva Maric, a former classmate at the Polytechnic with whom he already had a daughter (who was given up for adoption before the marriage). The couple later had two sons.

As early as 1902 Einstein had become consumed with the task of linking time and space, matter and energy. In 1905, at age twenty-six, he published a paper outlining his special theory of relativity, which mathematically demonstrated that the speed of light is constant (roughly 186,000 miles per second) and not relative to its source or to the speed of an observer. That same year he published papers on four other topics of note: quantum law and the emission and absorption of light (research that won him the 1921 Nobel Prize in physics), Brownian motion, the inertia of energy, and the electrodynamics of moving bodies.

When Einstein published his special theory of relativity it was met with scorn among the few scientists who bothered to pay attention. As the young theoretician published his other equally controversial papers, most concerning topics so advanced that only a handful of physicists understood them, an increasing number of his colleagues began to notice his genius. Einstein suddenly found himself in demand at universities throughout Europe. In 1913, after teaching at nearly a half-dozen institutions, he accepted appointments as head of the prestigious Kaiser Wilhelm Physical Institute, special professor at the University of Berlin (where he was afforded all the research time he required), and member of the Royal Prussian Academy of Sciences.

In April 1914, leaving his wife and sons behind in Zurich, he moved to Berlin. He and his wife divorced in 1919, at which time he married a cousin, Elsa Einstein. Comfortably settled into his new position and free of the distractions of family life, Einstein was able to devote himself entirely to research. During this time he built on some of his earlier findings and developed what is probably the best-known equation in science, the general theory of relativity: $E=mc^2$. In stating that energy (E) equals mass (m) times the square of the speed of light (c^2), Einstein proposed that an ounce of matter contains as much energy as that given off by the explosion of nearly a million tons of TNT. His theory challenged one of Isaac Newton's laws by predicting that observations of astronomical phenomena would prove that gravity can bend even light. Published in 1916, the theory was validated in 1919 by British astronomers who noted, in photographs of a solar eclipse, that the apparent positions of star images surrounding the sun changed position during the eclipse, their light deflected by the gravitational effects of the sun.

Noted Scientist and Pacifist

Although Einstein's scientific work was his most important life achievement, it was not his only concern. A pacifist who believed in the internationality of science, he was disappointed by the outbreak of World War I (1914–1918) and appalled by his colleagues' involvement in programs that developed weapons, airplanes, and poison gas for the German war effort. Denounced as a traitor, he was spared any serious consequences because of his fame. During the 1920s, as Germany struggled to reestablish itself after a humiliating defeat and punitive reparations outlined by the Treaty of Versailles, Einstein began speaking out on behalf of the Zionist movement and its demands for a Jewish homeland in Palestine.

Einstein was a target of anti-Semitic criticism and occasionally received death threats. The German public, along with members of the European scientific community, turned against Einstein, who resolved to stay in Germany and work for world peace. To demonstrate the depth of his commitment he renounced the Swiss citizenship he had held since 1901, once again becoming a German citizen. As conditions in his homeland deteriorat-

Leo Szilard Drafts Letter to Roosevelt

Leo Szilard was one of the earliest and most active campaigners for nuclear arms control, yet in 1939 he drafted a letter to U.S. President Franklin D. Roosevelt urging that the United States develop an atomic bomb before Germany could complete its own research on the weapon. Born in Budapest, Hungary, on February 11, 1898, he was the son of Louis Szilard, an architect and engineer, and Thekla (Vidor) Szilard. In 1922 he earned a Ph.D. in physics from the Technische Hochschule at Berlin-Charlottenburg, Germany, and went on to make significant contributions to research on thermodynamics, X-ray crystallography, and particle accelerators. As Adolf Hitler gained power in Germany, Szilard, who was Jewish, realized he had to leave the country.

In 1933 he fled first to Vienna and then to England, where he joined the physics department at St. Bartholomew's Hospital in London. In 1935 he moved to the Clarendon Laboratory at Oxford. During this period Szilard received news of Frederic and Irene Joliot-Curie's discovery of artificial radioactivity. He began to think about the possibility of a nuclear chain reaction. In addition to his research, Szilard continued his efforts to find new jobs for scientists fleeing the Nazi purges on the continent. Toward the end of 1938 he decided to move to the United States, where he took a position at Columbia University.

Then Szilard received startling news from Europe: Otto Hahn and Fritz Strassman had produced the first fission of an atomic nucleus, an event that was fully understood and explained by Lise Meitner in January 1939. With a colleague, Walter Zinn, Szilard set up a replica of the Hahn-Strassman experiment at Columbia. Conducting an experiment on March 3, 1939, Szilard and Zinn found that a nuclear chain reaction was possible. Szilard would later say he knew immediately that this discovery would cause the world great sorrow. News of the discovery of nuclear fission swept through the physics community like wildfire, but few failed to grasp the military potential of the discovery, particularly for Germany. A group of physicists in the United States became convinced that the U.S. government must take fast and aggressive action to see whether nuclear fission could be used in the development of weapons. Szilard composed a letter expressing the scientists' concerns to Roosevelt, who appointed an Adviso-

ed throughout the decade, Einstein spent increasing amounts of time abroad giving lectures and raising money for the Palestine Foundation Fund. When he was not traveling, he focused his research efforts on the problem that would occupy him for the rest of his life: the unified field theory (also known as the grand unified theory), a concept that would reconcile mathematically the apparent contradictions between general relativity and quantum mechanics and thus explain the behavior of everything in the universe.

During the 1930s, the rise of Adolf Hitler made life in Germany uncomfortable and even dangerous for Einstein, a Jew in a high-profile position, who continued to advocate peace and renounce rearmament and the rising tide of anti-Semitism.

In January 1933, while teaching at the California Institute of Technology in Pasadena, he learned that the Germans had elected Hitler as their new chancellor. Saddened by this turn of events, he once again renounced his citizenship and accepted a permanent position at the Institute for Advanced Study in Princeton, New Jersey. Einstein's repeated warnings about the Nazi threat mainly fell on deaf ears once he settled in the United States. Even his fellow pacifists scoffed and called him a traitor to the cause of world peace when he recommended that Europe re-arm itself and build up military forces to counter German preparations for war.

Feeling that no one was interested in his ideas, Einstein withdrew into his research. In 1939, however, Leo Szilard (see sidebar) and several other

ry Committee on Uranium to investigate the issue. The committee approved creation of the Manhattan Engineering District Project (Manhattan Project) to pursue the development of the world's first atomic bombs.

The first contract under the Manhattan Project went to a group of scientists at Columbia that included Szilard. In 1942 he left Columbia to become part of the Manhattan Project's Metallurgical Laboratory at the University of Chicago. Working there with Enrico Fermi, he witnessed the first controlled nuclear reaction on December 2, 1942, when the world's first atomic pile (nuclear reactor) was put into operation. The hopes and dreams—as well as the fears—that Szilard had long held for nuclear chain reactions had become a reality. Shortly thereafter, he began to argue for a cessation of research on nuclear weapons. He suggested that a demonstration test of nuclear weapons be held in an uninhabited area and that Japanese officials be present at the test. His proposal was ignored. Instead, on August 6 and 9, 1945, the first atomic bombs were dropped on Hiroshima and Nagasaki in Japan. World War II ended a week later.

In the post-war years, Szilard spent a major portion of his time working for the control of the demon he had helped release, atomic energy. He joined a large number of his fellow nuclear scientists in forming the Federation of Atomic Scientists, which worked to keep control of atomic energy out of the hands of the military and within a civilian department. He also made efforts to encourage mutual disarmament and the reduction of tensions between the United States and the Soviet Union. To this end, he was active in the formation and planning of the Pugwash Conferences on Science and World Affairs, a series of conferences on nuclear safety that met in the late 1950s and early 1960s. In 1962, he helped found the Council for a Livable World, a Washington, D.C.-based lobby for nuclear arms control. Szilard became a U.S. citizen in 1943. In 1951 he married Gertrud Weiss, whom he had first met in 1933 in Vienna, where Weiss was a medical student. The couple had no children. Szilard was awarded the Einstein Gold Medal in 1958 and the Atoms for Peace Award in 1959. He died of a heart attack on May 30, 1964, in La Jolla, California, where he had been a resident fellow at the Salk Institute.

prominent scientists persuaded him to end his silence and sign a letter they had written urging U.S. President Franklin D. Roosevelt to fund an atomic bomb project before Germany had a chance to develop the weapon. Nevertheless, Einstein harbored so many reservations about creating the bomb that he wrote a follow-up letter of his own stating that it should not be used against people. His plea was instrumental in convincing Roosevelt to approve the Manhattan Project. Although Einstein himself was never personally involved in the endeavor, his general theory of relativity provided the theoretical explanation for the research that spawned the first atomic bomb. He was horrified when the weapon was used against the Japanese in the bombings of Hiroshima and Nagasaki in August 1945.

Einstein officially retired from the Institute for Advanced Study in 1945 but continued to work on his elusive unified field theory. Several times he announced he was close to a breakthrough, but eventually he was forced to admit that he could not find a practical way of confirming his ideas through experimental evidence. In 1946 he became chairman of the Emergency Committee of Atomic Scientists, a group that encouraged countries to focus on developing peaceful uses for nuclear energy. During the late 1940s, Einstein began to suffer from health problems that doctors attributed to a heart aneurysm, but he ignored their advice to reduce his activities. Instead he maintained a full schedule: conducting research, raising money for war relief organizations, lobbying on behalf of the World Government Movement, speaking out on human rights and for civic and academic freedoms jeopardized by anti-communist hysteria, decrying the escalation of the arms race, and lending his support to Zionism. When Israel's founder and first president, Chaim Weizmann, died in 1952, Einstein declined an offer to succeed him.

Einstein's health took a turn for the worse in early 1955 and he died on April 18, after adamantly refusing to undergo surgery for a ruptured heart artery. In keeping with his instructions, he was not given a funeral or buried in a grave with a monument; his brain was donated to science and his body was cremated, the ashes scattered over a nearby river. Despite the fact that he was a public figure, Einstein was in many ways a personal enigma. He was close to only a handful of people, never divulging his innermost thoughts and feelings, and living a simple and secluded life that revolved around his work, the most significant portion of which he completed before he had turned thirty. The scientist was puzzled and rather annoyed by the fuss others made over him but learned to use it to advance his causes. In *Einstein in America,* author Jamie Sayen writes: "Einstein was a unique phenomenon: a theoretical scientist whose area of expertise was far removed from the everyday concerns of his fellow mortals, a man without interest or training in the workings of politics who, nevertheless, by the sheer force of his character, came to play a critical role in the public life of his epoch as preeminent moral figure of the Western world."

SOURCES

Books

Bernstein, Jeremy, *Einstein,* Penguin Books (New York), 1976.

Clark, Ronald W., *Einstein: The Life and Times,* Wings Books (New York), 1995.

Dank, Milton, *Albert Einstein,* F. Watts (New York), 1983.

Einstein, Albert, *Out of My Later Years,* Bonanza Books, distributed by Crown Publishers (New York), 1989.

French, A. P., editor, *Einstein: A Centenary Volume,* Harvard University Press (Cambridge, MA), 1979.

Ireland, Karin, *Albert Einstein,* Silver Burdett Press (Englewood Cliffs, NJ), 1989.

Sayen, Jamie, *Einstein in America: The Scientist's Conscience in the Age of Hitler and Hiroshima,* Crown (New York), 1985.

Periodicals

"Albert Einstein: Appraisal of an Intellect," *Atlantic,* June 1955.

"Death of a Genius," *Time,* May 2, 1955, pp. 5054.

"Einstein, at 75, Is Still a Rebel," *New York Times Magazine,* March 14, 1954.

"Einstein Sees Lack in Applying Science," *New York Times,* February 17, 1931, pp. 6; April 19, 1955.

"Unanswered Question," *Newsweek,* May 2, 1955, pp. 86–87.

"What Life Means to Einstein," *Saturday Evening Post,* October 26, 1929.

"The World of Albert Einstein," *Reader's Digest,* May, 1953, pp. 76-78.

Dwight D. Eisenhower

During World War II, General Dwight D. Eisenhower distinguished himself from other commanding officers with his even-tempered disposition and ability to rally the troops. His management skills were tested when, as commander of Allied forces in Europe, he led an alliance of men from all branches of military service and from many different countries to victory over the German army. At the outset of the war, Eisenhower was a lieutenant colonel; by war's end he had been promoted to five-star general. He overcame a lack of battle experience and used brilliant strategies and his calm demeanor to win the trust and loyalty of Allied politicians and military leaders as well as the men under his command. Eisenhower's accomplishments led to his election as the thirty-fourth president of the United States for two terms.

A Humble Upbringing

Eisenhower was the third of six sons of David Jacob and Ida Stover Eisenhower, who began their married life running a small grocery store in Hope, Kansas. When the store went bankrupt, David went to Denison, Texas, to find work and his family eventually joined him. Eisenhower was born in Denison on October 14, 1890, but his father soon moved the family back to Kansas when he took a job at a creamery in Abilene. The family lived an impoverished life as David Eisenhower did not earn more

Born October 14, 1890
    Denison, Texas, United States
Died March 28, 1969
    Washington, D.C., United States

U.S. Army general; thirty-fourth president of the United States

"There is no glory in battle worth the blood it costs."

(Reproduced by permission of AP/Wide World Photos)

than $100 per month. The boys sometimes had to defend themselves against taunting and ridicule from other children. The children were taught to work hard, be independent, and become self-reliant. David and Ida were members of a fundamentalist Christian group called the River Brethren, and religion was an important element in the Eisenhower household. In grade school and high school, Eisenhower was a good student who loved sports. At this time he earned the nickname "Ike," which remained with him throughout his life.

After graduating from high school, Eisenhower made an agreement with his older brother Edgar that he would work for a year while Edgar, who wanted to become a lawyer, attended college. The next year, Edgar would work while Eisenhower went to college. So, Eisenhower took a job at the Abilene creamery. One of Eisenhower's friends urged him to take the entrance examinations for both the U.S. Naval Academy and U.S. Army Military Academy at West Point, New York, which would provide him a free education. Torn by his religious upbringing, which opposed war, Eisenhower made the difficult decision to take the exams. Although he passed the tests, he exceeded the age limit for the Naval Academy, which was the facility he preferred to attend. Nevertheless, in 1911 Eisenhower entered West Point, where he pursued his interest in sports. He played halfback on the football team until an injury during his sophomore year ruined a promising athletic career. Disappointed, Eisenhower lost interest in school and spent much of his time earning demerits for smoking and playing cards. In 1915 he graduated sixty-first in a class of 164 students.

Eisenhower was assigned to the 19th Infantry Regiment at Fort Sam Houston in San Antonio, Texas. At a party he met Mamie Geneva Doud, the daughter of a wealthy Denver, Colorado, businessman who had brought his family to Texas for the winter. The couple were married in July of 1916 in Denver. They had two sons, Doud Dwight (who died in infancy) and John Sheldon Doud, who would become a career army officer. In 1917, as the United States prepared to enter World War I, Eisenhower was promoted to captain. He wanted to join the fighting in France but was assigned to command a tank training center in Camp Colt, Pennsylvania. Despite his frustration at being stateside during the war, Eisenhower earned a Distinguished Service Medal for his performance.

Eisenhower was promoted to major in 1920 and graduated from the Army Tank School at Fort Mead, Maryland, in 1921. In 1922 he was transferred to the Panama Canal Zone (now the country of Panama), to serve as executive officer to the 20th Infantry Brigade. There he met General Fox Conner, who took a great interest in his career. Conner instructed Eisenhower in military history and helped him sharpen his administrative and tactical skills.

Advice from a General

Conner told Eisenhower that American forces in the next war, which he predicted would be fought by a coalition of nations rather than one country against another, would be led by a colonel named George C. Marshall. He encouraged Eisenhower to try for an assignment with Marshall. Conner also helped him gain entrance into the Army Command and General Staff School in Leavenworth, Kansas. Eisenhower focused his energies on his studies and career, graduating first in a class of 275. From 1927 to 1933 he built a reputation as a resourceful, energetic staff officer.

In 1933, while working in the office of the assistant secretary of war, Eisenhower was assigned to serve under General Douglas MacArthur, a flamboyant, opinionated figure who appreciated Eisenhower's even temper and considerable administrative skills. When MacArthur was sent to the Philippines to serve as a military adviser, Eisenhower accompanied him. Eisenhower later said that working with the flamboyant McArthur was time that he spent studying "dramatics." Four years later Eisenhower returned to the United States and, now a lieutenant colonel, was made chief of staff for General Walter Krueger, commander of the Third Army at Fort Sam Houston. Just before the Japanese bombing of Pearl Harbor in late 1941, the Third Army participated in the largest session of war games ever conducted by the army. The brilliant strategies Eisenhower devised for this operation drew admiration from his superiors and he was promoted to brigadier general.

On December 8, 1941, one day after the Japanese bombed the U.S. naval base at Pearl Harbor, the United States declared war on Japan, which was met by an Axis declaration of war on the United States. Marshall, now the army's chief of staff, called Eisenhower to his office and asked for his advice on what course of action the United States should pursue in Asia. Eisenhower's answer impressed Marshall and he assigned Eisenhower to the War Plans Division. During the first months of

After his success in the war, General Dwight Eisenhower went on to become president of the United States. (Reproduced by permission of AP/Wide World Photos)

the war, Eisenhower's strategic talent, his skill in managing people, and his tendency to both share the credit for achievements and shoulder the blame for mistakes made him a valuable member of the team directing the U.S. military effort. His rapid rise through the ranks continued. In March 1942 he was promoted to major general and in June he was sent to London to take command of the U.S. forces in Europe. Meanwhile, General Douglas MacArthur and Admiral Chester Nimitz were in charge of the Pacific theater.

Eisenhower's first task was to meet with the heads of British and American military services to determine a course of action. Deciding the United States would invade Axis-occupied North Africa, Eisenhower took command of ground, sea, and air forces, launching Operation Torch in November 1942. It was followed by the Allies' victorious invasions of Sicily and Italy, respectively, in July and September 1943. Eisenhower was named the commander of the Supreme Headquarters Allied Expeditionary Forces in Europe (SHAEF). He returned to London in December to plan for the Allied invasion of Normandy on the northern coast of France. Nicknamed Operation Overlord and D-Day, this campaign had a profound impact on the course of World War II. Describing Eisenhower's role in Operation Overlord, Stephen E. Ambrose

wrote that it "bore his stamp. He was the central figure in the preparation, the planning, the training, the deception, the organization, and the execution of the greatest invasion in history."

D-Day: The Normandy Invasion

The invasion was to be carried out by 155,000 troops crossing the English Channel on boats and landing on the beaches of Normandy in France. They would be supported by 5,000-6,000 ships, thousands of airplanes, and a staff of 16,312 officers and enlisted men. The Allies planned to push the Germans back while the Russians flanked them from eastern Europe. In the event that the mission failed, Eisenhower prepared a press release in which he took full blame for the failure.

Operation Overlord, originally scheduled to begin on June 4, 1944, was stalled by a storm until June 6. Heeding the advice of his weather forecaster, Eisenhower gave the order to proceed. The storm did subside, allowing the men to land on the beaches. Eisenhower made regular visits to the battlefields, once straying behind enemy lines in his jeep. The Allies spent the next few months advancing through France, liberating Paris in August. In December the Germans made one last stand, now called the Battle of the Bulge, in the Ardennes region located at the border of France and Belgium. The campaign was so-named because the Germans were successful in pushing the Allies back in that region, causing a bulge in the front line. Although the German attack took the Allies by surprise, the Germans were fatally weakened and were forced to surrender on May 8, 1945.

Eisenhower spent another six months in Europe as head of the occupation forces—Allied troops who maintained order and provided assistance to the various European countries making transitions to peacetime. He then returned to Washington to replace Marshall as army chief of staff. Eisenhower had become so popular with the American public that both the Democratic and Republican parties urged him to run for president. He politely declined. In 1949 he was named president of Columbia University in New York City, but he left the job the next year to accept command of the North Atlantic Treaty Organization (NATO), which had recently been formed to help protect Europe from the threat of Soviet aggression.

The Thirty-Fourth President of the United States

As the election of 1952 drew near, the two major political parties continued their attempts to persuade Eisenhower to run for president. He decided to seek election as a Republican. Backed by moderate supporters, he won the nomination over his more conservative opponent, Senator Robert A. Taft. Eisenhower then won the national race against Illinois Democratic governor Adlai Stevenson, earning the highest number of popular votes to that time. He entered office as a talented administrator and foreign relations diplomat, but he was not highly experienced in domestic issues. As president he sought consensus, tending to avoid controversial policies and decisions.

One of Eisenhower's primary goals in his first term was to end the conflict in Korea, which had started in 1950. The Korean Conflict (1950–1953) involved the communists who occupied the northern part of the country and U.S.-backed South Korea. In July 1953 Eisenhower helped to negotiate a cease-fire and truce, stating that "There is no glory in battle worth the blood it costs." Several major events occurred in Eisenhower's first term. For instance, the 1954 Supreme Court declared that segregation in public schools was unconstitutional. In addition, Senator Joseph McCarthy waged his notorious anti-communist campaign,

seeking to remove suspected communists from the federal government, military, show business, and other realms of American life. Yet Eisenhower generally remained silent on such issues.

In September of 1955 Eisenhower suffered a heart attack while on vacation. His supporters feared he would be unable to seek re-election. However, Eisenhower recovered and won another term as president by defeating Adlai Stevenson. His Republican hold on the White House was met with Democratic control of the Congress. Despite a good relationship with congressional leaders of both parties, he faced mutual opposition on some of his legislative measures. He was forced to take action on the Supreme Court's segregation decision when a mob of angry white southerners blocked the integration of a high school in Little Rock, Arkansas. Eisenhower sent military units to enforce the court-ordered integration. Also, he had eased tensions between the United States and the Soviet Union, but his progress was shattered when Russian premier Nikita Khrushchev refused to take part in a planned summit meeting with Eisenhower. Khrushchev was angered after an American U-2 spy plane was shot down while taking photographs of military sites in Russia. Critics faulted Eisenhower for allowing such an espionage operation to jeopardize peace between the two countries.

In 1960, after two terms as president, Eisenhower retired and divided his time between his farm at Gettysburg, Pennsylvania, and a home in Palm Springs, California. He continued to speak occasionally on public issues and worked on his memoirs. Eisenhower suffered serious heart attacks in 1965 and 1968. In December 1968 a Gallup poll showed that he still led the list of the ten most-admired Americans. He died at Walter Reed Army Hospital in Washington, D.C., on March 28, 1969, and was buried in Abilene, Kansas, on the grounds of the presidential library he had established there a few years earlier.

SOURCES

Books

Ambrose, Stephen, *The Supreme Commander: The War Years of General Dwight D. Eisenhower,* Doubleday (New York), 1970.

Burk, Robert, *Dwight D. Eisenhower, Hero and Politician,* Twayne Publishers (Boston), 1986.

Darby, Jean, *A Man Called Ike,* Lerner Publications (Minneapolis, MN), 1989.

Eisenhower, Dwight D., *At Ease: Stories I Tell to Friends,* Doubleday (Garden City, NY), 1967.

Eisenhower, Dwight D., *Crusade in Europe,* Doubleday (Garden City, NY), 1948.

Eisenhower, Dwight D., *Dear General: Eisenhower's Wartime Letters to Marshall,* edited by Joseph Patrick Hobbs, Johns Hopkins University Press (Baltimore), 1999.

Eisenhower, Dwight D., *The Eisenhower Diaries,* edited by Robert H. Ferrell, Norton (New York), 1981.

Eisenhower, Dwight D., *In Review: Pictures I've Kept; A Concise Pictorial Autobiography,* Doubleday (Garden City, NY), 1969.

Eisenhower, Dwight D., *Letters to Mamie,* edited with commentary by John S. D. Eisenhower, Doubleday (Garden City, NY), 1978.

Eisenhower, Dwight D., *The White House Years,* 2 volumes, Doubleday (Garden City, NY), 1963–65.

Jacobs, William Jay, *Dwight David Eisenhower: Soldier and Statesman,* Franklin Watts (New York), 1995.

Sandberg, Peter Lars, *Dwight D. Eisenhower,* Chelsea House (New York), 1986.

Van Steenwyk, Elizabeth, *Dwight David Eisenhower, President,* Walker (New York), 1987.

Periodicals

"The Father Figure: Dwight Eisenhower," *U.S. News and World Report,* March 16, 1998, p. 59.

Other

Ambrose, Stephen, and George H. Mayer, *Dwight D. Eisenhower,* http://www.grolier.com/wwii/wwii_eisenhower.html (August 4, 2000).

Anne Frank

Born June 12, 1929
Frankfurt, Germany
Died March 1945
Bergen-Belsen concentration camp

German Holocaust victim; teenager who
wrote a diary depicting life as a Jew in
hiding from the Nazis

*"I still believe people are really
good at heart."*

*(Photograph by Rudolph Hess;
reproduced by permission of Archive Photos, Inc.)*

Although hundreds of thousands of children perished during the Holocaust because of their Jewish heritage, Anne Frank has become the most famous. Frank's diary chronicles her experience hiding from the Nazis and provides a moving insight into the anxieties of an adolescent girl. Her writing has become a symbol of all that was destroyed during the Holocaust, a constant reminder to the world of the hope and innocence that was lost during the Nazis' anti-Jewish campaign.

Anne Frank's Early Life

Anne Frank was born in Germany on June 12, 1929, about a decade after the close of World War I (1914–18). The war had left Germany in a shambles. According to the terms of the Treaty of Versailles, which ended the war, the German armed forces were drastically reduced and the country was forced to make reparations to the victorious countries. These terms of surrender left the German citizens humiliated and resentful. When Nazi leader Adolf Hitler began his ascent to power, he promised the German people he would once again restore Germany to a prominent position, as it had been before the war. Once he became dictator, Hitler began restructuring the German army. He convinced Germans that many of their troubles were caused by minority groups, especially the

Jews. Hitler's deliberate agenda of hate and intolerance paved the way for another terrible world war.

Frank was just a young child when Hitler became chancellor of Germany. The second daughter of Otto and Edith Hollander Frank, she and her family had a comfortable, prosperous life in Frankfurt, Germany, where Otto Frank continued to head the banking business that had been in his family for generations. By 1933, in the wake of a world-wide economic depression, the bank had failed and was forced to close its doors forever. That same year, Hitler came to power in Germany and began promoting his plan to control the Jews and other minorities. His anti-Semitic legislation, which included denying Jews the privileges of German citizenship and forbidding them to vote or hold public office, convinced Otto Frank to move his family to Amsterdam, Holland. Once in Holland, Frank opened a company to manufacture products used in making jam. For a while the Franks regained their sense of security. Anne Frank, who was only four years old at the time of the move, loved Amsterdam and made many friends. She was described by people who knew her as a bubbly, chatty girl, who was very curious about everything. She was a stark contrast to her sister, Margot, who was quiet and studious.

The family's life was disrupted once again when, in 1940, Hitler invaded Holland and continued the spread of his anti-Semitic policies. Frank had been receiving her education at a private school, but Hitler's new laws did not allow Jewish children to attend schools with non-Jews. The new law of the land also prohibited Jews from owning businesses, and Otto Frank had to turn his company over to one of his employees.

Writes Diary

On July 5, 1942—less than one month after Anne Frank's thirteenth birthday—her older sister, Margot, received orders to report to a work camp. Otto Frank anticipated this moment, having established a hiding place in the attic of his office building. Immediately after Margot received the summons, the family went into hiding in the attic, or the "Secret Annex" as Anne called it. During the next two years, Frank recorded her experiences in her diary—which she addressed as "Kitty." In the annex the Franks were soon joined by others—a Jewish couple named Hermann and Petronella van Daan, who were accompanied by their teenage son Peter, and a Jewish dentist named Albert Dussel.

A photo of Anne Frank at age five, one year after her family had moved to Holland. (Reproduced by permission of Archive Photos, Inc.)

(These were the aliases that Frank used when writing about them in her diary.) Everyone had to be absolutely silent during business hours and had to go to bed early in the evening so they would not attract the attention of anyone on the outside. Frank occupied herself by reading, taking lessons given by her father, listening to the radio, performing household chores, and writing in her diary.

At first Frank wrote the diary for herself. Then one day she heard a radio broadcast announcing that after the war, eyewitness stories about life in Holland during the Nazi occupation would be col-

Life in Close Quarters

Getting along with others for a long time in a small space can be difficult under normal circumstances, but when coupled with the constant fear of discovery and resulting death, it is even harder. Anne Frank had strong opinions about the people she lived with in the annex, and she described them in her diary.

> [My family are] always saying how nice it is with the four of us, and that we get along so well, without giving a moment's thought to the fact that I don't feel that way.

Later she had this to say about Peter van Daan:

> ....no one takes Peter seriously anymore, since he's hypersensitive and lazy. Yesterday he was beside himself with worry because his tongue was blue instead of pink.... His Highness has been complaining of lumbago [muscle pain] too.... He's an absolute hypochondriac!

Frank especially resented Petronella van Daan's comments about Frank's manners and upbringing. Frank had these comments to make:

> Mrs. van Daan is unbearable. I'm continually being scolded for my incessant chatter.... Some people, like the van Daans, seem to take special delight not only in raising their own children but in helping

others raise theirs.... More than once the air has been filled with the van Daans' admonitions and my saucy replies.... This is always how her tirades begin and end: "If Anne were my daughter.... " Thank goodness I'm not.

Frank had the typical teenager's mixed feelings about her own mother and her sister, Margot. About the two of them she wrote:

> At moments like these I can't stand Mother. It's obvious that I'm a stranger to her; she doesn't even know what I think about the most ordinary things.... Margot's and Mother's personalities are so alien to me. I understand my girlfriends better than my own mother. Isn't that a shame?.... Is it just a coincidence that Father and Mother never scold Margot and always blame me for everything?

When Albert Dussel, a dentist, sought refuge in the Secret Annex, Frank had to share a bedroom with him. Although she accepted this arrangement with good grace, she did not find Dussel an agreeable companion:

> Mr. Dussel ... has turned out to be an old-fashioned disciplinarian and preacher of unbearably long sermons on manners.... [S]ince I'm generally considered to be the worst behaved of the three young people, it's all I can do to avoid having the same old scoldings and admonitions repeatedly flung at my head and to pretend not to hear.... Really, it's not easy being the badly brought-up center of attention of a family of nitpickers.

lected so everyone could read them and know how the people had suffered. Frank decided that a book based on her diary would make a fine contribution to the collection, so she began to edit and rewrite it. From her hiding place, Frank could see the daily deportation of Jews, who were being led to either death camps or concentration camps. Frank knew what would happen to her and her family if the Nazis discovered their hiding place. In one diary entry she wrote: "Our many Jewish friends are being taken away by the dozen. The people are treated by the Gestapo [the German Secret Police] without a shred of decency, being loaded into cattle trucks.... We assume most of them are being murdered. The English radio speaks of their being gassed." In an entry dated July 15, 1944, Frank wrote: "I feel the sufferings of millions. And yet, when I look up at the sky, I somehow feel that everything will change for the better, that this cruelty too shall end, that peace and tranquility will return once more."

Sent to Concentration Camp

Frank did not live to see the end of the cruelty or the publication of her book. On August 4, 1944, after the Franks had lived undetected for twenty-five months, someone informed the police of their hiding place. As the war dragged on and on, many Dutch citizens who helped the Jews were having second thoughts. They were afraid of being punished if they were found out. Food was becoming scarce, and the Nazis were offering rewards for the betrayal of Jews in hiding. The Franks, the van Daans, and Albert Dussel were sent to the Auschwitz-Birkenau concentration camp in Poland. There Otto Frank was separated from his family and sent to the men's camp, while Hermann van Daan was immediately killed in the gas chambers. Peter van Daan and Albert Dussel were taken to other camps in Germany where they died of illness. Edith Frank died at Auschwitz-Birkenau on January 6, 1945. Petronella van Daan, Margot, and Anne were sent to the Bergen-Belsen concentration camp, where conditions were even worse than at Auschwitz. From there Petronella van Daan was sent to an unknown destination and did not survive. At Bergen-Belsen Margot and Anne developed typhus, which quickly spread under crowded, unsanitary conditions. Margot died in late February or early March 1945, and Anne died a few days later. It is likely that the bodies of both girls were placed in one of the camp's mass graves. If the eight residents of the Secret Annex had managed to remain hidden for only a few more weeks, they probably would have survived, for the camps were liberated in the spring of 1945.

Diary Published

Otto Frank was the only one of the Secret Annex refugees to survive his concentration camp imprisonment. When he returned to Amsterdam, Miep Gies, his former employee who had helped the family while they were hiding, gave Otto Frank Anne's diary, which Gies had saved. Otto Frank was urged to publish the diary, and the first edition was released in 1947. Since that time, the diary has become immensely popular because of its power as both a document of the suffering endured during Hitler's regime and a testimony of a girl becoming a young woman.

"I want to go on living after my death," Frank wrote. Her wish has been granted through her diary, which has sold twenty-four million copies in fifty-two editions, and has been translated into more than fifty languages. In an introduction to an early edition of Frank's diary, Eleanor Roosevelt, wife of U.S. President Franklin D. Roosevelt, wrote: "This is a remarkable book. Written by a young girl—and the young are not afraid of telling the truth—it is one of the wisest and most moving commentaries on war and its impact on human beings that I have ever read."

A Broadway play based on Frank's life called *The Diary of Anne Frank* opened in New York in 1955. New York theater critics described the play as "a lovely, tender drama," made from "what must have been one of the most heartbreaking documents of the ... war." When the play was performed in Germany, audiences were so moved that they could not even applaud and left the theater in stunned silence. A movie version of the play was released in 1959, and a made-for-television version was broadcast in 1967. An Academy Award-winning documentary film called *Anne Frank Remembered* was released in 1995. The documentary contained previously unknown information about the Frank family. While imprisoned at Auschwitz-Birkenau, Frank and her mother rediscovered their love for one another. Margot and Edith Frank also gave up a possible chance at survival by choosing to remain with Anne, who was too sick to travel.

Sources

Books

Bachrach, Susan D., *Tell Them We Remember: The Story of the Holocaust*, Little, Brown and Company (Boston), 1994.

Berenbaum, Michael, *The World Must Know: The History of the Holocaust as Told in the United States Holocaust Memorial Museum*, Little, Brown (Boston), 1993.

Brown, Gene, *Anne Frank: Child of the Holocaust*, Rosen Publishing Group (New York), 1991.

Frank, Anne, *The Diary of a Young Girl*, Globe Book Company (New York), 1988.

Frank, Anne, *The Diary of a Young Girl: The Definitive Edition*, edited by Otto H. Frank and Mirjam Pressler, translated by Susan Massotty, Doubleday (New York), 1995.

Hurwitz, Johanna, *Anne Frank: Life in Hiding*, Beech Tree (New York), 1993.

Leonard, William T., *Theatre: Stage-to-Screen-to-Television*, Scarecrow Press (Metuchen, NJ), 1981.

Tames, Richard, *Anne Frank*, Franklin Watts (New York), 1989.

Tridenti, Lina, *Anne Frank*, translated by Stephen Thorne, Silver Burdett (Morristown, NJ), 1985.

Hans Frank

After Germany invaded Poland starting World War II in 1939, Hans Frank was appointed as governor general of Poland. Historians have described Frank as a weak, unstable, and contradictory man. Although he made flowery speeches about furthering justice and honor, he became known for mistreating native Poles and Polish Jews, showing no semblance of justice or mercy. Frank venerated Nazi leader Adolf Hitler almost to the end of his own life, taken on the gallows. This devotion blinded Frank to the atrocities being committed by Hitler and his followers.

Youthful Years

Frank was born in Karlsrühe, Germany, in 1900, the son of Karl Frank, a lawyer who was disbarred. Historians note that Frank's father was a womanizer who wined and dined women with the promise of marriage, only to swindle them out of their money. Frank's mother had left her husband and child, running off to Czechoslovakia with another man. Growing up motherless, young Frank often had to fend for himself. Sometimes, his supper consisted of free leftovers from a neighborhood tavern. Frank's biographers assert that his family life contributed to a sense of insecurity, which later manifested itself in his overwhelming desire to please Hitler.

Born May 23, 1900
    Karlsrühe, Germany
Died October 16, 1946
    Nuremberg, Germany

Lawyer; government official; German-appointed governor general of Poland (1939–45)

"It is as though I am two people—me, myself ... and the other Frank, the Nazi leader. And sometimes ... this Frank looks at the other Frank and says, 'Hmm, what a louse you are, Frank!—How could you do such things?'"

(Lena Fagen/USHMM Photo Archives)

Frank graduated from high school in Munich, Germany, in 1918. While studying law at the University of Munich, he joined a military-style organization. In 1923 he joined the Nazi Party. His first role with the Nazis was with the Storm Troopers, also called the SA. The SA specialized in terrorizing people in an effort to help Hitler gain power in Germany. Frank was among Hitler's supporters during the Nazi leader's unsuccessful attempt to take over the German government in 1923. After the failed coup, Frank fled to Austria fearing arrest; Hitler was sentenced to five years in jail and the Nazi Party was banned in Germany. By 1924 Frank returned to Germany to complete his college studies. Hitler was released from prison after only serving nine months. He began to re-establish the Nazi Party in 1925. A year later, Frank began practicing law in Munich. He was also hired as an assistant professor of commercial and business law at the Munich Institute of Technology.

Rejoins Nazi Movement

Soon, Frank became involved with the Nazis again. He responded to an ad in a Nazi paper, which requested the services of a lawyer. The Nazis were looking for an attorney who could "take over the defense of poor, unemployed [Nazi] party members in court trial" without pay. Frank took the case and worked to reduce the charges against the Nazi defendants, who served minimal sentences. Eventually Hitler asked Frank to take on major cases for the Nazis, including some against Hitler himself. Frank was also given the task of searching Hitler's family tree to discover whether the Nazi leader had any Jewish ancestry. Speculation regarding Hitler's heritage was increasing. The anti-Semitic Nazis did not permit anyone of Jewish blood in their organization as they wanted to keep it "pure." The Nazis considered the Jews to be an evil, separate race that was inferior to the Aryan race—white, non-Jewish people. The Nazis believed intermarriage between Germans and Jews would taint German bloodlines. Frank found Hitler's heritage free of Jewish blood. However, some historians assert that Hitler might have been one-quarter Jewish.

Frank quit the Nazi Party in 1926 over a minor dispute, only to rejoin the following year. In 1929 he expressed his intent to start a career as a legal scholar, but Hitler persuaded him to remain working for the Nazis. In 1930 Frank was made head of the legal affairs department for the Nazi Party. Until 1933 he represented the Nazis in thousands of legal actions brought against party members. Once Hitler seized power in Germany in 1933, and no longer had to face his opponents in court, Frank's usefulness as a lawyer rapidly diminished.

Frank rose through the ranks of the Nazi Party. In 1934 Frank founded and appointed himself president of the Academy for German Justice, more popularly referred to as the Academy for German Injustice. The purpose of Frank's new institute was to reformulate German law on the basis of Nazi principles. This became virtually impossible, according to author Joachim C. Fest, because "the various drafts of a new legal code … never went beyond the first stages.… This was because of the regime's continued practice of intervening by force in the legal system, whenever it wished." Hitler preferred to govern not by principle, but by brute force.

Angers Hitler

On June 30, 1934, Hitler ordered Ernst Röhm, head of the SA, and several other high-ranking SA men arrested and jailed in Munich. This event is known as the "Night of the Long Knives." Hitler claimed that Röhm and his henchmen were conspiring to overthrow the government, planning to place themselves as the new rulers. Some historians note that Hitler really wanted to rid the party of the brutish SA, which had a reputation for bullying and brawling. He intended to replace them with the polished and calculating SS in an effort to change the party's image. Two of Hitler's personal bodyguards informed Frank that Hitler had personally ordered them to shoot all the SA leaders, at least 100 men, immediately. Frank refused, saying they were "standing on territory that belonged to Justice." The bodyguards called Hitler, who shouted at Frank over the telephone: "You hesitate to carry out one of my orders?" Frank's refusal infuriated Hitler. Frank later said that the event began his gradual decline as a political force. Hitler had little respect for attorneys, considering them weaklings and fools. For Hitler, the law was merely a tool useful in defeating political opponents. He once told Frank: "Here I stand with my bayonets. There you stand with your law! We'll see which counts for more!"

Reversal of Fortune

In 1939 Germany successfully invaded Poland, beginning World War II. It divided a conquered

Poland between itself and the Soviet Union. Frank's position greatly improved when Hitler appointed him governor general of Poland. He headed the central section of the country. Frank told his wife, a former secretary he married in 1924 named Brigitte, that she would become the "Queen of Poland." The Franks went to live in Kraków Castle, the traditional home of Polish royalty, with their young son, Niklas. Frank's wife was pleased with their new home. Frank filled the castle with art work and furniture looted from the Jews and Poles. Frank had a grand vision of himself as the head of Germany's eastern kingdom. According to writer Christopher R. Browning, Hitler considered Poland "a racial dumping ground, the slave-labor reservoir, and … the slaughter yard of the Third Reich."

Although Frank was the governor general of Poland, he was not in charge of the concentration camps located in the region, where Jews and other enemies of the Nazis were imprisoned. The SS and police were in charge of the camps. Frank objected to this, but not because he opposed the mass murders taking place there. He resented others having control of a major operation occurring in an area that he allegedly controlled.

Begins Anti-Jewish Measures

Shortly after his appointment as governor general, Frank published a regulation requiring all Jews ten years of age or older to wear an arm band with the six-pointed Star of David on their right sleeves. This emblem, a Jewish symbol of faith, was intended to identify the Jews from the rest of the population, making it easier for the Nazis to separate the Jews systematically when the time came. He also issued an order requiring forced labor for Jews, who would live in work camps, performing such tasks as paving roads, draining swamps, and building structures. Although they were required to do strenuous jobs, the Jews received very little food, and many died due to these conditions.

By November 1940 the Jews of Warsaw and other Polish cities were forced to live in ghettos—crowded, walled sections of cities fraught with inferior conditions. The population of the Warsaw ghetto reached nearly 400,000 at its zenith. It was fully operational from November 1940 to July 1942, when the Jews began to be deported en masse to concentration camps. In August 1942, Frank stated: "It is not necessary to dwell on the fact that we are sentencing 1.2 million Jews to death. That much is clear. And if the Jews do not

Hans Frank (left) and other Nazi officials review the troops during a military parade in Warsaw, Poland. (Rijksinstituut Voor Oorlogsdocumentatie/USHMM Photo Archives)

die of starvation, it will be necessary to step up anti-Jewish measures, and let us hope that too will come to pass."

Deterioration of Polish Life

After Frank became head of Poland, life in the nation changed dramatically. The mayor of Warsaw was arrested and shot, and nearly 200 professors of Poland's major universities were seized and taken to concentration camps. Universities, schools, libraries, publishing houses, and museums were closed. Polish monuments and works of art were looted, and music by Polish composers was banned. The purpose of these efforts was to break the spirit of the Poles. Frank himself declared that Poland would be treated as a Nazi colony, and its citizens would be "slaves of the Greater German

Frank's Son Condemns Him

In 1991 Niklas Frank, the son of Hans Frank, published a revealing book about his father. Niklas, who was seven when his father died in 1946, was raised by his mother to think of Hans Frank as a sensitive, cultivated intellectual. It took Niklas Frank years of research to uncover the true character of his father.

Niklas Frank's book, *In the Shadow of the Reich*, is written in the form of a letter to his father, condemning him for his evil life and deeds. At the beginning of the fourth chapter, Niklas Frank writes: "The snapping of your neck [during hanging] spared me from having a totally screwed-up life. You certainly would have poisoned my brain with all your drivel, the fate of the silent majority of my generation [the children of other Nazis] who did not have the good fortune of having their fathers hanged."

He continues: "That's why I am happy to be your son. How poor by comparison are all the millions of other children whose fathers spouted the same garbage filled with deceit and cowardice, with bloodthirstiness and inhumanity, but who were not so prominent as you. Their tirades were not worth recording, their journals not worth preserving. I have it good. I can scrape together the festering scraps of your life in the archives of Europe and America.... No matter how often I try to get to the root of them, with scalpel or hammer, the same typical German monster emerges."

Frank concludes: "There is no doubt about it: you will also lose the second Nuremberg Trial, this mini-trial with your son as prosecutor, judge, and hangman in one."

Empire." There was even talk of annexing Poland into Germany.

Under Frank's rule, the daily food allotment for each Polish citizen was gradually reduced. According to historian Keith Sword: "[T]he daily food rations in Warsaw [for non-Jews] provided ... 669 calories per day, compared to the Germans' 2,613 calories"; Jews were allotted only 184 calories. Disease flourished, as did the black market, which many Poles were forced to use to obtain food. Frank decreased the Polish birth rate by setting a higher minimum age for marriage and sending millions of people to work in Germany.

Frank frequently waffled between positions on various matters. He would agree that Jews should be kept healthy so they were strong enough to work, yet he also supported plans for the mass murder and starvation of the Jewish workers a short time later. Even though he was quoted as saying "You can depend on it that I would rather die than give up this idea of justice," unjust anti-Jewish laws were passed without the slightest protest from Frank. His contradictory policies extended into many areas under his control. He would publicly encourage the inclusion of Polish culture into Nazi life, only to institute policies that greatly suppressed the Poles.

His Power Diminishes

The power Frank enjoyed as governor general did not last very long. On March 5, 1942, he was brought before a court consisting of top-level Nazis, who relieved him of many responsibilities. This occurred, in part, because he had secretly enriched members of his family with goods looted from the Jews. His wife, Brigitte, loved furs. On more than one occasion she had pointed to a Polish woman walking down the street wearing a fur coat. That was the signal for her bodyguards to forcibly remove the coat from the woman and hand it over to Brigitte. In a 1942 diary passage, Nazi official Joseph Goebbels wrote that Frank had fallen out of favor with Hitler.

Soon after, Frank visited four different German universities and delivered speeches protesting the takeover of "German justice" by the Nazi police. He also sent Hitler a letter criticizing various Nazi policies. As a result, Hitler stripped Frank of all his power. Although he barred Frank from making public speeches, Hitler refused to accept Frank's resignation, preferring to keep him as the puppet head of Poland.

Arrest, Prosecution, Execution

When the Soviet Union began to take Poland from the Germans in 1945, Frank fled. He took with him a detailed daily account of activities and observations of the Third Reich that he had written. When he was arrested by the Americans, Frank surrendered these diaries, which also contained his speeches and notes about trips, receptions, meetings, and conferences. Passages from his diaries were used as evidence in the trials of other Nazi war criminals held in Nuremberg, Germany, after the war.

Frank was tried in Nuremberg in 1946 and found guilty of war crimes. At the trials, war crimes were defined as violations of the laws or customs of war, such as murder, ill-treatment, deportation, forced labor, or destruction not within military necessity. During the trial, Frank spoke of the guilt Germany had brought upon itself by its activities. He claimed that he had rediscovered God, and returned to the Roman Catholic faith of his youth. The judges were unmoved, and Frank was executed by hanging on October 16, 1946.

Near the end of his life, Frank wrote: "I could weep when I think of all the things I have done in absolutely the wrong way during my life, I, the number-one pupil at the [high school], number-

one student at the university, as Ph.D. [with highest honors, decorated] with medals and titles— and now, nothing left for me at all."

SOURCES

Books

Browning, Christopher R., "Hans Frank," in *The Encyclopedia of the Holocaust,* edited by Israel Gutman, volume 2, Macmillan (New York), 1990.

Fest, Joachim C., *The Face of the Third Reich,* translated by Michael Bullock, Weidenfeld and Nicholson (London), 1970.

Frank, Niklas, *In the Shadow of the Reich,* translated by Arthur S. Wensinger with Carole Clew-Hoey, Knopf (New York), 1991.

Gutman, Yisrael, *The Jews of Warsaw 1939–1943: Ghetto, Underground, Revolt,* translated by Ina Friedman, Indiana University Press (Bloomington, IN), 1982.

Snyder, Louis L., ed., "Hans Frank," in *Encyclopedia of the Third Reich,* Marlowe (New York), 1976.

Sword, Keith, "Poland," *The Oxford Companion to World War II,* edited by I.C.B. Dear, Oxford University Press (New York), 1995.

Zentner, Christian, and Friedemann Bedürftig, editors, "Hans Frank," in *The Encyclopedia of the Third Reich,* translated by Amy Hackett, volume 1, Da Capo Press (New York), 1991.

Viktor
E. Frankl

Born March 26, 1905
Vienna, Austria
Died September 2, 1997
Vienna, Austria

Psychotherapist; physician; university
lecturer; concentration camp survivor;
author; founder of logotherapy

*"The meaning of my life is to help others
find the meaning of theirs."*

Victims of torture, forced to witness their loved ones being taken off to their deaths during World War II, might be expected to emerge as bitter, doubting people. Though Viktor Frankl suffered through these events, his response was drastically different. Partly as a result of his experiences in the war, Frankl developed a unique way of looking at his life. He termed his method of response "logotherapy." The method has its foundations in the belief that every human situation has meaning.

Childhood in Vienna

Viktor Frankl was born to Jewish parents in Vienna, Austria, in 1905. As a young man, his father, Gabriel, wanted to be a doctor, but he could not afford to go to medical school. Assessing his situation, he became a civil servant in the Ministry of Social Service. Frankl's highly emotional mother was an educated and cultured woman. Frankl claimed he took after both his mother and his father, stating that his father gave him his sense of responsibility and perfectionism. These influences on Frankl's nature led a psychiatrist, who had done some testing of Frankl, to comment that he had "never seen such a range between rationality and deep emotions." At around age five, he realized that some day he would die. "What troubled me then," wrote Frankl, "was not the fear of dying, but the question of whether the [brevity] of life might destroy its meaning." Once, in a science class, a teacher offered the opinion that people are merely a mixture of chemicals. The young Frankl rose to his feet and demanded to know what significance life would have if this was one's view of humanity.

Frankl was raised in a traditional Jewish family, having his Bar Mitzvah at the expected age of thirteen. By then, he had decided his future was in medicine. While in school, he wrote letters about his aspirations to Sigmund Freud, and Freud answered him with encouraging replies. By age fifteen, Frankl was attending public lectures offered by socialist teachers. By the age of nineteen, he had published his first scholarly work—a paper that appeared in Freud's journal of psychology, which was read around the world. At twenty, he was president of an organization for socialist high school students throughout Austria.

University Career

During his college years, Frankl turned away from the theories of Freud. A majority of Freud's teachings were based on the principle that human behavior is a reaction to secret sexual impulses. Finding this view overly simplistic, Frankl embraced the theories of another Viennese doctor, Alfred Adler. Adler believed that human beings were motivated by the need for self accomplishment. Frankl's second scientific paper appeared in Adler's professional journal in 1925. He began traveling around Europe giving lectures on the topic of universal, equitable treatment of all social classes. Around this period of time, Frankl renounced his Jewish faith. By 1927 his enthusiasm for Adler's work was waning. Frankl and others founded the Academic Society for Medical Psychology and he was elected vice-president. By 1930 Frankl had developed a theory that there were three possible ways of finding meaning in life, including: "1) a deed we do, a work we create; 2) an experience, a human encounter, a love; and 3) when confronted with an unchangeable fate (such as an incurable disease), a change of attitude towards that fate."

Work as a Doctor

Frankl graduated from the University of Vienna Medical School in 1930 and became a practicing physician. He continued his studies in psychiatry and neurology, and worked with patients who, having lost their jobs because of a world-wide economic depression, suffered from feelings of apathy and hopelessness. According to writer Edward Hoffman: "[I]f they ... took up volunteer work and dwell[ed] less on their own woes, their depression often lifted considerably. [Frankl] became increasingly convinced that our underlying sense of purpose in daily life is a vital, and badly ignored, psychological factor."

In the early 1930s, Frankl organized counseling centers for young people in Vienna and in six other Austrian cities. Students were provided with an environment where they could talk over problems that were troubling them. With the increasing success of these centers, Frankl's work was recognized as new and effective. He was invited to lecture in Germany, Czechoslovakia, and Hungary. In 1937 Frankl went into private practice. A short time later, Adolf Hitler's Nazi party began its occupation of Austria. Seeking revenge for Germany's loss of World War I (1914–18), the Nazis blamed the Jewish people for the defeat. By claiming that Jews were out to take over the world, the Nazis were able to provide a scapegoat for a humiliating experience shared by the German people. Soon invading Austria, the Nazis began forcing Jews into concentration camps.

Frankl immediately applied for a visa to leave the country, but he was unable to obtain the necessary paperwork that would allow his family to flee. Remaining in Vienna, Frankl accepted a job as chief of neurology at Rothschild Hospital. As part of his work, he performed brain surgery, which was to remain an interest for the rest of his life. In 1938, Frankl began formulating the central ideas for his system of logotherapy. He published articles for medical journals, sharing his hypothesis with the scientific community at large. His system is based on the belief that people seek meaning in their lives, and when unable to find it, experience feelings of abject hopelessness and despair. Once they discover the special significance of their lives, they begin to experience a healing process.

Family Affairs and Marriage

In 1941 Frankl was granted a visa that would allow him to move to the United States. However, no such visas were available to his parents, who were likely to be sent to a concentration camp. Frankl gave a great deal of thought to the situation and decided to remain in Vienna with his family, and they remained safe for the better part of one year. While working at Rothschild Hospital, Frankl met a young nurse named Mathilde "Tilly" Grosser, whom he described as looking "like a Spanish

Psychological Impact of Living in Concentration Camps

Viktor Frankl spent more than three years in Nazi concentration camps. During this time, he observed that prisoners went through three phases of reaction. The first was the period just after being admitted, the second was when life settled into a daily routine, and the third was when the prisoner was freed from the camp.

Upon arrival at a concentration camp, people were stripped of their clothing; had all their body hair shaved off; and were forced to give up all of their possessions. Camp authorities provided a ragged shirt and pants that were to be worn every day. One eight-foot-wide wooden slab served as the bed for nine men, who had only two blankets to share among them. At first, most prisoners retained strong curiosity about what would happen next. Then an increasing number of people committed suicide. The most popular way was by touching an electrically charged barbed-wire fence that surrounded the camp. Frankl said that prisoners in the first few days did not fear death, for it meant that they would not have to take their own lives.

In the second phase, which began a few days later, most prisoners became apathetic. Prisoners had to deal with a number of difficult emotions, including a longing for home and family, and a disgust for the situation in which they were living. At first, prisoners looked away so that they would not have to witness others being punished. Prisoners were repeatedly struck by guards and forced to march for long hours. Within a few days or weeks, the prisoners no longer averted their eyes, and began to grow unmoved by the cruel acts they witnessed. Frankl said they were no longer capable of feeling "disgust, horror and pity," which helped to provide them with a protective shell.

Many inmates developed frostbite on their hands and feet, but had to continue working if they wanted to avoid being hit with a rifle butt. The daily rations provided to prisoners for their long days of work were about ten and one-half ounces of bread and one and three-fourths pints of a very watery soup. Occasionally prisoners received a dab of butter, a slice of cheese, or a bit of sausage. A central key of surviving the harsh realities of the camp was to avoid drawing the attention of the guards. At the camp, one surrendered individuality and existed as a mere number. For example, the skeleton-like bodies of sick people were placed on carts to be transported. If one of them died before the trip began, the corpse was still thrown on the cart to keep the numbers correct. The need for proper maintenance of lists mattered more than human life.

dancer." Admiring her kindness and good character, Frankl asked her to be his wife. They were among the last Viennese Jews permitted to marry before the Nazis passed restrictive legislation later in 1941. Designed to eliminate the Jewish race, the laws forbade Jews to marry, produce children, or become part of accepted society.

Sent to Concentration Camp

Any semblance of a normal life for the young couple was short-lived. Jews from all over Europe were being taken from their homes and transported to massive concentration camps. At first, these camps functioned as work camps to aid the German war effort. Eventually they turned into killing factories, where the targets of Nazi persecution met their deaths. Once inside the walls of the camps, male and female prisoners were separated. Shortly after the Frankls were wed, they were sent to Theresienstadt concentration camp. From there, Frankl was ordered to the Auschwitz death camp. His wife had been assured that she would not be sent to Auschwitz for two years because of her job

Prisoners frequently dreamed of warm baths, comfortable beds, and good food. Frankl observed that even among the large group of adult men, there was very little sexual interest or activity, as so much energy had to be focused on survival. The prisoners who seemed to survive best were not necessarily the most hardy, but the ones who had sensitivity and a rich intellectual life. Sometimes the prisoners put together entertainment made up of singing, joking, and poetry. Occasional humor also helped people to rise above their circumstances.

Most of the prisoners suffered from an inferiority complex. People who had once experienced success in their professional lives were now treated as if they did not matter at all. The tired and agitated state of the community increased the level of irritability among the prisoners, and fights frequently broke out. From witnessing the daily beatings of inmates, the "impulse to violence" also increased.

Frankl believed that even in the harshest of circumstances, like those he witnessed, people still have a choice of how to act. Throughout the camps there were people who went out of their way to comfort the suffering, and share their meager rations with others whose situation had taken a greater toll. Frankl believed that "any man can, even under such circumstances, decide what shall become of him—mentally and spiritually. He may

retain his human dignity even in a concentration camp." Frankl held that "Life ultimately means taking the responsibility to find the right answer to its problems.... Our answers must consist, not in talk and meditation, but in right action and in right conduct."

Frankl described the third stage of a concentration camp prisoner's mental reaction, which occurred after being freed. When the Allies liberated the prisoners, they were able to walk out of the camp into the countryside. Still numb to emotion, most people could not even feel any pleasure in freedom and life had a sense of unreality. Frankl observed that people exhibited obsessive behavior, eating and drinking to excess. With the sudden release from the mental pressure of living in the camps, some people became bitter and cruel to others, behaving as their captors had. Others suffered severe disappointment when they found out that the loved one they had dreamed of seeing for so many years no longer existed. Frankl pointed out that the best part for the person returning home was that, after all he had suffered, there was nothing he needed to fear any longer—"except his God."

as a munitions worker. Despite her husband's protests, she volunteered to go with him to Auschwitz. They were separated at the camp and never saw one another again. Frankl learned after the war that Tilly, who had been pregnant when she entered Auschwitz, had died there.

Frankl later wrote about his contact at Auschwitz with the notorious Nazi doctor Josef Mengele. When prisoners first arrived, Mengele separated them into two groups, in a process known as selection. Those sectioned off to the left

went to their deaths in gas chambers; those on the right went to work as laborers. Upon quick examination, Mengele indicated that Frankl should take his place in the left line. "Since I recognized no one in the left line," wrote Frankl, "behind Mengele's back I switched over to the right line where I saw a few of my young colleagues. Only God knows where I got that idea or found the courage." Frankl was forced to give up his good coat, which contained the manuscript for his first book in the pocket. He took an old, torn coat from a pile. In its pocket he found a page from a prayer book that

Frankl discussing the principles of logotherapy in his office. (Reproduced by permission of Bilderdienst Suddeutscher Verlag)

said, "Hear, oh Israel, the Lord our God is One." The prayer was an inspiration to Frankl during his time in the camps.

At the camp, Frankl survived an attack of typhus and respiratory problems. He always believed he was kept alive by his strong desire to reconstruct and publish his book. In that book he talked about a practice he used in the camps called self-distancing. For instance, one day when he was starving and in great pain from frozen feet, Frankl imagined how he would describe his reactions to an audience in a lecture hall. Years later, he gave talks on this very topic.

In addition to Auschwitz, Frankl also spent time in the Theresienstadt, Kaufering II, and Turkheim camps. Frankl's parents and his brother, Walter, all died in the camps. His sister, Stella, avoided the same fate by escaping to Australia.

Resumes Medical Career

By 1945 Hitler could no longer deny that Germany had lost the war. In order not to be captured by the Allies, Hitler committed suicide on April 30, 1945. Germany surrendered soon afterward under the authority of Admiral Karl Dönitz, Hitler's successor. With the end of the war, the concentration camps were liberated by the Allied forces. Following his liberation, Frankl returned to Vienna, where he alienated some colleagues by speaking against the then-popular concept of "collective guilt." That is, he rejected the notion that all non-Jewish people who lived under the Nazi shadow shared the guilt for the deaths of approximately six million Jews, as well as millions of other innocent people, who perished at the hands of the Nazis.

After his release, Frankl continued to grieve for his first wife and the family members he lost in the Holocaust, once stating that: "I lost all that could be taken away from a person except one thing—the last of the human freedoms—to choose one's attitude in any set of circumstances, to choose one's own way." He accepted a job as head of the neurology department at the Vienna Policlinic Hospital in 1946, a position he would hold for twenty-five years. He also finally wrote and published his first book, *The Doctor and the Soul.* In

1947 he married Eleonore Katharine Schwindt, a nurse at the hospital. The couple had a daughter named Gabriele.

Attains Worldwide Acclaim

Frankl developed a system of psychotherapy called the Third Viennese School. The title of Frankl's method was an homage to the systems developed by Sigmund Freud and Alfred Adler, his early mentors. Frankl's second and most famous book, *Man's Search For Meaning,* was written in nine days, selling nine million copies. The well respected work outlined the principles of logotherapy, and was followed by twenty-nine other books further detailing his theories. Worldwide interest in Frankl's work increased greatly in 1977, when he established the Viktor Frankl Institute of Logotherapy in Berkeley, California. In 1985, Frankl was granted the prestigious Oskar Pfister Prize by the American Association of Psychiatrists, the first non-American to be so honored.

Frankl died in Vienna of heart failure on September 2, 1997, at the age of ninety-two. He was a man of many talents and diverse interests, including mountain climbing, piloting airplanes, composing music, and designing commercial products. He had lectured at more than 200 universities around the world; many of his seminars were held in the United States. His books have been translated into twenty-four languages.

SOURCES

Books

Frankl, Viktor E., *The Doctor and the Soul: From Psychotherapy to Logotherapy,* (second expanded edition) translated from the German by Richard and Clara Winston, Vintage Books (New York), 1986.

Frankl, Viktor E., *Man's Search For Meaning: An Introduction to Logotherapy,* part one translated by Ilse Lasch, preface by Gordon W. Allport, Beacon Press (Boston), 1992.

Frankl, Viktor E., *Viktor Frankl: Recollections, An Autobiography,* translated by Joseph Fabry and Judith Fabry, foreword by Joseph Fabry, Insight Books (New York), 1997.

Frankl, Viktor E., *The Will To Meaning: Foundations and Applications of Logotherapy,* New American Library (New York), 1988.

Friedman, Maurice, "Viktor Frankl," *The Worlds of Existentialism: A Critical Reader,* edited with introductions and a conclusion by Maurice Friedman, Humanities Press International (Atlantic Highlands, NJ), 1991.

Ungersma, Aaron J., *The Search for Meaning: A New Approach in Psychotherapy and Pastoral Psychology,* Westminster Press (Philadelphia, PA), 1961.

Periodicals

Frankl, Victor E., "The Search For Meaning," *Saturday Review,* September 13, 1958.

Hoffman, Edward, "Viktor Frankl at 90: A Voice For Life," *America,* March 18, 1995, p. 17.

Varian M. Fry

Born October 15, 1907
New York, New York, United States
Died September 13, 1967
Easton, Connecticut, United States

Magazine editor; writer; teacher; rescuer
of 1,500 to 4,000 Jews, including famous
artists and scientists, from German-
occupied France

*"[I]t took courage [to stay in France], and
courage is a quality that I hadn't
previously been sure I possessed."*

Varian Fry is called "America's Schindler," a reference to German citizen Oskar Schindler who rescued 1,200 Jews during World War II and was the subject of a film directed by Steven Spielberg. Fry volunteered for a dangerous mission to help artists and intellectuals escape from German-occupied France during the war. At great personal risk, he operated an underground railroad that used false identity papers, disguises, and other means to get a number of well-known people out of France to safety. In 1941 Fry was ordered by the French government to leave the country. His heroic activities went unrecognized by the American people for many years. In 1983, sixteen years after Fry's death, extensive biographical information about the forgotten hero was made public. Writer Donald Carroll detailed the contributions of Fry in an article titled "Escape from Vichy" in *American Heritage* magazine, which is sponsored by the Society of American Historians.

Begins Life in New York

Fry was born in New York City in 1907. The son of a stockbroker, he was raised on the New Jersey side of the Hudson River in suburban Ridgewood. Described by Carroll as "moody" and "introverted," Fry was prone to hypochondria at a young age. Like other hypochondriacs, he felt the real pain of illness, yet there was nothing wrong with him medically. As a boy, Fry showed no interest in either his school work or his classmates, so his parents sent him to an elite private school in Connecticut when he was fourteen years old. There he faced his first real social and intellectual challenges, which he met with increasing introversion. He displayed a flair for languages, especially Latin. He had no tolerance for less gifted people, and he made conscious attempts to set himself apart from other students by wearing fancy clothing, affecting an interest in fine food and wine, and smoking. His seemingly elitist attitudes, wrote Carroll, "attracted few friends and much ridicule," so he "resigned" from school. Fry's parents sent him to another private school in Connecticut, which he liked better.

Fry earned a bachelor's degree from Harvard College (now Harvard University) in 1931, later continuing his education with graduate work at Columbia University in New York City. In college, he continued to display eccentric behavior. He became increasingly arrogant and his manner of dress even more unique. His intense individuality did not mask his talent, as he attracted some favorable attention when he founded a magazine in his sophomore year. He left the magazine in a fit of anger, however, after he and his partner disagreed about correct English grammar. Upon graduation, Fry married Eileen Hughes, a magazine editor who was seven years his elder. The couple moved to New York City, and for the next four years Fry earned a living as an editor and writer.

Visits Germany Prior to War

In 1935 Fry was offered a job as editor of a prominent magazine that published articles on international affairs. As a condition of employment, Fry was encouraged to visit Germany. During that time, Germany was in a state of transition. Adolf Hitler had recently come to power as head of the Nazi Party. Fry's assignment was to observe the changing climate of Germany. While in Berlin, the capital of Germany, Fry was stunned by the Nazis' severe violence against Jewish citizens. Fry described the early atrocities suffered by the Jewish people: "[I] saw with my own eyes young Nazi toughs gather and smash up Jewish-owned cafés, watched with horror as they dragged Jewish patrons from their seats, drove hysterical, crying women down the street, knocked over an elderly man and kicked him in the face." This violence had a tremendous impact on Fry.

As a result, the formerly solitary, introverted young man returned to the United States as a passionate and enraged advocate of the victims of Nazi violence. He immediately began informing the American public about the events in Germany, writing numerous articles on the sufferings of German Jews and others whom the Nazis considered "undesirable." He warned that Hitler was a dangerous threat to world peace.

War in France

As Fry cautioned others about the situation in Germany, France was being impacted by Nazi violence as well. France had long been regarded as a safe refuge for Europeans seeking to escape repression in their own countries. Since the early 1930s, intellectuals, artists, and refugees from Germany had been moving into France in great numbers to escape the Nazis. In 1939 the Nazis invaded Poland, swept through Denmark, Norway, and Belgium, and attacked France. On June 17, 1940, the French government, overwhelmed by the sheer power of the Nazi war machine, surrendered to Hitler. Under the terms of the armistice between the French government and Hitler, German troops would occupy the northern half of France and the area along the coast of the Atlantic Ocean. The French government would be left in control of the southern half of the country.

Seeing a momentary safe haven, numerous artists, intellectuals, and other refugees immediately fled to southern France, but they could go no farther without special travel papers. The armistice agreement included a provision requiring the new French government to "surrender on demand" any person wanted by the Nazis. This condition greatly concerned Fry. It was obvious that the Germans meant to call for the surrender of the artists and intellectuals who had been outspoken in condemning Nazi horrors. Fry later wrote *Surrender on Demand* (1967), a book about his experiences in France, in which he declared that "the fall of France, in June, 1940, meant … the creation of the most gigantic man-trap in history…. I could not remain idle as long as I had any chance at all of saving even a few [of Hitler's] victims."

Emergency Rescue Committee Formed

In New York, a group of shocked U.S. citizens immediately formed the Emergency Rescue Committee. The purpose of the group, wrote Fry, "was to bring the political and intellectual refugees out of France before the [German police] … got them." A

Fry at work in his office in France during his 1941 effort to rescue Jews from the Nazis. (Reproduced by permission of AP/Wide World Photos)

fundraising luncheon raised $3,500 for the cause. Yet the committee had still not decided who would be the liaison in arranging and executing the escapes. According to Fry: "After several weeks of fruitless searching for a suitable agent to send to France, the Committee selected me. I had had no experience in refugee work, and none in underground work. But I accepted the assignment because ... I believed in the importance of democratic solidarity."

The committee created a list of those people in the most danger in France. Fry spoke with Eleanor Roosevelt, wife of U.S. President Franklin D. Roosevelt. He worked to obtain special visas for the 200 people on his list. These visas were needed along with passports to help those trapped in the southern part of France to escape to another country. Fry arrived in France in the summer of 1940, and it soon became obvious that far more than 200 visas were needed. Refugees began coming to his hotel the day

after his arrival. "Many of them had been through hell," he wrote, noting that "their nerves were shattered and their courage gone." Fry attempted to find people who were in particular danger but they were hard to locate. Thus, Fry began trying to aid everyone who came to him for help.

An Order to Leave

Fry found a cartoonist who could create counterfeit identity papers and travel documents for the refugees. He bribed government officials and made deals with criminals. For more than a year he worked with ten other people to succeed in arranging the escape of prominent figures. Among them were novelist Heinrich Mann and Golo Mann, brother and son of Nobel Prize-winning author Thomas Mann; artists Marc Chagall, Andre Masson, Wilfred Lam, and Max Ernst; sculptor Jacques

American Heiress Helps

A few daring souls were brave enough to assist Varian Fry in his rescue efforts. One of them was American heiress Mary Jayne Gold (1909–1997) of Evanston, Illinois. After attending a finishing school in Italy, Gold headed to Paris, France, in 1930. She was armed with a small fortune, a pilot's license, and her own airplane. Gold was prepared to live a life devoted to parties and vacations, yet found her goals changed when German troops invaded France in 1940. Gold agreed to help Fry rescue Jews from France.

Gold's money paid for false passports and travel documents. Long after the end of the war, she told a journalist: "Women weren't taken too seriously in those days." The journalist added: "But when someone had to charm the commander of a French prison camp into freeing four [prisoners], Gold was sent to do the job."

Gold left France in 1941, shortly before Fry was ordered out of the country. She later wrote a book describing her adventures. Called *Crossroads Marseilles 1940*, it was published by Doubleday in 1980. (Marseilles was the town in southern France where Fry set up his rescue committee.) After the war, Gold returned to France, where she remained until her death in October 1997. She never married, nor had any children.

A few years before Gold's death, her friend, French filmmaker Pierre Sauvage, announced plans to make a movie based on her book. (Sauvage's parents were among those who sought help from the Fry committee.) Sauvage said of his friend: "She was a very shrewd woman whose heart was on the right side of issues and who at a crucial turning point in history understood what was called for.... [She always] felt that only one year in her life really mattered and it was the year she spent in Marseilles."

Lipchitz; poet and dramatist Franz Werfel; Nobel Prize-winning physicist Otto Meyerhoff; historian Konrad Heiden; writer and political scientist Hannah Arendt; historical novelist Lion Feuchtwanger; mathematician Emil Gumbel; journalist Hans Natonek; novelists Leonhard Frank, Alfred Polgar, and Hertha Pauli; harpsichordist Wanda Landowska; and Jaques Hadamard, called the "[Albert] Einstein of France." Estimates of the number of people Fry saved range from 1,500 to 4,000.

The new French government, based in the city of Vichy, was really just a puppet government of the Nazis. This fact complicated Fry's work, making his activities even more dangerous. He might have expected sympathy and even help from the French. Instead, he found that many French officials eagerly collaborated with the Nazis and carried out German orders. Fry was questioned by the French police several times, but always managed to avoid arrest. Eventually, the Vichy government ordered him to leave the country. The U.S. government refused to come to his aid. A U.S. official based in France told Fry: "We can't support an American citizen who is helping people evade French law." In September 1941 Fry found himself back in the United States.

Ignored in His Own Country

Fry began to write and give speeches about what he had seen and experienced in Europe. He warned of the impending massacre of European Jews, but few listened to his concerns. Fry wrote two books about his experiences in France, *Surrender on Demand* and *Assignment: Rescue*, which described his experiences for young readers. He told the story with little help from the people he had rescued. According to Carroll: "[Some] wanted to forget about the whole business and just get on with their lives. Some, including people who had once begged on their knees for Fry to save them, were too busy to be bothered by his modest requests for help." Both books sold poorly.

Fry experienced other setbacks as well. His marriage ended in divorce, though he remained on good terms with his former wife and was grief stricken when she died of cancer in 1948. He had trouble finding and holding jobs. By some accounts, his employment difficulties were due to concerns about a Federal Bureau of Investigation (FBI) inquiry into Fry's activities in France. When potential employers learned of the FBI file on Fry, they were unwilling to hire him. The U.S. army would not accept him because he had a weak stomach.

Fry remarried and had three children—Sylvia, Thomas, and James—with his second wife, Annette Riley. He took jobs teaching Latin and Greek and continued freelance writing. Nevertheless, Fry suffered from depression, in part, because of the way he had been treated. His frustrations eventually took their toll on his wife and children. His wartime heroism was finally acknowledged in 1967 when he received a medal from the French Legion of Honor. To his sorrow, however, he remained unrecognized by his own country. He died alone of a heart attack on September 13, 1967. He had been working on another book about his rescue missions. The policeman who discovered the body told a reporter that the book appeared to be a fictional account.

Honored Long After His Death

In 1991, twenty-four years after his death, Fry was honored in the United States with the Eisenhower Liberation Medal. An exhibit titled "Assignment: Rescue, The Story of Varian Fry and the Emergency Rescue Committee" was held at the U.S. Holocaust Memorial Museum from 1993 to 1994. On February 4, 1996, U.S. Secretary of State Warren Christopher planted a tree at Yad Vashem, the Martyrs' and Heroes' Remembrance Authority in Jerusalem. The tree honors Fry as one of the "Righteous Among the Nations," those "high-minded Gentiles who risked their lives to save Jews." Fry is the only American-born person to be so honored.

In 1996 a bill was introduced in the U.S. Congress proposing a combined Varian Fry-Raoul Wallenberg medal. As people became interested in learning more about Fry's wartime activities, both of his books were reissued. That same year the Varian Fry Foundation Project/IRC (International Rescue Committee) was formed to make his story more widely known in the United States, especially to school children. In 1997 Barwood Films, established by actor-singer Barbra Streisand, announced plans to make a television movie based on the life of Fry. The relatively unknown man who rescued more Jews than the famed Oskar Schindler is recognized today for his heroism.

SOURCES

Books

Fittko, Lisa, *Escape through the Pyrenees,* translated from the German by David Koblick, Northwestern University Press (Evanston, IL), 2000.

Fry, Varian, *Assignment:Rescue,* preface by Warren Christopher, Four Winds Press (New York), 1968.

Fry, Varian, *Surrender on Demand,* Johnson Books (Boulder, CO), 1997.

Gold, Mary Jayne, *Crossroads Marseilles, 1940,* Doubleday (Garden City), 1980.

Marino, Andy, *A Quiet American: The Secret War of Varian Fry,* St. Martin's Press (New York), 1999.

Periodicals

Carroll, Donald, "Escape from Vichy," *American Heritage,* June/July 1983, pp. 82+.

Chesnoff, Richard Z., "The Other Schindlers," *U.S. News & World Report,* March 21, 1994, pp. 56+.

Other

Varian Fry Foundation Project/IRC, 405 El Camino Real, No. 213, Menlo Park, CA 94025; telephone (650) 323-0530; e-mail fe.wem@forsythe.stanford.edu.

Varian Fry Website, http://www.almondseed.com/vfry (September 18, 2000).

Miep Gies

Miep Gies (pronounced Meep Geze) was one of more than 20,000 courageous Dutch citizens who helped hide Jews and others from the Germans during World War II. At tremendous personal risk nearly every day for more than two years, she brought food, companionship, and news of the outside world to eight Jewish people concealed in an attic in Amsterdam, Holland. Gies does not consider herself to be a hero, however. The eight people she tried to save are a symbol of courage today because one of them, Anne Frank, wrote a famous diary that was preserved through the efforts of Gies.

Rescued by the Dutch

Gies was born Hermine Santrouschitz in 1909 in Vienna, Austria, to working-class parents. When she was only five years old, World War I rocked Austria. The war caused a food shortage that did not end with the cessation of hostilities in 1918. By the age of ten, Gies was a scrawny, undernourished child. By 1920, with a new baby sister in the house, the family had even less food to share. Gies's parents were told that she would die if she did not get more nourishment. This situation was not uncommon: Children throughout Austria were starving. In response, a program was set up by the people of the Netherlands to help rescue the children of Austrian workers. Thus in 1920, Gies was taken in by a Dutch-speaking family in Leiden, Holland, headed

Born February 15, 1909
  Vienna, Austria

Resistance worker in Holland; provided food and friendship to Anne Frank's family in hiding during World War II

"My story is a story of very ordinary people during extraordinarily terrible times."

(Photograph by Bernard Gotfryd, reproduced by permission of Archive Photos, Inc.)

by a father who worked for a coal company. The family, who had five children of their own, treated Gies with great kindness and gave her the nickname "Miep," which is a term of affection in Dutch. They provided nutritional meals, which helped Gies regain her strength.

Gies attended a Dutch school in Leiden, where she quickly learned to speak the language. She developed a love for classical music, especially that of Wolfgang Mozart, and was encouraged to read the newspapers and discuss current events. When she was thirteen years old, Gies moved with her new family to the city of Amsterdam. Three years later she visited her birth family for the first time since 1920. By then, however, she had become so thoroughly Dutch that she felt out of place in Vienna. Her mother noticed this and believed her daughter would be happier living in Amsterdam with her new family. She gave her consent for Gies to return to Holland. No one thought to change Gies's citizenship from Austrian to Dutch, and this oversight proved to be a great mistake when World War II broke out in Europe in 1939.

At some point in her late teens or early twenties, Gies took her first job as an office worker. The blonde-haired, blue-eyed Gies had an active social life and spent her free time going to movies and dances. "I was one of the first girls in Amsterdam to learn the Charleston, the two-step, the tango, and the slow fox," she later wrote. At about five-feet tall, Gies was somewhat vain about her appearance and prided herself on dressing well. Like most of the rest of the world, Holland had not recovered economically from the effects of World War I, and unemployment was high. In 1933, when Gies was twenty-four, she was fired from her job. Yet she refused to be discouraged: "Being a young woman with an independent spirit," she later wrote, "I was longing to be working again."

Goes to Work for Otto Frank

Gies saw an advertisement in the newspaper for an office job only twenty minutes by bicycle from her home. In those days, many people rode bicycles to and from their jobs in Amsterdam. The advertisement directed her to apply to Otto Frank at Travies and Company, a firm specializing in products for homemakers. Gies was interviewed by Otto Frank himself. She found him to be a gentle, shy Jewish man, who had recently moved his family from Germany to escape the anti-Jewish campaign of Adolf Hitler. Otto Frank had witnessed

Hitler's persecution of the Jews and knew that the campaign of terror would only get worse. When Gies applied for a position with Otto Frank's company, she was asked to make jam with a new product called pectin during the interview process. Although she knew little about cooking, Gies soon proved herself adept at jam making. She got the job as head of the Complaint and Information Desk. When homemakers tried making jam with pectin and failed, their complaints were directed to Gies, who helped them.

Gies gradually developed a close relationship with the Frank family. She had also met a young man named Jan Gies, and they were invited to dine with the Franks on occasion. The tumultuous situation in Nazi-dominated Germany was a popular topic of dinner conversation. More and more Jews were fleeing Hitler's Germany to settle in Holland and other countries. Eventually, the population of such countries swelled to such a degree that many nations, including Holland, began turning away refugees. Until that time, Holland was one of the countries that had a reputation for being welcoming and tolerant toward refugees.

In March of 1938, as the Travies and Company staff listened to news via Otto Frank's radio, they learned that Hitler's troops had marched into Vienna, Austria—the city in which the Nazi leader had spent his youth. Gies wrote: "All of us were soon stunned when the news came that Viennese Jews had been made to clean out public toilets and to scrub the streets in an orgy of Nazi depravity, and that these people's possessions had been seized by the Nazis."

Shortly after the Germans took over Austria, Gies asked the police department to stamp her Austrian passport, which she was required to do annually. This time her passport was taken from her and she was issued a new German passport. She was told to consider herself a German citizen. However, Gies believed that "in my heart I was Dutch through and through." Several weeks later, she was visited by "a very blond young woman about my age wearing a sugary smile." The woman invited her to join one of the Nazi Girls' Clubs that were forming throughout Europe. Membership was a way of demonstrating loyalty to the Nazi Party. "How can I join such a club?" Gies asked. "Look at what the Germans are doing to the Jews in Germany." Gies did not know it then, but her refusal to join the club would be noted and remembered by Nazi officials.

War and Marriage

The news from Germany about Hitler's persecution of the Jews grew increasingly frightening. Gies was pleased to learn that an attempt had been made to assassinate Hitler. "I wanted Hitler to be put down, murdered, anything. Then, as I reflected on my gnawing feelings, I realized how much I had changed. I had been brought up never to hate.... And here I was, full of hate and murderous thoughts."

In September 1939, Hitler invaded Poland, marking the beginning of World War II in Europe. One after another, the countries of Europe fell to the mighty German army until finally, on May 10, 1940, Germany invaded the Netherlands. Four days later Holland surrendered. "Now, suddenly, our world was no longer ours," Gies wrote. As Dutch Jews experienced increasing pressure from Nazi restrictions, Gies, too, was having problems. One day she was summoned to appear before German officials in Amsterdam. When Gies admitted that she had refused to join a Nazi Girls' Club, her passport was marked with a black "X," which made it unusable. She was ordered to return to Vienna within three months. The only way she could free herself of this dilemma was to marry a Dutch citizen. Overcoming many obstacles related to her citizenship status and her invalid passport, she finally married Jan Gies on July 16, 1941. Among those present at the ceremony were Otto Frank; his daughter, Anne; and Hermann and Petronella van Daan.

Franks Go into Hiding

After her marriage, Gies continued to work for Otto Frank's company. Additional restrictions against Jews were enacted—these regulations were published in the local Jewish newspaper. "Perhaps the Germans thought that this way we Christians wouldn't know what was happening to the Jews. But word of every new measure spread like fire," Gies recalled. "At home, at night, the frustration and anger of the day left me drained dry."

In the spring of 1942 Jews were ordered to sew a yellow star—a Jewish symbol patterned after the Star of David—on their clothing to identify themselves as Jews. According to Gies, this order, "somehow so much more enraging than all the others, was bringing our fierce Dutch anger to a boil." Soon afterward Otto Frank informed Gies that he, his family, and the van Daans planned to go into hiding. He asked if she would care for the group

What Qualities Do Holocaust Rescuers Share?

The Holocaust was the central piece of the Nazi plan to establish a pure "master race." Millions of seemingly ordinary people stood by and did nothing while the Holocaust transpired. Some, like Miep Gies, helped and risked their own lives doing so. Experts who have studied Holocaust rescuers have found that these people had some common traits. Most came from warm, loving homes. Feelings of self-worth were encouraged and parents disciplined children through reasoning rather than punishment. As children, many Holocaust rescuers lost or were separated from a loved one but experienced caring from another. These experiences made future rescuers sensitive to others' suffering.

Gies, for example, lost her home and her family when she was sent to live in Holland. Yet she was welcomed by a warm and loving Dutch family, even though she was different from them. Thus she learned acceptance and tolerance for those who are different. She was able to take direct action when she saw that the lives of helpless victims were threatened.

and Gies quickly agreed. In July 1942 Gies and her husband helped the Franks move their belongings into the hiding place they had prepared in the attic of Otto Frank's office building.

For twenty-five months Gies helped the little group survive. Twice a day, except when she was sick, she visited the group, picking up their grocery list in the morning, and returning in the evening with provisions. The Franks and van Daans eagerly awaited her visits because she also brought news of what was happening outside. The news grew more and more grim. "Every time [I entered the hiding place], I had to set a smile on my face, and disguise the bitter feeling that burned in my heart. I would take a breath … and put on an air of calm and good cheer that it was otherwise impossible to feel anywhere in Amsterdam anymore," Gies remembered.

Food became increasingly difficult to obtain as the war continued because the Germans were shipping much of it home to "the Fatherland." Even soap was scarce. Gies grew close to Anne Frank, who was becoming a young woman while in hiding. "I felt a particular kinship with Anne," she wrote. "I became determined to find something grown-up and pretty for Anne in the course of my searches [for food]." Gies found a pair of second-hand, red leather shoes, which she presented to the girl—the first and only pair of high-heeled shoes Anne would ever have. "Never have I seen anyone so happy as Anne was that day." It was Gies who supplied Anne with writing paper after the girl's diary pages were filled.

The war waged on and on, and so did the scarcities. Winter was the worst time. Tempers flared and illnesses struck. Sometimes the only food Gies was able to obtain made people sick. The group lived through two terrible winters in their hiding place. At home, Gies and her husband concealed a young Jewish student, a boy named Karel. Gies wrote: "I'd cook the best dinner I could put together. [Jan], Karel, and I would sit down and eat. Often Karel would chatter away, hungry for company after another day of total isolation. [We] would listen silently."

Hopes Rise and Fall

The tides of war were soon to change. On June 6, 1944, U.S. and British forces landed on the beaches of Normandy in France. Known as D-Day, the event marked the first step toward Allied victory in the war in Europe. All Amsterdam was filled with excitement, sure that its rescuers would arrive soon. American General Dwight D. Eisenhower spoke on the radio, assuring his listeners that "total victory over the Germans would be coming within this very year, 1944." Otto Frank hung a map of Europe on the wall, marking with pins the daily advance of their potential rescuers. A little more than a month later, on July 20, 1944, everyone's hopes rose when they learned that yet another attempt had been made on Hitler's life by one of his own military leaders. But it failed and life in Amsterdam grew worse. On August 4, 1944, Gies was in her office when the Nazis came and took away the Franks and the van Daans. Someone had informed the police of their hiding place. Much later she wrote: "I could hear the sound of our friends' feet. I could tell from their footsteps that they were coming down like beaten dogs." After the war ended the following spring, only Otto Frank survived.

Otto Frank came to live with Gies and her family for a time after the war. Gies gave him Anne's diary, which she had saved but could not bring herself to read until long after it was published. Gies retired from her job in 1947 to devote herself to homemaking. In 1950, at the age of forty-one, she gave birth to a son, Paul. She remained anonymous until the publication in 1987 of her book *Anne Frank Remembered*. She wrote the book after the death of Otto Frank in 1980, when she and Jan realized that they were the only witnesses left to speak of the Frank tragedy. "It was very painful for us," she told an interviewer, "but we finally did it." In the 1990s, Gies toured the United States, giving lectures about her experiences hiding her Jewish friends from the Nazis. By that time she was well into her eighties. Her book was also made into a movie.

SOURCES

Books

Gies, Miep, with Alison Leslie Gold, *Anne Frank Remembered: The Story of the Woman Who Helped to Hide the Frank Family,* Simon and Schuster (New York), 1987.

Periodicals

Beauregard, Sue-Ellen, "In Search of the Heroes: Forget Me Not—The Anne Frank Story," *Booklist,* May 1, 1997, p.1509.

De Pres, Terrence, "Facing Down the Gestapo," *New York Times Biographical Service,* May 1987, p. 449–450.

Kauffmann, Stanley, "Anne Frank Remembered," *The New Republic,* March 4, 1996, p. 30.

Small, Michael, "Miep Gies, Who Hid Anne Frank, Adds a Coda to the Famous Diary," *People Weekly,* April 18, 1988, p. 123.

Mildred Gillars ("Axis Sally")

The morale of soldiers fighting a war is often vital in determining whether they will win or lose. During World War II, U.S. citizen Mildred Gillars was hired by the Axis countries and charged with the task of destroying the morale of U.S. soldiers. The radio programs of "Axis Sally," the name U.S. troops gave her radio personality, actually entertained American troops and ironically had a far more negative effect on her own life than on the morale of the soldiers.

A Transient Youth

Mildred Elizabeth Sisk was born in 1900 in Portland, Maine, to Vincent and Mae Hewitson Sisk. The couple divorced when Gillars was seven. Her mother then remarried a dentist, Robert Gillars, whose name both mother and daughter adopted. The family moved constantly, but settled long enough for Gillars to graduate from high school in Conneaut, Ohio, in 1917. She attended Ohio Wesleyan University in the town of Delaware, Ohio, from 1918 to 1922. Although Gillars did well in her study of speech and drama, she did not accumulate enough credits to graduate. After she left college, she held a variety of low-paying jobs, including sales positions and waiting tables, as she struggled to become a professional actress. In 1919 Gillars and her mother took a six-month trip to Europe, and Gillars was able to study in France.

Born November 29, 1900
   Portland, Maine, United States
Died June 25, 1988
   Columbus, Ohio, United States

Radio personality; English teacher; actress; model; made radio broadcasts for the Germans during World War II

"Hello, Gang. Throw down those little old guns and toddle off home. There's no getting the Germans down."

(Reproduced by permission of AP/Wide World Photos)

Other Radio Propagandists

Other women took to the airwaves to send potentially demoralizing messages to Allied soldiers. "Tokyo Rose" was a name applied to a number of female propagandists who broadcast radio programs on behalf of Japan to Allied troops serving in the Pacific. The women were of various nationalities, including Japanese, American, Australian, and Filipino.

The best known "Tokyo Rose" was an American citizen named Iva Toguri, who was born in 1916 to Japanese parents. After the war she was returned to the United States, and in 1948 she was tried and found guilty of treason. She was fined $10,000, and ordered to serve ten years in prison. She was released after six years and received a presidential pardon in 1977.

After returning to the United States, Gillars took some minor acting and dancing jobs in New York City while working as a nanny and in sales positions. During the 1920s, Gillars traveled to Germany to pursue an acting career. She reportedly worked as a model and a dressmaker's assistant in Paris, France, and studied music in Dresden, Germany. After arriving in Berlin, Germany, in 1934, she got a job teaching English at the Berlitz School of Languages. She fell in love with a married man named Max Otto Kosichwitz, who had taught at Hunter College in New York City. At the start of World War II, Kosichwitz began to work for the German foreign office, and served as program director at Radio Berlin.

"Axis Sally" Broadcasts

Kosichwitz convinced Gillars, who had already been working in German radio as an actress and a radio announcer, to do radio propaganda pieces. Her broadcasts for the Nazis were aimed at U.S. soldiers and designed to demoralize the troops. Gillars's broadcast, a program called *Home Sweet Home*, aired from late in the evening until early in the morning. Most of her shows were broadcast from Berlin, but sometimes they came from France or the Netherlands. After the Allies landed in North Africa, she broadcast her program from there. Although Gillars referred to herself as "Midge at the mike," U.S. soldiers nicknamed her "Axis Sally."

American GIs stationed all over Europe, North Africa, and the United States listened to Gillars's sexy voice as she played their favorite jazz recordings. Before starting the music, she sympathized with them about their loneliness and desire to return home. She also teased them about the possibility that their wives and girlfriends back home were going out on dates. In addition, "Axis Sally" would comment on information that was supposed to be secret, welcoming new arriving units by name, and bidding farewell to units on their way from North Africa to fight in Italy. She constantly liked to remind the Allied soldiers that they were fighting a losing battle. Another of Gillars's techniques was to read the serial numbers of American GIs who had been captured or killed. Nevertheless she may have done more good than harm; Allied troops enjoyed listening to the American jazz music and generally disregarded most of her propaganda messages. One of the songs she liked to play, "Lilli Marlene," became an international hit.

Postwar Capture

Gillars's program ran from December 11, 1941, through May 6, 1945. During the Soviet capture of Berlin in 1945, Gillars's lover, Max Kosichwitz, was killed. At the war's end, Gillars was found, near starvation, in the cellar of a bombed-out building. Before her identity was discovered, she received the help of charitable agencies in getting food and shelter. She was treated at an American hospital in Germany for three weeks, then spent some time at a camp for homeless people.

In late 1946 Gillars obtained a pass allowing her to live in Berlin's French Zone. The city had been divided up into sections run by various Allied countries. When she later traveled to Frankfurt, Germany, to renew her pass, U.S. agents took her into custody. A year later Gillars was sent to Washington, D.C., where she was jailed as she awaited trial for treason.

Goes On Trial

Gillars was one of only twelve Americans charged with treason after World War II. Her trial began in January 1949. The chief prosecutor began by pointing out that while working for Radio Berlin, Gillars had signed an oath of loyalty to Hitler and his Nazi Party. During the war, all of Gillars's programs had been recorded by representatives of the Federal Communications Commission, an American agency responsible for monitoring American radio. Prosecutors said that the broadcasts were "sugarcoated propaganda pills" whose purpose was to get GIs to defect to the side of the Nazis. The broadcasts failed miserably in their intended purpose as U.S. soldiers were often amused by the show.

The particular program that caused Gillars to be prosecuted was "Vision of Invasion," which she broadcast on May 11, 1944. It was aimed at the soldiers stationed in England awaiting the D-Day invasion, which was to take place on June 6. Americans also heard the program, which went out over U.S. airways. During the broadcast, Gillars assumed the role of the mother of an American soldier who dreamed that her son died while crossing the English Channel in a ship that went up in flames. She did an effective acting job as other entertainers pretended to be soldiers groaning in agony as they were fired upon from the beaches. The voice of an announcer intoned, "the D of D-Day stands for doom ... disaster ... death ... defeat...." In testimony at the trial, a German radio official stated that the purpose of the broadcast was to scare American soldiers out of taking part in the planned invasion.

Gillars had sometimes pretended to be a worker for the International Red Cross, and in that disguise often persuaded young soldiers to make recordings for people back home. She later added propaganda material to their messages, designed to undermine morale. In one message she was quoted as saying: "It's a disgrace to the American public that they don't wake up to the fact of what [President] Franklin D. Roosevelt is doing to the [non-Jewish people] of your country and my country."

At Gillars's trial, several ex-GI witnesses testified that she tried to get them to answer questions for recordings. One pointed at her, saying: "She threatened us as she left—that woman right there, that American citizen. She told us we were the most ungrateful Americans she had ever met and that we would regret this." Gillars's defense attorney pointed out that treason must be something more than the words one utters. He said: "Things have come to a pretty pass if you cannot make an anti-[Jewish] speech without being charged with

treason. Being against President Roosevelt could not be treason. There are two schools of thought about [him]. One holds he was a patriot and martyr. The other holds that he was the greatest [rascal] in all history, the greatest fraud, and the greatest impostor that ever lived."

Gillars's lawyer also defended his client by saying that she was heavily influenced to participate in the propaganda broadcasts by Kosichwitz, the older man with whom she was in love. Gillars took the stand three times, breaking down in tears on each occasion. She said she had lived with Kosichwitz in Berlin and was heartbroken when she heard reports that he had died. According to the *New York Times:* "Gillars fascinated the public and the press with her flamboyance and cool self-possession. She cut a theatrical figure in tight-fitting black dresses, long silver hair, and a deep tan. She had scarlet lips and nails."

Trial Ends in Conviction

In his closing statement, the prosecutor said that Gillars had taken great pleasure in doing the broadcasts, especially when reporting the agonies suffered by wounded soldiers before they died. He contended that Gillars thought Germany would win the war, suggesting that Gillars was selfish, only caring about her fame and what the broadcasts would do for her career. Gillars's six-week trial ended in March 1949. A jury of seven men and five women decided her fate. The lawyers had selected jurors who were neither Jewish nor could speak German. After deliberating for more than one hundred hours, the jury was unable to reach a verdict. The judge then had them sequestered in a hotel. After seventeen hours of further deliberation, Gillars was acquitted of seven of the eight counts and convicted on the count that involved the broadcast of the program "Vision of Invasion."

On March 26, 1949, Gillars was sentenced to ten to thirty years in prison and a fine of $10,000. She was declared ineligible for parole for ten years. "Axis Sally" was jailed in the Alderson, West Virginia, federal prison. She became eligible for parole in 1959 but, fearing the response of people outside the prison to her Nazi past, she waived the right to ask for her freedom. Two years later she did apply and was granted parole.

Life After Prison

In 1961, after her release from prison, Gillars went to live out of the public eye at the Sisters of the Poor Child Jesus Convent in Columbus, Ohio. At the convent school, she taught German, French, and music. Gillars returned to Ohio Wesleyan University when she was seventy-two—fifty years after dropping out—and earned her B.A. degree in speech. She died of colon cancer at the age of eighty-seven in Columbus.

SOURCES

Books

Boatner, Mark M., III, *Biographical Dictionary of World War II,* Presidio Press (Novato, CA), 1996.

Burgess, Patricia, editor, *The Annual Obituary,* St. James Press (Detroit), 1990.

Massakyo, Duus, *Tokyo Rose: Orphan of the Pacific,* translated from the Japanese by Peter Duus, introduction by Edwin Reischauer, Kodansha International, Ltd. (Tokyo), distributed in the United States through Harper & Row (New York), 1979.

Snyder, Louis Leo, *Encyclopedia of the Third Reich,* Marlowe (New York), 1998.

Joseph Goebbels

The life of Joseph Goebbels demonstrates that morality does not necessarily go along with high intelligence. This very well-educated man, who influenced the minds of millions of Germans, used his talents to spread hate and violence. Having no respect for ideas contrary to his own, Goebbels ordered the large-scale burning of books containing content he considered unacceptable or philosophies which differed from the stances of the Nazi party. He was also instrumental in organizing the assassinations of those opposing German leader Adolf Hitler, both prior to, and throughout the duration of, World War II.

Born October 29, 1897
    Rheydt, Germany
Died May 1, 1945
    Berlin, Germany

Minister of Culture and Minister of Propaganda for Nazi Germany; known as the "Little Doctor" and the "Father of Lies"

"It is almost immaterial what we believe in, so long as we believe in something."

A Difficult Childhood

Joseph Goebbels (pronounced Yo-seff Goor-bulz), the son of working-class German Catholic parents, was born on October 29, 1897, in Rheydt, Germany. Although his name was Paul Joseph Goebbels, he preferred to be called by his middle name, Joseph. His hard-working family of seven managed to budget its finances carefully in order to buy a small house. To maintain their middle-class status, the entire family manufactured wicks used in oil lamps for sale at the local market. Goebbels had a crippled left foot, which some historians believe was a birth defect commonly called a clubfoot, while others attribute it to a side effect of polio. Whatever the cause, and despite efforts to

(Reproduced by permission of AP/Wide World Photos)

Goebbels giving the Nazi salute. (Reproduced by permission of AP/Wide World Photos)

correct the problem, this disability prevented him from walking properly for the rest of his life. As a result, Goebbels developed an inferiority complex and spent a great deal of time alone reading in his room. Goebbels was an excellent student, and his parents encouraged him to develop his intellectual gifts. He was not popular at school; aloof to the other students, he showed an impressive talent for acting. According to writer Ralf Reuth: "Powerful displays of emotion, dramatic facial expressions and gestures were his [specialty]." A favorite teacher helped him develop his language skills, deepening his dramatic flair.

College Years and Brief Military Service

At the beginning of World War I (1914–18), Goebbels had eagerly volunteered to fight for Germany. He was deeply disappointed when he was rejected because of his severe limp; his height (five feet); and his weight (about one hundred pounds). These physical attributes were to remain unchanged for the rest of his life. In 1917 Goebbels enrolled at the University of Bonn in Germany to study literature. When he experienced money problems, a Catholic organization provided him with loans for several semesters. Later, the group found it very difficult to get the loans repaid. Later that year, with the war raging, the military was less selective and Goebbels was finally called. His place was not on the battlefield, but as a paper-pusher. He interrupted his college studies to serve his country.

After the war, Goebbels returned to college and wrote several plays and an autobiographical novel, titled *Michael Voorman's Youth*. In this book, he wrote about his own self-hatred, how he had worked so hard at school to try to make up for his physical disabilities, and his tendency to become "arrogant and tyrannical." Goebbels received his Ph.D. in literature from the University of Heidelberg in Germany in 1922, but his repeated attempts to become a playwright and a novelist proved to be failures.

Early Days with the Nazis

In 1924 Goebbels began to write and edit political journals, and he soon joined the Nazi party, led by Adolf Hitler. Goebbels was at first a follower of Gregor Strasser, a Nazi who believed Hitler was not extreme enough in his ideas for social and economic change. After meeting Hitler on several occasions, however, Goebbels became enchanted

with him. Hitler, realizing this, flattered Goebbels and cultivated his loyalty. Goebbels became the Nazi district leader for the Berlin-Brandenburg area in 1926. His task was to reorganize the Nazi party there. "I recognize [Hitler] as my leader quite unconditionally," he wrote. "He is the creative instrument of Fate and Deity … good and kind, but also clever and shrewd."

The stereotypical vision of the "yes-man" is a perfect description of Goebbels, at least in his relationship to Hitler. A story is told about the Nazi leaders viewing a film that Goebbels referred to as magnificent. A short time later, when Hitler entered the room and stated his opinion that it was absolutely no good, Goebbels was heard to exclaim, "Yes, my Führer. It was feeble, very feeble."

Rises in the Nazi Party

By 1928 Goebbels had become one of twelve Nazi deputies. The most intellectual of the Nazis, Goebbels was said to be charming and witty with a deep, musical voice. Hitler appointed the gifted communicator as head of party propaganda and public information in 1930. Goebbels was also in charge of the Nazis' chaotic election campaigns from 1930 through 1933. Goebbels's public speaking abilities earned him the office of Reichsminister of Propaganda following Hitler's rise to dictator in 1933. Goebbels was responsible for the impressive torchlight parades and well-orchestrated Nazi rallies. His job was to reinforce the Nazi hold on the minds of ordinary Germans. He controlled the media, and, in 1933, organized a burning of books disliked by the Nazis. He also imposed Nazification (the technical term for the promotion of Nazi values) on the artistic and cultural branches of German life. Goebbels helped fashion what has been referred to as the "Führer myth." This myth held that Hitler was superior to all other human beings, lived a simple life with no luxuries, and was infallible. Because this reputation of Hitler became widespread, criticism aimed at him was kept at a minimum. It was Goebbels's idea to have thousands of small record players produced so that supporters could listen to Hitler's speeches.

Anti-Jewish Hatred

Goebbels grew to be extremely anti-Semitic, although he was raised in a home with no particular anti-Jewish feelings. His strong anti-Jewish beliefs developed during the mid-1920s when he

Nazi Party Symbols

The swastika, a bent-arm cross, was an ancient symbol that first appeared in India, signifying good luck. In more recent times it was used by very conservative German political groups, including the Nazis. The Nazi swastika always appeared in black within a white circle and set on a red background. Hitler explained that red always captured people's attention.

Old movies about the Nazis are full of people raising their arms in a stiff fashion and declaring "Heil Hitler!" or "Seig Heil!" After Hitler's ascent to power, "Heil (meaning hail) Hitler" became the official greeting when Nazis met one another. The repetition of these two phrases at huge Nazi rallies came from the suggestion of a friend of Hitler. When Hitler's friend was in the United States attending Harvard University, he saw how cheerleaders whipped up enthusiasm among the crowd at Harvard football games by getting the spectators to clap and repeat cheers. Hitler copied the rigid outstretched arm salute used by the Nazis from Italian dictator Benito Mussolini. Hitler was known for being able to keep his own arm extended in the salute for very long periods. Some insiders attributed this to his wearing a collapsible spring under his sleeve.

began to see Jews as the perpetrators of economic ideas that he opposed. As the Nazis grew more powerful in the mid-1930s, Goebbels played a large role in fighting the Nazis' political opponents within Germany. By the time World War II began, Hitler was Germany's dictator and no longer had those enemies to fight, with one exception—the Jews. By then, Goebbels was known to be an extreme anti-Semite. He was responsible for an infamous event that took place in 1938 called *Kristallnacht* (meaning "Crystal Night" or the "Night of Broken Glass"). The name *Kristallnacht*

refers to the tons of windows from Jewish-owned stores and synagogues that lay shattered in the streets after several thousand Jews were brutally rounded up, had all their worldly goods taken from them, and were sent to concentration camps. According to the United States Holocaust Memorial Museum, "On November 9, 1938, the Nazis unleashed a wave of pogroms against Germany's Jews. In the space of a few hours, thousands of synagogues and Jewish businesses and homes were damaged or destroyed. Stormtroopers killed at least 91 Jews and injured many others." As an added injury, the Jews were made to pay an enormous fine for the damages, which were blamed on them. Goebbels took credit for the event. Historians have documented that Goebbels was the most persistent of the Nazi leaders in demanding the complete extermination of all the Jews.

Goebbels was said to have reveled in violence and did not hesitate to use the SA, or storm troopers, to attack and murder people. Once the war began, he did his best to worsen the living conditions of the Jews in Berlin. The first transport of Jews from Berlin to a ghetto in the city of Lódz, Poland, was in fulfillment of his promise to the führer to make Berlin "cleansed of Jews." The Nazis enjoyed being especially brutal to the Jews on Jewish holidays, and these days became known as "Goebbels's calendar."

Master of Propaganda

Like Hitler, Goebbels was very fond of the movies. He produced films that glorified Nazi heroes, and portrayed Jews as ugly and sinister. During World War II, Goebbels played a key role in influencing the minds of the German people through the use of the media and propaganda. Sometimes called the "Father of Lies," he was convinced that people would believe lies if they were repeated often enough. He also said that the bigger the lie, the more likely people were to believe it. Goebbels's campaigns were always built around causing the German people to hate some particular person or group, mainly the Jews, but other ethnic groups were frequently targets of his vitriolic speeches as well. Germans were kept from knowing the truth of how the war was progressing, saw defeats portrayed as victories, and heard an endless stream of official lies—for example, he purported that British Prime Minister Winston Churchill was a drunk and that U.S. President Franklin D. Roosevelt was Jewish. Goebbels's last big lie was that Hitler died near the end of the war, leading his troops in battle, rather than committing suicide in his underground bunker.

Goebbels became Hitler's savior in a situation that occurred in 1944. A group of German Army officers, realizing that the Nazis were losing the war, attempted to assassinate Hitler. They hoped to spark an overthrow of the Nazi government. They might have succeeded in their plans had Goebbels not stepped in and taken charge. He brought together troops for support, and soon had most of the plotters jailed or murdered.

Goebbels was married and the father of six children. Despite his external appearance as the model Nazi family man, he was known for having many romances with women—especially the young actresses under his control as head of the Nazi movie industry. At one point his adulterous behavior was so bold, his marriage was jeopardized and Hitler told him to cease his recklessness. Hitler said Goebbels was harming the image of wholesomeness that the Nazis liked to portray. Goebbels did as he was ordered for a short time, then secretly resumed his former behavior.

Murder and Death

Hitler's suicide took place on April 30, 1945, once it was obvious that the Nazis were going to lose the war. Goebbels intended to commit suicide right after Hitler, but could not bring himself to do so. Goebbels refused to accept the position of Reich chancellor, an appointment that Hitler had specified for him in his will. With the approach of the Soviets, he sent a Nazi general to talk with the Soviet troop commander in an attempt to negotiate a peace treaty. The Soviets were uninterested.

Before his death, Hitler had advised Goebbels's wife, Magda, to leave Germany by plane. Ever loyal to the führer, however, this was not what Joseph and Magda Goebbels wanted. On May 1, 1945, Goebbels and his wife sedated their children, and then killed each of them with injections of poison, finally killing themselves. Some accounts say Goebbels ordered the SS to perform the murders of his children, rather than performing them himself, and yet others claim it was the SS that killed Goebbels and his wife at Goebbels's request. As Goebbels had instructed before his death, his own body and that of his wife were then burned. Many historians believe that, as the war ended, the lives of Goebbels's six children could have been saved, though here is no doubt that the children, ages four to twelve, would have suffered some difficult times.

SOURCES

Books

Heiber, Helmut, *Goebbels,* translated by John K. Dickinson, Da Capo Press (New York), 1983.

Manvell, Robert, and Heinrich Fraenkel, *Dr. Goebbels,* Simon & Schuster (New York), 1960.

Reimann, Viktor, *Goebbels,* translated from the German by Stephen Wendt, Doubleday (Garden City, NY), 1976.

Reuth, Ralf Georg, *Goebbels,* translated from the German by Krishna Winston, Harcourt Brace (New York), 1993.

Riess, Curt, *Joseph Goebbels,* with a preface by Louis P. Lochner, Hollis and Carter (London), 1949.

Semmler, Rudolf, *Goebbels: The Man Next to Hitler,* AMS Press (New York), 1981.

Trevor-Roper, H. R., *The Last Days of Hitler,* University of Chicage Press (Chicago), 1992.

Other

United States Holocaust Memorial Museum, http://www.ushmm.org (July 13, 2000).

Hermann Göring

Born January 12, 1893
Rosenheim, Germany
Died October 15, 1946
Nuremberg, Germany

Field marshal and commander-in-chief of
the German Air Force

*"I pledge my destiny to you [Adolf Hitler]
for better or for worse...."*

(USHMM Photo Archives)

More than any other of the major German officials who worked for anti-Semitic dictator Adolf Hitler, Hermann Göring (also transliterated as Hermann Goering) is an excellent example of a decent man who became corrupted by power. During Göring's boyhood, at the end of the nineteenth century, Germany was a vigorous country, full of promise. As a young man, Göring saw his country, which was defeated in World War I (1914–18), grow frightened and desperate. A national feeling of despondency and frustration emerged, and people began listening to the political pontificating of Adolf Hitler, who seemed to provide answers that would pull Germany out of its economic and political recession. Hitler also identified a scapegoat for Germany's downfall—the Jewish people. Instead of systematic economic reform, Hitler involved Germany in a bloody and barbaric series of events, ending in national shame and defeat. Hermann Göring's fate was intrinsically tied to that of the nation and its hate-filled leader.

Troubled Beginnings

Hermann Wilhelm Göring (pronounced Hairmon Vil-helm Ger-ring) was born in a little town south of Munich, Germany, in January 1893. His father, Heinrich Ernst Göring, represented Germany's business interests in various foreign countries. Göring's mother, Franziska "Fanny"

Tiefenbrun, married Heinrich Göring when she was nineteen. Heinrich was a forty-five-year-old widower with five children. While fulfilling her role as a stepmother to these children, Fanny also gave birth to four children of her own. Hermann was the youngest.

When Göring was three months old, his mother went to join Heinrich in the country of Haiti, where he was stationed. Göring remained in the town of Furth, where a local family cared for him for three years. Göring spent his early years without his parents and it is purported that when the family was reunited, the enraged youth lashed out at his mother. Back in Germany, Göring's father watched his career disintegrate because he advocated equal rights for black citizens. This was a highly unpopular idea among the Germans at the time. Due to ostracism, he soon retired and died from alcoholism in 1913.

Childhood and Schooling

After his father's retirement, Göring went to live at the castle of his godfather, an Austrian physician named Hermann von Epenstein. While attending private school, teachers criticized Göring for writing an essay lauding his godfather. The teachers said that because von Epenstein was Jewish, it was inappropriate to write an essay praising him. That night the 11-year-old Göring packed his bags and returned home. He then attended two different military academies, where he showed a proficiency for mountain climbing and horseback riding. A loyal, self-confident boy, he dreamed of becoming a national German hero. He graduated in 1912 with highest honors and then served as a junior officer in the Prinz Wilhelm Regiment. Reputedly popular with young women, Göring had striking blue-green eyes and blond good looks that were later considered to be the ideal representation of Hitler's Aryan gentleman.

During World War I (1914–1918), Göring proved himself to be a brave pilot. He was awarded Germany's highest honor for an aviator, the Blue Max. On July 7, 1918, he was appointed the last commander of the famed Richthofen Squadron. This promotion allowed him to develop his excellent management skills, which would later attract Hitler's interest. After the war, Göring worked as a stunt pilot and as a commercial pilot for a Swedish airline. In Stockholm, Sweden, he met 32-year-old Swedish baroness Carin von Fock-Kantzoa, a married woman with an 8-year-old son. The baroness divorced her husband, a Swedish soldier, and married Göring in 1923.

Along with many other young German soldiers during the postwar period, Göring felt betrayed by his government. The political leaders of Germany never gave any indication they might be forced to surrender to the enemy. When the war ended in 1918, Germany's enemies enforced severe penalties and demanded reparations from the country. The payment of these reparations resulted in extreme economic hardships for the German people. High unemployment became a national problem. Poor and stripped of illusions promising a lucrative future, Göring was searching for answers.

Joins the Nazi Party

Adolf Hitler entered the life of Göring, and all of Germany, amidst national feelings of uncertainty and despair. As head of the Nazi party, Hitler preached that Germans were a superior race and should rule the world. Hitler's platform of German racial purity struck a chord with the public. His contention that Jews were a "poisonous" race that had caused Germany's defeat in the war provided a national scapegoat. He was emphatic that Jews must be removed. With growing support, Hitler rallied feelings of nationalism. He declared that the Treaty of Versailles, which ended World War I, contained unfair terms of surrender. Göring agreed with Hitler and pledged allegiance to the Nazi Party. At first, Göring resisted Hitler's strong anti-Semitic beliefs. However, as Göring became completely captivated by Hitler, he soon abandoned his own tolerant views and adopted those of the Nazi leader.

By 1923 the Görings' house had become the hub of Nazi social activities. It was at this house that the Nazis planned their first failed attempt to take over the German government. The failed coup would later be known as the Munich Beer Hall Putsch. In the confusion of the aftermath, Göring was severely wounded. He fled to Austria, later finding refuge in Switzerland. During Göring's slow recovery, his intense level of pain led to a severe morphine addiction, a problem that was to plague him on and off for the rest of his life. He finally recovered from his wounds by 1926, but the ordeal had disturbed his glandular system. The disorder slowed his metabolic rate, resulting in a lifelong condition of obesity. Thus he often became an object of ridicule for enemies. In 1927 Germany excused all political prisoners and Göring returned to his native land.

Göring receiving reports from plane crews during the war. (Reproduced by permission of AP/Wide World Photos)

A Change of Fortune

The Nazi party was gaining momentum by 1927, experiencing a great deal of support among the German people. Göring, who had not been invited to rejoin Hitler's staff, got a job selling BMW automobiles. Within a year, he was a successful businessman—a member of Berlin's social elite. Hitler, now aware of how to capitalize on Göring, selected him to head the ticket of the Nazi party in the 1928 elections. Although the party lost, Göring was able to prove his popularity. Hitler rewarded him with a handsome salary, and the Görings bought a large house in a prosperous district of Berlin.

During the next four years the Nazi party grew in political strength, and so did Göring. On January 29, 1933, Germany's president, Paul von Hindenburg, appointed Hitler chancellor. Göring convinced von Hindenburg that Hitler was the only man who could lead Germany out of the economic recession caused by the recent worldwide depression. His talent for persuasive speech made Göring the most important minister in Hitler's cabinet.

A political crisis required a new election to be held on March 5, 1933. The Nazis did well, but failed to earn a winning majority. On March 23, Göring demonstrated his political intelligence. Through elaborate political maneuvering, Göring had many of the Nazis' opponents arrested on questionable grounds. Their absence allowed the Nazis to drum up more than the two-thirds majority vote needed to place Hitler in charge of the government. In June a new law was decreed: "The [Nazi] Party constitutes the only political party in Germany." That same year, the former political police force was replaced by the Gestapo, or the Secret State Police. Thousands of Germans were arrested for being Jewish, Catholic, or for promoting opinions different from the Nazis'. The arrested groups were quarantined in concentration camps as "enemies of the state." Göring was held in contempt by the more brutish Nazis for his "squeamishness" when inflicting pain and suffering on others. His attempts to keep brutality out of the camps were unsuccessful. As his exposure to intense and brutish violence increased, Göring became numb to the practices of the Nazi soldiers throughout Germany.

Due to his passion for flying, Göring particularly enjoyed being Reichminister of Aviation. As head of the Luftwaffe, the German air force, he spent the years 1934 through 1936 strengthening the country's air power. By 1933 the Nazis maintained ultimate power over Germany. Hitler combined the office of president with that of chancellor, making himself head of state as well as commander-in-chief of the armed forces. Through his political maneuvering, Hitler was now dictator of Germany. Göring gathered his senior officers later that day, and all swore allegiance to Hitler.

Loss and Remarriage

Göring's wife, Carin, died in 1931 after a long illness, and in a northeast section of Berlin he built a grand mansion, named Carin Hall, in her honor. Göring, now a collector of fine art, furnished the home with priceless tapestries and paintings. By this time, he had begun sporting elaborate costumes, wearing rouge and expensive colognes. Beginning in 1933, Göring had a new companion, the German actress Emmy Sonnemann. The couple was married in 1935 at an elaborate ceremony attended by Hitler and other Nazi dignitaries. Emmy gave birth to their daughter, Edda, three years later.

Start of the War

In 1936 Hitler began planning for war, a secret which was quickly leaked to enemies. Hitler's aim was to consolidate all German-speaking territories under the Nazi flag. Göring, now second in command only to Hitler, was made head of economic matters. At the height of his powers in 1938 and 1939, Göring presided over the passage of legislation which reduced the freedom of German citizens, and destroyed the lives of millions of Jews.

In 1939 Germany attacked Poland, beginning World War II. After Germany's quick victory, Göring was treated as a hero. Germany's war machine made great gains with the fall of Holland, Belgium, and France in 1940. Hitler granted Göring the title of Reich Marshal and, in a speech, even referred to Göring as his successor.

Loss of Favor

Göring did not remain Hitler's right-hand man for long. During the course of World War II he fell into disfavor with Hitler over a variety of issues. As Hitler became unreasonable and increasingly ill-tempered, Göring grew disillusioned. When the Nazis started to lose ground in the Soviet Union, Hitler denied all responsibility. As head of the air force, Göring was blamed for the losses and he believed that his relationship with Hitler was deteriorating. He was also held responsible for the declining protection afforded by the Luftwaffe during the massive Allied bombing campaigns against German cities and industries. Hitler began to berate Göring and referred to him scornfully. Eventually, Göring assigned most of his duties regarding concentration camps and the Gestapo to various underlings.

By this time, Göring was pessimistic about the war and frightened about his family's fate if Germany lost. He continued to obey the orders of the führer, but avoided contact with the Nazi leadership as much as possible. He then spent most of his time at Carin Hall. When Hitler found out that Carin Hall was being protected by German paratroops, he ordered them to leave. Göring had his most precious possessions packed and taken to Bavaria. In February 1945, he and his aides left in a staff car, and had Carin Hall totally destroyed by dynamite.

Arrest and Imprisonment

Göring arrived in Obersalzberg, Bavaria, where he set up military headquarters. Hitler was wrongly informed by Göring's enemies that he had launched a coup d'etat. Hitler then stripped him of all his titles and had SS troops arrest Göring and his family at the castle where they were staying. In April 1945, Hitler committed suicide in order to avoid falling into the hands of Soviet troops who were closing in on his underground bunker. Göring, who by now had been freed, expressed regret that he would never have the chance to convince Hitler of his loyalty.

In May 1945, near the end of the war, Göring was arrested by the Allies. He still believed, however, that he would be able to charm his way back into a comfortable civilian life. At first he received special treatment, including fine food and wine, to encourage him to talk. He condemned Hitler, discussed Nazi policies and procedures at length, and did his best to make his own actions appear favorable to his Allied captors. He was soon placed in solitary confinement and treated as a common prisoner of war.

Göring's Testimony at Nuremberg

The courtroom was packed on March 13, 1946, the day Hermann Göring testified on his own behalf at the Nuremberg trials. During his testimony he was initially very nervous, indicative in his trembling hands. His voice gained strength and confidence with each question he answered. "He embellished his replies with [witty answers], attracting gales of laughter from the public in the courtroom, then subtly hushed the listeners with some throwaway self-incrimination of apparent sincerity," according to his biographer David Irving. Newspapermen in the courtroom were amazed by his brilliant performance on the stand. One prosecutor commented that it was evident why Göring had been so popular. One Nazi lawyer commented about him admiringly: "That Göring is quite a guy...."

Although arrogant, Göring handled himself very effectively against the U.S. prosecutor, smirking and making clever, sarcastic comments. The British prosecutor caused Göring to break out into a sweat when he asked why he had executed escaped British pilots. He questioned Göring's loyalty to Hitler in light of the atrocities ordered by Hitler. Proud of his own performance on the stand, Göring told his fellow defendants: "If you handle yourselves half as well as I did, you'll be doing all right." An attorney for one of the other defendants remarked: "Göring had nothing to lose. That's why he played the part to the very end—with [vigor] and shrewdness.... He won round after round against [the American] ... but he's as self-centered, vain, and pompous as ever."

In his final address to the Nuremberg court, Göring declared: "The German people trusted the Führer. Given his authoritarian direction of the state, [the people] had no influence on events. Ignorant of the crimes of which we know today, the people have fought with loyalty, self-sacrifice, and courage, and they have suffered too in this life-and-death struggle into which they were arbitrarily thrust. The German people are free from blame."

In 1946 the Allies put the Nazi criminals publicly on trial in Nuremberg, Germany. According to author Leonard Mosley, the Nuremberg Trials were meant "to draw a picture of Hitler's Germany in the fullest detail possible so that the German people themselves, and the rest of the world, could at least see what a horrendous spectacle it had been." Testifying at the trials, Göring tried to justify the rule of the Nazis, and surprised everyone with his intelligence and his masterful speaking skills. Nevertheless, the tribunal found "his guilt ... unique in its enormity" and sentenced him to death by hanging. Göring listened to the verdict stonefaced, but after returning to his cell he fought an emotional breakdown, asking to be left alone. Göring's written request to be executed by a firing squad, in the military tradition, was refused.

At around 11 p.m. on October 15, 1946, just a few hours before he was to be hanged, Göring swallowed a lethal dose of poison. He was found dead in his bed within minutes. How he procured the vial of poison remains a mystery. The next day, his body and those of the Nazi criminals who had been hanged the night before were burned in a crematorium. Their ashes were later poured into a muddy gutter.

Göring thought that he would be remembered as a hero in Germany. This never happened. Despite his many outstanding qualities, and his successful efforts to save a number of Jews who were family friends, he was guilty of moral cowardice. "All through his association with Adolf Hitler," author Leonard Mosley points out, "there were moments when he might have changed the course of National Socialism and Germany's race to [hell]—by arguing with and persuading the Führer to begin with, [and] by [seizing power from] him when that was no longer possible."

SOURCES

Books

Butler, Ewan, and Gordon Young, *The Life and Death of Hermann Göring,* Newton Abbot, Devon: David and Charles Publishers (New York), distributed in the United States by Sterling Publishing Company, 1989.

Hoyt, Edwin P., *Angels of Death: Göring's Luftwaffe,* Forge (New York), 1994.

Irving, David, *Göring: A Biography,* William Morrow (New York), 1989.

Lee, Asher, *Göring: Air Leader,* Hippocrene Books (New York), 1972.

Mosley, Leonard, *The Reich Marshal: A Biography of Hermann Göring,* Doubleday (Garden City, NY), 1974.

Shirer, William, *The Rise and Fall of the Third Reich: A History of Nazi Germany,* Simon & Schuster (New York), 1960.

Mendel Grossman

Born 1917
Poland
Died 1945
Germany (somewhere outside the
Konigs Wusterhausen work camp)

Photographer; recorded 10,000
photographs of life in Poland's Lódz
ghetto, where Jews were forcibly confined

"Such despair was never seen in the ghetto."

(Ghetto Fighters' House/USHMM Photo Archives)

Since the birth of photography in the 1800s, some of the most haunting pictures ever taken have been Mendel Grossman's photographs of life in Poland's Lódz ghetto, the crowded, walled section of the city where members of the Nazi party forced Jews to live in sub-human conditions. The pain-filled faces of children, mothers and fathers, and elderly people testify to the horrors imposed on their lives. The beauty of Grossman's work is in his ability to capture the fleeting glimpses of hope that sometimes remained in the hearts of his subjects. The work of Grossman eloquently defies those who deny that the Holocaust ever took place.

Youth in Lódz

Mendel Grossman was born into a family of Hasidic Jews in 1917. Hasidic Jews are extremely pious, religious people who adhere to the religious laws outlined in the Talmud and the Torah. Grossman was a short, slender young man who often wore an oversized topcoat. He walked slowly and carefully, and was frequently seen carrying a briefcase brimming over with papers. Young Grossman loved the theater, literature, and the arts. He was a painter, a sculptor, and a photographer. He took pictures of a wide variety of subjects, such as flowers, animals, landscapes, street scenes, and portraits. He often did paintings of these same types of subjects.

Why Were the Ghettos and Death Camps in Eastern Europe?

From their beginnings, the Nazis displayed, at their core, a hostility and severe hatred toward Jews. They blamed German Jewish industrialists for undermining German efforts to win World War I (1914–18). Adolf Hitler preached that the Jews were "parasites" on German society and that intermarriage with them poisoned the purity of German blood. Exactly when Adolf Hitler arrived at the *Endlösung* or "Final Solution"—the extermination of all European Jews—remains unclear. The first Polish ghetto was begun in 1939 in the town of Piotrkow. Next came the Lódz ghetto, wherein the second largest Jewish community in Poland was contained. By the end of 1940, ghettos were set up in almost all Polish towns that had significant Jewish populations. The Warsaw ghetto alone housed more than 400,000 people.

The ghettos were eventually emptied and their prisoners were sent to concentration camps. While concentration camps were spread throughout Europe, the major Nazi camps, whose primary purpose was the killing of their inhabitants, were located in eastern Europe. According to writer Barbara Rogasky, the three major reasons the Nazis set up ghettos and death camps in eastern Europe were: (1) because almost all of the Jews of Europe lived there; (2) the enormous land area and miles of forests separating communities allowed the Nazis to operate in secret; and (3) the Nazis, hoping that they would not meet much resistance among the local populations, wanted to take advantage of the longstanding anti-Jewish sentiment in eastern Europe.

During the 1930s, Grossman became especially interested in photographing humans on the move. His realized his interest in this particular type of photography while he was photographing members of a theatrical troupe who were performing in his home town of Lódz, Poland. The images he captured provided compelling behind-the-scenes images of the expressive faces and bodies of the actors and dancers. When he saw the pictures, he realized that he had an eye for capturing people in motion.

Photographs the Poor

Grossman then began to photograph people he encountered in the poorer sections of Lódz. He photographed men while they labored, children playing, and women preparing the family meals. His work became well known and respected. In 1939 a Jewish organization dedicated to promoting children's health hired him to take photographs of poor, but healthy, children in the neighborhoods of Lódz. That same year, Germany invaded Poland. Germany was already under the despotic rule of Adolf Hitler, notorious for his

anti-Semitic beliefs. He, and members of his Nazi party, believed that the Jews were a poisonous race that needed to be eliminated in order to maintain the purity of the German bloodline. After the invasion of Poland, the Nazis immediately began the persecution and systematic murder of Polish Jews. As the persecution of the Jews gathered momentum, Grossman's photographs were lost in the chaos. With the ever worsening conditions, Grossman realized his ultimate responsibility to his talent and to his people was to photograph them in their time of darkness.

Begins Recording Ghetto Life

The Lódz ghetto was a place where the Nazis forced Jews and other "undesirables" to live. Grossman brought his camera along as he moved into the ghetto. He captured on film images of the fear, suffering, and sickness of the ghetto inhabitants. In order to hide what he was doing, for he knew it was forbidden by the Nazi authorities, Grossman took a job in the photographic laboratory of the Lódz ghetto's department of statistics. He became aware of the vast amount of information about the ghetto

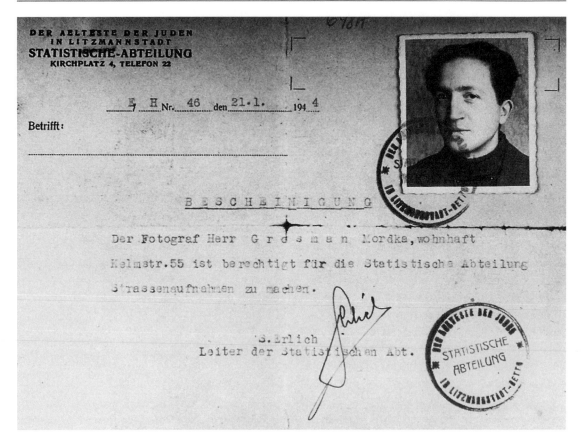

The permit issued to Mendel Grossman by the Statistical Division of the Lódz ghetto that allowed him to take photos. (YIVO Institute for Jewish Research)

that passed through the statistics office, since the Nazis kept track of all sorts of major and minor details about ghetto inhabitants. Grossman used this information to guide him to places and events especially worthy of being captured in pictures. Photography paper and chemicals were easily available at the laboratory, allowing Grossman to do his own developing. He took full advantage of the opportunity to photograph life in the ghetto.

Writer Arieh Ben-Menahem, whose essay entitled "Mendel Grossman—The Photographer of the Lodz Ghetto" appears in *With a Camera in the Ghetto: Mendel Grossman,* described the subjects of these photos. "There were children bloated with hunger … convoys of men and women condemned to death in the ovens of Chelmno [death camp] … public executions.…" Grossman shot one photo of a whole family wheeling a wagon of excrement through the streets. When Grossman requested permission to photograph the family, they responded: "Let it [the photo] remain for the future, let others know how humiliated we were." Ben-Menahem wrote: "He gave in to that urge

which motivated so many of the best of our [Jewish] people: to leave a record, to write down the events, to collect documents, to scratch a name on the wall of the prison cell, to write next to the name of the condemned the word vengeance."

Photographs Middle-Class Jews

Grossman was able to carry out his work partly because he had a bad heart, which prevented him from doing heavy physical labor. To avoid being observed and captured by the police, he hid his camera in his overcoat. To use it, he manipulated the camera through holes cut into the sleeves. At one point, prosperous Jews from other parts of Europe were brought to the Lódz ghetto. These people wore handsome coats and quality shoes, and carried suitcases stuffed with their personal possessions. They spoke an educated dialect and tried to bring to the ghetto, as much as possible, a higher quality of life. They also tried to avoid contact with other ghetto inhabitants. Grossman kept a pictorial record of the deterioration of these middle-class Jews. He recorded how they grew dirty and ill with ghetto diseases, and experienced physical and mental destruction. By the time they were forcefully loaded on the trains for the Chelmo death camp, the sad and painful stories of their lives were etched on their faces.

Decides to Proceed Despite Risks

After several unsuccessful attempts to photograph executions by the Nazis, Grossman succeeded in capturing the image of a young man who was hanged for trying to escape on a railroad train. When Grossman saw the power of this picture, he decided to abandon his more timid approach and risk all to take pictures that could most powerfully and painfully record the human suffering inflicted by the Nazis. As Ben-Menahem described: "....he climbed electric power posts to photograph a convoy of deportees on their way to the trains, he walked roofs, [and] climbed the steeple of a church that remained within the confines of the ghetto in order to photograph a change of guard at the barbed-wire fence."

Even though Grossman's own physical condition was becoming worse, he insisted on continuing his efforts. He photographed the Institute for Feather Cleaning. There, feathers from the stolen bedding of Jews on their way to the death camps were sorted and shipped to Germany for reuse by the Nazis. He photographed carts hauling off the corpses of Roma (more commonly called Gypsies) who had developed typhus (an intestinal disorder caused by living in unsanitary conditions) in their quarter of the ghetto. Grossman hid his negatives in circular tin cans, which grew in number daily. It was Grossman's desire, and that of almost all of the Jews in the ghetto, to record the horror of their daily lives for future generations to see.

Documents Those Exiled to Death Camps

The cruelty of the Nazis escalated in 1942 when the decision was made to send overwhelming numbers of people to Poland's death camps. Nazi authorities imposed a strict curfew, and over a five-day period, thousands of people were taken from their ghetto dwellings. In a diary written when he lived in the Lódz ghetto, Josef Zelkowicz describes the powerlessness of the ghetto-dwellers in trying to keep their loved ones from being carted off. He wrote: "It is to no avail that a child clutches its mother's neck with its two small hands.

It is to no avail that the father throws himself in front of the doorway like a slaughtered ox (saying only over my dead body will you take my child). It is to no avail that the old man clings to the cold walls with his gnarled [crooked] hands and begs, 'Let me die here in peace.'" Zelkowicz continues, "It is to no avail that the old woman falls on her knees, kissing the [policeman's] boots, and begs, 'I have grown-up grandchildren who are like you.' To no avail does the sick man bury his feverish head in the sweat-covered pillow and sob away his last tears...." These are the types of images that Mendel Grossman captured with his camera.

Photographs the Dead

In 1943, the Nazis forced a large number of the people living in the Lódz ghetto to leave the country. Those who tried to escape were shot, and soon the odor of rotting human flesh was overwhelming. Despite the peril, Grossman accompanied a group of grave diggers who were given permission to bury the bodies. He used his camera to photograph the mass grave. He took photos of corpses stored in a cemetery hall, marking each body with a number, so that their relatives could later determine where their loved ones were buried. (The numbers would show up on their grave markers.) Grave diggers lifted the head of each corpse so that Grossman could snap the image of the dead. They were people of all ages, with a variety of expressions frozen on their faces.

Uses Telescopic Lens

Grossman continued his photographic work until the great purge of the ghetto was completed. He returned to shooting the more placid images of daily life there. When another mass deportation of Jews started later in the year, friends warned him against taking pictures of the prisoners because of observant Nazi guards. It would take only one mistake for him to be found out. Despite the danger, Grossman persisted. He began to use a heavy, telescopic lens, made for him in a ghetto workshop, to photograph the large number of people being hauled away. Grossman was particularly interested in capturing the young people of the ghetto, with their youthful, hope-filled faces. Whenever possible he photographed the comfortable life of the Nazis running the ghetto, contrasting it with the horrible conditions of the people they ruled over.

Grossman was very generous in distributing his photographs to all in the ghetto who requested them. It was his hope that some would survive the war. He made many friends, and they did their best to help him accomplish his work, sometimes carrying his heavy satchel. He looked out for his friends, often taking them along to places where a little bit of food or warmth might be made available.

After four and one-half years of work, Grossman had amassed more than ten thousand negatives. In late 1944, when the Germans were close to defeat, Nazi headquarters issued an order to totally destroy the Lódz ghetto. Grossman knew that he must find somewhere to hide his negatives. He removed a portion of the window frame in his apartment, took out some bricks, and deposited a crate full of negatives inside the brick wall, then replaced the window frame. He could only hope that his vital negatives would be safe.

Ordered to German Work Camp

Grossman continued to take his photographs as the liquidation of the ghetto proceeded. He worked endlessly, taking pictures as the trains carried the prisoners off to unknown places. Grossman had already left the ghetto by the time Nazi officials realized what he had been doing. One of the last to leave the ghetto, he was sent to Konigs Wusterhausen work camp in Germany, his camera still intact and hidden under his coat. He continued to take pictures there, even though he could not develop and print them.

Shortly before the surrender of the Nazis in 1945, all the people confined in the German work camp with Grossman were ordered on a death march, an excruciating walk over great distances without much food or clothing. Exhausted by years of toil, his weak heart could not bear the strain of the march. He died on the road at age 32.

Negatives Retrieved Then Destroyed

After the end of World War II, Grossman's sister went to the ghetto and retrieved his photographs that were hidden in the wall. She sent them to Israel, where they were stored on a farm. During Israel's War of Independence in the late 1940s, they came into the possession of the Jews' Egyptian enemies and were destroyed. Most of the Grossman photos that remain today are those he had freely distributed to friends during their time in the Lódz ghetto. Nahman Sonnabend, a friend of Grossman's, was able to save some of the photographs, along with other documents, at the bottom of a well in the ghetto. This memorabilia can be seen at the Museum of the Holocaust in Israel and at the Ghetto Fighter's House in Israel.

SOURCES

Books

Adelson, Alan and Robert Lapides, ed., *Lódz Ghetto: Inside A Community Under Siege,* with an afterward by Geoffrey Hartman, annotations and bibliographical notes by Mark Web, Viking (New York), 1989.

Plank, Karl A., *Mother of the Wire Fence: Inside and Outside the Holocaust,* Westminster John Knox Press (Louisville, KY), 1994.

Rogasky, Barbara, *Smoke and Ashes: The Story of the Holocaust,* Holiday House (New York), 1988.

Szner, Zvi and Alexander Sened, eds., *With a Camera in the Ghetto: Mendel Grossman,* Schocken Books (New York), 1977.

Leslie Richard Groves

An officer in the U.S. Army Corps of Engineers, Leslie Groves directed the Manhattan Project during World War II. Although Groves's style of leadership provoked controversy, his ability to solve problems and to make difficult decisions at the risk of jeopardizing his own reputation was vital to the success of the program. In 1970 President Richard M. Nixon honored Groves for his work by giving him the Atomic Pioneers Award.

Born August 17, 1896
    Albany, New York, United States
Died July 14, 1970
    Washington, D.C., United States

Army officer; civil engineer

"When in doubt, act."

Coordinates Military Construction

Leslie Richard Groves was born in Albany, New York, on August 17, 1896, the son of Leslie Richard Groves, a chaplain in the U.S. Army, and Gwen Griffith Groves. In light of his father's army career, Groves could call no one place home. He entered the University of Washington in 1913 while his father was stationed at a post in Seattle. He then transferred to the Massachusetts Institute of Technology the following year, and in 1916 gained an appointment to the U.S. Military Academy at West Point. In November 1918 Groves graduated, fourth in his class, under an accelerated program instituted during World War I (1914–1918).

Commissioned too late to see combat in France during World War I, Groves joined the Army Corps of Engineers as a second lieutenant and completed basic and civil engineering courses

(Reproduced by permission of AP/Wide World Photos)

at the Engineer School at Camp Humphreys (later renamed Fort Belvoir), Virginia. In 1922 he married Grace Wilson and the couple eventually had two children. Between 1921 and 1925 Groves served at various posts, including Fort Worden in Washington, the Presidio in San Francisco, and Schofield Barracks in Honolulu. Afterward he became assistant to the district engineer in Galveston, Texas, and directed the opening of the silted-up harbor at Port Isabel.

He then served in Nicaragua surveying possible sites for a new canal. From 1931 to 1935 Groves worked in Washington, D.C., where he was attached to the Military Supply Division, the army agency that developed new equipment, from jack hammers to searchlights. He was promoted to captain in 1934 and made chief of the division. Over the next five years Groves, who was known as Richard or Dick to acquaintances, served with the Missouri River Division of the Corps of Engineers (1936–1938) and studied at both the Command and General Staff School (1935–1936) and the Army War College (1938–1939). Assigned in 1939 to the General Staff, Groves was promoted to major in July 1940 and four months later to lieutenant colonel (temporary). With a military defense buildup well underway by 1941, the army's construction expenditures were averaging in excess of $500 million monthly. Groves was named deputy chief of construction with a mandate to complete dozens of new camps and other army facilities throughout the United States. One of his many responsibilities was supervising the building of the Pentagon.

Heads Manhattan Project

By the time the United States entered World War II, important research on various aspects of nuclear fission had been ongoing at several major universities and other locations for more than a year. Enough was known by 1942 for authorities to believe that a nuclear weapon might be developed before the end of 1944. Since much of the nuclear program would involve immense construction tasks, some calling for unprecedented technical sophistication, the Army was given overall responsibility for the project. To direct the program, a new office, named the Manhattan Engineering District (later called the Manhattan Project), was established in Washington, D.C. Colonel James Marshall, the first head of the Manhattan District, began the search for sites for the various new facilities that would be needed. Once it became evident

that the army's task would be far greater than anticipated, Groves was given authority over the Manhattan District in September 1942 and promoted to brigadier general.

Groves soon put the stamp of his forceful, albeit abrasive, personality on the project. For instance, there was still considerable doubt over which of several enrichment technologies might be best suited for the task of making available uranium of sufficient quality for nuclear weaponry. Groves decided to pursue several promising options, including both gaseous diffusion and electromagnetic separation methods as well as thermal diffusion. He also ordered the construction of giant nuclear reactors where plutonium would be produced. "When in doubt, act," he reasoned.

Unlike the cautious Colonel Marshall, Groves did not hesitate in purchasing gigantic tracts of land at Oak Ridge, Tennessee, and Hanford, Washington, for the construction of these facilities and for town sites that would house the thousands of civilians and military personnel required to build and operate them. He considered services, such as schools, that would be needed for the children of residents. To do the work, Groves contracted with hundreds of firms, including such giants as du Pont, Union Carbide, and Eastman Kodak. Eventually more than 125,000 people would work under the aegis of the Manhattan Engineering District. Another of the Manhattan District's new facilities was the bomb laboratory at Los Alamos, New Mexico. This would be the site of the arduous work of designing and assembling the world's first nuclear bombs.

Several scientists resented Groves's hard-driving methods and emphasis on security. But the collaboration between Groves and J. Robert Oppenheimer, the theoretical physicist he chose to direct the laboratory, proved fruitful. Groves secured for Oppenheimer the personnel, equipment, and materials needed while the scientist guided work at the laboratory. Some formidable problems about the final design of the two types of atom bombs under development remained to be solved as 1945 began. By the spring, significant progress had been made, especially on the more complicated but more promising implosion bomb. Both Oppenheimer and Groves agreed that "the gadget," the name given to the atom bomb by project insiders, should be employed in combat. As chair of the target committee, Groves had a major voice in determining the timing and circumstances of the use of the A-bomb against Japan.

Vannevar Bush Mobilizes Scientists for War Effort

Vannevar Bush (1890–1974) was the recipient of more than twenty awards for his inventions and contributions to science; he was awarded twenty honorary degrees. Following a career as a professor and administrator at the Massachusetts Institute of Technology (MIT), in 1939 Bush was named president of the Carnegie Institution in Washington, D.C., and chairman of the National Advisory Committee for Aeronautics. Though he devoted much of his energy to the improvement of human life through his inventions, he was perhaps best known for his work on the atomic bomb and as director of the Office of Scientific Research and Development (OSRD) during World War II. It was Bush who first conceived the idea of a "system of national support for basic scientific research," and he is credited with its establishment.

In June 1940, in the wake of Hitler's advances in Europe, Bush feared the prospect that the Germans had begun working on atomic weapons and conferred with U.S. President Franklin D. Roosevelt about the possibility of a unified national effort to pool the energies and resources of America's scientists. Bush, and the presidents of the Massachusetts Institute of Technology (MIT), Harvard, and the National Academy of Sciences (Karl Compton, James B. Conant, and Frank B. Jewett, respectively), lobbied Roosevelt to create a federal agency to oversee scientific development and keep it out of the hands of politicians. Roosevelt agreed to form the National Defense Research Committee (NDRC) on June 27, 1940, and Bush became its chairman. This civilian organization of scientists and engineers was to develop new weapons for the military as a supplement to the military's own wartime research. Many politicians and military men opposed the NDRC, viewing it as a group of outsiders who had cornered the authority and money for defense research, but Roosevelt expanded this committee after a year, adding an Advisory Council and Committee on Medical Research, the Office of Field Service, the Scientific Personnel Office, and a liaison office to help coordinate scientific exchange among the Allies. The OSRD was created, and Bush was installed as its director, a post which he held for six years.

Through this office, Bush coordinated a vast network of industrial and academic research geared toward wartime science, including the early work conducted on the atomic bomb. When concern over the war in the Pacific reached its zenith, Bush discussed the use of the bomb and its effects with President Harry S Truman. Bush was scientific adviser to both Roosevelt and Truman, and dealt directly with Churchill and British scientists during the war. He always believed scientific research to be in the best interests of democracy and a free America. Under his leadership, more than 30,000 scientists worked together to upgrade America's defense system, and Bush is personally credited with advancements in the uses of radar, the proximity fuse, fire control mechanisms, and amphibious vehicles. Many medical advances also resulted from OSRD efforts, including antimalarial drugs, blood substitutes, and the large scale production of penicillin. After World War II, Bush played an important role in the federal government's financial support of basic research, including the establishment of the National Science Foundation.

The secrecy that cloaked the Manhattan Project was lifted only after the first bomb had actually been dropped on Hiroshima on August 6, 1945. Groves inevitably became the center of a flurry of media attention. After the war, he advocated the buildup of a stockpile of nuclear weapons ready to use should war develop between the United States and the Soviet Union. He remained head of the Manhattan Project until the end of 1946, when authority over the nuclear program was transferred to the newly created Atomic Energy Commission. Groves retired from the army in 1948 and became vice president of research and development at Remington Rand, where he was responsible for developing the UNIVAC computer. Groves retired in 1961. He died in Washington, D.C., on July 14, 1970. According to Los Alamos scientist Robert Bacher, Groves was "a genius at getting things done under very adverse circumstances."

The papers of Leslie Groves are at both the National Archives in Washington, D.C.—where they are accessioned to the Office of the Commanding General File—and at the Hoover Institution in Stanford, California. The work of the Manhattan Project was later dramatized in the film *The Beginning of the End* in 1947. In the movie, the role of Groves is played by Brian Donlevy. In addition, Groves wrote his recollections about the project in *Now It Can Be Told: The Story of the Manhattan Project* (1962).

SOURCES

Books

Gerber, Michele Stenehjem, *On the Home Front: The Cold War Legacy of the Hanford Nuclear Site,* University of Nebraska Press (Lincoln, NE), 1992.

Groves, Leslie, *Now It Can Be Told: The Story of the Manhattan Project,* new introduction by Edward Teller, Da Capo Press (New York), 1962.

Herken, Gregg, *The Winning Weapon: The Atomic Bomb in the Cold War, 1945–1950,* Princeton University Press (Princeton, NJ), 1981.

Lawren, William, *The General and the Bomb: A Biography of General Leslie R. Groves, Director of the Manhattan Project,* Dodd, Mead (New York), 1988.

Rhodes, Richard, *The Making of the Atom Bomb,* Simon & Schuster (New York), 1986.

Herschel Grynszpan

Born March 28, 1921
     Hannover, Germany
Died 1942 or 1943 (?)
     Germany

Jewish assassin whose shooting of a German official was used as the Nazis' official excuse for *Kristallnacht*

"Again and again I asked myself: 'What have we done to deserve such a fate?'"

Seventeen-year-old Herschel Grynszpan was a young Jewish man living illegally in Paris, France, when he learned of his family's deportation from their German home by the Nazi party. As his family sought refuge in Poland, Grynszpan retaliated by killing a minor German official stationed in Paris. Although large-scale persecution of German Jews was already planned by the Nazis, they used the assassination as their excuse for *Kristallnacht* (also known as "Crystal Night" or the "Night of Broken Glass"). The event was named for all of the broken glass scattered on the streets as the Nazis vandalized Jewish shops and burned synagogues. Although reports vary, the United States Holocaust Memorial Museum lists the damage done by the Nazis as follows. "In two days, over 1,000 synagogues were burned, 7,000 Jewish businesses were trashed and looted, dozens of Jewish people were killed, and Jewish cemeteries, hospitals, schools, and homes were looted while police and fire brigades stood by.... The morning after the pogroms 30,000 German Jewish men were arrested for the 'crime' of being Jewish and sent to concentration camps, where hundreds of them perished."

A Childhood in Poverty

Herschel Grynszpan was born in 1921, the sixth of eight children born to Sendel Siegmung and Rifka Silberberg Grynszpan. Herschel, an older

(Photograph by Morris Rosen, courtesy of USHMM Photo Archives)

brother, Mordechai Eliese (Marcus), and an older sister, Ester Beile (Berta), were the only three of the eight children who survived past childhood. Three other children were stillborn, one died of scarlet fever, and one died in an accident. Both of Herschel's parents were born in Poland. They fled the country in 1911, a year after they were married, because of rising anti-Semitic sentiments. They settled in Hannover, Germany, where Grynszpan's father opened a tailoring shop in an extremely poor and undesirable area of the city. For years they barely made ends meet. When Germany lost World War I in 1918, the country was forced to pay huge penalties to the victors of the war. The poor economic conditions worsened as the worldwide depression began in 1929. The elder Grynszpan was forced to give up his tailor shop and live mainly on welfare.

Grynszpan attended a public school until he was fourteen years old. His teachers considered him to be an intelligent young man, but lacking in motivation. He was considered rather surly, and despite his small physical stature (by the age of seventeen he was only five feet two inches tall and weighed one hundred pounds), he often instigated fights. He never received a diploma and later complained that his teachers had no interest in Jewish students, treating them as "outcasts." After leaving public school, he studied Hebrew for a year.

As Nazi leader Adolf Hitler established his dictatorship of Germany in 1933, he promised to reestablish Germany as the great world power it had been before the loss of World War I. He blamed the loss of that war on the Jews, claiming they were a "poisonous" race. Hitler declared that he would rid Europe of all Jews and win back the land lost by Germany in World War I. To succeed in these plans, Hitler began to build up the German army. This act was a direct violation of the Treaty of Versailles, the official agreement that ended World War I. Under Hitler's leadership, the economic situation in Germany began to improve, and Sendel Grynszpan was able to reopen his tailor shop.

For a while the Grynszpan family lived in relative comfort. By 1936 the comfort level of all Jews dramatically decreased as Nazi restrictions against German Jews began to take effect. These restrictions robbed virtually all rights from Jewish people, such as the right to own businesses. The family was once again reduced to extreme poverty. Although his siblings found work, Grynszpan did not seem willing or interested in doing so. He said no one would hire him because he was Jewish.

Leaves Germany

One day while at the synagogue, Grynszpan met an elderly man who told him to get out of Germany. "A boy like you can't stay here under such conditions. In Germany, a Jew is not a man, but is treated like a dog," the man said. Soon thereafter Grynszpan went to live with an aunt and uncle in Paris, who promised to teach him a trade and perhaps even adopt him. Complications quickly arose as Grynszpan tried to acquire travel papers. Although he had been born in Germany, he was a Polish citizen. Grynszpan finally left Germany by entering France illegally in late 1936. This illegal entry was later to cause him nightmarish problems. In Paris, Grynszpan lived with his Uncle Abraham, a tailor, and his Aunt Chawa. They were a relatively poor couple who nevertheless made Grynszpan welcome and provided him with spending money.

Grynszpan entertained himself by going to dances and movies, and by hanging out at a local coffee house. Again, he avoided looking for work because, he later wrote, "I didn't want to put myself in an illegal situation by working as an illegal immigrant." Grynszpan's aunt and uncle finally grew tired of supporting him. It was time for Grynszpan to return to Germany. French authorities had learned of his illegal entry into the country and ordered him to leave, but German authorities said he was not welcome in Germany. As a result, Grynszpan was forced to go into hiding.

The News from Germany

By 1937 the situation for Jews in Germany was growing increasingly worse. Moreover, Hitler decided in 1938 that all Jews in Germany who held Polish citizenship—some 15,000 to 17,000 people including the Grynszpan family—were to be deported back to Poland. The Polish government did not want these Jews either, and legislation was passed in Poland revoking the passports of all citizens who had lived out of the country for more than five years. Four days before that law went into effect, SS head Heinrich Himmler ordered that all Polish Jews in Germany should be rounded up and moved out. The SS, originally formed to act as bodyguards for Hitler, was now acting as a private, and brutal, police force.

Without warning, on a freezing and rainy October night, German police seized the Polish Jews. Herded into boxcars, they were taken across

The cable message that was sent to Berlin along with Grynszpan's photograph immediately after vom Rath's assassination. (Photograph by Morris Rosen, courtesy of USHMM Photo Archives)

the border and dumped into Poland. Each person was only allowed to carry one piece of luggage and a very small amount of money. They were left there without food or shelter. Grynszpan, who was already in a terrible predicament of his own, received a postcard from his sister on November 3, 1938. She wrote in part: "You have undoubtedly heard of our great misfortune.…We had to leave Germany before October 29.… I packed a valise [suitcase] with the most necessary clothes.… That is all I could save. We don't have a cent." Grynszpan's father later told his family's story at the trial of Nazi official Adolf Eichmann: "Finally we reached the border. We crossed it. The women went first because they began firing at us. The Poles had no idea why we were there or why there

were so many of us.…They saw that we were all Polish citizens—we had special passports and they decided to let us into Poland.… [We] were very hungry … they threw bread.… Then I wrote a letter to my son Herschel in Paris."

When he received the letter, Grynszpan decided to act. Although he knew nothing about weapons, he was able to buy a small handgun at a neighborhood shop. On November 7, 1938, he proceeded to the German embassy and asked to speak to the ambassador, claiming he had a secret document to hand over. He was instead directed to the office of a minor official, twenty-nine-year-old Ernst vom Rath. When vom Rath asked to see the secret document, Grynszpan cried: "You are a

Did Grynszpan Perform a Service?

Author Gerald Schwab was fourteen years old when he witnessed *Kristallnacht.* His father was arrested and spent five weeks in a concentration camp. Soon after his father's release, the family moved to the United States. In 1946 Schwab was asked to serve as a translator at the International War Crimes Tribunal in Nuremberg, Germany, where Nazi leaders were tried for their crimes against humanity.

While he was in Berlin, Schwab became interested in the case of Herschel Grynszpan, later publishing a biography of him. In his book, Schwab suggested that even though hundreds of Jews died as a result of Grynszpan's deed, many more lives were indirectly saved. The reason, he wrote, was that "many Jews who until that point [Crystal Night] had lived in the hope that Nazism would wither away or become more tolerant, suddenly found themselves face to face with another reality. They arrived at the realization that this evil was here to stay and that the conditions of Jews under Nazi domination could only get worse."

As a result, between 1933 and 1938, about 200,000 Jews left Germany, an action that saved their lives. Others argue, however, that Grynszpan's actions had no effect—that *Kristallnacht* would have happened with or without him.

filthy kraut [a slang word for a German] and here in the name of twelve thousand persecuted Jews, is your document!" He then drew his small weapon from his pocket and shot vom Rath five times.

To Grynszpan's horror, vom Rath did not die immediately. Instead, he called for help while Grynszpan stood and watched. When the police came, Grynszpan calmly surrendered. He told the police: "I've just shot a man in his office. I do not regret it. I did it to avenge my parents, who are living in misery...."

Kristallnacht

The next day Hitler was just leaving a party when his aide Joseph Goebbels informed him of the shooting of vom Rath, who later died on November 9. Hitler immediately promoted vom Rath, so the world would believe that Grynszpan had assassinated an important German official. Hitler saw the shooting not as the action of a desperate young man, but as a conspiracy against Germany by the entire Jewish race. For the Nazis, vom Rath's death was the perfect opportunity to stage an act of mass revenge against the Jews.

An order went out that read, in part: "Actions against the Jews and in particular against their synagogues will occur in a short time in all of Germany....The seizure of some twenty to thirty thousand Jews ... is to be prepared. Wealthy Jews above all are to be chosen." The order made it permissible to take money and goods from these individuals to be used by the Nazis. Thus, the Nazis launched the pogrom that came to be called *Kristallnacht,* or the "Night of Broken Glass." They vandalized Jewish businesses and synagogues, smashing doors and windows. Many Jews were rounded up and deported to concentration camps. Some were killed. The name *Kristallnacht* was in reference to the glow created by the broken glass.

Back in Paris....

French authorities were horrified by the shooting. French-German relations were already strained due to rumors of Germany's intended invasion of France. News of the shooting and its aftermath, *Kristallnacht,* spread around the world. Grynszpan, too, was horrified to learn that his act had apparently triggered the Germans' attack against the Jews. In the United States, fear that Grynszpan would be lynched led to the establishment of a fund to cover his legal fees. Preparations began for an elaborate trial that would be attended by journalists from all the major world newspapers. Grynszpan was placed in a relatively comfortable prison for young offenders. He began to keep a journal, enjoying his newfound celebrity status. "For the first time in his life, he felt important," according to authors Anthony Read and David Fisher.

The trial was postponed by a seemingly endless string of delays. Grynszpan's lawyers were unsure how to handle his case. If they presented him as a "boy avenger attacking a brutal regime," more Jews in Germany might suffer at the hands of the Nazis. Despite various suggestions by his legal team, Grynszpan was unwilling to heed any of their advice. He began to write letters to famous people complaining about his situation—including one to Hitler himself.

In September 1939, Hitler invaded Poland, beginning World War II. The Nazi war machine continued across Europe, poised for attack on the border of France in May 1940. Meanwhile, Grynszpan sat in jail. France surrendered to Germany on June 17, 1940. Uncertain what to do with Grynszpan, and afraid of angering the conquering Germans by seeming to protect him, French prison authorities released him. According to Read and Fisher: "Thus began what must be one of the most remarkable [wanderings] in [prison] history, as Herschel journeyed across France from prison to prison, from police station to police station, desperately seeking some jail that would take him in, some cell where he could be safely locked up" and hidden from the Nazis. He made no attempt to escape or save himself.

Even though they were preoccupied by a major war, the Germans had not forgotten about Grynszpan. Under the terms of the agreement signed by France and Germany, France would "surrender on demand" anyone the Germans asked for, and they asked for Grynszpan. On July 18, 1940, France handed the hapless Grynszpan over to the Germans. He was taken to a concentration camp near Berlin, Germany. The Nazis prepared to put him on trial for murder.

Grynszpan had spent enough time in jail that he was no longer a naive young man. He concocted a story, saying he had homosexual relations with vom Rath, who in return promised that Grynszpan's parents would not be deported to Poland. When they were deported despite the promise, Grynszpan said, he killed vom Rath. The Nazis were not at all pleased at the possibility of such a story coming out at trial. If vom Rath was shown to the world as a seducer of a young boy, it would be very embarrassing to the Nazis, especially after he had been buried with a hero's funeral. The trial was postponed until at least late 1942. Then Grynszpan simply disappeared. What happened to him is unknown, but it is unlikely he survived. His official date of death was later given as May 8, 1945, V-E Day—the day Germany surrendered in Europe.

SOURCES

Books

Imonti, Felix, and Miyoko Imonti, *Violent Justice: How Three Assassins Fought to Free Europe's Jews*, Prometheus Books (Amherst, NY), 1994.

Marino, Andy, *Herschel: The Boy Who Started World War II*, Faber and Faber (Boston), 1997.

Read, Anthony, and David Fisher, *Kristallnacht: The Nazi Night of Terror*, Times Books (New York), 1989.

Schwab, Gerald, *The Day the Holocaust Began: The Odyssey of Herschel Grynszpan*, Praeger (New York), 1990.

Thalman, Rita, and Emmanuel Feinermann, *Crystal Night: 9–10 November 1938*, translated from the French by Gilles Cremonesi, Thames and Hudson (London), 1974.

Odette Marie Celine Hallowes

Born April 28, 1912
Amiens, France
Died March 13, 1995
Walton-on-Thames, England

Radio operator; homemaker; spy for
Great Britain during World War II

*"I think the Germans are very obedient and
very gullible. Their tragedy—and
Europe's—is that they gladly allow
themselves to be hoodwinked into
believing evil to be good."*

There was a time when being a woman, especially the mother of three young children, exempted her from risking her safety in order to aid her country in wartime. For Odette Marie Celine Hallowes, duty and love of her native country, France, and her adopted country, England, compelled her to get involved. Even while in prison, subjected to fear, humiliation and torture, she conducted herself with dignity and honor.

A Difficult Childhood

Odette Marie Celine Hallowes (who married three times and was also known as Odette Marie Sansom and Odette Marie Sansom Churchill) was born Odette Marie Celine Brailly in 1912. She was the daughter of a French soldier, Gaston Brailly, and his wife, Yvonne. The family was Catholic and lived in Amiens, France. When Hallowes was only two years old, her father was killed by an exploding German shell while trying to help his wounded comrades during the first year of World War I (1914–18). Hallowes was a quiet child who loved horses and classical music. She was strongly influenced by her paternal grandmother, a patriotic woman who marched the family to the cemetery every Sunday to place flowers on the grave of her only son. Just before her eighth birthday, Hallowes was struck by temporary blindness, a condition that reversed itself after two years. Later in her childhood she was afflicted with rheumatic fever, an infectious disease causing fever and swollen joints, which left her partially paralyzed. Herbal treatments reportedly helped her regain her health. When her health improved, the young girl attended the local Catholic school until her mother decided to relocate the family to the large village of Sain Sens, France. In 1926, when Hallowes was fourteen, the family moved again, this time to the city of Boulogne, on the French coast.

War and an Invitation to Join "The Firm"

Hallowes completed her Catholic high school education and, in 1930, met Roy Sansom, an Englishman and old friend of the family. One year later they were married at a church in Boulogne. Their first daughter, Francoise, was born in 1932. Soon after, the family of three sailed across the English Channel to make their home in London, England. A second daughter, Lily, was born in 1934, and a third daughter, Marianne, was born two years later. The Sansom family lived in London until October 1940. By then Great Britain had been at war with Germany for a little more than a year following the German attack on Poland. Germany, under the leadership of dictator Adolf Hitler, planned to add to Germany's might by taking over Europe. The principal ingredient in Hitler's plan was the destruction of the Jewish people. Hitler was very adamant in his hatred of the Jews, as were his followers in the Nazi party. When Nazi bombing raids over London became frequent, Hallowes and her daughters took rooms at a little cottage in Devon, just a mile from her mother-in-law's. For a while, they were able to enjoy the quiet and security of country living.

In 1940 the British government was searching for photographs outlining the terrain of sites in France that might be useful to them in planning military operations against the Nazis. A request went out to the British people to report to a specific governmental office if they could provide such photos. Hallowes complied. After having her background checked, and being interviewed in great detail by military officials, she was invited to join "The Firm," which was part of the Special Operations Executive, or SOE. This was an organization of British officers who worked closely with French patriots. According to writer Jerrard Tickell: "The purpose of 'the Firm' was to organize and train a secret army in France, to supply this army with British weapons—and to teach them how to use

The Maquis

The Maquis was a name given to the group of young French citizens who, beginning in the autumn of 1942, hid in the forests and mountains of France to avoid being forced to work for Germany after the Nazis occupied France. Only a very small number of women were allowed to be in the Maquis. The word *maquis* referred to brushwood on the French island of Corsica, which resistance workers in another war used to hide behind. Members of the Maquis, armed and well trained, were successful in thwarting the Nazis following the landing of the Allies at Normandy, France, in 1944, and later on the French Riviera.

them—*when the time came.*" The organization kept in communication with England and disrupted Nazi plans in every way possible. The captain who recruited Hallowes said that, after examining her in detail, he believed she knew the "soft spots" of the German soul by reason and by instinct, and that she had an obvious singleness of purpose in defeating the enemy. She questioned whether she had sufficient knowledge and skill to perform the necessary tasks and wondered how she could hide what she was doing from her friends and family. The captain supplied her an alibi; she could say she was simply joining an organization of women who drove senior officers around and made themselves useful in various ways.

Begins Spy Duties

After much thought, Hallowes agreed to participate. She placed her three daughters in the care of nuns at a convent school and began her training as a radio operator. She also learned how to assume a new identity, concoct a flawless cover story, and perform other skills necessary for intelligence work. One of her instructors warned her about the dangers of being a spy: "It will be physically hard [and] mentally exhausting for you will be living a gigantic lie or series of lies, for months on end. And if you slip up and get caught, we can do little to save you." Small, dark-haired Hallowes was thirty years old in October 1942 when she assumed the identity of "Celine" and parachuted into France. She soon made contact with her team leader, Captain Peter Morland Churchill (no relation to British Prime Minister Winston Churchill). His job was to organize the delivery of supplies to French Resistance groups in the area. The French Resistance, a group of patriots, was trying to weaken Germany's army in France.

Hallowes agreed to assist Churchill while her own mission was still in the planning stage. Soon Churchill had convinced his superiors to let her stay and help him on a long-term basis. Hallowes was put to work carrying information. A bright, determined person, she was especially good at arranging pick-ups of secret agents and ammunition drops by plane. Her greatest contribution was supervising a major ammunition drop to members of the French Resistance who were in hiding in the mountains above the French Mediterranean coast.

Intrigue, Capture, and Torture

From February to mid-April, 1943, Churchill was called back to London to consult with his superiors. Upon his return he was disturbed to learn that Hallowes had been contacted by a German officer who had recently arrested one of their colleagues in Paris, France. The officer, Lieutenant Bleicher, had convinced an SOE colleague that he had information about negotiations between German anti-Hitler groups and the Allies. Bleicher had said that he needed only to make contact with London, and it was for this reason that the colleague had put him in contact with Hallowes. Upon hearing about the events that occurred while he was gone, Churchill decided that both he and Hallowes had to get away at once. However, before they could escape, Bleicher took them both into custody. After a few weeks in the local prison, they were taken to larger facilities in Fresnes, France, for interrogation. On the way they agreed to pretend that they were a married couple in hopes of diverting suspicion. After interrogation and torture, Churchill was transferred to a prison camp in Germany, where he stayed until it was liberated at the end of the war.

Hallowes was imprisoned for almost two years and was sent to the Ravensbrück concentration camp. She was tortured with red-hot irons and had all of her toenails pulled out. Neither torture nor starvation succeeded in getting her to reveal any secrets. At one point, one of her captors told Hallowes she was going to be shot because she had engaged in spying and disruption of Nazi plans, and because she was a Frenchwoman (they believed) married to an Englishman. This violated the Nazi policy that people should only marry within their same ethnic group. "You must take your pick of the counts," she replied. "I can die only once."

Stolen Moments

Hallowes and Churchill managed to communicate in prison. Occasionally Hallowes smuggled messages to her "husband" Churchill. Once Bleicher arranged a simultaneous interrogation of the two and they had an opportunity to converse privately for a brief time. On another occasion the clever Hallowes persuaded a Nazi captain to fingerprint them both at the same time. During the mass fingerprinting of seventy prisoners, they had a chance to talk together for three hours. While imprisoned, Hallowes made the acquaintance of several other female resistance workers who had been caught. They conversed when possible and gave one another messages to carry back to loved ones in the event that any of them survived the war.

Knowing that the war was lost for Germany, Adolf Hitler committed suicide on April 30, 1945. With the fall of the German capital of Berlin shortly thereafter, and the surrender of Italy, Germany's ally, it became clear that the war in Europe could only last a few more days. Grand Admiral Karl Dönitz became Hitler's successor. The surrender of Germany, authorized by Dönitz, took place on May 8, 1945. With the war at an end, Hallowes was released and reunited with her family in Great Britain. She personally delivered the messages of her deceased prison mates to their loved ones, as she had promised. Along with several of her fallen comrades, Hallowes was awarded the George Cross, a national honor given for bravery. The citation that went along with the cross said, in part, that she "drew [Nazi] attention from her commanding officer onto herself, saying that he had only come to France on her insistence. She took full responsibility and agreed that it should be herself and not her commanding officer who should be shot. By this action she caused [her captors] to cease paying attention to [him] after only two interrogations."

The British also honored Hallowes for refusing to divulge the whereabouts of a fellow radio operator, thereby saving his life. This she did despite extreme torture. "During the period of her two years in which she was in enemy hands," the citation read, "she displayed courage, endurance and self-sacrifice of the highest possible order." Hallowes's first husband, Roy Sansom, had died, and after World War II, in an interesting turn of events, Odette Hallowes and Peter Churchill, who had once pretended to be a couple, were married in real life. Apparently their shared war experiences had forged a close bond between them, though eventually they divorced. After their divorce in 1956, she married a wine merchant named Geoffrey Hallowes, who had also served (in a different division) in the SOE. She was married to him for thirty years until her death at age eighty-two in 1995.

SOURCES

Books

Churchill, Peter, *Duel of Wits,* Putnam, 1953.

Hoehling, A. A., *Women Who Spied,* Dodd, Mead and Co., 1967.

Tickell, Jerrard, *Odette: The Story of a British Agent,* Chapman, 1949.

Rudolf Hess

Born April 26, 1894
Alexandria, Egypt
Died August 17, 1987
Spandau Prison, Berlin, Germany

Soldier; pilot; deputy führer

"We believe that the Führer [Hitler] is obeying a higher call to fashion German history. There can be no criticism of this belief."

R udolf Hess, loyal member of German dictator Adolf Hitler's inner circle, is best known for his surprise airplane flight to Scotland in 1941. He claimed to have been sent by Hitler, charged with orders to make peace with the British by convincing them to fight with Germany against the Soviet Union. He was branded a madman and imprisoned by the British. After the war, he was taken from his British prison, tried by the victorious Allies, and sentenced to life imprisonment in Germany. He was still in prison when he died in 1987. Some called his death suicide; others called it murder.

Childhood in Egypt

Rudolf Hess was born in 1894, the first of three children of Friedrich and Clara Muench Hess. A brother, Alfred, was born in 1897; his sister, Margarete, was born in 1908. Hess's grandfather, who came from the German state of Bavaria, had started the family import-export business in Egypt. By the time Hess was born, his father had become wealthy from the business. The family lived in luxury, with a large home in Egypt and a summer home in Germany. Hess's father was a strict and formal man. His children did not speak to him unless spoken to first. This story about the senior Hess, told by authors Roger Manvell and Heinrich Fraenkel, illustrates the power he held over the

(Reproduced by permission of AP/Wide World Photos)

Hess greets Hitler at a Nazi conference in Nuremberg, Germany. (Reproduced by permission of AP/Wide World Photos)

Rudolf Hess, who served as deputy führer to Adolf Hitler, addresses a crowd. The Nazi deputy made a mysterious flight to England early in the war to convince Great Britain to side with Germany. His efforts proved unsuccessful. (Reproduced by permission of Archive Photos, Inc.)

household: "'I am not a goat,' he said once when served a salad, and no salad ever appeared again."

As was the German custom, Friedrich Hess oversaw the boys' education and directed their career choices. At the age of six, Hess attended a German school in Egypt. At age fourteen, he was sent to a Protestant boarding school in Germany. His teachers found him a "responsive and intelligent" young man. He was especially interested in German history, astronomy, physics, engineering, and mathematics. After three years at the boarding school, he requested permission to attend college. Instead, his father enrolled him in a Swiss business school to prepare him to take over the family company.

Young Manhood

Hess spent a year at business school and then signed on as a trainee at a German export house. Hess was rescued from an unwanted career in business by the start of World War I in 1914. He immediately volunteered for the German army. He was wounded twice and was transferred to the air corps, where he learned how to fly. When the war ended, 24-year-old Hess entered Munich University, where he fulfilled his dream of studying history, economics, and political science.

Like many young men who had served in the war, Hess was bitter about the conditions imposed on a defeated Germany. Forced to disband its army, give up territories it considered German property, and to pay reparations, Germany was left poverty-stricken. Many people, including Hess, blamed the Jews for such problems. They claimed that the Jews were "the enemies within" Germany who, for their own devious reasons, had brought about the loss of the war. Hess joined with others at the university who wished to see Germany restored to greatness. One of their activities was to distribute anti-Semitic literature. In 1919 Hess demonstrated that he was capable of more forceful action when he took part in the armed uprising that overthrew the government of Bavaria.

Hess Listens and Obeys Hitler

In 1920 Hess attended a meeting of the Nazi party and heard its leader, Adolf Hitler, speak for the first time. Hess was captivated and felt overcome. In Hitler, Hess saw the only man who could restore Germany to its rightful position in the world. Hess became the sixteenth person to join the Nazi party. According to author Eugene K. Bird, from that day forward, "he gave Hitler his loyalty and faith and followed him with a dog-like devotion."

Hess became a fixture at Nazi party meetings, often engaging in brawls with those who attempted to disrupt Hitler's speeches. In 1923 he took part in the party's failed attempt to seize control of Germany and was imprisoned together with his idol, Hitler. While the two were in prison, Hess acted as Hitler's secretary, typing Hitler's book *Mein Kampf* (translated as "My Struggle") and making suggestions and corrections. As a reward, Hitler appointed Hess his personal secretary after they were released from prison in 1925.

Between 1925 and 1933, Hess was promoted several times for his loyal and obedient service. Hitler assumed control of Germany in 1933, and in 1934 appointed Hess as deputy führer. Hitler began issuing demands on how to run the country. These demands passed through Hess's office, where they were delegated to those people responsible for carrying them out. As Hitler's deputy, Hess signed the Nuremberg laws. These racial laws, which took effect in 1935, stripped German Jews of their citizenship and barred them from engaging in most professions.

Although Hess's job involved mountains of paperwork, he preferred active labor to deskwork. At first, Hess tried to institute policies of his own, but Hitler usually issued contradictory orders. In time, Hess abandoned any attempts to issue his own legislation. He never had any major say in Hitler's decisions. Hess became something of a joke to other Nazi leaders. Authors Roger Manvell and Heinrich Fraenkel described how some viewed Hess's attitude to his job: "Come unto me all ye that are weary and heavy laden, and I will do nothing." Hess exhibited other behaviors that his colleagues found odd. He was a vegetarian who distrusted doctors and favored "nature cures and other weird beliefs," according to a Hess colleague quoted by Manvell and Fraenkel. He was, however, one of the few men Hitler trusted completely, and in 1939 Hitler chose Hess as the number two man, behind Hermann Göring, to succeed him as head of Germany.

Hess Takes Flight

World War II began when Germany invaded Poland in 1939. Great Britain and France, in accordance with Allied ties to Poland, then declared war on Germany. With the war in full swing by 1941, Hitler set his sights on the Soviet Union. Two years into the war, Great Britain was still battling Germany without assistance. Hitler made a peace offer to Britain, not wanting to have to fight a two-front war

What the Charges Meant

The military tribunal that tried the Nazi criminals charged them with the following crimes:

1. Conspiracy: secretly planning to commit crimes against peace, war crimes, and crimes against humanity;

2. Crimes Against Peace: planning, preparing, starting, or waging aggressive war;

3. War Crimes: violations of the laws or customs of war;

4. Crimes Against Humanity: murder, extermination, enslavement, persecution on political or racial grounds, involuntary deportment, and inhumane acts against civilian populations.

Hess was found innocent of all crimes except crimes against peace.

with Great Britain and the Soviet Union. His offer was rejected. Meanwhile, Hitler's circle of influence had expanded to include generals and others who fought for the supreme leader's attention. Hess began to feel left out. He longed to perform some great act that would help further Hitler's aims. Through this act, Hess felt he would restore himself to Hitler's esteem, and become a national hero.

Hess was an accomplished pilot with military experience. Two of his heroes of flying were American Charles Lindbergh and Great Britain's Duke of Hamilton, who had been the first pilot to fly over Mount Everest, the world's highest peak. Hess decided he would fly to the duke's home in Scotland and ask to be taken to see the King of England. There he hoped to persuade British Prime Minister Winston Churchill that it was in England's best interests to join with Germany in the fight against their common enemy, the Soviet Union.

On May 10, 1941, "the most loyal and unimaginative of Nazi leaders [attempted] a daring deed." Wearing an army uniform, Hess made the 900-mile flight to Scotland in five hours. About thirty miles from the home of the Duke of Hamilton, he

Hess's Son Defends Father

In 1991 Gerald L. Posner's book, titled *Hitler's Children: Sons and Daughters of the Third Reich Talk about Their Fathers and Themselves,* was published by Random House. In it Wolf Hess, son of Rudolf Hess, defends his father. Wolf Hess said his father always supported relocation of the Jews to their own homeland; he never favored the mass extermination that was actually implemented. Wolf Hess said his father had several Jewish friends, whom he helped escape from Germany. He pointed out that although his father held a powerful position in Hitler's cabinet, he never used it to enrich himself or his family, who lived very modestly. Wolf Hess believed his father's long imprisonment was "illegal." He stated that the courage his father displayed while imprisoned created a "spiritual bond between my father and myself [that] remained unsevered."

parachuted out of the plane, which crashed and burst into flames, and landed in the path of a Scottish farmer. "I have an important message for the Duke of Hamilton," he said. He was turned over to authorities and treated as a prisoner of war.

Back in Germany, radio broadcasts announced that Hess, "'apparently in a fit of madness,' had taken possession of an aircraft contrary to Hitler's orders and had disappeared." Churchill could hardly believe "that the Deputy Führer of Germany is in our hands." After listening to Hess's long and passionate praise of Hitler, as well as his demands and proposals for peace, it was decided that Hess should be imprisoned in the Tower of London. Due to devious Nazi actions since 1939—their broken treaties, their lies, and their murder of innocent people—the British did not feel inclined to negotiate a peace with Germany. The war with Germany would continue.

Hitler hated failures, and Hess knew that his mission was unsuccessful. Hess was declared insane by Hitler and disowned by Nazi leaders. He attempted suicide, but that too failed. Hess remained a prisoner of the British until the war ended. During this time he began to exhibit signs of mental instability and claimed that his food was being poisoned. At the war's end in 1945, Hess was returned to Nuremberg, Germany, to stand trial. Hess was tried along with other Nazi war criminals. The trial was adjudicated by a joint committee of Allied representatives.

Hess Stands Trial

On November 20, 1945, twenty-one Nazis appeared at the Palace of Justice in Nuremberg, Germany, to stand trial for conspiracy, crimes against peace, war crimes, and crimes against humanity. At the trial, Hess scarcely seemed sane, although there are some people who believe his behavior was an act. Eugene K. Bird described him as "a pathetic thin figure [who] huddled in the dock [where accused prisoners sit] reading books and mumbling.... When, at last, Hess had the chance to get up and tell his story, he gave only a rambling [speech] on 'secret forces' and 'evil influences' being used to destroy him. He sat down, and was convicted."

All of the Allies, except the former Soviet Union, were inclined to let Hess go. The Soviets, unwilling to forgive Hess for attempting to convince the British to fight against them, called for his execution. A compromise was reached, and Hess was sentenced to life in prison at Spandau—a huge, high-security prison intended to hold more than six hundred prisoners. Groups of guards and soldiers from the Allied countries took turns guarding the seven Nazi criminals confined there. One by one, the six other prisoners, "many of them no less guilty," according to Manvell, were released, until there remained only the aging Hess. For twenty years he was the sole prisoner at Spandau, although the number of guards and soldiers remained the same as before.

By 1973, write Manvell and Fraenkel, Hess was a "sick old man who while[d] away his time with books, gramophone records, and cups of instant coffee ... too old any longer to work in the prison garden." Hess lived for another fourteen years until his death in 1987 at the age of ninety-two. The official cause of death was listed as suicide.

His Legacy Lives On

Rudolf Hess remained loyal to Hitler to the end. He never expressed any remorse for the murders of millions of innocent people or for his part in the killing. He took with him the secret of whether his flight to England was the act of a madman, or an assigned mission on Hitler's behalf. Conspiracy theories about him continue to circulate. There are some, including Hess's son, who believe Hess was murdered. Yet another theory holds that Hess was executed while in England; it was a British secret agent, posing as Hess, who died at Spandau.

Hess has become a cult figure to neo-Nazis, who apparently believe he was acting for Hitler and was not a traitor to the Nazi cause. The neo-Nazi phenomenon is a reality throughout the entire world. Groups of them gather each August 17 in cities throughout Europe to mark the date of Hess's death. The Neo-Nazi movement is a small, but growing violent movement in Germany and other countries, including the United States. Devoted to the memory of Adolf Hitler, Neo-Nazis engage in such activities as the persecution of foreigners and the destruction of Jewish cemeteries.

SOURCES

Books

Bird, Eugene K., *Prisoner No. 7 Rudolf Hess: The Thirty Years in Jail of Hitler's Deputy Führer* (originally published in England under the title of *The Loneliest Man in the World* by the American director of Spandau), Viking Press (New York), 1974.

Costello, John, *Ten Days to Destiny: The Secret Story of the Hess Peace Initiative and British Efforts to Strike a Deal with Hitler*, Morrow (New York), 1991.

Douglas-Hamilton, James, *Motive for a Mission: The Story Behind Hess's Flight to Britain*, with a forward by Alan Bullock, Paragon House (New York), 1979.

Hutton, J. Bernard, *Hess: The Man and His Mission*, Macmillan (New York), 1971.

Manvell, Roger, and Heinrich Fraenkel, *Hess: A Biography*, Drake Publishers (New York), 1973.

Padfield, Peter, *Hess: Flight for the Führer*, Weidenfeld & Nicolson (London), 1991.

Posner, Gerald L., *Hitler's Children: Sons and Daughters of the Third Reich Talk about Their Fathers and Themselves*, Random House (New York), 1991.

Thomas, W. Hugh, *The Murder of Rudolf Hess*, Harper and Row (New York), 1979.

Reinhard Heydrich

Born March 7, 1904
Halle, Germany
Died June 4, 1942
Prague, Czechoslovakia

Head of the SD; deputy to SS leader
Heinrich Himmler; known as "The
Blonde Beast" and "The Hangman"

*"The Führer has ordered the physical
extermination of the Jews."*

(Reproduced by permission of AP/Wide World Photos)

R einhard Heydrich, one of the highest-ranking followers of Adolf Hitler, possessed the tall, fair-haired physical attributes of the Aryan superman. As a chief organizer for the Nazi plan of Jewish genocide, Heydrich displayed a cold, manipulative, and ambitious demeanor. Ultimately, he was responsible for the suffering and death of millions of people.

Born into Wealth

Reinhard Eugen Heydrich was born in Halle, Germany, in 1904. His father was an opera singer; his mother was a pianist and the daughter of his father's music professor. Heydrich had an older sister, Maria, and a younger brother, Heinz Siegfried. As a child, Heydrich excelled at the violin, which he enjoyed playing throughout his life. He and his brother experienced typical childhood adventures, enjoying such things as mock fights with wooden swords. Their childhood was spent in a handsome home, enjoying the comforts of life among the socially elite. Heydrich faced ridicule, partly because of his high-pitched voice and devotion to Catholicism in a predominately Protestant area. In an era when anti-Semitism was gaining popularity, Heydrich received negative attention from peers due to his grandmother's surname. She had remarried a man with a Jewish-sounding name, which caused some to speculate that Heydrich had Jewish roots.

Nazi Secret Police

During the Nazi era, the citizens of Germany were terrorized by a number of individuals who belonged to organizations which acted as a police force. The identities of these various units in the Third Reich can be confusing as they are commonly referred to by the initials of their German names.

The Gestapo is an abbreviation for the Geheime Staatpolizei or Secret State Police. The most famous of the German police groups, it was begun by Hermann Göring in Prussia in 1933. The Gestapo men, who wore black coats and slouch hats, were famous for their cruelty and violence. They had the power to follow, arrest, question, and imprison people, strictly on their own authority. The Gestapo inspired tremendous fear.

The SA stands for the Sturmabteilung, or Storm Troopers. The SA was founded at the very beginning of the Nazi party. The Storm Troopers were designed to be a "means of defense" for the Nazis and "a training school for the coming struggle for liberty." The members were often called the brownshirts, a reference to the clothing they typically wore. The organization was headed by Ernst Röhm. At its height, the SA numbered more than 4 million members. When the SA set up the first concentration camp at Dachau, they marched around Berlin and rounded up political opponents and trade unionists. Members were known to be exceptionally brutal and violent. Röhm eventually grew drunk on power and began talking about merging the SA with the army. In 1934 Hitler, allegedly concerned about a possible military takeover, had Röhm killed on what became known as the "Night of the Long Knives." Historians note that Hitler was actually trying to improve the party's image by dismantling the leadership of the unsophisticated, bullying SA. After that, the SA declined in number and importance.

The SS stands for the Schutzstaffel, the Security Squad. Members of the SS were Hitler's personal bodyguards. Led by Heinrich Himmler, the black-shirted group grew in size and importance following the murder of SA leader Ernst Röhm in 1934. Two years later, Himmler became head of all the police organizations in Germany, except the military intelligence group, the Abwehr. The SS provided guards at the various concentration camps and presided over the murders of millions of Jews, Roma (commonly called Gypsies), political prisoners, gays, and others the Nazis deemed undesirable.

The SD stands for the Sicherheitsdienst or Security Police. The SD, headed by Reinhard Heydrich, was started in 1931 to serve as the Intelligence Service of the SS. It was the job of the SD to spy on Hitler's enemies, especially those within the Nazi Party.

Heydrich was raised in a home where harsh attitudes and physical beatings were part of everyday life. His father taught him to be fiercely anti-Semitic. Heydrich was a shy, unhappy child who felt a need to excel at all he undertook. A gifted athlete, he was especially adept at fencing. When World War I began in 1914, Heydrich was too young to join the military. Instead, he banded with some anti-Jewish veterans in attacking communists in the streets. He welcomed becoming part of a group that idealized people who looked like himself, as it helped dispel rumors about his lack of "racial purity."

Joins Nazi Party

Like many Germans, Heydrich's family lost most of its fortune following World War I. A large contingent of the German people blamed Jews for losing the war, claiming that the Jews were attempting a worldwide takeover, starting with the defeated Germany. Such Germans were looking for a scapegoat and created many false theories about the role of Jews during World War I. In this political climate, the embittered, young Heydrich became a German naval cadet in order to get an education. He advanced quickly, becoming a second lieutenant in 1926. Unpopular with other officers because of his boastful ways, Heydrich was thrown out of the German navy for "conduct unbecoming an officer and a gentleman." When he found out that he had impregnated the daughter of a shipyard director, he refused to marry her. Not certain where to turn, he joined the Nazi party in 1931. That same year Heydrich married a 19-year-old student named Lina von Osten, who was also strongly anti-Semitic.

Heydrich's blue-eyed, typically Aryan looks helped him be accepted into the SS—the Schutzstaffel, or Security Squad, that acted as Hitler's personal bodyguards. Impressed with Heydrich's quick mind, SS leader Heinrich Himmler chose him for the task of building a new SS intelligence service, which became known as the SD. The service soon became a massive spy network that reported on Hitler's opponents, especially those within the Nazi party. Heydrich relished the use of secret cameras and hidden microphones. His success at this task skyrocketed his career. He became an SS major by the end of 1931, then an SS colonel with complete control of the SD by 1932. The following year, before he had even reached the age of 30, he was appointed SS brigadier general.

Despite recurrent rumors about Heydrich's alleged ancestry, Hitler decided not to force the general out of the Nazi party. Hitler described the six-foot-tall Nazi as "a highly gifted but also very dangerous man, whose gifts the movement had to retain." Noting that Heydrich would be grateful that the Nazis did not expel him from the party, Hitler believed that he could count on Heydrich to "obey blindly." Always haunted by the ever-present rumors about his roots, Heydrich became more intense in his hatred toward the Jews. He also was tormented by a severe lack of self-esteem. One report describes him returning home one night, drunk, seeing himself in the mirror, and using his pistol to shoot at his own reflection, shouting "filthy Jew." Some historians believe Heydrich's persecution of the Jews was his way of purging his own Jewishness.

At the beginning of 1933, Heydrich assisted Himmler in carrying out the large-scale arrest of opponents of the Nazis in Germany. These included religious leaders, communists, and trade union members who had spoken against Hitler. Great numbers of people were kept imprisoned at a converted munitions factory at Dachau, a town in southern Germany. Dachau became the Nazis' first concentration camp. Workers were forced to labor as long as 12 hours per day on very little food. They received lashings and other severe punishments for small crimes like stealing cigarettes. Similar camps for political prisoners were begun at Buchenwald and other sites around the country.

In April 1934 Himmler became head of a new secret state police force, popularly known as the Gestapo. Heydrich was made second in command. That same year, he and other top Nazis engaged in an event known as the "Night of the Long Knives." Writer Robert Leckie described the events of June 30: "SA [which stands for Sturmabteilung or Storm Troopers] leaders and Adolf Hitler's enemies—private and public, real or imagined—old friends of the early days ... co-conspirators and old collaborators, churchmen, generals and politicians, as well as enemies of [other top Nazi officials] were put to death." Heydrich drew up the list of those who were to be murdered that night. Among those killed was SA leader Ernst Röhm, head of more than 4 million Nazi storm troopers.

By 1936 Himmler controlled all of Germany's local police forces, including the SS and the Gestapo. The Gestapo was permitted to arrest anyone without providing a reason. People could be imprisoned if the Gestapo believed they might commit a crime in the future. The Gestapo and Heydrich's SD demanded bribes, using torture and blackmail to control anyone opposing the Nazis. As he grew in power, Heydrich became an object of fear throughout Germany. Even the highest-ranking Nazis shook in their boots when confronted by his menacing glare. A man with no personal friends, Heydrich generally kept out of the public eye as much as possible.

Heydrich's lust for power and love of political scheming went beyond Germany. In 1937 he forged documents that led to the overthrow of some important generals in the Soviet Union. The following year, Heydrich ousted two powerful German generals who had expressed opposition to Hitler. Devising phony scandals intended to embarrass the generals, Heydrich was able to force them into early retirement. He worked with Himmler to encourage pro-Nazi sympathizers in Austria to commit terrorist acts, causing political

Heydrich at work in his office at Gestapo headquarters. (KZ Gedenkstatte Dachau/USHMM Photo Archives)

unrest. When the Nazis gained rule over Austria in 1938, Heydrich's SD started the Gestapo Office of Jewish Emigration. Headed by an Austrian named Adolf Eichmann, the office issued permits to Jews who wanted to leave the country. The office soon became a gold mine for Heydrich and other Nazis who supplied the permits only after being bribed. More than 100,000 Jews sought the permits, many turning over all their goods and money to the SS. Heydrich set up a similar office in Berlin, Germany, further fattening the wallets of the SS.

On November 9 and 10, 1938, the Nazis vandalized Jewish businesses and synagogues. The event, commonly referred to as *Kristallnacht* (meaning "Crystal Night" or the "Night of Broken Glass"), marked the first widespread attacks and mass arrests of Jewish people in Hitler's Germany. At Heydrich's order, more than 30,000 people were sent to concentration camps. The name *Kristallnacht* referred to the vast amount of shattered glass from Jewish-owned stores that filled the streets.

In 1939 Hitler assigned Heydrich the responsibility of removing any "undesirables" from Poland. Heydrich was to imprison or execute them as the Nazis believed that Poles were inferior to Germans. Heydrich formed five SS Special Action groups (Einsatzgruppen) charged with the task of gathering up and shooting the leading citizens, professionals, and clergy of small Polish towns. They placed thousands of Polish citizens in jail on false charges, with some Poles being beheaded or burned alive. It is estimated that, by the end of 1939, between 50,000 and 100,000 Polish citizens were exterminated under Heydrich's command.

It was also Heydrich's task to decide the fate of the 3 million Polish Jews. Heydrich first deported the Jews to German labor camps, then moved them to Jewish ghettos. The ghettos were crowded, walled sections of cities where Jews were forced to live in poverty, quarantined from non-Jews. In the ghettos of Warsaw, Lódz, and Kraków, people were crowded together with very little food or medicine. By 1941 more than half a million Polish Jews had died there. Heydrich had Jewish leaders appointed to "Jewish councils" called the *Judenräte*. The work of such councils unwittingly led to the destruction of their own communities.

In 1941 after Hitler's invasion of the Soviet Union, Heydrich sent four Einsatzgruppe units there to kill all the communist officials, and anyone else the Nazis perceived to be a security risk. They entered into towns and villages, telling all the Jews to gather together in preparation for resettlement to another area. The Jews were commanded to relinquish their valuables, then to remove their clothing. Finally, they were marched to an area where trenches had been dug. Jews were shot and their bodies were thrown into the open ditches. By the end of World War II in 1945, more than 1.3 million people in the Soviet Union alone were executed this way.

On July 31, 1941, Hitler's right-hand man, Hermann Göring, gave the order which resulted in the extermination of millions of Jews. Göring's letter to Heydrich said, in part, "I hereby charge you with making all necessary preparations with regard to organizational and financial matters for bringing about a complete solution of the Jewish problem in the German sphere of influence in Europe."

Architect of "Final Solution"

On January 20, 1942, Heydrich met with other Nazi officials in the Berlin suburb of Wannsee. They discussed what they called the "Final Solution"—the systematic plan to eliminate all the Jews of Europe. As head of the project, Heydrich explained that able-bodied Jews would be worked to death building roads into the Soviet Union. The weak and sick would be put to death immediately. Heydrich also suggested that marriages between Jews and non-Jews be declared invalid so that the Jewish spouse could be sent to a concentration camp. He proposed that people who were partially Jewish be sterilized. Some report that following this meeting, Heydrich and SS Lieutenant Colonel Adolf Eichmann hopped up on the table and drank a toast.

In 1941 Heydrich had taken charge of Moravia and Bohemia, sections of what was then Nazi-controlled Czechoslovakia. Believing that Heydrich had been named Hitler's successor, the British launched operation "Daybreak." They sent two young, trained Czech men into the region of Prague by parachute with orders to assassinate Heydrich. In May 1942, as Heydrich rode in a car, his driver stopped at a red light in Prague and the gunmen ambushed the car. One of the men threw a grenade, severely injuring Heydrich. The young men were later captured and killed. The Germans in Prague had no penicillin to treat Heydrich's wounds, and his medical condition became very serious. Himmler sent his personal physician to Prague several days later to care for Heydrich, but it was too late. Heydrich died of his wounds shortly thereafter.

The impact of Heydrich's persecution of the Jews and other peoples did not end with his death. Hitler, enraged that Heydrich had been murdered, avenged his death. Many believed Hitler was so infuriated because Heydrich was slated to become his successor. Hitler consulted a map of Czechoslovakia, focusing on Prague and the surrounding area, and randomly placed his finger on the village of Lidice. He commanded that it be destroyed. As a result, all of the men of Lidice were murdered, the women were sent to concentration camps, and the children were relocated to Germany to be raised as Nazis.

SOURCES

Books

Burgess, Alan, *Seven Men at Daybreak,* Evans Bros. (London), 1960.

Calic, Edouard, *Reinhard Heydrich: The Chilling Story of the Man Who Masterminded the Nazi Death Camps,* translated by Lowell Bair, William Morrow (New York), 1985.

Deschner, Gunther, *Reinhard Heydrich: A Biography,* Stein and Day (New York), 1981.

Gilbert, Martin, *The Holocaust: A History of the Jews of Europe During the Second World War,* Holt, Rinehart & Winston (New York), 1986.

Graber, G. S., *The Life and Times of Reinhard Heydrich,* R. Hale (London), 1981.

Hutak, J. B., *With Blood and With Iron: The Lidice Story,* R. Hale (London), 1957.

Leckie, Robert, *Delivered from Evil: The Saga of World War II,* Harper & Row (New York), 1987.

Neville, Peter, *Life in the Third Reich,* edited with an introduction by Richard Bessel, Oxford University Press, (New York), 1987.

Wiener, Jan G., *The Assassination of Heydrich,* Pyramid Books (New York), 1969.

Whiting, Charles, *Heydrich: Henchman of Death,* Leo Cooper (S. Yorkshire, England), 1999.

Wighton, Charles, *Heydrich: Hitler's Most Evil Henchman,* Chilton (Philadelphia), 1962.

Wykes, Alan, *Heydrich,* Ballantine Books (New York), 1973.

Heinrich Himmler

einrich Himmler dreamed of becoming a soldier, but instead became one of the most notorious murderers in history. Though he was often ill, under his command the Schutzstaffel (or Security Squad, known as the SS) grew to be the most powerful and ruthless organization in Germany during World War II. The SS was composed of Hitler's personal bodyguards and those who acted as guards at the various concentration camps. Himmler became instrumental in the enslavement and murder of millions of innocent people through his command of the SS.

Childhood in Munich

Born in Munich, Germany, on October 7, 1900, Himmler was the second of three sons born to Gebhard and Anna Maria Heyder Himmler. Anna was a pious Catholic and dedicated homemaker. Gebhard was the son of an impoverished soldier, with family roots extending far back in German history. The family lived a comfortable life, employed a full-time maid, and was considered solidly middle class. Gebhard believed that it was important to establish relationships with higher social classes—a belief he passed on to his sons. He was especially proud to be employed as a tutor for a member of the royal family.

Himmler was often sick as a child and nearly died of a lung infection at the age of four. His

Born October 7, 1900
    Munich, Germany
Died May 23, 1945
    A British interrogation camp near
    Lüneburg, Germany

Farmer; fertilizer analyst; chief of the SS; Reichminister of the Interior; a chief architect of the *Endlösung* ("Final Solution")

"You see, I did not deem myself justified in exterminating the men … while allowing their children to grow up to avenge themselves on our sons and grandchildren. The hard decision had to be taken—this people [the Jews] must disappear from the face of the earth."

(Library of Congress)

father was a stern man who took an active interest in his sons' educations and insisted on excellence. Although Himmler was not an especially bright student, he worked hard and often managed to excel. When Himmler was ten years old, his father encouraged him to begin keeping a diary—his father even wrote the first entry in the diary as a model. Himmler dutifully followed his father's instructions; later, when he became a high-ranking member of the Nazi party, he used this early training to keep detailed records of his activities.

When Himmler was thirteen years old, his father became headmaster of a school in Landshut, Germany. A quiet town with its own castle, Landshut was located fifty miles from Munich. All three Himmler boys attended the school. The adolescent Himmler was short, plump, and a poor athlete. He wore thick glasses, attempting to remedy his severe nearsightedness. The discipline he put toward his studies was mirrored by attempts at exercise, hoping to overcome his physical shortcomings. He often complained in his diaries about his poor health.

World War I (1914–18) caused great excitement in Himmler, sparking a lifelong interest in the military. He managed to complete officer training, but not in time to serve in the war. He left the military, deciding to become a farmer. He was employed on a farm for a short time before he fell ill with typhoid fever, an infectious disease caused by unsanitary conditions. His doctor advised Himmler to engage in a less strenuous activity than farming for at least a year. Himmler resolved to continue his education.

Gets Involved in Politics

Himmler enrolled in the agriculture program at the University of Munich. He gave up his dream of a military career, but he spent his school breaks engaged in paramilitary exercises with various groups. Eager to be accepted socially, he took up fencing and dancing. Although he did not enjoy these activities, he felt they were required to get ahead. He was never comfortable socially, especially with women. A weak stomach, which plagued him for the rest of his life, prevented him from drinking beer with other male students, who in turn mocked him for his weakness.

It was during his college years that Himmler began to display anti-Semitic feelings, writing in his diary that Jews should be excluded from college clubs. His feelings were a direct representation of the political climate at the time. Himmler heard the popular political speeches blaming the Jews for Germany's loss of World War I, and he found himself drawn to politics. He also developed a mistrust of doctors, many of whom were Jewish, and turned to alternative forms of medical treatment for his frequent ailments. This interest in alternative medicine later led Himmler to authorize gruesome medical experiments on concentration camp prisoners by Nazi doctors such as Josef Mengele.

Himmler completed a degree in agriculture and obtained a job with a fertilizer company in 1922. He also continued his soldiering activities and, in 1923, joined the Nazi party. The party was considered quite radical at the time, due to its unsuccessful 1923 coup of the German government. As a result of Himmler's association with the party, he lost his job.

In 1927 Himmler met a Polish nurse, Margarete (Marga) Boden, who was seven years his elder. Marga, the owner of a Berlin nursing home, had an interest in herbal medicine and this attribute, coupled with her thrifty nature, greatly appealed to Himmler. The couple was married in 1928. With the proceeds from the sale of Marga's nursing home, they bought a small farm near Munich. There they kept hens and sold produce while Himmler continued his Nazi party activities. Although he had little social personality, Himmler was efficient and paid careful attention to detail. He was rewarded with a promotion to Reichsführer, a rank equivalent to a U.S. Army general, of the SS in 1929. That same year his daughter, Gudrun, was born.

Builds SS into Powerful Organization

During his sixteen years in power, Himmler built the SS into a vast and dominant organization. His success resulted in the death of millions of people. The SS was originally intended to protect Nazi leader Adolf Hitler and other important party members, as well as defend Germany against attack. Himmler transformed the SS into an agency that carried out anything Hitler ordered, including the punishment and murder of "enemies of the state." A timid man, Himmler became an object of fear to his countrymen as well as fellow Nazis. He quickly became one of Hitler's inner circle. In a mere four years, he expanded the SS, whose membership originally totaled 280, into an enormous military and economic empire totaling 50,000 members. Along the way, he acquired a number of

Himmler (second from the left) on an inspection of the Auschwitz concentration camp in Poland. (Main Commission for the Investigation of Nazi War Crimes/USHMM Photo Archives)

new titles, including Chief of Police, Reich Commissioner for the Solidification of German Peoplehood, and Commander of the Political Police.

Hitler assigned Himmler the special task of establishing the SS as an organization of carefully selected men who would become the leaders of the new German race. Himmler became obsessed with his assignment. Borrowing ideas from a book written by German agricultural expert Walter Darré, Himmler began by outlining the rules regarding marriage of SS members. Darré wrote that the future of Europe depended on the survival of the German race; the German race should reproduce at a greater rate than Jews and other ethnic groups. To help achieve this goal, SS men who wished to marry had to obtain a certificate approving their choice of brides. Only these approved couples would be guaranteed to produce children of pure, Aryan blood. Himmler established SS Bridal Schools, where brides were taught what was expected of

them in the new Nazi order. It was not long before the desire to build a master race included the extermination of everyone Himmler and Hitler considered "racially impure." These "racially impure" people included Jews, Roma (often referred to as Gypsies), Catholics, the physically and mentally impaired, homosexuals, and Jehovah's Witnesses.

The Move Toward a Pure German Race

The Nazi definition of a pure German person was tall, blond-haired, and blue-eyed. According to Elizabeth Wiskemann, writing in *Anatomy of the SS State*, "Himmler really believed that he could breed better Germans and arrange for all the subhumans to die out or rot away or, in plain language, be murdered." Author Robert E. Conot pointed out the irony in Himmler's idea of physical supremacy: "[Himmler] was a myopic, slopeshouldered, spindle-chested weakling who wanted

Albert Speer: Himmler's Partner in the War Factories

Albert Speer (pronounced Shpayr) was born into a wealthy family in Mannheim, Germany, in 1905. He lived in a luxurious home, with a full staff of servants. Speer was a gifted student from a young age. As the son and grandson of prominent architects, he wanted to continue the family tradition. Unable to find a job in his chosen profession, he became an architecture instructor. In his autobiography, Speer described himself as having no interest in politics as a young man. It was at the urging of some of his students that he went to hear Adolf Hitler, leader of the Nazi party, speak. At first Speer found Hitler "engaging" and full of "South German charm"; as he listened further, he became aware of Hitler's "hypnotic persuasiveness." "I was carried away," he wrote. Soon afterward, Speer joined the Nazi party with his mother.

With his professional life at a standstill, Speer became increasingly more involved in politics. He was given the task of redecorating a Nazi headquarters building; later he designed decorations for rallies that promoted the Nazi cause. Soon Speer's work was noticed by Hitler, himself a frustrated architect. Hitler had grand plans for buildings and monuments that would be suitable for his great German empire, and Speer became Hitler's chief architect. "For the commission to do a great building, I would have sold my soul," Hitler later wrote.

The building projects Hitler had in mind required laborers, and Heinrich Himmler's concentration camps were full of idle hands. So began the first collaboration between Himmler and Speer. In 1942 Hitler named Speer his Minister of Armaments, in charge of arms production. With all able-bodied Germans off fighting the war, Speer needed workers for mass production of weapons, and his projects required secrecy. Himmler suggested that a work force made up entirely of concentration camp prisoners would guarantee secrecy, since they had absolutely no contact with the outside world. Before the war ended, Speer had 14 million forced laborers under his control.

After the end of World War II, at the Palace of Justice in Nuremberg, Germany, twenty-one captured Nazi leaders were brought together for what became known as "the greatest trial in history." Among the men being tried for crimes against peace, war crimes, and crimes against humanity was Albert Speer. Like many of the Nazi criminals on trial, Speer tried to blame his crimes on the people who worked for him. He claimed that he was ill when many of the crimes occurred. In his autobiography *Inside the Third Reich*, Speer claimed that he was unaware of Hitler's anti-Semitism and his plans to expand the German empire. In his book about the trials, Robert E. Conot paints a picture of Speer as a "masterful liar," a manipulator of the truth, a man so attractive, intelligent, and convincing that he eventually received a sentence of only twenty years in prison for his crimes. His sentence paled in comparison to other war criminals, some of whom committed lesser crimes and were sentenced to hang. While in prison, Speer wrote his memoirs, which were later gathered together into a valuable insider's look at the Nazi reign. He went on to write several other books about his experiences. He died in 1981.

to be an eagle-eyed warrior; a darkhaired, stub-chinned ... [German] who dreamed of reincarnation as a ... blond.... " Himmler used Reinhard Heydrich, one of the most prominent in a string of cruel, cold men recruited for the SS, as the archetype for the perfect German man. Ironically, some speculated that Heydrich had Jewish blood.

On Himmler's orders, concentration camps were set up to interrogate, torture, and kill millions of "enemies of the state." The Jews, he maintained, were the cause of too much trouble in Europe. The sacrifice of these people was necessary for the future of the German people. According to biographers Roger Manvell and Heinrich Fraenkel, Himmler believed that: "Just as the Americans had exterminated the Indians [Native Americans], so the Germans must wipe out the Jews." Himmler, who preferred to remain in the background, had SS men act as his agents. In 1939 the Nazi reign of terror began. Gangs of SS soldiers dressed in black caps, swastika (a Nazi symbol) armbands with black borders, crisply pressed uniforms, and gleaming black boots rampaged through the Jewish ghettos. They raped, robbed, murdered, and rounded up people to send to concentration camps.

In spite of his many activities, Himmler found time to adopt a son, sell the farm, and move his family to a small town by a lake. Once the family relocated, he seldom visited. He bought himself a modest house in Berlin, Germany, and had two children by his secretary. He began to suffer from severe headaches and stomach cramps. Still distrustful of doctors, Himmler hired a masseur to treat him.

The "Final Solution" Begins

In 1941 Himmler and other Nazi leaders received the order to begin the *Endlösung* ("Final Solution"). The "Final Solution" was the Nazi code for the complete elimination of European Jews. Himmler's second-in-command, Reinhard Heydrich, headed the Wannsee Conference on January 20, 1942, a conference at which fifteen top Nazis agreed upon the terms of the "Final Solution." Until this time, the Nazi plan was to force European Jews to leave Germany and German-occupied territories in Europe. The "Final Solution," however, involved rounding up all Jews throughout Europe, transporting them to Poland, and organizing them into labor gangs at concentration camps. The camp conditions were so terrible that large numbers of Jews would die. Those too old or young to work would be "treated accordingly." This invariably meant death.

Himmler continued to make plans for carrying out the "Final Solution," stepping up the activity at the concentration camps. He showed a special concern for the feelings of SS men who had qualms about the unspeakably brutal acts taking place in the camps. He instructed there be no photographs, saying "in time of war, executions are unfortunately necessary. But to take snapshots of them only shows bad taste." To raise money for the war effort, he ordered that gold teeth be removed from the bodies of prisoners, both alive and dead. Himmler's passion for secrecy masked the full extent of the horrors. It was not worldwide knowledge until after the war ended in 1945.

War Winds Down

During the last days of the war, Himmler became concerned about Hitler's increasingly odd behavior, fearing it would lead Europe into disaster. It occurred to Himmler that if Germany were to lose the war, the Allies would overrun the concentration camps and inform the world of his role in the atrocities. Himmler hoped a friendly gesture on his part would lead the Allies to overlook his past activities, perhaps putting him in charge of a new Germany without Hitler. As the Allies approached Germany, Himmler decided to disregard Hitler's orders to blow up the concentration camps along with their inmates. His attempt to reach an agreement with the Allies failed, however, resulting in Himmler losing rank and office. On May 21, 1945, while disguised as a low-ranking soldier, Himmler was stopped by British military personnel as he attempted to flee the country. By May 23, when it became obvious to him that he was not going to receive special treatment, Himmler bit open a cyanide capsule concealed in his mouth. Despite efforts to revive him, he died fifteen minutes later. Himmler was buried in a secret grave so it could not become a gathering place for Nazi sympathizers.

SOURCES

Books

Breitman, Richard, *The Architect of Genocide: Himmler and the Final Solution,* University Press of New England (Hanover, NH), 1992.

Conot, Robert E., *Justice at Nuremberg,* Harper & Row (New York), 1983.

Krausnick, Helmut, Hans Buchheim, and others, *Anatomy of the SS State,* translated from the German by Richard Barry, Marian Jackson [and] Dorothy Long, introduction by Elizabeth Wiskemann, Walker & Company (New York), 1968.

Manvell, Roger, and Heinrich Fraenkel, *Himmler,* Putnam (New York), 1965.

Speer, Albert, *Inside the Third Reich: Memoirs by Albert Speer,* translated from the German by Richard and Clara Winston, introduction by Eugene Davidson, Bonanza Books, distributed by Crown Publishers, 1982.

Hirohito

Born April 29, 1901
Tokyo, Japan
Died January 7, 1989
Tokyo, Japan

124th emperor of Japan

"I come to you, General MacArthur, to offer myself to the powers you represent as the one to bear sole responsibility for every political and military decision made and action taken by my people in the conduct of war."

(Reproduced by permission of Archive Photos)

Hirohito's reign as emperor of Japan remains the longest of any monarch in modern times. Although he chose the name Showa (enlightened peace) as the name for his reign, he was emperor during one of the most turbulent and tumultuous periods in history. Hirohito's enemies considered him to be the leader of a brutal, militaristic country and called for his punishment as a war criminal for the atrocities committed by the Japanese military during World War II. During the late twentieth century, many historians reassesed Hirohito's role in the war. They contended that he was not in charge of military campaigns and that he personally opposed the war; his life had been dedicated not to governing a country as its ruler, but playing the symbolic role of emperor.

A Privileged But Lonely Childhood

Born at Aoynama Palace in Tokyo, Hirohito was the son of Crown Prince Yoshihito and grandson of Mutsuhito, known as the Meiji (enlightened ruler) Emperor. His mother was Princess Sadako, a member of a family that had provided royal brides for numerous centuries. When he was less than three months old, Hirohito was sent to live with foster parents, the Count and Countess Kawamura Sumyoshi. In accordance with a long-standing custom, he was to be raised in a normal family, away from the ceremonial trappings of palace life, where

Shinto

Shinto, the traditional religion of Japan, preceded the arrival of Buddhism and is still widely practiced today. Shinto is comprised of a pantheon of gods and forces called kami, which are honored with traditional ceremonies and festivals. The central deity is the goddess Amaterasu. Although there are no specific doctrines or scriptures, followers of Shinto believe their religion creates unity and harmony among the people of Japan. From ancient times until the reign of Hirohito, Japanese emperors were considered direct descendants of Amaterasu; their duties were therefore religious as well as political. In the nineteenth century the Meiji government took steps to establish Shinto as the national religion—despite the fact that the Japanese constitution guaranteed freedom of religion—by building shrines, teaching about Shinto in public schools, and making Shinto festivals national holidays. By 1945 there were 218 national shrines in Japan.

After World War II, however, the role of Shinto in Japanese life changed. An Allied occupation force arrived in Japan to assist the country in rebuilding itself as a democracy, and the new constitution called for the separation of church and state and freedom of religion. Hirohito announced to his people that he was not, in fact, a descendant of a Shinto goddess. The Japanese government had to break its affiliation with the church and cease public funding of the shrines. Some Japanese felt that this change was contrary to Japan's cultural traditions, while others attempted to find ways to maintain the role of Shinto in Japanese life without threatening religious freedom. By the 1980s there were approximately 80,000 Shinto shrines in Japan with seventy-five million followers of the faith.

---

he was treated like their other children. Count Kawamura Sumyoshi died when Hirohito was five years old and the boy was returned to his parents' official residence, Akasaka Palace. Hirohito and his two brothers rarely saw their parents while they were growing up and they had limited contact with children outside the family. Hirohito was an introverted child with an extremely solemn manner.

At the age of eight, Hirohito was sent to the Peers' School, becoming a member of a class of twelve boys whose parents were also members of the Japanese royalty. There he studied modern languages, military and technical sciences, politics, and history. He developed a special interest in marine biology, which provided him the opportunity for solitude while he conducted field research. Hirohito's headmaster, Count Maresuki Nogi, taught him to practice the values of discipline, hard work, loyalty, and bravery. With the death of the Meiji Emperor, Hirohito's father ascended the throne and Hirohito became the crown prince. He graduated from the Peers' School in 1914 and went on to the Crown Prince's Institute, located on the

palace grounds. His class was comprised of five other royal students. During his seven years of study, Hirohito began expressing doubt that his family was descended from gods, a belief deeply rooted in Shinto tradition.

In 1918 Hirohito became engaged to Princess Nagako, causing controversy because she was not a member of the traditional bridal family like his mother. Nevertheless, after a six-year engagement, in which they met nine times under the supervision of a chaperone, the two were married. Over the years they had seven children, one of whom died at age two. After graduating from the Crown Prince's Institute in 1921, Hirohito broke with tradition by becoming the first crown prince to go on a six-month tour of Europe. Following stops in Hong Kong, Singapore, and Cairo, he visited Belgium, France, and Italy. His favorite destination was England, where the family of King George V warmly welcomed him. Hirohito was especially impressed with Great Britain's constitutional monarchy, in which the role of royalty was to approve policies determined by other government leaders. This model strongly influenced Hirohito's ideas about his own position in Japan.

Declares Showa

Returning from his journey in November 1921, Hirohito found his father in poor health and was appointed regent. Yoshihito died in late 1926, with Hirohito ascending the throne that had been dominated by his family for more than 2,000 years. He chose Showa (enlightened peace) as the name of his reign. He was no longer regarded as a mortal; doctors used silk gloves when they treated him, tailors were not allowed to touch his body, and food tasters tested his meals. Soon after Hirohito became emperor, the Japanese economy went into a recession. The military continued to grow in strength, hoping to extend Japan's reach into other parts of Asia, especially China. Although Hirohito was emperor, his role in governing the country was limited to his silent attendance at Imperial Conferences, where his presence implied that the Imperial Will approved of whatever policy was being discussed.

Government matters were decided by the prime minister and other government and military leaders, mainly without Hirohito's involvement. He did take a more active role on a few occasions. For instance, in 1936 he recommended quick and harsh punishment for some military officers and soldiers who had attempted a coup. With Hirohito's approval, Japan waged war against China in July 1937. Hirohito took a great interest in the military conflict. After Germany invaded Poland in 1939, Japanese military leaders and future premier Hideki Tōjō began making plans for war against the West. Their main target was the United States, which had been attempting to halt Japanese expansion. The Japanese military believed that aggressive actions would force the United States into allowing Japan to control East Asia.

During an Imperial Conference on December 1, 1941, Hirohito's advisers recommended a declaration of war against the United States. While he approved the plan, he later claimed the decision did not reflect his own wishes. Since his visit to Great Britain, Hirohito had advocated a policy of cooperation with Western powers, including the United States, but according to his own ideal of constitutional monarchy, he did not think it was his right to intervene. He later wrote that opposition to military action would have resulted in his assassination. U.S. President Franklin D. Roosevelt sent Hirohito a personal note on December 6, urg-

ing Japan to keep the peace. Tōjō rejected the note, leaving Hirohito unable to reply. The next day Japan attacked the U.S. naval base at Pearl Harbor, Hawaii, decimating American ships and aircraft and killing thousands of people. Hirohito's request that the United States be given notice of the attack had been ignored.

During the war, Hirohito remained on the palace grounds in Tokyo despite frequent bombings by Allied planes. He was often confined to a stuffy, thick-walled air raid shelter adjacent to the royal library. By June 1942 Japan had suffered several major defeats in battle and it appeared that they might lose the war. Tōjō wanted the Japanese people to try harder to win, so he began to mention the emperor often in his public announcements, calling on citizens to make sacrifices in Hirohito's name. By the summer of 1945, it was obvious that Japan could not win the war, but many Japanese leaders wanted to continue the fight. On August 6 the United States dropped an atomic bomb on the city of Hiroshima, resulting in immediate and devastating effects. Another bomb was leveled on Nagasaki on August 9, one day after Soviet forces invaded Japanese-held Manchuria in northern China. In Tokyo, leaders debated whether to surrender or keep fighting. In a meeting that took place in the emperor's air raid shelter, Tōjō asked Hirohito what decision he would make. Convinced that Japan would be destroyed if the war continued, Hirohito chose to surrender. He knew his own fate would be dictated by the commander of the Allied occupation forces.

Japan Surrenders and Rebuilds

At 7:21 a.m. on August 15, the Japanese were informed that, for the first time in history, they were about to hear the voice of their emperor. In a barely audible radio transmission Hirohito told his people that they must "endure the unendurable" and surrender to the Allies. The officer chosen to head the occupation government in Tokyo, and establish democracy in the country, was U.S. General Douglas MacArthur. Speculation surrounded the fate of Hirohito. People all over the world debated whether he would be tried as a war criminal or be retained for the rebuilding of the government. Recognizing that Hirohito was revered by the Japanese, MacArthur decided the emperor could play an important role in creating a new government. Unaware of MacArthur's decision, Hirohito asked the general to meet with him and made the statement: "I come to you, General MacArthur, to offer myself to the powers you represent as the one to bear sole responsibility for every political and military decision made and action taken by my people in the conduct of the war."

MacArthur later wrote that he was impressed by Hirohito's courage, which could have resulted in his execution as a war criminal. The general informed Hirohito that he would not be held responsible for the war but would play an important role in Japan's recovery. Over the next few years, the two men met often, and MacArthur gave Hirohito credit for assisting the Japanese in their adjustment to a new government and way of life. Japan's new constitution abolished Shinto as the official state religion, and on January 1, 1946, Hirohito made a public statement declaring that he was not a descendant of gods. This declaration was a relief to Hirohito, who considered himself a scientist and had never believed the myth anyway. The emperor was now simply a symbol of the state and Japanese unity.

During the remainder of Hirohito's life, the Japanese government tried to bring the emperor into closer contact with the people. Though reputedly shy and self-conscious, Hirohito made many public appearances. He also found time to study marine biology; he published the first of his several books on the subject in 1962. In 1959 another long-standing Japanese tradition was broken when Hirohito's son, Crown Prince Akihito, married a woman who was a commoner. When Hirohito traveled to Europe in late 1971 and early 1972, he learned that some people around the world still considered him a war criminal. He received a friendly reception from U.S. President Richard M. Nixon, whom he met during a stopover in Anchorage, Alaska. In 1975 Hirohito made an official state visit to the United States. He was given a Mickey Mouse watch as a gift and it, along with his microscope, was buried with him when he died of stomach cancer in 1989.

Sources

Books

Behr, Edward, *Hirohito: Beyond the Myth,* Villard Books (New York), 1989.

Crump, Thomas, *Death of an Emperor: Japan at the Crossroads,* Oxford University Press (Oxford), 1991.

Hoobler, Dorothy and Thomas Hoobler, *Showa: The Age of Hirohito,* Walker (New York), 1990.

Hoyt, Edwin P., *Hirohito: The Emperor and the Man,* Praeger (New York), 1992.

Mosley, Leonard, *Hirohito, Emperor of Japan,* Prentice Hall (Englewood Cliffs, NJ), 1966.

Magnus Hirschfeld

Born May 14, 1868
Kolberg, Prussia (now Poland)
Died May 15, 1935
Nice, France

Physician; writer; promoter of
homosexual rights; prominent researcher
on sexology

*"[It should not be assumed] that reversed
sex drive is a sign of degeneration, just as
we do not assume this of a hare-lip."*

Even though known homosexuals existed among the highest-ranking officials of the National Socialist German Workers' Party, the Nazis publicly criticized homosexuals and sent tens of thousands to death camps. Magnus Hirschfeld, a German physician, pioneered large-scale research on human sexuality, especially homosexuality. Although he had gained worldwide acclaim for his work, Hirschfeld was threatened with harm by the Nazis and forced into exile.

Becomes Esteemed Scholar

Robert Magnus Alexander Hirschfeld was born into a Jewish family in Kolberg, Prussia (then part of Germany) in 1868. The son of a doctor, he was the seventh of eight children. As a student, young Hirschfeld could not decide if he wanted to be a physician or a writer. He received his medical degree after attending several different schools in Germany. Shortly after beginning his medical practice, Hirschfeld received a letter written by an army officer. After sending the letter, the soldier committed suicide the day before he was to be married. The soldier sent the letter to Hirschfeld hoping it would help other homosexuals who were experiencing similar stresses as they attempted to live heterosexual lives. In his letter, the soldier stated that he could no longer deny that he was a homosexual and could not go through with the marriage. He asked that his story be publicized so that others could benefit from

A frame from a Nazi propaganda film showing Hirschfeld. (Photograph by Roland Klemig, courtesy of USHMM Photo Archives)

it. This incident prompted Hirschfeld to begin a pioneering study of homosexuality, and ultimately a campaign for homosexual rights.

Hirschfeld's theories had first come to the world's attention in 1896 when, using the name Theodor Ramien, he wrote a now-famous article on human sexuality. Throughout his lifetime, Hirschfeld wrote many books and articles on human sexuality, particularly focusing on homosexuality. He also wrote on a variety of other subjects, including love, crime, prostitution, sex crimes, and alcoholism. He invented the term "transvestite" and was the first to explain the difference between cross-dressing and homosexuality.

On May 14, 1897, on his twenty-ninth birthday, Hirschfeld founded the Scientific-Humanitarian Committee—the first homosexual rights organization in the world. Its purpose was to conduct research on homosexuality and to promote the end of legal and social intolerance of homosexuals. Hirschfeld, himself a homosexual, conducted a thirty-year campaign to repeal the German law that had made homosexuality a criminal offense in Germany. Hirschfeld's committee also advocated birth control and making divorces easier to obtain. The committee's work was supported over the years by a number of groups in Germany, all with various political beliefs. It was opposed by conservative groups, including the Nazi party, which came into being years later. It should be noted, however, that Hirschfeld was very conservative himself. He was pro-German in most matters.

In 1899 Hirschfeld edited a 23-volume series regarding human sexuality. It was the world's first publication devoted to investigating all aspects of homosexual life. In 1908 he edited the *Journal of Sexual Science*, the first scholarly publication that dealt with a wide variety of sexual issues.

Continues Investigation

In Hirschfeld's younger days, he believed that homosexuals were a "third sex," intermediate between males and females. He based this idea on the work of two writers from the 1860s who had written that homosexuality was both natural and inborn. In order to advance his "third sex" theory, Hirschfeld had to ignore the fact that most homosexuals are not physically different in appearance from heterosexuals. As of 1910, Hirschfeld had established a medical practice in Berlin, Germany. By this time he was placing much less emphasis on his earlier "third sex" idea. He maintained that, at least physically, most homosexuals resemble others of their gender. From his own research Hirschfeld

Homosexuality Under the Nazis

Even in their earliest days, the Nazis declared that homosexuality was unnatural. They spoke against it on the grounds that it interfered with the natural increase in population and stood in opposition to proper family life. In 1935 the Nazi penal code declared friendship between males who were homosexuals, even with no sexual activity involved, was an offense. According to author Elisheva Shaul: "The Nazi position on homosexuality, however, was inconsistent.... Officially, homosexuality was sharply denounced, but its practice in certain Nazi circles was tolerated or ignored."

For years, Nazi leader Adolf Hitler ignored the fact that Ernst Röhm, head of the SA (the Storm Troopers who fought Nazi opponents in the early days of the Nazi Party) was a homosexual. Röhm was one of several prominent people whose sexual preferences were used as an excuse by the Nazis to execute them when they fell out of favor with party leaders.

The Nazis punished tens of thousands of people for being homosexuals. They were forced to wear pink triangular patches on their clothes, like the Jews were forced to wear the Star of David, a Jewish symbol, on their sleeves. Homosexuals were placed in concentration camps, where many of them died.

---

learned that homosexuals vary in terms of their mental makeup from those who possess characteristics like their own sex to those who display characteristics more common to the opposite gender. He believed that all varieties of these sexual preferences were normal and valid.

Hirschfeld's major publication, *The Homosexuality of Men and Women,* was published in 1914. Written after Hirschfeld had studied more than 10,000 homosexuals, it is one of the most comprehensive books ever written on the topic. Critics say the book and its three indexes contain everything that was known about homosexuality at the time the Nazis began their ascent to power.

In 1919 Hirschfeld was a consultant for, and acted in, the first film designed to inform people about homosexuality, *Different from Others.* That same year he founded the Institute for Sexual Science in Berlin. Located in an old mansion, the institute offered Germany's first marital counseling services, research facilities, a medical department, and a library on the topic of human sexuality. The library contained more than 20,000 books, 35,000 photographs, and 40,000 biographical letters. The institute also counseled homosexuals, which would become a concern to the Nazis. They called the institute "a singular breeding ground for

filth and dirt." During its first year, the institute served more than 4,000 people from around the world. In 1924 Hirschfeld turned the facility over to the government of Germany. He remained director of the institute, maintaining its policies.

Beliefs on Homosexuality

Believing that the causes of homosexuality should be the object of scientific investigation, Hirschfeld said that it was not homosexuality as such, but the secrecy that often surrounds it, that was unhealthy. He explained that it was very stressful to keep secret something that was so much a part of a person's make-up; especially something that has been considered sinful, abnormal, criminal, or even a sign of mental illness. He pointed out that some people spend much of their lives fighting their own homosexual orientation, in "the eternal battle between willing spirit and weak flesh; that the perpetual fear of being discovered, of blackmail, arrest, court sentences, loss of social status and respect from family and friends ... greatly affects one's disposition, must surely be nerve-racking, and could bring on [a nervous breakdown, depression] ... and thoughts of suicide."

Hirschfeld taught that most homosexuals are not sick. In fact, because most remain hidden, he wrote, it is only the most mentally unhealthy homosexuals who come to be known by the medical profession. Hirschfeld often quoted the English writer, Eduard Carpenter, who stated: "In the vast majority of cases, loving persons of one's own sex bears a character of normalcy and healthfulness."

Hirschfeld and his colleagues spoke glowingly of the period in ancient Greece when homosexuality was totally accepted, even seen as blessed by the pagan gods. Hirschfeld worked hard throughout his lifetime to promote a healthy and positive image of homosexual relationships between consenting adults. He also campaigned to have the age of legal consent in Germany raised from fourteen to sixteen, as he believed a person needed to reach an age of greater maturity to decide whether, and with whom, to become sexually active.

Efforts See Partial Success

Hirschfeld's efforts to promote homosexual rights were hard fought. The negative image of homosexuality that had existed for centuries in Europe made it almost impossible for Hirschfeld's movement to gain acceptance. The traditional theory, passed down by the Roman Catholic church, held that homosexuality was acquired by a lack of mature mental development during a childhood stage; or by a child's being seduced by a homosexual during adolescence. Instead, Hirschfeld contended that homosexuality was inborn, spontaneous, and unchangeable. During the 1920s Hirschfeld presided over the conferences of the World League for Sexual Reform on a Scientific Basis. The conferences took place in Berlin, Germany, in 1921; Copenhagen, Denmark, in 1928; London, England, in 1929; and Vienna, Austria, in 1930.

Between 1930 and 1931, with Nazi power on the rise in Germany, Hirschfeld left on a world tour, during which he lectured and collected material for Berlin's Institute for Sexual Science. He traveled to Japan, China, the United States, Egypt, India, and Palestine (now Israel), among other places, delivering both academic and public speeches.

Nazis Take Action

While Hirschfeld was still abroad, on May 6, 1933, Nazi soldiers broke into the Institute he had founded, causing major damage. The entire building was burned down four days later. The Nazis defended their actions, saying they were engaged in a fight against the undermining of "morality in sexual life." Fearful for his own safety, Hirschfeld fled to Switzerland, and then to Paris, France. In Paris, he founded the French Institute for Sexual Science, but it never attained the prominence of the institute in Germany. In 1934 Hirschfeld closed the French Institute and relocated to the French city of Nice, where he died the following year. He was cremated; his ashes were buried in Nice. Some of Hirschfeld's papers were saved and are now in the archives of the Kinsey Institute for Sex Research in Indiana.

Sources

Books

Bullough, Vern L., and Bonnie Bullough, editors, *Human Sexuality: An Encyclopedia,* Garland Publishing (New York), 1994.

Elisheva Shaul, "Homosexuality and the Third Reich," *Encyclopedia of the Holocaust,* Israel Gutman, editor in chief, Macmillan (New York), 1990.

"Magnus Hirschfeld," *Contemporary Authors,* volume 148, Gale (Detroit), 1996.

Russell, Paul Elliott, *The Gay 100: A Ranking of the Most Influential Gay Men and Lesbians, Past and Present,* Carol (Secaucus, NJ), 1995.

Wolff, Charlotte, *Magnus Hirschfeld: A Portrait of a Pioneer in Sexology,* Quarter Books (New York), 1986.

The Writings of Dr. Magnus Hirschfeld: A Bibliography, compiled and introduced by James D. Steakley, Canadian Gay Archives (Toronto), 1985.

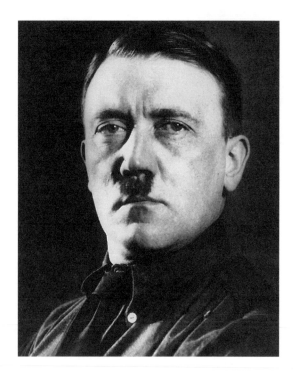

Adolf Hitler

Born April 20, 1889
Braunau, Austria-Hungary
Died April 30, 1945
Berlin, Germany

Dictator of Nazi Germany from
1934 to 1945

*"I feel myself the best of Germans, who
wanted the best for the German people."*

A dolf Hitler ascended to power in an era of confusion and anger in Germany. After being forced to pay large reparations as a result of World War I (1914–1918), the already financially stagnant Germany was soon crippled by the worldwide economic depression of the 1920s. As disenchantment with the government grew, Hitler began providing the German citizens with a national scapegoat, the Jewish people. While anti-Semitism gained increasing support throughout Europe, Hitler began a series of political maneuvers that swept his National Socialist German Worker's (Nazi) party into power. The once unemployed, drifter artist was appointed chancellor of Germany in 1933 and established an elaborate and well-organized military. Striving to rid Europe, and the world, of all those who were not part of his new Aryan nation, Hitler implemented one of the most devastating genocide programs in human history. A master orator, he promised to resurrect Germany and attain a position of world prominence through a policy of intolerance masked as nationalism. His twelve-year reign as dictator of Germany resulted in a world war and led to the deaths of 50 million people.

Dreams of Art

Born in 1889 in Braunau, a small Austro-Hungarian town located on the German border,

Hitler was the son of Alois Hitler, a customs inspector. His mother, Klara, was his father's second cousin who had served as a maid in the Hitler household. Alois was reputedly a harsh, demanding father who was severely disliked by his son. In contrast, Klara was a doting mother whom Hitler adored. He and his sister Paula were the only two of Klara's six children to survive infancy and were raised with two stepbrothers from their father's previous marriage. In 1899 the Hitler family moved to a small village near the town of Linz. As a child Hitler did well in school and enjoyed art, poetry, and music. As a teenager he expressed a desire to become an artist, a wish that was ridiculed by his father. Determined to pursue his own interests, Hitler began to rebel against his father and teachers. In 1903, when he was fourteen, his father died. Two years later, Hitler convinced his mother to let him quit school and spent three years wandering through the streets of Linz, visiting the library, opera, and theater. He developed a passion for the music of German composer Richard Wagner, whose operas portrayed gods and goddesses from old German legends.

At age eighteen Hitler traveled to Vienna, Austria. After taking the entrance exam for the Academy of Fine Arts, he was shocked and disappointed to learn that his drawings did not meet admission standards. Hitler refused the advice of the academy director, who suggested he enter the School of Architecture. Such a career path would require Hitler to return to conventional studies, a reality that he found unacceptable. Hitler's mother died in 1907, sending him into a deep depression. He applied to the academy again in 1908 but was rejected. For the next five years he drifted in Vienna, periodically making money by painting portraits, postcard scenes, and store posters. Austria, then part of the Austro-Hungarian Empire, was a socialist society struggling with the problems of modernization and rapid industrialization. As unemployment rose, dissension and conflict between the country's different ethnic groups increased with competition for jobs. As Hitler's personal dissatisfaction grew, he began blaming the Jewish population for the problems plaguing the nation. Such anti-Semitism was not new or unusual in Europe at this time; as Hitler gained more exposure to the use of political propaganda, he began formulating ideas for his own political platform.

When World War I erupted in Europe in 1914, Hitler had relocated to Munich, Germany. Not wanting to serve in the Austrian army, he volunteered for the German military. Accepted into the 16th Bavarian Reserve, Hitler left for France in 1914. He spent the next four years near the front lines as a message runner, later describing this period as the most memorable time of his life. He was a good soldier who enjoyed the orderliness and excitement of army life. Twice wounded, he was awarded the Iron Cross medal. In *Mein Kampf* (*My Struggle*), Hitler's autobiography, he documented an experience in the war that changed the course of his life. While temporarily blinded by poison gas, he envisioned himself as an Aryan hero called upon by the gods to lead his country into a glorious "1000-Year Reich." When World War I ended with Germany's surrender in 1918, the country was forced to sign the Treaty of Versailles. The agreement instituted severe conditions of surrender on Germany which included paying reparations, limiting the military, and forcing Germans to accept blame for starting the war. Like many Germans, Hitler was embittered by the outcome of the war, entirely convinced that Germany had been defeated because of socialists, liberals, and Jews.

The German Workers' Party

Hitler remained in the army and in 1919 he was chosen to become a special agent. Given the principal task of speaking to German troops about loyalty, he took the opportunity to voice his personal views, denouncing liberal attitudes that were gaining popularity at the time. He discovered the effect of his oratory prowess and retired from the army in 1920 to devote his energies to the German Workers' Party, a tiny group based on opposition to Jews and communists. Hitler began recruiting new members to the party, which was soon renamed the National Socialist German Workers' Party, or Nazi party. The Nazis' principal platform maintained that Jews were not Germans and therefore were not entitled to civil rights or residency within Germany. Realizing that the success of the party was contingent on his involvement, Hitler threatened to leave if he was not placed in charge. The members acquiesced to his demands, even agreeing to refer to him as *mein führer* ("my leader").

In November 1923 Hitler led a group of Nazi soldiers, called storm troopers, into a meeting of high-level government officials at a Munich beer hall and staged a putsch, or an attempt to seize power. When the coup proved unsuccessful, the rebels were arrested. While on trial, Hitler used the occasion to publicize his views, claiming his

"Father of Lies": Joseph Goebbels

The success of the Nazi party can be attributed to the use of printed propaganda that portrayed Jews as subhuman creatures who caused all of Germany's problems, and who would be eradicated by Adolf Hitler, Germany's savior. The mastermind and architect of this powerful literature was Joseph Goebbels, a novelist with a Ph.D. who was a dedicated follower of Hitler. Around 1924 he joined the Nazi party and was soon put in charge of one of the party's chapters by Hitler. By 1928 Goebbels had been appointed one of twelve Nazi deputies; Hitler made him head of party propaganda and public information in 1930. During the elections between 1930 and 1933, when the Nazis were gaining ground and winning increasing numbers of seats in the national legislature, Goebbels managed the party's campaigns. When Hitler became the dictator of Germany in 1933, Goebbels was named Reich Minister of propaganda. He seized control of the media, dictating what information was to be published; he arranged for the burning of books banned by the Nazis and limited all artistic and cultural expression to those deemed acceptable by the Nazi government.

Despite an upbringing that did not differentiate equality among races, Goebbels had adopted anti-Semitic opinions during the economic and political hardships of the 1920s. As anti-Jewish political groups gained popularity, Goebbels gradually saw the elimination of the Jewish race as the solution to Germany's domestic troubles. Goebbels launched a multifaceted attack against the Jews, utilizing propaganda to portray them as a sinister, ugly, and demonic race. Goebbels's crowning achievement was establishing a public image that portrayed Hitler as an omnipotent leader who lived a humble life, denying himself luxuries for the betterment of the German nation. Often referred to as the "Father of Lies," Goebbels falsified information given to German citizens, telling them that the Nazis were achieving victory when the war was actually slipping from Germany's grasp. After Hitler committed suicide in his underground bunker, Goebbels informed the public that the führer had died while leading his troops into battle. The day after Hitler's death Goebbels killed his six children and then committed suicide with his wife. Some accounts say Goebbels arranged to have the SS perform the killings rather than performing them himself.

---

accusers were the traitors. He stated: "I feel myself the best of Germans, who wanted the best for the German people." Hitler was sentenced to five years in jail, but he served only nine months due to a special amnesty for political prisoners. His fame and popularity surged while he was incarcerated at the Landsberg prison, where prisoners were allowed to drink beer and wine and entertain visitors. During this time, Hitler began working on *Mein Kampf*. Assisted by his devoted follower Rudolf Hess, Hitler explained his theory of racial superiority, which defined Aryans as "creators of culture" and the "Master Race." Jews were the "alien race" and "destroyers of culture" that needed to be eliminated. *Mein Kampf* was to become the most important document of Nazism.

Restructuring of the Nazi Party

Upon his release from prison in 1925, Hitler began rebuilding the Nazi party. He became increasingly popular among the desperate German people, who were suffering from the devastating effects of a worldwide economic depression. A powerful orator, Hitler addressed Germany's frustrations and fears, encouraging citizens to blame Jews for the poor condition of their country. His seemingly hypnotic speaking style produced strong emotion in his listeners, while his disciplined and brutal storm troopers terrorized his opponents. The failure of the Munich Beer Hall Putsch had convinced Hitler that his rise to power was to be implemented through legal maneuvers,

Adolf Hitler in Munich, 1931. (Reproduced by permission of AP/Wide World Photos)

not brute force. In the 1928 elections, the Nazi party won 2.6 percent of the votes, but by 1930 it had earned 18.3 percent. Surrounded by such supporters as Hess, Hermann Göring, Joseph Goebbels, and Heinrich Himmler, Hitler attracted more party members.

Chancellor of Germany

In the 1932 election Hitler ran against German president Paul von Hindenburg. He lost the election with 37 percent of the votes, but the Nazi party achieved a majority in the Reichstag. Meanwhile the German population grew increasingly angry and restless, threatening revolt and riot. To

prevent a civil war, Hindenburg appointed Hitler chancellor. Government leaders who opposed the violence of the Nazis believed that this promotion would constrain Hitler, allowing them to control his actions. The Nazi party continued building public support through propaganda and violence. When a February 1933 fire destroyed part of the Reichstag building, Hitler used the event to begin a series of terrorist acts against politicians who opposed him. Although there was never any proof linking any specific person or group to the fire, Hitler told the people that the fire was part of a communist plan to start a revolution in Germany. The next day he issued an emergency decree, approved by the nervous Reichstag and Hinden-

Italian dictator Benito Mussolini signed the "Pact of Steel" with Hitler in 1939. (National Archives and Records Administration)

burg, that gave him special powers to protect the nation against possible communist acts of violence. The decree, which empowered the government to strip German citizens of their constitutional rights, began the Third Reich.

The Nazis began a systematic elimination of civil rights, rendering the legal system powerless by allowing the Gestapo (Hitler's secret state police) to arrest and imprison any individual, regardless of reason. Laws no longer protected citizens and the Gestapo quickly arrested all of the members of the Reichstag. Hitler established the Nazi party as the only legal political party, and many of his opponents, including some from within his own party, were assassinated. The Nazis also implemented a series of harsh measures against the Jewish population in Germany. In 1933 Jews lost the right to

hold public jobs and their businesses were boycotted. As propaganda intensified hatred of the Jews, they were required to wear yellow six-pointed Stars of David (a Jewish religious symbol) on their clothing for identification. They were prevented from using public facilities and forced to attend segregated schools.

A majority of Europe observed the events occurring in Germany with trepidation and fear until Hitler withdrew Germany from the League of Nations. Uncertainty turned to anger when Hitler violated the terms of surrender outlined in the Treaty of Versailles, establishing a viable German army, navy, and air force. He eliminated uncooperative officers within the armed forces, started Hitler Youth movements that trained young people to become Nazi soldiers, and introduced a draft.

Hitler (standing) giving the Nazi salute during a meeting of the Reichstag in 1932. (Reproduced by permission of Bildarchiv Preussischer Kulturbesitz)

When Hindenburg died in August 1934, Hitler attained complete control of Germany. He became head of state, made himself commander of all military forces, and demanded that citizens refer to him as "Führer." He began making appearances before huge crowds in large halls, using military music, elaborate ceremonies, and dramatic speeches to demonstrate the glory of Germany under his leadership. A popular vote indicated that 90 percent of the population agreed with Hitler's policies, largely due to his eradication of unemployment and the doubling of the gross national income. Hitler's popularity was enforced by the Gestapo and the Schutzstaffel (the Security Squad known as the SS), who were free to torture, imprison, or kill anyone who did not agree with Nazi policy.

Germany Begins Policy of Aggression

By the late 1930s Hitler was ready to expand Germany's empire with the invasion of bordering countries. In 1938 he began by conquering Austria and specific German-speaking sections of Czecho-slovakia. Anxious to avoid war with Germany, Great Britain and France accepted these actions under the provision that Hitler refrain from invading any additional territory in Europe. They outlined the terms in the Munich Pact, which Hitler signed in 1938. He soon violated the agreement, however, by annexing the remainder of Czechoslovakia; in less than a year he had added ten million people to the population of Germany. In 1939 Hitler signed a "Pact of Steel" with Italy's dictator, Benito Mussolini, establishing the Axis powers; Japan joined the Axis in 1940. Great Britain and France responded, declaring that a German invasion of Poland would result in war; on September 3, 1939, the German army attacked Poland.

Hitler began formulating measures to achieve complete ethnic cleansing of German "enemies of the state." While numerous Jews had fled the country, approximately 500,000 Jews still remained in Germany proper, along with those who lived in areas Germany had conquered. Hitler began sending Jews, Catholics, Roma (also known as Gypsies), homosexuals, and political opponents to labor or concentration camps in Poland. In 1941 he ordered the implementation of the *Endlösung* ("Final Solution"), the systematic genocide of European Jews. In the camps, prisoners were often separated from their families, forced to work for no wages, given little food, and psychologically and physically tortured. A majority of Jews were killed in gas chambers and their bodies cremated; at the end of the war, an estimated 6 million Jews and approximately 1 million other people had been murdered by the Nazis.

The first few years of the war went well for Germany. The German army quickly conquered Denmark, Norway, Belgium, Luxembourg, and France while terrorizing Great Britain with a ceaseless barrage of aerial assaults. When the British bombed Germany, violating Hitler's contention that no enemy bombs would fall on his country, the Nazis continued their sweep of Europe by invading Bulgaria, Hungary, and Romania. Hitler's early success soon was overshadowed by his errors. In 1939 he had signed an agreement with Soviet leader Joseph Stalin that established a truce between the countries. In June 1940 Hitler broke the agreement by attacking the Soviet Union. At first the German army moved swiftly, making its way east toward the Soviet capital of Moscow. Hitler underestimated the strength of this new enemy, which challenged the Nazi attack through two bitterly cold winters. German troops were unprepared for the harsh weather and were unable to progress according to plan. The Soviets kept the Germans from taking Moscow, then retook the city of Stalingrad. With the Soviet victory at Kursk in mid-1943, the Germans were forced to retreat.

Reversal of Hitler's Fortunes

The entry of the United States into the war in December 1941 also greatly decreased the chances of a German victory, as did the defeat of seemingly unbeatable troops under General Erwin Rommel in North Africa. The Americans provided the additional men and supplies Allied forces needed to start pushing the German army back into Germany. After the Allies' successful D-Day campaign in Normandy in June 1944, it became clear that the German war effort was doomed. Yet Hitler refused to acknowledge defeat. By this time his opponents had made several attempts to assassinate him, and shortly after D-Day some of his own military officers implemented their own plot. They planted a bomb in a room where Hitler was conferring with other Nazi leaders. The bomb exploded but failed to kill Hitler and he ordered the execution of 5,000 people he suspected were involved. Hitler claimed that the foiled assassination was proof that he had been chosen by fate to conduct an important mission.

In January 1945, as the Allies pressed toward Germany, Hitler was forced to move into an underground bunker beneath his Berlin headquarters. By now his physical and mental health had declined sharply, conditions some historians believe were caused by syphilis. As the Soviet army was overtaking Berlin, the final blow in Germany's defeat, Hitler was in a state of extreme nervous exhaustion and his physical health was rapidly deteriorating. He had a leg rash, tremors in his extremities, and had suffered a minor stroke. It is reported that he was suspicious of everyone, repeatedly cursing all those in his life whom he believed had betrayed him. Pacing around the bunker stooped over and trembling, he talked incoherently, and planned new war strategies for divisions of the German army that had long been defeated. For Germany's defeat Hitler blamed not himself but the military leaders and the German people themselves, claiming they were all too weak to realize Germany's great destiny. He ordered a "scorched earth" policy to keep Germany out of Allied hands.

Though Hitler's seeming paranoia extended to many of those who had once been his closest confidants, he did believe in at least one person's steadfast devotion. Fifteen years before Hitler confined himself to the bunker, he had met a photographer's assistant named Eva Braun. She became his mistress and in 1936 she had moved into his Bavarian villa, Berchtesgaden. Though their relationship had gone through difficulties—Braun had attempted suicide twice—she remained loyal to Hitler. Now she joined him in the bunker and, on April 29, 1945, they were married. Hitler was urged to flee the bunker, but he refused and began preparations for his own death. He wrote a will in which he restated his hatred for the Jews, calling on Germany's future leaders to continue their opposition to the Jewish people. Several accounts exist describing Hitler's last moments. It is believed that the next day, as the Soviet Union bombed the area above the bunker, Hilter, Braun, and Hitler's dog Blondi went into the garden on the villa grounds. Hitler shot Blondi, then pulled the trigger on himself while Braun committed suicide by taking poison. The bodies were reportedly burned by Hitler's guards as Hitler had commanded.

Some people refused to believe the news of Hitler's death. For years rumors persisted that he was still alive and in hiding. In 1972 a dental forensic expert compared pictures of the dentures taken from a body found near Hitler's bunker with X-ray photos of Hitler's head that were taken in 1943. The two were a perfect match. The dental expert told the Sixth International Meeting of Forensic Sciences this was conclusive proof that Hitler had died in Germany as reported. Upon Hitler's death the Nazi government became a shambles. According to Hitler biographer John Toland, "without its true leader, it burst like a bubble." Germany surrendered to the Allies on May 8, 1945.

SOURCES

Books

Carr, William, *Hitler: A Study in Personality and Politics,* St. Martin's Press (New York), 1979.

Fuchs, Thomas, *The Hitler Fact Book,* Fountain Books (Los Angeles), 1990.

Haas, Gerda, *Tracking the Holocaust,* Runestone Press (Minneapolis), 1995.

Harris, Nathaniel, *Hitler,* B.T. Batsford Ltd. (London), 1989.

Marrin, Albert, *Hitler,* Puffin Books (New York), 1993.

Neville, Peter, *Life in the Third Reich,* edited with an introduction, by Richard Bessel, Oxford University Press (New York), 1987.

Shirer, William L., *The Rise and Fall of Adolf Hitler,* Random House (New York), 1961.

Speer, Albert, *Inside the Third Reich,* Galahad Books (New York), 1995.

Toland, John, *Adolf Hitler,* Anchor Books (New York), 1992.

Wepman, Dennis, *Adolf Hitler,* introductory essay on leadership, Arthur M. Schlesinger Jr., Chelsea House Publishers (New York), 1985.

Periodicals

Ryback, Timothy W., "Hitler's Lost Family," *The New Yorker,* July 17, 2000, pp. 46–57.

Oveta Culp Hobby

Born January 19, 1905
Killeen, Texas, United States
Died August 16, 1995
Houston, Texas, United States

Director of the Women's Army Corps
(WAC) and first secretary of the
Department of Health, Education,
and Welfare

*"The gaps our women will fill are in those
noncombatant jobs where women's hands
and women's hearts fit naturally. WAACs
will do the same type of work which
women do in civilian life."*

(U.S. Army)

Although women have played a role in every war in American history, most were relegated to functioning as nurses or in other supportive positions. World War II marked the first time women other than nurses served within the ranks of the U.S. Army. The original purpose of the Women's Army Auxiliary Corps (WAAC), which later became the Women's Army Corps (WAC), was to "free men for combat" by having women function in the realm of noncombat duties. The group also provided women the opportunity to demonstrate their abilities to perform as well as men in the same positions. When Oveta Culp Hobby became the first WAC director, she had already attained success as a lawyer and editor. She went on to manage the agency with dedication and energy, serving as an inspiration to the women under her leadership.

Heads WAACs

Born in 1905 in Killeen, Texas, Hobby later excelled as a student at Mary Hardin Baylor College for Women. When she decided to become a lawyer like her father, she attended the University of Texas Law School. By the time she was only twenty years old, Hobby had become assistant city attorney in Houston and the parliamentarian of the Texas legislature. In 1931, at the age of twenty-six, she married William Hobby, a former Texas governor and

"Rosie the Riveter": American Women at Work on the Home Front

As World War II escalated in Europe in 1939 and 1940, it appeared likely that the United States would eventually be drawn into the conflict. At that time the U.S. military was unprepared, lacking not only sufficient numbers of soldiers but also guns, ammunition, tanks, and airplanes. In May 1940 President Franklin D. Roosevelt announced that the United States must become the "great arsenal of democracy" for the rest of the world. The United States was charged with the task of producing the materials that would allow defenders of democracy to win the war over dictators Adolf Hitler and Benito Mussolini.

To accomplish this goal, Roosevelt authorized a huge buildup in the industrial production of war materials, while other products, such as automobiles, household appliances and bicycles, were put on hold. As increasing numbers of men joined the military after the Japanese bombing of the U.S. naval base at Pearl Harbor, Hawaii, the nation faced a crisis over who would fill jobs at munitions factories. The answer was women.

Shaking off the societal belief that their place was in the home, millions of women rallied to the call and began to work in industry and other areas. The U.S. government joined with industry to encourage women to take factory jobs. They distributed posters that showed strong, determined female workers who contributed to the war effort and whose husbands were proud of them. In February 1943 a song called "Rosie the Riveter" was broadcast on radio across the country. Written by Redd Evans and John Jacob Loeb and sung by a group called the Four Vagabonds, the song celebrated the historically significant role women were playing in the war. Soon the term "Rosie the Riveter," which the songwriters had chosen for its sound, not to honor any specific worker, came to be used as a fond nickname for the more than 6 million women who had joined the workforce.

Women were working in factories, shipyards, and steel mills; they were employed as welders, electricians, mechanics; engineers, and chemists; they operated heavy equipment, from cranes to streetcars; and even drove taxi cabs. Dressed in coveralls and heavy shoes, they were performing jobs that had previously been the domain of men, proving to themselves and the world that equality among the sexes resulted in a stronger nation. Two million women were employed in clerical jobs, about half of them with the federal government. Women also took charge of farms and many worked as Red Cross volunteers or with the Civilian Defense—serving as air raid wardens, messengers, drivers, and spotters who checked the skies for enemy airplanes.

The figures for total wartime production in the United States showed great improvements in efficiency: The country produced 296,429 airplanes, 102,351 tanks and self-propelled guns, 372,431 artillery pieces, 47 million tons of ammunition, and 84,620 warships, as well as other kinds of equipment. This massive output played a major role in the Allied victory and could never have been accomplished without the help of female laborers. After the war most of the women were laid off from their jobs, many unwillingly, due to a decrease in production and the return of men from the war. Nevertheless, the war years changed Americans' ideas about the capabilities of women, redefining the role of women in the workplace, and paving the way for the immense changes in women's rights over the next five decades.

World War II saw women entering the military in large numbers, thanks in part to the Women's Army Corps (WAC), which was directed by Oveta Culp Hobby. Here, Major Charity E. Adams and Capt. Abbie N. Campbell inspect the troops. (National Archives and Records Administration)

the publisher of the *Houston Post* newspaper. She worked at the *Post*, starting as a book editor and rising to the position of executive vice president. Between 1933 and 1941 Hobby held many jobs. While serving as parliamentarian of the legislature, she also helped her husband manage the *Post*, served as president of the Texas League of Women Voters, raised two children, and wrote a book on parliamentary practice (*Mr. Chairman*, 1936).

In 1941, as the United States prepared to enter World War II, Congresswoman Edith Nourse Rogers of Massachusetts introduced a bill to establish a separate women's corps of the army. Rogers knew that women would be instrumental in the upcoming war effort, just as they had been in World War I (1914–1918) and other conflicts. She wanted to ensure that women received the same benefits and protection as men, such as food, living quarters, legal protection, and medical care. Although many people believed that women should not be directly involved in war work, especially serving alongside men, Army Chief of Staff General George Marshall agreed that women would be well suited to perform office work and communication jobs that required manual dexteri-

ty and patience. He and other army leaders believed that if women could fill many noncombatant jobs, more men would be available to fight the enemy.

Congress passed the bill authorizing the Women's Auxiliary Army Corps (WAAC), although the final version of the plan contained changes that Rogers opposed. For example, women serving as WAACs would be paid less than men of the same rank and position and would not receive the same economic protection when they served overseas (including overseas pay, life insurance, veterans' medical coverage, and death benefits). Hobby was already in Washington when the bill was signed. Earlier, she had been assigned to head the new Women's Division of the War Department's Bureau of Public Relations. She had helped push the bill through Congress, testifying in its favor.

On May 15, 1941, the bill became law and Hobby was named director of the WAAC. Her record of personal achievement and experience in local and national politics qualified her for the job. It was also hoped that her attractive and "ladylike" demeanor would persuade conservative critics that the WAAC was a respectable organization. Public response to the WAAC bill was enthusiastic. By November, the goal

First Lady Eleanor Roosevelt in a ceremony with representatives of the women's armed forces: Dorothy Stratton (SPARS), Oveta Culp Hobby (WAC), Mildred McAfee Horton (WAVES), and Ruth Cheney Streeter (Women Marines). (Women in Military Service for America Memorial Foundation, Inc.)

of 25,000 recruits to the WAAC had already been met, so a new limit of 150,000 was authorized. When the first WAAC training center was established at Fort Des Moines, Iowa, more than 35,000 women signed up for fewer than 1,000 positions.

Soon after accepting her new appointment, Hobby appeared at a press conference to answer questions about the WAAC and its role in the military. Some questions were mundane and juvenile, such as what color underwear the women would wear under their uniforms and whether they would be able to wear makeup. Hobby answered them calmly and seriously. In other speaking engagements, she explained that "the gaps our women will fill are in those noncombatant jobs where women's hands and women's hearts fit naturally. WAACs will do the same type of work which women do in civilian life. They will bear the same relation to men of the Army that they bear to the men of the civilian organizations in which they work."

In July 1941 the first WAAC officer candidate training class, which included 440 recruits, started its six-week course at Fort Des Moines. The average officer candidate was a twenty-five-year-old college graduate, who had experience in office work or teaching. Many had friends and relatives already serving in the military. A separate platoon of forty African American officer recruits was also established; these women attended class and ate meals with the white women, but all of the post's service clubs, theaters, and beauty shops were segregated. In August the first class of auxiliary women reported for duty. Slightly younger than the officer candidates, these recruits had only a high school education and less work experience.

The first qualified WAACs were sent to the Aircraft Warning Service units of the U.S. Army Air Corps. Approximately half of the women filled office positions such as file clerk, typist, or stenographer; others were dispersed to various jobs,

Oveta Culp Hobby being sworn in as secretary of the Department of Health, Education, and Welfare by President Eisenhower. (Reproduced by permission of AP/Wide World Photos, Inc.)

including weather observer and forecaster, cryptographer, radio operator, parachute rigger, photograph analyst, and control tower operator. Women working for the Army Transportation Corps helped process men for overseas assignments; members of the Quartermaster Corps maintained supply depots; and women assigned to the Signal Corps operated telephone switchboards and served as photographers and map analysts.

Reactions to the Work of WAACs

The general response to work done by the WAACs was positive. For example, General Dwight D. Eisenhower, commander of the Allied forces in Europe and future president of the United States, commented in 1945: "During the time I have had the [WAACs] under my command they have met every test and task assigned to them…. [T]heir contributions in efficiency, skill, spirit, and determination are unmeasurable." A backlash of public opinion erupted in 1943 when rumors spread that most of the women were functioning as prostitutes and that a large number of them had become preg-

nant. The uproar demonstrated how uncomfortable many people were when women took on nontraditional roles. The furor eventually died down after Hobby testified before Congress and provided evidence that the rumors were untrue. She had always insisted that the WAACs maintain a high standard of performance, discipline, and morality in order to avoid such controversies.

The army's high regard for the WAAC was confirmed in July 1943, when the organization was assimilated into the army itself and its name was changed to the Women's Army Corps (WAC). This move provided women the same pay, privileges, and protection as men. By the end of the war, the WAC had served in a variety of positions in locations all over the world. For instance, 300 WACs assisted in the planning of the D-Day invasion of France, and an African American battalion worked in England and France to redirect the vast amount of mail sent to U.S. personnel fighting in Europe. More than 600 WACs were awarded medals and citations for their work during the war, including Hobby, who received the Distinguished Service Medal.

When the war ended, Hobby, then forty years old, resigned her command and returned to Houston. In 1953 President Eisenhower appointed her as the first secretary of the new Department of Health, Education and Welfare. This made Hobby the only female member of the president's cabinet and only the second female cabinet member in American history.

Hobby was responsible for the Public Health Service, the Food and Drug Administration, the Office of Education, and the Bureau of Old Age and Survivors Insurance. In 1955 she oversaw the distribution of the polio vaccine—the discovery by Jonas Salk that kept many people from developing the crippling disease. She then returned to Houston to care for her sick husband. When Hobby resigned, Treasury Secretary George Humphrey reportedly exclaimed that Washington was losing "the best man in the Cabinet." Hobby's husband died in 1964 and the following year she was appointed Chairman of the Board of the Houston *Post*. During the next few decades, she built the *Post* into a $100-million business. In 1983 Hobby was the only woman listed in *Texas Business* magazine as one of the twenty most powerful Texans. She died August 16, 1995, in Houston, Texas.

Lt. Col. Anna Walker Wilson served as the Women's Army Corps director of the European Theater of Operations. She points to her patch, which represents army, air, and ground forces. The lightning bolt symbolizes conquered countries that have been liberated. (Reproduced by permission of AP/Wide World Photos)

SOURCES

Books

American Decades: 1940–1949, Gale (Detroit), 1995, pp. 276 and 277.

Green, Anne Bosanko, and D'Ann Campbell, *One Woman's War: Letters Home from the Women's Army Corps, 1944-1946*, Minnesota Historical Society (St. Paul, MN), 1989.

Williams, Vera S., *WACs: Women's Army Corps*, Motorbooks International Publishers, 1997.

Periodicals

Time, August 28, 1995, p. 27.

Other

Bellafaire, Judith A., *The Women's Army Corps: A Commemoration of World War II Service*, U.S. Army Center of Military History, http://www.army.mil (August 4, 2000).

Rudolf Höss

Born November 25, 1900
Baden, Germany
Died April 16, 1947
Auschwitz concentration camp, Poland

Soldier; commandant at Auschwitz
who supervised the executions of at least
1.3 million Jews

*"The killing ... did not concern me much at
the time. I must even admit that this
gassing set my mind at rest."*

(Reproduced by permission of Archives Photos, Inc.)

Rudolf (or Rudolph) Höss served as a guard at Dachau, one of many such concentration camps that confined people regarded as "enemies of the state" by the Nazis. Höss' efficiency so pleased the Nazi party that he moved up the ranks swiftly. After only four years, Höss was promoted to oversee a camp. He converted a small army barracks in Poland into the Auschwitz-Birkenau camp, one of the largest and deadliest of all such facilities. Höss' superiors regarded him as a "a true pioneer ... because of his new ideas and educational methods."

Joins Army to Escape Home Life

Höss was born in 1900 in Baden, Germany, a small town near the border of France. He was the son of a German army officer who had served in Africa. Historians note that Höss had a peculiar childhood. According to author Robert E. Conot "his father had been a bigoted ... Catholic, who, after fathering Höss and his younger sister, had taken an oath of celibacy and dedicated [Höss] to God, intending that he should become a priest." The senior Höss declared his daughter was an angel. Höss developed a lasting hatred for both his father and sister, leaving home at the age of fifteen to become a soldier in the German army during World War I (1914–18).

After the war Höss joined a group of former soldiers who, he later wrote in his autobiography,

The gate to the Auschwitz concentration camp bearing the motto *Arbeit Macht Frei* ("Work Makes One Free"). (Main Commission for the Investigation of Nazi War Crimes/USHMM Photo Archives)

returned from the war to find themselves misfits in German society. In 1922 he joined the Nazi Party—a conservative, German-nationalist political group headed by Adolf Hitler. The party followed a strong anti-Semitic platform. In 1923 Höss participated in the execution of a schoolteacher suspected of being a traitor to the Nazi cause. Sentenced to serve at least ten years in prison, he was released after serving only five years. Although information is scarce, it appears he then married a woman named Hedwig.

Höss then joined a youth movement devoted to farming and country living. The group focused its attention in the east on land that belonged to Poland. Part of the Nazis' political agenda was to enlarge Germany by taking land from neighboring countries. Heinrich Himmler, future leader of the SS, was also a member of this group. It was at Himmler's suggestion that Höss later joined the SS. The unit served as Hitler's personal bodyguards and as guards at various concentration camps. When Himmler established the Dachau concentration camp in 1933, Höss was chosen to become one of its guards.

Guards the Camp

Dachau, located in the German state of Bavaria, was a former war materials factory. The factory was converted into a concentration camp intended to hold those imprisoned for actions or beliefs perceived to threaten the Nazi Party. They were termed "undesirables" by the Nazis, who believed that such people could be "reeducated" to fit back into society. Authors Debórah Dwork and Robert Jan Van Pelt note that Höss "saw it as his main task to teach them the value of hard work, which would bring structure and endurance to an unstable life." In his autobiography, Höss claimed he disliked the methods used against Dachau prisoners by the other guards, but he "had become too fond of the black uniform" to object. (Höss was referring to the black uniforms worn by the SS, which sometimes led the group to be called "the blackshirts.") He said he was too sensitive for the work at first. He recalled: "I wished to appear hard, lest I should appear weak." He soon adjusted to the brutality administered to the prisoners by the guards, and he executed his job with efficiency.

Dachau and other concentration camps were multifaceted institutions, serving as labor camps, farms, and killing centers. Höss never forgot the lessons he learned at Dachau. The phrase *Arbeit Macht Frei* ("Work Makes One Free") became his motto, even though most prisoners did not survive their confinement. When the Auschwitz concentration camp was established in 1940, Höss was put in charge. One of his first acts was to have this motto nailed above the entranceway.

Auschwitz was the name of a small town in Poland as well as the name of the Polish army barracks at the edge of town. The Nazis believed that the town was ideally situated for a concentration camp. The area was thinly populated, so few outsiders would know what was happening at the camp, and it was situated on a direct railroad line to Germany. When Hitler overtook Poland in 1939, Polish citizens who objected to German rule were sent to Auschwitz. The camp also served as a center where captured Poles and, later, Soviet prisoners of war were sent while the Nazis determined their suitability to work as slave laborers in other camps and factories.

Life at Auschwitz

As Hitler began work on his plans for expanding the German empire, the need for building materials became critical. Auschwitz had an abundance of sand and gravel, which could be made into concrete. Auschwitz was expanded and became an outpost of the German Earth and Stone Works. Höss' camp used slave laborers from conquered countries throughout Europe. A prison was built to hold the laborers, who were literally worked to death in many instances. A crematorium—a room with huge ovens—was constructed to burn the remains of the dead workers.

Höss complained that his co-workers at Auschwitz were untrustworthy, which made him uncomfortable. As his discomfort grew, he began drinking in secret. His wife tried to alleviate the situation by inviting people to their home outside the camp for social evenings. But Höss had little interest. He wrote: "I lived only for my work. I was absorbed, I might say obsessed.... Every fresh difficulty only increased my zeal.... [A]ll human emotions were forced into the background."

However, Höss continued to be interested in farming. Inspired by agriculture, he drew maps, plans, and diagrams for a farming complex to be built at Auschwitz. Höss took pride in his devotion

to his five children and his pets, and he designed the complex to include a farm for his family. Himmler supported the idea. When female prisoners began arriving at Auschwitz in 1942, they were set to work cultivating the heavy clay soil surrounding the camp. Working twelve-hour days with very little to eat, and beaten by guards if they faltered, the women and girls built greenhouses, barns, and roads. The male prisoners continued their work at the sand and gravel pits.

Soviet prisoners were also sent to Auschwitz. When Hitler poised his army for assault on the Soviet Union, Himmler ordered Höss to prepare Auschwitz to accept 100,000 Soviet prisoners of war. In December of 1941, 12,000 Soviet prisoners became part of the Auschwitz workforce and began expanding the facilities. The expansion was built in an area thickly covered with birch trees. The addition was called Birkenau ("in the birches"). By April of 1942, only 150 of the original 12,000 Soviets workers were still alive. But the expansion proved unnecessary. The Nazis' march into the Soviet Union failed, and large numbers of Soviet prisoners were never taken to Auschwitz.

Late in 1942, Höss began having troubles at home. Author Robert Conot described a defining incident in Höss' life that occurred during this time. While at a dinner party, a man asked Höss' wife what she thought of her husband's work. The man described the nature of the work for her since Höss' wife had only heard rumors about what her husband did for a living. Later in the evening, she confronted her husband, asking if what she had heard was true. When he admitted it was, she was so upset that she refused to sleep with him from that day forward. Soon after, Höss forced a camp inmate to become his mistress.

The "Final Solution"

In 1941 or 1942, according to Höss, he received orders from Himmler to transform Auschwitz into a killing site. This order was part of the Nazis' plans for the "Final Solution"—the Nazi code for the total elimination of European Jews. Höss claimed that Himmler said the Jews of Europe must be killed immediately or the Jews would later exterminate the German people. Höss later told a psychologist about this order: "I had nothing to say; I could only say *Jawohl!* [Yes, I will!]." Höss claimed he did try to get Himmler to improve the terrible conditions at the camp—the overcrowding, lack of drainage for sanitation purposes, and

Postcards from Auschwitz

William L. Shirer (1904–1993) was an American journalist and historian who was working in Berlin, Germany, as a radio correspondent when World War II began in 1939. He was often at Adolf Hitler's side during the dictator's rise to power. Shirer detailed his experiences in his massive book, *The Rise and Fall of the Third Reich: A History of Nazi Germany*. The volume won the National Book Award.

Shirer offered this description of the selection process that took place under Rudolf Höss' command, based on accounts given by jailers and inmates who survived the Auschwitz concentration camp:

> The 'selection,' which decided which Jews were to be [put to work] and which ones immediately gassed, took place at the railroad siding as soon as the victims had been unloaded from the freight cars in which they had been locked without food or water for as much as a week—for many came from such distant parts as France, Holland and Greece. Though there were heart-rending scenes as wives were torn away from husbands and children from parents, none of the captives, as Höss testified [at a trial after the war was over] and survivors agree, realized just what was in store for them.

Shirer noted that some of the new arrivals were given "pretty picture postcards ... to be signed and sent back home to their relatives with a printed inscription saying: 'We are doing very well here. We have work and we are well treated. We await your arrival.'"

---

lack of a reliable water supply—but Himmler was uninterested. It was through the will of Himmler, said Höss, that "Auschwitz became the greatest human [killing] center of all time."

By the winter of 1943, Höss had equipped the facility with four new crematoria, each with a gas chamber that could kill 2,000 people at one time. The gas chambers were sealed rooms that, when filled with poisonous gas, suffocated the people locked inside. New transports of "undesirables"— one term the Nazis used to describe Jews, Roma (often called Gypsies), homosexuals, and Jehovah's Witnesses—arrived at the camps frequently. Höss and his co-workers would select as many people as they needed for camp labor. The rest were executed. The selection for labor favored the young and strong, who were more capable of completing heavy field work. Those selected for the chambers were the sick, the elderly, and small children.

The Horrors Described

Later, when Höss testified at the Nuremberg Trials (1945–1946) of Nazi war criminals, he commented on the "Final Solution." According to author Robert Conot, Höss read his statement in a high-pitched, almost boyish voice. His sworn statement read, in part: "The 'final solution' of the Jewish question meant the complete extermination of all Jews in Europe. I had the order to produce extermination facilities in Auschwitz in June 1942." He added: "When I built the ... building in Auschwitz, I therefore used Zyklon B, a crystallized hydrocyanic acid, which we threw into the death chamber through a small opening. It took three to fifteen minutes, depending on the climatic conditions, in order to kill the people in the death chamber. We knew when the people were dead because their screaming stopped. We waited usually a half hour before we opened the doors and removed the bodies. After the bodies were brought forth, our special [troops] took off the rings and pulled the gold out of the teeth of the bodies." The jewelry and gold were stored to be transferred into money to support the German war effort.

Höss estimated that during his command of Auschwitz, which lasted until December 1, 1943, "at least 2.5 million victims were put to death and

---

exterminated there through gassing; at least a further half million died through hunger and sickness." Other estimates put the number of Jews killed under his command at more than 1.3 million. Höss performed his job so well that he was promoted to chief of the Central Administration for Camps, a job that took him to Berlin, Germany, where the Nazis' headquarters were located.

The War Winds Down

By the time Höss moved to Berlin, Germany was losing the war. The order came down to destroy the concentration camps in an effort to prevent the conquering Allied armies from learning of the horrors that had occurred in them. As the Soviets closed in on Auschwitz, officials were ordered to kill as many inmates as possible before the Allied troops arrived. The remainder were to be transported to other camps not in the path of the Allies. Höss tried to get to Auschwitz to supervise the killings, but then decided it was unwise to put himself in the path of the conquering Soviets. Instead, he joined a group that was fleeing toward Denmark. "It was a gruesome journey," he later wrote, "as the enemy's low flying planes continually machine-gunned the escape route." When the news reached them that Hitler had committed suicide, anything resembling order and discipline among the fleeing Germans collapsed.

Höss was captured by the British, but managed to conceal his identity and was released. He took a job on a farm and escaped arrest until March 1946, when the British—who had been looking for him—caught up with him. He was imprisoned and forced to testify at two trials of Nazi criminals. Author Abram L. Sachar described Höss' testimony at the Nuremberg Trials, asserting that the former commandant displayed as much emotion as a "robot." During his confinement, he wrote his autobiography. In it he denied responsibility for many of the crimes he was accused of committing, yet accepted responsibility for many horrific acts that he described in detail. He was handed over to authorities in Poland, where he had committed his crimes. In 1947 he was tried and condemned to death. He was hanged on April 16, 1947, at Auschwitz.

Sources

Books

Conot, Robert E., *Justice at Nuremberg,* Harper & Row (New York), 1983.

Dwork, Debórah, and Robert Jan Van Pelt, *Auschwitz: 1270 to the Present,* W.W. Norton (New York), 1996.

Höss, Rudolf, *Death Dealer: The Memoirs of the SS Kommandant at Auschwitz,* edited by Steven Paskuly, translated by Andrew Pollinger, Prometheus Books (Buffalo), 1992.

Manvell, Roger, and Heinrich Fraenkel, *Himmler,* Putnam (New York), 1965.

Sachar, Abram L., *The Redemption of the Unwanted,* St. Martin's/Marek (New York), 1983.

Franz Jaggerstatter

As Adolf Hitler and the Nazi party tightened their grip on occupied countries in Europe during World War II, greater numbers of men were required to serve in the German military. Failure to comply with Nazi orders could result in torture, deportation to concentration camps, and execution of objectors as well as their family members. Franz Jaggerstatter, an Austrian farmer with a wife and three young daughters, refused to comply with German policies that would force him into military service. Feeling that violent action on behalf of the Nazis would betray his religious beliefs, Jaggerstatter refused to enter military service knowing the severe consequences that would result from his actions. He was executed for his beliefs, and his death became a rallying cry for conscientious objectors.

Born May 20, 1907
    St. Radegund, Austria
Died August 9, 1943
    Berlin, Germany

Austrian farmer; conscientious objector during World War II

"We must love God even more than family, and we must lose everything dear and worthwhile on earth rather than commit even the slightest offense against God."

Religion a Foundation of His Life

Jaggerstatter was born in 1907 in the rural town of St. Radegund in northern Austria, located along the banks of the Salzach River. His parents were servants who were not married at the time of his birth. His mother, Rosalia, was working as a maid when his father, Franz Bachmeier, was killed while fighting in World War I (1914–1918). In 1917 Rosalia married a farmer named Jaggerstatter, who adopted the boy and introduced him to literature. Young Jaggerstatter attended the local

Conscientious Objectors

Conscientious objectors refuse to participate in war for various reasons, including religion, politics, and philosophy. Depending on an individual's personal reason for conscientious objection, he or she may perform different functions during times of war. Some conscientious objectors refuse to serve in combat but will accept noncombatant duties, while others also refuse noncombatant service but will work in civilian jobs. A third type of objector, often called an absolutist, refuses to fight or accept any alternative to fighting.

Conscientious objectors have existed throughout history. The ancient religions of Buddhism and Jainism are based on nonviolence, and early Christians refused to serve in the Roman army. During the Middle Ages, Christians began to differentiate between just and unjust wars. After the Protestant religions broke from the Roman Catholic church, some groups began to incorporate conscientious objection as a foundation of their beliefs. The Mennonites, the Society of Friends (Quakers), and the Church of the Brethren, among others, all continue to promote nonviolence. In the nineteenth and twentieth centuries, Jehovah's Witnesses and Seventh-Day Adventists began advocating policies of non-violence. Indian leader Mohandas K. Gandhi made a positive impact on the perception of conscientious objectors by taking a nonviolent stand as he campaigned for the independence of India from Great Britain. Now groups like the Fellowship of Reconciliation and War Resisters International provide support for those who refuse to fight in wars.

During the American Civil War conscientious objectors were excused from service if they were able to send someone else to serve in their place. In World War I, U.S. law recognized objectors if they were members of churches that declared nonviolence as an official belief. Although these objectors had to report to duty, they were assigned to noncombatant positions. Some of the absolutists who refused noncombatant service were sent to work on farms, while many were imprisoned. During World War I conscientious objectors in Austria-Hungary and Germany were sent to insane asylums, while those in France were often shot as deserters. In World War II approximately 100,000 Americans were classified as conscientious objectors.

U.S. law recognized those who refused to fight for religious reasons, but those who objected on political or philosophical grounds were not granted objector status. Objectors performed alternative service such as reforestation, flood control, soil conservation, dairy testing, and care of mental patients. About 6,000 absolutists were imprisoned. Great Britain utilized the same three categories of objectors as the United States, but conscientious objector status could be claimed on religious, political, or philosophical grounds. In Germany conscientious objectors were shot or sent to concentration camps, while in Japan some objectors entered the army and then refused to aim their guns at the enemy.

school in St. Radegund while pursuing extracurricular interests of games, dancing, and riding his motorcycle (the first seen in St. Radegund) loudly around the village streets. He left home at the age of twenty to work in the iron ore industry in Steiermark, Austria. After three years he returned home to pursue a life of farming. In 1936 he married a local girl named Franziska, and the couple traveled to Rome for their honeymoon. While in Italy, Jaggerstatter experienced a renewal of his Roman Catholic faith, and upon returning home, he attended daily mass and served as sacristan, a church officer in charge of priests' garments and other items used in the mass, in St. Radegund's small church. During the next few years the couple had three daughters. Jaggerstatter was known as a devoted and openly affectionate father.

As the Jaggerstatters tended to their farm and growing family, Hitler was becoming powerful in Germany. Prior to Hitler's appointment as chancellor, Jaggerstatter had a dream in which he envisioned a train on a track to hell. He maintained that the train represented National Socialism, the political philosophy of the Nazi party. He was distraught by the eagerness of the masses to board the train and join the Nazis. Jaggerstatter became increasingly alarmed as the events of his dream seemed to be taking shape in reality. He shared his distrust of Hitler with friends and neighbors at local gatherings.

In 1938 Austrians held a vote to decide if the country should join Hitler's Third Reich. Jaggerstatter was the only person in St. Radegund to vote against the *Anschluss,* or union of Austria and Germany. Jaggerstatter received his first call to military service in June 1940. Despite his doubts about Hitler and National Socialism, he reported for duty, only to be released in 1941 when his farm work was deemed more important than military service. Jaggerstatter used the time to reflect on his personal and religious beliefs about the use of violence in support of a system he did not advocate. He was not a pacifist; he stated that he would have become a soldier if Austrians had chosen to oppose, rather than join, the Nazis. However, it became increasingly clear to him that he could not kill in the name of Hitler.

In February 1943 Jaggerstatter received his second call to military service. Still struggling with his conscience, he consulted the Catholic bishop in the nearby town of Linz. He asked the bishop how one could remain a Christian while fighting for the Nazis. The bishop responded that Jaggerstatter's principal duties were to his country and to his family. Jaggerstatter's friends and relatives agreed with the bishop and urged him to join the military. Ignoring their advice, he went to the local induction center and informed the commanding officer that he refused to enlist in the army. Jaggerstatter was arrested and taken to prison in Linz, then transferred to the Brandenburg Prison in Berlin, Germany.

An Inspiration to Other Objectors

While awaiting trial, Jaggerstatter wrote several letters to friends and loved ones, explaining that he was upholding his commitment as a Christian and that God had granted him the grace and strength to die for his beliefs. Jaggerstatter's trial, held on July 6, 1943, was presided over by military judges from the regulation military, not Hitler's SS. Even the judges attempted to talk Jaggerstatter out of his position, but he reiterated his refusal to fight for National Socialism. He received the death sentence. On August 9, 1943, Jaggerstatter was beheaded at Brandenburg Prison. His remains were cremated and buried on the prison's grounds. In St. Radegund, he was regarded as a religious fanatic and his wife was criticized for not forcing him to change his mind. For almost twenty years Jaggerstatter was remembered only by his closest survivors.

Jaggerstatter might still be unknown today if not for the efforts of American sociologist and conscientious objector Gordon Zahn, who uncovered his story while conducting research in Europe on German Catholic support for World War II. In a book written by Father Kreuzberg, a Catholic priest, Zahn came across a reference to Jaggerstatter, whom Kreuzberg called "Franz II." Intrigued by Jaggerstatter's stand against the Nazis, Zahn traveled to St. Radegund and interviewed Jaggerstatter's widow and others who had known him. Zahn learned that after the war Jaggerstatter's ashes had been returned to his home village and buried near the door of the church in St. Radegund. Despite protests that Jaggerstatter was a coward who refused to fight while other men sacrificed their lives for their country, a sympathetic priest insisted that Jaggerstatter's name be added to a list of St. Radegund's war dead.

Zahn's book, *In Solitary Witness: The Life and Death of Franz Jaggerstatter,* was published in 1964. Public opinion about Jaggerstatter remained mixed in Austria, but much of the rest of the world embraced him as a religious martyr and role model for other conscientious objectors. His example helped to persuade the Catholic church to take an official stand to support a person's right to object to military service based on religious and moral grounds. In 1970 Jaggerstatter's name was cited when the United Nations expanded the Universal Declaration of Human Rights to include a provision for conscientious objection.

Although some continue to question Jaggerstatter's actions, he has come to be known as a hero in his homeland. Streets in Vienna, Linz, and other Austrian cities have been named for him; celebrations have been held in his honor; and a petition has been submitted to the Vatican to have him named a saint. The Jaggerstatters' old family farmhouse has been turned into a center for study and meditation. In a gesture of reconciliation and goodwill, a cycle of twelve etchings on Jaggerstatter by Austrian artist Ernst Degaspari has been displayed at Yad Vashem, the Holocaust memorial center in Israel. In an article in *New Statesman and Society*, Bruce Kent wrote that "Jaggerstatter's life continues to give courage to conscientious objectors around the world from many different religious and non-religious backgrounds."

SOURCES

Books

Balfour, Michael, "A Portrait Gallery: Franz Jagerstatter," *Withstanding Hitler in Germany 1933–45*, pp. 231–233, Routledge (London), 1988.

Zahn, Gordon, *In Solitary Witness: The Life and Death of Franz Jaggerstatter*, Holt, Rinehart, and Winston (New York), 1964.

Periodicals

Jabusch, Willard F., "A Tale of Two Towns," *America*, July 16, 1994, p. 4.

Kent, Bruce, "The Man Who Said No to Hitler," *New Statesman and Society*, May 6, 1994, p. 20.

Moore, Donald J., "Franz Jagerstatter: Conscience vs. Duty," *America*, February 19, 1994, p. 12.

Zahn, Gordon, "In Celebration of Martyrdom," *America*, February 19, 1994, p. 8.

Noor Inayat Khan

Like many people living in Europe at the time of the Nazi party's ascent to power, Noor Inayat Khan found her life drastically changed by the outbreak of World War II. A privileged young woman, Khan displayed artistic talent early in life and was educated at prestigious French schools. As Germany began invading and conquering countries throughout Europe, she became aware that the Nazis were establishing a repressive regime. Fearing a German victory, Khan joined the resistance effort by becoming a British spy in Paris, France. Her bravery and fortitude were overshadowed, however, by her lack of experience. While conducting espionage and intelligence work, she made a number of errors that would ultimately lead to her capture and execution by the Germans. The British government posthumously honored Khan with the George Cross, an award for patriotism.

Born January 1, 1914
Moscow, Russia
Died September 1944
Dachau, Germany

Student; writer; social worker; executed as a British spy by the Nazis

"There was no question as to her courage and loyalty. There was *as to her stability for the job."*
—WRITER A. A. HOEHLING

A Privileged Youth

Noor-un-Nisa Inayat Khan was born in Moscow, Russia, in 1914. Khan's mother was an American woman named Ora Ray Baker, a relative of religious leader Mary Baker Eddy, who founded the Christian Science church. Her father, Inayat Khan, was a musician and mystic from India, who had a close friendship with Russian novelist Leo Tolstoy. At the time of Noor Khan's birth, Inayat Khan was serving as a Sufi missionary in Russia,

The SOE Spy Operation

The Special Operations Executive (SOE) was initiated in Great Britain in July 1940 to disrupt enemy operations in Nazi-occupied territory. Many nations of the world participated in SOE activities, which had an important impact on the course of World War II. The smallest and most highly secretive section of the SOE was the London Controlling Section (LCS). According to historian M. R. D. Foot, part of the operation involved double agents who were to infiltrate and influence the higher levels of German intelligence, potentially even Hitler himself.

One story tells of a double agent, a citizen of Wales who had been recruited by the German military intelligence organization before the war. In 1939 the man went to his local police station and made his first radio report to the Germans, who mistakenly believed he was working for them. His efforts helped the British capture enemy agents the Nazis sent to Great Britain throughout the war.

attempting to better acquaint the other parts of the world with the mystical religion. Prior to the Russian Revolution, which began in 1917, he moved his family to London, England, where they remained until 1920. The Khans then settled north of Paris while Inayat went to Switzerland and founded the international headquarters of the Sufi movement. During a tour of Europe, he met a wealthy widow from Holland who bought a house for the Khans on the outskirts of Paris. Inayat died of pneumonia in Delhi, India, in 1927, leaving his wife with two sons and two daughters. Noor was only fifteen at the time, and she was devastated by her father's sudden death.

During the 1930s, Noor Inayat Khan attended a girls' college in Sursennes, France, and a music school in Paris. She then began studying at the world-famous Sorbonne college within the University of Paris. While pursuing a degree in child psychology and biology, she suffered a nervous breakdown. During her recovery she spent time in southern France, Spain, and Italy. In 1937, she returned to Paris to study Asian languages. By 1939, Khan was writing for the children's page of the *Sunday Figaro* newspaper, as well as young people's radio programs. Her story book *Twenty Jataka Tales* was published in 1939 in London. Hoping to distract children from the impending war, Khan established a new children's newspaper. She also studied first aid and nursing, and within a short time, she began working at a home for the pregnant wives of British officers. In November 1940, after her brother had joined the Royal Navy, she enlisted in the Woman's Auxiliary Air Force (the WAAF). The next year she requested a job in intelligence work. She was selected to be trained as a radio telegraph specialist.

Bungles Assignments as British Agent

In February 1943 Khan was invited to become an agent for the Special Operations Executive (SOE), the British Secret Service operation. Because of her expertise with radio telegraphing, it was decided that Noor would begin training as a wireless operator. Due to the urgent need for an English SOE agent in Paris, the SOE decided to send her into France before her training was complete. On June 16, 1943, under the cloak of darkness, she landed alone by parachute near Le Mans, France. Carrying only a handbag and no other supplies, Khan (using the alias Jean-Marie Regnier) found her way to Paris, which was under Nazi control. Her career as a secret agent was doomed as soon as she arrived in the city. She had been instructed to go to an apartment where she would meet a contact, who she assumed would be an elderly woman. When she was greeted at the door by a young man, however, she became confused, failed to give the password, and bungled the assignment. When Khan finally met up with the radio operator, she became part of an espionage team called "Prosper."

Soon Khan's incomplete training became glaringly obvious. According to writer Ronald Seth in *Encyclopedia of Espionage*, she displayed a number of social customs that identified her as having an English background, such as pouring her tea into milk, rather than the other way around. In addition, wrote Seth: "On one occasion she passed to another agent with whom she rendezvoused in the

A view of Dachau concentration camp where Khan was imprisoned. (Reproduced by permission of AP/Wide World Photo)

Luxembourg Gardens, in the middle of Paris, a map of a site where supplies were to be picked up; and she did so in full view of the public, and of any Gestapo agent who might have been in the vicinity. She left her note-books, in which were particulars of her code and coded messages, lying about the rooms of the flat [apartment] where she was staying, for anyone to pick up and read." In *SOE in France*, historian M. R. D. Foot wrote: "A fellow agent who trained with her put it still more directly: 'a splendid vague dreamy creature, far too conspicuous—twice seen, never forgotten—and she had *no* sense of security; she should never have been sent to France.'"

Close Calls

Khan quickly learned how to survive as a spy. Her principal contact in Paris was associated with a network of groups centered at the National School of Agriculture. Two weeks after Khan's arrival in France, the school was raided by Nazi soldiers. Although she had been instructed to stay away from the school on the day of the raid, she received some urgent materials from London that needed to be delivered. Khan arrived during the raid, and as she approached the building, she recognized a large group of Nazi soldiers. She managed to escape quietly on her bicycle. The raid on the school was followed by a nationwide German infiltration of French intelligence groups. Suspected spies from Paris and all parts of France were rounded up and imprisoned by the Nazis. Khan was the only member of the "Prosper" group who escaped the roundup. Advised by her British superior officer that she should return to England, Khan chose instead to remain in France.

For the next three months Khan single-handedly carried out almost all the radio work in Paris. Her acquaintances noted a nervousness and sense of urgency that disappeared only when she was seated at her transmitter. She became more efficient and conscientious as a spy. To avoid detection, she transmitted from different locations and frequently changed her places of lodging. Khan lived with constant danger and had several other close calls. She was once stopped aboard a subway car by a German soldier, who demanded to inspect the case containing her transmitter. Khan was able to convince the soldier that the transmitter was part of a film projector. Another time she was leaning from her window fixing a radio aerial that was mounted in a tree. An unsuspecting young German officer saw her struggling and helped her fasten the wire to the tree.

Death and Honor

Khan was captured by the Germans in mid-October 1943. She had been betrayed by a French woman living in her apartment building, who had reported her to the Nazis in return for a small sum of money. When Nazi authorities arrived at Khan's apartment, they found her surrounded by broadcasting equipment. Khan realized it would be pointless to deny her activities, yet she put up a fight while she was being arrested, biting one of her captors so hard that he began to bleed. After she was taken to prison, she gained the respect of her captors by refusing to speak, except to demand that she be shot as soon as possible. She further increased their admiration by making a risky attempt at escape: Khan was able to make contact with two other agents who were being kept captive in the same building, and by removing skylights and making ropes from sheets and blankets, the three managed to get out of the building. Then an air raid alarm sounded, and when prison authorities checked the location of all prisoners, they noticed that the three spies were absent. Khan and her comrades were recaptured almost immediately. Now considered extremely dangerous, they were transferred to a jail in Germany.

Khan was kept in solitary confinement and chained to a wall for ten months at the German prison Pforzheim. On September 13, 1944, she was taken with three other female prisoners by train to the Dachau concentration camp. According to writer A.A. Hoehling, one morning Khan and her prison mates "were awakened early, offered luke-warm weak tea [and] breakfast rolls, and [were] led out, in pairs, across the prison courtyard, toward a wall" covered with bloodstains. The women were permitted to hold hands while Nazi soldiers shot them in the back of the neck. "The whole bizarre episode was as casual and impersonal as though the executioner was firing at clay pigeons," wrote Hoehling. Khan was awarded the George Cross posthumously from the government of Great Britain. In *Encyclopedia of Espionage*, Ronald Seth cites this portion of the accompanying citation: "Assistant Section Officer Inayat Khan displayed the most conspicuous courage, both moral and physical, over a period of more than twelve months."

Sources

Books

Dear, I. C. B., and M. R. D. Foot, editors, *The Oxford Companion to World War II,* Oxford University Press (New York), 1995.

Foot, M. R. D., *SOE in France: An Account of the Work of the British Special Operations Executive in France, 1940–1944,* H.M.S.O. (London), 1966.

Franklin, Charles, *Great Spies,* Hart (New York), 1967.

Hoehling, A. A., *Women Who Spied,* Madison Books: distributed by National Book Network (Lanham, MD), 1993.

Seth, Ronald, *Encyclopedia of Espionage,* New English Library (London), 1975.

Beate and Serge Klarsfeld

Beate and Serge Klarsfeld are known for their tireless pursuit of Nazi criminals who escaped trial after World War II. The Klarsfelds are just as intent on memorializing victims of the Holocaust as they are on imprisoning and punishing Nazi war criminals. They have spent years conducting painstaking research, writing books, starting foundations, and establishing memorials to honor the Jews who died at the hands of the Nazis.

Different Heritages, Common Goal

Beate Klarsfeld was born in Berlin, Germany, in 1939, the year Germany invaded Poland and started World War II. Her parents were Kurt and Helen Kuenzel; her father worked as an insurance agent. Shortly after Beate's birth, her father quit his job and joined the German military. To escape the constant British bombing of Berlin, Helen took her daughter to the German village of Sandau. At the end of the war, the family returned to Berlin, where Beate attended elementary and secondary school. Losing the war was so painful for some Germans, like the Kuenzels, that they preferred not to discuss it. Beate's family busied itself in order to forget the German defeat. Beate later said that most people, including her own parents and their friends, complained about how bad things were for themselves after the war. They showed little pity, however, for the fate of the victims of Nazi crimes.

Beate Klarsfeld
Born 1939
    Berlin, Germany

Writer; secretary; child care worker; famous for her worldwide pursuit of war criminals

Serge Klarsfeld
Born September 15, 1935
    Bucharest, Hungary

Lawyer; writer; world-famous Holocaust scholar and anti-Nazi activist

"In my eyes … crimes against humanity are above all the crimes committed against innocents, those who threaten no one."
—SERGE KLARSFELD

Beate Klarsfeld has devoted her life to exposing Nazi war criminals. (Reproduced by permission of AP/Wide World Photos)

At age eighteen, Beate began working as a secretary for a large drug firm. In 1960, when she was twenty-one, she moved to Paris, France, and worked as a nanny. During this time she met Serge Klarsfeld, who was then a law student in his twenties.

Serge Klarsfeld was born in Hungary in 1935, the son of a Jewish couple, Arno and Raissa Klarsfeld. In 1939, after taking Raissa, Serge, and Serge's sister Tanya to France to escape Nazi persecution, Arno joined the French Foreign Legion. He was captured by the Germans, then escaped from a prison camp and joined the French resistance. In the middle of World War II, the Klarsfelds were living in Nice, France. Although they had planned to flee the country to avoid being taken to concentration camps, the family found refuge hiding in a large closet in a friend's apartment. The Klarsfelds lived behind a false panel in the closet until the day the building was raided by the Nazis. When Arno heard German soldiers come into the apartment, he left the closet in order to divert attention from his family. He was taken prisoner and eventually killed in the gas chambers of the Auschwitz concentration camp in Poland. Hours after his departure, Raissa and the children fled the

closet and made their way to the home of a neighbor, who took them in. Serge, his mother, and his sister moved several times during the war and managed to avoid capture by the Nazis.

As a young man Serge studied at the University of Paris, where he received a diploma in political science in 1960, the year he met Beate Kuenzel. As their friendship grew, Serge encouraged Beate to read and to attend lectures and plays. He also acquainted her with the history of the Nazis in Germany, about which she knew very little due to the lack of open discussion of World War II in Germany. Beate and Serge were married in 1963. Beate took a position as a secretary for an organization called the OSA, which promoted good relations between French and German young people. The Klarsfelds had a baby son, Arno, and a daughter, Lida.

The Klarsfelds' Mission: Expose Former Nazis

In 1967 Beate inadvertently initiated the couple's long campaign to expose Nazi war criminals. That year Kurt-Georg Kiesinger was running for chancellor of the Federal Republic of Germany. Although several French newspapers revealed that he had once held a high-level Nazi post, there was very little protest among the Germans or mention of his past in German newspapers. By now Beate had become well informed about the actions of the Nazis, and she believed it was wrong for former party officials to be eligible for prosperous postwar positions in Germany. Much to her dismay, Kiesinger was elected chancellor. Although the Karsfelds were living in Paris, Beate's conscience demanded that she respond to the German election in some way. So she wrote two letters of protest that were printed in a French newspaper. On August 30, 1967, she was fired by the OSA because her public statements about Kiesinger were controversial. This event became a turning point in the lives of the Klarsfelds, who were now determined to make exposing former Nazis and bringing them to justice their number one priority. Beate did extensive research, preparing a study that exposed Kiesinger's past as a Nazi. She said that as a high-level Nazi, Kiesinger had intimate knowledge of the suffering and mass murder of the Jews. Kiesinger claimed he had joined the Nazi party because, as a Catholic, he had hoped to work from within the movement to establish Christian ideals. He said he quit the party in 1934, merely serving as a low-ranking scientific aide during the war.

Denouncing Kiesinger as a liar, Beate traveled to Germany to confront him. In early November 1968 Beate joined a session of the National Congress of the Christian Democratic Union where Kiesinger was giving a speech. During the speech, she rose, shouting "Nazi, Nazi!," stepped up to Kiesinger, and gave him a hard slap across the face. After being escorted out of the hall by several policemen, Beate was arrested and tried for her actions. In court she defended herself by continually referring to Kiesinger's Nazi past. The case was dismissed when Kiesinger failed to appear at the trial on his own behalf. Within a few months, a new election was held and Kiesinger lost his post as chancellor to an anti-Nazi candidate. The Klarsfelds considered Kiesinger's defeat a personal triumph.

Mission Expands

Enraged by the hundreds of former high-level Nazis who were enjoying complete freedom in Germany, the Klarsfelds continued their mission to track down war criminals. In 1971 Beate made arrangements for the kidnapping of Kurt Lischka,

What Happened to Records about the Jews of Europe?

The Nazis intended to erase all traces of the Jews who disappeared in the concentration camps, and succeeded in this effort to a great extent. Those seeking information about loved ones after the war found the task nearly impossible. As Beate and Serge Klarsfeld searched for written documentation about French Jews murdered by the Nazis, they learned that in many cases, there were no records to be found. After France was liberated from Nazi rule in 1945, the Paris police destroyed any evidence linking French involvement to the Nazi persecution of French Jews. In concentration camps throughout Europe, the Nazis also systematically eliminated individual identities. After tattooing serial numbers on victims' arms that replaced the individual's name, the Nazis destroyed the identification papers of Jews who entered the camps. Plans were implemented so that, in case of a German defeat, all camp records would be burned. For the most part, this burning of records did take place.

who was then a bank clerk in Cologne, Germany. As former head of the Nazis' Bureau of Jewish Affairs, Lischka was involved in the torture and murder of countless victims. Beate wanted him brought to France and put on trial for his crimes. According to German law at that time, Lischka could not be sent to France or even tried in a German court, so Beate contacted four men who agreed to kidnap him. The plot failed, however, when the kidnappers were scared off by Lischka's shouts. Reports of the event were published around the world. Not to be discouraged, the Klarsfelds continued their exposé, this time singling out Herbert Hagen and Ernest Heinrichsohn. Hagen had been an officer in charge of capturing all Jews in one region of France, and Heinrichsohn was instrumental in sending Jews to the death

Serge Klarsfeld displays photos of former Nazi Alois Brunner for the press. (Reproduced by permission of AP/Wide World Photos)

camps. Along with Lischka, Hagen and Heinrichsohn were brought to trial in Germany in 1979.

The most famous Nazi identified by the Klarsfelds was Klaus Barbie, known as the "Butcher of Lyon." Barbie actively participated in torturing Jews, and authorized the murders of thousands of

people. After the war he was kept under the protection of the United States because he had given secret information to U.S. agents. In 1951 Barbie escaped from the United States, fleeing to Bolivia. He was discovered in 1971 after the Klarsfelds sent photographs of him around the world. Their successful efforts to bring him to justice took more than ten years. Barbie was arrested in 1983, returned to France, and placed on trial in 1987. He was convicted and sentenced to life in prison. Several years later, ill with cancer, he died in prison.

Books Written

As a result of Serge's careful research, the Klarsfelds have produced dozens of books that document Nazi crimes. *Vichy-Auschwitz* (1983 and 1985) links the Vichy (French Nazi) government to attempts to exterminate the Jews of Europe. Another book, *Auschwitz: Technique and Operation of the Gas Chambers* (1989), describes the gas chambers used by the Nazis, refuting claims that the gas chambers were not large enough to carry out mass murder. *The Children of Izieu: A Human Tragedy* (1989) commemorates the forty-four children taken from a group home in France and deported to Auschwitz concentration camp in 1944. Serge's book in English, *French Children of the Holocaust: A Memorial* (1996), features the pictures, names, and addresses of 2,500 of the 11,400 French children who were deported to Auschwitz, where many met their deaths.

Ongoing Efforts

The Klarsfelds have continued their efforts to bring Nazis to justice, traveling around the world. Beate has carried out on-site operations against Walter Rauff, the inventor of movable gas chambers, who was found hiding in Chile, and has also tracked down Alois Brunner, trusted henchman of Adolf Eichmann, who had been living in Syria. Writer Peter Hellman finds it astonishing that although the Klarsfelds have "[put] their bodies on the line in many unfriendly [places] … the only casualty has been their car—destroyed by a bomb in its garage in 1979." The Klarsfelds' work is supported by the Beate Klarsfeld Foundation, which funds such items as international telephone books distributed free to libraries and the press, and human rights campaigns. The Klarsfelds began another organization in 1979 called the Sons and Daughters of Jews Deported from France. This group was instrumental in the creation of the French Holocaust Memorial, a long, curving wall that displays the names of 76,000 French victims of the Nazis.

SOURCES

Books

Klarsfeld, Beate, *Wherever They May Be,* translated from the French by Monroe Stearns and Natalie Gerardi, Vanguard (New York), 1975.

Klarsfeld, Serge, *The Children of Izieu: A Jewish Tragedy,* foreword by Beate and Serge Klarsfeld, translated by Kenneth Jacobson, Abrams (New York), 1985.

Klarsfeld, Serge, *French Children of the Holocaust: A Memorial,* edited by Susan Cohen, Howard M. Epstein, Serge Klarsfeld, translated by Glorianne Depondt, Howard M. Epstein, New York University Press (New York), 1996.

Periodicals

Hellman, P., "Hunting a Nazi," *New York,* March 19, 1984, pp. 44–50.

"Just and Unjust," *Time,* July 22, 1974, p. 47.

Other

Au Revoir les Enfants (video), Orion Pictures Corporation, 1987.

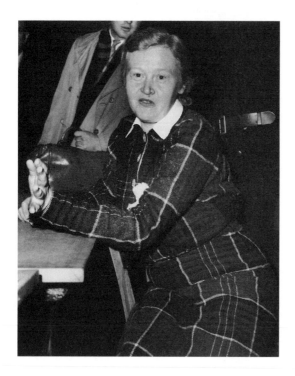

Karl and Ilse Koch

Karl Koch
Born 1897
Darmstadt, Germany
Died 1945
Buchenwald camp, Weimar, Germany

Soldier; bookkeeper; commandant of
Buchenwald concentration camp

Ilse Koch
Born September 1906
Dresden, Germany
Died September 1, 1967
Aichach women's prison,
Upper Bavaria, Germany

Secretary; wife of the commandant of
Buchenwald concentration camp; SS
supervisor; known as the "beast [or bitch
or red witch] of Buchenwald"

"You are to call me 'gracious lady.'"
—ILSE KOCH

(Reproduced by permission of AP/Wide World Photos)

Karl Koch was the commandant of the Buchenwald concentration camp, where nearly 60,000 people were sent to their deaths during the Holocaust. At the end of World War II he was singled out by the Nazis as one of the most depraved camp commanders and tried as a war criminal. Yet Koch did not act alone in committing acts of barbarism: He was joined by his wife, Ilse, who earned the nickname "beast of Buchenwald," in part because she kept a collection of handbags and lamp shades made from the skin of murdered concentration camp prisoners. Ilse Koch was also tried for war crimes, once by the Nazis and twice by the Allies. She finally committed suicide in prison after several failed attempts to win her freedom.

Marriage Begins at Buchenwald

Karl Koch was born in 1897 in Darmstadt, Germany. The son of a civil servant, he became a bookkeeper after serving in World War I (1914–1918). An unsuccessful first marriage ended in divorce in 1927. That same year he joined both the Nazi party, which had recently been built up by Adolf Hitler, and the party's bodyguard unit, known as the SS (the Schutzstaffel, or Security Squad). Koch worked his way through the ranks of the Nazi party and was put in charge of several concentration camps. He became head of the new Buchenwald camp near Weimar, Germany, when it opened in 1937, the

Buchenwald Concentration Camp

The Buchenwald concentration camp was built by German prisoners on the grounds of a wooded estate near the German city of Weimar. Opened in 1937, the camp was entered via a gate over which was inscribed the words: "My country, right or wrong." Buchenwald held Germans, both Jewish and non-Jewish, who were needed as laborers for Nazi factories. Later, the camp took in prisoners of war, such as Roma (Gypsies), Soviets, and homosexuals.

Between 1937 and 1945, an estimated 238,979 people were admitted to Buchenwald; 56,545 died from starvation, disease, torture, and overwork. Unlike the more famous Auschwitz camp in Poland, Buchenwald did not have equipment or buildings for gassing its victims. Instead, the daily murder of inmates took place by hanging, firing squad, and beatings.

Buchenwald was liberated in 1945 by the U.S. Third Army under the command of General George S. Patton. Upon learning of the U.S. Army's approach, the 5,000 Nazi soldiers on duty fled Buchenwald. Three hours before the arrival of American troops, the greatly weakened inmates took control of the camp from the few German soldiers left behind. Although Patton was an especially hardened veteran of war, he vomited when he saw the pitiful condition of the prisoners. The storehouse building at Buchenwald was made into a museum in 1985.

same year he married Ilse Köhler and moved into a mansion near Buchenwald. Ilse had been born in 1906 in Dresden, Germany, the daughter of a factory foreman. A young woman with green eyes and flaming red hair, she worked as a secretary in Berlin, the capital of Germany. Both Ilse and Karl had reputations for being non-traditional, having many lovers after their marriage. Their wedding was said to have been a riotous affair.

Terror Under the Commandant and His Bride

The Kochs' four-year term as commanders of Buchenwald was a reign of terror. Prisoners were brutally beaten, with both Karl and Ilse actively participating. Many examples of their cruelty are given in *The Buchenwald Report,* created in 1945 shortly after the liberation of Buchenwald by an Allied intelligence team in order to document conditions at the camp. According to the report, on one occasion:

The Gypsy was placed in a wooden crate that had wire netting in the place of wood on one side. The poor victim had to sit in this crate in a bent-over position. In addition the crate was held together by long nails driven from the outside to the inside, so that with his slightest movement the nails dug deep into his flesh. In this cage the Gypsy was placed on display in roll call square for two days and three nights. His horrible cries no longer sounded human. Finally, on the morning of the third day, he was put out of his misery with a lethal injection.

Ilse Koch was an accomplished horsewoman, and according to *Encyclopedia of the Third Reich,* "she liked to ride on horseback, with whip in hand, through the prison compound, lashing out at any prisoner unfortunate enough to glance in her direction." At home, she was a fearsome employer. One servant, Kurt Dietz, provided this testimony in *The Buchenwald Report*: "I had to perform all the work in the house. At a prescribed time I had to wake the children, wash and dress them, take them to the toilet, and wipe their bottoms. Then the dog had to be fed and taken for a walk and the coffee made and brought to the 'gracious lady' [the name Ilse insisted that her servants call her] in her bed.... I was locked into the children's room.... I was not allowed to use the toilet.... I was not allowed to leave the house.... Thus I had to relieve myself in the cellar, hiding among the coals."

Many Nazi camp officials and their wives had a taste for luxury, and the Kochs were no exception.

Irma Grese, Angel of Death

Irma Grese (1923–1945), Ilse Koch's counterpart in cruelty, was stationed at the Auschwitz concentration camp, one of the largest and deadliest camps in Poland. She also worked at Bergen-Belsen where she earned the nickname "the Bitch of Belsen." She was born in 1923, one of five children of a poor farmer. She had a strict upbringing, and, like many other German girls, joined Adolf Hitler's Bund Deutscher Mädel or BDM (League of German Maidens) when she was only ten years old. There she received her first lessons in hating Jews. Grese left school at the age of fourteen and found work at a medical clinic, hoping to become a nurse. The clinic was run by a famous Nazi doctor, Karl Gebhardt, who was a friend of Nazi official Heinrich Himmler. Many high-ranking Nazis went to Gebhardt's clinic for treatment. Leaving the clinic in 1941, Grese was unable to secure work in her field and took a job at a dairy. A year later she began training as a concentration camp guard at Ravensbrück in Germany, where female trainees were instructed on methods for beating women prisoners. One female prisoner noted that it might take anywhere from a few days to a month before the brutality came naturally to the trainees. After eight months of thorough instruction, Grese was found to be ready for Auschwitz.

During her two years at Auschwitz, Grese rose through the ranks until she became the person who selected women for medical experiments or death in the gas chambers. Grese was remembered for her physical beauty, so much so that some prisoners had a hard time believing such an angelic-looking, blonde-haired, blue-eyed woman could be capable of such cruelty. Grese served at two other camps. In 1945, when she was only twenty-one years old, she went on trial as a war criminal. She admitted she had beaten prisoners, but claimed she had not enjoyed it. Nevertheless, a witness at the trial noted that she did not seem remorseful for her actions.

Irma Grese, commonly called the "Bitch of Belsen," oversaw a compound of 18,000 women, treating them harshly. Grese was executed for war crimes on December 13, 1945, when she was 21 years old. (Imperial War Museum/United States Holocaust Memorial Museum Photo Archives)

While ordinary German citizens faced a scarcity of food, and camp inmates were nearly starving, Ilse and Karl lived like royalty. When not involved in torture, the couple stole the money and possessions of their prisoners. The inmates were supposed to be put to work in order to assist the German war effort, but their labor was often focused on making life pleasant for the Kochs. For instance, Ilse had a riding hall built for her personal use. As many as thirty prisoners died from overwork during its construction. According to *The Buchenwald Report:* "After its completion Frau Koch held her morning ride there for a quarter to a half an hour a few times a week, during which the SS band had to provide the musical accompaniment." Another source cited in *The Buchenwald Report* describes the basement of the Koch mansion as filled with fine food: "at least thirty whole hams, about fifty to sixty smoked sausages … hanging on a stick, and several hundred jars of fruits and vegetables…. 'Last but not least,' about 500 to 600 bottles of the finest wines and champagnes were stored in special cabinets." Ilse was said to be fond of bathing in Madeira, a sweet white wine.

In spite of such extravagances, however, the Kochs were nearly always broke. Karl Koch's barber is cited in *The Buchenwald Report* as saying that "Commandant Koch never seemed to be able to make ends meet, despite his high salary, he never rejected enormous bribes." His highhanded methods made him unpopular with the men under his command. The barber further reported: "Once a truck full of lemons for SS members came to Buchenwald. Koch seized the entire shipment, kept most of it for himself, and gave only a few lemons to some of the higher-ranking officers."

Tried by Nazis and Allies

In 1941 Karl and Ilse left Buchenwald when Karl was appointed commandant at Majdanek, a Soviet prisoner of war camp in Lublin, Poland. Here, as at Buchenwald, the couple reportedly worked on their collection of artifacts made from tatooed human skin. Their behavior was finally found to be too extreme, even by the standards of the Nazis. An investigation was carried out by a high-ranking Nazi authority, who found Karl guilty of corruption. Due to his friendship with Hitler, however, he escaped punishment until sometime in 1945, when his superiors had him shot.

The investigator also reported that Ilse was a woman totally without morals, a "power-mad demon." Finding that "she had personally killed or fatally beaten and tortured hundreds of prisoners," he also speculated that she "had been responsible for the deaths, beating and starving of hundreds of others." Despite these claims, Ilse was set free. In 1945 Germany surrendered and brought an end to the war in Europe.

In 1947 a military court made up of Allied judges from the United States, Great Britain, the Soviet Union, and France put Ilse on trial for war crimes. Hundreds of former prisoners testified against her, and more than forty volumes of written evidence was offered at the trial. Although Ilse was found guilty, she was saved from a sentence of death by hanging because she had become pregnant while awaiting trial (she later gave birth to a son). International law prohibited the execution of a pregnant woman, so Ilse was sentenced to a life of imprisoned hard labor. The sentence was eventually reduced to four years' imprisonment on the basis of insufficient evidence. Across the world, victims of the Nazis protested the reduced sentence. The U.S. Senate conducted a three-month investigation, concluding, according to the *Encyclopedia of the Third Reich*, that "[T]his bestial woman's guilt in specific murders is irrefutably established." Ilse was tried again, this time for murder, attempted murder, and the mistreatment of German citizens who were inmates at Buchenwald. On January 15, 1951, she was once again sentenced to life imprisonment. Ilse reportedly commented at one point that she found it absurd to have so much emphasis placed on herself while some war criminals walked free.

Ilse Ends Own Life

While in prison, Ilse began to study English, hoping that she might be freed and allowed to move to Australia. When her wish was not granted, she committed suicide in her cell. On September 1, 1967, she was found hanging from a noose fashioned out of bedsheets. She left behind a farewell letter to Uwe Köhler, the son she had birthed in prison. According to author Louis L. Snyder, the note read in part: "I cannot do otherwise. Death is the only deliverance." Ilse also had two children with Karl Koch. According to her death notice, which appeared on the front page of the *New York Times:* "Witnesses said Mrs. Koch neglected their two children, who were brought up in abject poverty and denied a higher education." Other reports indicate that Ilse was nonetheless particular about some aspects regarding her children. On one occasion, when her son expressed a desire to play the piano, a piano was obtained. The pianos in Weimar did not fulfill Ilse's strict requirements, so a soldier was sent to Braunschweig, a distant city, to procure a better one. Even when that piano arrived, it still did not suit Ilse. The soldier had to return to Braunschweig and procure another one.

Ilse Koch testifying on her own behalf during her trial for war crimes. (Reproduced by permission of AP/Wide World Photos)

Uwe Köhler had grown up in various foster homes, never meeting his natural parents. When he was eight years old, however, he saw Ilse Koch's name on his birth certificate and committed it to memory for future reference. When he was nineteen, he read a newspaper headline announcing the denial of Ilse Koch's request for a pardon. Recognizing the name, he began to visit his mother in prison in 1966 and continued to do so until she hanged herself the next year. After Koch's death, Köhler began a campaign to clear her name. Like many other Nazi criminals, Koch had claimed she was not guilty. Her son, while admitting he was not absolutely convinced of her innocence, believes that Ilse, like many other Nazis, was helplessly sucked into the concentration camp world.

SOURCES

Books

The Buchenwald Report, translated and edited by David A. Hackett, Westview Press (Boulder, CO), 1995. The original report was produced in 1945 by the Intelligence Team of the Psychological Warfare Division of the Supreme Headquarters of the Allied Forces.

Manvell, Roger, and Heinrich Fraenkel, *The Incomparable Crime: Mass Extermination in the Twentieth Century: The Legacy of Guilt,* Heinemann (London), 1967.

Snyder, Louis L., *Encyclopedia of the Third Reich,* McGraw-Hill (New York), 1976.

Periodicals

Binder, David, "Ilse Koch's Posthumous Rehabilitation Sought by Son," *The New York Times Biographical Edition,* May 13, 1971, p. 1531.

"Ilse Koch Hangs Herself in Cell: Nazi 'Beast of Buchenwald' Was Serving Life Term," *New York Times,* September 3, 1967, pp. 1+.

Janusz Korczak

Born July 22, 1878
Warsaw, Poland
Died August (?) 1942
Treblinka concentration camp,
Malkinia Gorna, Poland

Polish-Jewish doctor; writer; teacher; radio
personality; children's rights activist;
directed orphanages; perished in a
concentration camp with two hundred
orphans when he refused to abandon them

*"You do not leave a sick child in the night,
and you do not leave children at a time
like this."*

(Ghetto Fighters's House/USHMM Photo Archives)

Janusz Korczak, a Polish author and early advocate for children's rights, has become a legend in Europe. By the time World War II began in 1939, he was already famous for his classic children's story *King Matt the First.* The director of a Jewish orphanage and host of a children's radio program in Warsaw, he had also become a respected authority on child psychology. In 1942 Korczak achieved heroic status by refusing to abandon his orphans to the Nazis. He and the children all died in the Treblinka concentration camp. Korczak's ideas about children and child-rearing have lived on: Many organizations continue to promote his theories. The centenary of Korczak's birth, 1978, was declared by UNESCO to be the Year of Korczak.

Becomes Authority on Children

Korczak was born Henryk Goldszmit in Warsaw, Poland, in 1878. At that time Poland had been part of the Russian empire for more than 100 years. Korczak and his younger sister, Anna, came from a distinguished and prosperous Jewish family. Korczak's grandfather was a surgeon and his father, Jozef, was a lawyer. His mother, Cecylia, was greatly concerned with appearances, and the family lived in a large home in an affluent area of Warsaw, the capital and cultural center of Poland. Betty Lifton, who in 1988 published the only English-language biography of Korczak, described him as a

Korczak poses with some of his orphans. (Ghetto Fighters' House/USHMM Photo Archives)

dreamy, solitary child who enjoyed playing with dolls and building blocks. His father disapproved of these activities, but in his later professional life, Korczak would stress the importance of children's games as developmental tools.

Korczak's father, who often had spells of madness, died in a mental institution when Korczak was eighteen years old. Deeply affected by his father's illness, Korczak vowed never to marry or have children of his own; instead he would spend his life working with the abandoned and unfortunate children of others. He exhibited many talents early in life. In 1899, for example, he won a prize for a work he submitted under the pen name Janusz Korczak, after a character in a popular Polish novel; he decided to keep that name. In 1901 he published *Bankructwo Malego Dzeka* (*Children of the Streets*), and in 1906 his semi-autobiographical first novel, *A Child of the Salon,* was published. His books dealt with children and how to help them lead full, happy lives, which became his lifelong interest. While writing novels he also attended medical school at Warsaw University. Upon graduating in 1904, Korczak took a position as a doctor in a children's clinic. He was immediately called to serve in East Asia as an army doctor in Russia's war with Japan.

In 1906 Korczak took a job at a children's clinic located in a poor district of Warsaw. He earned extra money by giving medical advice to wealthy patients. He began to work with orphans in 1908, and four years later was named director of a large new orphanage for Jewish children. Soon he became an expert in child psychology. Korczak believed children were the hope of humankind; he wanted to teach children that there was justice and kindness in the world, even if it did not always seem so. He published books and articles denouncing the commonly held view that children were hindrances, not assets. He also voiced concern about the way parents regarded children as obstacles to their work and put their own pleasure before the well-being of their children. Working closely with his orphans, he developed strong, loving relationships with them. He encouraged children to discipline themselves, and delegated responsibility to older children, who were to look after the younger ones. In a society where harsh punishment of children was common, Korczak instituted a system of rewards to those who were successful in breaking their own bad habits. His methods of dealing with children were new, and his success brought him respect as a revolutionary in the field of child psychology.

Respected Expert on Children

Korczak's duties at the orphanage became his chief concern. He reduced, and eventually completely ceased, his activities as a doctor—except when he was needed in times of war. During World War I (1914–1918) he served as a doctor in the Russian army. It was at this time that he wrote one of his most important books, *Jac Kochac Dzieci* (*How to Love a Child*). His time as a medic was cut short by typhus, which Korczak caught while living in unsanitary army barracks. He returned home to be cared for by his mother, who died when she caught the disease as well. Korczak became so distraught that he contemplated suicide. He willingly performed military duty again in 1920, though, when he enlisted in the Polish army and served briefly in the war with Russia.

The years between World War I and World War II were extremely busy for Korczak. He was asked to take charge of another orphanage, this one for Polish children, and to apply the methods he had developed at the Jewish orphanage. In 1923 he published his first book for children, *Krol Macius Pierwszy*, or *King Matt the First*, the story of a boy king who dreams of leading an army of children to make the

world a better place. The book was enormously popular, and he followed up with the best-selling *Krol Macius Na Wyspie Bezludnej*, or *King Matt on the Desert Island*. During this period he founded the *Little Magazine*, the first newspaper edited by children for children, which was published as a weekly attachment to the daily Polish-Jewish newspaper.

During the 1920s, while continuing to write books and articles about children, Korczak taught at boarding schools, summer camps, and colleges. In the 1930s he hosted a popular radio show for children called *The Old Doctor*. He used this name instead of his own for the show because of strong anti-Semitism in Poland—even government officials objected to the idea of a Jew influencing children through radio broadcasts. Korczak's orphans were actors on the show, which became extremely popular with both children and adults. Unrest was growing in Poland, however, and Korczak aroused strong feelings among groups who did not trust Jews or Korczak's new ideas about how to value children. In 1936 he was forced to give up his radio show.

Into the Ghetto

Between 1934 and 1936, Korczak made several trips to Palestine (now Israel). A growing movement called Zionism sought to establish a separate Jewish state in the region, and Korczak thought seriously about moving to Palestine. He kept procrastinating as he struggled with the decision. On the one hand, Korczak saw Palestine as a land of great potential promise. "He dreamed, in moments of enthusiasm, of what Jews, once independent, would do to help the oppressed…. Perhaps Palestine would become a League of Nations…" wrote Marie Syrkin of the *New Republic* about Korczak. On the other hand, however, Korczak's orphans were in Warsaw and he was hesitant to abandon them. In 1939 Germany invaded Poland, removing Korczak's option to emigrate. As the Germans marched on Warsaw, the city erupted in flames, and bombshells hit Korczak's orphanage. Soon both Poles and Jews were being imprisoned, forced into labor, or executed by the Germans. Korczak was determined to protect his orphans.

In 1940 the Nazis ordered the Jews of Warsaw to build a ghetto. Its boundaries did not include Korczak's orphanage, which meant that he and the children were forced to move into a new home, a high school located within the ghetto zone. By this time Korczak was not in the best of health, and friends urged him to go into hiding. Korczak declined, however, when no one else could guarantee the safety of the 170 children. He still believed that he was too well known and respected, even by the Germans, for harm to come to the orphans. On the way to their new home, Korczak was stopped by a German soldier who demanded to know why he was not wearing the armband the Nazis required for identification of Jews. Not satisfied with Korczak's answer, the soldier arrested him and took him to jail. Korczak emerged a month later, even weaker and more frail than before. Despite tremendous obstacles, he managed to take care of his orphans, keeping them clothed, fed, and clean.

The Last Walk

On July 22, 1942, Korczak's sixty-fourth birthday, Adam Czerniaków, chairman of the Warsaw ghetto, received the German order to evacuate all Jews from the city. They were told they were to be resettled at the concentration camp called Treblinka. The Jews knew that being sent to a camp often meant a death sentence from starvation, overwork, or murder. On August 6, 1942, Korczak and his orphans—by now numbering nearly 200—were transported to Treblinka. This trip has become the subject of legends, for no one survived to tell exactly what happened at the death camp during the last hours of Korczak and his orphans.

Hanna Mortkowicz-Olczakowa discussed the event in her story "[Janusz] Korczak's Last Walk." She wrote:

> Somehow or other, Korczak's children were always distinguished from the general poverty around them. Even on ordinary days their clothing was clean and neat. That was why the impression made by the small, quiet and well-behaved group, which was following the doctor with complete confidence, was so pleasant....

> [Janusz] Korczak walked at their head. We know that at the time he was weak and that he had been ill. His feet were swollen and his heart was giving him trouble. I doubt whether he had the strength to carry two of his charges in his arms—even the tiniest ones—as the legend alleges.

> They were pulled, stopped, crowded together and pulled along again in the burning heat of August, accompanied by cruel cries and rifle-blows.... It is possible that Korczak held the feverish, tired, sweating hands of two children, as they drummed with their little feet to his right and his left....

"Part of His Nature"

In 1978, while doing research for her biography of Korczak, Betty Jean Lifton spoke to Michal (Misha) Wroblewski, a teacher at Korczak's orphanage. Wroblewski was away when Korczak and the children were seized by the Nazis. But he told Lifton: "You know, everyone makes so much of Korczak's last decision to go with the children to the train. But his whole life was made up of moral decisions. The decision to become a children's doctor. The decision to give up medicine and his writing career to take care of poor orphans. The decision to go with the Jewish orphans into the ghetto. As for that last decision to go with the children to Treblinka, it was part of his nature. It was who he was. He wouldn't understand why we are making so much of it today."

....It is ... almost certain that to the very last moment he assured the children of something which he himself no longer believed—that they were going to work in agriculture, in the forest, felling trees.

SOURCES

Books

Lifton, Betty Jean, *The King of Children: A Biography of Janusz Korczak,* St. Martin's Griffin (New York), 1997.

Mortkowicz-Olczakowa, Hanna, "Yanosz Korczak's Last Walk," *Anthology of Holocaust Literature,* Jacob Glatstein, Israel Knox, and Samuel Margoshes, editors, Jewish Publication Society of America (Philadelphia), 1969.

Periodicals

Syrkin, Marie, review of "The King of Children," *The New Republic,* June 6, 1988, pp. 44+.

Other

Janusz Korczak Communication-Center, http://korczak.com/englisch.htm (July 25, 2000).

Fred T. Korematsu

Born 1919
Oakland, California, United States

Japanese American working as a welder at the onset of World War II

"I still remember forty years ago when I was handcuffed and arrested as a criminal here in San Francisco.... I would like to see the government admit that they were wrong and do something about it so this will never happen again to any American citizen of any race, creed, or color."

(Copyright 1998 Shirley Nakao. Reproduced by permission of the Asian Law Caucus)

Between 1941 and 1944, approximately 120,000 Japanese Americans were forced to evacuate their homes and move into internment camps. The U.S. government claimed that those quarantined represented a threat to the internal security of the country, yet critics felt the underlying reason was racism. Fred Korematsu refused to be forced into a camp and challenged the evacuation order in court, charging that it violated his constitutionally protected rights. By fighting the policies of the government, Korematsu soon became an important figure in the ongoing battle for the rights of non-Caucasian citizens in the United States.

Family Sent to Internment Camps

Toyosaburo Korematsu was a nisei, or child born in America to Japanese immigrants. His parents had settled in Oakland, California, where they ran a flower nursery. Although the family spoke only Japanese at home and observed some Japanese holidays, Korematsu and his three brothers also enjoyed traditional American sports such as tennis, basketball, and football. He was first called "Fred" by a teacher who found his real name difficult to pronounce; he liked this new name and continued to use it. By June 1941, it seemed inevitable that the United States would get involved in World War II. Korematsu and some friends went to enlist in the armed forces, only to be refused an application. The officer in charge claimed that his orders did not allow Japanese Americans to sign up.

On December 7, 1941, the Japanese bombed Pearl Harbor, Hawaii, killing thousands of American service personnel and destroying many planes and ships. A wave of anti-Japanese hysteria swept the country, particularly the West Coast, where curfews restricted the activities and travel plans of Japanese Americans. Some military and political leaders pressured President Franklin D. Roosevelt to take action against the "threat" posed by Japanese Americans. One of the most vocal was General John DeWitt, who issued a report stating that the United States could expect another attack from Japan; Japanese Americans living on the West Coast were therefore a potential threat, and it was necessary to evacuate them into camps.

On February 19, 1942, Roosevelt issued an executive order directing that all Japanese Americans and resident Japanese aliens be sent to inland internment camps. The first camp was established at Manzanar in southern California; nine more camps were set up in California, Arizona, Wyoming, Colorado, Utah, and Arkansas. On March 31 evacuees were ordered to report to control stations to register the names of all members of their families, and then were told where and when to report for relocation to temporary holding areas, and from there to the internment camps. Given between four days and two weeks to move, they were allowed to bring only what they could carry with them. They had to make last-minute decisions about what to do with property and possessions. Many were forced to sell their businesses, homes, cars, and other belongings at low prices. In some cases these items were illegally confiscated. Estimated losses totaled between $810 million and $2 billion.

When the United States entered World War II, twenty-two-year-old Korematsu was working in the defense industry as a welder. His family was ordered to go to the Tanforan assembly area, a former racetrack where internees had to camp in empty horse stalls. Korematsu refused to go. He was dating an Italian American woman whose parents disapproved of their mixed-race relationship, and he urged her to go with him to Nevada, where they could get married and avoid the internment order. His girlfriend decided she did not want to leave her family, so Korematsu stayed in Oakland, planning to flee to Nevada later.

Fighting for Rights in Court

He moved into a boarding house and changed his name to Clyde Sarah, presenting himself as a person of Spanish and Hawaiian heritage. He even had surgery on his eyelids so he would appear more Caucasian. On May 30, 1942, Korematsu was recognized by an acquaintance who reported him to the authorities. He was arrested in San Leandro, California, and imprisoned in the San Francisco County Jail. Ernest Besig, a lawyer who worked for the American Civil Liberties Union (ACLU), read about Korematsu's situation in the newspaper and went to visit him in jail. He asked Korematsu if he would be willing to test the legality of the internment order in court and Korematsu agreed. Freed on bail, Korematsu joined his family at Tanforan; they were later sent to the Topaz camp in the Utah desert. Other internees, fearful of more trouble, tried to talk Korematsu out of taking legal action.

At Korematsu's trial, the judge agreed that the executive order was racially biased, but still found Korematsu guilty of defying the law. He was sentenced to five years probation and returned to Topaz with his family. Korematsu's attorneys filed a suit in the Ninth Circuit Court of Appeals, but their argument that the executive order was unconstitutional was again rejected. Korematsu's legal team then took the case to the U.S. Supreme Court. When the Supreme Court reached its decision in December 1944, the government had already closed down the internment camps. The Court came to a split decision: Only three of the nine judges ruled in Korematsu's favor and he lost the case.

New Evidence Resurrects Case

After the war, Korematsu moved to Detroit, Michigan, in search of a new start. Over the next forty years, he married, raised two children, and worked as a draftsman. In 1982 Korematsu was contacted by Peter Irons, a lawyer and historian who had uncovered new evidence in the case against the camps. Irons learned that government attorneys had intentionally disregarded reports from the FBI and Naval Intelligence that concluded Japanese Americans were not security risks. Korematsu and others who had fought the internment order agreed to retry the case, aided by a group of two dozen pro bono attorneys from California, Washington, and Oregon. The attorneys filed suit in the San Francisco federal court on January 19, 1983, arguing that the judgment in *Korematsu vs. United States* should be overturned due to the government's falsification,

Nisei Prove Their Loyalty

After the December 7, 1941, bombing of the U.S. naval base at Pearl Harbor, Hawaii, anti-Japanese hysteria swept the United States and thousands of Japanese Americans living on the West Coast were forced to move into internment camps. At the same time, many young Japanese Americans were eager to prove their loyalty to the United States by joining the fight against the Axis nations. In response to their pleas, the U.S. Congress authorized the formation of the U.S. Army 442nd Regimental Combat Team, made up entirely of nisei, the first generation of Japanese to be born in the United States to immigrant parents, who had volunteered to serve. This 3,000-member team, comprised primarily of young men from Hawaii and from internment camps on the mainland, was to become the most decorated army unit in U.S. history.

After training at Camp McCoy in Wisconsin and Camp Shelby in Mississippi in September 1943, the Japanese American soldiers were sent to North Africa and then to Italy, where Allied troops were preparing for an invasion. They participated in rigorous combat throughout the following spring; they lost one-fourth of the regiment but performed valiantly, living up to their motto, "Go for Broke." The 442nd Regiment then moved on to France, where they rescued the "Lost Battalion," a unit of 211 Texas soldiers that had been surrounded by Germans in a mountainous region. By the end of the war, the 442nd Regiment had earned 18,143 individual decorations, including more than 3,600 Purple Hearts, and had been responsible for 9,486 enemy casualties.

One member of the 442nd Regiment was Daniel Ken Inouye, the son of a Honolulu file clerk, who had dropped out of the premedical program at the University of Hawaii to join the unit. While fighting on Mount Nebbione in Italy, Inouye lost his arm in an assault on a German infantry position but destroyed three enemy machine-gun nests after being wounded. For his bravery in combat, Inouye won the Distinguished Service Cross, the Bronze Star, and the Purple Heart.

Soon after the war, Inouye encountered overt racism within his own country. One day, for example, he walked into a San Francisco barbershop for a haircut. Even though he was wearing his army uniform, heavily decorated with ribbons and medals, with its empty right sleeve pinned up, Inouye was denied service because he was of Japanese descent. He returned to Hawaii and became a lawyer, later entering politics. In 1959, after Hawaii became a state, he was elected to the state's first seat in the U.S. House of Representatives. The first Japanese American to serve in Congress, Inouye was a strong supporter of civil rights and a spokesperson for the Asian American community. He spoke out against racism in an important speech at the 1968 Democratic convention and played a key role in the 1974 Watergate hearings, which led to the resignation of President Richard M. Nixon.

Daniel K. Inouye (Courtesy of Daniel K. Inouye. Reproduced by permission.)

suppression, and withholding of evidence that demonstrated there was no necessity to banish Japanese Americans to the camps.

At an October 4 hearing attended by a large number of Japanese Americans, Judge Marilyn Hall Patel overturned Korematsu's conviction, arguing that it had been based on racism and unsubstantiated evidence. After the trial, Korematsu moved back to San Francisco, where he became active in the Japanese American community. In 1983 he received the Earl Warren Human Rights Award from the ACLU. In 1988 Congress passed a bill formally apologizing to Japanese Americans for the internment and offered a one-time payment of $20,000 to any living person who spent time in the camps. In 1998 Korematsu was honored with the nation's highest civilian award, the Presidential Medal of Freedom. Korematsu's daughter Karen has established a civil rights fund in her father's honor.

U.S. President Bill Clinton presents Fred Korematsu with a Presidential Medal of Freedom in 1998. (Photograph by Dennis Cook. Reproduced by permission of AP/Wide World Photos.)

SOURCES

Books

Chin, Steven A., *When Justice Failed: The Fred Korematsu Story,* Raintree Steck-Vaughn (Austin, Texas), 1993.

Fremon, David K., *Japanese-American Internment in American History,* Enslow Publishers (Springfield, NJ), 1996.

Irons, Peter, *Justice at War: The Story of the Japanese American Internment Cases,* Oxford University Press (Oxford), 1983.

Levine, Ellen, *A Fence Away from Freedom,* Putnam's (New York), 1995.

Other

Honoring Fred Korematsu and the Day of Remembrance, http://www.aclunc.org/opinion/9802223-internment.html (May 5, 2000).

Alfried Felix Alwyn Krupp

Born August 13, 1907
Essen, Germany
Died July 30, 1967
Essen, Germany

German industrialist and
arms manufacturer; major contributor
to Germany's military strength during
World War II

*"We take great pride in the fact that our
products have come up to expectations
during the war…"*

(Reproduced by permission by Archive Photos, Inc.)

A lfried Felix Alwyn Krupp was descended from a line of extremely wealthy German weapons manufacturers. Some members of his family even had the nicknames "Cannon King" and "Cannon Queen." During World War II, Krupp headed the family business, which fueled the German military effort. After the war, the Allies tried him on charges of plundering conquered countries and forcing prisoners to work in his factories. Although Krupp was found guilty and sentenced to twelve years in prison, he served barely three years. Following his release, he once again became the wealthiest man in Europe.

Krupp Dynasty Flourishes

The Krupp dynasty originated in the city of Essen, Germany, in 1587. The family began amassing considerable wealth in 1811 when Friedrich Krupp founded the family's steel company, which he named Fried Krupp. The Krupp works manufactured bayonets for European soldiers. The company grew in size and wealth as its weapons production became more sophisticated and powerful. As each succeeding generation of hardworking, dedicated Krupp sons carried on the family tradition, the Krupp name became synonymous with Germany. Eventually there were no more Krupp sons, only daughters. When Bertha Krupp inherited her father's huge empire in 1902 at the age of sixteen, she became known as the "Cannon Queen" and was the wealthiest heiress in Germany.

By Bertha's time, the Krupp family was famous for its great loyalty and sense of duty to Germany. The German ruler, Kaiser Wilhelm, took a personal interest in the future of the Krupps' empire. His interest was due, in part, to fact that the Krupp works was a vital factor in the German economy, but his chief concern was appearances, as he did not consider it proper for a woman to have so much power, or for men to be forced to report to her. Wilhelm solved the problem by choosing a husband for Bertha Krupp—thirty-six-year-old Gustav von Bohlen und Halbach, a diplomat who was nicknamed "Taffy." Gustav was known for his absolute devotion to his country's leader, whoever that might be at any given time. The wedding of Bertha and Gustav took place in 1906 at the Krupp family castle in Essen. Known as the Villa Hügel, it was a sprawling 300-room structure. After the couple exchanged wedding vows, Kaiser Wilhelm announced that Gustav's new last name would be "Krupp von Bohlen und Halbach."

The Dynasty Continues

Bertha bore her first son, Alfried, on August 13, 1907, at Villa Hügel. Kaiser Wilhelm was the boy's godfather. Alfried was quickly followed by four more sons and two daughters. Although the family was extremely wealthy and the children might have lived like royalty, their home life was not luxurious. Both Bertha and Gustav were thrifty; they kept the castle so cold that family members had to wear fur coats indoors to keep warm. Bertha busied herself with the welfare of the 63,000 (and later, up to 200,000) employees of the Krupp works. The employees were grateful, and her memory was cherished in Germany long after her death in 1957. Gustav, on the other hand, devoted his time to expanding the empire and its holdings, and increasing its efficiency.

The family placed their hopes for the continuation of the Krupp dynasty on Alfried Krupp, the eldest son. He was an earnest, serious, lonely, and friendless boy; he remained so throughout his life. The young Krupp was tended to by a large staff of maids and footmen, who reported on his life to Gustav. Alfried learned French prior to learning German, and at the age of five he began a daily regimen of horseback riding instruction. Once a week, he and his brothers and sisters were allotted sixty minutes to spend with their father, time that was often spent playing with his toy trains.

Throughout his childhood, Krupp was constantly reminded that as eldest son, he was destined to carry on both the family name and the empire.

Krupp Works During World War I

When World War I was sparked in 1914 by the assassination of the heir to the throne of Austria, Germany fought against the Allies (Great Britain, France, Russia, Italy, and the United States). The Krupp works was Germany's foremost arms producer. As a boy, Krupp observed firsthand his father's pride in supplying the beloved Fatherland with weapons. Millions of Allied soldiers were killed by the most modern and fearsome weapons ever seen—Krupp submarines, machine guns, cannons, torpedoes, armored cars, anti-aircraft guns, howitzer cannons, and more. According to Krupp tradition, particularly exemplary weapons were named for family members, so it came about that two weapons were called "Fat Bertha" and "Fat Gustav." Orders for weapons poured into the Krupp works.

Despite the tremendous output of Krupp weapons, Germany lost the war in 1918. For single-handedly supplying the German war effort with weapons of mass destruction, Gustav's name was placed on the Allied list of war criminals. He was so vital to the German government that officials refused to hand him over. Rather than folding the Krupp business empire when the Treaty of Versailles called for Germany to disband its weapons factories, Gustav switched many of the Krupp factories over to producing peacetime products, such as railroad locomotives and steel bridges. The Krupps actually benefited from the Allied demand that weapons factories be destroyed, because obsolete facilities were gutted and rebuilt for other purposes. Some plants were left intact but idle with the assumption that someday weapons would be needed to help make Germany great again. By the 1930s, the Krupp works were operating with highly modern facilities and equipment, and the family was making huge profits. In 1933 Adolf Hitler promised to restore Germany to greatness as his Nazi party gained control of the government. Gustav Krupp felt he had reached the most important point in his career: Finally the German people were ready to rearm, and Krupp was ready to make it happen.

Krupp Heads War Effort

Alfried Krupp attended college in Munich, Germany, majoring in engineering. In 1937 he married

The Krupps Celebrate Hitler's Birthday

In 1939, shortly before the Nazis invaded Poland, Gustav and Alfried Krupp delivered a special present to Hitler on his fiftieth birthday. The gift was a table made of Krupp steel and decorated with swastikas and iron crosses. The top was engraved with a quotation from Hitler's famous autobiography, *Mein Kampf* (*My Struggle*), in which he outlined his plan for the revival of Germany and blamed Germany's problems on Jews and others. Under a trick lid on the table was an engraving of the humble home in which Hitler had been born. Hitler was reportedly delighted with the gift.

Annelise Bahr, who bore him a son, Arndt, in 1938. The couple divorced in 1941 when Bertha objected to her son's alliance with Annelise, who had previously been divorced. Arndt would be Krupp's only child. During the 1930s, Krupp went to work in the family firm, first in a rather lowly position and then as a director in 1938. He shared his father's feelings of loyalty to Hitler and the Nazi party. In the Krupp factories, the special stiff-armed Nazi salute was part of the workers' daily routine. Krupp helped raise money for the party and joined several Nazi organizations, including the Flying Corps. In 1935 a grateful Hitler named both Alfried and Gustav "War Economy Leaders," in charge of keeping German industry moving in the war effort. When Germany invaded Poland in 1939, the Polish army, which was fighting on horseback, was completely overwhelmed by the awesome modern weapons manufactured by Krupp. The same year, all Krupp employees received a generous Christmas bonus. As Gustav fell deeper into senility, his son took charge of the company, though he was not officially named to succeed Gustav in the Krupp works until 1943. Hitler demanded that Krupp get the huge empire working at maximum efficiency.

In 1938 Hitler began his sweep across the European continent. Alfried Krupp benefited from Hitler's policy of depriving Jews of their property. Jewish factories, coal mines, ore pits, hotels, banks, cement works, and farms all over Hitler's expanding empire were turned over to Krupp. Entire factories were sometimes dismantled and moved to Germany to become part of the Krupp works. The empire was so vast that Krupp could barely keep track of it. More and more workers were needed for factories and mines. In 1942 Hitler and Krupp decided to employ 120,000 prisoners of war, 45,000 Soviet civilians, and 6,000 other civilians as forced labor. Their working conditions did not meet even the minimum health standards required for German workers. When more workers were needed, Krupp asked that Jews from concentration camps be put in his employ.

Krupp employees were sent to the concentration camps to locate and acquire the healthiest prisoners for work in the factories. Krupp was informed by members of his own medical staff of the appalling living and working conditions at his plants. Laborers were overworked in cold, wet weather, with no shoes and scant clothing, and were given barely enough food to survive. Krupp passed these complaints on to underlings, neither knowing nor caring if conditions changed. His foremen brutally worked the laborers, some as young as six years old, who were regarded by Krupp as "Jewish livestock" and "Russian slaves." According to David Segal of the *Washington Post*, one Krupp worker, Rachel Grunebaum, "ended up in a Krupp factory in Essen, cleaning up debris after British bombardments and working a smelting press. Beaten frequently during 12-hour shifts, she was paid nothing and each day was fed a single piece of bread, some watery soup and a paper-thin slice of sausage."

Alfried Krupp on Trial

Krupp traveled throughout Europe, looking for plants, equipment, and raw materials to feed Germany's mighty war machine. When not piloting his own plane, he made business trips from factory to factory in his expensive sports car. At home in the castle, he spent his evenings accompanied only by his servants, drinking and smoking. During this time Krupp's name was placed on the Allied list of Nazi war criminals. As the war drew to a close and Germany's defeat seemed assured, Krupp had a bunker built beneath the castle, where he could retreat from Allied efforts to arrest him. The bunker was furnished with a marble-tiled swimming pool and a red-and-black "Chinese

Room." There he often sat alone in the dark, the only illumination coming from his cigarette.

In spite of his efforts to elude capture, Krupp was immediately arrested when the war ended in 1945. Along with eleven other directors of the Krupp works, he was placed on trial two years later as a major war criminal. Though Krupp maintained that his father was in fact the guilty party, an Allied prosecutor laid the blame firmly on Alfried's shoulders. An excerpt from the proceedings of the International Military Tribunal stated that: "There is ample evidence that in Krupp's custody and service [enslaved laborers and prisoners of war] were underfed and overworked, misused, and inhumanly treated." Despite the harsh charges against him, Krupp was sentenced to only twelve years in prison and forfeiture of all property. He was released in 1951 after serving only thirty months, and his property (including a personal fortune of 10 million dollars) was restored to him. According to the *Jewish Bulletin of Northern California*, William Wilkins, the judge who originally sentenced Krupp, reportedly wrote: "Imagine my surprise one day in February 1951 to read in the newspaper that John J. McCoy, the high commissioner to Germany, had restored all the Krupp properties that had been ordered confiscated."

The Rise and Fall of the Krupp Works

Krupp had sworn never again to manufacture weapons. Yet during the next two decades he reigned as the wealthiest man in Europe, his personal assets estimated at more than 1 billion dollars. Considered respectable once again, he was visited at his castle by kings and queens from around the world. Most Germans regarded him as a martyr, not a criminal. In 1952 Krupp became captivated by Vera Hossenfeldt Wisbar. They were soon married, but Wisbar was not content with her new life. She had been divorced three times, so she was scorned by Krupp's mother Bertha. Wisbar was also dismayed by the fact that her husband spent most of his time working, and she disliked the industrial town of Essen. At first she tried to soothe her loneliness by enjoying Krupp's wealth in wild shopping sprees, but when this no longer helped, she became one of the first members of the "jet set," flying around the world to expensive resorts and hobnobbing with movie stars. The couple divorced in 1956.

In the late 1950s Krupp's fortunes changed again. A man who had been present at his trial read

Krupp (middle) listening to workers testify about their mistreatment at Krupp plants during World War II. (Reproduced by permission of AP/Wide World Photos)

estimates of Krupp's wealth in *Time* magazine. He wondered why Krupp was not required to pay reparations to people who had been forced to work for him, and took action. In 1959, after much wrangling and repeated delays, it was announced that Krupp would pay $1,250 to any surviving Krupp employee. Krupp was shocked when far more people than he anticipated appeared to collect the money. His advisers had wrongly assumed that most were dead. The promised amount fell to $750, then $500 per person. He finally informed the remainder of the former slaves that the money had run out, and no more reparations would be paid.

Krupp's son Arndt was destined to carry on the Krupp tradition, but he was completely uninterested in the business, although he did enjoy spending the profits. Living on a plantation with his mother in South America, he hosted lavish parties and flirted with actresses and fashion models. Ultimately, his conduct proved to be so embarrassing that, in 1967, Krupp forced Arndt to renounce his right to the company. The 380-year-old dynasty was at an end, and the business became a publicly held company. Soon after, on July 30, 1967, Krupp died suddenly. Several different causes of death were released to the press. According to one report, he died from cancer caused by cigarettes. On his bedside table was a copy of Adolf Hitler's autobiography, *Mein Kampf*.

Reparation Controversy Continues

Even after Krupp's death, the question of reparations owed to former workers continues to be a thorn in the side of the Krupps' business, now known as Krupp AG. An article in the *Washington Post* discusses the ongoing efforts of Krupp workers to achieve compensation from Krupp AG. According to the *Post*'s David Segal: "Both sides in the dispute have a reason to push for a quick resolution. If the cases go to trial, they could take years to litigate. Many victims are old and near death. The companies, meanwhile, are eager to put an end to a looming public relations fiasco."

Sources

Books

Gutman, Israel, editor, *Encyclopedia of the Holocaust*, Macmillan Library Reference (New York), 1990.

International Military Tribunal, *The Trial of the Major War Criminals before the International Military Tribunal, Blue Series,* Volume 1, (Nuremberg), 1947–1949.

Manchester, William, *The Arms of Krupp*, Little, Brown and Company (Boston), 1968.

Periodicals

"Nuremberg Judge William Wilkins, 1998," *Jewish Bulletin of Northern California*, September 22, 1995.

Segal, David, "Past vs. Future: Nazi-Related Suits Put Law Firms on the Defensive," *Washington Post*, March 9, 1999.

Isabella (Katz) Leitner

Isabella (Katz) Leitner was a vital, energetic young woman when she and her family were taken from their Hungarian home and sent to a concentration camp during World War II. During her years of detention at various camps, Leitner was an attentive observer. She later wrote her memoirs, relaying to readers of all ages both the horrors and the triumphs of Jewish life under Hitler's Nazi regime.

Born May 28, 1924
  Kisvarda, Hungary

Concentration camp survivor; writer of three books about her life during and after concentration camp imprisonment; lecturer

"Most of us are born to live—to die, but first to live."

Situation in Hungary

The Hungary into which Isabella Leitner was born was a country in turmoil, particularly for Jews. Six years prior to Isabella's birth, the Austro-Hungarian kingdom had been disbanded. The newly independent Hungarian kingdom, with nearly half a million Hungarian Jews among its citizens, was experiencing a surge of civil rights demands from the Jewish community. The Jews requested legislation that would protect them as a minority, and guarantee equal rights in education and jobs and full participation in economic life. The rise of the Nazi party in Germany influenced the civil rights of Jewish citizens in surrounding countries, however, as the anti-Semitic speeches of Nazi leader Adolf Hitler penetrated Europe. By 1938, Hungary had passed the first of many laws drastically restricting the economic, social, and political life of Jews. Although local Hungarian newspapers carried no official record of anti-Jewish violence in Nazi-occu-

(Reproduced by permission of Isabella Leitner)

The Role of the Red Cross in Hungary

The International Committee of the Red Cross (ICRC) was founded in 1863. It is a private organization comprised of citizens from Switzerland, a country that adopted a policy of neutrality in World War II. The ICRC originally provided for the establishment of societies to provide aid to wounded soldiers. These groups are today known as the Red Cross and Red Crescent Societies. Today the goals of the ICRC are to maintain consistency among the various Red Cross societies around the world, to act as a go-between with countries involved in wars, and to ensure that laws designed for the relief of human suffering are obeyed by all countries. During World War II, the ICRC provided help to Hungarian Jews.

In spring 1944 thousands of Hungarian Jews were deported from Hungary and imprisoned in concentration camps. Representatives of the ICRC began to implement ways to relieve their suffering, such as bringing food to the camps. In July 1944 the ICRC asked the regent of Hungary, Miklós Horthy, to suspend the deportations. He agreed, though by that time all of Hungary, with the exception of Budapest, was *judenrein*, or "cleansed of Jews." Friedrich Born, a representative of the ICRC, arranged for lodging and food for thousands of Jews still in Budapest, Hungary. Born also arranged for Budapest Jews to receive Latin American immigration papers, which, while they would not help Jews leave Hungary, might provide them some protection. These travel papers were handed out by Swedish diplomat Raoul Wallenberg and Swiss diplomat Carl Lutz, acting independently. The Nazis did everything possible to interfere with the Jews' attempts to reach neutral countries.

On September 7, 1944, Hungarian authorities permitted Otto Komoly, a hero of World War I, to rent several buildings in Budapest for the protection of Jewish children, with the approval and supervision of the International Red Cross. With the help of two Polish Jews, who were refugees in Hungary, more than five thousand children were protected in some thirty-five buildings.

In October 1944 the ruling party of Hungary was overthrown. During this chaotic time, several thousand lives were saved from Nazi violence by the ICRC before Budapest was liberated by the Russian army.

---

pied countries, travelers relayed stories of anti-Semitic occurrences in Germany.

Early Rescue Foiled

Into this chaotic place and time, Isabella Leitner was born Isabella Katz in 1924 in Kisvarda, a small town in northeastern Hungary. She had one brother, Philip, and four sisters: Regina, Chicha, Cipi, and Potyo. During Leitner's childhood, the family lived in the town's Jewish area. In 1939, at the beginning of World War II, Leitner's father emigrated to the United States after a group of youths assaulted Jewish merchants, breaking windows in their shops and threatening the lives of customers. He believed he could obtain travel visas that would allow his entire family to escape to the United States, but the application process took two years. By that time, Germany, which was an ally of Hungary, had declared war on the United States, and it became impossible for Hungarian immigrants to get visas. On March 20, 1944, Hitler invaded Budapest, Hungary's capital, and took control of the radio station and the newspapers. The Nazis decreed that all Jewish people, including children, were to identify themselves. They were commanded to wear yellow Stars of David on their outer clothing, were prohibited from appearing in public places after 7 p.m., and Jewish children were banned from attending school. Soon Jews were forbidden to own radios, ride bicycles, or even talk to non-Jews in public.

Kapos unload the property of Hungarian Jews after their arrival at Auschwitz. (Yad Vashem Photo Archives/USHMM Photo Archives)

Family Sent to Ghetto

When two Hungarian policemen came to the Katzes' house, they gave the family ten minutes to prepare for relocation. Leitner's mother and the six children quickly complied with the order, packing bedclothes, food, clothing, soap, cleaning utensils, and cooking pots. Along with hundreds of other families, the Katzes marched to their new home in a rundown, crowded, unsanitary section of the city called the Jewish ghetto. Thirty or forty people resided in a space meant for three or four. Leitner's mother insisted that the children help her scrub out their quarters in an attempt to rid them of any disease-causing bacteria.

Deportation to Auschwitz

On May 28, 1944, the families in the ghettos were told to prepare for immediate deportation. There was no mention of their destination. Each of the Katz children took his or her finest possessions; twenty-year-old Isabella brought her camel hair coat, despite the warm weather. Armed Nazis, accompanied by dogs, assembled the families into lines and marched them to the railroad station.

Leitner later said that as the Jewish families of Kisvarda were marched past their non-Jewish neighbors, none of the neighbors seemed to display any sympathy. Some smiled, though they must have known or suspected the Jewish families were destined for the camps. The Jewish people, including babies and the elderly, were packed into unventilated cattle cars. They were provided with neither food nor water, and were given no way of tending to their physical needs. Several of the most vulnerable, including infants and the old, died during the trip, which ended three days later in Poland at the Auschwitz concentration camp.

The Jews were noisily hurried off the train by *Kapos*—prisoners dressed in striped uniforms who worked for the Nazis. The Nazis took away all their personal belongings. As the people marched away from the train, a uniformed man in white gloves inspected them. He pointed his thumb either right or left—those sent to the right were put to work; those sent to the left went to their deaths. In *People Weekly*, Leitner described the scenario: "As we alighted from the cattle car—my mother, my brother and my four sisters—there was [Josef] Mengele, looking magnificent with his dog, his pistol, his riding crop. He stood there as his henchmen separated the men and the women. Then with his thumb he would motion to the left or right, the ultimate god, choosing those who lived and those who died. He sent my mother to the crematorium immediately.... And my youngest sister, 'Potyo,' she was too young for him at 13. Because the crematoriums were filled, they built big, open fires for the children."

Those who were selected to die were killed in a brutally systematic way. They were taken to a "bathhouse," told to remove their clothing, and given a bar of soap. The doors were closed and sealed, but instead of water, the showers were filled with poisonous fumes, and the people inside were gassed to death. Their bodies were hauled to large nearby crematoria, where they were burned. Between 10,000 and 20,000 people were killed in this way every day during summer 1944.

When Leitner and her three other sisters, Cipi, Chicha, and Regina, stood before Josef Mengele, he motioned them to the right, away from the death chambers to which their mother and sister had been sent. They were taken to a big room, where they were stripped of their clothing and all the hair on their bodies was cut or shaved off. The sisters were humiliated and terrified. Suddenly their brother, Philip, popped through a window to tell them that no matter what occurred, they must eat and survive.

Life and Death in the Camps

The conditions awaiting those not selected for the gas chambers were harsh. Housed in a block containing 1,000 prisoners, Leitner and her sisters, along with ten other girls, slept on wooden boards that were stacked in groups of three. It was impossible to sleep well. Sometimes the shoddy shelves broke, sending people toppling upon one another. The sparse food supplied by the Nazis generally consisted of dirty, watery soup and bits of bread. Standing through two long roll calls a day, the girls were lined up in groups of five and told they must not move or they would be beaten. Although males and females were kept apart, Philip managed to communicate with his sisters daily. After writing a short note on a piece of wood, he would jot down instructions that anyone who found the wood should toss it over the fence in the direction of the place where the girls were being kept. Every day the sisters waited for his words of encouragement. One day the messages stopped coming. The girls waited in vain for more messages, but unbeknownst to them, their brother had been moved.

Near the end of 1944, Leitner and her sisters were transported to the Birnbaumel camp in Germany. Although they had to sleep in huts with earthen floors, they were relieved to be there. Birnbaumel was a work camp, not a death camp like Auschwitz. Each morning, the girls were marched to a site where the Nazis expected the approach of enemy Soviet troops. They were told to dig holes in the cold, often frozen, earth to impede the progress of Soviet tanks. Leitner stopped digging as soon as those in charge looked away. She did not want to contribute to the Nazis' success.

Difficulty Adjusting to Normal Life

In January 1945 the inmates were lined up and told they must make the five-mile march to the nearby concentration camp Bergen-Belsen. People too weak to complete the march were ruthlessly shot by the Nazis. On the third day of the march, Leitner's sister Chicha got out of line and ran toward a nearby farmhouse in the German village of Jagadschutz. Leitner and Regina followed, immediately hiding in a doghouse. They assumed that their fourth sister, Cipi, was with Chicha, but she was not. After hearing the soldiers retreat, the three girls ran into the farmhouse and ate the food they found there. Afraid they might be captured, they peeked out the window only to see soldiers and equipment being rolled down the road under the red flag of the Soviet Union. They realized they were now in the hands of the Soviet army; they were no longer prisoners of the Nazis. The Soviet soldiers allowed them to stay in the farmhouse, providing them with food in exchange for tending a herd of cows. It was very difficult for the girls to adjust to their new reality. In the concentration camp they had had to become desensitized to the bodies of the dead in order to survive emotionally. Once they were liberated, they had to readjust to a normal way of life.

Over the next month and a half, Leitner and her sisters watched refugees from many countries march through the town on their way to a place called Oelsk. Finally they too set out for Oelsk, hauling their clothes and belongings in a small wagon. After two weeks of difficult travel, they reached Oelsk and boarded a train for an unknown destination. The girls' chief wish was to get as far away from Nazi Germany as possible. In April 1945 they arrived at the Russian city of Odessa, where they met a young foreign Jewish pilot. Hoping to help them get to the United States, he took the sisters to the American embassy. After only two days the girls, along with the soldier, were aboard the SS *Brand Whitlock* on their way to America.

A New Life

Leitner and her sisters arrived in Newport News, Virginia, on May 8, 1945—the day the fighting in Europe came to an end. The first survivors of Auschwitz to reach the United States, they were interviewed by FBI representatives about their experiences in the camps. Two days later they reached Baltimore, Maryland. With the help of a Jewish American judge they were able to locate their father, whom they had not seen for six years. Traveling to his home in Brooklyn, New York, Leitner and her sisters looked forward to starting a new life.

Adjustment problems between the girls and their father soon overshadowed the joy of the reunion. Their father was an extremely spiritual man, and wanted his daughters to embrace religion with piety and dedication equal to his own. Having witnessed the horrors of the concentration camps, however, the girls felt unwilling and unable to comply with his wishes. In a few months they were reunited with their brother Philip, who had recovered from a leg wound in a German hospital before flying to the United States. The sisters also began to create new family ties. The young soldier who aided the girls in coming to the United States had captured the heart of Chicha. Against the wishes of her father, who opposed the relationship due to religious differences, Chicha married the young man. During the next few years, Leitner and Regina also married. Leitner's husband, Irving A. Leitner, whom she married in 1956, is a writer from New York City. They have two sons.

Leitner Tells Her Story

In 1978, more than thirty years after her arrival in the United States, Leitner finally learned what had happened to her sister Cipi. While trying to escape with her sisters, Cipi was captured by the Nazis. Deeply depressed by her loneliness, she rejected escape offers from other inmates. She was taken to the concentration camp in Bergen-Belsen, where she was eventually liberated by the British. She died shortly thereafter.

The same year she learned Cipi's fate, Leitner wrote about her personal experiences in the book *Fragments of Isabella,* which was nominated for the Pulitzer Prize. The famed Abbey Theater in Dublin, Ireland, created a one-woman dramatic presentation adapted from the book, which was presented in Vienna, Austria, on the fiftieth anniversary of *Kristallnacht* ("Night of Broken Glass"), a pogrom by the Nazis against German Jews on November 9, 1938.

Leitner's second book, *Saving the Fragments,* which tells of her liberation and her life after the camps, was published in 1985. In 1992 these two books, with added material, were combined into *Isabella: From Auschwitz to Freedom.* The same year, Leitner published *The Big Lie,* a poetic book for children. The title refers to the Nazi practice of blaming the Jews for the world-wide economic depression of 1933.

Even after having written several volumes about her experiences in Auschwitz and throughout World War II, Leitner is still struggling with these memories. In an interview with *People Weekly* magazine in 1985, Leitner said: "On the subway during rush hour, I'm never sure I'm not sitting next to [Josef Mengele] or one of the henchmen who killed my mother or who butchered 128 members of my family—just counting my first cousins and aunts and uncles. It's harder to live with now than in the beginning. I carry this unbearable luggage in my head—what Mengele did to me.... For me it happened yesterday, or tomorrow."

Sources

Books

Leitner, Isabella, with Irving A. Leitner, *The Big Lie,* illustrated by Judy Pederson, Scholastic Inc. (New York), 1992.

Leitner, Isabella, *Fragments of Isabella: A Memoir of Auschwitz,* edited and with an epilogue by Irving A. Leitner, Thomas Y. Crowell (New York), 1978.

Leitner, Isabella, *Saving the Fragments,* with an introduction by Howard Fast, New American Library (New York), 1985.

Periodicals

Broadburn, Frances, *Wilson Library Bulletin,* December 1993, p. 118.

Kaminow, Susan, *School Library Journal,* December 1992, p. 123.

Publishers Weekly, August 10, 1992, p. 71.

Rochman, Hazel, *Booklist,* February 1, 1993, p. 982.

"Witnesses to a Nightmare," *People Weekly,* June 24, 1985, p. 65+.

Douglas MacArthur

Born January 26, 1880
Little Rock, Arkansas, United States
Died April 5, 1964
Washington, D.C., United States

American general who commanded
Allied forces in the southwest Pacific and
served as civilian administrator of
occupied Japan

"I shall return."

(Reproduced by permission of Archive Photos, Inc.)

Douglas MacArthur established himself as an impressive and colorful figure during World War II, with his hallmark achievements being the successful campaign to liberate the Philippines from Japanese control and a term as civilian administrator of Japan after the war. An active self promoter, MacArthur was often featured in newspaper articles and newsreels, usually wearing sunglasses and smoking an oversized corncob pipe as he commanded the Allied forces in the Pacific. MacArthur was a complicated person who could be charming and modest or vain and arrogant, often clashing with his superiors.

A Boy Bound for Glory

MacArthur was the third child of General Arthur MacArthur, who earned a Congressional Medal of Honor during the American Civil War, became the top-ranking officer in the U.S. Army in 1906, and once served as military governor in the Philippines (under American control since the Spanish-American War in 1898). Douglas MacArthur's mother, Mary Pinkney Hardy, was devoted to her son and used her social connections to help him advance his career. Instilling values of duty and honesty in all her children, she saw and nurtured special potential in MacArthur. He spent his childhood at a variety of army posts and was attracted to military life at an early age; he claimed to have learned to ride horses and shoot before he was able to read and write. He was close to his older brother, Arthur, who died of appendicitis in 1926 while pursuing a promising career in the navy. In 1897, the family moved to St. Paul, Minnesota, which MacArthur always referred to as home. His father decided that MacArthur should attend the U.S. Military Academy at West Point, New York.

MacArthur entered West Point in 1899 at age nineteen. During his years at the academy, he maintained an excellent academic record; he also played baseball, managed the football team, and served as president of the student body during his senior year. Upon graduating in 1903, MacArthur was ranked first in his class and was appointed first captain, the school's highest military honor. After graduation, he was made second lieutenant of engineers and served briefly in the Philippines before being transferred to San Francisco. In 1905 he was assigned to be an aide to his father, who was an official observer for the U.S. Army in the Russo-Japanese War (1904–1905). The following year, MacArthur returned to Washington to work as an aide to President Theodore Roosevelt, who was a friend to his father. Over the next ten years, MacArthur performed a number of assignments.

World War I

When the United States entered World War I (1914–1918) in 1917, MacArthur was working in the office of the Army General Staff in Washington, D.C. In response to the call to unite the country behind the war effort by recruiting more men into the armed forces, MacArthur suggested the formation of a "Rainbow Division," which would be comprised of National Guard volunteers from each state. Assigned to lead this division, MacArthur was given the temporary rank of colonel. In June 1918, when he was thirty-eight years old, MacArthur was promoted to the rank of brigadier general, and in August he was given command of the Rainbow Division's 84th Infantry Brigade. Leading several major battles in France, including those at St. Mihiel, Meuse-Argonne, and Sedan, he earned seven Silver Stars, four other U.S. medals, and nineteen honors from Allied countries. He was notorious for his individuality, which he demonstrated by wearing a non-standard uniform: riding breeches, a turtleneck sweater, a four-foot-long scarf, and a soft cap. He also smoked cigarettes in a long holder. Called the "Fighting Dude" by his troops, MacArthur was once taken

prisoner by an American soldier who thought he must be a German because of his unusual garb.

Between Wars

Upon returning to United States in 1919, MacArthur became the youngest officer to be appointed superintendent of West Point. During his three-year tenure at the academy, he modernized the curriculum, reorganized the athletic program, and doubled the enrollment. In February 1922 he married Henrietta Louise Cromwell Brooks, a wealthy divorcée, and the following August he was posted to the Philippines. After three years, MacArthur returned to the United States to command the U.S. Army 3rd Corps Area in Baltimore. In 1928 he was named president of the U.S. Olympic Committee and spent a summer in Amsterdam overseeing the games. When he returned to the Philippines, his wife did not join him; they were later divorced.

In 1930 MacArthur returned to Washington, D.C., and was named army chief of staff by President Herbert Hoover. At the age of fifty, MacArthur became a four-star general, a rank achieved by only eight other generals in U.S. history. The American military budget was reduced during the Great Depression, yet despite this lack of funds, MacArthur managed to modernize and strengthen the army in his five years as chief of staff. The only controversy during his term occurred when he was accused of taking a personal role in a troop action during the "Bonus March," a demonstration by impoverished World War I veterans demanding assistance from the government. MacArthur was accused of trying to promote his personal interests by appearing on the scene; his troops were also charged with using excessive force against the veterans.

Career in the Philippines

MacArthur was then appointed military adviser to the newly formed Philippine Commonwealth, an independent nation under the military protection of the United States. His job was to create and train military forces for the Philippine government. A young Dwight D. Eisenhower, who would later achieve sucess as commander of Allied forces in Europe during World War II, accompanied MacArthur on the trip. In April 1937 MacArthur wed Jean Faircloth, a Tennessean he had met on the ship to the Philippines. Later that

During the landings at Leyte, General Douglas MacArthur wades ashore as he makes good on his promise that he would return to the Philippines. (National Archives and Records Administration)

year, he retired from the army, but remained in the Philippines. The couple's son, Arthur MacArthur III, was born in early 1938. By the middle of 1941, Japan's aggressive actions in the Pacific region alarmed the American government. President Roosevelt recalled MacArthur from retirement and appointed him head of army forces in the Pacific area, including the army of the Philippines, which was immediately assimilated into the U.S. Army. MacArthur quickly began making preparations, increasing the number of soldiers from 22,000 to 180,000, most of whom were untrained troops.

On December 7, 1941, Japan bombed Pearl Harbor, Hawaii, and the United States declared war on Japan. Three days later, Germany and Italy declared war on the United States. Believing the Philippines would be unaffected by the Japanese war effort, MacArthur made no moves to secure planes and equipment at Clark Air Field, a U.S. base there. Shortly after Pearl Harbor, Japan struck Clark and then launched a full-scale invasion of the Philippines. By Christmas, MacArthur and Manuel Quezon, president of the Philippines, were forced to abandon Manila, the country's capital. They took refuge on Corregidor, an island fortress at the

entrance to Manila Bay. Combined U.S. and Filipino forces moved the battle into the jungles of the Bataan peninsula, but it was soon clear that they would be unable to save the Philippines. Roosevelt therefore ordered MacArthur to evacuate all American troops. Accompanied by his family, a few staff members, and fellow officers, MacArthur escaped to Australia, first traveling 560 miles by PT boat, then taking a flight in a B-17 Flying Fortress airplane with Japanese war planes in pursuit. As he left he made a promise: "I shall return."

Determined to Return

MacArthur felt the United States had broken its promise to protect the Philippines and was determined to rescue the country from Japan. In order to do this, he had to convince other Allied military commanders, who were focused on the defeat of Germany, that conquering the Japanese should be a high priority. He would then have to convince the leaders not to bypass the Philippines on their way to attack Japan.

As the Japanese continued their assault in the Pacific, Australia became increasingly vulnerable to attack. MacArthur was named Supreme Commander of the Southwest Pacific Area in April 1942. From October to December that year, he led Australian and American troops in a campaign in New Guinea, successfully keeping the Japanese at bay. By 1943, the United States was sending more troops and planes to the Pacific. As part of a grand battle plan, the U.S. War Department divided the region into two theaters of attack: Admiral Chester Nimitz would lead the navy west across the central Pacific toward Japan while MacArthur and the army would move north from Australia. MacArthur utilized a unique and highly successful "leapfrogging" strategy, in which troops moved their attacks from island to island, bypassing areas where enemy troops were waiting in large numbers, and attacking where they were least expected. In this way, MacArthur was able to work his way toward the Philippines, minimizing casualties, by making eighty-seven amphibious landings, involving the joint action of land, sea, and air units.

In October 1944, as the Allies prepared to retake the Philippines, MacArthur waded ashore with his troops at Leyte island, and made his way to the mainland at Luzon three months later. MacArthur was viewed as a hero by many Filipinos, and his fellow officers and soldiers began to feel he was taking sole credit for the entire mission. After Allied forces cleared the Philippines of all remaining Japanese soldiers, they prepared to invade Japan. MacArthur was named commander of all U.S. ground troops in the Pacific, with Nimitz heading the naval forces. These plans were rendered unnecessary, however, when the United States dropped atomic bombs on Hiroshima and Nagasaki in August 1945. On August 15 Japan surrendered to the Allies and MacArthur was promoted to Supreme Commander of the Allied Powers. He flew to Tokyo, where he formally received the Japanese surrender aboard the USS *Missouri* on September 2, 1945.

MacArthur was made civilian administrator of occupied Japan. The position involved helping the country recover from the devastating effects of war and encouraging a move from Japan's traditional imperial/military form of government to a more democratic one. MacArthur set up headquarters in the Dai Ichi Building in Tokyo, where he issued rules and regulations to disarm the country, restore the economy, begin land reform, and create labor unions. Emperor Hirohito was allowed to remain as a symbol of Japanese unity and tradition, but was stripped of almost all his power.

Although detractors viewed MacArthur as a dictatorial ruler who did not listen to criticism, most observers praised the evenhanded approach he used in winning the trust of the Japanese people. MacArthur himself felt this was his most successful role and greatest accomplishment. In 1948, he was mentioned as a possible presidential candidate. He did not discourage his supporters, and was said to be disappointed when Thomas Dewey beat him out of the Republican nomination.

"Old Soldiers Never Die"

After World War II, Korea was divided into two countries: South Korea, which had an authoritarian government, and communist North Korea. Wanting to reunite Korea under communist rule, North Korea attacked South Korea on June 25, 1950. The United States was concerned about the spread of communism throughout Asia. President Harry S Truman placed MacArthur in charge of the U.S. troops in the region, directing him to protect South Korea. Soon MacArthur was made commander of United Nations forces sent to help South Korea. His personal determination to fight communism led him to ignore the advice of other military leaders and launch a bold strike against North Korea with an amphibious landing at Inchon in September 1950. His troops succeeded in pushing the enemy back across the 38th parallel into North Korea, and they continued driving the North Koreans toward the Yalu River, which formed the boundary between North Korea and China. MacArthur ignored warnings that the Chinese might join the North Koreans in their struggle, and when the Chinese did join the fight, American and United Nations troops had to withdraw. MacArthur asserted that instead of retreating, the United States should bomb strategic sites in China. He thought that the spread of communism in Asia could be stopped only by crushing China, the largest communist country. Truman and other Western leaders opposed MacArthur's proposal, not wanting to risk another major war. Unwilling to accept this judgment, MacArthur publicized his conflict with Truman over U.S. policy in Korea. Truman firmly believed that a military officer must not question the commander in chief of the United States, and so relieved MacArthur of his command on April 11, 1950.

A week later, MacArthur returned to the United States for the first time in fifteen years. He received a hero's welcome, with approximately 20,000 admirers waiting to greet him. He made a speech before Congress, quoting a line from an old ballad, "Old soldiers never die, they just fade away." MacArthur spent his remaining years living with his wife at the Waldorf Astoria Hotel in New York City. Upon the death of General George C. Marshall in 1959, MacArthur became General of the Army, the top-ranking officer. He remained on active duty, without assignment, until his death in 1964. MacArthur was buried in one of the old uniforms, adorned with the insignia of a five-star general, that he had worn during his days in the Pacific.

Sources

Books

Darby, Jean, *Douglas MacArthur*, Lerner (Minneapolis, MN), 1989.

Devaney, John, *Douglas MacArthur: Something of a Hero*, Putnam's (New York), 1979.

Finkelstein, Norman H., *The Emperor General: A Biography of Douglas MacArthur*, Dillon Press (Minneapolis, MN), 1989.

Perret, Geoffrey, *Old Soldiers Never Die: The Life of Douglas MacArthur*, Random House (New York), 1996.

Scott, Robert A., *Douglas MacArthur and the Century of War*, Facts on File (New York), 1997.

Wittner, Lawrence S., editor, *MacArthur*, Prentice-Hall (Englewood Cliffs, NJ), 1971.

Periodicals

"The Emperor: Douglas MacArthur," *U.S. News & World Report*, March 16, 1998, p. 54.

George C. Marshall

General George C. Marshall played an intrinsic role in Allied success during World War II. Neither so flashy nor so famous as military leaders like George Patton and Douglas MacArthur, Marshall has been compared to George Washington. Like Washington, Marshall was a rare combination of soldier and statesman who believed a democratic government required a civilian-controlled military. Marshall was an adept organizer with a keen perception of people, qualities that served him well in his job as army chief of staff. He transformed a small, under-equipped U.S. Army into a powerful fighting force. As secretary of state, Marshall led the effort to help European nations recover from the devastation of World War II, an effort for which he was awarded the Nobel Peace Prize in 1953.

A Family Legacy

Marshall was born into an old Virginia family descended from John Marshall, the third chief justice of the U.S. Supreme Court. Lance Morrow of *Smithsonian* reported that George Marshall noted in later years that he often tired of his father's references to this fact, feeling it was "about time for somebody else to swim for the family." Marshall decided to become a soldier when he witnessed the enthusiastic greeting of troops returning from duty in the Philippines during the Spanish-American War (1898). The outpouring of respect and

Born December 31, 1880
   Uniontown, Pennsylvania, United States
Died October 16, 1959
   Washington, D.C., United States

American general and army chief of staff from 1939 to 1945

"There had been considerable comment over the awarding of the Nobel Peace Prize to a soldier. I'm afraid this does not seem quite so remarkable to me as it quite evidently does to others."

(Library of Congress)

admiration he witnessed had a lasting effect on Marshall.

A Military Education

Several men in Marshall's family, including his older brother Stuart, had attended Virginia Military Institute (VMI). Marshall and Stuart had a less than amicable relationship. When Marshall heard Stuart telling their mother that he hoped George would not attend VMI, he decided to attend out of spite. Marshall earned adequate, though not excellent, grades at VMI and demonstrated his potential for leadership. He graduated in 1901 with the rank of first captain of his class, a high honor at the school, and was commissioned as a second lieutenant in the army. In 1902 Marshall married Elizabeth "Lily" Coles, a woman several years his elder who had previously been courted by his brother. Lily stayed in the United States when Marshall went to serve his first assignment in the Philippines, but joined him when he was transferred to Oklahoma.

In 1907 Marshall graduated at the top of his class from the army's Infantry and Cavalry School at Fort Leavenworth, Kansas. For a year he then attended Staff College, which retained his services as an instructor until 1911. After serving assignments in Massachusetts, Arkansas, and Texas, Marshall was posted to the 13th Infantry in the Philippines, where he was an aide to General Hunter Liggett. Upon returning to the United States he was appointed aide to General J. Franklin Bell. Although his performance was lauded by numerous commanding officers, Marshall did not feel his assignments matched his potential and considered leaving the army.

Assignments During and After World War I

When the United States entered World War I in 1917, Marshall was called into active service. Promoted to captain with the First Division, he left on the first boatload of troops headed for France. There he worked in operations, quickly gaining a reputation as a brilliant organizer of men and supplies. He served as chief planner of the St. Mihiel battle and supervised the transfer of 600,000 soldiers and 900,000 tons of supplies into the Meuse-Argonne area, where another battle took place. During the war, Marshall was given the temporary rank of colonel, but when the war was over he returned to his former rank of captain.

From 1919 to 1924, Marshall served as aide to U.S. Army Chief of Staff General John J. "Black Jack" Pershing. Marshall had impressed the general during the war when he angrily defended his superior officer, whom Pershing had criticized. Marshall's friends predicted that his career was doomed after this incident, but Pershing respected Marshall's honesty and loyalty and wanted him to join his staff. Marshall assisted Pershing in drawing up legislation and preparing reports on World War I, and participated in many high-level meetings with government leaders. These years gave him experience in dealing with politicians and other officials, providing him with lessons that would serve him well in later years.

Revolutionizes Military Education

In 1924 Marshall was sent to Tianjin, China, where he served as the executive officer of the 15th Infantry for three years. In 1927, after Marshall had returned to the United States and was teaching at the Army War College, his wife died suddenly. Marshall coped with his loss by dedicating himself to his work and was soon made assistant commandant in charge of training at the Infantry School in Fort Benning, Georgia. This was an important period in Marshall's career, as he was able to play a major role in restructuring the army. He oversaw what came to be known as the "Benning Revolution": Faculty members were reassigned, manuals rewritten, and the curriculum redesigned to emphasize the new mobile warfare required by modern conflicts. Marshall taught his students not to rely on the "school solution," or standard response to problems, but to be bold and innovative.

During Marshall's tenure, approximately 150 future generals came through the Infantry School as students and fifty more served as instructors. Among them were such famous World War II figures as Omar Bradley, Joseph W. Stilwell, Matthew Ridgway, and Walter Bedell Smith. Marshall entered the names of the most promising officers in a "little black book," a record-keeping process that he would utilize a decade later in the promotion of commanding officers for the wartime army. In 1930 Marshall married Katherine Tupper Brown, a former Shakespearean actress and widow with three children, with General Pershing acting as his best man at the wedding. During the 1930s, Marshall served a number of assignments, including director of Civilian Conservation Corps camps in Georgia, Florida, South Carolina, and Washington.

The Normandy Invasion: D-Day, June 6, 1944

The largest amphibious invasion in military history utilized ground, air, and naval forces that had been gathering in England for months. About 5,000-6,000 ships and landing craft were used to carry 155,000 troops (50,000 of whom would make the initial assault on the beaches) and 1,500 tanks to the area. The aerial assault included 10,000 fighter planes, bombers, transports, and gliders, which provided protection for the ground troops. Troops crossed the English Channel to land on a fifty-mile stretch of beaches in the Normandy region in northern France. The U.S. First Army landed on western beaches code-named Utah and Omaha, while the British Second Army landed on eastern beaches code-named Gold, Juno, and Sword.

Forty-seven Allied divisions participated in the invasion. Of these, twenty-one were American; the remaining divisions were comprised of British, Canadian, Polish, French, Italian, Belgian, Czech, and Dutch troops. All were under the supreme command of General Dwight D. Eisenhower. General Bernard Montgomery headed up the overall ground forces, with General Omar Bradley in charge of the American First Army and General Sir Miles Dempsey in charge of the British Second Army.

Facing the Allied onslaught were sixty Germany divisions in France and the Low Countries—the Netherlands, Belgium, and Luxembourg. In the area the Allied troops invaded were nine Germany infantry divisions and one tank division. The Germans were aware of Allied plans for the invasion, but thought they would land on the coast near Calais rather than Normandy. In order to deceive German intelligence the Allies stationed landing craft off Calais, formulating a fake unit called the First United States Army Group under the supposed command of General George S. Patton. Architects of the attack used weather and tide forecasts to plan the exact date of the invasion. Originally scheduled for June 4, stormy weather forced Eisenhower to postpone the invasion until June 6. Prior to the landing of troops, British and American paratroopers dropped into France behind German lines to capture bridges, roads, railroads, and airfields the Allies would need for their advance.

At 6:30 a.m. on June 6 the Allied troops began their landing. The well-entrenched Germans mounted a blinding counterattack, resulting in a high number of Allied casualties. The Americans who landed at the beach code-named Omaha were the worst hit, suffering some 2,500 casualties—as opposed to about 200 at the beach code-named Utah. Allied D-Day casualties totaled approximately 15,000, and the number of German casualties was about the same. The Allies moved inland and by the end of the month German field marshal Erwin Rommel reported that the Germans had lost twenty-eight generals, 354 field commanders, and 250,000 men.

Soldiers help a wounded soldier ashore during the Normandy invasion. (Reproduced by permission of AP/Wide World Photos)

The Corps was a Depression-era measure designed to create jobs while improving the environment. He had now advanced to the rank of colonel.

Before, During, and After World War II

At the close of the 1930s, war loomed in Europe and Asia as Germany and Japan moved aggressively to expand their empires. In summer 1938, President Roosevelt called Marshall to Washington to head the War Department's War Plans Division and promoted him to major general. Only three months later, Marshall was appointed deputy chief of staff for the army. He made a strong impression on Roosevelt when, during a White House conference, he respectfully but decisively disagreed with the president on a policy issue. Many people at the meeting again told Marshall his career was doomed; yet like Pershing before him, Roosevelt respected Marshall's honesty and conviction. In spring 1939 Marshall was nominated for the chief of staff position; after serving for four months as acting chief, he was sworn in on September 1—the same day Germany launched World War II by invading Poland. Marshall began the arduous task of preparing the U.S. Army and the Army Air Corps for combat in the event that the United States had to enter the war.

The U.S. Army at that time had fewer than 200,000 soldiers, putting it on par with much smaller countries like Portugal and Bulgaria. Its weapons were outmoded, and U.S. military bases were neglected. Marshall lobbied an already financially inundated Congress to allocate more funds to the army. As the navy and the Lend-Lease Program (which allowed the United States to send troops and supplies to assist countries fighting Germany) continued submitting requests, Congress approved a draft that required qualified men to serve in the armed forces, and also allocated funds to assist the army in training and equipping recruits. Marshall was central in pushing through legislation that removed older officers from command in favor of the rapid promotion of younger, more capable men. While this practice offended some of Marshall's old colleagues, he believed the success of the modern army was contingent on this new blood.

On December 7, 1941, when Japan bombed the U.S. base at Pearl Harbor, Hawaii, Marshall was again called upon to use his skill. One of the leading planners of Allied strategy, Marshall was an integral part of Allied military conferences, including those at Casablanca, Morocco, and Tehran, Iran, in 1943; Quebec, Canada, in 1944; and Malta,

Yalta, U.S.S.R., and Potsdam, Germany, in 1945. Marshall often demonstrated his intelligence and analytical ability by inviting forty or fifty reporters to ask him questions one after another, then giving a long response in which he tied all the issues together in a logical way.

Along with secretary of war Henry Stimson, Marshall was in favor of a "Germany First" approach to winning the war in Europe. He thought the Allies should regain France, which had been occupied by the Nazis since 1940, and then attack Germany. The British plan, which called for starting an attack in North Africa then driving through Italy and finally to Germany, won out. Marshall continued to push for an attack across the English Channel on the Germans in France, however, and the plan was approved at the end of 1943. Formally called Operation Overlord and nicknamed D-Day, the strategy involved landing Allied troops and equipment on the beaches of Normandy in northern France. The attack was originally scheduled for June 4, 1944, but was postponed for two days because of inclement weather. Roosevelt had to decide who would direct the D-Day campaign, and asked Marshall for advice. Marshall refused to suggest himself, even though such an assignment would have been the crowning achievement in his military career. He left the decision to Roosevelt, who chose General Dwight D. Eisenhower for the job, telling Marshall he was needed in Washington. The D-Day campaign was a success (see box), and in May 1945 the Germans surrendered. The war continued in the Pacific theater until the United States dropped two atomic bombs on Japan in August, forcing the Japanese to surrender.

Marshall retired in November 1945, but a few days later President Harry S Truman called him to serve as a special envoy to China. The ruling Nationalist Party, or Kuomintang, led by Chiang Kai-Shek, and the Communists, led by Mao Zedong, were vying for control of the country in a situation that threatened to explode into a bloody civil war. Although Marshall was able to halt the hostilities temporarily, he finally had to return to the United States in defeat.

Marshall's abilities and experience were recognized once again when Truman appointed him secretary of state in 1947. In June of that year Marshall made a momentous speech at the Harvard University commencement ceremony, where he proposed that the United States establish an aid program to help European nations recover from the war. Warning that economic and political chaos in Europe could result in another war, Marshall stated the new plan would not be political, but instead would alleviate hunger and poverty and facilitate reconstruction. Through the European Recovery Act, usually called the Marshall Plan, sixteen countries received 13 billion dollars in assistance.

Postwar Accomplishments

Prior to leaving his position as secretary of state in 1949, Marshall helped to lay the foundation for the North Atlantic Treaty Organization (NATO), an alliance established to shield Europe from the threat of the Soviet Union's expansion plans. After briefly serving as head of the American Red Cross, Marshall was again summoned by Truman. The outbreak of war in Korea had resulted in the need for strong leadership, and Truman appointed Marshall secretary of defense. Marshall succeeded in expanding the army, increasing weapons production, and helping enact NATO agreements. His fifty-year career in public service came to an end on September 1, 1951, when he retired for the last time. As a five-star general, he remained the highest-ranking officer in the U.S. military. In 1953 Marshall was awarded the Nobel Peace Prize for his efforts to assist Europe's recovery, becoming the first member of the military to receive the prize.

Marshall refused to write his memoirs, which he considered a self-centered activity, but he did agree to be interviewed by historians from the Marshall Foundation. He died in October 1959 after having suffered a stroke earlier in the year, and was buried in Arlington National Cemetery.

Sources

Books

Cray, Ed, *General of the Army,* Norton (New York), 1990.

Pogue, Forrest C., *George C. Marshall,* 4 volumes, Viking Press (New York), 1963–1987.

Stoler, Mark, *George C. Marshall,* Macmillan (New York), 1989.

Periodicals

Morrow, Lance, "George C. Marshall: The Last Great American?," *Smithsonian,* August 1997, p.104.

Mulvoy, Thomas F., Jr., "George Marshall's Influence Was Felt Through World War II and on Into the Cold War," *Knight-Ridder News Service,* August 25, 1994.

"The Straight Shooter: George Marshall," *U.S. News & World Report,* (Special Report: The Strategists of War) 124, number 10, p. 64.

(Library of Congress)

Bill Mauldin

Born October 29, 1921
Mountain Park, New Mexico,
United States

Cartoonist

*"Just gimme a coupla aspirin. I already got
a Purple Heart."*

When confronted with the grim realities of World War II, American soldier Bill Mauldin used his talents as an artist to describe the experience. Mauldin expressed his frustrations and feelings about the common infantryman's tour of duty, combining serious subject matter with his unique brand of humor. In the process, he crafted a popular series of cartoons featuring two scruffy GIs named Willie and Joe. Through his art, Mauldin commented on a range of subjects, including the never-ending quest for a dry pair of socks, the prevalence of bombed out towns and villages, his characters' tangles with the military brass, and the camaraderie of soldiers bonded by war. The Willie and Joe cartoons were a smash with fellow soldiers, although U.S. army leaders were not always among Mauldin's fans. Today, Mauldin's World War II work is regarded as among the most memorable and accurate depictions of the GI experience.

Born William Henry Mauldin on October 29, 1921, in Mountain Park, New Mexico, the future cartoonist was the son of Sidney Albert and Edith Katrina (Bemis) Mauldin. He attended public schools in New Mexico and Arizona. A lean child, he was often confined to bed by rickets. As he recuperated, he expressed his daydreams in drawings of himself as a cowboy or other heroic figures. In his teens, he began to draw posters for

"*Just gimme a coupla aspirin. I already got a Purple Heart.*"

(Reprinted by permission of Bill Mauldin and the Watkins/Loomis Agency)

local merchants. He also dabbled with newspaper work at his high school in Phoenix and signed up for a correspondence course in cartooning. Then, in 1939, he headed off to study at the Chicago Academy of Fine Arts. Mauldin returned to Phoenix, where he began drawing gag cartoons for *Arizona Highways* magazine. Although he was able to find work, he had a difficult time supporting himself during the economic hard times of the Great Depression.

Enters the Army

To earn extra money, Mauldin joined the National Guard in September of 1940. As war raged in Europe, Mauldin found that his unit was quickly activated for service in the U.S. Army—five days later to be exact. He ended up in a truck unit before being assigned to the infantry. As a member of the U.S. Army's 45th Division, Mauldin was sent overseas in 1943 to Sicily, where he joined the Mediterranean edition staff of *Stars and Stripes,* the army's wartime newspaper. Mauldin covered the fighting in Sicily, Salerno, Monte Cassino, and Anzio before being sent to France and Germany. He was wounded at Salerno and received the Purple Heart—the military's prestigious medal awarded to those wounded in the service of the United States.

Mauldin's cartoons for *Stars and Stripes* featured the experiences of ordinary, unheroic GIs, wearily slogging on, getting the job done, and wanting to go home. Like Ernie Pyle's prose, the cartoons vividly and realistically portrayed GI life, intimately expressing the GI's hopes, dreams, fears, hardships, and triumphs. For many Americans, Mauldin's combat-weary team of characters—named Willie and Joe—became the archetypical GIs of the war in Europe. Disenchanted yet dignified, dirty and bearded, the battle-hardened Willie and Joe were more interested in dry socks than in the lofty rhetoric of war aims, and they hated officers almost as much as they despised the war. The cartoons were featured in a strip named "Up Front" that was also syndicated in more than 100 newspapers in the United States.

Cartoons Portrayed Real Army Life

While most of the Army hierarchy approved of Mauldin's cartoons as a healthy outlet for the average conscript's emotions, some officers—particularly General George S. Patton—objected to the grimy, realistic public image Willie and Joe were projecting of the U.S. Army. Patton threatened to ban the *Stars and Stripes* from his area of command unless Mauldin "cleaned up" his depiction of the common soldier. Nevertheless, Mauldin's melancholy pen-and-ink commentaries on GI life continued. They were also collected in several books, including *Star Spangled Banter* (1941) and *Mud, Mules and Mountains* (1944). Other cartoons were issued in a book bearing the same name as the famous strip—*Up Front* (1945). Mauldin's most famous book, *Up Front* earned the artist a Pulitzer Prize in 1945 at the age of twenty-four.

In *Up Front,* Mauldin's commentary about the war experience accompanies many of his memorable cartoons. Although Mauldin opens the book with a declaration that he is an artist not a writer, his text further illuminates the common soldier's experience. He describes how he approached his work, noting that "nobody who has seen this war can be cute about it while it's going on. The only way I can try to be a little funny is to make something out of the humorous situations which come up even when you don't think life could be any more miserable. It's pretty heavy humor, and it doesn't seem funny at all sometimes when you stop and think it over."

But Mauldin's cartoons and descriptions did bring smiles and a sense of appreciation from his fellow GIs. Civilian readers could also see the irony of the situations that Mauldin presented. For example, in one cartoon, Willie tells Joe to take his jeep to the top of a mountain again because the engine is still not hot enough. Willie is shown draining water from the jeep's radiator, with his shaving supplies by his side. In another cartoon, Willie and Joe hug the ground as bullets whiz over their heads. Joe remarks that he just can not get any closer to the ground because his buttons are in the way.

Mauldin comments on many other subjects in *Up Front,* including a soldier's fondness for liquor and card playing; the experience of liberating a town; the naive attitudes of new recruits; the importance of mail from home; and the treatment of soldiers by officers. He also discusses the blandness of GI food on the front lines. "Our army is pretty well fed behind the lines—as well fed as an army can be.... The abundance of food in our big ration dumps amazes Europeans. But the advertisers make one mistake. They always show the soldier wallowing in goodies at the front. He doesn't wallow in anything but mud up there." Mauldin also notes that soldiers did a little foraging to supplement their meals. "The soldiers killed a lot of cows. One rifleman at Anzio insisted that a cow had attacked him and he had fired in self-defense.... It's astounding how many soldiers before cleaning their rifles squeezed off a couple of rounds to loosen the dirt in the barrels and a cow just happened to be standing there. Anyone who objected to this sort of thing either didn't like fresh meat or hadn't been living on front-line rations."

Cartoons Syndicated to Newspapers

Mauldin was released from the army in June 1945. He received a lucrative contract to continue

Braving Battle as a War Correspondent: Quentin Reynolds

War correspondents often risk their lives, dodging bullets and explosives, to bring news of the conflict to those at home. Such was the case of Quentin James Reynolds, an American journalist who began covering World War II for *Collier's* magazine in 1940. In order to secure his story, he journeyed into the thick of battle. To observe the action and uncover the facts, he braved voyages aboard naval destroyers and traveled to the front lines. Known for his dramatic writing style, Reynolds witnessed the raid on Dieppe as well as action in Italy, the Pacific, and North Africa. His fearlessness earned him the respect of Allied readers as well as military commanders such as Dwight D. Eisenhower and political leaders like British Prime Minister Winston Churchill.

Born on April 11, 1902, in New York City, Reynolds initially pursued a law degree before committing to a career in journalism. He joined the staff of the International News Service (INS) in 1932 as a reporter and foreign correspondent. His work with the INS took him to Berlin, Germany, where he witnessed the activities of Adolf Hitler and the Nazi party. During that time, Reynolds became critical of the Third Reich. In 1933 Reynolds took a job with *Collier's* magazine as an associate editor and war correspondent. He left Germany to return to New York City. His work at the magazine was to encompass fifteen years and more than 380 articles and short stories.

Standing more than six feet tall and weighing about 250 pounds, the red-headed Reynolds was known as a hard-drinking man. He wrote on a variety of subjects, which he later conceded were not matters of vital importance. That soon changed when Reynolds was sent to cover World War II in Europe, which began in 1939 when the Nazis invaded Poland. Heading abroad in March 1940, Reynolds soon discovered he would be denied accreditation to the German army. The reason? The Nazis remembered the articles he wrote for the INS in 1933. Reynolds headed for France, only to find the nation being overpowered by the German war machine. As France surrendered to the Germans, Reynolds fired off his report and fled to Great Britain.

While in England, Reynolds used his journalistic talents to describe the perseverance of the British people. Witnessing the Battle of Britain, during which time the Germans bombed England again and again, day after day, Reynolds vividly recorded what he saw and heard. In 1941 he issued *The Wounded Don't Cry,* which paid tribute to the determined British spirit. He tried to help the British maintain their positive outlook, lending his speaking talents to the British Broadcasting Company (BBC). During his assignment in London, he also found time to narrate two British documentaries—*London Can Take It* and *Christmas Under Fire.* In 1941 Reynolds headed out on assignment to Moscow, where he was to serve as press officer for W. Averill Harriman. He resigned from the position in protest against Soviet censorship.

Reynolds's contributions to war correspondence during World War II were vast. In all, Reynolds penned seven books about World War II. In his autobiography, titled *By Quentin Reynolds,* he recorded some of his experiences covering Sicily, Tehran, England, North Africa, and Palestine during the war. Reynolds died of cancer on March 17, 1965.

"Joe, yestiddy ya saved my life an' I swore I'd pay ya back. Here's my last pair of dry socks."

(Reprinted by permission of Bill Mauldin and the Watkins/Loomis Agency)

the "Up Front" series as "Willie and Joe," which dealt with the characters' return to civilian life. He joined the United Features Syndicate, which distributed his cartoon strips to more than 180 newspapers in the United States. In addition to *Up Front,* the cartoons were released under the following titles: *Sweating It Out* and *Back Home.* Although his first postwar collection, *Back Home,* won critical acclaim, the angry, bitter tone of Mauldin's liberal cartoons soon led him to be dropped by one newspaper after another. In 1950 he went to Hollywood to try his hand as an actor and technical advisor in several films, including the Civil War drama *Red Badge of Courage,* which also starred Audie Murphy, the most highly decorated soldier of World War II. Early in 1952 he went to the war front in Korea. His report of the experience was published as *Bill Mauldin in Korea* (1952). In 1956 he ran for Congress as a Democrat in New York's heavily Republican 28th Congressional District and was trounced by the incumbent Katherine St. George.

Mauldin joined the staff of the St. Louis *Post-Dispatch* as editorial cartoonist in 1958 and won another Pulitzer Prize for his cartoons the next year. His wry satires on the politics of Eisenhower's last years in the presidency were collected in *What's Got Your Back Up?* (1961). *I've Decided I Want My Seat Back* (1965) summed up his liberal commentaries on the desegregation struggles of the early 1960s. In June 1962 Mauldin moved to the Chicago *Sun-Times,* where his editorial cartoons were syndicated to more than 200 newspapers. Continuing "to buck power," as he put it, to satirize the high and mighty, Mauldin earned the reputation as a worthy successor to Herblock, the editorial cartoonist for the *Washington Post.*

Continuing to produce books, Mauldin wrote *The Brass Ring* (1971) and *Mud and Guts* (1978). An avid flying buff, Mauldin described his air experiences in articles for *Sports Illustrated.* Throughout his career, he has received many honors, including the 1962 Cartoonist of the Year Award from the National Cartoonists Society and Sigma Delta Chi (journalism fraternity) awards for editorial cartooning in 1963, 1969, and 1972. Mauldin's work was also featured as part of an exhibit at the National Archives in Washington, D.C., in 1992. The exhibit, called *Draw! Political Cartoons from Left to Right,* featured Mauldin and five other prominent political cartoonists. A fiftieth-anniversary edition of his classic *Up Front* was published in 1995.

SOURCES

Books

Blum, John Morton, *V Was for Victory: Politics and American Culture During World War II,* Harcourt Brace Jovanovich (New York), 1976.

Jakes, John, *Great War Correspondents,* Putnam (New York), 1967.

Mauldin, Bill, *Back Home,* W. Sloan Associates (New York), 1947.

Mauldin, Bill, *Bill Mauldin in Korea,* Norton (New York), 1952.

Mauldin, Bill, *The Brass Ring,* Norton (New York), 1971.

Mauldin, Bill, *I've Decided I Want My Seat Back,* Harper and Row (New York), 1965.

Mauldin, Bill, *Star-Spangled Banter,* Universal Press (San Antonio, TX), 1941.

Mauldin, Bill, *Up Front,* Henry Holt (New York), 1945.

Mauldin, Bill, *What's Got Your Back Up?,* Harper (New York), 1961.

Rechnitzer, F. E., *War Correspondent: The Story of Quentin Reynolds,* J. Messner (New York), 1943.

Reynolds, Quentin, *By Quentin Reynolds,* McGraw-Hill (New York), 1963.

Reynolds, Quentin, *Only the Stars Are Neutral,* Blue Ribbon (Garden City, NY), 1943.

Reynolds, Quentin, *The Wounded Don't Cry,* Dutton (New York), 1941.

Wepman, Dennis, "Bill Mauldin," in *The Encyclopedia of American Comics,* edited by Ron Goulart, Facts on File (New York), 1990.

Periodicals

American History Illustrated, March/April 1992.

The Atlantic Monthly, June 1995.

Time, March 26, 1965.

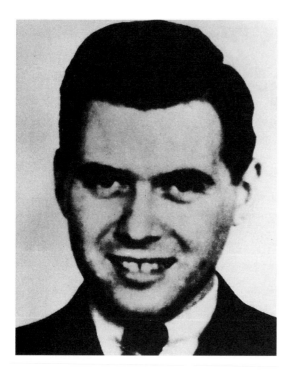

Josef Mengele

Born March 16, 1911
Gunzburg, Germany
Died February 7, 1979
Bertioga, Brazil

Doctor who performed barbaric
experiments on prisoners during World
War II; known as the "Angel of Death"

*"There are only two gifted peoples in the
world, Germans and Jews, and it's a
question of who will be superior."*

*(State Museum of Auschwitz-Birkenau/
USHMM Photo Archives)*

Doctor Josef Mengele was the chief Nazi physician responsible for human testing during the Holocaust. A man of high intelligence and unethical behavior, Mengele promised to give medical treatment to Auschwitz-Birkenau inmates while actually participating in the largest attempt at human genocide in recorded history. After engineering experiments of incredible cruelty, Mengele escaped punishment by fleeing to South America at the end of the war. Hunted by several governments and privately funded groups, Mengele lived his remaining years plagued by fear and illness. The discovery of his death brought an end to a massive worldwide manhunt.

Rejects Family Traditions

Born in 1911 in the small town of Gunzburg, Germany, Josef Mengele was the eldest of three sons of Karl and Walburga Mengele. Soon after Josef's birth, the family experienced great financial success when Karl became sole owner of a farm equipment foundry. The business prospered and the Mengele family flourished. Mengele's parents spent most of their time working, however, and their absence caused tension in the home. Early in life, Mengele expressed a desire to succeed outside of the family business. As a teenager, he excelled at his studies and continued to distance himself from his family, finally renouncing his Catholic faith.

While Mengele finished high school and began studying medicine at Munich University in 1930, Nazi leader Adolf Hitler was stirring up German patriotism in Bavaria. Although Mengele did not join the Nazi party, in 1931 he became a member of Stahlhelm, a youth group that marched in military-style uniforms at public events. At the university he became interested in anthropology and genetics, which intensified his fascination with Nazi attempts to create a perfect society. Writers Gerald L. Posner and John Ware suspect that Mengele's mind was corrupted by "a combination of the [pro-Nazi] political climate and that his real interest in genetics and evolution happened to coincide with the developing concept that some human beings afflicted by disorders were unfit to reproduce, even to live."

Promotes Nazi Theories

In 1935 Mengele completed his Ph.D. thesis, which maintained that differentiation among racial groups could be assessed through the shape of an individual's jaw. After earning his degree, he went to Leipzig, Germany, where he worked at a medical clinic and in 1937 joined the Nazi party. Mengele embraced the Nazi theory that racial supremacy was a biologically determined fact and that a race of people could be further improved by selecting individuals who would be allowed to mate. He became a research assistant at an institute for heredity, biology, and racial purity at the University of Frankfurt in Germany. By 1938, Mengele had received his medical degree and had also made connections with high-ranking officials within the Nazi Party. At age twenty-seven, he joined the SS (Schutzstaffel, or Security Squad) as part of a Nazi physicians' group. Five weeks prior to Germany's invasion of Poland in 1939, Mengele married a woman named Irene Schoenbein, a businessman's daughter whom he met in Leipzig, Germany, while working at a medical clinic there. He continued his genetic research, completed basic training for the military, and joined the German army in 1940.

While stationed in the Soviet Union, Mengele earned the Iron Cross for rescuing two wounded soldiers from under a burning tank. At the end of 1942, he was sent to Berlin, the German capital and headquarters of the Nazi party. By that time, Hitler was finishing the details of the *Endlösung,* or "Final Solution," his plan for the systematic elimination of European Jews. In May 1943 Mengele became the senior doctor in the women's section

of the Auschwitz-Birkenau concentration camp in Poland. Located in swampland an hour outside of Kraków, Auschwitz originally served as a labor camp for prisoners deemed "undesirable" by Nazi legislation—Jews, Roma (Gypsies), political opponents, and homosexuals. When the camp was equipped with crematoria and gas chambers, it became the center for Jewish genocide; about 1.5 million people lost their lives at the camp. Through a special selection process, the strongest prisoners were forced to work for the German war effort, while those deemed weak and useless were immediately sent to the gas chambers.

As the workers starved to death, Nazi officers were served gourmet meals with fine beer and wine while they watched plays and concerts presented by artistic prisoners. The only Nazi doctor to have engaged in combat, Mengele liked to wear his Iron Cross and other decorations on his uniform. Efficient, cruel, and cynical, he worked with other staff physicians to meet exhausted prisoners arriving at Auschwitz by train. Mengele would look at each incoming prisoner and direct them either to the right or to the left. Those directed to the left were sent to the crematoria to die. Prisoners Mengele directed to the right lived—for the moment. In many cases, these prisoners became the subjects of Mengele's horrifying experiments. It has been estimated that Mengele sent 400,000 prisoners directly to the gas chambers to die—and that number does not include the many more who perished while participating in his experiments.

Performs Experiments

Auschwitz became Mengele's laboratory, providing him an unending supply of human research subjects—especially Roma, deformed people, and twins. While he performed a number of disturbing experiments, his particular interest was twin research. He hypothesized that if the Nazis could consistently duplicate multi-zygotic births, the European population could rapidly attain Aryan "perfection," a Nazi standard that included blond hair, blue eyes, and perfectly formed bodies. Mengele therefore would not allow twins to be executed in the gas chambers. Instead, he fed them well, providing them with clean clothes and comfortable living conditions. After they regained their strength, all parts of their bodies were measured and every minute detail was recorded. He and his assistant then performed crude surgery, including amputations. They deliberately infected the twins

A reproduction of a poster advertising the reward for Mengele's capture. (Reproduced by permission of Archive Photos, Inc.)

with diseases in order to observe their reactions. One night Mengele himself injected fourteen children in order to see if patterns existed in twin deaths. After they expired, he autopsied the bodies. Mengele also performed experiments on other prisoners, using methods involving electricity and radiation. Witnesses recalled that he shot prisoners, struck some with an iron bar, and even burned children alive. After performing these violent acts, Mengele calmly resumed his scientific routine. He did not show any remorse and later his son, Rolf, claimed that even privately, Mengele never expressed feelings of shame or regret.

On the Run

As the end of the war approached and the Nazis faced defeat, Mengele sank into a depression. He continued his barbaric experiments until he left Auschwitz for the last time on January 17, 1945, taking his records with him. The SS was ordered to destroy all remaining records and to shoot any prisoners who were unable to walk unassisted. When

the Soviets approached Auschwitz, Mengele moved westward to other camps. After placing his files in the care of a friend, Mengele was captured with his medical unit by U.S. forces in Bavaria. As large numbers of prisoners were quickly processed, Mengele slipped through the hands of Allied forces, despite being listed as a major criminal by the United Nations War Crime Commission. He was able to obtain a duplicate set of release papers in another name.

Mengele was protected by private citizens once he arrived home in the Gunzburg area. Believing the stories of his work were merely rumors spread by the enemy, locals gave Mengele a job as a farm hand. He and his wife, Irene, met secretly at a vacation resort in Bavaria. Irene and Mengele's father, Karl, were very effective at deceiving the Allies. On January 19, 1948, Brigadier General Telford Taylor, U.S. Chief of Counsel for War Crimes in Nuremberg, Germany, announced that records indicated Josef Mengele was dead. Amidst great confusion, Mengele and other Nazi war criminals were able to avoid Allied efforts to capture them. Although

The Mock Trial of Josef Mengele

In 1985 a final effort was made to expose the failure of any government to locate Josef Mengele. A mock trial of the Nazi doctor was held in Jerusalem, Israel. The result of the extraordinary efforts of Nazi-hunter Simon Wiesenthal, the trial occurred before a distinguished panel that included Wiesenthal; the chief prosecutor at the trial of Nazi criminal Adolf Eichmann; and Telford Taylor, the American prosecutor at the Nuremberg trials. The enormously successful event was televised for four consecutive nights around the world. It featured testimony by people who related their suffering as victims of Mengele's crimes. More than 100 witnesses were gathered and prepared to participate. A week earlier, the forty-year anniversary commemoration of the liberation of Auschwitz had been televised. Auschwitz survivors wanted to focus public attention on the need for governments to continue pursuing Mengele. A month prior to the reunion, Wiesenthal publicized recently released American documents showing that Mengele may have been in American hands in 1947. The documents were later proven to be false.

These three events—the mock trial, the forty-year anniversary of the liberation of Auschwitz, and the release of the documents—placed pressure on the U.S. government, which ordered the Justice Department to examine every aspect of the Mengele case and make an effort to locate him. The Israeli government was also mobilized to find him at all costs. The Israeli and German governments, as well as privately funded Nazi-hunting organizations, greatly increased the rewards for news pertaining to Mengele's whereabouts. The increase of public awareness fueled "Angel of Death" stories until well after Mengele's death.

claims have been made that Mengele was arrested and later mistakenly freed by the Americans in 1947, there is no written proof.

Escapes to Buenos Aires

In 1948, convinced that capture by the Allies would mean certain death, Mengele used funds from his family business to flee to Argentina under an assumed name. He asked Irene to bring their son, Rolf, and join him once he got settled. Uncertain about life on the run in a foreign country, Irene refused to leave Europe and the people she loved. The couple later divorced, Irene remarried, and Mengele only saw his son, Rolf, a few times during his remaining years.

After bribing officials, Mengele was able to leave for Buenos Aires, Argentina, on the ship *North King* in July 1949. He quickly found employment as a carpenter and lived in a small room in the city. After surrounding himself with Nazi sympathizers who helped him find gaping loopholes within the corrupt Argentine government, Mengele easily bribed officials. He moved to a comfortable house, bought an automobile, and settled into a new lifestyle. In 1956 the now-divorced Mengele returned to Germany, where he met his deceased brother's wife, Martha Mengele. Wishing to marry her, he decided to obtain Argentine papers in his own name. Even though the name Josef Mengele appeared on numerous international lists of Nazi criminals, no one alerted the authorities, and Mengele obtained the papers.

Death in Brazil

In July 1958 Mengele married Martha and became the stepfather to her son, Karl Heinz. There are strong suspicions that Mengele made his living in Argentina at that time by selling farm equipment manufactured by his family's company in Germany. His comfortable life in Buenos Aires soon came to an end, however, when local police began an exhaustive search for Mengele. In 1961 he fled to Paraguay, where he lived for several years in the home of a family named Stammer, and later with a family named Bossert. Over time, many of his new friends discovered his true identity, but chose not to turn him over to the authorities. As Martha did not wish to move with him to Paraguay, the Mengeles separated and never lived together again. Nevertheless, he maintained regular contact with Martha and Karl Heinz. After a while, Mengele's family in Germany reduced the amount of funds they provided for his support. Fearing capture, Mengele fled to Brazil in 1978. Now sixty-seven years old, he fell in love with Elsa Gulpian de Oliveira, who did his cooking and cleaning. He tried to introduce her to classical music and art. Mengele was dejected when she turned down his offer to move in with him; she chose to marry a younger man.

Near the end of his life, Mengele became depressed and anxious, and he longed for his childhood home in Germany. He suffered from high blood pressure, the effects of a stroke, degenerative spinal disease, and other illnesses. On February 7, 1979, he went for a swim in the Atlantic Ocean at the seaside cottage of friends. While swimming, he suffered another stroke and, despite efforts to save him, he drowned. Mengele was buried in the town of Bertioga. His friends and family in Germany, not wanting further publicity, kept the death a secret.

Mystery Uncovered

In 1985 portions of a mock trial of Mengele held in Jerusalem, Israel, and organized by Simon Wiesenthal were televised around the world (see box). The testimony of victims of his Auschwitz experiments made a tremendous impact on viewers. In February 1985 the U.S. Justice Department began to investigate all aspects of Mengele's life to ascertain whether he was alive or dead. The Israeli government soon followed suit. Organizations around the world offered millions of dollars in rewards for information that would lead to his capture.

The renewed interest in the notorious war criminal yielded "Mengele sightings" throughout the world. The Israelis, Germans, and Americans decided to share their information in an effort to bring the case to a close. After many false leads, letters to and from Mengele were found hidden in the house of a friend named Sedlmeier, who had protected Mengele's secret over the years. These letters indicated that Mengele had died. Pictures and papers of Mengele were also found at the home of two other Mengele protectors, Wolfram and Liselotte Bossert. Finally his grave site was revealed by the Stammer family, who had housed Mengele for fourteen years. Experts in forensic science from around the world were sent to Brazil to examine Mengele's body. They looked at partial fingerprints and graying hairs and used an electronic process to superimpose photographs over the bones of the face for comparison. On June 21, 1985, Mengele's remains were examined at the Sao Paolo police station. Bones showing his height, a broken finger, the gap between his teeth, and signs of spinal degeneration all acted as proof that the skeleton found in Brazil was that of Josef Mengele. The mystery of the "Angel of Death" had finally been solved.

SOURCES

Books

Astor, Gerald, *The Last Nazi: The Life and Times of Dr. Josef Mengele,* Donald I. Fine (New York), 1985.

Gutman, Israel, editor, *Encyclopedia of the Holocaust,* Macmillan Library Reference (New York), 1990.

Lengyel, Olga, *Five Chimneys,* Howard Fertig (New York), 1983.

Perl, Gisella, *I Was a Doctor in Auschwitz,* Arno Press (New York), 1979.

Posner, Gerald L., *Hitler's Children: Sons and Daughters of Leaders of the Third Reich Talk About Their Famous Fathers and Themselves,* Random House (New York), 1991.

Posner, Gerald L., and John Ware, *Mengele: The Complete Story,* McGraw-Hill (New York), 1986.

Periodicals

Harmon, Jeff B., "Bowling with Dr. Mengele," *Harpers,* July 1982.

Kanfer, Steffan, with Peter Carlson, "I Knew Josef Mengele," *People,* June 24, 1985.

Lifton, Robert J., "Who Made This Man Mengele?" *New York Times Magazine,* July 21, 1985.

Schreiber, Flora, "The Satanic Dr. Mengele," New York Times Syndication Service, May 4, 1975.

Glenn Miller

With his orchestra, bandleader Glenn Miller synthesized all the elements of big band jazz and gave a generation of young people the perfect example of smooth, sophisticated dance music. Miller's popularity as a music maker began in the late 1930s and continued with standards such as "Moonlight Serenade," "In the Mood," and "Tuxedo Junction." Miller was one of the most popular musicians of his time. Moreover, he was extremely patriotic and took his personal definition of "duty" very seriously. He used his power to create a successful military band on his terms. Then, just as he finally convinced the military to send his band to places where it could truly boost morale, he disappeared. Rumors circulated almost immediately, but Miller's fate remains a mystery.

Born March 1, 1904
    Clarinda, Iowa, United States
Died December 15 (?), 1944
    English Channel

Bandleader; musician

"…I knew [the band] was playing like I wanted it to. It sounded wonderful. I didn't say anything—just drove home and told the wife. But I prayed it would last."

Becomes Big-Band Phenomenon

Alton Glen (later changed to Glenn) Miller was born on March 1, 1904 in Clarinda, Iowa. His parents, Lewis Elmer and Mattie Lou (Cavender) Miller, raised four children. The family moved quite often during his youth, to places including North Platte, Nebraska, and Grant City, Oklahoma. In the latter town, Miller milked cows at the age of thirteen in order to earn enough money to purchase a trombone. It is said that he inherited his strong character and love of music from his mother. Miller did not, apparently, count on music to be his career, because

(Reproduced by permission of AP/WideWorld Photos)

Bob Hope Starts Tradition

ob Hope is perhaps the most widely known and loved standup comedian in America. In addition to his successes on radio, in movies, on television, and in live shows, Hope has developed a reputation for the numerous appearances he has made in the name of various charities and his untiring efforts to entertain and boost the morale of American military personnel stationed all over the world. His devotion to his country and the armed forces was made clear after America entered World War II following the bombing of Pearl Harbor in 1941. Hope, who was born in England, became dedicated to the United States after immigrating. He delivered a radio broadcast several days after the bombing and informed Americans of his patriotism and his confidence that America would be victorious. When he was asked in 1942 to lead an entertainment tour of Alaskan army bases, he quickly found several other performers willing to go on tour. From that point on, Hope made many tours overseas to entertain the Allies, covering Europe, Africa, and the Pacific, and also performed at home to entertain troops both during war and peacetime, on battleships, in hospitals, and anywhere he felt the troops needed entertainment. He continued his efforts though wars in Vietnam, Korea, and the Middle East.

In 1995, the fiftieth anniversary of the end of World War II, Hope published a multi-media series commemorating the event, entitled *Bob Hope Remembers World War II: The European Theater and D-Day*. In a review by Michael Allen in the *Saturday Evening Post* (May/June 1995), the following excerpt from Hope's book appeared: "I was there. I saw your sons and your husbands, your brothers and your sweethearts. I saw how they worked, played, fought, and lived. I saw some of them die. I saw more courage, more good humor in the face of discomfort, more love in an era of hate, and more devotion to duty than could exist under tyranny." Along with professional acclaim and honors, Hope received awards and medals for his humanitarian services from American and British leaders. An air force C-17 was named after him; he was honored with a Congressional Gold Medal by President John F. Kennedy and a Medal of Freedom by President Lyndon B. Johnson; he received the title "Honorary Veteran" from the U.S. Congress; and he was given a British knighthood in 1998 for his services to troops in several wars. Hope began performing with the USO during World War II and continued to entertain American servicemen and women, in wartime and peacetime, throughout the twentieth century.

---

he finished high school and began attending classes at the University of Colorado. During his time in college, though, he devoted little time to his studies, continuing to play the trombone and working briefly with Boyd Senter's band in Denver during the mid-1920s. The lure of music proved too strong and Miller left the university after three terms to try his luck on the West Coast.

Miller played with a few small bands in Los Angeles until 1927, when he joined Ben Pollack's orchestra as trombonist and arranger. This was a wonderful opportunity for Miller, since Pollack's band was well-known and respected. Pollack and his musicians moved to New York, and Miller was able to find so many opportunities to perform that he decided to strike out on his own. In addition to playing the trombone, he did arrangements for Victor Young, Freddy Rich, and many others. Miller felt optimistic enough about his burgeoning career by 1928 that he decided to marry Helen Burger, a woman he had met in his student days at the University of Colorado. They later adopted two children.

For the next ten years Miller gained experience by organizing bands and arranging or playing for

Entertainer Bob Hope tries to bring a little levity to hundreds of Allied soldiers who eagerly listen to his comedy routine. Most of the soldiers are patients recuperating at a hospital in New Caledonia. (Reproduced by permission of AP/Wide World Photos)

them. This included serving as the trombonist and arranger for the Dorsey Brothers, as well as organizing a band for the internationally famous Ray Noble, who had come to the United States from Great Britain. Miller not only organized a band for him, he also arranged and played for it. Despite his success with Noble, Miller wanted to have a big band of his own, and turned down a lucrative job with the Metro-Goldwyn-Mayer film company to work on this project. In March 1937 Miller's dream became a reality when he put together musicians such as Charlie Spivak, Toots Mondello, and Maurice Purtill to form the Glenn Miller Orchestra. Though Purtill soon left to perform with Tommy Dorsey, the orchestra carried on for the rest of the year, playing one-night stands in various cities.

In 1938 Miller temporarily suspended the band. Purtill's absence brought about problems with the

orchestra's rhythm section that continued to plague its leader. The members were not meshing with one another the way Miller had hoped. He wanted to achieve a full ensemble sound, rather than spotlighting a soloist. Miller decided to reorganize, using only a few of the band's original members. Later that year the Glenn Miller Orchestra added singer Marion Hutton to its roster. By 1939 the band was playing to standing-room-only crowds in New York City. They made radio broadcasts and recordings, which did much to spread the Glenn Miller sound across the country. Their most famous recordings included "Moonlight Serenade," "In the Mood," and "Chattanooga Choo Choo." Miller's orchestra was famous for its well-blended balanced sound. Critics have noted that it was not a vehicle for star soloists, but rather that emphasis was placed on the output of the entire band. Miller was known to discourage musicians who stood out from the rest of the orchestra, and praise those who combined well with their fellows. The Glenn Miller Orchestra was acclaimed by a large variety of fans because it played many different types of big band music—everything from hot jazz to popular ballads. Miller and his band had appeared in two motion pictures for Twentieth Century Fox: *Sun Valley Serenade* and *Orchestra Wives*. They had achieved both fame and wealth.

Contributes Talents to War Effort

In 1942, during World War II, Miller decided to break up his orchestra in order to accept the rank of captain in the U.S. Army Air Corps. He was past the age when he might expect to be called to service. Nonetheless, Miller felt that he could and should do more to contribute to the war effort than play on the radio, safe from the action. He did not want to use his fame to excuse himself from what he felt was his patriotic duty. On October 7, Miller enlisted in the army and invited members of his band to join him. They declined. Upon his induction into the Army Air Force (AAF), Miller was named director of bands training for the Technical Training Command. He was initially thwarted from implementing some of his more creative plans. He was interested in incorporating string instruments in order to transcend the conventional sound of a dance band, which usually only included brass, reed, and rhythm sections. This was a highly innovative concept, and not all of the military bandleaders were open to his idea. In fact, he was reprimanded for an interview he gave to *Time* magazine, which was printed September 6, 1943, in which he criticized army band music of the time. He asserted that it should be up-to-date, so that the soldiers could enjoy it. He was also quoted as specifically criticizing the compositions of Sousa, which were standards for the army bands. Naturally bandleaders who were admirers of Sousa's works took offense. Miller later claimed he had been misquoted, but the magazine declined to print a retraction. Several months later, though, after helping to organize almost fifty other bands, he was permitted to form a band of his own, the Glenn Miller Army Air Force Band.

In November 1943 Miller was released from his other band responsibilities, leaving him free to concentrate on the growth and development of his own band. He wanted an ensemble sound, so improvisation by individual musicians was not tolerated. Miller also refused to give furloughs for band members. He felt that they were living the easy life, compared to soldiers out on the front lines. On the other hand, he was always willing to help musically talented servicemen find their way into a band, if he could manage it. His band entertained World War II service personnel in America and in England with live concerts and dances and radio performances.

Overseas Assignment and a Mysterious Disappearance

Miller was anxious to go overseas. After repeated requests, he received permission in June 1944 to take his band to England. The group performed in conjunction with the British Broadcasting Corporation (BBC). Wartime London was the site of air raid warnings, rationing on most items, and demolished buildings. Appalled by the conditions and concerned for the safety of his band, Miller made arrangements to move to nearby Bedford. Besides its weekly BBC broadcasts, the band also visited military hospitals and airfields to perform. The applause they received gave Miller and his band immense satisfaction, but Miller again grew restless. His next mission was to have the band sent to France. Once more, he met with opposition from the AAF, not to mention the BBC, which was concerned about their weekly program featuring the band. By November 15 he finally received approval.

Miller decided to fly to Paris to make arrangements before the arrival of his band. Colonel Baessell was leaving for France and offered to let Miller ride along. They took off in a Norseman plane on the stormy afternoon of December 15, 1944. The plane, the pilot, and its passengers were never seen again. According to flight records, the plane never landed in France, nor was any wreckage found. The most widely accepted theory asserts that the plane went down over the English Channel. Two months after his disappearance, the Bronze Star was presented to Miller's wife in recognition of his contribution to the war effort. On June 5, 1945, Glenn Miller Day was declared in the United States as a national tribute.

SOURCES

Books

Encyclopedia of World Biography Supplement Vol. 19, Gale Group (Detroit), 1999.

Simon, George T., *Glenn Miller and His Orchestra*, Thomas Y. Crowell Company (New York), 1974.

Other

The Glenn Miller Birthplace Society, http://www.glennmiller.org (August 2000).

Bernard Montgomery

Considered by some historians to be the premier British general of modern times, Bernard Montgomery was the most notorious and successful officer to lead British troops during World War II. He transformed the demoralized 8th Army into a skilled fighting machine that defeated the Afrika Korps, commanded by German General Erwin Rommel, in the North African desert. Although Montgomery was a hero to many, he was also a controversial figure; his bluntness, egotism, and stubborn disposition frequently embroiled him in conflicts with fellow officers. Still, whatever Montgomery's reputation with colleagues, his careful planning and desire to minimize casualties enamored him to the soldiers who served under him.

Born November 17, 1887
London, England
Died March 24, 1976
Alton, England

British field marshal

"Here we will stand and fight; there can be no further withdrawal.... [W]e will stand and fight here. If we can't stay here alive, then let us stay here dead."

Launching a Military Career

Montgomery was born on November 17, 1887, in London, England, the fourth of nine children of a clergyman and his wife. Montgomery's mother, a stern woman, was sometimes more involved with church work than parenting. When Montgomery was two years old, the family moved to Tasmania, an Australian island in the southern Pacific Ocean, where his father had been appointed bishop. After their return to London in 1901, Montgomery attended St. Paul's School. Five years later, already planning a military career, Montgomery entered the Royal Military Academy at Sandhurst, where his

(Reproduced by permission of AP/Wide World Photos)

Admiral Mountbatten: Allied Commander in Southeast Asia

While Montgomery dominated the scene in North Africa and Europe, the supreme commander of Allied forces in Southeast Asia, Admiral Louis Mountbatten, successfully led his troops on several offensives against Japan. A member of the British royal family, Mountbatten was the great-grandson of Queen Victoria and Prince Albert. Born in 1900, he joined the British navy and served as a midshipman during World War I, specializing in the use of signals. Prior to the outbreak of World War II, he was assigned to command the Fifth Destroyer Fleet. Mountbatten assumed command of the battleship HMS *Kelly* in August 1939 and was soon involved in several conflicts with German submarines. In spring 1940 the *Kelly* was almost sunk several times during torpedo attacks launched from German aircrafts. Eventually, while fighting off the Greek island of Crete, the ship was sunk and Mountbatten nearly drowned.

After a short period as commander of the aircraft carrier *Illustrious,* Mountbatten was appointed an adviser on combined operations by British Prime Minister Win-

ston Churchill. He was in charge of commando units that staged raids against German positions in Norway and France. After the United States entered the war at the end of 1941, British military leaders began preparations for an eventual invasion of France. Mountbatten's experience in conducting amphibious landings became a valuable asset to the operation. In March 1942 he was named chief of combined operations and promoted to the rank of vice admiral. In August, Mountbatten oversaw a raid on the German position at Dieppe, France. While the mission was a failure (3,336 of the 5,000 men who participated were killed), it did provide crucial information that assisted in the planning of the Normandy invasion.

In 1943 Mountbatten was transferred to Asia and named Supreme Commander of Allied Forces in Southeast Asia. The Japanese had overtaken the country of Burma (now Myanmar) and Allied troops stationed in India were suffering from despondency and a variety of tropical diseases. They felt ignored and called themselves the "Forgotten Army." Much like Montgomery, Mountbatten knew personal attention from high-ranking commanders could lift the men's spirits, so he began visiting numerous units in attempts to convince the troops that they were important and appreciated.

grades demonstrated his interest in sports and leisure pursuits over academics. During the latter part of his education, he improved his grades, and in 1908 he graduated thirty-sixth in a class of 150. Commissioned as a lieutenant, Montgomery requested a post in India where he could support himself on low pay. His low grades did not allow him a station assignment in the Indian army, so he signed up for service with the Royal Warwickeshire Regiment, which had a battalion in India.

In 1912, after several years in India, Montgomery returned to England. When World War I began in 1914, he was immediately called to battle in France. After two months in active combat, he

was shot in the chest. He was saved by another soldier who, while coming to his aid, was himself shot; the dead man's body fell over Montgomery and shielded him from further danger. Assumed dead for several hours, Montgomery finally showed signs of life and was rescued and taken to a hospital in England. He was promoted to captain and awarded the Distinguished Service Order, then returned to the fighting in France in 1916. He was a staff officer for the remaining two years of the war, serving as a lieutenant colonel in command of the 17th Battalion Royal Fusiliers.

Montgomery's experiences during World War I strongly affected his attitude toward the military,

As U.S. leaders pushed for an invasion of Burma, a key strategic location due to its proximity with China, Mountbatten led the Allied charge to recapture the country in July 1945.

Maj. Gen. George S. Patton confers with Vice Admiral Lord Louis Mountbatten. (Library of Congress)

The following month, the United States dropped two atomic bombs on Japan, forcing the official Japanese surrender in September. Mountbatten soon received the surrender of all Japanese forces in Southeast Asia and the war was over. Named Earl Mountbatten of Burma in 1947, he was appointed viceroy of India. He was involved in negotiations that led to India's independence from Great Britain in 1947, as well as the establishment of Pakistan, an Islamic state created from Indian land as a separate country. Mountbatten served as governor-general of India until 1948, when he returned to England to rejoin the navy. Over the next several decades, Mountbatten served in various command positions in the British navy. From 1959 to 1965, he was chief of the United Kingdom Defense Staff and chairman of the Chiefs of Staff Committee. Upon retiring in 1965, Mountbatten had reached the rank of admiral of the fleet. In 1979, while on holiday in Ireland, he was assassinated by members of the Irish Republican Army wishing to make a political statement.

especially in regard to commanding officers' treatment of troops. He had witnessed suffering and death that he deemed unnecessary, concluding that soldiers were needlessly sacrificed by officers attempting to win a futile battle. As a result Montgomery advocated careful, detailed planning prior to the deployment of troops, who he felt should always be well trained and equipped for the mission. He believed that open dialogue between officers and soldiers about the purpose and methods of the mission would produce loyalty and rapport. In later years, Montgomery would be criticized for his refusal to begin battles before his plans, troops, and equipment were ready. Those fighting under his command, however, appreciated his concern for their lives.

In the years between World War I and World War II, Montgomery was assigned to a number of locations around the world, rising steadily through the ranks of the army. After serving with the occupation forces in Germany, he attended the army's Staff College at Camberley before spending time in Ireland. In 1926 he became an instructor at the Staff College and in 1929 was put in charge of the committee rewriting the manual on infantry training. Montgomery created internal conflict when he dismissed suggestions from other committee members in favor of his own. When he was thirty-nine years old, Montgomery married Betty Carver, the widow of an officer who had died in World War I. The couple had a son,

Bernard Montgomery (right), head of the land forces for the D-Day invasion, is pictured en route to Normandy with Bertram Ramsey (left), head of the naval forces for D-Day, and Dwight D. Eisenhower (center), commander in chief of the operation. (Reproduced by permission of AP/Wide World Photos)

David, in 1928. After ten years of marriage, Betty died from an insect bite. Devastated by her death, Montgomery internalized his grief by committing himself to his work. During the 1930s, he served in India, Egypt, and Palestine. By 1939 he was in command of the British Army Third Division, one of the few combat-ready units. In September 1939, World War II broke out as Germany invaded Poland, and in 1940 the Nazis moved into France. In summer 1940, Montgomery was deployed to France as part of the British Expeditionary Force sent to repel this German invasion. The unsuccessful campaign resulted in British troops being evacuated from Dunkirk on the northern shore of

France. The French surrendered to the Germans on June 22, 1940.

With England under the threat of German invasion, Montgomery was assigned to lead the 5th Corps in protecting the coastal Dorset and Hampshire regions. Instead of adhering to conventional military tactics that concentrated primarily on beach areas, Montgomery dispersed his troops to several locations, transporting them in double-decker buses that normally functioned as tourist vehicles. He focused his efforts on training and physical fitness to keep his men ready for possible attack. Though Montgomery's abrasive personality and arrogance made him unpopular with some people, his skills and experience were noted by his superior officers. By December 1941, he had been promoted to lieutenant general and placed in charge of the entire South East Command.

Fighting Rommel in the Desert

A primary German stronghold was North Africa, where the Afrika Korps, under the command of German General Erwin Rommel, threatened to take tactical control of the Suez region of Egypt. The British 8th Army, having engaged in extensive conflict with Rommel's troops, was exhausted and demoralized. British Prime Minister Winston Churchill placed Montgomery in charge of the unit after his original choice, General William Henry Ewart "Strafer" Gott, was killed in a plane crash en route to the assignment. Montgomery took his forces to northern Egypt and immediately began implementing strategies to lift the morale of his troops. His initial step was to adopt a distinctive hat, first wearing an Australian bush or slouch hat, and eventually the black beret that became synonymous with his image. Montgomery claimed the beret was worthwhile as it made him immediately recognizable during his daily visits to the troops.

Montgomery left a majority of the detailed battle planning to his staff, especially his chief of staff Francis de Guingand, and concentrated instead on building up his men's fighting spirit. Rallying them with motivational speeches, he called upon their sense of duty. The soldiers were so inspired by Montgomery's own determination that they won a decisive victory against Rommel's troops at Alam Halfa, Egypt in late August and early September. In October, during the battle of El Alamein, Egypt, the 8th Army engaged the Afrika Korps in twelve days of vigorous and fierce fighting. They emerged victorious after chasing the Germans 2,000 miles across the desert into Tunisia, thus validating Montgomery's approach to combat leadership. England's King George VI recognized his efforts by inducting him into the British knighthood.

Military Victories and Personality Conflicts

After the North African victory, Montgomery had less success in Sicily and Italy. In the Sicily campaign, he worked alongside General George

In early 1946, Montgomery was made viscount of El Alamein.

S. Patton, an overbearing and tenacious American leader. Montgomery resented being forced to work with Patton and being given a lesser role in the fighting of the Sicilian campaign. Montgomery also encountered personal conflict while conducting a combined operation in Italy with General Mark Clark, another American. Clark openly accused Montgomery of stalling his troops so that Clark's American troops would take the brunt of the fighting. In December 1943, prior to the completion of the Italian campaign, Montgomery was called away to participate in planning the Normandy invasion. Code-named Operation Overlord, or D-Day, the plan involved the Allies establishing a foothold on the northern shores of France, then driving the Germans out of French territory and back into Germany. The D-Day landing took place on June 6, 1944, with Montgomery in charge of land forces and General Dwight D. Eisenhower of the United States in overall command. During the Normandy battle, Montgomery demonstrated his usual energy, organizational skills, and ability to cut to the core of problems. He focused on bolstering morale by traveling around Normandy during and after the initial invasion to meet with the soldiers. It is said that he was personally seen by as many as 1 million men, whose lives he promised not to waste

Giving Viscount Bernard Law Montgomery a hero's welcome, thousands crowd the streets in Copenhagen, Denmark. (Reproduced by permission of © Hulton Getty/Liaison Agency)

and whom he encouraged to have faith in an eventual victory.

With the initial phase of the successful Normandy invasion over, the Allies made preparations to move across France toward Germany. This strategy resulted in changes in the command structure. Eisenhower was placed in direct command of the land forces, while Montgomery was assigned to head a section of the invasion brigade called the 21st Army Group, comprised of one British and one Canadian army. Promoted to field marshal, the highest rank in the British army, Montgomery continued to have difficulty cooperating with his Allied colleagues, especially Eisenhower. While Eisenhower favored a "broad front" approach to moving the troops forward, Mont-

gomery pushed him to adopt a "single thrust" approach. In September, Montgomery's plan, nicknamed Operation Market Garden, was implemented, and Allied troops landed behind the northernmost section of the German front line. The goal of the mission was to create a gap through which more Allied troops could pour in and surround the German army from behind. The Allies faced stronger than expected resistance from the Germans, however, and the operation resulted in more than 17,000 Allied casualties. Montgomery's strategy had been a failure.

Montgomery further inflamed the temper of Eisenhower in December after the Battle of the Bulge, which was fought in the Ardennes region of Belgium. In a desperate move to gain ground, the Germans managed to repel the Allied momentum along one portion of the front, thus creating a "bulge" in the line. Eisenhower was forced to put Montgomery in command of two American units that had been caught above the northern bulge. The Allies eventually won the battle and, at a press conference held after the victory, Montgomery implied that he had rescued the Americans and was solely responsible for repulsing the German stand. De Guingand managed to soothe Eisenhower's temper, preventing Montgomery from being charged with insubordination.

Montgomery's troops participated in the Allied advance across northern Europe, liberating the Netherlands and sweeping into Germany. On May 4, 1945, Montgomery accepted the surrender of 500,000 Germans. The remaining German forces surrendered to the Allies on May 8. The war in Europe was over, and Montgomery took command of Great Britain's Army of Occupation in Germany. In early 1946 he was named viscount of El Alamein and appointed chief of the Imperial General Staff, a position he retained until 1948. He was then named chairman of the Western European Union's Commanders in Chief Committee (with representatives from Great Britain, the Netherlands, France, Belgium, and Luxembourg). From 1951 to 1958, Montgomery served as deputy supreme allied commander in Europe for the North Atlantic Treaty Organization (NATO), training, equipping, and integrating the forces. Montgomery retired in 1958 and went to live with his son at Isington Mill in Alton, Hampshire, England, where he worked on his memoirs. Montgomery died in 1976 and was buried in a country churchyard near his home.

Sources

Books

Hamilton, Nigel, *Monty: The Battles of Field Marshall Bernard Montgomery,* Random House (New York), 1994.

Howarth, T. E. B., editor, *Monty at Close Quarters,* Hippocrene Books (New York), 1985.

Lewin, Ronald, *Montgomery as Military Commander,* Stein and Day (New York), 1971.

Thompson, R. W., *The Montgomery Legend,* Ballantine Books (New York), 1967.

Heinrich Müller

Born April 28, 1901?
Munich, Germany
Died May 17, 1945?
Berlin, Germany

A commander of the Gestapo during
World War II; responsible for carrying out
the "Final Solution"

*"Everything we [the Nazis] do is half-
attempted and half-done."*

Heinrich Müller began his career as a Bavarian police officer. When the Nazi party assumed power in Germany, Müller quickly ascended the ranks of the Gestapo, becoming commander in 1939. Intimately involved in the organization of the *Endlösung,* or "Final Solution," which called for the total elimination of European Jews, Müller ordered the deaths of millions of people. He disappeared after the war, becoming the "second most-wanted Nazi fugitive" (after Martin Bormann).

A Model Bureaucrat

Little is known about the personal life of Heinrich Müller. He was a reserved and solitary man who had little social interaction outside of work. He was born in Munich, the capital of Bavaria (a state in Germany), to Catholic parents. Sources cite different birth dates, but April 28, 1901, is considered the most likely. Müller attended school only through the elementary years, dropping out to become an apprentice at the Bavarian Aircraft Works in Munich, where he learned to be an aircraft mechanic. When World War I began in 1914, Müller was seventeen years old. He joined the German army as a fighter pilot for the Central powers—the Austro-Hungarian Empire, Germany, Bulgaria, and Turkey. The Allied powers (Great Britain, France, Russia, Italy, and the United States) won the war in 1918. Müller received the Iron Cross medal for bravery.

Müller has been described as a meticulous and imposing man. Constantly observing his surroundings, Müller was concerned only with his personal advancement. He found purpose in following and carrying out orders, whatever those might be. Author Jacques Delarue described him as being "entirely wrapped up in red tape and statistics. He was only at home in a world of notes, memos, and regulations." After leaving the army, Müller began a civil service career in the Bavarian police force. Within a short time Adolf Hitler and his Nazi party attempted and failed to take over the Bavarian government in Munich, in an event that has become known as the Munich Beer Hall Putsch. As a member of the Munich State Police, Müller was obligated to protect the government, which meant working against the Nazis. Sensing an impending change of political power, Müller quietly made himself known to high-ranking Nazi officials. When Hitler was able to assume power after the German elections of 1933 and Bavaria became a Nazi stronghold, Müller was recognized for his allegiance. In the 1930s he was appointed a chief in the Gestapo, the newly created State Secret Police. In light of Müller's earlier anti-Nazi activities, however, his application for membership in the Nazi party was turned down. His superiors believed he would work harder for them if they held the threat of non-admission over him. He was finally admitted in 1939.

"Gestapo" Müller

The Gestapo was initially formed to protect Hitler as the Nazi party began its ascent to power. It gradually grew into an organization that terrorized citizens, carrying out the anti-Semitic policies Hitler preached at his political rallies. Countless numbers of people deemed "enemies of the state" were arrested by the Gestapo and sent to concentration camps. Müller was named sole head of the Gestapo in 1939, earning him the nickname "Gestapo" Müller.

When the Nazis were ready to begin the conquest of Europe and the elimination of Jews, they decided to launch their grand plan by invading Poland. They needed a pretext for going into Poland, however, so they put Müller in charge of the event that started World War II: Müller drove a group of concentration camp inmates, whom the Nazis called "canned goods," to the Polish border.

Did Müller Conceal a Murder for Hitler?

Author William Stevenson, in his book *The Bormann Brotherhood,* suggested that Heinrich Müller earned the gratitude of high-ranking Nazi leaders by covering up a possible murder. Müller was working as a detective for the Bavarian police on the night of September 18, 1931, when news came of the mysterious shooting death of Adolf Hitler's niece, Geli Raubel. The death was officially ruled a suicide, but rumors persisted that she might have been murdered by her Uncle Adolf, with whom she was living.

Stevenson claimed that Hitler became enraged when Geli confessed she was having an affair with a Jewish man. Hitler's gun caused the death of the girl, leading some to the conclusion that Hitler actually murdered her. To avoid any embarrassment to Hitler, who would take control of Germany two years later, authorities secretly buried the girl. Nazi leaders were said to have been grateful for Müller's help in keeping the whole matter quiet.

He promised the men they would be pardoned and released after they performed their patriotic duty. Instead, the prisoners were murdered and their dead bodies, dressed in Polish army uniforms, were left on the German side of the border. Upon "discovering" the bodies, German troops publicly claimed that Polish soldiers had illegally crossed into German territory.

With Müller providing Germany with the excuse it desired to invade Poland, World War II began on September 1, 1939. Soon Germany was invading other countries in eastern Europe. At that point, the Gestapo stepped up its terror tactics and suppressed anti-Nazi activities in the conquered countries by torturing and imprisoning the perpetrators. Members of the Gestapo were included in the Einsatzgruppen—death squads that followed the German army into Poland and the Soviet Union to kill Jews and other "undesirables." The actions of the Gestapo could not be challenged in court, and anyone could be subjected to the whim of Gestapo officers at any time.

Helps Draft "Final Solution"

On January 20, 1942, Müller was one of fifteen top Nazis who met in the Wannsee suburb of Berlin to plan the "Final Solution" to the "Jewish question." Prior to this time, Nazi policy had been to force European Jews to leave Germany and German-occupied territories in Europe. The new plan involved rounding up all Jews throughout Europe, transporting them to Poland, and organizing them into labor gangs at concentration camps where they would work to aid the war effort. Those deemed unable to work would be executed in gas chambers. Only a few men, Müller among them, were selected to sign the actual orders that sent millions to the camps. According to historian Richard Breitman, "There cannot have been many people in Nazi Europe better informed about what was actually happening to the Jews than Heinrich Müller." Müller's Gestapo was largely responsible for the entire project.

Daily luncheons were held by the Nazis and presided over by Müller's boss, Heinrich Himmler. According to author Jacques Delarue, who interviewed members of the Gestapo after the war, "all the men who made Europe tremble" gathered round this lunch table. Müller would often take the opportunity to ask for advice on methods of genocide. "Thus between the dessert and the cheese, or enjoying a glass of brandy brought from France," Delarue reported, "the decision was [made] to suppress or spare a certain category of prisoners, and whether a certain form of execution was to be chosen in preference to another. This monstrous type of conversation seemed to these men entirely commonplace."

Faithful to the End

On July 20, 1944, an assassination attempt was made on Hitler in Rastenburg, Germany. Colonel Claus (Schenk Graf) Von Stauffenberg placed a suitcase containing a bomb, with the fuse activated, under a table close to Hitler. Excusing himself to make a phone call, Stauffenberg then left the room. The briefcase was inadvertently moved across the room and the following explosion, while killing some people, missed its intended target. Müller was put in charge of investigating the attempt on Hitler's life. The conspirators, some of them Müller's friends, were caught and ordered to appear before a "People's Court." They were all condemned to death and hanged. Müller was awarded the highest award for excellence, the Knight's Cross, for his tireless efforts in the search for the perpetrators.

Müller faithfully served the Nazi party until the end of the war. He was present at the underground bunker where Hitler withdrew to escape Soviet bombings in 1945, staying until the Nazi leader committed suicide on April 30, 1945. Immediately after Hitler's death, Müller disappeared.

Müller's fate remains a mystery. It has been suggested that he was a spy for the Soviet Union all along and defected to the Soviet Union after World War II. An admirer of Soviet police methods, Müller reportedly felt communism offered more hope to the world than did the new German empire. Witnesses reported that he was living in South America with Hitler's secretary, Martin Bormann. Still others claimed they had seen him in the Middle East. In 1963 a grave located in Berlin was believed to hold the body of Müller. The grave was dug up and experts examined the bones contained inside. The bones were found to belong to three different men, none of whom was Müller.

SOURCES

Books

Breitman, Richard, *The Architect of Genocide: Himmler and the Final Solution,* University Press of New England (Hanover, NH), 1992.

Delarue, Jacques, *The Gestapo: A History of Horror,* translated from the French by Mervyn Savill, Paragon House (New York), 1987.

Stevenson, William, *The Bormann Brotherhood: A New Investigation of the Escape and Survival of Nazi War Criminals,* Barker (London), 1973.

Edward R. Murrow

Edward R. Murrow was a pioneer of radio and television news reporting. Though he was never formally trained as a reporter, Murrow succeeded in bringing to radio a level of intelligence and professionalism that helped make it, for the first time, a major news medium. His career in media broadcasting began when he covered the invasion of Austria by Germany in 1938, and two years later he became well-known around the world for his coverage of the Battle of Britain. The pace of events during World War II gave broadcast journalism much of its importance, but the high quality of Murrow's reporting gave it much of its character. He is considered one of the most eminent of American journalists and still serves as a model for newscasters.

Born April 25, 1908
    Polecat Creek, North Carolina,
    United States
Died April 27, 1965
    Pawling, New York, United States

Television journalist; radio journalist; news anchorperson

"I pray you to believe what I have said about Buchenwald. I have reported what I saw and heard, but only part of it. For most of it I have no words."

Reporter for Events of the War in Europe

Edward R. Murrow was born Egbert Roscoe Murrow (he legally changed his name later) in 1908 in Polecat Creek (near Greensboro), North Carolina, the son of Roscoe C. Murrow, a railroad engineer for a logging company, and Ethel Lamb Murrow. The family moved in 1913, and Murrow grew up in Washington state. He worked off and on as a logger to earn money to go to college. In 1930 Murrow graduated with a bachelor's degree in speech from Washington State College (now Washington State University) in Pullman, Wash-

(Reproduced by permission of Archive Photos, Inc.)

William Shirer: Eyewitness to History

An eyewitness to many of the critical events in Europe in the 1930s, William L. Shirer reported key developments leading to World War II and wrote widely on the history of Nazi Germany. Born in Chicago, Illinois, on February 23, 1904, he was the son of Seward Smith (a lawyer) and Josephine (Tanner) Shirer. After graduating from Coe College in 1925, Shirer left his home in Cedar Rapids, Iowa, to set out for Paris, France, planning one last youthful fling before settling down to work in the United States. Crossing the Atlantic on a cattle boat, Shirer dreamed of becoming a poet and novelist. Hundreds of other American men and women with similar dreams were then going to Paris, however, and Shirer could not find work with the major American newspapers that published Paris editions. On the morning of what he thought was his last day in France, he had become resigned to returning to the United States, when the editor of the Paris edition of the *Chicago Tribune* offered him a job. The next day he was sitting at the *Tribune* copy desk next to a fellow expatriate-turned-copywriter, James Thurber.

For the next two years, Shirer wrote sports and human interest stories for the *Paris Tribune* and studied European history at the College de France. Increasingly, he turned away from fiction and poetry, preferring to write reports on world events for American readers. His *Tribune* editors agreed, and from 1927 to 1932, Shirer served as a foreign correspondent for the home newspaper, roaming from one European capital to another. He worked subsequently for the Paris edition of the *New York Herald,* the Universal News Service, and the Columbia Broadcasting System (CBS), where famous correspondents such as Edward R. Murrow were employed. Shirer spent much of his time in Berlin, Prague, and Vienna, reporting on the rise to power of Hitler and the Nazis. His dramatic radio reports on the coming of World War II won him the Headliners Club Award in 1938 and 1941. His observations of the tumultuous events in Europe in the 1930s formed the basis of his best-known books, each one a blend of journalism and history: *Berlin Diary: The Journal of a Foreign Correspondent, 1934–1941* (1941), *The Rise and Fall of the Third Reich: A History of Nazi*

ington. Two years later, he married Janet Huntington Brewster, with whom he had one son.

Murrow began his career in international student exchange, but after his marriage, he joined the Columbia Broadcasting System (CBS) in 1935 as director of talks. In 1937 he went to London as the CBS representative in Europe, arranging speeches and concerts for the American radio network. His job was non-journalistic, since he was not trained as a reporter and had never worked on a newspaper. In 1938, however, he was plunged into news broadcasting when Adolf Hitler annexed Austria to Germany. CBS had no experienced radio reporters ready to cover the story, so Murrow chartered a plane to Vienna to document the entry of German troops into the city. He then covered the events leading to World War II and became famous for his broadcasts from London during the Battle of Britain.

Murrow soon became one of the most respected war correspondents in Europe, pioneering a new style of journalism grounded in the immediacy of eyewitness accounts. He was devoted to accuracy and objectivity, but he was equally concerned with the qualities of human experience, with what the war felt like to those whose lives it touched. He utilized innovative techniques to convey those feelings to Americans, interviewing citizens as well as officials and telling of the courage of civilians as well as soldiers. He insisted on experiencing as much as he could, and was known for his willingness to take risks to get a story. Such "eyewitness"

Germany (1960), and *The Nightmare Years, 1930–1940* (1984).

Shirer returned to the United States in December 1940, continuing to work as a radio commen-

William Shirer. (Library of Congress)

tator for CBS until 1947, when he joined the Mutual Broadcasting System. His support for the Hollywood Ten during the postwar "Red Scare" caused him to be blacklisted from broadcasting, and in 1950 he turned to lecturing and writing to support his family during the McCarthy era. Shirer spent much of the next decade utilizing his own reports on the events of the 1930s, transcripts of the Nuremberg Trials, and captured German documents to write his panoramic *The Rise and Fall of the Third Reich,* which won the 1961 National Book Award and the Sidney Hillman Foundation Award. His major works after 1960 included a memoir of Indian spiritual leader Mohandas K. Gandhi, an analysis of the fall of the third French Republic in 1940, a book on Russian novelist Leo Tolstoy, and a memoir of his own life and times. Married in 1931 to Theresa Stiberitz and divorced in 1970, Shirer had two daughters. He lived in Lenox, Massachusetts, and died in Boston in 1993, a few months prior to his ninetieth birthday.

reporting, then considered dramatically unconventional, is now standard in radio and television.

In pursuit of colorful stories, Murrow flew on a bombing run over Berlin and, in defiance of orders from CBS, took a cruise on a North Sea minesweeper. The German "blitz" against London in 1940 made Murrow the best-known American radio voice from overseas, identified by his powerful and articulate speaking, his incisive personal reporting from rooftops and airfields, and his social and political probing behind the wartime headlines. He faced an unusual challenge when he decided to do a live broadcast from a rooftop during one of the air raids. British censors feared that such a broadcast might provide information that would help the bombers find their targets, so

Murrow had to choose his words carefully and describe the raid without revealing where the bombs fell. His London broadcasts were commended by other journalists as exemplary journalism; his style as well as the substance of his reporting won praise. These and other broadcasts from 1939 and 1940 were collected in the book *This Is London.* After America entered the war, Murrow won renown for his broadcasts describing a bombing raid against Berlin, the liberation of the Buchenwald concentration camp, and the American capture of Leipzig. Murrow's reports were an important influence on American public opinion, helping to overcome isolationist sentiment. Murrow continued to broadcast throughout the war, assembling a staff of highly talented correspondents, including William Shirer and Eric

Sevareid, and made CBS the foremost American news network.

Move to Television Reporting

After the war, Murrow undertook a brief stint as CBS vice-president in charge of news, but he found his talents and temperament unsuited to administration and returned to reporting in 1947. Along with daily news broadcasts, he started the popular radio program *Hear It Now,* a weekly documentary interpreting current events and probing social and political problems, in 1950. He also began a program entitled *This I Believe,* on which people discussed their philosophies of life. Herbert Hoover, Thomas Mann, and dozens of others, not all of them prominent, were featured on the five-minute show.

Murrow was at first suspicious of television. He considered it too unsubtle to be a good medium for ideas, and he preferred radio's flexibility. Nevertheless, he turned to the new medium in 1951 and inaugurated in-depth television journalism in 1951 with the weekly program *See It Now,* which followed the format established by its radio predecessor. *See It Now* stirred controversy as it explored various national concerns, and Murrow included a diversity of topics, from world to film news and interviews with political figures. The program was often controversial, never more so than in March 1954 when Murrow challenged the nation's most feared demagogue at that time, anti-Communist Senator Joseph McCarthy, examining McCarthy's career and criticizing him strongly for his chilling effect on civil liberties. The Washington State University website on Murrow refers to his conclusion on the show, when he stated, "We will not be driven by fear into an age of unreason if we remember that we are not descended from fearful [people, people] who feared to write, to speak, to associate and to defend causes which were, for the moment, unpopular." The McCarthy program is considered the most dramatic moment in Murrow's lifelong defense of freedom of speech and of the press. Nonetheless, CBS executives were upset by the controversy and attempted to restrict Murrow's autonomy. Murrow found himself embroiled in conflicts that led eventually to the cancellation of *See It Now,* despite the fact that it had won an Emmy Award.

Murrow also helped anchor and produce several other television programs, one of which was a one-hour documentary show called *CBS Reports,* and another called *Small World,* which featured several people in different locations who would communicate via remote links and have discussions. His good looks and forceful personality made Murrow a well-known public figure, especially after anchoring the extremely popular television program *Person to Person,* which featured interviews with celebrities in their homes. Some critics felt that *Person to Person* was superficial, lowbrow, and unworthy of Murrow's talent and stature. Murrow himself once called the show "demeaning," but it brought him widespread popularity that enabled him to withstand the attacks that followed the McCarthy show and other controversial *See It Now* documentaries.

Leaves Broadcasting

Murrow became disappointed with the widening mass nature of television, with its increasing commercialism, and with the fact that costs put the emphasis on entertainment programs that won audience ratings. Murrow began to reconsider his role. He became increasingly frustrated by the political and commercial constraints on television news. The brand of purposeful news broadcasting he had pioneered found less and less time on the air. A notable speech to the broadcasting industry in 1958, accusing the industry of "escapism" and appealing for better programs, found little response. Finally he left CBS for government service under the John F. Kennedy administration. His last broadcast was his report on Kennedy's inauguration on January 20, 1961. Murrow become director of the U.S. Information Agency (USIA), where he restored the USIA's morale and effectiveness, damaged in the McCarthy years, but found conflict between his role as government propagandist and his independent journalistic past. Ill health compelled his resignation, and he died of cancer on April 27, 1965. Many of Murrow's broadcasts have been transcribed and published in books, including *This I Believe* and *See It Now.* A posthumous anthology, *In Search of Light,* covers the whole of Murrow's career, from the earliest radio newscasts to his departure from broadcasting.

SOURCES

Books

Boddy, William, *Fifties Television: The Industry and Its Critics,* University of Illinois Press (Urbana and Chicago), 1990.

Persico, Joseph E., *Edward R. Murrow: An American Original,* McGraw-Hill (New York), 1988.

Periodicals

Wertenbaker, Charles, "The World on His Back," *The New Yorker,* December 26, 1953, p. 28–45.

Other

Edward R. Murrow: A WWW Information Source, http://www.wsu.edu/Communications/ERM (August 2000).

"Edward R(oscoe) Murrow," *Contemporary Authors Online,* The Gale Group (Detroit), 1999.

(Reproduced by permission of the Gale Group)

Benito Mussolini

Born July 29, 1883
Predappio, Italy
Died April 28, 1945
Milan, Italy

Italian general and dictator for 21 years (1922–1943); known as *il Duce* ("the leader")

"My objective is simple. I want to make Italy great, respected and feared."

Benito Mussolini was the founder of fascism, a form of government he instituted in Italy in the 1920s. Many of Mussolini's ideas were adopted by German leader Adolf Hitler, and the two men made Italy and Germany allies prior to World War II. At first beloved by Italians, Mussolini was so hated by the end of the war that when he tried to escape from Italy, he was captured and shot by some of his own countrymen. His body was hung by the feet and displayed to jeering crowds.

Before 1861, Italy was geographically divided by rivers and mountains and organized into separate states. As a poor country devoid of natural resources, Italy was controlled by a few wealthy landowners, and most Italians were peasants who lived in poverty, finding work as farm laborers only at harvest time. In 1861 Italy was united for the first time under one king, Victor Emmanuel II. But this did not solve Italy's problems. Taxes were high under the new king, his advisers were inexperienced, and citizen riots were commonplace.

A Violent, Stubborn Bully

Into this despotic and chaotic country, Benito Mussolini was born on July 29, 1883. He was the first of three children of Alessandro Mussolini, a blacksmith and an atheist, and Rosa Maltoni, an elementary school teacher and devout Roman

Catholic. He was named in honor of three revolutionary leaders admired by his father. From a young age, Benito was inundated with revolutionary jargon by his angry father. Alessandro taught his son that the world was an unjust place and that rebellion against authority was the only solution. Author Laura Fermi described the young Mussolini as a violent, stubborn, restless, and sullen bully with few friends.

Mussolini's mother had high aspirations for her children; she valued education and hoped to see them succeed in the world. Unable to control him, though, Mussolini's mother sent him to a Roman Catholic boarding school when he was nine years old. He was enrolled with students from a variety of social classes, and at mealtimes he was assigned to the poor children's table, where the food was inferior to that served to the wealthier students. This was Mussolini's first real exposure to injustice, and the bitter lessons he learned at school stayed with him for the rest of his life. After two years, an unhappy and rebellious Mussolini was expelled. Despite a violent disposition, Mussolini continued his schooling and graduated with honors, earning a diploma that allowed him to teach in elementary school. While at home on weekends and holidays, he absorbed his father's revolutionary diatribes, then carried those ideas back to the schoolyard, dazzling his schoolmates with his public speaking skills.

Finds Work as a Journalist

At the beginning of the twentieth century, many Italians, including Mussolini, were forced to leave the country because of high unemployment rates. Mussolini moved to Switzerland in 1902, where he was eventually arrested for vagrancy and sent to jail. Upon his release, he fell in with a group of Italian socialists who helped him launch his career as a journalist. The socialists' beliefs in both an economic system in which the production and distribution of goods is controlled by the government and the primacy of cooperation over competition appealed to Mussolini, and he began to write about the difficulties experienced by Italians who left home to find work, only to be treated cruelly and underpaid. In an attempt to organize worker protests he gave speeches promoting the use of violence by the working classes against government authorities. In 1904 Mussolini returned to Italy and joined the army, where he served for two years. After being released, he continued his anti-govern-

ment work. In 1910 Mussolini married Rachele Guidi, the daughter of poor peasants; they eventually had four children. (Mussolini also fathered at least one child by one of his many mistresses.)

A few years later, he was named editor of *Avanti!* ("*Forward!*"), an Italian socialist party newspaper. He took extreme positions on issues, and was soon recognized as a leader among socialists. When he spoke in favor of Italy entering World War I (1914–1918) on the side of the Allies, the Socialist party expelled him for violating their policy of neutrality. Mussolini then started his own newspaper, the pro-war *Il Popolo d'Italia* ("*The People of Italy*"). He served for seventeen months in the Italian army during World War I and was wounded by an exploding shell.

Rise of Fascism in Italy

Italy had entered World War I in the hopes of acquiring land and international respect. Despite an Allied victory, the Italians were unhappy when their share of the spoils did not save the country from financial ruin. This national feeling of discontent allowed Mussolini and his followers to rally the Italian people against countries that had emerged strong and rich from the war. In 1919 they formed the *Fasci di Combattimento* ("Union for Struggle" or "Fighting Leagues"), an army of young, black-shirted war veterans who were supplied with weapons by Mussolini. They sought supporters throughout the country, promising the revitalization of Italy through political power. Despite this following, Mussolini lost his first attempt at election to public office. The loss prompted Mussolini to reexamine his political ideas. Having failed in his attempt to rally the peasant class, Mussolini believed he could attain victory through the support of landowners and the army. He thought these groups should unite, seize power, and form a new government. Although Mussolini promised rewards for everyone, his new cause became personal power; he sought to place himself in the position of dictator. This is believed to be the real beginning of the fascist movement.

The fascists, who employed brutal tactics against their opponents, acquired power so quickly that by 1922 they were threatening to march on Rome and seize the government. The king of Italy, Victor Emmanuel III, was alarmed by the possible coup and appointed Mussolini prime minister. At the age of thirty-nine, Mussolini became the youngest person in Italian history to hold the posi-

Mussolini's war aims cost many Italian lives.
(Reproduced by permission of AP/Wide World Photos)

tion. In a matter of only four years, Mussolini took control of the government and established a puppet regime, retaining the king to curry public favor. He was given the nickname *il Duce*, meaning "The Leader." He began building roads, restoring crumbling statues of Roman heroes, and making improvements to help farmers. He even appointed a transportation commission to ensure the trains ran on time. Mussolini also encouraged people to have more children in order to increase the Italian population so devastated by the recent war. He instituted social reforms to aid unmarried mothers and conquer diseases. Building up the army and navy with intentions of conquering foreign lands, he promised to return Italy to the glory it had known during the Roman Empire. His popularity soared.

Mussolini called his form of government fascism, a word which derives from the Latin *fasces,* a bundle of rods tied around an ax with the blade projecting from the top of the bundle. The *fasces* symbolized the supreme power of the government in ancient Rome. Under fascism, Mussolini held absolute power. All citizens were expected to work together for the betterment of the country. No one had protection from their dictator, even if the dictator was unreasonable or unjust. Mussolini's slogan, cited in *Encyclopedia of the Third Reich,* was "Believe! Obey! Fight!" At one point, Mussolini

gave this as his own definition of fascism (cited in the same source):

> Fascism is a religious conception in which man is seen in his immanent relationship with a superior law and with an objective will that transcends the particular individual and raises him to a conscious membership of a spiritual society.... Fascism besides being a system of government is also, and above all, a system of thought.... Fascism is opposed to all the individualistic abstractions of a materialistic nature like those of the 18th century.... Against individualism, the Fascist concept is for the State; and it is for the individual in so far as he coincides with the state.... Liberalism defines the State in the interests of the particular individual; Fascism reaffirms the State as the true reality of the individual.

As his fascist government supported violence against private citizens by the secret police and military, public opinion began to turn against him. Mussolini focused his efforts on expansion abroad, engaging Italy in a war with the African country of Ethiopia. Although he triumphed over Ethiopia, the war cost Italy lives and money, but the victory did stabilize Mussolini's waning popularity. Peasants in the fields knelt before him, women held up their babies for him to bless, and government-controlled newspapers referred to him as the divine leader. Mussolini began to believe his own propaganda, and refused to take advice or criticism.

Mussolini Influences Hitler

In Germany, Hitler was keeping a close eye on the fascist takeover of Rome. He began to borrow from Mussolini's speeches, telling Germans they should be nationalistic despite their defeat in World War I. In time, Hitler's respect for Mussolini's ideas evolved into admiration for Mussolini himself. The two leaders agreed to join forces and establish their respective countries as world powers. While visiting Germany, Mussolini marveled at the numerous rows of disciplined Nazi soldiers marching in unison. He attempted to achieve this same "goose stepping" with his own troops. Mussolini spent more time on appearances than on preparing his army for war, and accordingly, his troops suffered greatly.

Reiterating Mussolini's contention that hard work could restore a country to its former greatness, Hitler added a new, German component to fascism:

Mussolini and Hitler in 1939. (Reproduced by permission of Archive Photos, Inc.)

the idea of racial purity and the superiority of the Aryans. Hitler viewed the Jews as a poisonous race who weakened the purity of the Aryan blood. Mussolini, however, did not share Hitler's hatred for Jews. He had many Jewish friends, some of whom had helped him found the fascist movement. Mussolini had denied the very existence of anti-Semitism in Italy. Jews and Italians alike were therefore stunned when Mussolini adopted anti-Jewish laws in 1938. As his friendship with Hitler grew closer, Mussolini felt that Italian Jews were becoming too vocal in their objections of the relationship with Germany. Mussolini hoped that an alliance with Germany would win power and respect for Italy. When Germany's aggressive policies led to the outbreak of World War II, Italy did not have the military prowess to fight. Mussolini initially proclaimed a policy of "non-belligerency," but entered the war on the side of Germany in 1940, despite the complaints of Italian citizens about Mussolini and his repressive policies. Mussolini began showing the physical and mental effects of a disease (possibly syphilis), losing weight, and experiencing severe stomach pains. Soon the Germans, who had never been popular with Italians, were controlling affairs in Italy, and Mussolini was taking orders from Hitler.

Most Hated Man in Italy

The Allies invaded the southern Italian island of Sicily in 1943, increasing the Italian public's disenchantment with Mussolini. Even Mussolini admitted that he was the most hated man in Italy. Disgraced, and on the verge of physical and mental collapse, Mussolini was dismissed and imprisoned by the king. He was quickly rescued by the Germans at Hitler's request in a move called "Operation Oak" and was taken to Hitler's headquarters in Germany. Hitler ordered Mussolini back to northern Italy, where he was to reestablish control. By then, Mussolini was extremely ill and dependent on morphine to relieve his severe stomach pain, and he held no real power when Hitler's "Final Solution" moved into northern Italy. During this campaign, more than 8,000 Italian Jews were sent to German concentration camps.

From Sicily, the Allies invaded the Italian mainland. On September 3, 1943, a devastated Italy surrendered, and then declared war on Germany. With the Allies, the Italian army began a bitter, bloody march northward in attempts to drive out the Germans and find Mussolini. He was captured by his countrymen near Como and shot, together with his lover, Clara Petacci, who had insisted on joining him in his final moments. He left behind his wife, two sons, and a daughter. One son later wrote a book describing his father as a cold man who showed little affection for his children.

After the war ended in 1945, many Italians wanted to forget Benito Mussolini and his fascist party politics. For nearly fifty years, Italian politics was controlled by socialist parties. As the old parties were increasingly beset by scandals, quarrels, and chaos, new parties emerged in the late 1980s and 1990s. In 1992 the Italian Social Movement, a neo-fascist party favoring black shirts and military-style salutes, successfully propelled Benito Mussolini's twenty-nine year old granddaughter, Alessandra Mussolini, to the Italian Parliament.

Sources

Books

Bayne-Jardine, Colin Charles, *Mussolini and Italy*, foreward by William J. Jacobs, McGraw-Hill (New York), 1968.

Collier, Richard, *Duce!*, Viking Press (New York), 1971.

DiMeo, Guido, "Mussolini," *McGraw-Hill Encyclopedia of World Biography*, McGraw-Hill (New York), 1973.

Fermi, Laura, *Mussolini*, University of Chicago Press (Chicago), 1961.

Hartenian, Larry, *Benito Mussolini*, Chelsea House (New York), 1988.

Joes, Anthony James, *Mussolini*, F. Watts (New York), 1982.

Kirkpatrick, Ivone, *Mussolini: A Study in Power*, Hawthorn Books (New York), 1964.

Mulvihill, Margaret, *Mussolini and Italian Fascism*, Franklin Watts (London/New York), 1990.

Smith, Denis Mack, *Mussolini: A Biography*, Vintage Books (New York), 1983.

Smith, Denis Mack, *Mussolini's Roman Empire*, Penguin (New York), 1977.

Snyder, Louis L., *Encyclopedia of the Third Reich.*, McGraw-Hill, 1976.

Other

Delzell, Charles F., "Mussolini, Benito," *Microsoft Encarta*, Funk & Wagnalls, 1994.

Benito Mussolini, http://gi.grolier.com/wwii/wwii_mussolini.html (July 25, 2000).

The Navajo Code Talkers

A number of crucial conflicts during World War II occurred on islands located in the western Pacific Ocean. Not only were the Allies in this arena faced with a formidable Japanese military, they also had to contend with dense jungle terrain on the islands. Secure Allied radio and telephone communications were vital to controlling the region successfully and winning the war, but Japanese intelligence was adept at cracking codes, and quickly deciphered every new code developed by Allied agents. Caught in a quagmire, the U.S. Marines finally discovered an unbreakable code when a World War I veteran recommended recruiting members of the Navajo nation, a tribe of Native Americans living in the American Southwest. Called the "Code Talkers," the Navajo participated in every battle fought by the Marines in the Pacific from 1942 to 1945. Although their contributions to military intelligence are not widely known, the Navajo Code Talkers were an integral part of the Allied victory over Japan.

Code Problem Solved

During the war in the Pacific, the Allies employed a "leapfrogging" strategy, moving troops from island to island and attacking where least expected while bypassing areas with high concentrations of Japanese forces. Covert Allied communications were essential to the success of the strate-

Approximately 400 young Navajo men were recruited from their reservation (which includes parts of Arizona, New Mexico, and Utah) to join the U.S. Marine Corps and become "Code Talkers." The Navajo Code Talkers developed a code based on the Navajo language that was never deciphered and played an important role in military communication.

"*Without the Navajo Code Talkers the Marines would never have taken Iwo Jima.*"
—MAJOR HOWARD CONNOR, SIGNAL OFFICER OF THE 5TH MARINE DIVISION

(Reproduced by permission of Archive Photos, Inc.)

During World War II, Native Americans also served in the U.S. Army Air Corps. Here, a group of airmen perform steps from a traditional dance. (National Archives Trust Fund Board)

gy, but the Japanese had become highly adept at infiltrating codes. The U.S. military had to institute a "twenty-four-hour rule": A code would be abandoned after one day in case it had been cracked by the Japanese.

The Allies were given a solution to this dilemma by World War I veteran Philip Johnston, who in 1896 had traveled with his family into Navajo country where his father served as a Christian missionary. Johnston was raised in the Navajo culture and was fluent in the language. At the age of nine, he had traveled with his father and representatives of the Navajo and Hopi nations to Washington, D.C., to request that a reservation be set aside for the Native Americans. He had served as a translator when the group met with President Theodore Roosevelt. During World War II, Johnston learned about the Allies' problem of finding a safe code. He thought the Navajo language would be an ideal choice because it was spoken almost exclusively by Navajo (a population of about 50,000 in 1942) living in an isolated area, with fewer than thirty non-Navajo speaking the language at that time. Navajo is an essentially oral language with no written alphabet and highly complex tonal qualities and dialects that make it difficult to learn.

Early in 1942 Johnston presented his idea to Major J. E. Jones, a communications officer at Camp Elliot in San Diego, California. Initially doubtful about the plan, Jones told Johnston to bring Navajo to San Diego for a demonstration. Johnston contacted four men from the reservation and one who was already serving in the Marine Corps. They conducted the experiment under the supervision of General Clayton B. Vogel, commander of the Amphibious Corps, Pacific Fleet. The Navajo were given forty-five minutes to translate six military messages into their native language. There were many terms with no equivalents in Navajo, so simple translations had to be created. The Navajo demonstrated their ability to translate either a written or verbal message into Navajo and transmit it by radio to another Navajo in a different room, who would then translate the message back into English. The men proved that they could encode, transmit, and decode a three-line message in only twenty seconds, a feat that required thirty minutes on a coding machine.

Recruiting and Training Code Talkers

The Marines immediately accepted the proposed project and made plans to recruit Navajo men as Code Talkers. Recruiters were met with suspicion when they visited the reservation until Chee Dodge, chairman of the Navajo nation, informed the community that the Marines needed special communications agents. As notices were placed around the reservation, volunteers came forward to offer their services. In February 1942 twenty-nine Navajo, known later as "The First 29," were inducted into the Marines. They boarded trains in Flagstaff, Arizona, and Gallup, New Mexico, to attend boot camp in California. Four of the men began devising a code they taught to the others. The Navajo Marines were required to memorize the entire code during their training period as there would be no written reference in battle. The

The Code Talker Alphabet

Letter	Navajo Word	Meaning
A	Woh-la-chee	Ant
B	Nov-hash-chid	Badger
C	Moasi	Cat
D	Be	Deer
E	Dzeh	Elk
F	Ma-e	Fox
G	Klizzie	Goat
H	Lin	Horse
I	Tkin	Ice
J	Tkele-cho-gi	Jackass
K	Klizzie-yazzie	Kid
L	Dibeh-yazzie	Lamb
M	Na-as-tsosi	Mouse
N	Nesh-chee	Nut
O	Ne-ahs-jah	Owl
P	Bi-sodih	Pig
Q	Ca-yeilt	Quiver
R	Gah	Rabbit
S	Dibeh	Sheep
T	Than-zie	Turkey
U	No-da-ih	Ute
V	A-keh-di-glini	Victor
W	Gloe-ih	Weasel
X	Al-a-as-dzoh	Cross
Y	Tsah-as-zih	Yucca
Z	Besh-do-gliz	Zinc

—McClain, S., *Navajo Weapon,* Books Beyond Borders, 1994.

Some Terms Used By The Code Talkers

Term	Navajo word	Meaning
Major General	So-na-kih	Two Stars
Colonel	Astah-besh-legai	Silver Eagle
Fighter Plane	Da-he-tih-hi	Hummingbird
Transport Plane	Astah	Eagle
Aircraft Carrier	Tsidi-ney-ye-hi	Bird carrier
Destroyer	Ca-lo	Shark

—McClain, S., *Navajo Weapon,* Books Beyond Borders, 1994.

An Example of a Translated Order

The order in English...
    Request for artillery and tank fire at 123 B, Company E move fifty yards left flank of Company D.
Would be translated into Navajo words that meant...
    Ask for many big guns and tortoise fire at 123 Bear tail drop Mexican ear mouse victor elk 50 yards left flank ocean fish Mexican deer.

—McClain, S., *Navajo Weapon,* Books Beyond Borders, 1994.

The experiences of King Mike are an example of the work executed by the Code Talkers. Mike traveled from remote Monument Valley in Arizona, where he was living on his wife's family sheep farm, to participate in some of the bloodiest battles in the Pacific. After Mike was the only survivor from his brigade in an attack on the island of Guam, he was reassigned to the 6th Division of the 22nd Regiment just before the U.S. invasion of Okinawa. He was assigned to a five-person regimental intelligence team comprised of a demolition specialist, a soldier fluent in Japanese, a communications expert, a technician, and a Navajo Code Talker. After the U.S. Navy had bombed a particular area of the shore, the team would land on the beach and infiltrate enemy lines, sending back information via radio on estimated enemy damage and timetables for the deployment of U.S. forces. Much of this work was done under the cloak of darkness in constant danger of capture and death. The information gathered by Mike's team was crucial to the Allies' success on Okinawa and in other battles.

Another Code Talker, Teddy Draper, Sr., participated in the battle of Iwo Jima. The bloody thirty-six-

code, soon proven successful in combat, was authorized to be learned by another 300 Navajo recruits. Despite his age, Johnston was admitted into the Marines to assist in the recruiting and training of Code Talkers. Recruits from boot camp were sent directly to Johnston, who was now a staff sergeant, for training in utilization of the code. In early 1943 he worked with experts to develop an even more sophisticated code.

The Navajo Code Talkers used from one to three Navajo words to represent each letter of the English alphabet. For instance, the Navajo word for ant, "woh-la-chee," stood for a; "nov-hash-chid" or badger was b; and "moasi" or cat was c. Words would then be spelled out letter by letter. For nearly 400 military words and expressions, the Code Talkers devised symbolic Navajo names: The Navajo word for "chicken hawk" meant dive-bomber, "iron fish" meant submarine, "fast shooter" was machine gun, and "hummingbird" was fighter plane.

The Navajo code proved so ingenious that Navajo untrained in its usage could not decipher it. One Navajo soldier captured while fighting in the Philippines was unable to translate when ordered by his Japanese captors to decipher the code. Two American code-breaking specialists who were called in to test the code could not even transcribe the sounds of the words, much less decipher their meaning.

In addition to the Navajo, other Native American groups saw service during World War II. Here, Lt. Woody Cochran, a Cherokee, holds a Japanese flag captured in New Guinea. (National Archives and Records Administration)

General Colin Powell at an exhibit honoring the Navajo Code Talkers at the Pentagon in Washington, D.C., 1992. (Reproduced by permission of AP/Wide World Photos)

day battle utilized the Navajo code as the exclusive language for communication. During the initial two days of the battle, six Code Talkers worked around the clock to send and receive 800 messages, which they relayed with no mistakes. Major Howard Connor, signal officer of the 5th Marine Division, is quoted on the Navy and Marine Corps World War II Commemorative Committee's web site as saying: "Without the Navajo Code Talkers the Marines would never have taken Iwo Jima." During a battle on the island of Saipan, Code Talkers successfully redirected American troops who were accidentally firing on their own men—they were not convinced they were firing at Americans until the Code Talkers confirmed the fact.

Upon hearing the story of the Navajo Code Talkers after the war, Japanese intelligence chief General Setzo Avisue said, "Thank you, that is a puzzle I thought would never be solved" (as quoted on the web site *Passages West: The Navajo Code Talkers* by Gerald Knowles). Some believe that the code devised and carried out by the Navajo may have been the only unbreakable code in military history.

The Code Talkers returned to the reservation and underwent the traditional Navajo "Enemy Way" ceremony to cast away painful memories and chase away any lingering ghosts of fallen friends or enemies. It would be many years before their contribution to the Allied victory was openly acknowledged by the U.S. government, which classified any information pertaining to the role of the Code Talkers until 1968. Officials feared a premature disclosure would remove any chance of using the code in future conflicts.

Honoring the Code Talkers

By the end of World War II, around 400 Navajo had served as Code Talkers. In 1969 the 4th Marine Division held a reunion for World War II veterans, inviting the Code Talkers along with Philip Johnston. They were presented with special bronze medallions depicting a Native American on a pony next to the well-known depiction of Marines in Iwo Jima raising an American flag. A representative of President Richard Nixon read a message honoring the Code Talkers for their role in the war. In 1971 the Code Talkers held their own reunion at Window Rock, Arizona, headquarters of the Navajo Nation, where they gave demonstrations of their skills to an audience of younger Navajo. In 1981 President Ronald Reagan praised them for their service and dedication. In September 1992 thirty-five surviving Navajo Code Talkers attended the dedication of a special exhibit at the Pentagon in Washington, D.C. Placed on permanent display were photographs, equipment, the original code, and explanations of

the code. A monument honoring their contributions resides near the natural arch called Window Rock, in the Arizona city of the same name.

SOURCES

Books

Aaseng, Nathan, *Navajo Code Talkers,* Walker and Company (New York), 1992.

Kawano, Kenji, *Warriors: The Navajo Code Talkers,* Northland Publishing Company (Flagstaff, AZ), 1990.

Lagerquist, Syble, *Philip Johnston and the Navajo Codetalkers,* Council for Indian Education (Billings, MT), 1996.

McClain, S., *Navajo Weapon,* Books Beyond Borders (Boulder, CO), 1994.

Paul, Doris A., *The Navajo Code Talkers,* Dorrance & Co. (Philadelphia), 1973.

Other

The Navajo Code Talkers, http://wae.com/webcat/navajos.htm (May 5, 2000).

The Navajo Code Talkers, http://www.unink.com/passages/Monument-Valley/Ledgends/Code Talkers.html (May 5, 2000).

Chester W. Nimitz

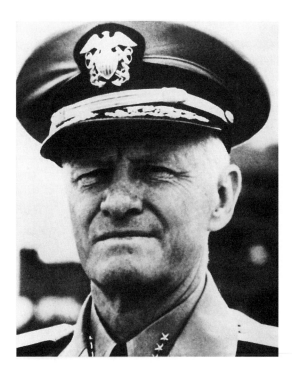

Chester W. Nimitz, commander of the U.S. Pacific Fleet in World War II and one of the strategists who oversaw the defeat of Japan, directed devastating naval campaigns that involved more military power than had been wielded by any commander in a previous war. Though he rarely captured headlines, Nimitz remains one of the most outstanding naval commanders in history. Showing little emotion and seldom raising his voice, Nimitz commanded a theater of war 65 million square miles in area through a combination of proven ability, personal simplicity, and quiet determination.

An Affinity for Leadership

Nimitz was born in 1885 in Fredericksburg, a German-American community in the hill country of central Texas. His father was a cattle drover who joined drives from Texas to Nebraska, a profession that aggravated his weakened heart and lungs. He died five months before Nimitz was born, and Nimitz's mother married her late husband's younger brother. At the age of eight, Nimitz earned one dollar per week as a delivery boy at his uncle's meat market and received high grades in the local schools. After living a few years in Fredericksburg, Nimitz moved to Kerrville, Texas, where his mother and stepfather, William "Uncle Willie" Nimitz, managed the small St. Charles Hotel. Though he had hoped to attend West Point, he learned there

Born February 24, 1885
　Fredericksburg, Texas, United States
Died February 20, 1966
　Berkeley, California, United States

Admiral and commander of the U.S. Pacific Fleet in World War II

"In those falling bombs at Pearl Harbor, Japan was hearing the sound of defeat. Perhaps nothing else could have brought Americans together so completely."

(Reproduced by permission of © Hulton Getty/ Liaison Agency)

were no vacancies. Then his congressman told him about an opening at the U.S. Naval Academy in Annapolis, Maryland, an institution that was unfamiliar to him. In 1905 Nimitz graduated seventh in his class of 114, with the rank of midshipman.

Nimitz was immediately sent to Asia, where he spent four years on battleships, advancing to the rank of lieutenant. After returning to the United States in 1909, he served on the submarine *Plunger.* Although the first submarines were extremely primitive, Nimitz foresaw the day when they would become lethal weapons. In 1912 he commanded the Atlantic Submarine Flotilla, which was comprised of all the submarines in the Atlantic. Soon considered the foremost expert on diesel engines in the United States, Nimitz was sent to Hamburg in 1913 to become familiar with the larger German diesel engines. He sought to install diesel engines in all submarines; the gasoline engines, he noted, emitted poisonous fumes and had a tendency to explode. In 1916, after having built a diesel engine for the oil tanker *Maumee,* Nimitz became the ship's chief engineer and executive officer. In August 1917, just five months after the U.S. entered World War I (1914–1918), he joined the staff of Captain Samuel S. Robison, who commanded the submarine force in the Atlantic Fleet. As Robison's protégé, Nimitz shifted the direction of his career from engineering to command positions at sea. During the 1920s, he had a variety of assignments, ranging from executive officer of the battleship *South Carolina* to building a submarine base at Pearl Harbor, Hawaii. In 1922 he attended the Naval War College at Newport, Virginia.

Displays Tactical Genius

From 1926 to 1935, Nimitz directed the Naval Reserve Officers' Training Program at the University of California, Berkeley, commanded Submarine Division 20 in San Diego, and commanded the heavy cruiser *Augusta.* He was assistant chief of the Navy Department's Bureau of Navigation, stationed in Washington, D.C., from 1935 to 1938. Promoted to rear admiral in June 1938, he was named chief of the Bureau of Navigation (now the Bureau of Navy Personnel) the following year. Congress had enacted a naval construction program amounting to billions of dollars per year, thereby embarking the United States on a great naval race. Nimitz was assigned to recruit and train the sailors required for that enterprise. He streamlined the chain of command and eliminated archaic practices. Acquainted with every senior officer in the navy, he proved invaluable to President Franklin D. Roosevelt, who relied heavily on his advice. In early 1941 Roosevelt offered Nimitz the second highest position in the navy (after chief of naval operations), commander in chief of the U.S. Fleet. Nimitz turned it down, considering himself too junior an officer.

On December 16, 1941, Nimitz replaced Admiral Husband E. Kimmel, commander in chief of the Pacific Fleet (CINCPAC), who had been relieved of his position pending investigation of the surprise Japanese air attack on Pearl Harbor on December 7. When Nimitz assumed command, the Japanese possessed twice the number of battleships and over twice as many carriers as the United States. Nimitz refused to either blame Kimmel for the Japanese raid or to fire high-ranking naval officers stationed there, raising morale at the base. Nimitz realized that the battleships sunk at Pearl Harbor would have been superfluous in the new conflict—too vulnerable to operate without air cover and too slow to operate alongside carriers.

By early January 1942, the Western powers were in full retreat in the Pacific. The small U.S. Asiatic Fleet had fled from the Philippines to the Java Sea. With the U.S. Pacific Fleet in shambles, Japan occupied both Hong Kong and Manila and was advancing on Java and Singapore while shelling Midway. Nimitz urged the American public to be patient and, knowing that an offensive action was necessary to restore the navy's confidence, authorized a series of carrier strikes on Japanese positions. The most famous strike, commanded by Lieutenant Colonel James H. Doolittle, was on Tokyo. The raid inflicted minimal damage on the Japanese but helped restore American morale and made the Japanese realize that their homeland was not safe from attack. In early 1942 Nimitz was promoted to commander in chief of the Pacific Ocean Area (CINCPOA), gaining command of the Pacific Fleet and designated army ground and air units. His responsibility was equal to that of General Dwight D. Eisenhower in Europe and General Douglas MacArthur in the Southwest Pacific, but the title was inaccurate insofar as MacArthur exercised independent command over Nimitz's jurisdiction. This division of Pacific power between Nimitz and MacArthur would later prove troublesome, causing competition between the two men for the limited resources available. In early May 1942 Nimitz ordered the Pacific Fleet to the Coral Sea. The battle was the

Fleet Admiral William F. Halsey

The popular and aggressive American naval officer Fleet Admiral William F. Halsey (1882–1959) commanded major Pacific Fleet units during World War II. The son of a navy captain, he entered the Naval Academy in 1900. Most of Halsey's early sea duty was on destroyers. At the age of fifty-one, he began flight training, and after graduation assumed command of the aircraft carrier *Saratoga*. In 1938 he was given command of Carrier Division 2 and was promoted the following year to vice admiral and appointed commander of the Aircraft Battle Force. After the U.S. Navy's battleships had been crippled in the Japanese attack on the naval base at Pearl Harbor, Hawaii, on December 7, 1941, Halsey's carrier force became the heart of the American fleet in World War II. Early in 1942 he led his ships on daring strikes against Japanese bases that culminated in a raid on Tokyo. While the damage inflicted by these raids was minor, they did much to bolster American morale and to make Halsey a popular hero. On October 18, 1942, Halsey was appointed commander of the South Pacific Area. He thus commanded America's initial Pacific offensive, the battle for Guadalcanal in the Solomon Islands. Operations had reached a critical

(Library of Congress)

stage, and the appointment of Halsey, with his reputation for audacity and aggressiveness, was welcomed by the beleaguered marine and navy units. In a series of fierce engagements, Japanese naval forces in the area were defeated and American victory on Guadalcanal assured. President Franklin D. Roosevelt promptly promoted Halsey to admiral. Throughout 1943 and early 1944, Halsey commanded naval operations around the Solomons, overrunning or isolating Japanese garrisons.

On June 15, 1944, Halsey was relieved as commander of the South Pacific Area and named commander of the 3rd Fleet. This force was the most powerful aggregation of naval striking power in American history. Halsey and his staff began planning for reoccupation of the Philippines. However, his operational performance failed to match his good planning. During the crucial battle for Leyte Gulf, he sent his main force after a Japanese decoy fleet; this allowed powerful enemy surface units to penetrate the Philippine Sea. Only frantic resistance by a small escort carrier group and a sudden Japanese retreat saved the American landing forces from major damage. Two months later, the admiral's reputation suffered another blow when he maneuvered directly into the path of a typhoon, losing three destroyers. In early summer 1945 Halsey maneuvered the fleet into the path of another typhoon. Despite these errors, he retained command until the end of the war, directing the final successful air and sea attacks upon the Japanese home islands. Following the Japanese surrender in 1945, Halsey was promoted to fleet admiral and assigned what were essentially public relations duties until his retirement in 1947. In subsequent years, he held several business positions and led an unsuccessful drive to raise funds for the preservation of the carrier *Enterprise*.

first great aircraft carrier conflict, and no surface ship on either side ever sighted the enemy. Tactically, it was close to a draw: The Japanese lost more planes, but the Americans lost more naval craft, including the valuable *Lexington*. Yet by halting a possible Japanese assault on Port Moresby, Nimitz may have gained a strategic victory by saving Australia and New Zealand.

The Battle of Midway, fought just a month later, was an overwhelming success for the United States. The Japanese had deployed the major part of their navy, outnumbering Nimitz's fleet. Although Rear Admiral Raymond A. Spruance and Rear Admiral Frank Jack Fletcher were also involved in the engagement, Nimitz planned the strategy, picked the commanders, and ordered the plan into execution. Acting on intelligence supplied by naval code-breaker Commander Joseph J. Rochefort, Jr. and estimates made by Lieutenant Commander Edwin T. Layton, Nimitz estimated the time, location, and strength of the Japanese strike. The Japanese steamed into a trap, bearing losses, particularly in carriers and experienced pilots, that reversed the course of the Pacific war. For Nimitz, Midway was a gamble that paid off: Had Admiral Yamamoto Isoroku of Japan been able to win, the U.S. supply line to Australia and the South Pacific would have been severed. With Yamamoto able to raid Hawaii and the West Coast of the United States, the American public might have demanded a "Pacific-first" strategy, which in turn might have forever postponed invasions at Casablanca and Normandy.

Deprived of the initiative after the Battle of Midway, Japan was forced on the defensive. Retaining its newly won empire became increasingly difficult. Serving as a gateway to Australia and providing direct access to Japan, Guadalcanal was a strongly contested battlefield, and in mid-July the Americans launched campaigns in the area. Upon visiting U.S. forces there, Nimitz called for reinforcements and gave William E. "Bull" Halsey (see box on page 341) command. On November 12, 1942, in one of the bloodiest confrontations in the South Pacific, the Japanese naval force was turned back at Guadalcanal, thus permitting an armed U.S. convoy to get through. In January 1943 Nimitz contracted malaria, but recovered by November, when he launched a legendary offensive in the Central Pacific. Utilizing a two-pronged approach, Nimitz struck at sea while MacArthur's ground forces moved up from New Guinea. Nimitz used the famous "leapfrogging" technique, by which strongly held Japanese positions would be first bypassed and then neutralized by air attack and naval blockade. By combining devastating carrier attacks, amphibious assaults, and the leapfrog strategy, Nimitz's forces took only nine months to advance thousands of miles. Moving from Tarawa on Japan's defensive perimeter to the Marianas, the United States' B-29 bombers were now in striking distance of Japan.

First Conflict, Then Cooperation, between Two Military Leaders

During the war, Nimitz continually clashed with General Douglas MacArthur, though they were on amicable terms in the last phases of the Pacific campaign. The flamboyant MacArthur envisioned victory only through an army offensive, with his forces striking at Japan via New Guinea and the Philippines. Such a strategy would relegate the navy to transport status, moving MacArthur's men to various islands under army air cover. Nimitz, on the other hand, believed that to defeat Japan, the army, navy, and marines should be sent directly across the Central Pacific, a strategy he claimed was swifter and cheaper. A meeting held at Pearl Harbor in July 1943 was particularly significant in this conflict. MacArthur explained his strategy, which involved first taking Luzon, then the other Philippine islands, then recapturing the Netherlands East Indies (modern-day Indonesia), all the while moving toward Japan. Backed by Chief of Naval Operations Ernest J. King, Nimitz's plan called for moving west to the Caroline chain, then taking in sequence the central Philippines, Iwo Jima, and Okinawa, before invading Japan. In Nimitz's scheme, the conquest of Formosa held the key to victory. The 14,000-square mile island in the South China Sea could block the flow to Japan of needed oil, tin, rubber, and quinine from the East Indies, aid the Chinese in their effort to erect an air base poised at the Japanese, and possibly serve as the launching pad for an invasion of Japan itself.

At the Pearl Harbor meeting, MacArthur pleaded for his Philippine strategy, stressing American moral commitment to the Philippines, promising fewer casualties, and claiming the Filipinos would offer more resistance to Japan than the Formosans. According to Nimitz biographer E. B. Potter, Nimitz changed his mind at the meeting, in part because of the heavy American losses at Tarawa, a logical stopping place on the way to Formosa. Other factors favoring MacArthur's plan included

Admiral Chester Nimitz, who commanded the U.S. Pacific Fleet, uses confiscated Japanese binoculars to get a look at Guadalcanal. (Reproduced by permission of AP/Wide World Photos)

the estimate of 90,000 to 200,000 fresh American troops needed to take Formosa—men who were unavailable until the war in Europe ended—and Japanese control of most air bases in eastern China, which made strikes from China impossible.

In December 1944 Nimitz was made fleet admiral, enabling him to wear five stars and giving him rank equal to that of MacArthur. Instructed to support MacArthur with his Third Fleet, in late October 1944 Nimitz participated in the Allied assault on the island of Leyte in the Philippines. In the battle of Leyte Gulf, considered by some the greatest naval battle in history, Japanese kamikaze ("divine wind") pilots launched suicide attacks. American strikes made Leyte Gulf a graveyard for Japanese warships. Nimitz gave Halsey orders to cover the Leyte operation and, if the opportunity arose, to attack the enemy fleet. Vice Admiral Thomas C. Kinkaid and his Seventh Fleet, under MacArthur's control, were able to stave off disaster. Overall, Leyte Gulf resulted in a victory for the United States and Nimitz. Realizing that Halsey was still the navy's most inspiring leader, Nimitz kept him in his post.

The conquests of Iwo Jima in March 1945 and Okinawa the following June put CINCPOA forces within a few hundred miles of Japan. By August, the

Pacific Fleet was operating off Japan's shores. Like MacArthur, Nimitz recommended the invasion of Kyushu, the southernmost island of Japan, but warned of heavy casualties. The invasion plan was rendered moot by the atomic bombs dropped on Hiroshima and Nagasaki in early August and the entry of the Soviet Union into the Pacific war. Japan signed surrender documents on September 2, 1945. Nimitz signed the surrender on the battleship *Missouri* as official representative of the U.S. government. MacArthur signed in his capacity as supreme commander of the Allied forces. Largely through the efforts of Secretary of the Navy James V. Forrestal, October 5, 1945, was designated "Nimitz Day." Nimitz was honored by a parade and presented with his third Distinguished Service Medal by President Harry S Truman. Offering a highly unorthodox interpretation of how the Pacific war ended, Nimitz told the U.S. Congress that neither atomic weapons nor Soviet participation had ended the conflict. Instead, according to Nimitz, Japan sought a peace accord because its supply routes had been blocked and its air power decimated.

In December 1945 Nimitz succeeded Ernest J. King as chief of naval operations. During two years in office, he oversaw post-war demobilization of forces. Deploring the rapid disarmament, he warned that the navy was becoming too weak to protect U.S. overseas interests and support American foreign policy. In a bitter dispute over service unification, Nimitz defended continued naval control over carrier aviation. Prior to relinquishing his post, Nimitz claimed that American naval strength had been seriously depleted. In 1949 he retired, moving to Berkeley, California. He confided to his family that the military had become too dominated by technocrats and that U.S. defense policy relied too much on a strategy of mass destruction. As a regent of the University of California, he was unsuccessful in preventing a loyalty oath from being imposed upon its faculty. He was named plebescite administrator for the United Nations Commission on Kashmir, and from 1949 to 1952 he acted as a roving "goodwill ambassador" for the United Nations, advancing the UN cause in speeches throughout the country. He died on February 20, 1966, after a series of small strokes. His contributions to the Navy are recorded at the Chester Nimitz Museum, part of the Museum of the Pacific War, in Fredericksburg, Texas.

SOURCES

Books

Driskill, Frank A., and Dede W. Casad, *Chester W. Nimitz: Admiral of the Hills,* with an introduction by Ernest M. Miller, Eakin Press (Austin, TX), 1983.

Holt, Edwin P., *How They Won the War in the Pacific: Nimitz and His Admirals,* Weybright and Talley (New York), 1970.

Morison, Samuel Eliot, *The Two-Ocean War: A Short History of the United States Navy in the Second World War,* Galahad Books (New York), 1997.

Potter, E. B., *Nimitz,* Naval Institute Press (Annapolis, MD), 1976.

Potter, E. B., editor, *Sea Power: A Naval History,* Prentice-Hall (Englewood Cliffs, NJ), 1960.

Potter, E. B., and Chester W. Nimitz, editors, *The Great Sea War: The Story of Naval Action in World War II,* Bramhall House (New York), 1960.

Potter, E. B., and Chester W. Nimitz, editors, *Triumph in the Pacific: The Navy's Struggle against Japan,* Prentice-Hall (Englewood Cliffs, NJ), 1963.

Spector, Ronald H., *Eagle Against the Sun: The American War with Japan,* Easton Press (Norwalk, CT), 1989.

J. Robert Oppenheimer

Due to J. Robert Oppenheimer's brilliant research in the field of quantum mechanics, the study of the energy of atomic particles, he was appointed as director of the weapons laboratory at Los Alamos, New Mexico, where scientists from throughout the world secretly convened to develop an atomic bomb. The successful formulation of this weapon resulted in the bombing of Hiroshima, Japan, on August 6, 1945, and Nagasaki, Japan, on August 9, 1945, ending the conflict with Japan. Oppenheimer was not only central in the Manhattan Project but was also recognized for his work as a researcher and teacher, and for his assistance to the government in post-war research on utilization of nuclear energy and weapons.

Born April 22, 1904
    New York, New York, United States
Died February 18, 1967
    Princeton, New Jersey, United States

American physicist; helped develop the first atomic bomb

"What we do not know we try to explain to each other."

Makes Contributions to Physics

Julius Robert Oppenheimer was born into a wealthy, cultured family and grew up in a spacious apartment in New York City. His father, Julius Oppenheimer, emigrated from Germany as a young man and became a successful entrepreneur by building a thriving textile importing company. Oppenheimer's mother, Ella Friedman, was a noted painter. Oppenheimer showed unusual intelligence and inquisitiveness early in life. At the age of eleven, he assembled a vast rock collection and became the youngest member of the New York Mineralogical Society, presenting a paper to the society at age

(Library of Congress)

Enrico Fermi

One of the most famous scientists to participate in the Manhattan Project was Italian physicist Enrico Fermi, who defected to the United States after winning the Nobel Prize in 1938. Born in Rome, Italy, on September 29, 1901, Enrico Fermi grew into a talented, bright teenager, learning more about physics while still in high school than many graduate students learned in universities. He earned his Ph.D. in physics in Italy at the age of twenty-one, going on to study at the German universities of Göttingen and Leiden. In 1924 he returned to Italy and became a professor at the University of Florence. While teaching in Florence, Fermi wrote an important paper about the actions of subatomic particles. Now recognized as a leader in physics, he was named to the newly created chair of theoretical physics at the University of Rome, where for the next six years he collaborated with a number of leading physicists and promising students.

During the early 1930s, while studying the atomic nucleus, Fermi discovered a new particle called a "neutrino" and a new kind of force called "weak force." Later he experimented with bombarding atoms in various chemical elements with neutrons, demonstrating that this process could produce radioactive forms. He then discovered that a uranium atom bombarded with neutrons would split, resulting in nuclear fission. This work won him the Nobel Prize in 1938; after accepting the award in Sweden, Fermi and his Jewish wife fled with their family from the repressive regime of Italian dictator Benito Mussolini to the United States, where Fermi accepted a position as a professor of physics at Columbia University in New York City.

In August 1939 President Franklin D. Roosevelt received a letter from physicists Leo Szilard and Albert Einstein warning that the Germans were trying to develop nuclear weapons. Roosevelt responded by establishing the Manhattan Project, allowing American scientists to devote their attention to the development of an atomic bomb. On December 2, 1942, in his lab housed

twelve. Oppenheimer attended the liberal and academically challenging Ethical Culture School in New York City. The summer after he graduated, he traveled to Europe, where he contracted dysentery and spent the next year recovering. In 1922 he entered Harvard University. Studying a wide range of subjects, he was especially drawn to physics, which became his major. Oppenheimer graduated summa cum laude in only three years.

Oppenheimer graduated during a prolific time in the field of physics. Resolving to further his studies in theoretical physics in Europe, he first attended Cavendish Laboratory at Cambridge University in England. In 1926 he transferred to the University of Göttingen in Germany to work with physicist Max Born. The pair ended up developing the "Born-Oppenheimer Theory" of molecular activity. Oppenheimer earned his doctorate in 1927 and went on to conduct further research in Leiden,

Holland, and Zurich, Switzerland. In Switzerland, he worked closely with another famous scientist, Wolfgang Pauli. During these years of study, Oppenheimer demonstrated his ability to conceptualize and analyze ideas, draw connections between established theories, and detect problems. On his return from Europe, Oppenheimer was offered teaching positions at ten universities. In 1928 he accepted offers from the University of California at Berkeley and the California Institute of Technology (Cal Tech) at Pasadena. For the next thirteen years, he divided his time between these two schools, establishing Berkeley as a major American center for the study of quantum physics, the study of the energy of atomic particles, and conducting independent research.

Oppenheimer earned a reputation as an excellent instructor. He led fast-paced discussions, typically holding a cigarette in one hand and a piece of

under the Columbia squash courts, Fermi produced the world's first self-sustaining nuclear chain reaction. He continued his work on nuclear fission at a Chicago laboratory until 1944, when he and his wife, now citizens of the United States, moved to Los Alamos, New Mexico, allowing Fermi to join scientists working under the direction of J. Robert Oppenheimer.

Fermi was placed in charge of his own division, which was assigned to resolve any special problems that might arise as work on the first atomic bombs continued. The bombs were finally tested and dropped on Japan, effectively ending the war in Asia. Fermi returned to the University of Chicago, where he remained as a professor and researcher for the rest of his life. He received the Civilian Medal of Merit in 1946 for his work on the Manhattan Project. After his death in 1954, the U.S. Atomic Energy Commission named Fermi the first recipient of its Enrico Fermi Award.

Enrico Fermi. (Los Alamos National Laboratory.)

chalk in the other, that sparked student interest in theoretical physics to such a degree that many followed him from one campus to another, sometimes to repeat courses they had already taken. Although Oppenheimer continued to pursue a wide range of interests, until the mid-1930s he lived a sheltered life with no telephone, little contact with the media, and no concern with politics. The advent of the worldwide economic depression and the rise of dictatorships in Europe captured his attention, however, and he became active in several groups working for social reform. Although some of these groups had ties to the Communist party, Oppenheimer never became a Communist.

Heads Manhattan Project

As the threat of war in Europe loomed in 1934, Italian physicist Enrico Fermi (see box) devised a method to bombard uranium, a radioactive metallic element, with neutrons, atomic particles, creating a reaction called nuclear fission. Many scientists contended that the utilization of a large enough amount, or "critical mass," of uranium would result in a chain reaction, instantly triggering a massive explosion of energy. Various physics laboratories began studying this possibility in hopes of creating an atomic bomb to be used in combat situations.

After the United States entered World War II on December 7, 1941, Allied intelligence agents learned of German efforts to create an atomic bomb. President Franklin D. Roosevelt ordered the immediate formulation of an atomic research program called the Manhattan Project. Oppenheimer's recruitment to the program was due more to his reputation for brilliance in the field of physics than for any particular interest in the project itself. Oppenheimer participated in a number of initial meetings that explored

Oppenheimer, third from left, with other scientists working on the Manhattan Project, 1945. (Photograph by Popperfoto. Reproduced by permission of Archive Photos)

the possible uses of an atomic bomb, and in early 1942 he was asked to direct research on the bomb at Berkeley. Soon the government placed the project under the jurisdiction of the U.S. Army, with Brigadier General Leslie Groves in charge. Work on the bomb was conducted at numerous laboratories in various locales until Oppenheimer recommended establishing a single lab where scientists could work together. Groves then decided that Oppenheimer, despite his lack of administrative and management experience, was the best candidate to direct the lab.

Oppenheimer suggested the laboratory be built at Los Alamos, New Mexico, near an area where he went on vacation. The location was geographically isolated and transportation was difficult, thus helping to ensure secrecy. Groves and Oppenheimer supervised the construction of the huge complex (which, by the end of World War II, housed 5,000 workers) and the collection of equipment needed for research. Oppenheimer was put in charge of assembling a team of leading scientists, convincing them to move to Los Alamos until the end of the war, and helping them work together harmoniously. Oppenheimer established an atmosphere of hard work and free exchange of information at the laboratory. His home became a social center where scientists and staff were frequently entertained.

Creating and Testing an Atomic Bomb

The principal obstacle the team had to overcome was achieving critical mass: how to bring two pieces of uranium together quickly enough to create a chain reaction and produce an explosion. Another stumbling block was the length of time it took to refine uranium to the required purity. Uranium was processed in two factories in Oak Ridge, Tennessee, and Hanford, Washington, but production moved more slowly than expected. By summer 1945, the technical problems had finally been resolved and the atomic bomb was ready for testing. At 5:30 a.m. on July 16 on the Alamogordo Bombing Range, the bomb was detonated, raising a cloud of sand and debris 40,000 feet into the air. Observing the explosion from five miles away, Oppenheimer was reminded of two lines from the Bhagavad-Gita, a Hindu sacred text he had read in the original Sanskrit (one of eight languages he could read). One line referred to the "radiance of a thousand suns," and the other was "I am become death, the Shatterer of Worlds." He called the site Trinity after a poem by John Donne.

Like others present at the test, Oppenheimer's feelings were a mixture of pride in the success of their efforts, terror at the bomb's immense destructive power, and anxiety about what the bomb meant for the future. By this time, Germany had surrendered, ending the conflict in Europe, but the Japanese theater was still active with no apparent imminent conclusion. Oppenheimer met with scientists Ernest Lawrence, Enrico Fermi, and Arthur Compton to discuss the use of the atomic bomb against Japan. The government maintained the only alternative to the bomb was the invasion of Japan, which would cost many American lives. On the other hand, the detonation of the bomb on a military target would undoubtedly kill an unprecedented number of Japanese civilians. Although Oppenheimer would later regret his decision, claiming that the killing of civilians could and should have been avoided, he and the other scientists recommended that the United States use the atomic bomb against Japan.

The final decision to use the bomb in Japan was made by President Harry S Truman. On August 6, 1945, the first bomb, nicknamed "Little Boy," was dropped on Hiroshima, Japan. The city was instantly destroyed: more than 70,000 people were killed and 60,000 buildings were demolished. During the next weeks and months, thousands more died of sickness caused by the radioactive particles released by the explosion. On August 9, a second bomb, referred to as "Fat Man," was dropped on Nagasaki, Japan, killing about 35,000 people and also resulting in many deaths later from radiation sickness. Japan formally surrendered on September 2, ending World War II.

Post-War Career

The existence of the atomic bomb had been classified until the Hiroshima bombing. Afterward, Oppenheimer became famous as the "Father of the A-Bomb." Secretary of War Henry Stimson claimed that Oppenheimer's leadership and genius were critical factors in the bomb's development. Oppenheimer continued to have reservations about the bomb, wanting to ensure it was properly controlled and used to prevent rather than start wars. After the war, he was asked to advise the government on methods to control and manage atomic energy and weapons. In 1947 he was appointed to the General Advisory Committee of the Atomic Energy Commission, which had been established the previous year to place atomic energy under civilian control. He remained in this position until 1952. In 1947 Oppenheimer became the director of the Institute for Advanced Study at Princeton University, overseeing its development into a first-rate physics research center with a lively atmosphere that attracted a growing number of young scientists.

During this period, Oppenheimer wrote and lectured on atomic energy and the relationship between the scientist and society. His interest in making science accessible to the general public was the topic of his book *Science and the Common Understanding* (1954). Despite the praise he received for his performance as director of the Manhattan Project, his advocacy of arms treaties over weapons development angered many, including the developer of the H-bomb (a more powerful weapon using hydrogen rather than uranium or plutonium), Edward Teller. During the mid-1950s, anti-communist sentiment was spreading throughout the United States. Joseph McCarthy and his senate committee crusaded to rid the government of people they considered to be Communist sympathizers, Oppenheimer among them. In 1954, when Oppenheimer was informed that his security clearance was being withdrawn, he requested a hearing to defend his position. At the three-week hearing, Oppenheimer's past connections with communist-related groups and his opposition to the H-bomb were given as grounds for canceling his security clearance. The outraged scientific community openly supported Oppenheimer, and although he never again worked for the government, he continued his work at Princeton. Many saw this as the government's way of making amends with Oppenheimer. In 1963 the Atomic Energy Commission gave Oppenheimer the Enrico Fermi Award, which was presented by President Lyndon B. Johnson. Four years later, Oppenheimer died of cancer at the age of sixty-two.

SOURCES

Books

Driemen, J. E., *Atomic Dawn: A Biography of Robert Oppenheimer,* Dillon Press (Minneapolis, MN), 1989.

Goodchild, Peter, *J. Robert Oppenheimer: Shatterer of Worlds,* Fromm International (New York), 1985.

Kunetka, James W., *Oppenheimer: The Years of Risk,* Prentice-Hall (Englewood Cliffs, NJ), 1982.

Larsen, Rebecca, *Oppenheimer and the Atomic Bomb,* Franklin Watts (New York), 1988.

Periodicals

"Brotherhood of the Bomb: Two Flinty Physicists Struggle Over Their Terrifying Legacy," *U.S. News & World Report* Special Report: Masters of Discovery: The Great Inventions of the 20th Century, August 17, 1998, p. 64.

George Smith Patton, Jr.

Born November 11, 1885
    Pasadena, California, United States
Died December 21, 1945
    U.S. military hospital, Heidelberg,
    Germany

General; military genius; liberated France during World War II then led the U.S. Third Army into Germany to end the war in Europe

"All my life, I have wanted to lead a lot of men in a desperate battle. I will leave the beaches either as a conqueror or a hero."

Considered one of the greatest combat generals of modern times, George S. Patton, Jr.—or "Old Blood and Guts," as he was often called—remains a controversial figure. A colorful, sometimes vulgar and arrogant man, Patton was sometimes regarded as selfish and only interested in personal fame and glory. Nevertheless, men under his command were inspired to perform feats of enormous courage. No military force in history has ever moved with the speed of Patton's Third U.S. Army as it swept across France and into Germany to win the war in Europe. The Germans believed him to be America's finest general, and it is often said he was the only man feared by German leaders.

Privileged Upbringing

George Smith Patton, Jr. was born into an aristocratic family on November 11, 1885, near Los Angeles, California. He was the first child and only son of George and Ruth Wilson Patton; his sister, Anne, was two years younger. Patton's maternal grandfather, who had once been mayor of Los Angeles, owned a ranch near the city. Called Lake Vineyard, the ranch was one of the largest wine and brandy producers in California. Patton's father served as district attorney in Los Angeles County before quitting his law practice to run Lake Vineyard, which became the family's permanent home. The Patton family could trace its military ancestry back to a soldier who had fought

(Library of Congress)

The Germans believed that Patton was America's finest general. (Library of Congress)

for the Scottish rebel Bonnie Prince Charlie in 1746. Many of Patton's relatives had fought for the South during the U.S. Civil War (1861–1865), and he always felt that the family war heroes were judging his actions from above.

As a child, Patton apparently suffered from dyslexia, which impaired his ability to read and caused him to feel insecure about his intelligence. Afraid that other children would mock Patton for being slow, his aunt educated him at home until he was nearly twelve years old. A large part of his home-schooling consisted of reading from the Bible, myths and legends, Greek tragedies, and military histories. His family believed him to be gifted with second sight, the ability to see things beyond the range of normal human experience. He liked to reenact great battles from history; when asked how he knew the details of these battles, he would respond that he had been there. Patton learned from his father how to ride horses, shoot, fish, and hunt. He was accident-prone, however, and suffered many sporting injuries. Some people have theorized that skull injuries sustained by Patton in his twenties may have caused a blood clot that contributed to his notoriously short temper throughout his life. When Patton began formal education at a private school for boys in Pasadena, California, in 1897, he still

could not read or write. He now faced the scorn and mockery of his schoolmates instead of the praise and flattery of his aunt. Exhibiting the determination that would later be characteristic of him, Patton got through his years of schooling by memorizing vast amounts of material. In 1902 seventeen-year-old Patton met sixteen-year-old Beatrice Ayer, daughter of a wealthy entrepreneur, and married her in 1910.

Cultivates Patton Legend

Patton had long dreamed of attending the prestigious U.S. Military Academy at West Point, New York, which he called "That Holy Place." Fearing he would fail the treacherous entrance exam, Patton opted to attend the Virginia Military Institute in 1903. After his first year of study, he was able to transfer to West Point without taking the exam. Throughout Patton's six-year stay at the academy, members of his family took turns living nearby so he would not get homesick. Although Patton failed mathematics his first year at West Point and had to repeat the entire year, he finally established himself as a student leader and athlete. He became known for his rigid attention to the military code, and became convinced that military service was the only way he might leave his mark on society.

After graduating in 1909, Patton was assigned to Fort Sheridan, near Chicago, Illinois, then moved to several different posts over the years. Throughout his military career, he remained an active sportsman, and he used his wife's family's money to support such interests as playing polo, raising thoroughbred horses, writing poetry, and ballroom dancing. He participated in the Stockholm Olympics of 1912, placing fifth in the military pentathlon, an event that included pistol shooting, fencing, swimming, steeplechase riding, and a 500-meter foot race.

Patton also studied swordsmanship in France with the professional champion of Europe. His design for a straight cavalry saber was adopted by the U.S. Army. Assigned to Fort Riley, Kansas, in 1912, to study at its Mounted Service School, he was also appointed instructor in fencing. He held the title Master of the Sword, making him the foremost expert on the subject in the U.S. Army.

Patton deliberately suppressed his softer qualities in order to create a war-like image. His cursing, scowling, and boisterous behavior were calcu-

Actress Befriends General

Marlene Dietrich (c. 1901–1992) was a famous film actress who met General George Patton after she volunteered to entertain U.S. soldiers during World War II. Born Maria Magdalen von Losch in Berlin, Germany, she first achieved fame in a 1930 German film called *The Blue Angel.* The same year that film was released, Dietrich was offered a contract to make movies in Hollywood, California, and departed for the United States. For years the Nazis had been making life in Germany uncomfortable, especially for Jews, whom they often attacked in speeches and with beatings. Although Dietrich was not Jewish and not subjected to Nazi abuse, she recognized the tense situation in Germany. Due to her Hollywood movies, she had become famous throughout the world. When the Nazi party rose to power in Germany in 1933, Nazi officials offered Dietrich a large sum of money to return and make films in Germany. When she refused, the Nazis banned *The Blue Angel* in Germany, claiming the film was immoral.

The German press criticized her severely for leaving her native country to make movies in a foreign land. Her biographer, Donald Spoto, author of *Blue Angel: The Life of Marlene Dietrich,* quoted the reaction in one Berlin publication: "As long as she opts for the dollar and has shaken the dust of her fatherland from her feet, can the new Germany place any value on the importance of her movies?" When Dietrich applied for U.S. citizenship in 1937 (and lied about her birth date, giving it as 1904 instead of 1901, according to Spoto), an anti-Semitic German newspaper columnist complained: "Marlene Dietrich, the film actress of German origin, has spent so many years with the cinema Jews of Hollywood that she has become an American citizen. The association with Jews has made her character quite un-German." He also accused her of betraying "her Fatherland."

In 1944 Dietrich decided to contribute to the U.S. war effort against the Nazis by joining the United Service Organization (USO), which had been founded in 1941 to provide entertainment to American soldiers at home and abroad. Many famous stars were volunteering to entertain the troops, often appearing near battle sites at great personal risk. Dietrich put together a one-woman show in which she sang, accompanied herself on a musical saw, and performed a mind-reading act. She departed for North Africa, where the Allies had landed in 1942, and began a grueling schedule, performing twice a day for American and British soldiers. From there she traveled through Italy and on to London, England, reaching liberated Paris, France, in the autumn of 1944. Through that winter she entertained Patton's troops, and became a friend of the general.

Rumors began to circulate that Dietrich and Patton were having an affair, although such gossip was never proven. In her autobiography, Dietrich described Patton as "a great man." In his book about his grandfather, Robert H. Patton noted it was certainly true that "Dietrich and Georgie [General Patton] shared a mutual regard." The author noted that the general's only written comment was an evaluation of Dietrich's show for the troops. George Patton described it this way: "Very low comedy, almost an insult to human intelligence."

Dietrich's shows for the troops and her radio broadcasts, in which she expressed her anger at Nazi Germany, outraged the Nazis. She was considered a traitor to Germany and regarded as such long after the war. A grateful U.S. War Department awarded her the Medal of Freedom, a high honor, in 1947. Dietrich continued to make films, including *Judgment at Nuremberg* (1961), which told the story of the trial of Nazi criminals that took place after the war. Later in life she became increasingly withdrawn and was seldom seen in public. She wrote three volumes of memoirs: *Marlene Dietrich's ABC* (1961), *My Life Story* (1979), and *Marlene* (1987). She died in 1992.

Patton talking with American soldiers in Europe. (Reproduced by permission of AP/Wide World Photos)

lated to create a Patton legend. He had his first combat experience in 1916, as part of a Texas Cavalry regiment led by General John J. "Black Jack" Pershing against rebel Mexican leader Pancho Villa in New Mexico. During World War I, Patton briefly served with Pershing's forces in Paris, France. Far from the front, Patton quickly grew bored and so quit Pershing's staff in order to join the U.S. Tank Corps. In 1918 he was promoted to lieutenant colonel and put in charge of a tank unit. Two days later, however, he was wounded in battle and taken out of action for the rest of the war. He was awarded the Distinguished Service Medal and the Distinguished Service Cross. After the war, he held various staff positions and continued to study military history and tank warfare. But he was so generally bored with life during peacetime that he lapsed into depression.

"We Shall Surely Win"

In 1939 the German invasion of Poland pulled Patton out of his depression. The following year, he was placed in command of a tank division and promoted to the rank of general. By February 1942, shortly after the United States entered the war, Patton was put in charge of the First Armored Corps. He was instrumental in Operation Torch, the November invasion of North Africa that provided the Allies a base for taking over German-occupied Sicily. Patton biographer Carlo D'Este records Patton's advice to his men: "When the great day of battle comes, remember your training … you must succeed, for to retreat is as cowardly as it is fatal. Americans do not surrender.… The eyes of the world are watching us. The heart of America beats for us. God is with us. On our victory depends the freedom or slavery of the human race. We shall surely win." Patton was soon recognized for his energy and belief in speed, movement, and an indirect approach to combat.

By July 1942, Patton had been promoted to lieutenant general and was focusing his attention on Sicily. By the end of the successful Sicilian campaign, he was recognized as the best battle general in the U.S. Army. Patton's sensational victory was marred by an incident in which he slapped two soldiers who were hospitalized for combat exhaustion. Though he later claimed he had merely been trying to shock the men, the event nearly ended his career. General Dwight D. Eisenhower, Patton's superior and the future

The "G.I.'s General": Omar Bradley

General Omar Bradley was General George Patton's fellow commander and one of his closest colleagues, yet the two men had entirely different personalities. Where Patton swaggered, swore, and slapped soldiers, Bradley was a calm, cautious leader who understood his men, so much so that he became known as the "G.I.'s General." Born into a poor family in Clark, Missouri, on February 12, 1893, Bradley graduated from the U.S. Military Academy at West Point, New York, in 1915. After serving in World War I, he held various military positions and was promoted to the rank of brigadier general. He earned another star soon after the U.S. entered World War II, when he was put in command of the army's 82nd and 28th Divisions.

Bradley took over for Patton as commander of the 2nd Corps in Tunisia when Patton left to prepare for the invasion of Sicily. In 1943 he helped plan Operation Overlord, the Allied invasion of France. Appointed commander in chief of the American ground forces for the invasion, he led the First Army when it landed on the beaches of Normandy in northern France in June 1944.

Two months later, Bradley headed the Allied 12th Army Group, which played a major role in the push across western Europe and eventual defeat of Germany. After the war, Bradley was appointed head of the Veterans Administration. In 1948 he succeeded Eisenhower as chief of staff of the army, and three years later he became the first chairman of the newly created Joint Chiefs of Staff. After retiring from the army in 1953, Bradley was appointed chairman of the board of the Bulova Watch Company, published his memoirs (*A Soldier's Story*, 1951), and headed a presidential committee on veterans' benefits. He died in New York City on April 8, 1981.

---

president of the United States, ordered Patton to apologize publicly to the men, the hospital personnel, and the rest of his army. Patton willingly carried out the order and Eisenhower did not send him home. Patton was needed for the invasion of western Europe.

On D-Day, June 6, 1944, the Allies invaded Normandy, France, a move that took the German military completely by surprise. In August Patton took command of the Third Army, a tank unit, and made a dramatic sweep across France into German territory. He had accomplished an unprecedented feat. Following the official German surrender on May 8, 1945, he issued a victory order to his troops, and is cited in Carlo D'Este's Patton biography as writing: "The one honor which is mine and mine alone is that of having commanded such an incomparable group of Americans, the record of whose fortitude, audacity, and valor will endure as long as history lasts." Despite a desperate last stand at the Battle of the Bulge, the Germans were outwitted and outmaneuvered, and surrendered by the tens of thousands.

From D-Day to Victory

Patton's Third Army liberated the Buchenwald concentration camp in April 1945. Learning of the approach of Patton and the U.S. Army, the 5,000 Nazi soldiers on duty fled Buchenwald. Three hours before the arrival of U.S. troops, the greatly weakened inmates took control from the few soldiers left behind. Although Patton was a hardened veteran of many battles, he vomited when he saw the desperate condition of the prisoners in the camp.

By the end of World War II, Germany was in a shambles. In a famous speech to the American public, Patton compared the wrecked remains of Germany, Austria, and other places liberated by the Third U.S. Army to Hell. Patton was put in charge of trying to restore the ruined land, but the general was not well suited for the job. Patton's strength lay in military campaigns, not political campaigns.

Patton's Behavior Questioned

With the end of the war, Patton immediately realized that he had become obsolete. He told his

---

wife that the ideal death for a soldier is a death right at the end of the battle. His public statements became increasingly embarrassing to the army high command. Defending his decision to hire former Nazis to help restore Germany, he compared the vast majority of Nazi party members to average American Democrats and Republicans, relieving them of responsibility for their actions. He angered the parents of dead soldiers by remarking that a soldier killed in battle was frequently a fool. He began to express strong anti-Semitic sentiments, making insulting and insensitive comments about the ways Jews had survived the concentration camps and their behavior after liberation. Soon people were questioning Patton's sanity, and Eisenhower transferred him from the Third Army. Knowing he had essentially been fired, Patton became despondent. His change of command ceremony was held on October 7, 1945, and two months later he died after an automobile accident. Eisenhower thought it appropriate for soldiers to be buried were they had been killed, so Patton's grave was dug by German prisoners of war in a military cemetery in Luxembourg, Belgium. He was laid to rest among the soldiers of the Third Army. There were so many visitors to his grave, however, that it was later positioned at the head of his men.

Sources

Books

Ambrose, Stephen E., *Citizen Soldiers: The U.S. Army from the Normandy Beaches to the Bulge to the Surrender of Germany*, G. K. Hall (Thorndike, ME), 1998.

Blumenson, Martin, *The Patton Papers*, volumes 1 and 2, illustrated with photographs and with maps by Samuel H. Bryant, Da Capo Press (New York), 1998.

Blumenson, Martin, *Patton: The Man Behind the Legend*, William Morrow (New York), 1985.

Codman, Charles R., *Drive*, Little Brown (Boston), 1957.

D'Este, Carlo, *Patton: A Genius for War*, Harper-Collins (New York), 1995.

Devaney, John, *"Blood and Guts": The True Story of Gen. George S. Patton, USA*, J. Messner (New York), 1982.

Farago, Ladislas, *The Last Days of Patton*, McGraw-Hill (New York), 1981.

Patton, George S., Jr., *War as I Knew It*, annotated by Paul D. Harkins, with a new introduction by Rick Atkinson, Houghton Mifflin Company (Boston), 1995.

Patton, Robert H., *The Pattons: A Personal History of an American Family*, Brassey's (Washington, DC), 1996.

Peifer, Charles, Jr., *Soldier of Destiny: A Biography of George Patton*, Dillon Press (Minneapolis), 1989.

Semmes, Harry H., *Portrait of Patton*, Appleton-Century-Crofts (New York), 1955.

Other

George Patton, http://www.gi.grolier.com/wwii/wwii_patton.htm (May 5, 2000).

Philippe Pétain

At age fifty-eight, Philippe Pétain was considering retirement from a long career in the French army when he was thrust into battle during World War I (1914–1918). Promoted to the rank of brigadier general, he organized the successful defense of Verdun against German forces in 1916. An advocate of cautious defense instead of risky combat charges, Pétain acquired a reputation as the most humane of the French military leaders. He emerged from the war a national hero, and in 1918 he was named marshal of France. During the German invasion of France in 1940, eighty-four-year-old Pétain used his prestige to gain leadership of the government. Securing an armistice from the Germans, he then led an authoritarian regime based in Vichy, France, that cooperated with the Nazi war machine until the liberation of France by the Allies in 1944. Upon the defeat of the Axis powers in 1945, Pétain was taken to Germany, where he refused to head a French government in exile. He then returned to France, where he was tried for collaborating with the enemy in wartime and sentenced to death. Because of his World War I record and his advanced age, however, his sentence was commuted to life imprisonment. He died in 1951.

Born April 24, 1856
   Cauchy-à-la-Tour, France
Died July 23, 1951
   Île d'Yeu, France

French general; head of Vichy regime

"It is with honor and in order to maintain French unity, a unity ten centuries old, in the framework of a constructive activity of a new European order that I have today entered the path of collaboration.… It is I alone who will be judged by history."

War Heroism Leads to Political Career

Henri-Philippe Benoni Omer Pétain was born in 1856 into a peasant family in Cauchy-à-la-Tour,

(Reproduced by permission of AP/Wide World Photos)

---

a small village in the Artois region of northern France. He attended a local primary school and in 1867 enrolled in the Collège Saint-Bertin at nearby Saint-Omer. In 1876 Pétain entered the French Military Academy at Saint-Cyr, where he graduated two years later as a second lieutenant. After serving in the French army at Villefranche-sur-Mer and in Besançon, he entered the War College in Paris in 1888. In 1895 Pétain joined the staff of the military governor in Paris, in charge of the defense of the city in the event of war, and in 1901 he returned to the War College to teach first infantry tactics and later military tactics. In 1911 he became a full colonel and was placed in command of the 33rd Infantry Regiment at Arras in northern France, where he met young Charles de Gaulle, who would succeed Pétain as French leader more than thirty years later. At the beginning of World War I, Pétain was promoted to brigadier general and named commander of the Fourth Infantry. He went on to become a national hero at the Battle of Verdun in 1916, when French forces held the city of Verdun for months, preventing a German occupation. Pétain further endeared himself to the French people by quelling a mutiny in the French army the following year.

After the war, in 1920, Pétain was appointed vice president of the Higher War Council, and two years later, he was appointed Inspector General of the Armies; both positions gave him authority over French military planning. In 1920, at age sixty-four, he married Eugénie-Alphonsine Hardon, with whom he had had a long relationship; the couple settled on a small estate at Villeneuve-Loubet, overlooking the Mediterranean. In 1927 Pétain supervised the initial construction of a chain of fortifications connected by underground passages along the border between France and Germany (but which excluded the border between France and Belgium). Named for André Maginot, the war minister who promoted the project, it came to be known as the Maginot Line. Four years later, Pétain was elected to the Academie Française, one of the highest honors in France. He was also appointed Inspector General of Air Defense and began urging increased spending on air power, despite France's financial woes from the Great Depression, its radical government's advocacy of military budget cuts, and a general European desire for disarmament.

Political events further enhanced Pétain's public career. A series of government scandals, combined with economic depression, culminated in a crisis on February 6, 1934, when an angry mob marched across the Pont de la Concorde toward the Chamber of Deputies (part of the French parliament), threatening to throw the deputies into the Seine River. When counter-demonstrations took place several days later, the French premier, Édouard Daladier, resigned, and the chamber called upon former president Gaston Doumergue to form a government of national unity. Doumergue appointed Pétain minister of war, and in this new position Pétain once again requested increased resources for air power. He also argued that the Maginot Line was sufficient in its coverage of only the border between France and Germany and not the border between France and Belgium, for he anticipated that in a future war French forces would be able to defend the nation in the Low Countries. Noting the fascist policies of Benito Mussolini in Italy and Adolf Hitler in Germany, Pétain contended that the French needed a moral regeneration that would emphasize authority and military preparedness. The Doumergue government fell in late 1934 without achieving significant political reform; although Pétain resigned his position, he was still popular with the public. Press campaigns depicted him as a man who could save France from economic depression, threats from fascist countries, and parliamentary stagnation. Pétain expressed distaste for a coup against the constitution, yet was also willing to assume leadership of France.

By this time, Pétain was nearly eighty years old—in 1938 he even made a will in which he stated that he wished to be buried at the Douaumont fort near Verdun, the site of his 1916 military victory. Pétain was again called into service, however, in March 1939 as ambassador to Spain, where Francisco Franco's forces were about to win the civil war that had been in progress since 1936. It was believed that Pétain's military prestige might encourage Franco to disassociate his country from the Axis powers, which had helped him gain control of Spain. Pétain was in Spain in September 1939 when Nazi Germany invaded Poland and initiated World War II, and he remained there until May 1940.

On May 10, 1940, the Germans invaded France through Belgium at the gap in the Maginot Line. Within days, French forces were in a state of collapse. Desperately trying to shore up the government and public morale, Reynaud named Pétain vice-premier on May 17. Pétain called for an armistice. Historians have differing accounts of the eighty-four-year-old marshal's actions during this

When Marshal Philippe Pétain visited southern France after its fall to the Nazis, members of the French Legion and Volunteers of the National Revolution marched past his reviewing stand and saluted him. (Reproduced by permission of AP/Wide World Photos)

period. Some picture him as being deeply pessimistic or senile, while others depict him as robust and alert. He remained physically strong, but his lack of intellectual concentration betrayed his years. In his biography *Pétain, Hero or Traitor: The Untold Story*, Herbert R. Lottman notes that other French officials gradually took advantage of Pétain's diminishing powers of concentration. The exact degree to which he was manipulated by politicians seeking their own advancement under the terms of an armistice may never be known.

Clearly, however, the aging leader was convinced that a continuation of the war would result in the physical ruin of France. Pétain believed an armistice was urgently needed to keep the French army intact as a force for order in the country. He was especially worried about the possibility of revolutionary activity in Paris. Again he urged a moral regeneration that would return France to its agrarian, spiritual, and martial roots, and lead it away from cosmopolitanism and materialism. He attributed the French defeat to a failure of French spirit

and education during the years between World War I and World War II. On June 17, 1940, Pétain was named premier of France; in his first speech as the new leader, he formally requested an armistice, which was granted by Germany. The next day, General Charles de Gaulle, who refused to accept defeat, broadcast a radio appeal from London, calling upon the French to defend their national honor and resist the Nazis.

Vichy Government Aligns France with Germany

Under the terms of the armistice, Germany occupied roughly the northern three-fifths of France, including Paris, and France was required to pay the costs of the war. The French government would remain in place, with control, theoretically, over domestic order; in reality, however, the Germans ran the occupied zone. The French did manage to keep their fleet, their major remaining military asset, from falling into German hands, but the French army was drastically reduced to 100,000

Pierre Laval Urges Collaboration

Pierre Laval (1883–1945), chief minister of the French Vichy regime during World War II, made his greatest impact on French foreign policy before 1940, acting as foreign minister four times between 1932 and 1936. He sought accommodation with Benito Mussolini, the fascist leader of Italy, against the rising power of Nazi Germany. Coauthor of the abortive Hoare-Laval Agreement, which was meant to appease Mussolini at the expense of Abyssinia, Laval was overruled when the British cabinet rejected the arrangement. Since his dream of a united Franco-Italian front against Germany had been rendered impossible, Laval did an about-face and began to urge an understanding with Führer Adolf Hitler. Laval argued that France could not survive the ordeal of another war, and thus advocated peace at any price.

After the fall of France in June 1940, Laval joined the government of Marshal Philippe Pétain, in which he was instrumental in securing parliamentary ratification of the armistice terms and the granting of full powers to Pétain. Laval urged that France must accept German victory and through collaboration find a place in Hitler's "New Order." His fellow ministers rejected this approach, however, and he was ousted from power in a revolt on December 13, 1940. Laval remained out of office until April 1942, when the Nazis pressured Pétain into reappointing him, in order to obtain greater supplies of French workers than they had been getting from his predecessor. At that point engaged in a massive confrontation with the Soviet Union, the Germans knew that a collaborationist regime in France under Laval guaranteed their security in western Europe. Laval continued to urge collaboration, saying that a German victory could avoid a communist takeover of Europe.

Finally realizing that the end of the Vichy regime was near in the summer of 1944, Laval called for a national assembly at Paris, but the maneuver was too little too late; Laval was ignominiously carried off by the retreating Germans. After escaping his captors, he was found by Americans in Austria and handed over to the French. Laval was put on trial for treason by the provisional government of Charles de Gaulle in Paris on October 4, 1945. The trial was mismanaged by government prosecutors, but nevertheless, Laval was convicted and sentenced to death. De Gaulle personally refused to grant him a new trial. Though he nearly escaped execution by swallowing poison, Laval was revived by a team of doctors and a few hours later, on October 15, 1945, he was executed by firing squad.

Laval is one of the most controversial figures in recent French history. His detractors portray him as the archvillain of wartime France who sold his countrymen to the Nazis. His admirers claim he was an unsung hero who single-handedly kept French losses to a minimum after April 1942 by playing a double game with the Germans. There may be partial truth in both views. Laval had a pragmatic view of the French national interest and, convinced of an ultimate German victory, saw collaboration as the only recourse. This calculation may have resulted from the fact that the political strategies Laval had used successfully during the Third Republic were rendered irrelevant when France became a German satellite state in June 1940. From this perspective, Laval may be seen as much the prisoner of his own narrow opportunism as he was the captive of his German sponsors.

men. As the Germans consolidated their hold on northern France, Pétain's government moved to the spa resort of Vichy in the unoccupied zone and tried to cope with problems such as severe economic dislocations, German demands, and the flight of millions of refugees from German invaders. In the meantime, former premier Pierre Laval (see box) and other political leaders were

As Admiral François Darlan arrives in Berghof, Nazi leader Adolf Hitler salutes him. (National Archives/USHMM Photo Archives)

restructuring the government to enhance Pétain's role and align France more closely with the victorious Axis powers. On July 10 the French Parliament (the combined Senate and Chamber of Deputies) voted 569 to 80 to give Pétain full authority to prepare a constitution for the French state. Pétain outlined this "National Revolution," the base of which would be an authoritarian state, with the motto "Work, Family, Fatherland," rather than the traditional "Liberty, Equality, Fraternity."

From July 1940 until the liberation of France by Allied forces in summer 1944, Pétain remained in France as head of state. He addressed four major themes: (1) a moral rejuvenation; (2) a social order based on the peasantry; (3) a corporate worker-employer social solidarity that would be neither capitalist nor socialist; and (4) the elimination of the "non-French" influences of Freemasons and Jews. In October 1940 Jews were legally prohibited from holding public office, teaching, and serving as military commanders. Jews could not be officials in businesses receiving government funds, and, with limited exceptions, they were also barred from the press, film, theater, and the radio. After meeting with Hitler in the town of Montoire in October 1940, Pétain ordered the French to collaborate with the Nazis.

The political situation during the four-year Vichy regime was byzantine, even though Pétain himself had complained about the parliamentary intrigues of the Third Republic. Pierre Laval, who advocated close collaboration with the Germans, served as vice-premier until December 1940. Then, for reasons still being debated today, he was fired by Pétain. Early in 1941, Admiral François Darlan succeeded to the vice-premiership, only to be replaced in April 1942, under German pressure, once again by Laval, who occupied the post through the end of the Vichy years. During Darlan's tenure the Vichy cabinet had included technocrats who, despite Pétain's "return to the soil" campaign, pushed industrial planning as a government priority. Once Laval was back in office, he used his newfound influence with the Germans to write a constitutional clause giving him control of all policy, subject only to the approval of Pétain.

In November 1942 the Allies landed in Algiers, then a French colony. Pétain ordered French forces to refrain from interfering with the Germans, who were deploying against the Allies in Tunisia, another French colony. Within six months, however, the Allies had taken control of the French empire in North Africa. Allied landings brought on the German occupation of the remainder of metropolitan France, and the French scuttled their fleet. Without the fleet and with the Germans now at Vichy, Pétain's government lost the last vestiges of independence. Although he was then eighty-six years old, Pétain chose to remain in Vichy. As the Allies continued their assaults, the Vichy government first encouraged, then forced, French laborers to work in Germany, where the Nazis needed foreign labor for the war effort. Pétain's reputation as a humane military leader had obvious limits as the Vichy police helped round up resisters and thousands of French Jews for deportation to German extermination camps. By 1944, Pétain's government was acting as a proxy for Germany. After the Allied liberation of France, the Germans installed Pétain at the Sigmaringen castle on the Danube in Germany, but he refused to have anything to do with the French government-in-exile that the Nazis had set up there.

Judging Pétain

With the final defeat of Germany in May 1945, Pétain returned to France to face trial by a special High Court established by the new Provisional Government under de Gaulle. In a highly charged courtroom atmosphere, Pétain defended his course of action from 1940 until the liberation, arguing that he had come to power legitimately and had helped France resist the power of the Germans. Found guilty of collaboration with the enemy, however, he was sentenced to death. In light of Pétain's advanced age and service record during World War I, de Gaulle commuted the sentence to life imprisonment and had Pétain transferred to a military fortress at the Île d'Yeu, where he died, at age ninety-five, in 1951. Contrary to his wishes to be interred at Douaumont, Pétain was buried, by government order, on the Île d'Yeu. His wife remained with him until his death, after which she moved back to Paris, where she died in 1962.

Since the end of World War II, Pétain's legacy has been hotly debated. Some argue that Pétain's actions may have spared France an even worse fate during the German occupation—perhaps one similar to that of Poland. Some claim that chief minister Pierre Laval, not Pétain, was the true collaborator with the Germans. On the other hand, Pétain's critics say the Vichy government policies of collaboration and anti-Semitism would have been inconceivable without Pétain. Adolf Hitler's goal during the occupation was to keep France pacified enough to be exploited for the German war effort, and Pétain lent his personal prestige to that cause. Journalist Jean-Pierre Rioux noted that Pétain was part of the "sinister rendezvous" of collaboration: the meetings with Hitler, the deportation of Jews, the fervent wish for German victory, and the creation of a militia to squash resistance. De Gaulle once observed, in effect, that had Pétain died in 1925, he would have been remembered as one of the country's greatest heroes.

SOURCES

Books

Commire, Anne, editor, *Historic World Leaders*, Gale Research (Detroit), 1994.

Ferro, Marc, *Pétain*, Fayard (Paris), 1987.

Gordon, Bertram M., *Collaborationism in France During the Second World War*, Cornell University Press (Ithaca, NY), 1980.

Lottman, Herbert R., *Pétain, Hero or Traitor: The Untold Story*, W. Morrow (New York), 1985.

Marrus, Michael R., and Robert O. Paxton, *Vichy France and the Jews*, Stanford University Press (Stanford, CA), 1995.

Webster, Paul, *Pétain's Crime: The Full Story of French Collaboration in the Holocaust*, I. R. Dee (Chicago), 1991.

Pope Pius XII

Eugenio Pacelli, the man who became Pope Pius XII, was the head of the Roman Catholic church when Adolf Hitler came to power in Germany in 1933. A long-time admirer of the German people, Pacelli hoped Hitler would stop the spread of anti-Christian ideas in Europe. As pope, he adopted a policy of neutrality during World War II while Hitler carried out the extermination of Jews. Many years after his death, Pope Pius XII remains a controversial figure. Many people still feel that he should have spoken out more forcefully against the Nazi regime.

Becomes Vatican Official

Eugenio Maria Guiseppe Pacelli was born in Rome, Italy, on March 2, 1876. He was the second of four children of Filippo Pacelli, a lawyer, and Virginia Graziosi Pacelli. The Pacellis were an old Roman family with a long tradition of service to the Vatican (the state within Rome where the Roman Catholic church is headquartered). Although he excelled in his studies, the young Pacelli was a weak and sickly boy who was often bullied by his peers. First educated at home, he began attending a Roman college, then transferred to Gregorian University. Sister Pascalina, a Roman Catholic nun who was a friend and aide to Pacelli for more than forty years, recalled that just before Pacelli entered the priesthood he proposed mar-

Born March 2, 1876
    Rome, Italy
Died October 9, 1958
    Castel Gandolfo, Italy

Head of the Roman Catholic church during World War II; often the subject of controversy over whether he did enough to help Jewish victims of the Holocaust

"…the blood of countless human beings … has been shed and cries out to heaven.…"

Vatican Defends Pius XII

Controversy continues over whether Pope Pius XII did everything in his power to save the Jews during World War II. In March 1998 the Vatican released a document titled "We Remember: A Reflection on the Shoah" addressing the role of the Catholic church in the Holocaust. "We cannot know how many Christians in countries occupied or ruled by the Nazi powers or their allies were horrified at the disappearance of their Jewish neighbors and yet were not strong enough to raise their voices in protest," the document states. It also maintains that Pius XII was a "wise diplomat."

Jewish leaders criticized the Vatican for taking ten years to issue an official position on the issue. Many felt that the statement came far too late, more than 50 years after the war, and that it also portrayed Pius XII as almost blameless. Many Jews continued to maintain that Pius XII's actions cost lives during the Holocaust. Cardinal Edward I. Cassidy, whose Commission for Religious Relations with the Jews produced "We Remember," said that eleven volumes of documents in Vatican archives supported the Vatican's conclusions about the pope's actions.

---

riage to a young woman named Lucia. She refused him, and he became a priest in 1899. Pacelli rose rapidly through the ranks in the church. In 1918 he was selected to serve as the pope's first ambassador to Germany, a post he held until 1929. Pacelli did a great deal to assist the German people, who were suffering after World War I, and mutual affection developed. While in Germany, Pacelli was exposed to communism in the nearby Soviet Union and came to despise that economic and political system.

Upon his return to the Vatican from Germany in 1929, Pacelli was named a cardinal by Pope Pius XI. The following year, he was appointed Vatican Secretary of State, a position he still held when Hitler became Chancellor of Germany in the early 1930s. In the same year, Pacelli signed a concordat, proposed by Hitler himself, with the German government. (Agreements between the church and individual nations were common, and a refusal to sign one might have placed German Catholics in danger.) German Catholics were granted various rights, such as the continuing operation of Catholic schools and state recognition of Catholic marriages. In return, German Catholic officials recognized the Nazi party as a lawful authority. Many people believe that the concordat allied the Vatican with Germany during World War II. It was widely regarded as a victory for Hitler, because it seemed to indicate that the Vatican supported his policies.

Elected Pope

When Pope Pius XI died in 1939, Pacelli was elected to succeed him as supreme head of the Catholic church. Taking office on March 12, 1939, Pacelli chose the name Pius XII. One of the first people to be notified of his election was Hitler, to whom the new pope sent his regards, expressing his desire for peace. In September, the Nazis invaded Poland, a largely Catholic country, marking the beginning of World War II. This aggression against a Catholic-dominated country, coupled with the recent ascension to power of Italian dictator Benito Mussolini, placed Pius XII and the Vatican in a difficult position. Mussolini, an avid anti-Christian dictator, had allied Italy with Hitler's Germany. Pius XII watched in horror as the population of Catholic Poland suffered under German occupation. At some point—historians do not know precisely when—Pius XII learned about Hitler's "Final Solution," the plan for the extermination of European Jews. Despite his pity for the victims of the Nazis, Pius XII decided the interests of Catholic Europe required that the Vatican maintain its neutrality. He adhered to this position throughout the war.

Defenders and Detractors

Debate still surrounds Pius XII's actions, or lack of action, during the Holocaust. His defenders maintain that the pope did not have complete

Future Pope Saved Jews

Angelo Roncalli succeeded Pius XII and took the name of Pope John XXIII. Born in Bergamo, Italy, in 1881, Roncalli was the son of poor peasant farmers. A career in the church was one of the few options available to a gifted child of his social class, so Roncalli was sent to a special school for religious training before he was ten years old. He became a priest in 1903. While on a mission for the Roman Catholic church in Turkey during World War II, Roncalli urged Pius XII to listen to the pleas of a Jewish religious leader to aid in the rescue of Jews; Pius XII refused. For his efforts, Roncalli became famous in Turkey for saving tens of thousands of Jews in Romania, Hungary, and Bulgaria. He provided them with phony certificates "proving" they had been baptized as Catholics.

At the time he became pope, Roncalli was seventy-seven years old. A bald, robust, and cheerful man, Roncalli was regarded by his colleagues as dim-witted, even clownish; it was generally felt that his reign would be short and uneventful. As it turned out, his intelligence, political skill, and good humor made him beloved throughout the world by Catholics and non-Catholics alike. Among his many accomplishments during his short reign (1958–1963) was the establishment of better relations between Roman Catholics and Jews. He declared that the crucifixion of Jesus Christ could not be blamed indiscriminately on modern Jews, and that Jews should no longer be referred to as "Christ killers."

---

knowledge of Hitler's plan to exterminate the Jews. If he had spoken out against Hitler, he would have endangered Catholics trapped in Nazi-occupied countries. An estimated 1.5 million refugees, including Jews, were helped by Pius XII, who granted them Vatican citizenship. This is a far greater number of war victims than were helped by either Great Britain or the United States. The pope's defenders also point to the many radio speeches in which he condemned Hitler's aggression.

Critics of Pius XII maintain that he ignored his moral duty by not speaking out more forcefully in his radio addresses—as the spiritual leader of nearly 400 million Catholics, his words would have carried a lot of weight. They say it is unacceptable to claim ignorance of Hitler's plan to exterminate the Jews, and some accuse the pope of remaining silent due to the Roman Catholic belief that Jews were responsible for crucifying Jesus. Despite the controversy, many prominent Jews publicly thanked Pius XII after the war for his assistance to victims of the Holocaust.

Life's Work Overshadowed

The actions of Pius XII during World War II have overshadowed the achievements of the rest of his tenure as pope. He was the author of numerous encyclicals, or letters, about church policies on religious, moral, and political issues. He is highly respected for his efforts to persuade all warring nations to settle their differences peaceably. He also spoke out in favor of social justice for the poor and the persecuted throughout the world, promoting the belief that every individual has dignity, and that the individual and the family are more important than any country. His convictions stood in direct opposition to the fascism exercised by Mussolini and Hitler in which the state took precedence over the individual. Under Pius XII's leadership, the influence of the Roman Catholic church reached around the world, extending into Africa and China. Millions of people were converted to the Catholic faith and the prestige of the church was greatly enhanced during his papacy.

By 1954 the seventy-eight-year-old pope, who had long been plagued by poor health, stood nearly six feet tall but weighed only 105 pounds. He continued a demanding schedule of writing and delivering speeches on church matters, but grew gradually weaker and began seeing visions of Jesus of Nazareth at his bedside, a revelation that caused astonishment worldwide. He died on October 9, 1958. Vatican

---

radio made the official announcement, and the Roman Catholic church has since begun the lengthy process of recognizing him as a saint.

Sources

Books

Falconi, Carlo, *The Silence of Pius XII,* translated by Bernard Wall, Little, Brown (Boston), 1970.

Friedländer, Saul, *Pius XII and the Third Reich: A Documentation,* translated from the French and German by Charles Fullman, Octagon Books (New York), 1980.

Hochhuth, Rolf, *The Deputy,* translated by Richard and Clara Winston, preface by Albert Schweitzer, Johns Hopkins University Press (Baltimore), 1997.

Lewy, G., *The Catholic Church and Nazi Germany,* Da Capo Press (Boulder, CO), 1999.

Martin, Malachi B., "Pius XII," *McGraw-Hill Encyclopedia of World Biography,* McGraw-Hill (New York), 1973.

Minerbi, Sergio I., "Pius XII," *Encyclopedia of the Holocaust,* Israel Gutman, editor in chief, Macmillan (New York), 1990.

Murphy, Paul I., and R. Renè Arlington, *La Popessa,* Warner Books (New York), 1983.

"Pius XII," *The Holocaust,* Grolier Educational, 1997.

"Pius XII, Pope," *New Catholic Encyclopedia,* prepared by an editorial staff at the Catholic University of America, J. Heraty (Palatine, IL), 1981.

Periodicals

Taubman, Howard, "Deputy: Drama About Pius XII at the Brooks Atkinson," *New York Times,* February 27, 1964.

Taubman, Howard, "Time of Inquest," *New York Times,* March 8, 1964.

Ernie Pyle

Even before he became famous as a war correspondent, journalist Ernie Pyle had attracted millions of American readers with newspaper columns that depicted the lives of ordinary people. During World War II, he went overseas and lived with American soldiers, using his talents to present vivid accounts of their experiences on the battlefield. Pyle's critics claim he whitewashed events and softened the brutal realities of war; his champions argue that Pyle's reports helped Americans adjust to the war and gave them a sense of purpose. According to biographer James Tobin, Pyle was "America's eyewitness to the 20th century's supreme ordeal."

Beginning a Career

Ernest Taylor Pyle grew up on a farm near the small town of Dana, Indiana. His father, William C. "Will" Pyle, was a quiet man who became a farmer when he was unable to support his family by working as a carpenter. Pyle was raised in a household dominated by confident, hardworking women. His mother, Maria, raised her only child with a mixture of rigorous discipline and tenderness, aided by her sister, Mary, who lived with the family. When Pyle went to school, he felt inferior to the other boys, and was not interested in farm work. He kept a scrapbook of postcards from around the world, dreaming of the day he could leave Dana. In 1917 the United States entered

Born August 3, 1900
  Dana, Indiana, United States
Died April 18, 1945
  Ie Shima, Japan

American journalist

"No statesman … or general or admiral or movie star ever got a quicker or more complete bath of fame than this thin man from Indiana."

(Reproduced by permission of Archive Photos, Inc.)

World War I (1914–1918), and Pyle was greatly disappointed that he was too young to join the army. In 1919 he entered Indiana University in Bloomington and declared a major in economics. Developing a keen interest in journalism, he was a reporter and editor on the university's newspaper, the *Daily Student.* In the middle of his senior year, he dropped out of college to take a job as reporter at the *Daily Herald* in La Porte, Indiana.

Pyle did well enough at the *Herald* to be noticed by an editor at the Scripps-Howard newspaper company who was looking for talented young writers. He offered Pyle a job at the *Washington Daily News* in Washington, D.C., giving the young man a pay increase of two dollars and fifty cents per week and an opportunity to leave Indiana. Pyle quickly earned praise for his clearly written stories and ability to edit the work of others. In 1923 he met Geraldine "Jerry" Siebolds, an unconventional young woman from Minnesota, whom he married in 1925. A year later, they left for a long camping trip across the United States, settling in New York City, where Pyle found work copyediting for several area newspapers. Unhappy with his job and living conditions, Pyle returned to the *Washington Daily News.*

During the 1920s, aviation was a relatively unknown and exciting field; daring pilots performed thrilling feats at airshows and airline travel was becoming popular. In 1928 Pyle convinced his editors that an aviation column would attract readers, so he was given the assignment. He spent the next four years visiting airfields around Washington, D.C.; interviewing pilots, mechanics, and other industry people; and reporting on such issues as passenger safety, airplane design, and new airports. In these widely read articles, Pyle established the loose, highly descriptive, and personable style that would make him famous during World War II. Although Pyle enjoyed writing about aviation, he accepted an offer to become managing editor of the *Washington Daily News.* He worked for three years in this capacity but longed for his previous location assignments. By this time, his marriage had also become difficult, as Jerry was having emotional problems and struggling with alcohol addiction.

Becomes a Roving Reporter

After taking a three-week vacation in the southwestern United States, Pyle recorded his experiences in a special eleven-article series that was an immediate hit. This gave him the idea of becoming a "roving" reporter—he would travel around the United States and write stories about places he visited and people he met. A high-level editor at Scripps-Howard, who had admired Pyle's southwestern stories, approved the idea. Pyle and his wife packed a few belongings into a Dodge convertible coupe and set out on the road. For a time, Pyle wandered across the United States, visiting all forty-eight states plus Alaska and Hawaii (which were not yet states), Canada, Central America, and South America. Encountering thousands of people from all walks of life, he wrote about what he saw and heard in columns that were published in more than forty newspapers. Pyle created what biographer Tobin called a "forgotten but magnificent mosaic of the American scene in the Great Depression."

Pyle's vivid descriptions of American life and landscapes captured the imagination of the public, who liked the friendly, self-deprecating voice he used in the articles. He often mentioned his own family members, though during the seven years they were continually on the road, Pyle became tired and ill and Jerry grew even more depressed and isolated as she abused pills and alcohol. Finally the couple decided to build a house in Albuquerque, New Mexico, and settle down. By the end of 1939, the war in Europe was often in Pyle's thoughts. When Germany started bombing raids on London, Pyle decided to go overseas to write a column in which he would share experiences in war-torn Europe with the American people. He arrived in London on December 9, 1940, and nine days later, from a hotel balcony, he witnessed one of the most severe bombing raids of the war, as German aircraft bombarded London. He later wrote that the scene was both horrible and beautiful, and expressed his admiration for the bravery and determination of the British people, suggesting that Americans should support British efforts against the Germans.

In the pre-television era, Pyle's columns helped the general public understand events in England. His readership grew, and upon his return to the United States in March 1941, he received an unexpected and enthusiastic welcome. His columns were published in a book, *Ernie Pyle in England* (1941). Pyle's plans for a trip to Asia were halted by the Japanese attack on the U.S. naval base at Pearl Harbor on December 7, 1941. The next day the United States declared war against Japan, and with reciprocal war declarations against the United States by the remaining Axis powers, America became fully involved in World War II. Pyle attempted to enlist in the U.S. Navy but did not meet the physical requirements. In April 1942 he and Jerry divorced, and in June she entered a hospital for treatment of physical and emotional ailments. With nothing left to keep him in the United States, Pyle decided to spend six months touring war zones.

With the Troops in North Africa

Pyle first went to Great Britain, where U.S. troops were preparing for future campaigns. He roamed from camp to camp, talking to soldiers and recording details of their daily routines. An invasion nicknamed Operation Torch was launched in November, in which American forces landed in North Africa to join the British army already engaged in fighting the experienced and efficient Afrika Korps. Pyle soon followed, joining American troops in Tunisia. Instead of living among officers and keeping away from the front lines, he remained close to the GIs, living the life of a soldier—sleeping on the ground, eating in a mess tent, wearing dirty clothes, and going without hot baths. The troops appreciated his efforts to see the war from their viewpoint, and they responded to him warmly. He accompanied the men into combat, often putting himself in harm's way as they collided with the Germans in desert battles. The columns Pyle sent home to eager American readers were full of intimate details about what the soldiers were doing, thinking, and feeling. He focused entirely on enlisted infantry men rather than officers. With riveting descriptions and graceful writing, he told of their transformation from ordinary men into warriors. On the home front, Pyle gained recognition as America's top war correspondent. Between November 1942 and April 1943, his column appeared in 122 newspapers, and its readership increased from 3.3 million to 9 million. He received a flood of letters from readers who thought of him as a personal friend; many sent him gifts and cookies. Pyle was often asked to establish contact with particular soldiers, but he explained in his columns that the task was impossible to perform. His African columns were collected in a book called *Here Is Your War* (1943).

In the European Theater

Once the Allies had taken North Africa from the Germans, they were ready to conquer Italy, which had aligned itself with the Axis nations. The invasion was launched in Sicily and Pyle accompanied the troops, traveling on the battleship USS *Biscayne*. He joined the 7th Army, which was under the command of General George S. Patton, as its troops fought their way north toward the town of Messina and witnessed some of the most intense, bloody fighting of the war. Overwhelmed by the death and chaos that surrounded him, Pyle suffered from the same battle fatigue that many soldiers experienced when the reality of war became too much to bear. He felt both physically and emotionally exhausted. When the Sicily campaign ended in an Allied victory, Pyle decided to go home and recuperate.

Although he had been told that he was immensely popular in the United States, he was still unprepared for the attention he received upon landing in New York. He was besieged by people who wanted to meet him, ask him about the war, or offer him jobs and speaking engagements. In Hollywood, work had begun on a film entitled *The Story of G.I. Joe*, based on Pyle's book, *Here Is Your War*. Having no desire to stay in the United States while the film was being made, Pyle decided to return to Europe. On his way overseas, he stopped in Washington, D.C., and had tea with First Lady Eleanor Roosevelt at the White House. Despite his embarrassment about having only a shabby suit to wear to the meeting, he had a long, pleasant chat with the first lady.

Pyle then left for Italy, where he would spend five months with American troops struggling under terrible conditions, including heavy rain, bone-chilling cold, and fierce resistance from German and Italian soldiers. This experience only deepened his admiration for the American troops. Pyle is credited with contributing to the heroic image of the American soldier, described by Tobin as "the long-suffering G.I. who triumphed over death through dogged perseverance." Pyle's hallmark column, which he wrote during this period, told the story of a young soldier who went into an occupied area to retrieve the body of his company commander, Captain Henry Waskow. In simple, graceful prose, Pyle told of soldiers paying their respects to the fallen captain. By February 25, the troops had reached the town of Anzio, where casualties were especially high. On March 17 the house in which Pyle was staying was shelled, and he barely escaped injury. In April he went to London, where the Allies were planning "Operation Overlord," the invasion of Normandy, France, that would become known as D-Day. Pyle learned that he had won the Pulitzer Prize for his journalism.

Ernie Pyle working on a column in Normandy, France. (Reproduced by permission of AP/Wide World Photos)

Witnessing the Normandy Invasion

Pyle was invited to travel to Normandy, France, with General Omar Bradley on the command ship *Augusta,* which would have allowed him to witness the arrival of the first troops on the beaches of northern France in relative safety among top army officers. Pyle declined, opting to go aboard an LST (landing ship, tank) with regular soldiers. The massive invasion began on June 6, and Pyle went ashore the next day. Unsure how to describe the scene to his readers, he took a long walk on the beach. The focus of his columns was what he saw during his walk: bodies floating in the calm water, wrecked equipment, and piles of personal gear, such as toothbrushes, Bibles, and photographs, that had belonged to soldiers killed in the fighting.

For a few weeks, Pyle remained at the center of Allied movements as troops fought their way into France. His energies again drained by battle fatigue, he left the front to report on other army units. During this period, a photograph of Pyle was featured on the front cover of the July 17, 1944, issue of *Time* magazine. After witnessing an Allied assault near the town of Saint-Lô, France, being caught in heavy bombing there, and observing the liberation of Paris on August 25, Pyle returned to the United States. At that time, he had approximately 40 million devoted readers around the world. Although he was courted by various newspaper companies, he remained loyal to Scripps-Howard. Pyle also turned down several offers to have his columns broadcast on radio. While he was in North Africa, Pyle and his wife had been remarried (long distance), and he returned to their house in Albuquerque. Although Jerry seemed at first to have recovered from her illness, Pyle's hectic visit and his plans to go to the Pacific upset her greatly. She attempted suicide and was hospitalized again. Though worried about Jerry, Pyle left for the Pacific in January 1945. He was compelled to cover the war in the Pacific even though he sensed that he had used up all of his luck.

Into the Pacific Theater

After a short stay in Honolulu, Hawaii, Pyle flew to Guam and then on to Saipan, two islands in the Marianas chain in the South Pacific. There he relaxed for a few days with a relative named Jack Bales, an airplane radio operator, and pilots who were conducting regular bombing raids on Japan. Pyle also went for a cruise on a light aircraft carrier, the USS *Cabot*, writing that the life of troops in the South Pacific seemed much easier than that of soldiers in Europe. He noted that the weather was pleasant, living conditions were comfortable, and everything moved at a slower pace. For the first time, Pyle's work drew negative criticism, especially from enlisted men who claimed he had spent all his time with officers and had not tried to see or

portray the grittier realities of the war in the Pacific. Pyle promised he would try to gain a more accurate perspective.

As the Allies made plans to invade the Japanese island of Okinawa, Pyle decided to accompany the marines. He traveled to Okinawa aboard the ship *Panamint* and went ashore on April 1. On April 17 Pyle went to Ie Shima, a tiny island that the Marines had invaded the previous day. He spent the night on the island, and the next morning climbed into a jeep with several other men to go inland. After driving a short distance they heard the rapid firing of a Japanese machine gun. The men jumped out of the jeep and into a ditch, but when Pyle raised his head, he was shot in the left temple and killed instantly. President Roosevelt had died only six days earlier, and the new president, Harry S Truman, expressed an entire nation's grief anew at Pyle's death. Pyle's body was initially buried on Ie Shima, but was later moved to lie among army and navy dead in the National Memorial Cemetery of the Pacific at Punchbowl Crater in Honolulu. Soldiers placed a simple plaque on Ie Shima that referred to Pyle as the "buddy" of the 77th Infantry Division.

Sources

Books

Miller, Lee G., *The Story of Ernie Pyle*, Greenwood Press (Westport, CT), 1950.

Nichols, David, editor, *Ernie's War: The Best of Ernie Pyle's World War II Dispatches*, Random House (New York), 1986.

O'Connor, Barbara, *The Soldier's Voice: The Story of Ernie Pyle*, Carolrhoda Books (Minneapolis, MN), 1996.

Tobin, James, *Ernie Pyle's War: America's Eyewitness to World War II*, Free Press (New York), 1997.

Wilson, Ellen Janet Cameron, *Ernie Pyle, Boy from Back Home*, Bobbs-Merrill (Indianapolis, IN), 1962.

Other

"Ernie Pyle," *Access Indiana Teaching & Learning Center*, http://tlc.ai.org/pyle (August 2, 2000).

Vidkun Quisling

Born July 18, 1887
Fyresdal, Norway
Died October 24, 1945
Oslo, Norway

Soldier; politician; executed as a traitor by
the Norwegian government

*"If my activity has been treason ... then I
wish to God for Norway's sake that a good
many of Norway's sons should become
traitors like me, only that they be not
thrown into jail."*

(Reproduced by permission of Archive Photos, Inc.)

Vidkun Quisling is possibly Norway's best-known political figure. His name has become synonymous with traitor: The term "quisling" is now used to describe a person who betrays his or her country by cooperating with the enemy. After showing brilliant promise as a patriotic student and young army officer, Quisling was charged and executed as a traitor to his country during World War II.

Begins Military Career

Vidkun Abraham Lauritz Jonsson Quisling was born in the southern Norwegian village of Fyresdal in 1887. He was the son of Jon (a Lutheran minister) and Anna Quisling. His parents stressed the importance of education and encouraged their children—Vidkun, his two younger brothers, Jorgen and Arne, and his younger sister, Esther—to be strong individualists. After deciding against a career as a priest or scientist, Quisling graduated from junior school and enrolled at the Royal Norwegian Military Academy. Patriotism was booming in Norway after the country earned its independence from Sweden in 1905, and Quisling was caught up in the nationalist spirit. In 1908 he graduated at the head of his class and became a lieutenant in the army. He taught school for a year to earn money to continue his education, then returned to study for two more years at the military academy, specializing in engineering. He received the highest grades

Quisling reviewing his bodyguard unit. (Reproduced by permission of AP/Wide World Photos)

anyone had ever achieved at the school, and was invited to meet the king of Norway.

In 1911 Quisling joined the general staff of the Norwegian military. Young officers were expected to become knowledgeable about a particular country and master its language; Quisling chose Russia. In 1918 he was appointed to a post with the diplomatic staff stationed in Petrograd (now St. Petersburg), Russia. He arrived just after Czar Nicholas II was overthrown by communists and Russia became part of the Soviet Union. The young Quisling observed the Russian Revolution from the center of power, and he came to admire the revolutionary leaders. In 1919 he took a post with the Norwegian embassy in Finland.

Quisling was still in the military when he returned to Norway in 1921 and began working for world-famous Norwegian explorer Fridtjof Nansen, who had been appointed to head a relief program for people in Russia and bordering countries who were suffering from starvation, disease, and the ravages of war. In need of someone who knew the Communist leaders and could speak

Russian, Nansen chose Quisling as his administrative assistant and translator. From 1922 to 1927, Quisling participated in Nansen's relief efforts. While working in the Ukraine (also part of the Soviet Union), Quisling married a young woman named Maria Vasilievna Pasek. He then served at the Norwegian embassy in Moscow, Russia's capital, during 1928 and 1929. As a result of broken diplomatic relations between Great Britain and the Soviet Union, Quisling also attended to the interests of British citizens living in Russia. He retained the position until the two countries resumed amicable relations. In gratitude, the British honored Quisling by making him a member of the British Empire. Soviet dictator Joseph Stalin had completely seized power by 1929, and made it clear that all foreigners were unwelcome in his country. By this time, Quisling had lost his affection and respect for the Soviet Union's communist ideals.

Enters Politics

After his return to Norway in 1930, Quisling retired from the military with the rank of major.

The Nazis Exploit the Norwegian Economy

Prior to World War II, the Norwegian economy had been dependent on mining, the export of fish and forestry products, and the import of food and machinery. When the Germans took over the country in April 1940, they took control of Norway's exports and became responsible for the Norwegian food supply. As the war escalated, Germany ruthlessly exploited the country's resources, and the Norwegian standard of living plummeted. Food and other goods were rationed, and more than one-third of the national income went to pay for the huge German army occupying Norway. (There was one German soldier for every ten Norwegian citizens.)

He became involved in politics and was appointed minister of defense in 1931. Like the rest of the world, Norway suffered mightily as a result of the worldwide depression of the 1930s. As defense minister, Quisling was held partly responsible for the shootings of workers striking for better working conditions; he was also blamed for the overfunding of the military. He attempted to oust trouble-making communists from the Norwegian military, calling them paid "stooges" of Joseph Stalin. He believed that the leader of his own party had become too willing to compromise with members of other political groups, and unsuccessfully tried to get himself appointed the new head of the party. Instead, he was forced to resign his post in 1933.

In 1931 Quisling had cofounded the Nordic Folk Awakening movement, a group that believed in many of the ideas and principles of Adolf Hitler's Nazi party. Seeking new solutions to Norway's problems, Quisling started the Nasjonal Samling (NS) party, or National Unity party, two years later. He suggested a concordance of business and government programs and called for a return to basic values of religion, patriotism, and family life. In 1934 Quisling organized a group of young men, called the Hird, to serve as the party's bodyguards. Asserting that the Norwegian elite was vital to a stronger country, he regarded the Hird as a breeding ground for a new brand of leaders. Like Hitler, Quisling and the NS blamed Jews for Norway's problems: Jews were "impure" and their very existence was a threat to the ideals embraced by the NS. These ideas did not gain much popular support, however, and Quisling was unable to win a seat in the Norwegian parliament.

Encourages Nazi Takeover of Norway

In December 1939 Quisling decided it was his job to save Norway. He met with Hitler and warned of a possible invasion of Norway by the British. Quisling advised Hitler to head off the British by occupying Norway himself. During their talks, Hitler assured Quisling that Germany would give financial and moral support to the NS. Hitler realized that Norway would be beneficial as a site for Nazi naval bases, from which German submarines could disrupt British trade routes. In addition, Norway was the home of one of the only factories in the world that produced heavy water, a substance vital to the building of atomic bombs and reactors.

On the night of April 8–9, 1940, the Germans began their assault on Norway. As German troops came ashore, King Haakon VII and chief Norwegian government officials fled to Sweden and eventually to Great Britain. Still, Haakon maintained cooperation with many Norwegians at home, including members of the Norwegian military. The Allies considered the remaining members of Haakon VII's government the legitimate representatives of order within the independent kingdom of Norway.

After the Nazis arrived in Oslo, the capital city of Norway, Quisling went on the radio and proclaimed himself prime minister. The conquering Germans then announced that the NS was the only legitimate political party in Norway. Quisling's speech was not well received by his countrymen, however, and German and Norwegian leaders joined forces to wrest power from him. In addition, Quisling was disdained throughout the world as a dangerous Nazi sympathizer. The Norwegian and British governments—who themselves had done a poor job of responding to the invasion—blamed Quisling for the German takeover. Thus his name became synonymous with the term "traitor."

Executed for Treason

On April 15, 1940, Josef Terboven, a senior German official, assumed power as the highest-ranking Nazi in Norway. He formed a "shadow" government made up of members of the Norwegian royal government who had chosen to remain in the country. The Nazis soon became disenchanted with Quisling, in part because he could not convince his fellow Norwegians to follow his orders, and removed him from office within a week. As the shadow government continued to take control, Quisling was forced to the sidelines, where he remained in charge of the NS. On February 1, 1942, Hitler appointed Quisling puppet prime minister, a post he would retain until the end of the war. Quisling hoped he could negotiate a treaty with the Germans that would give his government legal independence from Nazi power. This never happened. Instead, he used harsh measures against his opponents and had open disputes with Terboven. Quisling advocated the arrest and deportation of Norwegian Jews to camps in Germany. He also tried to place Norway's teachers and the state church under the jurisdiction of NS leaders. When the teachers rebelled, he had several hundred of them arrested and shipped to labor camps in the north.

In time, Quisling's countrymen hated him more than the Nazis. Near the end of the war, there were rumors of an assassination plot against him. King Haakon expressed a popular sentiment when he suggested that upon his return to power, Quisling would be hanged. The king further suggested that the rope could be fixed to break "accidentally" during the first two attempts and Quisling could be returned to prison twice, thus prolonging his torment. Instead, Quisling was arrested on May 9, 1945, and put on trial for a lengthy list of crimes, including treason, murder, making illegal changes to the Constitution, and aiding an enemy during wartime. Throughout the trial he maintained his innocence, claiming his actions had been in the best interests of the country. During closing arguments, Quisling gave an eight-hour speech, reviewing his illustrious career and justifying his actions. His testimony was unconvincing, however, and on September 10, 1945, he was found guilty of all charges and sentenced to death.

Quisling appealed the decision to the supreme court, but after a two-day hearing the court dismissed the appeal and upheld the death sentence. Although Quisling refused to appeal to the king of

Norway Resists the Nazis

Throughout the war, a strong resistance movement flourished in Norway to oppose the Nazis. Secret missions were carried out to disrupt the German war efforts, sometimes by Norwegian special forces sent from Great Britain. In the Vemork Raid of November 1942, thirty-four British engineers were sent into Norway on glider planes. Assisted by local resistance agents, they vandalized the Norwegian hydroelectric plant that produced the only heavy water available for use in Germany's atomic bomb program, rendering it inoperable.

Norway's liberation from the Nazis began in 1944, when Norwegian troops gained control of two northern counties. The country remained under Nazi control until May 8, 1945, when King Haakon VII returned and restored Norway's legitimate government.

Despite the attempts of the Norwegian resistance to undermine the German occupation of Norway, during the war more than 40,000 Norwegians were imprisoned by the Nazis and more than 2,000 were killed in death camps, including about 700 Norwegian Jews.

Norway for mercy, his wife did so on his behalf. Her petition was rejected. While awaiting execution, Quisling maintained that he was innocent. On October 24 he was taken from his prison cell and driven to an old Norwegian castle, where he was blindfolded and shot by a firing squad. To the end, Quisling maintained his innocence and suggested his death would make him a martyr.

Sources

Books

Hayes, Paul M., *Quisling: The Career and Political Ideas of Vidkun Quisling 1887–1945,* Indiana University Press (Bloomington, IN), 1972.

Hewins, Ralph, *Quisling: Prophet Without Honor,* John Day (New York), 1966.

Hoidal, Oddvar K., *Quisling: A Study in Treason,* Oxford University Press (Oxford), 1989.

Larsen, Karen, *A History of Norway,* Princeton University Press (Princeton, NJ), 1948.

Petrow, Richard, *The Bitter Years: The Invasion and Occupation of Denmark and Norway, April 1940 to May 1945,* Morrow (New York), 1974.

Jeannette Rankin

The first woman to serve in the U.S. Congress, Jeannette Rankin was elected at a time when most American women were not even allowed to vote. Throughout her life, she was a staunch advocate of women's rights, a leader in the campaign for women's suffrage, and a champion of social reforms for the poor and working classes. Rankin was also a pacifist, a position that endangered her political career when she voted against American entry into both World War I (1914–1918) and World War II. She disregarded the overwhelming tide of public opinion to become the only member of Congress to vote "no" on a resolution to enter World War II proposed by President Franklin D. Roosevelt.

Born June 11, 1880
    Missoula, Montana Territory
Died May 18, 1973
    Carmel, California, United States

American politician; feminist; pacifist

"As a woman I can't go to war, and I refuse to send anyone else."

Works for Women's Suffrage

Jeannette Rankin was the eldest of seven children of John Rankin, a wealthy rancher and land developer who had immigrated to Montana from Canada, and Olive Pickering Rankin, a schoolteacher. When Rankin was born in 1880, Montana was still a territory and Missoula was a frontier town. Though a quick learner, Rankin was not especially fond of school and preferred to spend her time riding horses and sewing her own clothes. When the University of Montana opened in Missoula in 1898, she was one of its first students. After graduating four years later with a degree in biology, she tried a variety of careers—teaching

(Reproduced by permission of Archive Photos, Inc.)

elementary school, apprenticing as a seamstress, and taking a correspondence course in furniture-making—but none of them appealed to her. In 1904 Rankin left Montana for the first time and traveled to Boston to visit her brother Wellington, who was a student at Harvard University. Shocked by the poverty and miserable conditions of people living in the city's slums, she began reading the works of various social reformers to learn how to alleviate these problems. Rankin soon decided she would become a social worker.

Heading to the West Coast, Rankin worked in a San Francisco settlement house, a community-service center located in a poverty-stricken inner-city neighborhood. In 1908 she left this job to attend the New York School of Philanthropy (later the Columbia University School of Social Work) in New York City. A year later, Rankin moved to Seattle, where she conducted social work while studying economics, public speaking, and sociology at the University of Washington. As the women's suffrage movement gained momentum, Rankin began to work with local activists. When these activists discovered her oratory skills, they sent her around the state to campaign.

In November 1910, Washington voters approved an amendment guaranteeing women the right to vote. Using the organization and coordination skills she had acquired in the Washington campaign, Rankin returned to Montana to continue working in the suffrage movement. She organized the Equal Franchise Society to push for the immediate passage of a state amendment granting women the right to vote, and she became the first woman ever to address the Montana state legislature when she gave a speech in favor of women's suffrage. Although the amendment initially failed, Rankin helped establish a powerful lobby that applied enough pressure to the state legislature to win women in Montana the vote in 1914. Rankin served as legislative secretary of the National American Woman Suffrage Association and promoted the cause in several other states, including New York, California, and Ohio.

During a long vacation in New Zealand, where women already had the right to vote, Rankin decided her efforts would be better served by running for office in the U.S. Congress. Her brother Wellington agreed and supported her decision. Rankin's experience in social reform and campaigning helped her as she prepared to run as a Republican in a predominantly Democratic state.

She presented a platform advocating women's suffrage, child protection law, prohibition (an issue she did not focus on so as to avoid opposition from Montana's liquor companies), and pacifism. Rankin won the Republican nomination over seven male candidates when a large number of female Democrats crossed party lines to vote for her. Rankin campaigned across Montana, and became the only victorious Republican winner in the Montana election, winning one of only two seats in the House of Representatives.

Rankin's victory was an accomplishment for the women's rights movement, as she became the first woman elected to Congress in an age when the majority of American women did not even have the right to vote. Upon taking office, Rankin vowed to use her position as a forum to speak out for women's rights and other issues in her campaign platform. As Congress opened its session on April 2, 1917, Rankin was escorted to the Capitol by a group of excited supporters, including the prominent feminist leader Carrie Chapman Catt, amidst cheers and applause. A mere four days later, the mood in Congress darkened when President Woodrow Wilson proposed the United States declaration of war against Germany that would involve the United States in World War I (1914–1918).

Advocates Pacifism

Relations between the United States and Germany had been growing steadily more tense for several years and a German attack on several American merchant ships increased the hostility. Germany was already at war with Great Britain and France, but until 1917, the United States had maintained a policy of isolationism, a position many Americans felt should be rescinded in favor of war. Rankin was outspoken in her pacifism. She did not believe the United States should go to war and felt most of her fellow Montana residents agreed with her. At a special session on April 6, the Senate approved Wilson's resolution and sent the bill to the House. Rankin's brother and suffragist advocates urged her to vote in favor of the resolution, fearing her opposition would damage the cause of women's rights. Rankin disagreed, saying she wanted to support her country but could not vote for war. Despite Rankin's opposition, the resolution passed and the United States declared war against Germany.

Approximately fifty male members of Congress voted against the resolution, but Rankin

Rankin was a staunch pacifist who worked to promote peace after World War I and was the only member of Congress to vote against declaring war on Japan in 1941. (Reproduced by permission of AP/Wide World Photos)

received more attention for her decision than any of the men. Some people saw her vote as a stereotypical "woman's" vote, and there were even calls for her resignation. Some suffrage groups canceled her speaking engagements. Despite her opposition to the conflict, Rankin sold Liberty Bonds to support the war effort. She voted in favor of the draft but against the Espionage Act, which cast suspicion on foreign residents of the United States and made it dangerous to disagree openly with government policy. During her two years in office, Rankin also introduced a bill to make women into citizens independent from their husbands. She promoted government-sponsored aid for mothers and children while helping to bring about better working conditions for employees of the Bureau of Engraving and Printing. She also worked to resolve the problems of Montana copper miners, which included trying to settle a strike.

In 1918 Rankin decided to run for the Senate. When she failed to win the Republican nomination, she ran as a candidate of the liberal National party. She was defeated by the Democratic nominee, who had the support of the powerful Anaconda Copper Company. Over the next twenty years,

Rankin focused her energy on a variety of social reform efforts. In 1919 she became involved with numerous international groups that were working to promote women's rights and world peace. In 1923 she bought a farm in Athens, Georgia, becoming a part-time resident of the state and founding the Georgia Peace Society in 1928. She advocated international peace by supporting the International Court of Justice, the General Disarmament Conference, and the London Naval Conference.

By 1939 Great Britain and France were embroiled in a war with Germany, and the United States was supplying weapons to the British and French. Despite the prevailing sentiment that the United States would eventually be drawn into the conflict, Rankin remained a strong pacifist. In 1940 she was once again elected to Congress as a representative from Montana. Running on an antiwar platform, Rankin conducted an effective campaign, visiting fifty-two of the fifty-five high schools in her district and achieving a landslide victory. Despite the nation's continuing support of isolationism, more people were becoming aware of the fascism that was spreading across Europe. On December 7, 1941, the Japanese launched a surprise attack on the U.S. naval base at Pearl Harbor, Hawaii, killing thousands of people and destroying battleships, airplanes, and other equipment. The next day President Franklin D. Roosevelt, at the urging of the American public, brought before Congress a proposal to declare war on Japan. Just as she had done more than twenty years earlier, Rankin took an unpopular stand and voted against the resolution. The only member of Congress to vote no, Rankin caused a great furor: She was booed and cursed and had to be escorted by police back to her office, where she remained under guard for the rest of the day. In the weeks that followed, she received vast amounts of hate mail.

Rankin's non-violent stand ended her political career. She returned to social reform work, establishing a cooperative homestead for women in Georgia. Interested in and inspired by Indian leader and pacifist Mohandas K. Gandhi, an advocate of peaceful resistance who led his country to independence in 1947, Rankin visited India seven times between 1946 and 1971. In 1962 she ignored the atmosphere of suspicion and hostility between the United States and the Soviet Union and traveled to Moscow to act as an observer at the World Peace Congress. During the 1960s, the United States became involved in the Vietnam conflict, in which communist North Vietnam attempted to take over South Vietnam, which was supported by the United States. Rankin strongly opposed U.S. involvement in the conflict and took an active role in the protest movement, which gathered strength toward the end of the decade. On January 15, 1968, at age eighty-eight, she led a procession of 5,000 women, calling themselves the Jeannette Rankin Brigade, to the U.S. Capitol. Rankin was one of fifteen women allowed to enter the building and meet with lawmakers to express opposition to U.S. involvement in Vietnam.

In 1972 the National Organization for Women (NOW) honored Rankin as the first member of its Susan B. Anthony Hall of Fame, which emphasizes the achievements of American women. Even into her nineties, Rankin remained active in public life, pushing for changes in the methods used to elect presidents, and supporting the work of consumer advocate Ralph Nader. She even considered running for Congress again, but was prevented by failing health. She died in her sleep on May 18, 1973, just before her ninety-third birthday. In 1985 a bronze statue of Rankin was placed in the U.S. Capitol building.

Sources

Books

Block, Judy Rachel, *The First Woman in Congress: Jeannette Rankin*, C.P.I. (New York), 1978.

Giles, Kevin, *Flight of the Dove: The Story of Jeannette Rankin*, Touchstone Press (Beaverton, OR), 1980.

Josephson, Hannah, *First Lady in Congress: Jeannette Rankin*, Bobbs-Merrill (Indianapolis, IN), 1974.

Morin, Isabel, *Women of the U.S. Congress*, Oliver Press (Minneapolis, MN), 1994.

Other

Jeannette Rankin: The Woman Who Voted No (video), PBS Video, 1984.

Leni Riefenstahl

German film director Leni Riefenstahl achieved fame and notoriety for her propaganda movie *Triumph of the Will* and her two-part film about the 1936 Olympic Games, *Olympia,* both made for the Third Reich, the government headed by Adolf Hitler. Riefenstahl remains one of the most controversial figures in the world of film. A talented and ambitious dancer, actress, and director, she had already established a name for herself in her native Germany and abroad when Hitler ascended to power in 1933. They shared a mutual respect, and through Hitler's support she gained even more fame. In spite of her attempts to continue as a filmmaker after the fall of the Third Reich and her protestations that she was nothing but an apolitical artist, she never managed to complete another film. Eventually she turned to still photography, producing two books on the African tribe of the Nuba (*The Last of the Nuba,* 1974, and *The People of Kau,* 1976). She also published a collection of underwater pictures (*Coral Gardens,* 1978), for which she learned to scuba dive while in her seventies. These photographs continued her life-long fascination with the beauty and strength of the human body, especially the male form, and her early interest in natural life outside modern civilization.

Born August 22, 1902
 Berlin, Germany

Film director

"I was finished by this Nazi business. All the time, they kept saying I was Hitler's favourite or that I promoted Nazism. I made films, that's all, and I won lots of prizes for them."

(Reproduced by permission of AP/Wide World Photos)

Early Career as Dancer, Actress, and Finally Director

Helene Berta Amalie Riefenstahl was born in Berlin, Germany, on August 22, 1902. Her father, Alfred Riefenstahl, owned a plumbing firm and eventually died in World War II, as did her only brother, Heinz. Early in life she decided to become a dancer and received thorough training both in traditional Russian ballet and in modern dance with Mary Wigman. By 1920, Riefenstahl was a successful dancer touring such cities as Munich, Frankfurt, Prague, Zurich, and Dresden.

Riefenstahl became interested in cinema when she saw one of the then-popular mountain films of Arnold Fanck. With characteristic decisiveness and energy she set out to meet Fanck and entice him to offer her the role of a dancer in his *Der heilige Berg* (*The Holy Mountain*, 1926). The film was so well-received that Riefenstahl decided to stay with the relatively new medium of motion pictures. Over the next seven years, she made five more films with Fanck: *Der grosse Sprung* (*The Great Leap*, 1927), *Die weisse Hölle vom Piz Palü* (*The White Hell of Piz Palü*, 1929), *Stürme über dem Mont Blanc* (*Storms over Mont Blanc*, 1930), *Der weisse Rausch* (*The White Frenzy*, 1931), and *S.O.S. Eisberg* (*S.O.S. Iceberg*, 1933). She also tried a film with a different director, *Das Schicksal derer von Hapsburg* (*The Fate of the Hapsburgs,*1929). In Fanck's films Riefenstahl was often the only woman in a crew of rugged men who were devoted to capturing the beauty and the dangers of the still untouched high mountains (and for *S.O.S. Eisberg,* of the Arctic) in adventure films. Not only did she learn to climb and ski well, she also absorbed all she could about camera work, directing, and editing.

Eventually, Riefenstahl conceived of a different kind of mountain film, more romantic and mystical, in which she would be both the central character and the director. This film, *Das blaue Licht* (*The Blue Light,* 1932), was based on a mountain legend about Yunta, an innocent mountain girl who falls to her death after greedy villagers steal crystals from a grotto high up on a mountain that had once been accessible only to Yunta. The crystals are the source of a mysterious blue light that sustains Yunta and fatally attracts the young men of the village. The film was shot in remote parts of Tessin and the Dolomites, and both demanded and received a great deal of dedication from cast and crew, many of whom were former associates of Fanck. Riefenstahl also obtained the help of well-known avant-garde author and film theoretician Bela Balazs, a Marxist and Jew, who collaborated on the script and served as assistant director. The theme, lighting, and camera angles of the film show the legacy of German Expressionism. Riefenstahl aimed at fusing the haunting beauty of the mountains with her legendary tale and, as she would continue to do in later films, experimented technically with special film stock, special lenses, soft focus, and smoke bombs to achieve the desired mystical effect. *The Blue Light* won acclaim both abroad, where it received the silver medal at the 1932 Biennale in Venice, and at home, where it attracted the attention of Hitler.

Films for the Third Reich

In 1933 Hitler asked Riefenstahl to film the Nazi party rally in Nuremberg. That film, *Sieg des Glaubens* (*Victory of Faith,* 1933), has been lost, presumably destroyed because it showed party members who were soon afterward liquidated by Hitler. The Nazi leader wanted Riefenstahl to film the 1934 rally as well, a task she claims to have accepted only after a second "invitation" and the promise of total artistic freedom. The resulting *Triumph des Willens* (*Triumph of the Will,* 1935) is considered by many to be the ultimate propaganda film, despite the fact that its director later maintained it was simply a documentary. Carefully edited from more than sixty hours of film, with concern for rhythm and variety rather than chronological accuracy, it emphasizes the solidarity of the Nazi party, the unity of the German people, and the greatness of their leader who, through composition, cutting, and special camera angles, is given mythical dimensions. Albert Speer's architectural spectacle, which prominently displayed Nazi icons, flags, lights, flames, and music, made a powerful appeal to the emotions of the German people when filmed by Riefenstahl. *Triumph of the Will* was awarded the German Film Prize for 1935, and was also given the International Grand Prix at the 1937 Paris World Exhibition.

Riefenstahl's next film, the short *Tag der Freiheit: Unsere Wehrmacht* (*Day of Freedom: Our Armed Forces,* 1935) was in a way a sequel to *Triumph of the Will.* It was shot to placate the German armed forces, who were displeased about having received little attention in *Triumph of the Will.* Another major assignment from Hitler followed in 1936: the filming of the Olympic Games held in Berlin. *Olympia* Part 1: *Fest der Völker* (*Festival of Nations*) and Part 2: *Fest der Schönheit* (*Festival of*

Bertolt Brecht, Anti-fascist Playwright

During the rise of Adolf Hitler, before Leni Riefenstahl began making films glorifying the Third Reich, Bertolt Brecht was staging anti-fascist plays that resulted in his exile from Germany. Probably the greatest German playwright of the first half of the twentieth century, Brecht created works that were often considered controversial because of his revolutionary dramatic theory and political beliefs.

Brecht was born on February 10, 1898, in Augsburg, Germany. Although he was the son of a Catholic businessman, he was raised in his mother's Protestant faith. In 1917 he enrolled at the University of Munich to study philosophy and medicine. In 1918, during World War I, he served as a medical orderly at a military hospital in Augsburg. The unpleasantness of this experience confirmed his hatred of war and stimulated his sympathy for the unsuccessful Socialist revolution of 1919. Brecht returned to his studies but devoted himself increasingly to writing plays that emphasized the artificiality of the theatrical medium and disregarded conventional psychological motivation. By 1924, he had moved to Berlin, and for the next two years was associated as a playwright with Max Reinhardt's Deutsches Theater; he also began a serious study of Marxism. During this period, the director Erwin Piscator was teaching Brecht the techniques of experimental theater, such as the onstage use of films, projections, and slides. Brecht then entered into collaboration with composer Kurt Weill on *Mahagonny* (or *Kleine Mahagonny*) and *Die Dreigroschenoper* (*The Threepenny Opera*, 1928), which made Brecht

famous. He wrote several more plays with music in collaboration with Weill and with composer Paul Hindemith. Notable are *Aufstieg und Fall der Stadt Mahagonny* (*The Rise and Fall of the City of Mahagonny*, 1929) and *Das Badener Lehrstück vom Einverständnis* (*The Didactic Play of Baden: On Consent*, 1929).

In 1933 Brecht's books were among those publicly burned in the Reichstag fire in Berlin. The next day, he went into exile, finally settling in Skovbostrand, Denmark. In 1935 he was stripped of his German citizenship, and until after the war, his new plays were performed in German only in Zurich. Becoming involved in the anti-fascist cause, in 1936 he wrote *Furcht und Elend des Dritten Reiches* (*Fear and Misery of the Third Reich*), a string of naturalistic scenes of life under Hitler. He moved to the Soviet Union before settling in the United States in 1941. He continued to write in exile, completing such great plays as *Mutter Courage* (*Mother Courage*, 1939), *Der gute Mensch von Setzuan* (*The Good Person of Szechuan*, 1941), and *Der kaukasische Kreidekreis* (*The Caucasian Chalk Circle*, 1943). In 1948 Brecht moved to East Berlin, where he remained until his death. He and his wife, actress Helene Weigel, founded the Berliner Ensemble the following year. Brecht died of a heart attack in August 1956.

Beauty) premiered in 1938, again to great German and international acclaim. Elaborate and meticulous preparation, technical inventiveness, and eighteen months of laborious editing helped Riefenstahl elevate sports photography, until then a subject for newsreels, to the level of art. From the naked dancers in the opening sequence and the emphasis on African-American athlete Jesse Owens

to the striking diving and steeplechase scenes, the film celebrated the beauty of the human form in motion in feats of strength and endurance.

Career Ruined by Nazi Ties

Immediately after completing *The Blue Light*, Riefenstahl had made plans to film *Tiefland* (*Low-*

lands), a project that was to be interrupted by illness, Hitler's assignments, and the war. Upon its completion in 1954, all the fire had gone out of this tale of innocence and corruption, high mountains and lowlands, based on the opera by pianist and composer Eugene d'Albert. Many of Riefenstahl's other projects, most notably her plan to do a film on Penthisilea, the Amazon queen, were never completed. Though this was due partly to the fact that she was a woman in a man's profession, it was mainly her role in Hitler's empire that ruined her postwar film career. She visited Africa many times in hopes of making a film, but eventually these trips resulted instead in two books of still photography (*The Last of the Nuba,* 1974, and *The People of Kau,* 1976). Once again, her work was praised for its beauty and castigated by some for a perceived fascist aesthetic. Susan Sontag, for example, wrote in the *New York Review of Books*: "In celebrating a society where the exhibition of physical skill and courage and the victory of the stronger over the weaker have … become the unifying symbol of the communal culture … Riefenstahl seems only to have modified the ideas of her Nazi films." Bill Marvel of the *National Observer* wrote: "If the essence of fascism is the glorification of strength and violence, Miss Riefenstahl's Kau qualify.… Yet there is undeniable beauty here.… The most beautiful book of the year, if beauty alone counted." In her seventies, Riefenstahl learned to scuba dive and concentrated her photography on underwater coral life, resulting in a book of photos called *Coral Gardens* (1978).

In 1993 German director Ray Müller made a film biography of Riefenstahl called *The Wonderful, Horrible Life of Leni Riefenstahl.* The release of the film in the United States in 1995 coincided with the English translation of her autobiography,

Leni Riefenstahl: A Memoir. In both the film and the book, Riefenstahl proclaimed her innocence and mistreatment. In his review of the film, *New York Times* film critic Vincent Canby concluded, "Ms. Riefenstahl doesn't come across as an especially likable character, which is to her credit and Mr. Müller's. She is beyond likability. She is too complex, too particular and too arrogant to be seen as either sympathetic or unsympathetic. There's the suspicion that she had always had arrogance and that it, backed up by her singular talent, is what helped to shape her wonderful and horrible life."

SOURCES

Books

Berg-Pan, Renata, *Leni Riefenstahl,* Twayne (Boston), 1980.

Encyclopedia of World Biography, second edition, Gale Research (Detroit), 1998–1999.

Hinton, David B., *The Films of Leni Riefenstahl,* Scarecrow Press (Lanham, MD), 1978.

Infield, Glenn B., *Leni Riefenstahl, the Fallen Film Goddess,* Crowell (New York), 1976.

Riefenstahl, Leni, *Leni Riefenstahl: A Memoir,* Picador USA (New York), 1995.

Periodicals

National Observer, November 27, 1976.

Sontag, Susan, "Fascinating Fascism," *New York Review of Books,* February 6, 1975.

Other

The Wonderful, Horrible Life of Leni Riefenstahl (video), Kino on Video, 1995.

Róza Robota

Róza Robota was instrumental in the Auschwitz uprising of October 7, 1944. Risking certain death, she lent her support to an elaborate plan to destroy the crematoria used for disposing of the bodies of gas chamber victims. The carefully planned revolt was doomed to failure, however, and Robota was executed for her role in the plot.

Early Experience in Polish Resistance

Very little is known about the early life of Róza Robota. She was born into a middle-class family in Ciechanów, Poland, around 1921. None of her family members are believed to have survived the Holocaust. Adamant in her religious beliefs at a young age, Robota joined an underground Zionist youth group. The Zionists believed that Jews should have their own nation (which eventually occurred in 1948 with the formation of Israel). Robota's association with the group placed her in danger of Nazi persecution. The activities of Polish Jews were conducted secretly after the German occupation of Poland in 1939, when all forms of Jewish expression were outlawed by the Nazi Party. Jews who were considered in violation of Nazi policy faced extreme penalties. The efforts of the underground groups to retaliate against Nazi aggression were complicated by informants, sometimes fellow Jews who wished to gain Nazi favor.

Born 1921 (?)
　Ciechanów, Poland
Died January 6, 1945
　Auschwitz concentration camp,
　Oświęcim, Poland

Polish-Jewish underground activist; Holocaust victim who participated in the Auschwitz uprising in October 1944

"Vengeance will come."

(Yad Vashem Photo Archives/USHMM Photo Archives)

Robota (first on the left, in the back row) and members of a youth Zionist organization. (Eliyahu Mallenbaum/USHMM Photo Archives)

A number of Jewish activists who had been instrumental in previous political movements fled Poland, giving way to a new generation of resistance fighters such as Robota. Underground groups, like the one to which she belonged, began intercepting shipments of food and weapons intended for the Nazi forces. They also gathered news and information for publication in periodicals declared illegal by the Nazis. Resistance groups were usually composed of five to seven members who were known to be absolutely trustworthy. Robota's experience in this movement laid the foundation for her assistance in the 1944 uprising in the Auschwitz camp in Poland.

The removal of the citizens of Ciechanów, including Robota, to the Auschwitz concentration camp took place from November to December 1942. If the people being deported did not know their status in the eyes of the Nazis already, the soldiers made sure that they learned quickly. Townspeople described an incident that occurred during a roundup of Jews on November 5, 1942, when a woman's baby began to cry. One of the German SS men asked the woman politely for the child. She was reluctant to give her child to him, but after a moment, she did as he requested. In front of everyone there, he threw the infant headfirst into the road and it died.

Auschwitz was the largest and most deadly of the Nazi death camps. A multifaceted unit, it consisted of a killing center, a concentration camp, and a complex of slave labor camps. During the camp's existence, between 1940 and 1945, approximately 1.25 to 1.5 million people died there. Upon her arrival, Robota experienced the selection process, in which Nazi doctor Josef Mengele decided the fate of incoming prisoners. As he inspected the new arrivals, Mengele indicated whether they should take their place in the right line, where they would serve as slave laborers, or in the left line, where they would be exterminated in the gas chambers. It is likely that an orchestra, comprised of prisoners, would have been playing during the process. According to eyewitnesses, post-selection protocol included shaving the inmates' hair, stripping them of their clothing, dressing them in rough prisoners' clothing (sometimes leaving them without shoes), and examining them for hidden jewelry or valuables. The inmates suffered complete degradation, which some described as being treated like animals. Robota was put to work examining and sorting the clothing of gas chamber victims.

Participates in Plot

Many male inmates, members of the Sonderkommando (Special Squad), were forced to haul the bodies of gas chamber victims to the crematoria, where they were burned. According to Fayge Silverman in the book *Women of the Holocaust*, these men "worked in a world of terror beyond the scope of human imagination. They witnessed the greatest evil of Auschwitz and were unable to help." Sometimes they even encountered the remains of parents, friends, or relatives. Having no choice but to do the job, the men worked only a few months until they, too, were killed because they knew too much about Nazi activities. Desperate to stop the genocide, several of the Sonderkommando workers secretly formed a group that plotted to blow up the crematoria. They needed gunpowder as an explosive, but it could be obtained only by women who worked in the gunpowder factory. The Sonderkommando contacted Robota, who began organizing women willing to take the risk. One of them was Rose Meth, a Polish-Jewish woman, who later described her own role in the plot as a means of resistance against her captors. She stated that she and the other women were unafraid of the danger posed. They began collecting powder by putting small amounts into tiny pieces of cloth and hiding them in pockets or on their bodies. If the women saw that there was a chance for a search, they would dump the powder on the ground and grind it into the dirt. A person could collect a little less than a teaspoon per day using this method.

The powder passed from hand to hand until it reached Robota, who turned it over to the Sonderkommandos. They in turn gave it to the Soviet prisoners of war, who made hand grenades and even bombs, which were buried in cans around the crematoria until needed. Every person involved in the plot knew he or she would be killed if discovered. There are several versions of what happened at Auschwitz on the day of the inmates' revolt, October 7, 1944. It is known that a riot broke out. Guards were attacked with stones, axes, and crowbars. Prisoners set mattresses aflame, and the fire spread to one of the crematoria. The Sonderkommandos thought the fire was the signal to begin their revolt. While the rest is unclear, a popular version states that a lone Jewish man took the explosives into a crematorium, sacrificing himself as he incinerated the building. Other men cut the wires of the prison fence and fled into the countryside, but they all were found and shot. Finally the revolt was suppressed.

The Nazis rounded up several of the women who had access to explosives, including Robota. All of the women were tortured without mercy, but none revealed any information implicating their accomplices. One of Robota's co-conspirators managed to visit her in jail. He could barely recognize her features because she had been so badly beaten and bruised. She reportedly told him of the brutal means that had been used to coerce information from her, but said that despite the pain, she had not submitted to the Nazis' demands for the names of others involved. Robota and three other women were sentenced to death. On January 6, 1945, they were hanged. Jewish women in the camp were excused from their work and forced to watch. The condemned women "held their heads up high as they stood on the scaffold, and their last call was '*Zemsta!*'" ("Revenge!"). The camp was liberated only three weeks later, on January 27, 1945.

Sources

Books

Gilbert, Martin, *The Holocaust: A History of the Jews of Europe During the Second World War,* Holt, Rinehart and Winston (New York), 1985.

Gutman, Yisrael, and Michael Berenbaum, editors, *Anatomy of the Auschwitz Death Camp,* editorial board, Yehuda Bauer, Raul Hilberg, and Franciszek Piper, Indiana University Press in association with the United States Holocaust Memorial Museum (Bloomington, IN), 1994.

Langbein, Hermann, *Against All Hope: Resistance in the Nazi Concentration Camps 1938–1945,* translated by Harry Zohn, Continuum (New York), 1996.

Rittner, Carol, and John K. Roth, editors, *Different Voices: Women and the Holocaust,* Paragon House (New York), 1993.

Silverman, Fayge, Jehoshua and Anne Eibeshitz, editors and translators, *Women in the Holocaust: A Collection of Testimonies,* Remember (Brooklyn),1993.

Ernst Röhm

A close friend and early political supporter of German dictator Adolf Hitler, Ernst Röhm headed the Nazi military faction known as the Sturmabteilung (SA), also known as storm troopers, an organization that grew to become millions of members strong. The storm troopers, who were recognized by the brown shirts of their uniforms, physically assaulted opponents of Nazi policies. Röhm eventually became more powerful and ambitious, and Hitler began to perceive him as a threat. When Röhm disagreed with Hitler's policies, causing dissension among the party members, Hitler personally ordered Röhm's execution.

Gains Hitler's Confidence

Ernst Röhm was born into a family of government workers in the German region of Bavaria in 1887. He dreamed of being a soldier during his childhood and joined the German army in 1914, shortly before World War I began in Europe. He was wounded several times in combat and rose to the rank of captain. At the conclusion of the war, Röhm joined a group of ex-soldiers in Munich who had difficulty adapting to civilian life. They engaged in warlike activities, marching in their uniforms and causing political unrest. Röhm met Hitler in 1919 and was so impressed by the Nazi leader's speeches that he became one of the first members of the Nazi party. Retiring from the German army in 1923,

Born November 28, 1887
    Munich, Germany
Died July 1, 1934
    Munich, Germany

Professional soldier; traveling salesperson; military instructor; organized, trained, and commanded the military force known as the SA, or storm troopers

"Since I am an immature and wicked man, war and unrest appeal to me more than [middle-class] good order."

(Photograph by H. Hoffmann, courtesy of Bildarchiv Preussischer Kulturbesitz; reproduced by permission)

Röhm assisted Hitler in his unsuccessful attempt to overthrow the German government—an event known as the Munich Beer Hall Putsch. Hitler was imprisoned for nearly a year, and Röhm was placed on probation for fifteen months. Realizing that direct military action against the government would not achieve his desired goals, Hitler began formulating a more gradual approach. Röhm disagreed with Hitler's plan, wanting to initiate a larger and more forceful coup.

By the end of 1924, the relationship between Röhm and Hitler became strained, largely due to Röhm's opposition to Hitler's slow-moving legal tactics. Disillusioned, Röhm withdrew from politics in 1925. The ex-soldier wandered about and took a number of unsatisfying jobs, from working as a traveling salesperson of patriotic publications to toiling in a machine shop. In 1929, Röhm accepted an offer to go to Bolivia as a military adviser. He later referred to this period in his life as "leading the life of a sick animal." After the Nazis achieved some success in the elections of 1930, Hitler summoned Röhm back to Germany. Hitler envisioned a new and powerful country with himself at its head. He knew Röhm's abilities would be useful in rebuilding Germany. After receiving an oath of loyalty from Röhm and his associates, Hitler placed Röhm in charge of organizing and training the Sturmabteilung, also called the SA.

Heads Brutal Storm Troopers

Well organized and practical, Röhm believed in action over philosophy. As Hitler called for the forceful removal of Jewish citizens from public and private German society, Röhm began assembling his military faction. Within three months, he had enlisted 170,000 men into the SA; by the end of 1933, the number had grown to three million. The men who joined the SA were looking for adventure and were anxious to fight. Some of those who joined were veterans of World War I who had held low-ranking positions. They had returned home from battle to face a poor German economy and massive unemployment. The organization also appealed to other unemployed men, who were often restless, agitated, and unmotivated. Röhm and the Nazis seized the opportunity to offer such men a purpose and an outlet to renew their motivation. The SA provided a quasi-military structure as well as the confidence that comes from wearing a uniform. The storm troopers were allowed to use their own discretion in apprehending and punishing German citizens that the Nazis considered enemies. They used brutal tactics that made this Nazi, brown-shirted, private army the terror of the times. Hitler noted and appreciated Röhm's ruthlessness.

The SA became Hitler's private army, carrying out violent assaults against his opponents. Hitler rewarded Röhm's success with the SA by naming him minister of the Bavarian state government and appointing him to a position in the Nazi cabinet. Hitler wrote Röhm a glowing letter thanking him for "immeasurable services rendered to the movement and to the German people." Röhm was a homosexual and practiced a lifestyle that was frowned upon by Hitler and the Nazi party. Official Nazi policy stated that homosexuality interfered with the natural increase in population and the development of "proper family life." However, Hitler and other Nazi leaders tolerated or ignored Röhm's private activities. Thousands of homosexuals who were not in the Nazi party, however, were tortured, imprisoned, and killed.

Night of the Long Knives

Relations between Hitler and Röhm began to sour once again. Röhm accused Hitler of being a mere artist and dreamer, and he denounced Nazi foreign policy, anti-Semitic activities, the destruction of workers' trade unions, and the stifling of "free expression." In 1933, Röhm organized large parades of people who shared his ideas. Writer Joachim Fest noted: "[Röhm] turned bitterly against [Hitler's highest-ranking aides] and … antagonized the generals, who were jealous of [the SA's] privileges." Röhm's actions earned him enemies among the military elite. He requested that he be placed in command of a "people's army," which would combine his SA troops with the larger German army. However, the military elite of the German army, made up of aristocratic officers, wanted no part of Röhm's troops, whom they perceived as a brutish band of unsavory characters. Hitler recognized that the support of wealthy military officers would be instrumental if he hoped to take over Germany, so he concluded that Röhm was a serious threat to that plan. Hitler claimed that Röhm was trying to take control of the country and using the SA to establish his own government. Hitler met with Röhm for five hours, promising that he had no intentions of disbanding the SA, which then numbered 4.5 million members. Sending Röhm and his chief aides on vacation for the month of August, Hitler decided to cleanse the SA of Röhm sympathizers. The list of those to be killed included about 100 names.

The night of the executions, later known as the "Night of the Long Knives," occurred on June 30, 1934. Hitler secretly flew to a resort near Munich, where Röhm and his top aides were vacationing. Roused out of bed and herded off to a Munich prison to join other jailed SA officers, scores of Röhm's chief aides were murdered. The next evening, two high-ranking Nazis entered Röhm's cell and placed a pistol next to him on a table. They left him alone for ten minutes but heard no shots. The officers sent a guard to retrieve the pistol, then they entered Röhm's cell, guns ablaze, and killed him. After Röhm's death, a military group that had been part of the SA became the independent Schutzstaffel (SS) or Security Squad. This group of highly disciplined men was put under the command of Heinrich Himmler, who was to serve as one of Hitler's most important and trusted col-

leagues. Well organized and precise, the SS enacted ruthless policies that instilled fear throughout Germany and Europe.

SOURCES

Books

Fest, Joachim C., *The Face of the Third Reich: Portraits of the Nazi Leadership*, translated by Michael Bullock, Pantheon (New York, NY), 1970.

Gallo, Max, *The Night of Long Knives*, translated by Lily Emmet, Harper and Row (New York, NY), 1972.

Keegan, John, *The Second World War*, Hutchinson (London), 1989.

Merkl, Peter H., *The Making of a Stormtrooper*, Princeton University Press (Princeton, NJ), 1980.

Erwin Rommel

Born November 15, 1891
Heidenheim, Germany
Died October 14, 1944
near Herrlingen, Germany

German field marshal known as the
"Desert Fox"

*"A very daring and skillful opponent
and, may I say across the havoc of war,
a great general."*
—WINSTON CHURCHILL

(Library of Congress)

Erwin Rommel was renowned for his leadership of Germany's Afrika Korps, which he commanded in numerous victories against the Allies in the deserts of North Africa. His ability to keep the enemy off balance, utilizing surprise attacks and quick movements, earned him the nickname "Desert Fox." Rommel was admired by friends and enemies alike, but toward the end of World War II, Rommel had fallen out of favor with Adolf Hitler, telling the Nazi leader that Germany could not defeat the Allies.

An Impressive Young Soldier

Rommel was the second of four children born to middle-class parents—Erwin (a schoolteacher) and Helene Rommel—in Heidenheim, a town in southern Germany. As a boy, Erwin Rommel was well-behaved, with a dreamy manner; as a teenager he became more active, spending much of his time on his bicycle or skis and studying mathematics, his favorite subject. He developed an interest in airplanes and gliders, but his desire to study aviation engineering was thwarted by his father, who wanted him to enter the military. In July 1910 Rommel joined the 124th Wurtemberg Infantry Regiment as a cadet. Two years later, he was commissioned as a lieutenant. In 1914 he married Lucie Mollin, whom he had met several years earlier.

Rommel (pointing) led the Afrika Korps in many successful battles against the British 8th Army in North Africa. (Reproduced by permission of Archive Photos)

While serving in World War I (1914–1918), Rommel impressed his superior officers with his boldness, courage, determination, and ability to act quickly and decisively. He participated in battle in Romania, France, and Italy, where in 1917 he led the capture of Monte Matajur near Caporetto. For his bravery, twenty-seven-year-old Rommel received the Pour le Merite, or Iron Cross, the highest award granted by the German military. As Germany's defeat in World War I plunged the country into a period of economic hardship, Rommel decided to stay in the army, even though the terms of the Versailles Treaty had greatly reduced the role of the German military. By 1921, Rommel's son, Manfred, had been born while he was serving as a company commander with a regiment

based near Stuttgart. Rommel was appointed an instructor at the Infantry School in Dresden. The lectures he gave during his four-year tenure at the school were collected and published as *Infantry Attacks,* which featured vivid descriptions of Rommel's war experiences. Used by the Swiss army to train its troops, the book was also admired by Adolf Hitler, who took control of the German government in 1933.

In 1935, while Rommel was a lieutenant colonel, he became an instructor at the Potsdam War Academy, assisting in the training of Hitlerjügend, or Hitler Youth, clubs. The assignment ended when Rommel had a disagreement with the Nazi officer in charge of the program. In 1938 Germany conquered Czechoslovakia using a method of warfare called blitzkrieg, or "lightning war"—troops in vehicles made swift, surprise attacks while planes dropped bombs on the enemy. In order to show the Czechs that he was a strong leader, Hitler made plans to personally visit Prague in October. Rommel was chosen to command the group providing security for Hitler during the trip, and again impressed the führer. With Germany's annexation of Austria, Rommel became commandant of the Austrian war academy in Wiener Neustadt. Less than a year later, German troops pushed across the Polish border, staging an invasion that caused Great Britain and France to declare war on Germany. Rommel was promoted to major general and given command of Hitler's field headquarters in Poland.

Rommel had grown to greatly admire Hitler, whom he regarded as an idealistic and devoted patriot striving to strengthen Germany. Only later did Rommel recognize the depth of Hitler's anti-Semitism and the measures he would take to destroy the Jews. As Germany prepared to attack France, Rommel was placed in command of the 7th Panzer (Tank) Division, which he led into France from Belgium. His troops were known as the "Ghost" or "Phantom" division because they moved with such swiftness that they appeared to materialize from nowhere. Rommel devised many bold, clever military moves and played an important role in the successful takeover of France, for which he was awarded the Knight's Cross medal.

Leads Afrika Korps

After victory in France, Rommel was appointed to lead the Afrika Korps—the German force that would fight the British army in North Africa, where troops from Italy were struggling to maintain control. Beginning in 1941, Rommel commanded the Afrika Korps in a series of battles against the British 8th Army, utilizing the blitzkrieg method that had proven so effective previously. The Germans were able to push the British from Libya to the Egyptian border, a distance of approximately 1,500 miles, bringing them close to the Suez Canal. This region was strategically important because the Canal would make it easier to ship supplies to the area.

His overwhelming method of swift bombardment earned Rommel the admiration of friends and foes alike, as well as the nickname "Desert Fox." One British general had to warn his own officers about revering the German general too much. Rommel's reputation with Allied troops was due in

part to his humane treatment of prisoners of war, which was uncommon in other parts of the world. His combat command location at the center of conflict won him the admiration of his troops, but often kept him away from headquarters, where decisions were made. As news of the Afrika Korps' victories reached Germany, Rommel became a hero in his own country. Hitler publicized Rommel's accomplishments, using Rommel as a popular figure to promote the overall war effort. This was "safe" for Hitler as Rommel had no political ambitions and therefore posed no threat to Hitler's power. In June 1942 Rommel was promoted to field marshal, making him the youngest officer to reach the highest rank within the German military. Upon hearing of his promotion, Rommel commented he would have preferred deployment of another division to assist him in fighting the British.

As 1942 progressed, the British began to improve their position and performance in North Africa, due partly to the dynamic leadership of General Bernard Montgomery. Rommel was unable to get the supplies, equipment, and troops he needed to take the Suez Canal, and the Afrika Korps lost several battles against the British 8th Army. A pivotal defeat occurred at El Alamein, located a few hundred miles west of Cairo, Egypt; as a result, Rommel's troops were driven back 2,000 miles across the desert to Tunisia. With the March 1943 loss at Medenine against American troops led by General Dwight D. Eisenhower, the Germans had to accept defeat in North Africa. By that time, Rommel had developed stomach and other health problems and had left the country to seek medical treatment in Germany.

Further Military Service in Europe

After Rommel recovered from his illness, he was sent to northern Italy to assist Benito Mussolini against the Allies—the Allies had invaded Sicily and were making their way onto the Italian mainland. As the troops pushed north, Italian partisans overthrew Mussolini and arrested him. The Germans saved him from the partisans and established him as leader of a new government in northern Italy, which was still under Axis control. By the end of 1943, the Germans were expecting the Allies to launch an invasion of Europe. Now in command of all German troops from the Netherlands to the Loire River in northern France, Rommel took his forces to France in 1944 to prepare for possible invasion.

The Plot to Kill Hitler

As the war raged on and Nazi Germany seemed to have no prospect of beating the Allies, many of Adolf Hitler's former supporters began to think the country would be better off without him. Claus (Schenk Graf) Von Stauffenberg, who had served as a staff officer in the German invasions of Poland, the Netherlands, and France, regarded Hitler as a failure. Born into a wealthy family, Stauffenberg was a devout Catholic horrified by the Nazi brutalities he witnessed. In April 1943 Stauffenberg was serving with a tank division in North Africa when the car in which he was traveling came under fire. He was seriously wounded, losing his left eye, his right hand, and two fingers on his left hand. While recovering in a German hospital, he decided that Hitler must be swiftly executed. He and other officers conspired in a plot to assassinate the Nazi leader.

Stauffenberg and his co-conspirators planned the assassination for July 20, 1944. Hitler was hosting a military conference at one of his headquarters, called Wolf's Lair. When Stauffenberg arrived at the conference, he was carrying a captured British time bomb, fitted with a triggering device, in his briefcase. Stauffenberg armed the bomb just before entering the conference room. Claiming he had poor hearing, he requested a seat close to Hitler. He then placed the briefcase six feet from Hitler before excusing himself to make a phone call. He fled to his car and was headed for the airport when he heard the bomb explode. Stauffenberg was unaware, however, that after he left, someone moved his briefcase away from Hitler, causing the explosion to kill four other men while only slightly injuring Hitler. After reaching his Berlin headquarters, Stauffenberg learned that Hitler was not dead. He tried to convince other army officers to overthrow Hitler, but they refused. Stauffenberg and several others were soon arrested and taken to Hitler's military headquarters. In a courtyard, lit only by truck headlights, they were executed by firing squad.

Rommel believed the secret to repulsing an Allied attack was to ambush the troops as soon as they landed, while others thought that more troops should be placed inland to catch the Allied forces as they moved into the French countryside. Hitler insisted on an assimilation of the two ideas. Rommel was able to establish a few defenses on the beaches where the Germans thought the Allies might try to invade. Rommel used defenses such as underwater explosives and devices called "Rommel's asparagus"—stakes driven in to the ground, draped with barbed wire and land mines—to prevent Allied boats and airplanes from landing safely. On June 6, 1944, the massive Allied D-Day invasion began with the landing of 155,000 troops on the beaches of Normandy in northern France. After the successful landing, Rommel realized that Germany could not win the war. Upon being informed of the concentration camps Hitler had established in Europe, Rommel met with Hitler, urging him to close the camps and take other measures to improve Germany's chances of winning the war. Hitler refused to listen, leaving Rommel disillusioned and bitter.

On July 17 Rommel was traveling along a French road when his car was machine-gunned by a British warplane. The driver was killed and Rommel received a skull fracture. He was unconscious for a week and was flown home to Germany to recover. Meanwhile, a group of German officers who were unhappy with Hitler's leadership made a plan to assassinate him. Due to his outspoken denunciation of Hitler's actions, Rommel was suspected of being involved in the bomb plot, even though he had been lying unconscious in a hospital bed at the time. Rommel may have known about the plot but probably had no active involvement; he had advocated the arrest and trial of Hitler, not assassination. Rommel was summoned to Nazi headquarters in Berlin on October 7, 1944. Convinced that his life was in danger, he stayed home.

On October 14 two Nazi generals arrived at Rommel's house and asked to speak to him privately. Afterward Rommel said good-bye to his wife and son, telling them that within fifteen minutes, he would be dead. The generals had delivered a message from Hitler stating that Rommel was to make a choice: He could either commit suicide or go before the Nazi "people's court" to face charges of being involved in the assassination plot. If he chose suicide, Rommel's family would not be harmed. Rommel left with the generals. Fifteen minutes later, his wife, Lucie, received a phone call informing her that Rommel had died of a heart attack. Hitler, worried about public reaction, announced that Rommel had died of his war wounds. Rommel was given a grand state funeral with fine speeches and stirring music. Rommel's wife, finding the ordeal unbearable, refused Hitler's offer to establish a memorial in her husband's honor.

Sources

Books

Blanco, Richard L., *Rommel, the Desert Warrior: The Afrika Korps in World War II,* J. Messner (New York), 1982.

Douglas-Home, Charles, *Rommel,* introduction by Lord Chalfont, Weidenfeld and Nicolson (London), 1974.

Fraser, David, *Knight's Cross: A Life of Field Marshal Erwin Rommel* HarperCollins (New York), 1993.

Irving, David, *The Trail of the Fox,* Dutton (New York), 1977.

Mitcham, Samuel W., Jr., *Triumphant Fox: Erwin Rommel and the Rise of the Afrika Korps,* Cooper Square Press (New York), 2000.

Rommel, Erwin, *Rommel: In His Own Words,* Pimlott, John, editor, Stackpole Books (Mechanicsburg, PA), 1994.

Young, Desmond, *Rommel,* with a foreward by Sir Claude Auchinleck, Collins (London), 1950.

Franklin D. Roosevelt

Considered one of America's greatest leaders, Franklin D. Roosevelt was the only U.S. president to be elected to four terms. Both beloved and controversial, he took office during a turbulent period in American history. The Great Depression, an economic recession that affected most of the world, resulted in widespread unemployment, bankruptcy, and doubts about the future of democracy in the United States. Roosevelt reacted by implementing the "New Deal," a set of programs and reforms, many of which have survived to the present day. Though elements of his institutionalized reforms were unsuccessful, Roosevelt's commitment to maintaining a democratic form of government inspired many Americans to support his platforms. He led the country through World War II, all the while assuring citizens that sacrifices were necessary to halt the Axis powers, who were seeking world domination.

Born January 30, 1882
    Hyde Park, New York, United States
Died April 12, 1945
    Warm Springs, Georgia, United States

Thirty-second president of the United States

"The only thing we have to fear is fear itself."

Dedicated to Public Service

Born on his wealthy family's estate in Hyde Park, New York, in 1882, Franklin Delano Roosevelt was the only child of Sara Delano and James Roosevelt. He was a distant cousin of Theodore Roosevelt, who was to serve as U.S. president from 1901 to 1909. Franklin had a close relationship with his mother, but his father (twenty-six years his mother's senior) was often ill and emotionally distant. Roosevelt led a sheltered, pleasant child-

(Franklin D. Roosevelt Library)

hood. He was tutored at home and frequently accompanied his parents on trips to Europe. At the age of fourteen Roosevelt went to the Groton School in Massachusetts, an elite academy noted for its emphasis on public service, which Roosevelt took seriously. In 1900 Roosevelt entered Harvard University to study history and government. He was not an outstanding student, focusing instead on social activities such as serving as editor in chief of the *Harvard Crimson*, the university's undergraduate newspaper.

During his years at Harvard, Roosevelt developed leadership abilities and strong political beliefs. In his senior year he became engaged to his distant cousin Eleanor, the niece of Theodore Roosevelt. Despite his mother's efforts to discourage the wedding, the couple married on March 17, 1905, with Eleanor's famous uncle walking her down the aisle. During their marriage, Eleanor would prove to be an asset to her husband's career as well as an exceedingly accomplished woman in her own right. Over the years, the Roosevelts would have six children (one of whom died in infancy). After graduating from Harvard, Roosevelt attended Columbia University Law School in New York. In 1907 he joined a New York law firm, leaving in 1910 after becoming the first Democratic senator elected to the New York Senate in fifty years. As a senator, Roosevelt worked to reduce corruption in government.

In the presidential election of 1912, Roosevelt supported the Democratic candidate, Woodrow Wilson, even though Wilson was running against Theodore Roosevelt. After Wilson's victory, Roosevelt was appointed assistant secretary of the navy, a position he held throughout World War I (1914–1918) and which allowed him to acquire valuable political skills. At the 1920 Democratic convention, Roosevelt was nominated to be the vice presidential candidate under James M. Cox, who was seeking the presidency. Although Cox lost the election to Republican Warren G. Harding, the campaign provided Roosevelt with experience in running for office and public speaking. After the election, he returned to New York to practice law. A year later, while vacationing at his family's summer home on Campobello Island near New Brunswick, Canada, Roosevelt contracted polio. As a result, his legs were paralyzed and movement was limited in his back, arms, and hands.

At first Roosevelt was deeply depressed by his illness, but eventually he regained a positive outlook. His mother believed he should retire, but

Eleanor convinced him to continue in public service. Through a program of vigorous exercise, Roosevelt overcame the partial paralysis of his back, arms, and hands, eventually gaining enough strength to walk occasionally with the aid of canes and braces. For the rest of his life, he spent a majority of his time in a wheelchair. The public remained largely unaware of this fact because the press published photographs that showed Roosevelt standing or sitting behind a desk. In some respects, Roosevelt's condition was beneficial, as it helped him develop patience and self-control, increasing his awareness of problems suffered by other people. Roosevelt was often admired for his courageous manner of dealing with his physical challenges. For instance, at the 1924 Democratic convention, he made his way to the podium supported by his sixteen-year-old son James, receiving a standing ovation from the audience.

A New Deal for America

With Eleanor's help, Roosevelt remained politically connected during his recovery, and also maintained his interest in social problems. In 1928 he won the governorship of New York in a close election. The onset of the Great Depression followed the next year when the stock market crashed, plummeting millions into unemployment, bankruptcy, and despair. Faced with a high unemployment rate in his state, Roosevelt established a system of direct relief for workers who had lost their jobs. His popularity soared and he was reelected in 1930, gaining a nationwide reputation as a leader with bold new ideas. During the first years of the depression, Roosevelt was mentioned as a possible presidential candidate, and in 1932 he was nominated by the Democratic Party. He broke a long-standing tradition by traveling to the convention to accept the nomination in person. In his acceptance speech, he promised the delegates a "new deal" for American citizens. This new deal would include both direct financial relief and reform measures to prevent future economic depressions.

During the presidential campaign, Roosevelt appeared in thirty-eight states, dispelling any concerns about his physical health. He won a substantial victory over incumbent president Herbert Hoover, whom many Americans blamed for the country's problems, and was inaugurated on March 4, 1933. Prior to being sworn into office, Roosevelt began to assess the nation's problems, which included approximately 15 million unem-

The Roosevelt family estate in Hyde Park, New York. (Library of Congress)

ployed workers—one-quarter of the work force. Numerous banks had closed, causing many people to lose their life savings. An overwhelming number of people were homeless, with charities unable to feed or house a majority of them. Young people lacked the funds to attend or finish college, and many of them took to the roads looking for work. After evaluating the situation, Roosevelt concluded that the government should assume responsibility for solving these problems.

A Popular President

In his first inaugural address, Roosevelt promised Americans that the country would recover from hard times. Pledging he would find new solutions to social problems, he urged people to remain calm and courageous. In now-famous words, he announced: "The only thing we have to fear is fear itself." Roosevelt immediately inspired confidence by sharing his own hope and optimism. His willingness to give the federal government a larger role in American life made him different from previous presidents and he gained the support of a wide range of citizens, including farmers, poor and middle-class city dwellers, and labor union members. Many African Americans even

switched their loyalty from the Republicans—the party of Abraham Lincoln—to support Roosevelt.

The new president's popularity was partly the result of his excellent communication skills. He promoted good relations with reporters by holding two press conferences a week and making transcripts of the meetings available to the public. One of Roosevelt's major accomplishments was understanding the power of radio and the central role it played in American homes. Each week he made a radio broadcast called a "Fireside Chat," in which he established a sense of intimacy by addressing his listeners as "my friends" and conveyed an informal, relaxed manner while discussing important issues.

Roosevelt's first term as president began with a special 100-day session of Congress, which passed an unusually high number of measures. Roosevelt declared a "bank holiday," temporarily closing all banks to provide relief for financial institutions and panicked investors. He then pushed through a law that permitted the reopening of only the most financially stable banks and later established the Federal Deposit Insurance Corporation, which protected bank deposits up to $5,000. Roosevelt tackled the problem of unemployment by implementing programs such as the Civilian Conserva-

"First Lady of the World" Eleanor Roosevelt

Prior to Franklin D. Roosevelt, the United States had never had a president who served four terms, nor had the nation experienced a politically active first lady like Eleanor Roosevelt. Born into a wealthy family in 1884 in New York City, she was the niece of Theodore Roosevelt, who was president of the United States from 1901 to 1909. She was an awkward and shy girl, who became lonely after both her parents died before she was ten. At age eighteen, like all wealthy young women, she was required to enter society by attending parties and dances. This painful prospect was eased by the attentions of her fifth cousin, Franklin Delano Roosevelt, who was a student at Harvard University. The two fell in love and were married on March 17, 1905. Their first child was born a year later, and over the next nine years they had five more children, including one who died in infancy.

In the summer of 1921, Franklin contracted polio, which paralyzed his legs and endangered his political career. Political adviser Louis Howe suggested that Eleanor become more active in public life so that her husband would not be forgotten during his recovery. She soon became a leader in the Democratic Party. While maintaining her husband's political connections, Eleanor was also able to establish a name for herself. Increasingly concerned about the problems of the disadvantaged, she wrote newspaper articles, started a special school for poor children, and helped set up a furniture factory for unemployed workers. When Franklin was elected governor of New York, Eleanor traveled around the state and reported back to him on the conditions of the general public.

After Franklin was elected to his first term as president in 1932, Eleanor began earning a reputation as the most active, outspoken first lady in American history. She was passionate about civil rights, continually encouraging her husband to consider equal opportunities for African Americans in his New Deal programs. In 1939 she resigned her membership in the Daughters of the American Revolution (DAR) when the organization would not permit Marian Anderson, an African American opera singer, to appear at Constitution Hall in Philadelphia. Eleanor then arranged for Anderson to give a concert at the

tion Corps, which put 2.5 million young men to work in parks and forests; the National Youth Administration, which gave part-time work to 2 million high school and college students; and the Works Progress Administration, which employed 8 million people in the building of roads, schools, dams, and other projects. Roosevelt passed the Agricultural Adjustment Act to help farmers increase their income by reducing surpluses and raising prices. He also implemented the Tennessee Valley Authority to build dams for flood control and to produce low-cost electricity.

In 1936 Roosevelt ran for president against Governor Alf Landon of Kansas, winning by a landslide—gaining sixty-one percent of the popular vote. At the beginning of his second term, he was criticized for reorganizing the U.S. Supreme Court, which had opposed a number of his New Deal measures. Soon after his reelection, the Supreme Court approved a number of important programs, including the National Labor Relations (Wagner) Act, which guaranteed workers the right to join unions; the Social Security Act, which offered citizens protection from poverty in old age, sickness, and unemployment; and the Fair Labor Standards Act, which established a minimum wage for workers. Roosevelt was criticized by some business leaders and Republicans, who claimed his policies were wasteful and gave the government too large a role in people's lives. Roosevelt became even less popular when he cut government spending, producing another economic downturn and the loss of approximately two million jobs. Despite these set-

After her husband's death in 1945, Eleanor Roosevelt continued to play a public role in American life. (Franklin D. Roosevelt Library)

Lincoln Memorial in Washington. She also encouraged women to fight for their rights, establishing the White House Women's Press Corps. Since only women reporters were allowed to attend her press conferences, newspapers were forced to hire at least one woman.

Having witnessed the devastating effects of World War I, Eleanor was a staunch promoter of international peace. During World War II she made several goodwill tours as her husband's representative in England, the South Pacific, and the Caribbean. After Franklin died in 1945, Eleanor continued to play a role in American public life. She was appointed a member of the first U.S. delegation to the newly formed United Nations by President Harry Truman, who called her the "First Lady of the World." Eleanor was instrumental in writing the United Nations Declaration on Human Rights and took part in the formation of UNICEF, the U.N.'s fund for children. She continued to write articles and books and remained involved in Democratic politics. She died in 1962.

backs, his supporters continued to credit him with making improvements in the economy and maintaining calm during the escalating war in Europe.

Democracy and Dictators

Roosevelt was well aware that Nazi dictator Adolf Hitler, Italian fascist leader Benito Mussolini, and Japanese military leader Hideki Tōjō were gaining power through the restriction of civilian freedom. Roosevelt advocated American involvement in the war, but the American public was still recovering from World War I and wished to remain isolationist. In 1940 Roosevelt became the first president elected to three terms, a victory he achieved by a slim margin. Despite increasing public resistance, he urged greater assistance to Great Britain and France,

the Allies, in the war against the Nazis. When France was defeated by the Germans in May 1940, Great Britain was left to face the Germans alone. Roosevelt persuaded Congress to approve a program whereby the United States gave Great Britain fifty destroyers in exchange for American use of British naval bases close to the United States.

As Great Britain withstood months of heavy German bombing raids, Roosevelt continued to promote support for the Allies. He pushed through a law setting up the Lend-Lease Program, through which supplies and weapons sent from the United States to those fighting against the Axis nations could be paid for after the war. In August 1941 Roosevelt met with British Prime Minister Winston Churchill to sign the Atlantic Charter, an agree-

Winston Churchill, Roosevelt, and Joseph Stalin at the Yalta Conference in the Soviet Union, 1945, where the leaders discussed how to bring the war to a close. (National Archives and Records Administration)

ment in which Great Britain and the United States expressed their common opposition to tyranny and their commitment to establishing an international peace-keeping organization. In the meantime, Japan was attacking China and other areas of Asia that had been controlled by Great Britain and France. In an effort to halt Japanese aggression, Roosevelt ceased trade relations with Japan. In retaliation, Japan launched a devastating surprise attack on the U.S. naval base at Pearl Harbor, Hawaii, on December 7, 1941, sinking and damaging battleships and killing more than 2,400 people. Referring to December 7 as "a date which will live in infamy," Roosevelt signed a declaration of war against the Japanese the next day. A few days later, under the provisions of the Tripartite Pact, Ger-

many and Italy declared war on the United States. Just as Roosevelt had rallied Americans to overcome the Great Depression, he now called upon them to resist military aggression and dictatorship.

Preparing the Nation for War

During the early months of the war, Roosevelt assembled a team of top-ranking generals and admirals to lead the U.S. war effort while he presided over important strategic decisions. He began to prepare the U.S. economy for war, starting agencies to handle such tasks as processing recruits into the armed forces and producing weapons, tanks, and other equipment needed by the military. Upon learning of Nazi efforts to build an atomic bomb, Roosevelt started the Manhattan Project, which coordinated the efforts of leading scientists to produce nuclear weapons. He also persuaded twenty-six countries to join the United Nations. Although Roosevelt and his military commanders thought the Allies should first invade Europe and attack Germany on its own soil, they were finally persuaded by the British to attack first in North Africa, where British troops had been battling the Afrika Korps under the able command of German General Erwin Rommel. The Allies also invaded Sicily and pushed their way into Italy. In the Pacific theater of the war, which involved only fifteen percent of Allied resources, Allied forces fought their way through vast island chains toward Japan.

The Allies carried out a successful military campaign in Europe, defeating the Germans in Sicily and Italy, as well as in North Africa. On another front, the Soviet Union was reeling from a German invasion that had taken place in June 1941, resulting in the loss of approximately 20 million Soviet lives. Despite this immense devastation, the Soviet army had prevented the Germans from overtaking the entire country. Soviet leader Joseph Stalin, who had used brutal policies against his own people, joined Roosevelt and Churchill at several major conferences. At Casablanca in early 1943, Roosevelt and other Allied officials declared that they would accept only "unconditional surrender" by the Axis nations. In August 1943, at another conference in Quebec, they began planning a massive invasion to liberate France, called Operation Overlord, which was to take place the following spring.

After six months of preparation under the direction of U.S. General Dwight D. Eisenhower, Operation Overlord, popularly known as D-Day, was staged on June 6, 1944. Approximately 155,000 Allied troops landed on the heavily defended beaches of the Normandy region in northern France. Within a month a million soldiers were pushing across France toward Germany, stopped only briefly by a German counteroffensive (called the Battle of the Bulge) in December in the Ardennes region. In March 1945, the Allies crossed the Rhine River into Germany and by May the Germans were forced to surrender.

In November 1944 Roosevelt had been elected to a fourth term as U.S. president. By now the massive spending of the wartime period had eradicated the Great Depression and many of Roosevelt's New Deal reforms had been eliminated. Most Americans appreciated the president's strong leadership during the crisis of World War II. His critics claimed he had made some serious mistakes, including relocating Japanese Americans to internment camps, not ordering desegregation of the military, not providing enough assistance to Jewish refugees, and even allowing the Japanese to attack Pearl Harbor. In February 1945 Roosevelt traveled to a conference at Yalta in the Soviet Union, where Allied leaders discussed methods for ending the war and beginning the recovery of Europe. Critics later faulted Roosevelt for placing too much trust in Stalin and giving the Soviet Union control of Eastern Europe. At the time, however, Roosevelt believed the measures were necessary to ensure that the Soviet Union would continue to support the Allies.

After returning from Yalta, Roosevelt went to Warm Springs, Georgia, where he owned a small home and had established a foundation to help polio victims. Plagued by heart problems and other ailments, Roosevelt died from a cerebral hemorrhage on April 12, 1945. Later the same day, Vice President Harry S Truman was sworn in as the nation's thirty-third president, left with the responsibility of leading the nation out of war and into peacetime. Thousands of Americans gathered along the railroad tracks as Roosevelt's body was taken by train from Georgia to New York. He was buried on the grounds of his estate at Hyde Park under a simple headstone that bore his name and the dates of his birth and death.

SOURCES

Books

Davis, Kenneth S., *FDR: Into the Storm, 1937–1940,* Random House (New York), 1993.

Freedman, Russell, *Franklin Delano Roosevelt,* Clarion Books (New York), 1990.

Freidel, Frank Burt, *Franklin Delano Roosevelt: A Rendezvous with Destiny,* Little, Brown (Boston), 1972.

Goodwin, Doris Kearns, *No Ordinary Time: Franklin and Eleanor Roosevelt: The Home Front in World War II,* Simon & Schuster (New York), 1994.

Heinrichs, Waldo H., *Franklin Delano Roosevelt and the American Entry into World War II,* Oxford University Press (Oxford), 1988.

Morgan, Ted, *FDR: A Biography,* Simon & Schuster (New York), 1985.

Potts, Steve, *Franklin D. Roosevelt: A Photo-Illustrated Biography,* Bridgestone Books (Mankato, MN), 1996.

We Can Do It!

WAR PRODUCTION CO-ORDINATING COMMITTEE

"Rosie the Riveter"

Millions of American and British women went to work during World War II, providing much-needed wartime labor

"… [W]hen a big four-motored, double-ruddered airplane flies overhead … we say … 'That's a Liberator!' Maybe it's one we helped to build."

—CONSTANCE BOWMAN

(National Archives and Records Administration)

Although there were exceptions, the people doing the actual fighting in World War II were predominantly men. Back on the home fronts of the Allied countries, the result of this lack of manpower was a rise in "womanpower." Women had to take over many of the tasks that had previously been done by men as well as new tasks created by the war, all the while keeping wartime economies going. The epitome of the woman worker was "Rosie the Riveter," a composite of all women's efforts.

A Labor Crisis

When the Japanese bombed Pearl Harbor in December 1941, the United States needed to meet the demands of war head on. In the first eight days after war was declared, the U.S. Navy gained more than 11,000 recruits. Thousands of men joined other branches of the services as well, and throughout the war, more than10 million men were drafted. Such a huge military demand drained the labor force.

The war itself also created a heightened need for workers to supply ordnance for the war, such as munitions, planes, and ships. Donald Nelson, head of the War Production Board, said, "For nine years before Pearl Harbor, Germany, Italy and Japan prepared intensively for the war, while as late as 1940 the war production of peaceful America was virtually nothing. Yet two years later the output of our

One Woman's Experience

In 1941 Nathalie "Nat" Engdahl was a twenty-six-year-old wife and mother of two young children living in York, Pennsylvania. Her husband, James ("Jim"), owned and operated a small machine shop. During World War II, demand for machinery needed to supply American troops soared, and Jim Engdahl received a draft deferment so that Engdahl Machine & Tool, Co. could produce small tools for repairing airplanes and presser feet for sewing machines, needed to make military uniforms.

Jim sometimes worked twelve hours a day, seven days a week. In an unpublished autobiography, Nat Engdahl explains how she also helped out in the shop, running a lathe, milling machine, or drill press, with her two sons riding tricycles around the machines as she worked. Her husband set up a lathe and drill press in the cellar of the couple's home so that Engdahl could also work when she was unable to come to the shop.

When Engdahl was not doing machine work, she was participating in the same activities as many other American women. She would pick up yarn at the Red Cross and knit mittens, stockings, caps, scarves, and blankets for the soldiers. Engdahl's family, like most of the other families in York, had a plot of land that served as a victory garden to provide food beyond that allowed by rationing. The garden had to be tended and the food harvested, and then cooked or preserved to be eaten later. The entire family, including the two young children, helped out with the garden.

"I just needed to help out because they were so busy; it was hard to get help because all the young men were at war," said Engdahl in a 1999 interview with Patricia Poist-Reilly of the *York Dispatch.* "Everybody was working at the time, it was the patriotic thing to do."

war factories equaled that of the three Axis nations combined." From 1940 on, the federal government and private industry combined to create an unprecedented surge in production. Many commercial companies received defense contracts. For instance, the H. J. Heinz company of Pittsburgh, Pennsylvania, best known for its ketchup and relishes, began making airplane parts, and Kleenex began making machine-gun mounts. Construction companies were commissioned to build military camps, hospitals, shipyards, and munitions plants. Men who worked in vital military industry positions received draft deferments, but when millions of workers left their jobs to become soldiers, America found itself with a dangerous labor shortage on its hands.

American Women Go to Work

As it was necessary that these jobs be filled, women stepped up to the challenge. During the Great Depression, when jobs were scarce, many companies actively discriminated against women in their hiring practices. Once the war began, the government considered passing measures drafting women into the work force. Though these measures were defeated, millions of women voluntarily entered both the armed forces and the labor force, encouraged to do so by an intense government-sponsored propaganda campaign. One poster, featuring an attractive young woman on a motorcycle, declared, "This Is No Time To Be Frail! … The dainty days are done for the duration."

Female participation in the American labor force increased significantly between 1941 and 1945. During the war years, approximately 6 million women went to work. The average American work week increased about 24 percent between 1939 and 1943. Unemployment virtually disappeared in the early 1940s, and worker productivity rose.

Some women took on jobs in such previously male-dominated domains as meat-packing and metal-smelting. In New Hampshire, the U.S.

The Petticoat Army

In May 1942 registration opened for the newly created United States Women's Army Auxiliary Corps (WAAC). On the first day of registration at Fort Des Moines, Iowa, an enlisted man was assigned to administer smelling salts—to help the recruits through the enlistment and inoculation process. His services were not required.

More than 13,000 women volunteers showed up at Fort Des Moines that day, and eventually more than 60,000 women served in the WAC (the word "Auxiliary" was dropped from the title in 1943). They underwent rigorous boot camp training similar to that of enlisted men, although there were no weapons drills, and the women were never assigned to combat duty. They repaired trucks, deciphered Morse code, served as combat nurses, and acted as couriers and chauffeurs with the motor pool. Although the WAC was never large, its members were so useful in freeing male soldiers for the front lines that soon other branches of the service were allowing women to take support roles. Women pilots served in the WAFS, the Women's Auxiliary Ferrying Squadron, and the WASPs (Women's Airforce Service Pilots). The WAVES were Women Accepted for Volunteer Emergency Service. And the Coast Guard auxiliary was called SPARS, a contraction of *semper paratus,* Latin for "always ready."

The women in service were not widely accepted. The WACs and other auxiliary corps members were soon stereotyped as either brazen strumpets or lesbians. In 1942 the *Miami News* compared military women to "the naked Amazons ... and the queer damozels of the isle of Lesbos." However, Colonel Don C. Faith of Fort Des Moines said, "They're a damn sight better than we ever expected they would be. I honestly didn't believe they could do it."

Department of Agriculture hired women to work in a sawmill. At the Mellon Institute of Industrial Research in Pittsburgh, the number of women chemists on the staff increased 500 percent. Perhaps the most famous incursions of women into men's sacred domain were the women's professional baseball teams. However, for the most part, the work women took on fell into two major categories: office jobs and munitions. As the *Oxford Companion to World War II* argues, the image of Rosie the Riveter doing traditionally male work was a propaganda device. The real Rosies either did traditional women's work, like assembling radios, or else they did new sorts of jobs that no one had ever done before. For example, they riveted airplanes or welded the hulls of ships. Many of the positions in the military industry being filled by women workers had not previously been filled by men simply because such positions had never before existed.

Women flocked to the munitions jobs in particular, in part out of patriotism, and in part because these jobs usually paid better. For instance, women taking on the dangerous job of manufacturing anti–tank ammunition could expect to be paid 40 percent more than women in other factories. Hundreds of laundries went out of business in the 1940s because so many women employees left for more profitable war work. Munitions work paid better because it was dangerous. Women workers were exposed to the extreme heat of welding arcs, heights, heavy machinery, and explosive chemicals. In 1944 the *New York Times* reported that between the Japanese attack on Pearl Harbor and January 1, 1944, some 37,500 women and men were killed in industrial accidents—7,500 more than were killed in action.

No matter what the job, and no matter how intense wartime demand for labor became, women were almost always paid less than men, in spite of the War Manpower Commission's official policy of equal pay for equal work. According to a newspaper account, the daily wages for apprentices at the U.S. Armory in Springfield, Massachusetts, were as follows: "$5.28 for men, $3.36 for boys, and $3.12 for women."

African-American women went to work as well. Before the war, their only employment opportunities were usually as servants or farm laborers. Even during the war years, many employers did not want to hire them. Most companies hired white women first, then African-American men, then African-American women. African-American women often found themselves in the dirtiest, most difficult, and most dangerous jobs—ones that no one else wanted to do. Nevertheless, as one African-American woman reported, "The war made me live better, it really did. My sister always said that Hitler was the one that got us out of the white folks' kitchens."

Great Britain Utilizes Female Workers

Great Britain, beleaguered by savage aerial bombings, was even more effective than the United States at utilizing women in both its workforce and its armed forces during World War II. In 1939, some 5 million British women were employed; by 1943, that number had jumped to 7.75 million. In March 1941 a law was passed that allowed women to be directed into war work. In December of that year another piece of legislation allowed single women between the ages of twenty and thirty to be conscripted. Between 1942 and 1945, 125,000 women were given the choice of working in British women's auxiliary services, civil defense, industry, or the Women's Land Army (WLA).

The WLA was designed to provide crucial agricultural and forestry workers in Britain. It had first been created during World War I, and was reestablished in 1939 to accomplish the same function during World War II. At its height, the WLA had over 80,000 members (not counting part-time workers), both voluntary and drafted. The women did work such as cultivating, planting, and harvesting crops, or cutting timber needed for the war effort. In 1939 there were 55,000 "Land Girls" in Great Britain; in 1944 the number had risen to 229,000, a jump of more than 400 percent.

By December 1942, approximately 300,000 British families were living in potentially structurally unsafe houses, and thousands more were homeless and bedded down in subway tunnels. The Women's Voluntary Service (WVS), tried to help before, during, and after air raids by evacuating children and supplying food and clothing to those rendered homeless by the bombing. At its height, the WVS had an all-volunteer membership in the hundreds of thousands.

With so many men away fighting the war, American farms faced a shortage of workers. If farms failed to produce sufficient crops, the country would experience a severe food shortage. The government put out a call for help and established the Women's Land Army. A similar program existed in England, where female farmers were called "Land Girls." (Library of Congress)

The Domestic Front

For the first time in history, many of the American and British women entering the work force were married or had children. These wives and mothers had concerns that their single compatriots did not share, such as child care. A few companies, like Kaiser Industries in Oregon, built day care centers for employees' children, and the federal government also built some child-care centers, but these efforts were not sufficient to meet the demand. Many groups of women made arrangements to work in shifts, taking care of one another's children during their off hours.

The war also changed the lives of homemakers as radically as it did the lives of their working and fighting peers. Rationing put strict controls on food and other resources available to stay-at-home women, and drives were held constantly to find resources, such as scrap metal, to support the war industry. A moratorium went into effect on the

Women donned clothing traditionally considered to be men's attire, to work in factory jobs. Some women experienced discrimination because they dared to wear trousers. (Reproduced by permission of Corbis-Bettman)

production of durable goods like cars, appliances, and houses. Despite the new opportunities for women in the workforce, the prevailing attitude at the time was that women should remain at home and raise the children, while men were responsible for bringing home the paycheck. Still, the role of housekeeper was given enormous importance even in times of labor shortage. The *Oxford Companion to World War II* cites this comment from the magazine *Good Housekeeping*: "If those who keep house went on strike, the war would be lost in a week."

Changing Images of Women

Although women were working in difficult and often dangerous jobs, wearing trousers and heavy-toed boots, their roles were almost invariably presented in the media in a way that reinforced ideas of the traditional, "feminine" roles of women. This reflects the deep discomfort felt in both the United States and Great Britain over the idea of women doing men's jobs. *Life* magazine published a detailed description of a Boeing Aircraft worker named Marguerite Kershner: "Now, at day's end, her hands may be bruised, there's grease under her nails, her makeup is smudged, and her curls out of place. When she checks in the next morning at 6:30

a.m., her hands will be smooth, her nails polished, her makeup and curls in order, for Marguerite is neither drudge nor slave but the heroine of a new order." Close inspection of the famous poster of a female worker, bicep flexed, and topped with the slogan "We Can Do It," shows nail polish, makeup, and plucked eyebrows.

With the end of the war in the summer of 1945, propaganda directed at American women changed. New posters and magazine articles emphasized the desirability of leaving one's job and making a home for the returning soldiers. The October 31, 1944, edition of the Boeing Aircraft newsletter featured an article about a riveter named Lorraine Blum: "'As soon as it's curtains for the Axis, it's going to be lace curtains for me,' says Lorraine. 'I want to establish my own home and stay put.'" The consensus opinion of the propaganda was that the experience gained by women during the war would be most beneficial in marriage and in raising the next generation. Many women agreed and left the work force in droves.

By 1946, over 3 million women had left the workforce. Although many women quit voluntarily, the majority of them had been laid off. Many wanted to continue doing the work they had been trained for—but this was to be impossible. Out-of-work women picketed the Ford plant in Highland Park, Michigan, carrying signs demanding an end to sexual discrimination. It didn't work. Women who wanted to do "men's work" were seen as unpatriotic and unfeminine. Former welders and riveters could only find jobs as typists, laundresses, and grocery clerks.

Although American culture after the war years and throughout the 1950s insisted upon a rigid demarcation between the sexes, there were still more women in the workforce than before the war. The percentage of working women has also steadily increased since 1945, but many of the jobs that were open to women during World War II are still male-dominated.

SOURCES

Books

Bowman, Constance, and Clara Marie Allen, *Slacks and Calluses: Our Summer in a Bomber Factory,* Smithsonian Institution Press (Washington, DC), 1999.

Dear, I. C. B., editor, *The Oxford Companion to World War II,* Oxford University Press (Oxford), 1995.

Kelsey, Marion, *Victory Harvest: Diary of a Canadian in the Women's Land Army,* McGill-Queen's University Press (Montreal), 1997.

Litoff, Judy Barrett, and David C. Smith, *American Women in a World War: Contemporary Accounts from World War II,* Scholarly Resources (Wilmington, DE), 1997.

Lynn, Vera, Robin Cross, and Jenny de Gex, *Unsung Heroines: The Women Who Won the War,* Sidgwick & Jackson (London), 1990.

Nicholson, Mavis, *What Did You Do in the War, Mummy?: Women in World War II,* Chatto & Windus (London), 1995.

Parrish, Thomas, editor, *The Simon and Schuster Encyclopedia of World War II,* Simon and Schuster (New York), 1978.

Pearsall, Phyllis, *Women at War,* Ashgate Editions (Aldershot, Hampshire, UK), 1990.

Weatherford, Doris, *American Women and World War II,* Facts on File (New York), 1990.

Wise, Nancy Baker, and Christy Wise, *A Mouthful of Rivets: Women at Work in World War II,* Jossey-Bass (San Francisco), 1994.

Periodicals

Poist-Reilly, Patricia, "York Plan Known Worldwide," *York Dispatch,* December 27, 1999, p. A1-A4.

Other

Free a Man to Fight!: Women Soldiers of World War II (video), A & E Home Video, 1999.

The Life and Times of Rosie the Riveter (video), Direct Cinema Limited, 1987.

A String of Pearls (video), PBS Video, 1990.

Renée Roth-Hano

Born August 16, 1931
Mulhouse, Alsace, France

Holocaust survivor; writer; psychiatric
social worker; therapist; French Jewish
child hidden by Catholic nuns during
World War II

*"Dear God, you've got to end this
horrible war! What more will it take to
convince you?"*

Renée Roth-Hano was only nine years old when the Germans invaded France, forcing her family to flee from their home in Alsace to Paris, where they lived in constant fear in a cramped apartment. As wartime tensions mounted, Roth-Hano's parents placed their three children in hiding at a women's shelter run by Catholic nuns, where for two years they lived apart from their parents and were reunited only after the end of the war. Roth-Hano wrote about her wartime experiences in *Touch Wood: A Girlhood in Occupied France* (1988), a book for young readers. *Touch Wood* and its sequel *Safe Harbors* (1993), which details Roth-Hano's life since the war, are the primary sources of biographical information about Roth-Hano.

Childhood During Wartime

Roth-Hano was born Renée Roth in 1931, the oldest of three daughters (Renée, Denise, and Liliane, nicknamed Lily) of Oscar and Marguerite Roth. Roth-Hano's father, a tailor, was originally from Poland, and her mother was Hungarian. The elder Hanos, who were Jewish, had left their native lands and settled in Alsace, then a province of eastern France, hoping for the freedom and equality long enjoyed by citizens of that country. Oscar owned a shop and provided a financially stable life for the family. When France fell to the Germans in 1940, Jewish citizens were ordered to leave Alsace.

The area had long been coveted by the Germans, and the Nazis planned to "Germanize" the province. Roth-Hano's immediate family and members of her extended family fled Alsace for a new start in Paris. They had been assured by friends that Paris was safe for Jews and that Oscar would easily find work.

Roth-Hano's account of her childhood begins in August 1940. Her father obtained work in a raincoat factory, and he sometimes brought work home to finish. As living conditions grew steadily worse, Roth-Hano's mother struggled to put food on the table. By the time the family arrived in Paris, some restrictions had already been placed on Jews, and conditions only worsened over the next two years. Jews were forbidden to own radios, they could not speak to non-Jews on the street, and their food was rationed. In June 1940 newly passed legislation required Jews to wear identifying yellow stars on their clothing. The stars, patterned after the Star of David religious symbol, exposed Jews to increasing anti-Semitic violence. Only three girls in Roth-Hano's class at school had to wear the stars; Roth-Hano herself felt as though the star physically weighed her down.

Food shortages grew worse as the Nazis used food from conquered lands to feed its own people. Some French citizens blamed Jews for the shortages and came to regard them as "foreign" and "the enemy." To the dismay of the Roths, French police began to carry out German orders to round up and deport their Jewish neighbors, including children. The situation grew so tense that Roth-Hano's aunt, uncle, and two cousins fled Paris. By chance, Roth-Hano's mother made the acquaintance of a Roman Catholic nun who offered to take the girls in if the situation became more dangerous. In July 1941 Roth-Hano's parents decided to accept this offer.

Sheltered by Catholic Nuns

Sister Pannelay, the mother superior of La Chaumière, a Catholic women's shelter, took the girls into the facility, despite potential danger to herself. Located in Normandy, France, on the English Channel, the shelter was occupied primarily by single women commuters in their twenties who lived there during the work week and then returned to nearby small villages and towns on weekends. At first, Roth-Hano and her sisters were the only children at the convent, but the nuns then began to take in groups of orphans from Paris for weeks during the summer. As the war progressed, the

Restrictions Vexing to a Child

As a child sheltered by nuns during World War II, Renée Roth-Hano did not have to endure as severe a reality as many other European victims of the war. Nevertheless, lack of freedom, daily humiliation, and outright fear for herself and those around her took their toll on the child. The curfews kept her from visiting friends and made her a virtual prisoner in her home. She and other Jews had to ride on the last car of the train. They were not allowed to attend movies or shop in certain areas; in time they were allowed to leave their houses for only an hour a day. In the end, the Roths were afraid to stay home at night for fear the French police would take them away, as they had thousands of others. They took to splitting up and sleeping at the homes of various neighbors. As the situation grew increasingly desperate, Oscar and Marguerite Roth made the decision to break up the family.

nuns also sheltered Jewish families with children. In the beginning, Roth-Hano and her sisters lived quite comfortably in the strange surroundings. They were treated kindly and fed well, but missed their parents. The girls attended a local Catholic school, where they received gold medals for excellence in their studies. To conceal their identity as Jews, they tried to blend in with the local girls by attending religious services. In late 1942, as German soldiers neared Normandy, it was decided the girls should be baptized in the Catholic faith.

Roth-Hano's parents had delayed the girls' religious training, reasoning that Jews were having enough trouble simply surviving during the war. Living in La Chaumière, Roth-Hano found herself drawn to many aspects of the Catholic faith, such as reverence for Mary, mother of Jesus. On being baptized a Catholic, Roth-Hano felt torn between

Aristides de Sousa Mendes Saved French Jews

After Adolf Hitler and his Nazi party occupied France, many people tried to escape the country. To leave legally, they needed a visa issued by the country where they planned to settle. In Bordeaux, a French port on the Atlantic coast, thousands of refugees were desperate to obtain these documents so they could board outgoing ships. Aristides de Sousa Mendes, a deeply religious Portuguese Catholic lawyer, was the consul general in Bordeaux at the time. He began to issue huge numbers of Portuguese transit visas to French refugees, including Jews. The Portuguese government formally remained neutral in the war, but was friendly to Germany and forbade Sousa Mendes from issuing further visas. He ignored these orders. From June 17 to June 19, 1940, Sousa Mendes approved 30,000 transit visas, 10,000 of them to Jews.

For these actions and his insubordination, Sousa Mendes was arrested and sent back to Portugal, where he lost his job and his pension, and was barred from practicing law. He died in poverty in 1954. He said that he had disobeyed his government's orders because he acted as a Christian. In fact, some of Sousa Mendes's own ancestors were Portuguese Jews who had been forced to convert to Catholicism in 1497 during the Inquisition.

More than ten years after his death, he was honored by Israel as "Righteous Among the Nations," a non-Jew who had acted to save Jews. In 1987 the Portuguese government officially named him a hero. Sousa Mendes probably saved more Jews from the Holocaust than any single individual except Raoul Wallenberg.

---

her new religion and her Jewish faith. In January 1944 the girls saw their mother for the first time since they had left home. She and their father had since assumed a new, more French-sounding name. As the year went on, Roth-Hano was afflicted with one ailment after another, including jaundice and scabies, some of them caused by lack of proper nutrition. She began to wonder if she and her family would ever escape from the Germans.

On June 6, 1944, American and British troops landed on the beaches of Normandy, France, in an invasion called D-Day, which marked the beginning of the Allied victory in Europe. In the dangerous military chaos, with bombs dropping all around, people fled Paris. The nuns took the Roth sisters and other convent occupants to an abandoned farm some distance outside the city. German soldiers fleeing the Allied troops took shelter nearby. Since food was scarce for everyone—French and German alike—the soldiers struck a bargain with the nuns whereby the nuns would mend their uniforms in exchange for food. This uneasy situation continued for two months until Allied troops arrived and the German soldiers surrendered. Two weeks later, the Roth sisters were reunited with their parents in Paris. Roth-Hano notes in *Touch Wood* that her father had aged and her mother had lost weight. The happiness of the reunion was tempered by Roth-Hano's concern for her parents' health.

Goes to America

When Roth-Hano was nineteen, she went to the United States to serve as governess for a wealthy Jewish family in New York City. Wanting Roth-Hano to embrace her Jewish heritage, her mother adamantly supported her new job. Initially, Roth-Hano continued to feel more comfortable with Catholic rituals, but as time passed, she began to attend a Reform Jewish temple. She married a Parisian, but divorced after six years. She received a master's degree in social work at Hunter College and became a psychiatric social worker, a therapist, and a faculty member at the New York University School of Social Work. In 1968 Roth-Hano married John R. Hano, an accountant. Roth-Hano's mother came to the United States in the early 1960s.

The publication of *Touch Wood* in France caused a sensation among the people of Normandy who had known Roth-Hano and her sisters. One of them was Sister Madeleine Malolepszy, a nun at La Chaumière who had been especially kind. In 1993 Sister Madeleine was awarded the Medal of the Righteous Gentiles by Yad Vashem, the Martyrs' and Heroes' Remembrance Authority in Jerusalem. It honors the "Righteous Among the Nations," non-Jews who put their own lives in danger to help Jews.

SOURCES

Books

Roth-Hano, Renée, *Safe Harbors,* Four Winds Press (New York), 1993.

Roth-Hano, Renée, *Touch Wood: A Girlhood in Occupied France,* Puffin Books (New York), 1989.

Oskar Schindler

Born April 28, 1908
Zwittau, Austria-Hungary
Died October 9, 1974
Frankfurt, Germany

Nazi spy; factory owner; salesman; farmer; saved 1,200 Jews from death at the hands of the Nazis

"I just couldn't stand by and see people destroyed. I did ... what my conscience told me I must do."

(Prof. Leoppold Pfeffergerg-Page/ USHMM Photo Archives)

Oskar Schindler has been described as a benefactor of slave labor, a crook, an alcoholic, and a womanizer. Yet this wealthy factory owner took on the mission of protecting as many Jews as possible from death at the hands of the Nazis. A luxury-loving man, he risked his life and spent his fortune saving the lives of at least 1,100 Jewish people during World War II.

Joins Nazi Party

Oskar Schindler was born in 1908 into a German Catholic family in Zwittau, a small town of the Austro-Hungarian Empire, an area later known as Czechoslovakia. Schindler and his younger sister, Elfriede, were raised by their father, an uneducated man who sold electric motors and battled problems with alcohol; their mother died when Schindler was young. His parents emphasized their German heritage at home, where only German was to be spoken, so Schindler grew up identifying himself as German. While working in the family business, Schindler met twenty-year-old Emilie Pelzl in 1927 in a small town where he was selling electric motors. They were married the following year. In 1935 Schindler took a job as sales manager for an electrical engineering firm in a small Czechoslovakian town, where he joined the Nazi party. Emilie Schindler later wrote: "Not every German was a Nazi ... but the pressure to conform was intense, and very few dared to be themselves. Hitler had been very clear: 'whoever is with me will be able to live in a great Germany. But whoever is against me will find instant death.'" In the mid-1930s Oskar Schindler became a spy for the Germans. In 1939 he was arrested by the Czechs and condemned to death, but soon afterward the Nazis took over Czechoslovakia, which saved his life.

In 1939 the Germans conquered Poland, starting World War II. As Germans rushed into Poland to take over businesses there, Schindler acquired a bankrupt factory that made enamel products. He hired a Jewish accountant named Itzhak Stern. By paying bribes to the right people, Schindler was able to acquire lucrative army contracts, and his factory soon began turning out pots and pans for the German army. In 1940 all the Jews of Kraków, Poland, had been forced to move into a ghetto. Most of the Jews who lived in this ghetto worked for Schindler, and were marched to and from work under armed guard. Instead of paying wages directly to his Jewish laborers, Schindler was required to give the money to the Schutzstaffel (Security Squad), or SS.

Helps Jewish Employees

It is unclear when Schindler became sympathetic to the plight of the Jews. By the end of his first year in business, Schindler had a work force of about 300, half of them Jews. Herbert Steinhouse, who interviewed Schindler after the war, wrote: "Although [Schindler's Jewish workers] could not understand the reasons, they recognized that [he] was somehow protecting them [from the Nazis]. An air of [partial] security grew in the factory and the men soon sought permission to bring in families and friends to share in their comparative haven." By the end of 1942, Schindler was employing 370 Jews. He succeeded in protecting his workers by keeping false records. According to Steinhouse: "Old people were recorded as being twenty years younger; children were listed as adults. Lawyers, doctors, and engineers were registered as metalworkers, mechanics, and draughtsmen—all trades considered essential to war production." In late 1941 Schindler was arrested by the SS under the suspicion that he was illegally selling goods, and his account books were examined. Nothing out of the ordinary was found, and he was released.

In February 1943 SS officer Amon Goeth was ordered to clear out the Kraków ghetto and send all healthy workers to the nearby Plaszów labor camp, which he was to head. The night the ghetto was closed, Goeth and his men searched for anyone who might have stayed behind. The 4,000 people they found hiding were executed. Soon after, Goeth held a meeting with major factory owners in the area. When he proposed that all factory work be moved into the Plaszów labor camp, Schindler objected. He was able to convince Goeth to allow his factory to continue operating as usual. From then on, wrote Steinhouse, Schindler began "the conspiring, the string-pulling, the bribery and the shrewd outguessing of Nazi officialdom which finally were to save so many human lives." Schindler told Nazi officials that an increasing amount of work had to be done. Thus he was able to have relatives of his Jewish workers sent to the plant, avoiding their deportation to the Auschwitz concentration camp.

Intervenes to Save Workers

Schindler is said to have been a very charming and witty man. He spent many of his evenings entertaining local SS officers and strengthening his position. As Nazi treatment of the Jews grew more brutal, however, Schindler pretended to be even friendlier with the German soldiers. He began to take more risks to protect his workers. When his two closest associates were placed aboard a train bound for a concentration camp, he went to the station and demanded their return, claiming they were engaged in work that was essential to the war effort. As a result, their lives were saved and they returned to work at the factory.

Schindler then made a bolder move: He bribed Goeth to have a large labor camp built on his factory premises. Called Emalia, Schindler's facility was more luxurious than the typical Nazi labor camp. Although it was surrounded by a nine-foot fence with watchtowers, it contained latrines, barracks, a medical clinic, a dental office, a bath house, a delousing complex, a barber shop, a food store, a laundry, and a guard block. Schindler spent a great deal of his own money on raw materials for Emalia, and he insisted on the ethical treatment of the workers who lived there. Guards were expected to stay in their own areas and not bother the laborers. Workers were given wholesome meals averaging 2,000 calories a day, nearly twice the amount fed to prisoners at Plaszów. When the food supply ran short, Schindler spent his own money to supplement the rations. He also bribed Nazi officials

Schindler (second from right in top row) poses with a group of Jewish survivors he helped save. (Prof. Leoppold Pfeffergerg-Page/USHMM Photo Archives)

to keep the camp from being closed. There were confrontations between the guards and the prisoners. At one point a Nazi guard threatened to shoot an old man who was mourning the loss of his entire family. Schindler quickly offered the soldier a bottle of liquor if he would spare the man. The soldier laughed and agreed to the bargain.

"Schindler's List"

By 1944, Schindler was being forced to give Nazis expensive presents—jewels, caviar, cigarettes, and liquor—in order to retain his Jewish workers. Later that year, the German Army High Command ordered the dismantling of the Emalia camp. Schindler's workers were instructed to return to the Plaszów camp for relocation to Auschwitz, which would mean almost certain death. When Schindler was offered the management of a weapons factory in Czechoslovakia, he and his associates began making the famous

"Schindler's List" of workers who would be needed at the new plant. Among them were more than 1,000 Jews who either worked at the enamel factory or lived in the Plaszów labor camp; the rest were recommended by prominent local residents. Schindler did not have complete control of his list: Somewhere in the Nazi organization, the list was obtained by people who added or removed names for their own financial gain.

As Schindler's new factory was under construction, workers began arriving by train. When one train brought only men, Schindler discovered that female workers and a number of children had been sent to Auschwitz. He then bribed officials with a bag of diamonds to have these people returned to his factory, insisting that he needed the children because their small fingers were better at polishing bomb parts that the new factory was to produce. Once the women and children arrived, they were in such terrible condition that the Schindlers nursed them back to health. The couple lived in fear of what would happen if the Nazis discovered they were providing food and medicine to Jews. Although the Schindlers had been provided with a handsome apartment in the town, they chose to live in the factory so they could intercede if there was trouble. During the seven months of its existence, the factory produced nothing of use to the German army. Schindler claimed that everything turned out by his workers failed quality control tests because of "start-up problems." Although he kept insisting production would improve, it never did. The only weapons Schindler sold were produced by other ammunition makers and passed off as his own.

On May 7, 1945, Schindler heard via British radio that Germany surrendered to the Allies and that the war was to end on midnight of the following day. He had loudspeakers installed in the factory and assembled the workers in the central courtyard to listen to radio speeches. Announcing that the factory would be closed, Schindler told his workers they were free to go wherever they wished. He presented each worker with three yards of fabric and a bottle of vodka, which would be valuable to trade for other items. In return, the workers gave Schindler a letter they had composed in Hebrew describing his good deeds. They told him he might need it for his defense if he were to be captured and tried by the Allies as a criminal for operating a slave-labor factory. They also presented him a gold ring made from the dental bridgework of a prisoner, which was inscribed with this verse (in Hebrew translation) from the Jewish religious text, the Talmud: "He who saves a single life saves the entire world."

Lost Wealth

The Schindlers fled from the approaching Soviet army and from the Czechs, who were still pursuing Schindler as a spy. After a short stay in Switzerland, the couple moved to a small apartment in the German city of Regensburg, which was under the administration of the Americans. By this time they were no longer wealthy: They had spent an estimated 2 million dollars in their efforts to save their Jewish workers. In order to procure funds, they resold goods provided by relief agencies to needy victims of the war. The Schindlers stayed in Regensburg for five years, all the while trying to obtain visas to leave Germany. In 1949, with the help of Jewish friends, they received two passes on a ship taking refugees to South America.

The Schindlers settled in Argentina, where they worked as caretakers of a house in the area of San

Survivors of the Shoah Visual History Foundation

Jews sometimes refer to the Holocaust by its Hebrew name, Shoah. Filmmaker Steven Spielberg, director of the movie *Schindler's List,* founded the Survivors of the Shoah Visual History Foundation in 1994. Its purpose is to videotape eyewitnesses' accounts of the Holocaust and to develop the largest media archive of survivor testimonies ever assembled. The accounts are being fully catalogued and made available to museums and other educational institutions, using the latest interactive computer technology, books, and CD-ROMs. The archive will be used to educate people all over the world about the Holocaust, and to promote racial, ethnic, and cultural tolerance. The Foundation hopes to help future generations learn the lessons of that period in modern history from those who survived it.

Vicente and raised chickens and hens. After eight years, Schindler decided they could make a better living breeding nutrias (a type of rodent) and selling their fur for coats. In 1958 the German government passed a law allowing compensation to victims of the Nazis who had lost their property during World War II. That spring, Schindler departed Argentina, leaving his wife behind. He collected money from the German government and never returned to South America. When the nutria farm went bankrupt, Schindler's wife was given a house by a Jewish charitable organization. The couple never reunited. Emilie Schindler later wrote a book in which she claimed that her husband worked to keep the Jews out of concentration camps because he was greedy and needed their cheap labor.

Honored for Heroism

Schindler settled in Frankfurt, Germany, where he opened a tile factory backed by loans from the *Schindlerjuden,* an organization made up of people whose lives had been saved by Schindler. This venture, too, eventually ended in bankruptcy. In 1961 Schindler was invited to Israel at the expense of the *Schindlerjuden.* On his fifty-third birthday, the city of Tel Aviv dedicated a plaque to Schindler in the Park of Heroes. Yad Vashem, the Martyrs' and Heroes' Remembrance Authority in Jerusalem, named Schindler "Righteous Among the Nations," a non-Jew who put his own life in peril to help Jews. He also received honors from the Catholic church. By then, Schindler had become an alcoholic and had no source of income. He sold the gold ring given to him by his Jewish workers for liquor. For the rest of his life, he spent six weeks each year in Israel. He lived on funds supplied by the *Schindlerjuden* until 1968, when a group in Tel Aviv petitioned the German government to provide him with a monthly pension. Schindler died in 1974 in Germany while undergoing heart surgery. At his request, he was buried outside the Jewish cemetery in Jerusalem, Israel. In 1993 filmmaker Steven Spielberg released *Schindler's List,* an acclaimed film about Schindler's efforts to save his Jewish workers.

SOURCES

Books

Brecher, Elinor J., *Schindler's Legacy: True Stories of the List Survivors,* Dutton (New York), 1994.

Fensch, Thomas, editor, *Oskar Schindler and His List: The Man, the Book, the Film, the Holocaust and Its Survivors,* with an introduction by Herbert Steinhouse, Paul S. Eriksson (Forest Dale, VT), 1995.

Keneally, Thomas, *Schindler's List,* Wheeler (Hingham, MA), 1982.

Schindler, Emilie, with Erika Rosenberg, *Where Light and Shadow Meet: A Memoir,* translated from the original Spanish by Dolores M. Koch, W. W. Norton & Company (New York), 1997.

Periodicals

Alter, Jonathan, Mark Miller, and Laura Shapiro, "After the Survivors," *Newsweek,* December 20, 1993, p. 116.

Corliss, Richard, "Topping Spielberg's List," *Time,* December 13, 1993, p. 77.

Ottenhoff, John, "Naming the Dead," *Christian Century,* February 16, 1994, p. 172+.

Steinhouse, Herbert, "The Real Oskar Schindler," *Saturday Night,* April 1994, p. 40+.

Hans and
Sophie Scholl

When World War II started in 1939, Hans and Sophie Scholl were university students in Germany. The Scholls were brother and sister, former members of Hitler Youth organizations. They watched in horror as the Germans carried out Hitler's "Final Solution," which involved the total extermination of European Jews. Although the Scholls were not Jewish, they joined a small group of students who demanded passive resistance to the war and the overthrow of Nazi leader Adolf Hitler. For these activities Hans and Sophie were seized by German officials, tried, and beheaded.

Hans and Sophie Reject Nazism

Hans and Sophie Scholl were the second and third of five children of Robert and Magdalene Scholl; they had two sisters, Inge and Elisabeth (Lisel), and a brother, Werner. All the siblings were within about five years of each other in age. The family lived in Ulm, a farming region along the Danube River, where Robert was a tax and business consultant. He had previously served as mayor in several small towns before moving to Ulm. Magdalene had been a deaconess in a Protestant nursing order before her marriage and remained devoutly religious throughout her life. Both Robert and Magdalene encouraged the children to think for themselves and to speak their minds, and the family often discussed books, art,

Hans Scholl
Born September 22, 1918
     Ingersheim, Germany
Died February 22, 1943
     Munich, Germany

Sophie Scholl
Born May 9, 1921
     Forchtenberg, Germany
Died February 22, 1943
     Munich, Germany

German students; founders of the protest organization known as the White Rose; executed for protesting the actions of Adolf Hitler

"Somebody, after all, had to make a start.... What we did will make waves."

Sophie (against fence) bids farewell to Hans (second from right) and other members of the White Rose resistance group as they depart for the Russian front. (Photo by George J. Wittenstein; reproduced by permission)

music, and current events. Robert was a pacifist who refused combat duty during World War I (1914–1918), serving instead as a medic. Robert later served a prison term after making insulting remarks about Hitler.

Hans was born in 1918, the year World War I ended and Germany was forced to accept the terms of the Treaty of Versailles as punishment for its role in the war. As Germany plunged into economic hardship, Hitler began promising to return the nation to its former glory. Hitler blamed Jews for the country's problems, and he used the Nazi party to promote anti-Semitism. Like other non-Jewish, German schoolboys, Hans was expected to join the Hitlerjugend, or Hitler Youth, a militaristic club that trained young Nazis. Being an idealistic young man, Hans jumped at the chance to participate in the "rebuilding of Germany," despite the misgivings of his father, who distrusted Hitler. At a week-long Nazi rally, though, Hans was disgusted by the Sturmabteilung (storm troopers), or SA—young soldiers who marched by the tens of thousands with bands playing and their voices raised in war-like songs. Deciding to break from the Hitler Youth, Hans formed Young Germans, a non-military group for boys age twelve to seventeen.

In 1937 Hans passed the qualifying exams for college, but first had to fulfill the National Labor Service requirement imposed by the Nazi party on all young people. He built roads for the Autobahn, a vast freeway system that still exists today, and then served in a military cavalry unit for two years. During this time, the Nazi party decided to round up members of youth groups not affiliated with the Hitler Youth. Young people throughout Germany were arrested; among them were Hans' siblings Inge and Werner, who spent a week in a Gestapo jail. Sophie was also taken in for questioning, the first of many times this would happen. Hans was not questioned because he was serving in the military, but a few months later he, too, was arrested and spent a month in jail. He would remain an object of suspicion to the Nazis for the rest of his short life. In 1939 Hans enrolled at the University of Munich, but the following year he was called back into military service as World War

Treason

The Treason Law, passed by the Nazi government, made even the slightest criticism of the Nazi regime an offense punishable by imprisonment, torture, or death. The penalties were particularly harsh during wartime. To enforce the law, some 40,000 Gestapo agents shadowed every aspect of German social life. The Nazi party also assigned *Blockwartes,* or block wardens, to watch German citizens for signs of disloyalty. In return for each captured traitor, block wardens received awards. (Janitor Jakob Schmid, who turned in Hans and Sophie Scholl, was such a block warden.) Surveillance became so commonplace in Germany during the war that citizens coined the expression the "German look" to refer to a shifty glance.

Accused traitors appeared before a special court in Berlin known as the *Volksgericht,* or People's Court. Proceedings were held under bright lights and filmed by camera. Ronald Freisler, known as the "hanging judge," presided over the court, wearing a bright red robe and frequently shouting abuse at the defendants. Few lawyers dared to defend the accused actively, and no appeals were permitted. Those sentenced to death would either hang or be sent to the guillotine, an instrument of death that the Nazis had reinstituted soon after they came into power.

When Hans and Sophie Scholl went to trial, Freisler himself flew from Berlin to Munich to conduct the proceedings. Freisler was killed on February 3, 1945, during an air raid by American bombers while he was presiding over a treason trial in Berlin.

II escalated in Europe. In 1941, still in the army, he was ordered back to continue his medical studies in Munich.

Sophie Scholl was born on May 9, 1921. Idealistic like her brother, Sophie grew to enjoy pursuits such as writing, drawing, and dancing. As a young teen, she joined the Bund Deutscher Mädel, or League of German Girls, the female equivalent of the Hitler Youth. Although she wanted to attend college to study philosophy and biology, she was taught that motherhood should be the ultimate goal of all German girls. She quickly rose in the ranks of the League and soon became a group leader. As Sophie observed the results of Hitler's policies in Germany, she, like Hans, became disillusioned with the Nazi regime. She was shocked when artists began to leave the country rather than conform to Hitler's concept of art; she saw some of her favorite books banned because they had been written by Jewish authors. In 1940 Sophie finished secondary school. Like Hans, she had to perform some type of public service before she could enter college. Hoping to satisfy the requirement by becoming a kindergarten teacher, she enrolled in a training course. As the war continued, Sophie struggled to reconcile her feelings as a pacifist with the militarism that surrounded her.

White Rose: A Subversive Group

After a year of training, Sophie was denied admittance to college because kindergarten work was not recognized as a substitute for national service. When she tried to return home after six months of service, she was informed that new legislation required her to give an additional six months of her time. In 1942, twenty-one-year-old Sophie was finally allowed to begin attending the University of Munich, where twenty-four-year-old Hans was also a student, nearing the completion of his medical studies. He introduced her to his friends, who shared an interest in art, literature, music, and nature. They also discovered they had a mutual disgust for Hitler and the war. The group became an underground resistance group called *Die Weiße Rose,* the White Rose. The incorporation of such a group was an illegal action punishable by death. In summer 1942, the White Rose began distributing pamphlets in which the Nazis were called immoral criminals. Soon the White Rose was targeting private citizens who stood

Members of the White Rose student resistance group in Munich, Hans Scholl is on the left; Alexander Schmorell is second from the left (hidden from view); and Sophie Scholl and Christoph Probst are on the right. (Photograph by George J. Wittenstein; reproduced by permission)

by and watched as the Nazis committed atrocities. In a dangerous campaign, a series of anti-Nazi pamphlets was sent to people chosen randomly from the telephone directory.

From July to October 1942, Hans, his younger brother, Werner, and several other members of the White Rose served a tour of duty on the Russian front. When they returned, White Rose activities continued. The University of Munich campus became a hotbed of political activity. One day a Nazi-sponsored speaker announced that women should abandon their college plans in order to bear children for the German empire. Female students in the crowd loudly protested and were arrested, immediately triggering a small riot. When the German army suffered a humiliating defeat in the Soviet Union, the White Rose took advantage of increasing anti-Nazi public sentiment to spread its message to several other universities and cities, including the academic community of Hamburg.

On February 16, 1943, the group printed its sixth and final pamphlet, which Hans and Sophie volunteered to distribute on campus two days later. Carrying a suitcase filled with 1,700 copies of the leaflet, Hans and Sophie walked through the corridors of the main building on campus, depositing small piles of the pamphlets at doorways and on windowsills. In the few remaining minutes before classes ended, the two dropped the last copies from the top-floor gallery, showering the empty hall with paper. A janitor, Jakob Schmid, noticed the flying leaflets, quickly locked the building doors, and phoned for assistance. The president of the university, an SS officer, called the Gestapo, and the Scholls were arrested.

Nazis Execute White Rose Activists

Hans and Sophie remained steadfast in their convictions throughout intense questioning, but they were put on trial along with their friend Christoph Probst. The Scholls' composure in the face of an extremely hostile and volatile judge impressed even their Nazi interrogators. Sophie repeatedly rejected the Gestapo's offer to lighten her sentence if she repented for her treasonous actions. At the end of the trial, the judge ruled that the Scholls and Probst should be executed. The method of execution was to be the guillotine, which had not been used in Germany for many years, but had been recently resurrected by Nazi official Hermann Göring. Fearful that more pro-

White Rose members Hans Scholl and Alexander Schmorell on the train bound for military service in Russia. (Photo by George J. Wittenstein; reproduced with permission)

testers might rise up to challenge the ruling, the Nazis hurriedly and quietly carried out the executions on February 22, 1943. As soon as the sentence was handed down, the three young people were handcuffed and taken to the guillotine. That same afternoon they were beheaded.

Five days later, Kurt Huber, a professor and author of the last White Rose pamphlet, was arrested. Soon afterward the Gestapo also picked up students Willi Graf and Alexander Schmorell. Huber and Schmorell were executed by guillotine on July 13, 1943. On October 12, 1943, after enduring months of brutal questioning without giving any information, Graf was also beheaded. In total, seventeen members of the White Rose were killed or forced to commit suicide.

Soon after the execution of the Scholls and Probst, the underground resistance began circulating a new version of the last White Rose leaflet. An added line on the cover declared in boldfaced type: "DESPITE EVERYTHING, THEIR SPIRIT LIVES ON." Throughout the city of Munich, the same slogan appeared on walls and pavements. By the end of 1943, RAF planes were dropping millions of White Rose pamphlets over Germany. They printed a new headline on the front page, proclaiming the leaflet to be a "Manifesto of the Munich Stu-

dents." Copies of the leaflets were also circulated in Sweden, Switzerland, the United States, and the Soviet Union—news of the resisters and their handbills even reached concentration camp inmates in Germany and other occupied countries. Thomas Mann, German author and Nobel laureate, learned of the Scholls' actions while living in exile. He praised them on the radio program *Voice of America,* saying "Good, splendid young people … you shall not be forgotten."

The Scholl family was the first victim of *Sippenhaft,* the Nazi party's new policy of arresting and punishing the relatives of anti-Nazi dissidents. Robert Scholl was sentenced to the longest prison term of any of the family members, two years of hard labor (though he was released before he had served his full sentence). When the war ended, he became Lord Mayor of Ulm. Many schools and streets in Germany have been named for Hans and Sophie Scholl and other members of the White Rose. The square in front of the main building at the University of Munich, for example, is known as Geschwister-Scholl Platz (*Geschwister* is German for "brother and sister").

After the war, the Scholls' sister Inge began to organize the writings of Hans and Sophie. In 1953 she published *Die Weisse Rose,* an account of her siblings' courageous battle against tyranny. An opera of the same name opened at the Dresden State Theatre to ovations and praise. Sophie has also been immortalized in the book *The Short Life of Sophie Scholl* by Hermann Vinke, which won the Buxtehuder Bulle award for an outstanding children's book promoting peace. In the 1960s both the German Democratic Republic (the former East Germany) and the Federal Republic of Germany (the former West Germany) issued commemorative stamps featuring the Scholls.

SOURCES

Books

Forman, James, *Ceremony of Innocence,* Hawthorn (New York), 1970.

Hanser, Richard, *A Noble Treason: The Revolt of the Munich Students Against Hitler,* G.P. Putnam's Sons (New York), 1979.

Innocenti, Robert, *Rose Blanche,* translated by Martha Coventry and Richard Graglia, Creative Education (Mankato, MN), 1985.

Jens, Inge, editor, *At the Heart of the White Rose: Letters and Diaries of Hans and Sophie Scholl,* translated from the German by J. Maxwell Brownjohn, preface by Richard Gilman, Harper & Row (New York), 1987.

Scholl, Inge, *Students against Tyranny: The Resistance of the White Rose, Munich, 1942–1943,* translated from the German by Arthur R. Schultz, Wesleyan University Press (Middletown, CT), 1970.

Vinke, Hermann, *The Short Life of Sophie Scholl,* with an interview with Ilse Aichinger, translated from the German by Hedwig Pachter, Harper & Row (Cambridge, MA), 1984.

Other

Die Weiße Rose (video), MGM/UA Home Video, 1983.

Eduard Reinhold Karl Schulte

Eduard Reinhold Karl Schulte was a German industrialist who opposed the policies of Adolf Hitler and the Nazi party. At the outset of World War II, he began doing undercover work for the Allies, passing along information about Nazi activities that he acquired through business contacts in Europe. Schulte is credited with being the first person to alert the Allies to Hitler's plans for the *Endlösung*, or "Final Solution"—the mass extermination of European Jews. Schulte's role as a spy remained a closely guarded secret for more than forty years. Some historians suggest that the Allies wanted to conceal the fact that they failed to act quickly enough to prevent the deaths of millions of Jews. Considered a traitor in his own country, Schulte was honored in Israel as a "Righteous Gentile" who risked his own life to save the Jews.

Born January 4, 1891
   Düsseldorf, Germany
Died January 6, 1966
   Zurich, Switzerland

Industrialist; lawyer; spy; the first person to inform the Allies about Nazi plans for the destruction of European Jews

"I have received information ... that Hitler's headquarters is considering a plan to kill all remaining European Jews."

Opposes Hitler

Eduard Reinhold Karl Schulte was born in 1891 into a wealthy Protestant family in Düsseldorf, Germany, where he, his older sister Erna, and his younger brother Oskar had a privileged upbringing. (A second brother, Reinhold, died as an infant.) An excellent student, Schulte was always seen as a leader at school and the same distinction followed him into adulthood—writers Walter Laqueur and Richard Breitman include among Schulte's leadership qualities the ability "to

A door to a Nazi gas chamber that reads "Harmful gas! Entering endangers your life." (Stanislaw Luczko/Main Commission for the Investigation of Nazi War Crimes/USHMM Photo Archives)

dissect a problem with lightning speed, almost intuitively, and to express the essentials, verbally or on paper, with great clarity." While serving an apprenticeship at a geological drilling company, Schulte had an accident that nearly killed him and eventually resulted in the amputation of one of his legs. He received a doctorate in law in 1912 at age twenty-one, and then became a banker. During World War I, he served in the War Office for Raw Materials; following the war he became an executive with a major soap company. In 1917 Schulte married Clara Luise Ebert, a teacher and writer. The couple lived in Breslau, Germany, and had two sons. In 1925 Schulte became the managing director of Germany's largest zinc company, which also produced lead, coal, and sulfur. Eventually the firm acquired a business in Switzerland, and Schulte made frequent visits to that country. The Schultes did not like the politics of the emerging Nazi party and its leader Adolf Hitler.

As Hitler's policies became increasingly dictatorial and ruthless, Schulte decided to oppose the Nazis. He believed the only hope for his country was peace with the Allies and the destruction of the German military class. Schulte's business activities put him in touch with important people, so he began passing information about Nazi activities to the Poles and the French. Schulte's information was extremely valuable to the Allies. According to writers Richard Breitman and Alan M. Kraut, in January 1942 Schulte "transmitted the operational plans of the German armies in Russia, predicting their thrust toward the Caucasus (a Russian mountainous region). [He] also described in detail internal frictions that were pitting Hitler and the Nazi Party against the German general staff." The Poles passed the information along to Great Britain, which shared some of it with the United States. Despite the squabbles among the Nazis, Schulte did not think the German army would overthrow Hitler.

Warns of "Final Solution"

In late July 1942 Schulte heard some shocking news that sent him immediately to Switzerland to meet with Gerhart Riegner, the Swiss representative of the World Jewish Congress. Although the source of Schulte's information is unknown, he reported that the Nazis were planning to implement a "Final Solution"—the slaughter of all European Jews through the use of massive gas chambers. The number of people killed was expected to reach millions. Schulte told Riegner to pass this

information on to appropriate groups in Switzerland, Great Britain, and the United States. He asked Riegner to keep his source secret, since Schulte planned to return to Germany and wished to protect his identity from the Gestapo and German military intelligence. Allied officials could not believe Schulte's revelation. Unbeknownst to Schulte, however, the Holocaust had already begun, and reports from Paris, Holland, Berlin, Vienna, and Prague testified to the fact that large numbers of Jews were being deported to eastern Europe under brutal conditions. Hitler had even begun to speak openly about the "Final Solution." Despite continuing reports received by Washington, D.C., from various sources around the world, the United States failed to respond to Schulte's information. Some U.S. officials were horrified by the news, and others merely chose to ignore it. Most considered military victory over the Nazis the top priority.

Allies Fail to Act

According to Breitman and Kraut, some U.S. officials believed that rescuing the Jews was a "humanitarian effort that the [United States] could not afford in the midst of a war for the survival of Western civilization." Despite his disappointment at America's limited response, Schulte continued to assist the Allies throughout the war. In 1943 U.S. authorities feared he might be in danger when an unnamed European secret agent radioed Schulte's name to a colleague in London, England. Though it remains unclear if the Nazis ever found out about Schulte's spying, he fled to Switzerland in fear for his life. His wife and two sons joined him there, and the family remained in Switzerland until the end of the war. Schulte occupied his time working on an economic plan for postwar Germany, the details of which were passed along to U.S. officials. When the war was over, some of his Allied contacts suggested that he participate in the reformation of the German government. Other Allies questioned Schulte's role in wartime Germany, however, so he retired to Switzerland. In 1956, following the death of his wife, Schulte married a long-time friend, a Jewish woman who operated a boutique. To the surprise of many who knew him as a dynamic businessman, he seemed to enjoy spending his days balancing the books at his wife's shop.

Schulte received certificates of appreciation from the governments of France, Great Britain,

Why the U.S. Government Failed to Help the Jews: One Opinion

In *The Abandonment of the Jews: America and the Holocaust, 1941–1945*, historian David S. Wyman discusses how President Franklin D. Roosevelt of the United States dealt with the massive execution of European Jews by the Nazis. According to Wyman, Roosevelt and his advisers developed four main reasons for failing to take action to help European Jews. Wyman, however, feels that none of these reasons were fully valid.

The first reason was the unavailability of a sufficient number of boats to transport Jewish refugees. Wyman calls this explanation a fraud. He says that it was not that shipping resources were unavailable but that "the Allies were unwilling to take the Jews in." He continues: "The [U.S.] War Department admitted to the War Refugee Board in spring 1944 that it had 'ample shipping' available for evacuating refugees; the problem, it agreed, was to find places where [the Jews] could go."

Secondly, Roosevelt and his advisers suggested that the Nazi government planted agents among refugees. Wyman claims this problem was "vastly overemphasized and could have been handled through reasonable security screening."

A third reason for maintaining non-involvement was that aiding the Jews would improperly single out one group for help when many people were suffering under Nazi brutality. Wyman notes that several Allied governments regularly refused to admit that the Jews were unique in being the targets of mass extermination.

The final reason supposed that rescue efforts would take attention and resources away from the war effort, thereby prolonging it. In fact, Wyman maintains, no rescue proposal would have taken away from the war effort so much that the war would have lasted longer, and none of the proposals would have caused more injuries or deaths to soldiers or civilians.

Wyman concludes that an insufficiently strong desire to save the Jews of Europe was the real reason for the United States' lack of action. The question of how much more the United States and Roosevelt could or should have done to combat the Holocaust remains highly controversial.

---

non-Communist Poland, and the United States, but he succumbed to stomach cancer in 1966 and died in relative obscurity. Literary critic Henry Ashby Turner wrote on the events following his death: "Only years after Schulte's death did anyone in his homeland again take notice of his wartime activities. This occurred when his heirs entered a claim with a German court for compensation in view of the property he had lost … at the end of the war." The German court dismissed the claims. The court ruled that by passing information to the Allies, Schulte had committed a crime.

For forty years, Schulte's story remained unknown to the public. In the 1980s Breitman, a professor of German history at American University, began investigating the identity of a mysterious German industrialist who had been the first to inform the United States and Great Britain about the Holocaust. Breitman interviewed Riegner, the Jewish man who had brought the industrialist's report to the Allies. Even after four decades, Riegner would not reveal the identity of the informant. Breitman knew only that the man's name started with "S" and that he had employed more than 30,000 people. By researching American documents and German industrial histories, he determined that there was only one man who fit the description: Eduard Schulte. Breitman and fellow historian Walter Laqueur documented Schulte's contributions in their book *Breaking the Silence* (1986). Soon afterward, Schulte was honored on Israel's Avenue of the Righteous, where carob trees are planted to commemorate Gentiles who risked their lives to save Jews during the Holocaust. Schulte's family also received a medal.

Sources

Books

Laqueur, Walter, and Richard Breitman, *Breaking The Silence,* Simon and Schuster (New York), 1986.

Wyman, David S., *The Abandonment of the Jews: America and the Holocaust, 1941–1945,* Pantheon Books (New York), 1984.

Periodicals

Breitman, R., and A. M. Kraut, "Who Was the Mysterious Messenger?" *Commentary,* October, 1983, pp. 44–47.

Markham, J. M., "Unsung Good Germans: Fame Comes at Last," *New York Times Biographical Service,* November, 1983, pp. 1394–1395.

Turner, H. A., "Herr S's Secret," *New York Times Book Review,* June 22, 1986, p. 19.

Hannah Senesh

Born July 17, 1921
Budapest, Hungary
Died November 7, 1944
Budapest, Hungary

Poet; pioneer; Hungarian Jewish
resistance fighter

*"I want to believe that what I have done, and
will do, [is] right. Time will tell the rest."*

(Beit Hannah Senesh/USHMM Photo Archives)

Hannah Senesh (also transliterated as Szenes) was a Hungarian Jew whose short life spanned the rise of German Nazi dictator Adolf Hitler and most of World War II. She moved to Palestine in 1939 to join the Zionist movement and to escape the anti-Semitism that was spreading across Europe. Overwrought with concern for her mother when Hungary fell to the Germans, Senesh returned to her native country in 1944 as a spy for the British. After being betrayed by one of her own guides on a spying mission, Senesh was executed by the Nazis.

Life Changed by Jewish Laws

Hannah Senesh was born in 1921 in Budapest, Hungary, the second child of Catherine Salzberger Senesh and Bela Senesh, a popular playwright, theater critic, and journalist. Hannah and her brother, George, were close to their father, who died in 1927. After graduating at the top of her elementary school class, Senesh enrolled at a recently secularized private Protestant high school for girls. When Senesh was thirteen, she started keeping a diary. As she grew older, she wrote poetry and plays, hoping to become a writer. When Hannah proved herself a gifted student, her mother negotiated a reduction in her tuition rate; instead of the tripled rate that Jewish girls normally paid, she was required to pay only double.

The War in Hungary

Prior to Adolf Hitler's ascent to power in 1933, there were about 800,000 Jews in Hungary. One-quarter of them lived in Budapest, the capital city. During the 1920s, Budapest resembled a fairy-tale city, with graceful bridges over the Danube River, a royal palace, beautiful architecture, and tree-lined streets. While the economy relied mainly on agriculture, Budapest was the cultural center of the country. Jews such as Hannah Senesh's father were prominent figures in the cultural, economic, and scientific life of the city. Like other European countries defeated in World War I, Hungary was affected by deep social and political unrest. Anti-Semitism raged as Hungary maintained close relations with Germany during the 1930s. When Hitler took over parts of nearby Czechoslovakia in 1938 and 1939, Hungary was rewarded with some of the new territory.

When World War II began, Hungary officially declared neutrality, but its actions were sympathetic to Hitler's goals. The country was more interested in being given land than in seeing Jews eliminated, but Hungarian officials did nothing while 50,000 Jews died in the new territories. In 1941 Hungary declared war on the Soviet Union. After suffering heavy losses in battles, Hungary's government, headed by Admiral Miklós Horthy, secretly approached the Allies about making peace. Horthy delayed the deportation of Jews that had been ordered by Hitler, thus enraging the Nazis. In March 1944 German troops began a campaign of terror to rid Hungary of Jews. Adolf Eichmann, who was in charge of eliminating Jews, worked quickly. Between March and July 1944, an estimated 440,000 Hungarian Jews were sent by train to Auschwitz. When the war ended in 1945, only one-quarter of Hungary's prewar Jewish population was alive. Much of the beautiful city of Budapest was also destroyed during the war.

Like Hannah Senesh's mother, many Jews in Hungary simply could not believe that they would meet the same fate as Jews in other occupied European countries. Convinced that Hitler would be defeated, Hungarian Jews put up very little resistance. Opposition efforts were mainly left to small Zionist groups whose members were shunned by mainstream Hungarian Jews. Zionist colleagues of Hannah Senesh who were killed for their resistance efforts include Abba Berdichev, Peretz Goldstein, Zvi Ben Jacob, Chaviva Reik, Rafael Reis, and Enzo Sereni.

The Senesh family lived in a large house in one of the city's finer neighborhoods. Although Hungary had long been known for its tolerance toward Jews, the country had begun to change in the 1920s. Nevertheless, the Senesh family continued to enjoy the comfortable life of assimilated Jews. In 1937 Hannah Senesh first experienced outright discrimination—she had been nominated as secretary of her school literary society, but lost the election when several girls objected to a Jew holding office. Although the teacher lectured the girls for their behavior and encouraged Senesh to stay in the club, she dropped out and alienated herself from classmates. She was acutely aware of what was happening around her.

Her diary entries refer, for example, to the Nazi overthrow of the Austrian government and the tension this caused in Hungary. By 1938, the Senesh family could no longer ignore the anti-Jewish atmosphere. Senesh's brother encountered anti-Semitism when he was rejected from an Austrian university because of quotas on Jewish applicants and was forced instead to attend a French college.

The First Jewish Law, which was passed in May 1938, limited the Jewish workforce within certain industries to 20 percent and declared it the "national duty" of Hungarians to banish Jews from public and private life. The Second Jewish Law, passed the

Senesh greets her brother, George, on his arrival in Palestine at what would be their last meeting. (Beit Hannah Senesh/USHMM Photo Archives)

following year, further decreased Jewish employment to 6 percent and authorized seizure of land owned by Jews. The laws strictly defined who should be considered Jewish. For instance, anyone who had converted from Judaism to Christianity now had to obey both laws. When Hungarians expressed minimal opposition to the legislation, the Nazis began calling for the deportation of all European Jews. Passage of the first Jewish bill confirmed Senesh's pride in her heritage. She made plans to join the Zionist movement as soon as she graduated from high school. By the time the second bill went into effect, she was already participating in a Zionist discussion group and studying Hebrew. She confided in her diary that she was proud of being a Jew and wished to move to Palestine. Her mother was troubled by the situation in Hungary, but she was convinced that Jews were still safe there. Although Senesh pleaded with her mother to go to Palestine, Catherine was reluctant to leave her life behind. When Senesh was accepted at an agricultural school in Nahalal, Palestine, Catherine gave her permission, and Senesh set sail in September 1939.

Becomes Spy for Britain

For more than two years, Senesh was able to distance herself from events in Europe by studying poultry farming and childhood education and writing plays. After graduating from the Nahalal Agricultural School in September 1941, she joined a kibbutz, a communal farm, called Sedot Yam. There she learned to do farm and kitchen chores, a kind of work her privileged childhood had not prepared her to do. As she continued to write poetry, she felt a conflict between her desire to become a writer and her commitment to the kibbutz. In the meantime, reports about the progress of the war in Europe grew more alarming.

The Germans had conquered France; Senesh was unable to receive letters from her brother George. Then the Nazis occupied Greece and began bombing Palestine. By January 1943, Senesh could no longer sustain her enthusiasm for the peaceful life at Sedot Yam. Worried about what might happen to Palestine if the war continued, and fearful for her mother in Hungary, Senesh was faced with a dilemma. She decided to return to Hungary in an effort to persuade her mother to flee to Palestine. In February 1943, she met a young man named Yonah Rosen, a fellow Hungarian who lived at another kibbutz who was organizing a rescue mission to Europe. The plan was to convince the British to parachute Jewish volunteers into the German-occupied countries of

Europe. There they would form resistance movements and rescue Jews trapped by the Nazis.

Senesh was one of the first to volunteer. Along with 240 other Jewish youths chosen for their outstanding physical and mental abilities, she went to Egypt to be trained by the British in the use of weapons, parachutes, and radio transmitters. The plan called for the youths to be dropped behind enemy lines, where they would gather information about German troop movements, plan escape routes for imprisoned fliers, and rescue as many Jews as possible. Just before Senesh's group left, her brother George paid her a surprise visit. He informed her of his decision to move to Palestine. This meeting would be the last time the two ever saw each other. On March 13, 1944, Senesh and three young men parachuted into Yugoslavia, landing about 200 miles from the Hungarian border. The war had reduced Yugoslavia to a state of severe chaos, and for three months they were able to do little more than observe as battles raged and towns were destroyed. They were able to radio valuable information about the location of German troops to British headquarters.

Goes on Fatal Mission

In June 1944 Senesh learned that Hungary had fallen to Germany and that Nazi official Adolf Eichmann was working to cleanse the entire country of Jews. She grew even more determined to go into Hungary to save her mother and other Jews held captive there. She crossed into Hungary, only to be betrayed to the German police by one of her own guides. When Senesh did not reveal the code to her transmitter, she was severely beaten and sent to military prison in Budapest. Soon she was transferred to another prison. When she refused to divulge information, the Germans took her mother prisoner and threatened to kill her if Senesh did not talk. Catherine later described her daughter's

tangled hair, black eyes, and bruised and wounded skin. Despite such extreme treatment in the prison, Senesh told the Germans nothing.

Finally, Senesh was taken to the Margit Boulevard Prison. Her trial began on October 28; over a week later she was sentenced to death, with no possibility of appeal. Senesh was told that the sentence would be set aside if she confessed to spying and pleaded for mercy, but she refused to capitulate. On November 7, 1944, one hour after the death sentence was handed down, Senesh was executed by a firing squad. She refused to wear the customary blindfold. Three months later, the war in Hungary ended. In 1950, three years after the Jews established the state of Israel, Senesh's body was buried in Israel, near the Sdot-Yam kibbutz, with full military honors. Her diary and poems have been published and translated into many languages. One of her poems has been set to music and has become an Israeli national folk song.

SOURCES

Books

Atkinson, Linda, *In Kindling Flame: The Story of Hannah Senesh, 1921–1944,* Lothrop, Lee & Shepard (New York), 1985.

Ransom, Candice F., *So Young to Die: The Story of Hannah Senesh,* Scholastic (New York), 1993.

Sachar, Abram L., *The Redemption of the Unwanted: From the Liberation of the Death Camps to the Founding of Israel,* St. Martin's/Marek (New York), 1983.

Senesh, Hannah, *Hannah Senesh: Her Life and Diary,* translated from the Hebrew by Marta Cohn, Vallentine, Mitchell (London), 1971.

Whitman, Ruth, *The Testing of Hanna Senesh,* with a historical background by Livia Rothkirchen, Wayne State University Press (Detroit), 1986.

Raymond A. Spruance

Born July 3, 1886
Baltimore, Maryland, United States
Died December 13, 1969
Pebble Beach, California, United States

U.S. Navy admiral

"Some people believe that when I am quiet that I am thinking some deep and important thoughts, when the fact is that I am thinking of nothing at all. My mind is blank."

(Reproduced by permission of AP/Wide World Photos)

On June 4, 1942, the U.S. Pacific Fleet defeated a massive concentration of Japanese vessels and aircraft at the Battle of Midway. Coming six months after the Japanese attack on Pearl Harbor, Hawaii, which had provoked U.S. involvement in World War II, the victory boosted American military and public morale. Historians consider the battle a crucial turning point in the war. Raymond A. Spruance, the rear admiral in charge of strategy at Midway, is credited with successfully repelling the Japanese invasion through effective deployment of aircraft carriers and introducing a new dimension in naval warfare. Thrust into a commanding role on the spur of the moment, Spruance acted quickly and decisively, thus keeping American losses to a minimum while devastating the enemy. Yet, in keeping with his reserved and private nature, he was reluctant to accept the status of hero.

Given Crucial Role in the Pacific

Born in Baltimore on July 3, 1886, Raymond Ames Spruance was the son of Alexander and Annie Spruance. He grew up in East Orange, New Jersey, and Indianapolis, Indiana. After graduating from high school in Indianapolis, he briefly attended Stevens Preparatory School in Hoboken, New Jersey. In 1903 he entered the U.S. Naval Academy at Annapolis, Maryland, where he graduated twenty-sixth in his class three years later.

Spruance served tours of duty aboard several battleships until 1921, when he took the first of a series of administrative positions with the U.S. Navy. Frequently returning to sea duty as a battleship commander, he was promoted to the rank of rear admiral in 1939; the following year he was posted to the Tenth Naval District in the Caribbean. In 1941, at the age of fifty-five, Spruance was transferred to the Pacific and assigned command of a division of cruisers under Admiral Chester W. Nimitz.

The situation was bleak when Spruance arrived in the Pacific. Nimitz had recently replaced Admiral Husband E. Kimmel, commander in chief of the U.S. Pacific Fleet, who had been relieved of his position pending investigation of the Japanese attack at Pearl Harbor on December 7. By early January 1942, the Western powers were in full retreat in the Pacific, and the small U.S. Asiatic Fleet had fled from the Philippines to the Java Sea. With the U.S. Pacific Fleet in shambles, Japan occupied both Hong Kong and Manila and was advancing on Java and Singapore while shelling American installations on Midway Island. In early 1942 Nimitz was promoted to commander in chief of the Pacific Ocean Area. In May he ordered the Pacific Fleet to the Coral Sea. The ensuing battle between the Americans and the Japanese was the first great aircraft carrier conflict, but there was no real winner because surface ships on both sides were unable to sight the enemy. The Japanese had lost more planes, yet the Americans had lost more naval craft, including the valuable USS *Lexington.* After the Battle of Coral Sea, the entire Pacific Fleet was left with only three aircraft carriers, eight cruisers, fifteen destroyers, twelve submarines, and 353 fighter planes. At this point most of the fleet was positioned north of Midway Island. Spruance had also received an unexpected promotion: Vice Admiral William F. "Bull" Halsey, commander of Task Force 16, was in the hospital for treatment of a skin disease, so Nimitz appointed Spruance to succeed him. The stage was thus set for Spruance's unexpected victory at Midway.

Spruance at the Battle of Midway

On the morning of June 4, 1942, 108 Japanese fighters, dive-bombers, and torpedo bombers launched an assault on Midway. The Japanese had planned their strategy with great deliberation: deploying fleets commanded by admirals Isoroku Yamamoto, Chuichi Nagumo, and Nobutake

Admiral Chuichi Nagumo, who gave the order to attack Pearl Harbor in December 1941, later fought against Spruance at the Battle of Midway. (Reproduced by permission of AP/Wide World Photos)

Kondo, they would first take the Aleutian Islands. With 200 ships and 700 aircraft, the Japanese knew they outnumbered the Americans, so they thought they could easily invade Midway, which would be left virtually unprotected as American ships struggled to reach the area. By defeating the Americans in a subsequent pincher action between two powerful fleets under Yamamoto and Nagumo, the Japanese would then achieve total dominance in the Pacific. Conquest of the Aleutians took place as planned on June 3, yet the Japanese did not realize that on June 2 the Americans had spotted their ships 600 miles west of Midway and were moving toward the island. Japanese reconnaissance flights had failed to detect the American presence, so Yamamoto and Nagumo assumed the Pacific Fleet was at Pearl Harbor. Consequently, the Japanese were confident of victory when they staged the air strike on Midway on June 4. In fact, as they bombarded the island for twenty minutes, they were careful not to damage the runways because they expected to use the facilities for their own planes. At first it seemed they would prevail; a small detachment of American marines on Midway were caught off guard. Marine fighter planes and antiaircraft artillery soon rallied, however, bringing

Admiral Frank Jack Fletcher

Rear Admiral Frank Jack Fletcher (1885–1973), like Rear Admiral Raymond A. Spruance, was a seasoned sailor by the time he was transferred to the Pacific in 1941. After graduating from the U.S. Naval Academy in the class of 1906, Fletcher went on to command five destroyers, a battleship, and three other ships during the next thirty years. He was promoted to rear admiral in the late 1930s. In December 1941, after the United States entered World War II, he led a failed relief expedition at Wake Island. The following month he was placed in command of a carrier task force with the USS *Yorktown,* which engaged in actions against the Japanese in the South Pacific islands, the Central Pacific, New Guinea, and the Solomons. Fletcher was the senior officer at the Battle of Coral Sea in May 1942. When the *Yorktown* was hit in the Japanese assault on Midway in June, Fletcher transferred to the cruiser *Astoria* and turned command duties over to Spruance. In November 1942, Fletcher was named commander of the Thirteenth Naval District and commander of the Northwestern Sea Frontier. The following year he was put in charge of the Northern Pacific area, a position he held for the duration of the war. After the Japanese surrender in August 1945, Fletcher's forces occupied northern Japan. Now a vice admiral, Fletcher was appointed chairman of the General Board. Upon retirement in 1947, he was promoted to the rank of full admiral and the USS *Fletcher,* built in 1980, was named in his honor.

For more information on Admiral Frank Jack Fletcher, see the Naval Historical Center's page on him at http://www.history.navy.mil (July 13, 2000).

down or severely damaging about one-third of the Japanese planes.

In the meantime, as the Japanese were making a second air strike at Midway, Spruance had been placed in charge of the American offensive after one of the three American aircraft carriers, the USS *Yorktown,* which was part of Task Force 17 under Rear Admiral Frank Jack Fletcher (see box), had been hit at Midway. Although Fletcher and Spruance were equal in rank, Fletcher had seniority and was in command. When the *Yorktown* was damaged, Fletcher took over the cruiser *Astoria* and gave tactical responsibilities to Spruance. American carriers were now within 175 miles of the enemy fleets and, knowing there was no time to waste, Rear Admiral Spruance decided to send out as many planes as possible on search-and-destroy missions. He ordered the immediate launching of Grumman F-4 Wildcat fighter planes, Douglas SBD-3 Dauntless dive-bombers, and Douglas TBD-1 Devastator torpedo bombers from the carriers USS *Enterprise* and USS *Hornet.* Soon planes were also taking off from the repaired *Yorktown.* Shortly after 9 a.m., the Pacific Fleet was engaged in a full-scale offensive against the Japanese fleets. Commanders Yamamoto and Nagumo were taken totally by surprise. Most of their planes were either at Midway or out on patrol, so their ships were essentially unprotected. For a brief time the Japanese thought they had won the battle after they destroyed the VT-8 torpedo bomber squadron launched from the *Hornet.* Their fighter planes were finally overcome by American torpedo bombers and dive-bombers, however, and by afternoon Yamamoto had suspended the assault on Midway.

The Imperial Japanese Navy suffered debilitating losses, including four carriers, a heavy cruiser, and 322 airplanes; a second cruiser, three destroyers, an oil tanker, and a battleship were heavily damaged. In contrast, the Americans lost the *Yorktown,* the destroyer *Hammann,* and 147 planes. The Battle of Midway provided a tremendous boost to American morale, and historians consider it the first step in the ultimate defeat of the formidable Japanese navy. For his performance, Spruance was awarded the Distinguished Service Medal and received a series of promotions. In November 1943, after Nimitz named him commander of Central Pacific Forces, he planned the

U.S. Pacific Fleet Commander, Admiral Chester Nimitz, honors Admiral Raymond A. Spruance with a medal for his heroism during the war in the Pacific. (Reproduced by permission of AP/Wide World Photos)

successful attack on the Gilbert Islands. Two months later Spruance executed what some historians consider to be the most powerful naval strike force in history. Starting in the Marshall Islands, he attacked the Marianas, then led the Fifth Fleet on to the Battle of the Philippine Sea. During the campaign, Spruance used ships in a new way by positioning them so that enemy planes could be shot down before they attacked. Now a full admiral, he also directed a group of battleships, cruisers, and destroyers that pursued Japanese ships; reportedly this was the first time a four-star admiral had taken part in action aboard a vessel engaged in conflict. The American strike was devastating to the Japanese, who began a retreat from the Pacific.

After the Philippine Sea campaign, Spruance handed over command of the Fifth Fleet to Halsey and went to Pearl Harbor to plan future operations. In January 1945 he returned to sea duty and participated in the invasions of Iwo Jima and Okinawa, which lasted three months and contributed to the Japanese surrender the following August. Spruance was awarded the Navy Cross for heroism in the battles. In November 1945 he replaced Nimitz as commander in chief of the Pacific Fleet and the Pacific, remaining in that position until February 1946, when he was appointed president

of the Naval War College at Newport, Virginia. Later that year, the U.S. Army awarded him the Distinguished Service Medal for his achievements in the Marshall and Mariana islands. After retiring from the U.S. Navy in 1948, he lived in Pebble Beach, California, with his family. In 1952 President Harry S Truman appointed him ambassador to the Philippines, a position he held for three years. Spruance died in Pebble Beach in 1969 and was buried in a military cemetery overlooking San Francisco Bay. The USS *Spruance* was launched in 1973, and a building at the Naval War College was named in his honor.

Sources

Books

Andidora, Ronald, *Iron Admirals: Naval Leadership in the Twentieth Century,* Greenwood Press (Westport, CN), 2000.

Buell, Thomas B., *The Quiet Warrior: A Biography of Admiral Raymond A. Spruance,* Naval Institute Press (Annapolis, MD), 1987.

Fuchida, Mitsuo, and Masatake Okumiya, *Midway: The Battle That Doomed Japan: The Japanese Navy's Story,* with an introduction by Thomas B. Buell, edited by Clarke H. Kawakami and

Roger Pineau, foreward by Raymond A. Spruance, Naval Institute Press (Annapolis, MD),
1992.

Prange, Gordon W., *Miracle at Midway,* edited by
Donald M. Goldstein and Katherine V. Dillon,
Easton Press (Norwalk, CT), 1982.

Other

Hull, Michael D., "Modest Victor of Midway,"
World War II, http://www.thehistorynet.com/
WorldWarII/articles/1998/0598_cover.htm
(May 5, 2000).

Joseph Stalin

Joseph Stalin became the leader of the Soviet Union after the death of Vladimir Lenin, who led the Bolshevik revolution that removed the Russian czar from power and established a communist regime in 1917. Under Stalin, the Soviet Union ascended to world prominence, an escalation achieved through a reign of terror that caused millions of citizens to be executed or deported to labor camps called "gulags." During World War II, Stalin rallied the Soviet populace to repel a German invasion and defeat Germany, a victory that cost the lives of 21 million Russians.

Drawn to Marxism

Stalin was born Iosef (Joseph) Vissarionovich Dzhugashvili in 1879 in Gori, Georgia, then part of the Russian Empire. He was the only child (three siblings died in infancy) of Vissarion and Yekaterina Dzhugashvili. Stalin's father was a shoemaker and an alcoholic who died from wounds he received in a fight; his mother was a housekeeper. Stalin endured several serious childhood illnesses. Called "Soso" as a boy, he spoke the Georgian language exclusively until the age of eight, when he went to school and was given instruction in Russian. Although his mother could neither read nor write herself, she felt he was destined for the priesthood and hoped he would one day be ordained as a bishop. In 1894 Stalin was awarded a scholarship to the theological seminary in Tbilisi, the largest

Born December 21, 1879
Gori, Georgia, Russia
Died March 5, 1953
Moscow, Soviet Union

Dictator of the Soviet Union from 1928 to 1953

"The triumph of one man turned into the tragedy of an entire nation."
—DIMITRI VOLKOGONOV

(Reproduced by permission of UPI/Corbis-Bettmann)

city in Georgia. Initially, he was a serious student, but during his second year, he began rebelling against the strict confines of the school. He smuggled banned literature into the seminary and refused to obey school officials. During this time Stalin began reading works by Marxist writers, followers of Karl Marx's theory calling for the working class to revolt and create a classless society. Stalin was especially interested in the writings of Vladimir Lenin, who would later lead the Russian Revolution.

In 1899 Stalin was expelled from the seminary, a failure his mother would never forgive, even after Stalin became leader of the Soviet Union. He continued to dream of revolution and began referring to himself as "Koba" (the "Indomitable") after a hero from Georgian folk tales. Stalin took a job as a bookkeeper at the Tbilisi observatory. There he met members of the Social Democrats, who advocated communism—a political system in which property is owned by groups rather than by individuals. Although an illegal political party in Russia, communism appealed to Stalin. After losing his job when he became a party member, Stalin devoted all his time to the revolutionary activities of the Social Democratic party's militant wing, attempting to convince industrial workers to support the group. In 1894 he married a peasant girl, Yekaterina Svanidze, who died after giving birth to a son, Jacob. Arrested in 1902 for revolutionary activities, Stalin was sent to Siberia; he escaped two years later and returned to Georgia. In 1905 he attended a political meeting in Finland where he was introduced to Lenin. A split in the Social Democratic party resulted in the formation of the Mensheviks, who believed in gradual change and compromise, and the Bolsheviks, led by Lenin, who called for immediate revolution. Recognizing Stalin's loyalty and organizational skills, Lenin put him in charge of raising money for the Bolsheviks by robbing banks and government money transports—activities that were carried out quietly to avoid disapproval from other Bolsheviks.

Stalin disappeared, then resurfaced in Baku, Azerbaijan, near the Caspian Sea, where he tried to convince oil workers to join the Bolsheviks. Constantly in and out of trouble with the police, Stalin spent several periods of exile in Siberia. In 1912 Lenin broke his ties with the Social Democrats and formed his own party. Knowing that Stalin's ruthlessness and intelligence were invaluable, Lenin nominated him to the party's central committee. Stalin was arrested again and detained in

Siberia until March 1917, when the Russian Revolution toppled the czarist regime. By this time, Stalin had adopted the name he would keep for the rest of his life, a derivation of the Russian word *stal,* meaning steel.

Prior to the revolution, Russia was comprised of a collection of individual republics ruled by a provisional government. After the revolution, the government was composed of several political parties that had collaborated to overthrow the czar. In April 1917 Lenin announced his dissatisfaction with the new government. After issuing a demand for peace, bread, and land for the Russian people, Lenin and his followers organized a revolutionary committee and began urging urban workers, peasants, and members of the military to lend their support.

Over the next few months, members of Lenin's group gradually gained influence. In October 1917 they staged a bloodless takeover of the provisional government. Lenin was named leader of the Soviet Union. Lenin appointed Stalin as Commissar of Nationalities, in charge of positioning Communists within various ethnic groups to increase the party's power. Stalin began attracting his own supporters—although he was not considered an intellectual leader, he was capable of making difficult decisions. Between 1918 and 1921, the Communists and their Red Army fought a civil war between advocates of a return to the czarist regime and others who wanted a more democratic government. Stalin served as a military commander during this conflict. In 1919, when Lenin established agencies to perform various government tasks, Stalin was appointed Commissar of the Workers and Peasants Inspectorate; he also became a member of the policy-making and executive committee of the party, known as the Politboro. At this time Stalin married his second wife, Nadezhda Alliluyeva, the sixteen-year-old daughter of an old friend. The couple had two children, Vasili and Svetlana; Nadezhda killed herself in 1932, leaving a note that expressed disapproval of Stalin as a man and leader.

Building His Own Power

In 1922 Lenin named Stalin the general secretary of the Central Committee of the Communist party. This was an important position that enabled Stalin to staff the party's higher levels with his supporters. In May 1922 Lenin suffered a stroke and his health steadily declined. He became increasingly

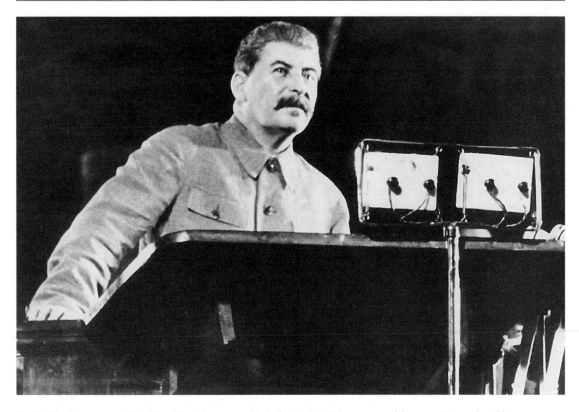

In 1928 Stalin presented his Five-Year Plan to establish the Soviet Union as a world power. (Reproduced by permission of UPI/Corbis-Bettmann)

disgruntled with the power Stalin and others had managed to acquire and was largely disregarded by party members who accused him of forgetting the original ideals of the Communist party. After Lenin's death in January 1924, the country was headed by a provisional government composed of five men: Stalin, Leon Trotsky (the head of the Red Army), Lev Kamenev and Grigori Zinoviev (Moscow and Leningrad party chiefs), and Nikolai Bukharin (the party's theorist). Each man vied for power, but Stalin emerged as the new leader.

Stalin initially allied himself with Kamenev and Zinoviev in a plot to oust Trotsky. As a result, Trotsky went into exile in Mexico and was eventually killed by Stalin's agents there. Then Stalin and Bukharin collaborated to rid themselves of Kamenev and Zinoviev. Finally Stalin turned against Bukharin. In less than ten years, Stalin was the only one of the five leaders left alive. Stalin seized complete control of the Soviet Union, which he ran with the help of a brutal police force. His main objective was to develop the country's industry and agriculture to a point where they could compete with those of other advanced countries. In 1928 he proposed an initial Five-Year Plan to achieve his goals.

Five-Year Plan Succeeds

The first phase of the Five-Year Plan involved building factories, dams, and other major projects. Within five years, the Soviet Union was producing steel, machine tools, tractors, and other industrial products. As industry continued to thrive, Stalin turned his attention to the de-privatization of family farms, which he absorbed into larger state-owned collectives for greater government control. Farmers who resisted giving up their farms were labeled *kulaks* (tightwads) and were either executed or sent to *gulags* (labor camps). Other farmers starved when the government punished them by taking their grain. By the late 1930s, most Soviet agriculture had been collectivized, but some rules changed to allow people to keep their own houses and tools in order to grow private gardens for personal use.

These rapid changes were hard on the Russian people. Factory workers could afford to buy only basic necessities, and food and goods were sometimes hard to acquire. Workers had to obtain permission to change jobs, and all citizens were required to have special passports when they traveled. People were afraid to express themselves freely,

A Great Russian General

The general in charge of the Soviet Union's key victories against the Germans at Moscow, Leningrad, Stalingrad, and Kursk was Georgy Zhukov. Considered one of the greatest generals in World War II, Zhukov was born in 1896 in Strelkovka, a small village located sixty miles from Moscow. As a young boy, he worked as a furrier's apprentice, and in 1915 joined the Russian army. During the revolution and civil war that followed, Zhukov was part of the new Red Army, serving as a squadron commander until 1920. In the 1920s he attended schools for military commanders while rising through the ranks.

During the 1930s, Zhukov established his military prowess. In 1939 he went to Upper Mongolia (now part of China), where the Japanese were conducting an undeclared war along the border. After leading the Soviet First Army Group to victory against the Japanese Sixth Army at the Khalkhin-Gol River, he was promoted to the rank of general in May 1940. In February 1941 Zhukov became chief of the Soviet General Staff and deputy commissioner for defense. In August 1942 he was made deputy supreme commander in chief of the Red Army and Navy, placing him second in command only to Stalin. He led the defense of Leningrad against German attack in summer and fall 1941, then returned to Moscow in December to successfully defend that city. He went on to coordinate Soviet victories at Stalingrad in 1942 and 1943 and Kursk in July and August 1943.

With the end of the war in Europe in sight, Zhukov led his troops across eastern Europe toward Germany, capturing Berlin in May 1945. He was at the head of the delegation that accepted Germany's unconditional surrender on May 8, 1945. Immediately after the war, Zhukov was put in charge of the Soviet occupation of Germany; he was removed a year later. Zhukov had won three Gold Medals as a "Hero of the Soviet Union" during the war and was probably the second-most respected figure to the Soviet people, after Stalin. Stalin gave Zhukov jobs commanding the Odessa and Ural military districts, far from the center of Soviet political life. Upon Stalin's death in 1953, Zhukov became deputy defense minister, and acted as defense minister from 1955 to 1957. Zhukov's close relationship with Communist party leader Nikita Khrushchev resulted in his being named a member of the party's Central Committee. A few months later he left public office.

Zhukov retired to his country home and began working on his memoirs, which were initially published in a censored form. The full version of Zhukov's memoirs appeared in 1989, fifteen years after his death, and in 1995 a statue was erected in his memory.

Georgy Zhukov. (Library of Congress)

especially if they disagreed with the government, knowing the penalty would be swift and severe.

Stalin created a public image of himself as a great hero. Cities, towns, villages, and even the tallest mountain in Russia were named after him, and he was mentioned in the national anthem. Yet he was increasingly fearful of enemies and suspicious of everyone around him. In the mid-1930s he initiated a series of purges, during which an estimated 17 to 25 million people were sent to gulags; approximately 1 million were executed and 7 million died in the gulags. Stalin also purged the Soviet armed forces, killing most of the country's marshals, generals, and admirals. This dismantling of the military would prove a mistake when the Germans invaded the Soviet Union in 1941.

During the 1930s, Nazi leader Adolf Hitler became dictator of Germany and began expanding his empire with the annexation of Czechoslovakia and Poland. In August 1939 Stalin was also interested in expanding his territories; he signed an agreement with Hitler in which the Soviet Union and Germany divided the countries of eastern Europe between them and promised not to attack one another. Lithuania, Latvia, Estonia, and (after a short war of resistance) Finland were forced to join the Soviet Union. Despite warnings from advisors who claimed Hitler would not honor his agreement, Stalin was stunned when the German army invaded Russia in June 1941. Realizing the gravity of the situation, Stalin took personal command of the Soviet armed forces. On July 3, 1941, he addressed the Soviet people in a radio broadcast (the first time most of them had heard their leader's voice) and called on them to resist the enemy. The Soviet Union entered World War II on the side of the Allies.

World War II

The Germans quickly swept through the province of Russia until they reached the outskirts of two of its largest cities, Moscow and Leningrad (formerly St. Petersburg). They had confiscated half of Russia's industry and agriculture, and placed approximately 40 percent of the population under German control. In response, Stalin shifted many Soviet industries to the eastern part of the country where they would be safer from the Germans. He arranged to borrow supplies and equipment from other Allied countries and built morale by stirring up the religious and patriotic feelings of Soviet citizens. He even relaxed some of the restrictions he had imposed, letting people practice traditional religion more openly and allowing more artistic expression. Stalin advocated a "scorched earth" policy, in which the Soviets destroyed crops and property rather than allow them to fall into the hands of the Germans. With Germans entrenched around Moscow, Stalin ignored brutal winter weather and called for a counterattack. The Red Army gained ground despite massive casualties. In July 1942 Stalin issued an edict proclaiming that any Soviet soldier taken prisoner would be considered a traitor. When his own son Vasili was captured by the Germans, he responded by disowning him and later refused an offer by the Germans to exchange Vasili for a captured German officer.

Stalin used the threat of severe punishment to intimidate citizens, foot soldiers, high-ranking officers, and government officials. Despite his despotic rule, most agreed that he ran the war effort well, planning strategies that worked, promoting capable commanders, and representing the Soviet Union at several important Allied conferences. In January 1943 the Red Army won another important battle, reclaiming the city of Stalingrad (now Volgograd). That summer, the Soviets defeated the Germans at Kursk, then began pushing German forces out of the Soviet Union. These victories boosted Stalin's image both at home and abroad. Allied troops referred to him as "Uncle Joe" and considered him an enemy of Nazism, even though he had made agreements with the Nazis prior to the war.

In April 1945 Russian troops were the first to enter Berlin, where Hitler was hiding in an underground bunker. When Hitler committed suicide on April 30, the Germans soon surrendered to the Allies. As the war drew to a close, Stalin used his newfound popularity and the Russian contribution to the Allied victory to gain Soviet control over most of Eastern Europe. He soon returned to his ironfisted methods, beginning the Cold War between the Soviet Union and the Western countries that would last till the 1980s. In March 1953, Stalin suffered a stroke and died of internal bleeding.

SOURCES

Books

Caulkins, Janet, *Joseph Stalin,* Franklin Watts (New York), 1990.

Conquest, Robert, *Stalin: Breaker of Nations,* Viking Penguin (New York), 1991.

Hoobler, Dorothy, and Thomas Hoobler, *Joseph Stalin,* Chelsea House (New York), 1985.

Kallen, Stuart A., *The Stalin Era: 1925–1953,* Abdo & Daughters (Edina, MN), 1992.

Marrin, Albert, *Stalin,* Viking Kestrel (New York), 1988.

Whitelaw, Nancy, *Joseph Stalin: From Peasant to Premier,* Dillon Press (New York), 1992.

Other

Joseph Stalin, http://www.grolier.com/wwii/wwii_stalin.html (May 5, 2000).

Franz Stangl

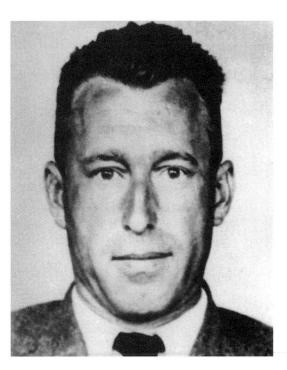

Franz Stangl headed two German death camps, Sobibór and Treblinka, during World War II. He was responsible for establishing the Treblinka camp as one of the most efficient killing stations in the Nazi empire. Despite years of flight after the war, Stangl was captured, placed on trial, and found guilty of his crimes. He defended his actions at the death camps by claiming he only did his duty.

Early Life

Franz Stangl was born in the small town of Altmünster, Austria, in 1908. He and his older sister were the children of a night watchman and his much younger wife. As a child, Stangl was frightened of his father, who ran the house with military precision. When Stangl was eight, his father died, and his mother married a widower who had two children. Young Stangl became close to his stepbrother, Wolfgang, who was the same age. At fifteen, Stangl left school to become an apprentice weaver. By eighteen, he was the youngest master weaver in Austria. He worked at the trade for several years, and contributed 80 percent of his earnings to the family household. He supplemented his pay by giving lessons on the zither, a musical instrument he had taught himself to play. Concerned about dust-related illnesses associated with the weaving industry, Stangl decided to find another trade. He became a policeman in 1931,

Born March 16, 1908
    Altmünster, Austria
Died June 28, 1971
    Düsseldorf, Germany

Policeman; weaver; captain of the Schutzstaffel (SS); commandant of the Treblinka and Sobibór death camps

"I have nothing on my conscience. I did nothing but my duty."

(American Jewish Archives/USHMM Photo Archives)

1943 Rebellion at Sobibór

A rebellion took place at the Sobibór death camp on October 14, 1943, a little more than a year after Franz Stangl was transferred to another camp. The event was organized by Alexander Perchersky, a captured Jewish Soviet soldier. In order to reach the camp's arsenal, the rebels had to distract head Nazi officers. On the day of the revolt, a dozen Nazi officers were lured separately into camp workshops and silently killed with hatchets. Although the rebels were unable to seize the arsenal, they did manage to cut the phone lines into the camp. This delayed the arrival of Nazi reinforcements to put down the revolt. Two-thirds of Sobibór's 600 inmates ran into the woods. Half of them were killed by land mines surrounding the camp, while others were shot by Nazis and Polish Nazi-sympathizers. Perchersky was among sixty rebels who escaped and joined Soviet troops nearby. Two days after the rebellion, Nazi official Heinrich Himmler ordered that Sobibór be dismantled.

and joined the political division of the criminal police department, which investigated anti-government activities, in 1935. When the Austrian chancellor was assassinated, Stangl discovered a secret supply of German weapons while searching for clues in a forest. He turned the weapons over to the Austrian authorities and was awarded a medal.

Joins Nazi Party

By 1937 the Nazi party was experiencing strong support in Austria. Fearful of possible Nazi retaliation for his earlier discovery and disposal of German armaments in Austria, Stangl joined the party in 1938, the same year the Nazis overtook the country. By 1939, Stangl was assigned to the state police in Linz, Austria, and served in the Jewish Bureau. In accordance with Nazi deportation policy at the time, Stangl's duty in the Jewish Bureau was to convince Jews to emigrate from Austria. Jews who chose to leave were required to surrender all private property while also paying for necessary exit permits. Nazi leader Adolf Hitler objected to anyone in the Nazi party remaining loyal to the Catholic church, seeing this commitment as a threat to his power. Stangl was required to sign a paper that affirmed his faith in God but stated that he was not a Catholic. Stangl later claimed his subsequent involvement in the Nazi party was due to fear. In 1935 Stangl married a woman named Therese, with whom he had three daughters. As Stangl became increasingly entangled in Nazi activities, however, Therese distanced herself from him.

Heads Death Camps

From 1940 to 1942, Stangl was the superintendent in charge of maintaining security for the Nazis' Euthanasia Institute at Schloss Hartheim, Germany (near Linz). This top-secret agency was in charge of the "mercy-killing" of mentally and physically disabled people, and eventually had a central role in the extermination of Jews. In 1941 Stangl was sent to Bernburg, another euthanasia center, where he later claimed to have handled insurance, property rights, and other matters for families of people killed by the Nazis—he denied having any knowledge that political prisoners were being gassed there at the time. In 1942 the Sobibór concentration camp was opened in Poland, and Stangl was named commandant. More than 100,000 people were gassed at Sobibór within the first two months. The Nazi death camps at Chelmno, Belzec, Treblinka, and Sobibór were different from the other concentration camps, where inmates were put to work supporting the German war effort—and where they had at least a small chance to survive. In contrast, about 100 people survived the four death camps, where approximately 2 million Jews and Roma (Gypsies) were murdered. According to writer Gitta Sereny: "The killings were organized systematically to achieve the maximum humiliation and dehumanization of the victims before they died."

In 1942 Stangl's wife and daughters came to live with him at Sobibór. Therese did not know about the genocide until one of Stangl's drunken colleagues told her. When she became extremely upset and confronted Stangl, he claimed that he was merely in charge of construction and did not personally carry out the murders. Eventually, Therese

Stangl at his war crimes trial in 1970. (Reproduced by permission of AP/Wide World Photos)

convinced herself that his role was merely administrative and tried to resume a normal life. In September 1942 Stangl was placed in charge of Treblinka, a position he held for eighteen months. Conditions at Treblinka were even worse than at Sobibór, and Stangl later claimed that on numerous occasions he unsuccessfully tried to get transferred out of Treblinka. Writer Tom Segev disagrees: "Had [Stangl] wanted to, he could have gotten up and gone." Segev admits that leaving would not have been without risk for Stangl—it could have ended his career, or resulted in him being sent to the front lines to fight. Still, writes Segev: "All the assignments [Stangl] performed prepared him psychologically [mentally] for what came next. He toughened and felt more and more apart from those led to death. At some point he ceased to see [the prisoners] as human beings like himself."

In 1942 Stangl ordered the construction of a phony railway station at Treblinka. It had a fake clock with hands that did not move, and false ticket-windows displaying train connections to other areas of Poland. The purpose was to trick newly arriving prisoners into thinking they were going to be sent to work camps, thus making them more easily controllable. Upon arrival at the death camps, the prisoners were stripped of their clothes and marched naked to their deaths, sometimes beaten with whips as they went. When asked if he could have changed the mode of execution, Stangl claimed he could not. It has been estimated that during Stangl's tenure at Treblinka, nearly 900,000 Jews were killed there. Despite an apparent alcohol addiction, Stangl was highly praised by Nazi headquarters for being so efficient in his work. According to Franz Suchomel, a former SS member, Stangl cared more about efficiency than about the treatment of the Jews. Stangl claimed the primary reason for exterminating the Jews was to obtain their money and valuables, and that anti-Semitic policies merely provided an excuse to claim these material possessions.

The Treblinka Uprising

On August 2, 1943, Jewish prisoners at Treblinka staged a major uprising. For reasons that remain in dispute, shots rang out from the lower portion of the camp. A gasoline storage building exploded, and numerous fires were started around the camp. The shooting lasted somewhere between ten and thirty minutes. Groups of prisoners tried to escape, but only seven or eight succeeded. Several who fled lived in a nearby forest for more than a year, while others survived by pretending to be Gentiles. At the time of the revolt, Stangl ordered the camp surrounded, and hundreds of prisoners were returned at gunpoint. Despite damage to the camp, the gas chambers remained intact. Stangl was planning repairs to Treblinka when an order came from the Nazi high command that stated that the camp was to be closed and the staff reassigned.

Escape and Recapture

In 1943 Treblinka was torn down to destroy any evidence of genocidal activity. Stangl was not punished for the revolt that took place under his command, but instead was sent to Trieste, Italy, where he worked for a short time in the San Sabba concentration camp. He also served as a procurement officer, in charge of buying shoes, clothes, and food for German soldiers, mostly on the black market. After becoming ill in 1945, he was hospitalized in Italy. By the time Stangl was told to report to headquarters in Berlin, the Nazi government was in disarray. Knowing that Germany had lost the war, Hitler committed suicide on April 30, 1945. Shortly thereafter, Berlin fell to the Allies. Grand Admiral Karl Dönitz, who was appointed Hitler's successor, authorized the surrender of Germany a week later. Stangl fled during the subsequent confusion, but was soon caught by U.S. forces and placed in prison at Glasenbach. Stangl's wife and family remained at their home in Wels, Austria.

In 1948 Stangl escaped from the prison. Using forged identity papers, he made his way to Rome, Italy, and from there to Damascus, Syria, where he was joined by his family. In 1951 they traveled to South America. By the mid-1960s, Stangl was working as a safety official at a Volkswagen auto plant in São Bernardo do Campo, near São Paolo, Brazil. He was finally apprehended when his former son-in-law reported his whereabouts to Austrian Nazi-hunter Simon Wiesenthal. In 1967 Stangl was taken to Düsseldorf, Germany, to stand trial for war crimes. In 1970 one of the last major Nazi war crimes trials was held in Germany, and Stangl was sentenced to life imprisonment for his involvement in the murder of nearly 900,000 Jews. Testimony at the trial charged that he had raised the death toll at Treblinka to 10,000 per day. In June 1971 sixty-three-year-old Stangl died of a heart attack in prison while awaiting a federal court appeal. He had also been scheduled to face trial in Austria for his part in the euthanasia program at the Euthanasia Institute. Following his death, his wife and three daughters continued to live in Brazil.

Sources

Books

Segev, Tom, *Soldiers of Evil: Commandants of the Nazi Concentration Camps,* translated by Haim Watzman, McGraw-Hill (New York), 1988.

Sereny, Gitta, *Into That Darkness: From Mercy Killing to Mass Murder,* Deutsch (London), 1974.

Wiesenthal, Simon, *The Murderers Among Us,* edited by Joseph Wechsburg, Heinemann (London), 1967.

Edith Stein

On October 11, 1998, Edith Stein became the first person in modern times who was born a Jew to be declared a saint by the Roman Catholic church. Stein was a respected writer and philosopher when she converted to Catholicism at the age of thirty. Twelve years later she entered a convent as a nun; she was executed by the Nazis at Auschwitz in 1942. Stein's canonization immediately caused controversy within the Jewish community. Many Jews claimed the canonization, coming as it did while the church maintained silence on atrocities committed by Nazis during the Holocaust, undermined the memories of the millions of Jews who died during World War II.

An Exceptional Intelligence

Edith Stein was born on Yom Kippur, the Jewish holiday known as the Day of Atonement, in 1891. She was the youngest of seven children of Siegfried and Auguste Stein, a Jewish couple. The Steins lived in Breslau (now Wroclaw, Poland), then one of the largest Jewish communities in Germany. Upon Siegfried's death in 1893, Auguste took over the family lumber business. Edith's intelligence and aptitude became evident when she was still quite young; at age six she asked her mother if she could bypass kindergarten and start school immediately. When she was fifteen, Stein renounced her Jewish faith, proclaiming herself an atheist. She dropped out of school for six

Born October 12, 1891
   Breslau, Germany (now Wroclaw, Poland)
Died August 9, 1942
   Auschwitz, Poland

German Jew who converted to Catholicism and became a nun

"In my dreams I always foresaw a brilliant future for myself.… I was convinced that I was destined for something great.…"

(Reproduced by permission of UPI/Corbis-Bettmann)

months, but later returned to her studies. In 1911 she entered the University of Breslau for two years before transferring to the University of Göttingen. Initially, she studied psychology, but finally turned to philosophy. She became a student of Edmund Husserl, a leader in the field of phenomenology, a branch of philosophy that concerns the nature of thought and experience. While pursuing her doctorate at Göttingen, Stein associated with a circle of exceptional students, several of whom would later become noted philosophers. When Germany entered World War I (1914–1918), Stein volunteered to serve in a hospital run by the Red Cross. In 1915 she spent six months at the Weisskirchen Epidemic Hospital in Moravia nursing Austrian soldiers who suffered from dysentery and cholera. After the war, Stein returned to Breslau and accepted a brief teaching position at her former high school. Relocating to Göttingen to complete work on her doctoral thesis, she took a position as Husserl's teaching assistant, conducting classes for his beginning students and preparing his papers for publication.

In 1917 Stein's friend Adolf Reinach was killed in the war. Intending to lend her support to Adolf's widow, Anna, Stein was awestruck when Anna consoled her instead. A recent convert to Christianity, Anna claimed faith allowed her the serenity to accept her husband's death. Deeply moved by this expression of belief, Stein made the conscious decision to become a Christian. In 1918, after earning her Ph.D., Stein returned to Breslau to write and publish articles about philosophy. She applied for teaching positions at numerous German universities, none of which would hire a female philosophy professor. Three years later, while visiting a friend, Stein was left alone when everyone else went out. To occupy her time, Stein began reading the autobiography of Theresa of Avila, a Catholic saint who lived from 1515 to 1582. Stein was immediately captivated by Theresa.

Becomes a Catholic

Despite the strong objections of her mother and many of her friends, who felt she had turned her back on her own heritage, Stein was baptized into the Catholic faith on January 1, 1922. She wanted to enter a convent, but a spiritual advisor recommended she wait, claiming it would be too difficult for her family to accept. She spent the next eleven years as a teacher while continuing to write and lecture. Although she was not yet a nun, she privately took vows of chastity, poverty, and obedi-

ence. From 1923 to 1931, Stein worked at a teacher's college, where she helped high school girls and nuns prepare for teaching careers. In 1932 she was hired to teach at the German Institute for Scientific Pedagogy in Münster. In 1933 Stein's teaching career was cut short by the Nazis, who banned Jews from holding public positions. She had to leave her job and stop publishing her work. Feeling uncomfortable in the secular world, Stein chose to enter the convent, a decision that was not understood by her family. Her mother was especially upset, knowing that she would probably never see her daughter again. Asked why she was abandoning the Jewish people in their time of greatest need, Stein replied that her actions were not a rejection of her heritage but instead a way to help others by praying for them within the convent.

On October 14, 1933, Stein took the name Teresa Benedicta of the Cross and entered the Cologne Carmel (a convent of the Carmelite order of nuns). Recognizing Stein's gifts, her superiors provided her time to study and to write about religious and philosophical topics. She continued work on her autobiography, which she hoped would honor her mother and demonstrate that the lives of Jews were different from the negative stereotypes portrayed by the Nazi party. Stein was well aware of what was happening to Jews in the outside world, and, like other German Jews, was made to wear a yellow Star of David on her clothing. She wrote a letter to Pope Pius XII, head of the Roman Catholic church, asking him to publicly condemn the Nazis, but received no reply. On November 9, 1938, the Nazis carried out their *Kristallnacht* ("Crystal Night," or the "Night of Broken Glass") pogrom, during which Jewish homes, businesses, and synagogues were destroyed and 30,000 Jews were sent to concentration camps. For her protection, Stein was sent to a convent in Echt, Holland, where she hid for nearly three years. On August 2, 1942, the Nazis entered the convent and arrested Stein and her sister Rosa, who had also converted to Catholicism. Stein spent approximately a week in two transport camps in Holland before being sent to Auschwitz. She arrived on August 9 and was killed in the gas chambers that day, along with her sister and about 700 Dutch Catholics.

At a ceremony held in the Cologne soccer stadium in May 1987, Pope John Paul II beatified Stein, declaring her a holy person to be admired and respected, and saying she remained faithful to both her Jewish heritage and her Catholic faith. Rumors that Stein would eventually be made a saint stirred up controversy among some Jews, who were troubled by her conversion at a time when it was so dangerous to be Jewish. Others felt that the vast majority of Holocaust victims were Jews, and Stein's sainthood was an attempt to deflect attention from accusations that the Catholic church failed to condemn Nazism adequately. Some believed that Stein was not killed by the Nazis because of her Catholicism at all, but instead solely because of her Jewish lineage. The Catholic church responded by claiming that Stein and the other Catholics killed at the same time were probably murdered in revenge for a statement against Nazism that Holland's Catholic bishops had made a month earlier. When Stein was canonized on October 11, 1998, the top church official for Jewish-Catholic relations, Cardinal William Keller, made it clear that her sainthood should not take attention away from the fact that Jewish people were the main targets and victims of the Holocaust. The church honored Stein in this way, they said, because she had promoted understanding between Christians and Jews and because she died a martyr to both her heritage and her faith.

SOURCES

Books

Herbstrith, Waltraud, *Edith Stein,* Harper & Row (San Francisco), 1985.

Oben, Freda Mary, *Edith Stein: Scholar, Feminist, Saint,* Alba House (New York), 1988.

Periodicals

Donohue, John W., "Edith Stein, Saint," *America,* June, 21 1997, p. 8.

Gordon, Mary, "Saint Edith?," *Tikkun,* March–April 1999, p. 17.

Jerome, Richard, "The Convert: Born a Jew, Edith Stein Is Tapped for Sainthood," *People Weekly,* May 19, 1997, p. 161.

Michael, Eleanor, "Saints and Nazi Skeletons," *History Today,* October 1998, p. 4.

Payne, Steven, "Edith Stein: A Fragmented Life," *America,* October 10, 1998, p. 11.

Penner, Martin, "A Martyr, But Whose?," *Time,* October 19, 1998, p. 16.

Karl Stojka

Born April 20, 1931
Wampersdorf, State of
Burgenland, Austria

Austrian Roma (Gypsy) who survived
imprisonment in three concentration
camps; painter of autobiographical art;
Oriental rug specialist

*"God made me a Gypsy in this life, and for
that I thank God, and shall always be
proud to be a Gypsy."*

Largely overlooked or forgotten in studies of the Holocaust are the estimated quarter-million Roma, or Gypsies, who lost their lives at the hands of the Nazis. Gypsy artist Karl Stojka was one of the fortunate survivors. In 1990 an exhibition of his paintings brought worldwide attention to the imprisonment, persecution, and murder of Gypsies in Nazi death camps.

Nazis Restrict Gypsies

Karl Stojka was born on April 20, 1931, the fourth of six children of Karl Wackar Horvath Stojka and his wife. The Stojkas, descendants of a Gypsy family that had lived in Austria for more than 200 years, were well-known traveling horse traders; sometimes Stojka's mother supplemented the family income by telling fortunes. Stojka was born in his family's caravan. The Stojka children enjoyed a life of considerable freedom, but because the family was poor, they were expected to contribute to the household at a young age. The children gathered wood for meals prepared at the campfire, carried water, and fed and groomed the horses. When times were especially hard, the family had to beg for help from farmers.

In 1938 the Stojkas' life changed dramatically with the German annexation of Austria. Almost immediately after the takeover, the family moved their caravan into the city of Vienna, converted it

Prejudice Against Gypsies

Until the twentieth century, the Gypsies lived a nomadic existence. The Gypsy people are believed to have originated in India, arriving in Europe by the fifteenth century. While some joined the Muslim faith, more European Gypsies became Roman Catholics; a majority also retained elements of their old beliefs. Wherever they roamed, the Gypsies encountered prejudice because of their dark skin and unfamiliar language. Coupled with their nomadic lifestyle, the belief that Gypsies had the ability to foretell the future sparked superstitious distrust. They were often accused of stealing and general dishonesty, and the term "gypsy" itself was used in an unflattering way to describe a person who cannot settle down or a thief. Many Gypsies today prefer to be called Roma or Sinti.

In 1899 anti-Gypsy policies became official when Bavaria established an office for Gypsy affairs. This office dictated anti-Gypsy regulations until the Nazis started their rise to power in the 1920s. In 1935 the Nazis passed the Nuremberg Laws, which were designed to keep the German race "pure" by forbidding marriages between Germans and Jews and Germans and Gypsies. After 1936, Gypsies, like Jews, had to be registered. The records were used in the deportation of Gypsies and Jews in the late 1930s. Later, killing replaced deportation as Nazi policy.

The Jews, too, had originally been a nomadic people, and both groups, the Gypsies and the Jews, have faced considerable prejudice throughout their history. The Nazis regarded both groups the same way, as racially inferior and worthless.

into a house, and tried to adjust to a settled existence, acting on their belief that Gypsies who traveled around or lived in wagons were more likely to be persecuted by the Nazis than those with fixed homes. As members of the family secured factory employment, seven-year-old Karl began attending school despite Nazi legislation forbidding Gypsies to receive an education.

Stojkas Sent to Camps

In 1938 the Nazis sent a quarter of Austria's estimated 12,000 Gypsies to concentration camps. By 1940, some 30,000 Gypsies had been expelled from Germany and relocated in recently conquered Poland. On December 16, 1942, Nazi official Heinrich Himmler issued an edict to send all Gypsies (with a few exceptions) to the Auschwitz concentration camp in Poland. Auschwitz was the largest and most deadly of the Nazi death camps, consisting of a killing center, a concentration camp, and a group of slave labor camps. In late 1941 or early 1942 Karl Sr. had become the first member of the family to be sent

to a concentration camp. Some time later, Stojka's mother received a container filled with the cremated remains of her husband. Although an attached note explained that he had died of a heart attack, the family later learned he had been beaten to death.

Stojka's fifteen-year-old sister Kathi was the next to be relocated. A year later, in spring 1943, she joined the rest of her family, including twelve-year-old Stojka, at the special Gypsy "family camp" at Auschwitz, where they had to perform pointless and mundane labor. Along with several hundred other Gypsy children, Stojka had to carry rocks from one place to another, and sometimes return them to their original positions. As Stojka grew older, he was assigned to work in the guards' cafeteria and had greater access to food. Despite the hardship, the Stojka family was fortunate to be kept together during their imprisonment, which allowed them to help each other procure food and clothing.

In 1944 Stojka was accused of stealing soap. After being whipped for his crime, he returned to his rock-hauling duties. From their housing unit,

A group of Roma, or Gypsy, prisoners await instructions from their German captors in a concentration camp. (USHMM Photo Archives)

the family could see the fires from the crematoria and watch Jews walk by on their way to be murdered. In late 1943 Stojka's youngest brother died of typhus, a disease caused by unsanitary conditions and malnutrition. Fearing an epidemic of the disease, the Nazis soon closed down the "family camp" and killed more than 3,000 of the inmates.

Stojka and his brother Hansi were sent to the Buchenwald concentration camp in Germany, but when Stojka arrived at Buchenwald, he was deemed unfit to work because of his small size and weakness due to malnutrition. When the Nazis threatened to send Stojka back to Auschwitz, where he would have faced certain death, Stojka's brother and uncle convinced them that Stojka was a dwarf. Believing he was healthy, the Germans decided to let him stay at Buchenwald to continue work carrying rocks. In early 1945 Stojka and Hansi were transferred to another concentration camp, just ahead of the advancing Allied armies. Conditions in the camps grew worse as the Allies drew nearer. To conceal the camp conditions and avoid worldwide condemnation, the Nazis con-

stantly moved prisoners out of the Allies' path on long death marches. On April 24, 1945, during their own death march from a third to a fourth camp, Stojka and Hansi were liberated by the U.S. Third Army under the command of U.S. General George Patton. After liberation, Stojka was found to be suffering from injuries sustained during many beatings by Nazi camp guards. He was hospitalized and operated on several times. Stojka's father, youngest brother, and thirty-five other family members died in the Holocaust. Stojka, his mother, three sisters, and a brother survived.

Documents Experience in Paintings

The surviving Stojkas returned to Vienna, where Karl Stojka operated a thriving business in Oriental rug sales and repair. Inspired by the beautiful colors in the rugs, he decided to take up painting. Beginning in 1970, he expressed his wartime experiences through a series of paintings that earned him a reputation as a leading amateur artist. In 1990 more than 100 of Stojka's paintings were featured in an exhibition called *The Story of*

Karl Stojka: A Childhood in Birkenau, presented at the Documentation Archives of the Austrian Resistance in Vienna. The exhibition catalog, which reproduced twenty of the paintings and contained Stojka's unpublished German-language autobiography, has become an important tool in educating the world about the Holocaust.

SOURCES

Books

Friedman, Ina R., *The Other Victims: First-Person Stories of Non-Jews Persecuted by the Nazis,* Houghton, Mifflin Company (Boston), 1990.

Wiesenthal, Simon, *Justice Not Vengeance,* translated by Ewald Osers, Weidenfeld and Nicolson (London), 1989.

Other

The Story of Karl Stojka: A Childhood in Birkenau, U.S. Holocaust Memorial Museum, exhibition at the Embassy of Austria, April 30–May 29, 1992.

Remembering the Holocaust's Gypsy Victims

Famous Nazi-hunter Simon Wiesenthal took up the cause of the Gypsies after the end of World War II, and he continues to speak out on their behalf, often lamenting that the world has forgotten the Gypsies. The United States Holocaust Memorial Museum in Washington, D.C., which seeks to educate the American public about the history of the Holocaust, has also recognized the Gypsy cause. Its efforts to develop educational materials about the fate of the Gypsy victims helped bring Karl Stojka and his art to public attention.

Chiune Sugihara

Born January 1, 1900
Yaotsu, Gifu Prefecture, Japan
Died July 31, 1986
Tokyo, Japan

Japanese diplomat

"I thought as follows: 'I can issue transit visas ... by virtue of my authority as consul. I cannot allow these people to die, people who had come to me for help with death staring them in the eyes. Whatever punishment may be imposed on me, I know I should follow my conscience.'"

In July 1940, a few months after Germany invaded Poland, Chiune Sugihara was running the tiny Japanese consulate in Soviet-occupied Kaunas, Lithuania. Thousands of Jewish refugees were flooding to the gates of the embassy and appealing for transit visas so they could flee through Russia to another country. Sugihara was confronted with a dilemma; as the representative of the Japanese government, which would soon be allied with Nazi Germany in World War II, he would be violating official policy by assisting the Jews. Yet he had always been true to his own conscience, and he felt a moral obligation to help people in distress. Although Sugihara's decision to issue the transit visas ultimately ruined his career, his selfless act made him a hero to Jews throughout the world.

Rises in Diplomatic Corps

Chiune Sugihara was born in Japan on January 1, 1900. (He changed his name to Sempo Sugihara after World War II.) Although his father wanted him to be a doctor, he entered Waseda University in Tokyo to study English. Working at such part-time jobs as longshoreman and rickshaw-puller, Sugihara financed his own education. While he was still a student at Waseda he was accepted into the Japanese foreign service program at a university in Harbin, China, where he specialized in Russian studies. Upon graduating with honors he was assigned to a government post in Manchuria, which was then controlled by Japan. Within a few years Sugihara had risen to the position of vice minister of foreign affairs and he was in line for appointment as minister. During his tenure in Manchuria, however, he had become increasingly alarmed at the harsh treatment of Manchurians by the Japanese. In 1934 he resigned his job in protest and returned to Tokyo. His knowledge of the Russian language qualified him for a post at the Japanese embassy in Moscow, but his transfer was prevented by a dispute he had with Soviet officials in Manchuria over the purchase of a railroad.

In 1939 Sugihara was sent to Lithuania to open a one-person Japanese consulate in the city of Kaunas (also known as Kovno). His job was to monitor the activities of the Soviet Union—the Japanese government was staunchly anti-Communist and therefore suspicious of the Soviets—and report on German preparations for war in Europe. In September 1939 Germany invaded Poland. Under the terms of the Nazi-Soviet Pact, a non-aggression treaty between Germany and the Soviet Union, the Soviets annexed Lithuania. The Nazis immediately began implementing their racial cleansing programs in Poland, deporting thousands of Jews to concentration camps. Thousands more people were fleeing for their lives. The only route out of Poland was through the Soviet Union, and the way to reach that destination was to cross into Soviet-controlled Lithuania. Yet the Soviets would not allow safe transit without proof that another country would provide asylum.

Issues Thousands of Visas

By late July 1940 crowds of refugees were gathering at the gates of Sugihara's consulate. Although he had heard stories about the atrocities the Nazis were committing against Jews, he had never witnessed their plight firsthand. Morever, he did not know what he, as a lone Japanese official, could do for them. On July 27 Sugihara met with Zorach Warhaftig, a representative of the Jewish Agency Palestine Office. Warhaftig explained the situation: the other embassies in Lithuania were either closed or were not interested in assisting the refugees; the people were therefore asking Sugihara to grant them transit visas that would enable them to cross Russia and find safety in another country. Sugihara told Warhaftig that he wanted to help, but he would first have to get permission from the Japanese government in Tokyo. Both men knew this could present a problem because Japan was negotiating a formal alliance with Germany in the war.

Deciding to take the risk, Sugihara sent a cable to Tokyo. Two days later he was informed that he could not issue a visa to anyone who could not state a specific destination. After discussing the matter with his wife, Yukiko, who was sympathetic to the Jews, Sugihara sent another cable requesting that Japan grant the visas on the understanding that the refugees would stay only thirty days in Japan. Since it would take at least twenty days for them to cross Russia, Sugihara argued, that meant they would have fifty days to find a destination country, and he was confident they would be able to do so. The Japanese government would not be moved, even after Sugihara's third appeal. Finally he realized he would have to disobey his country in order to do what he knew was right. Once again talking over the problem with his wife, he decided to take the latter course. On August 1, 1940, he went outside the consulate and announced that he would grant visas to anyone who wished to apply.

As people clamored into the embassy, Sugihara began processing the applications. The refugees still had to declare a destination country, an obstacle that had been cleared by Warhaftig. He had secured a document stating that the Dutch-controlled island of Curaçao in the Caribbean would not require a visa for entry. Refugees continued to stream into the embassy that first day, and every day for the next three weeks. Sugihara worked around the clock until he was exhausted, waiving rules and improvising hand-written forms when he ran out of applications. By this time government officials in Tokyo, alarmed at the number of Polish refugees entering Japan, were demanding that he stop issuing visas. He refused. At the end of August the Soviets shut down the embassy and the Sugiharas and their sons were ordered to go to Berlin. On August 30, the night before they were to leave Kaunas, they stayed at a hotel. They were met by a huge crowd because Sugihara had promised to continue processing visas from the hotel room; the next morning even more people were waiting at the train station. While sitting in the train car Sugihara wrote as fast as possible, finally scribbling his name on blank pieces of paper and tossing them into outstretched hands as the train moved away from the platform. Sugihara later said he had issued around 3500 visas (other estimates place the number at 1600 and 6000).

Honored by Israel

For the duration of the war Sugihara ran embassies in Czechoslovakia, Romania, and

Polish Jews Saved by Sugihara

After obtaining visas from Chiune Sugihara, Polish Jews traveled east through Lithuania into Siberia, where they boarded ships bound for Japan. They encountered no discrimination in Japan, and when their visas expired they were permitted to go to Shanghai for the duration of the war. Although Sugihara had been assured that the refugees could emigrate to Curaçao, the island was actually not open to them. After the war many Jews remained in Japan, while most settled in the United States, South America, or Palestine. Among those who went to the United States were 300 people from the rabbinical school Mirrer Yeshiva, including faculty, students, and family members, who eventually started a new school in New York City. They all had escaped from Mir, Poland, and were granted visas by Sugihara. In celebration of its fiftieth anniversary, the school established the Sempo Sugihara Educational Fund.

Germany. In 1945, when the Japanese surrendered to the Allies, Sugihara and his family were living at the consulate in Bucharest, Romania. They were arrested by Soviet soldiers and taken to a prison camp, where they were held for twenty-one months. After being released, the Sugiharas returned to Japan. Certain that the visa incident in Lithuania had long ago been forgotten, Sugihara applied for an ambassador position. When they reached Tokyo, however, the vice foreign minister asked for Sugihara's resignation. For a time he could find no real work. Eventually he was hired as branch manager of a trading company in Moscow, a job that required him to be away from his family for extended periods of time. Sugihara was working in Moscow in 1967 when Yehoshua Nishri, an Israeli embassy official, contacted Sugihara's son, Hiroki, in Tokyo. Nishri had been one of the refugees who received a visa in Kaunas, and he told Hiroki that Israel wanted to honor his father. When Hiroki relayed the message, Sugihara replied that he was too busy to make the trip. Nishri managed to persuade him, however, and three months later he went to Tel Aviv, where he was given a hero's welcome.

Sugihara met many of the people he had helped flee from Poland; for the first time in twenty-seven years he also saw Warhaftig, who had been involved in drafting the Israeli declaration of independence and was serving as the nation's minister of foreign affairs. In 1984 Sugihara was given the title "Righteous Among the Nations" by Yad Vashem. He was too ill to travel to Israel, so his wife accepted the award for him. Sugihara died two years later in Tokyo. In 1991 the Japanese government issued a formal apology to his family for firing him from his job.

SOURCES

Books

Levine, Hillel, *In Search of Sugihara: The Elusive Japanese Diplomat Who Risked His Life to Rescue 10,000 Jews from the Holocaust,* Simon & Schuster (New York), 1996.

Mochizuki and Dom Lee, *Passage to Freedom: The Sugihara Story,* afterword by Hiroki Sugihara, Lee & Low Books (New York), 1997.

Periodicals

Tracey, David, "Visas for Life," *Reader's Digest,* January 1994, pp. 69–74.

Telford Taylor

As World War II drew to a close, the Allied powers decided that top-ranking Nazis and Japanese officials should be tried for their war crimes in an international court of law. Initially selected as a member of the U.S. legal staff, U.S. Brigadier General Telford Taylor eventually became chief counsel at the war crimes trials held in Nuremberg. Aided by his experiences and extensive knowledge of international law, Taylor has written at length about Nazi Germany.

Joins Nuremberg Trial Staff

Telford Taylor was born in 1908 in Schenectady, New York, the son of an electrical engineer, John, and his wife, Marcia Estabrook (Jones) Taylor. After earning both bachelor's and master's degrees from Williams College in Massachusetts, Taylor received a law degree from Harvard University in 1932. That year, he took a position as a law clerk to a U.S. Circuit Court judge. He then went to Washington, D.C., where he performed legal work for various departments of the federal government. In 1935 Taylor began a four-year tenure as associate counsel for the U.S. Senate Committee on Interstate Commerce. In 1937 he married Mary Eleanor Walker, an attorney; the couple, who had three children, later divorced. Taylor became a special assistant to the U.S. Attorney General in 1939, and worked for the Federal Communications Commission (FCC) from 1940 through 1942.

Born February 24, 1908
    Schenectady, New York, United States
Died May 23, 1998
    New York, New York, United States

Brigadier general of the U.S. Army; lawyer; law professor; author; chief counsel at the Nuremberg war crimes trials

"A nation in which the individual means nothing will find few leaders courageous and able enough to serve its best interests."

(Reproduced by permission of Corbis)

Taylor (front right) seated at the prosecution table with his staff during one of the Nuremberg trials. (Hedy Epstein/USHMM Photo Archives)

In December 1941 the United States joined the Allies in their fight against the Axis powers. Taylor entered the U.S. Army in 1942, quickly advancing to the rank of colonel. From 1943 to 1945, he was stationed in London, England, analyzing enemy messages gathered and decoded by the U.S. Army. In 1945, with the war in Europe over, Taylor joined the staff of Robert H. Jackson, an associate justice of the U.S. Supreme Court. Jackson had been appointed by President Harry S Truman to serve as chief prosecutor at Nazi war crimes trials held in Nuremberg. The Nuremberg war crimes tribunal (1945–1949) was composed of delegates from Great Britain, France, the Soviet Union, and the United States; the trials were conducted by judges and chief prosecutors from the various member countries.

In preparation for the trials, Taylor researched all possible sources of evidence against the Nazis that could be located in Washington, D.C. Then, in autumn 1945, he went to Nuremberg. During his first months in the city, Taylor outlined the procedure for gathering and processing evidence to be used at the trials. Working closely with the Soviet

Union, he prepared part of the indictment on war crimes and crimes against humanity in eastern Europe. The crimes against humanity included murder, ethnic extermination, enslavement, persecution on political or racial grounds, involuntary deportation, and inhumane acts against civilian populations. At Taylor's suggestion, the tribunal held a series of trials instead of a single trial. The first to be tried were prisoners against whom prosecutors had gathered substantial evidence. Despite a petition challenging the legality of the proceedings filed by the defense, the Nuremberg trials opened on November 20, 1945. On the first day, prosecutors read the full indictments against the prisoners, who included such Nazi officials as Hermann Göring, Rudolf Hess, Joachim von Ribbentrop, General Alfred Jodl, Franz von Papen, Albert Speer, and others. All the defendants pleaded not guilty.

Appointed Chief Prosecutor

Robert H. Jackson made the opening statement for the prosecution. Taylor wrote that no other legal

Nazi Doctors on Trial

In November 1946 an international military tribunal with Brigadier General Telford Taylor of the United States as chief counsel opened criminal proceedings against twenty-three prominent German physicians and administrators for their voluntary participation in war crimes and crimes against humanity. Their offenses included the "Euthanasia" program, in which the mentally, emotionally, or physically impaired were systematically killed. Other Germans were prosecuted for their roles in thousands of scientifically improper experiments that were conducted on concentration camp prisoners without their consent. Many people died or were permanently injured as a result of the experiments. Two of the major defendants were Nazi doctor Karl Brandt, Adolf Hitler's personal physician, whom he appointed Reich Commissioner for Sanitation and Health, and Paul Rostock, Brandt's immediate subordinate, who headed the Office for Scientific and Medical Research.

During his presentation, Taylor noted that a small number of German doctors and scientists had spoken out against the medical experiments. But, Taylor maintained, the calling of a doctor is to protect life, and so the majority of medical personnel, who had either remained silent or actively participated in the Nazis' crimes, bore more than an average load of guilt. Nearly 1,500 documents were presented at the trials, which lasted almost five months. Eighty-five witnesses gave personal testimony. Sixteen of the doctors were found guilty, and seven were sentenced to death. Their executions took place on June 2, 1948.

speech he had ever heard matched the power of Jackson's. Taylor had at first been suspicious of reports of the Nazis' atrocities, but his opinion changed as the trials progressed and more and more evidence of massacres and mass exterminations at concentration camps came to light. Jackson prosecuted the first thirteen trials before returning to his duties at the U.S. Supreme Court in 1946. By now, Taylor was a brigadier general; he took Jackson's place as chief counsel and handled twelve trials. One particularly noteworthy trial (see box), conducted under the jurisdiction of the military government of the United States, concerned cruel and barbarous experiments conducted by Nazi doctors, such as Josef Mengele. In all, Taylor obtained indictments against twenty-three German physicians, scientists, and medical administrators; several German industrialists who had financed the Nazis, including Alfried Krupp; fifteen judges; thirteen SS guards; and several Nazi generals. He wanted to indict 200 to 400 more Nazi leaders, but the U.S. Army could not afford the expense.

Postwar Career

In 1951 Taylor became a partner in a New York law firm. He was a visiting law lecturer from 1957 to 1976 at Yale University and from 1958 to 1963 at Columbia Law School; he became a full law professor at Columbia in 1963. Taylor served as counsel for the Joint Council for Educational Television during the 1950s, and headed the New York City Advisory Board of Public Welfare from 1960 to 1963. In 1974 he was married for a second time, to Toby Barbara Golic, an attorney; they had two children.

Taylor has written a number of books on law and justice in modern states. In *The Anatomy of the Nuremberg Trials* (1992), Taylor provided an eyewitness account of the Nazi war crimes trials, proclaiming them fair, humane, and an international success. Taylor's other books include *Sword and Swastika: Generals and Nazis in the Third Reich* (1952), *Grand Inquest: The Story of Congressional Investigations* (1955), *The March of Conquest* (1958), *The Breaking Wave: The German Defeat in the Summer of 1940* (1967), *Two Studies in Constitutional Interpretation* (1969), *Nuremberg and Vietnam: An American Tragedy* (1970), *Guilt, Responsibility, and the Third Reich* (1970), *Munich: The Price of Peace* (1979), *Perspectives on Justice* (1975) (with Alan Dershowitz, George Fletcher, Leon Lipson and Melvin Stein), and *Courts of Terror: Soviet Criminal Justice and Jewish Emigration* (1976).

SOURCES

Books

Gilbert, G. M., *Nuremberg Diary,* Da Capo Press (New York), 1995.

Polmar, Norman and Thomas B. Allen, *World War II: America at War, 1941–1945,* Random House (New York), 1991.

Snyder, Louis L., *Louis L. Snyder's Historical Guide to World War II,* Greenwood Press (Westport, CT), 1982.

Taylor, Telford, *The Anatomy of the Nuremberg Trials: A Personal Memoir,* Knopf (New York), 1992.

Taylor, Telford, *Guilt, Responsibility and the Third Reich,* Heffer (Cambridge, MA), 1970.

Taylor, Telford, *Nuremberg and Vietnam: An American Tragedy,* Quadrangle Books, (Chicago), 1970.

Trials of War Criminals Before the Nuremberg Military Tribunals under Control Council Law No. 10. Nuremberg, October 1946–April 1949, U.S. Government Printing Office (Washington, D.C.), 1949–1953.

Corrie
ten Boom

In 1940 Corrie ten Boom was nearing the fiftieth year of her life. Employed as a watchmaker in her father's shop, the first woman in the Netherlands to be licensed in that field, she had for many years devoted her spare time to religious activities. She and her older sister, Betsie, lived with their widowed father in rooms above the watch shop. When Germany invaded neutral Holland and conquered the entire country in only five days, the Nazification of the Dutch people began. Ten Boom risked her life to shelter Jews from the Nazis, for which she was arrested and sent to a concentration camp. Upon her release, she dedicated herself to founding support groups for those displaced by the Nazis, tirelessly lecturing across the world in support of Holocaust victims. She also wrote a number of books about Christian topics and about her experiences during World War II. After settling in California, she remained active in her community until her death in 1983.

A History of Generosity

Cornelia Arnolda Johanna ten Boom was born in Amsterdam on April 15, 1892, to Casper ten Boom, a jeweler and watchmaker, and Cor Luitingh ten Boom. The family, who moved to Haarlem after Corrie's birth, lived a strictly Calvinistic and impoverished life, but was happy, offering shelter, food, and money to anyone in need. Casper was highly regarded in the community as a kind

Born April 15, 1892
    Amsterdam, Netherlands
Died April 15, 1983
    Placentia, California, United States

Evangelist; author

"I believe that God delights to use His children in the fulfillment of His plans for the world. I am sure He loves to use small people to do great things."

(Reproduced by permission of Russ Busby)

and generous man who, like his father before him, had a deep respect for the Jews, regarding them as God's ancient people who required special consideration from all Christians. Casper in turn passed this belief on to his children. Corrie supplemented the religious instruction she received at home from her parents with additional studies at a local Bible school. After a failed romance left her disappointed, Corrie decided to learn the watchmaking trade and join her father in the family business. She apprenticed briefly in a Swiss watch factory and then returned to Haarlem, working by day with her father to perfect her skills while devoting her evenings to helping her sister Betsie care for their ailing mother and aunts.

Throughout the 1920s and 1930s, the ten Booms opened their home to German war refugees and the children of missionaries who could not take them into the field. Affectionately dubbed the Beje (short for Barteljorisstraat, the name of the street it was on), the house was constantly overflowing with guests, some of whom stayed for years and grew to adulthood under the guidance of Casper, Betsie, and Corrie. In addition to working in the watch shop and caring for the children in the Beje, Corrie conducted Bible classes in public schools and taught Sunday school, making a special effort to reach out to the mentally challenged. With the financial support of several wealthy citizens of Haarlem, she organized youth clubs for teenage girls that provided religious instruction as well as lessons in music, singing, folk dancing, gymnastics, sewing, and handicrafts.

Initially, the German occupation of Holland had little impact on the daily routine of most Dutch people. However, by the end of 1940, the Nazis began imposing curfews and food rationing, confiscating property, and harassing Jews. When rules went into effect requiring Jews to wear yellow armbands, Corrie and Betsie had to convince their father that it would not be safe for him to wear one in protest. As the situation grew increasingly dangerous, the ten Booms began harboring resistance fighters and *onderduikers* (literally "those who dive under"—Dutch Jews and young men wanted by the police). Over a period of four years, dozens of refugees used the Beje as a stopover on their way to other places, and approximately six or eight people stayed permanently. Under the bottom shelf of Corrie's closet was a door leading to a secret room, a cramped but essential hiding place in case the Gestapo came. To assist those they could not shelter in Haarlem, the ten Booms also established a network of safe houses in the country. Corrie was the overseer of all these operations, which may have saved 700 Jewish lives.

Discovered by the Nazis

On February 28, 1944, the Beje was raided by the Gestapo. Everyone inside the house was arrested, as was anyone who came to the shop that day. Thirty-five people were taken into custody with Corrie, Betsie, their brother Willem and his family, their sister Nollie and her family, and eighty-four-year-old Casper. Six people who had hidden in the secret room stayed there for nearly three days before managing to escape. The ten Booms were split up and subjected to endless questioning by the Gestapo. Casper quickly grew weak and confused, dying only ten days after his arrest; all of the other people arrested in the Beje, with the exception of Corrie and Betsie, were eventually released. Corrie, extremely ill with bronchitis, was relocated to a prison at Scheveningen. When she was strong enough to attend a hearing on the charges that had been brought against her, the judge assigned to her case was deeply moved by her strength, courage, and her unwavering devotion to her faith. He later did what he could to help the ten Booms, even destroying incriminating papers that the Gestapo had found in the Beje.

Shortly after D-Day in June, 1944, Corrie was reunited with Betsie, and the two sisters were moved to the Vught concentration camp. To bolster morale and counter boredom and fear among their fellow prisoners, the women formed prayer groups and held discussions, making use of a Bible that Corrie had hidden in her clothes and smuggled into camp. As the Allied armies drew closer, rumors of an impending release swept through the barracks; it soon became clear, however, exactly how the Nazis planned to empty Vught. First the men and boys were shot, then the women were shipped to Germany to perform hard physical labor at the Ravensbrück concentration camp. Corrie continued her Bible studies as best she could, but conditions at Ravensbrück were considerably harsher than they had been at Vught. There was little time, energy, or opportunity to do much more than pray with and for other prisoners. Betsie, who had never been physically strong, died on December 16, 1944. Prior to her death she told Corrie of a dream she had about establishing a home for people who had suffered during the war and needed a safe, quiet place to recover before moving on with their lives. Betsie wanted Corrie to fulfill this wish.

Two weeks later, on New Year's Day, 1945, Corrie was handed her release papers and abruptly told to leave the camp. She later learned that a clerical error was responsible for her freedom; while some Dutch prisoners were indeed released at that time, Corrie was not supposed to be among them. Within days of her departure, all of the remaining women in Ravensbrück went to the gas chambers. Corrie made her way back to Holland and, after a brief convalescence, began speaking to small groups about her experiences at Ravensbrück and about Betsie's dream. At the conclusion of the war, Corrie increased her efforts, soliciting donations and banding together with friends to establish a rehabilitation center that housed displaced persons and former prisoners. The facility also served as a training center for evangelical workers.

Corrie presented her personal message of hope and faith to a wider audience in 1947, when she made her first trip to the United States. Over the next thirty years, until age and illness began to take their toll, she was on the move almost constantly, visiting nearly seventy countries. She also became a prolific author, particularly well-known for her 1971 autobiography *The Hiding Place.* Corrie used the royalties from this best-selling title to fund missionary work through an organization she founded called Christians, Incorporated. In 1977, at the age of eighty-five, Corrie settled in Placentia, California, her first real home since she had been taken from the Beje in 1944. She continued to write books and started a neighborhood Bible-study group, remaining active until August 1978, when she suffered a severe stroke that left her unable to move or speak. A succession of strokes over the next few years left her weaker still, and she died on April 15, 1983, her ninety-first birthday.

Sources

Books

Brown, Joan Winmill, *Corrie: The Lives She's Touched,* F. H. Revell (Old Tappan, NJ), 1979.

Browne, Ray B., editor, *Contemporary Heroes and Heroines,* Gale Research (Detroit), 1990–1998.

Carlson, Carole C., *Corrie ten Boom: Her Life, Her Faith,* F. H. Revell (Old Tappan, NJ), 1983.

ten Boom, Corrie, with John and Elizabeth Sherrill, *The Hiding Place,* Revell (Old Tappan, NJ), 1971.

ten Boom, Corrie, and Jamie Buckingham, *Tramp for the Lord,* Christian Literature Crusade (Fort Washington, PA), 1974.

ten Boom, Corrie, and Carole C. Carlson, *In My Father's House: The Years before "The Hiding Place,"* F. H. Revell (Grand Rapids, MI), 2000.

Other

The Hiding Place (video), Republic Pictures, 1975.

Dorothy Thompson

Born July 9, 1893
Lancaster, New York, United States
Died January 30, 1961
Lisbon, Portugal

American journalist

"She has shown what one valiant woman can do with the power of a pen. Freedom and humanity are her grateful debtors."

—WINSTON CHURCHILL

Dorothy Thompson established herself as a world-famous reporter in the 1920s and 1930s. Writing for newspapers and magazines, Thompson also made radio broadcasts informing audiences about the rise of Nazism and fascism in Europe. As one of the first to speak out against the Nazi party's political agenda, she was credited with promoting greater public awareness of the causes and events of World War II.

Early Career

Thompson was born in the rural town of Lancaster, New York, in 1893. Her family, which included her parents, Peter (a Methodist minister) and Margaret Thompson, and her two siblings, was poor but charitable. She was only seven when her mother died. Three years later, Peter Thompson remarried; his young daughter did not get along with her stepmother, and in 1908 she was sent to Chicago to live with two aunts, who lavished her with attention. She attended the Lewis Institute, which combined high school courses with a two-year college program. She entered Syracuse University as a junior in 1912, her tuition paid by a scholarship for the children of Methodist ministers. Thompson graduated in 1914 with a reputation as a well-spoken young woman.

Thompson's first job after college was working for the women's suffrage movement, which was gaining strength in many parts of the United States. For eight dollars per week, she worked at the New York State Women's Suffrage party headquarters. In 1917, the year New York women won the right to vote, Thompson began to give lectures on suffrage. These experiences sparked her interest in becoming a writer, and she wrote articles, published in local newspapers, on various political and women's issues. After an unhappy six months working as a copywriter for an advertising agency and a short stint as a publicity director for a social reform agency, Thompson decided to travel to Russia in search of reporting opportunities. In 1920 she boarded a boat headed for London, where she met a group of Zionists working to establish a Jewish state in Palestine (now Israel). Interested in their cause, she interviewed them while conducting research on Zionism. Twelve days later, when Thompson reached London, she wrote an article that was published by the International News Service. Soon inundated with assignments, she decided to remain in Europe, where there was an abundance of work.

The following year, at the age of twenty-eight, Thompson traveled to Vienna, Austria, to report on events in central Europe. Economic depression had resulted in social unrest and outbursts of violence in many central European countries. In 1921 Thompson was shot at during a riot in Bulgaria. By 1924 the *Philadelphia Public Ledger* and the *New York Evening Post* had made Thompson their central European bureau chief. From her headquarters in Berlin, Germany, she covered events in that city as well as Vienna and Warsaw, Poland. Numerous interviews with famous people, including the psychiatrist Sigmund Freud, brought her recognition as a journalist. In 1927 Thompson divorced her husband, a Hungarian writer named Joseph Bard whom she had married five years earlier. She traveled to the Soviet Union and published a series of articles that were later released as a book titled *The New Russia* (1928).

In 1928 Thompson married Sinclair Lewis, American author of the novels *Babbitt* (1922) and *Main Street* (1920), among others. After only a few years, though, the marriage was in trouble. Lewis had lost some of his popularity as a novelist and developed an alcohol addiction. He resented the time Thompson spent with her friends and accused her of caring more about her career than her family. In 1930 the couple hoped the birth of their son, Michael, would help their marriage. Lewis also won the Nobel Prize for literature that year. The couple separated in 1931.

Margaret Bourke-White: Photographer of War

A talented photographer who created photo-essays on numerous events and topics, Margaret Bourke-White provided visual images to accompany written descriptions given by Thompson and other journalists. She was in Moscow, Russia, with her husband, writer Erskine Caldwell, when the Germans attacked the city in 1941. The only foreign correspondent in Moscow at the time, Bourke-White photographed the event while Caldwell wrote about it. After the United States entered World War II in December 1941, Bourke-White became an official Army Air Corps photographer whose work was used both by the military and *Life* magazine. At one point, following American pilots en route from England to North Africa, the ship Bourke-White was aboard was torpedoed. In January 1943 she was allowed to go along on a bombing mission in Tunisia. When the Allies invaded Italy, Bourke-White photographed the bloody combat in the Cassino Valley, and as the war drew to a close she traveled with the Third Army of General George Patton into Germany. Bourke-White took many photographs inside the Nazi concentration camps as they were liberated, creating such unforgettable images as "The Living Dead of Buchenwald." (See full entry.)

Tracks the Rise of the Third Reich

In December 1931 Thompson went to Germany to interview Adolf Hitler for *Cosmopolitan* magazine. Finding Hitler to be an unpleasant, unimpressive person, she predicted he would never achieve the power he was seeking. While in Germany, Thompson observed the German people's support for Hitler and the Nazis and was alarmed to see a Hitlerjügend (Hitler Youth) camp, where approximately 6,000 young boys were being trained to fight for the Nazi cause. Through her articles and a book entitled *I Saw Hitler!* (1932), Thompson attacked the Nazis, ridiculing their methods and quest for power. Her publications increased her fame and she was in great demand on the lecture circuit. By 1933, Hitler had taken control of Germany, to Thompson's embarrassment and dismay. She remained in Germany and continued to condemn the Nazis, begging the rest of the world to prevent them from gaining more power. On August 25, 1934, Hitler sent a Gestapo agent to Thompson's hotel room with an order giving her twenty-four hours to leave the country. Thompson quickly departed for the United States, the first of many foreign journalists to be expelled by Hitler.

Back home, Thompson received a warm welcome from her fellow journalists and admirers, who praised her for her courage in criticizing Hitler. Thompson went on a lecture tour around the country as an expert in international affairs and an enemy of dictators. Two articles published in *Foreign Affairs* magazine gave her a reputation as a serious political commentator. Sinclair Lewis, inspired by his estranged wife's work, wrote a novel called *It Can't Happen Here* (1935), about the possibility of a dictator taking over the American government. In 1936 Thompson's popularity as a speaker led to her being hired as a radio commentator for NBC (National Broadcasting Company), a job she held throughout World War II. She also began writing a column, "On the Record," that appeared in 170 newspapers, including the *New York Herald Tribune*. It was read by an estimated 8 million to 10 million people every day. In 1937 she started a column in the monthly *Ladies Home Journal* magazine.

As the 1930s drew to a close, imminent war in Europe was of great concern to the American public. Every Monday evening, 5 million listeners gathered around their radios to hear Thompson report news and personal commentaries denouncing Nazism. With the outbreak of World War II in September 1939, a flood of refugees began pouring out of Europe, leading Thompson to open her own home to some of these displaced people. Nicknamed Cassandra, after the character from Greek myth who stands on the walls of Troy and predicts war, Thompson wrote articles urging governments to take the refugees' plight seriously and provide international aid. Thompson was called on to advise President Franklin D. Roosevelt in 1940. She continued to lecture and write, taking care to make her work easy to read and understand. On December 8, 1941, the day after Japan bombed the Ameri-

can naval base at Pearl Harbor, Hawaii, the United States entered World War II. Thompson's contribution to the war effort included broadcasting into Germany by short-wave radio. Hoping to reach a wide variety of Germans and inspire them to rebel against Hitler, she pleaded for an end to the fighting. She also continued to show concern for refugees, working as a member of the Emergency Rescue Committee. In 1942 Thompson was divorced from her estranged husband, Sinclair Lewis, and in 1943 she married Maxim Kopf, an Austrian-born artist to whom she remained married until his death in 1958.

Soon after Germany surrendered in May 1945, Thompson went to Europe to visit some war-torn areas, including the concentration camp at Dachau, Poland, and the heavily bombed city of Dresden, Germany. She was already back in the United States when two atomic bombs were dropped on Japan in August 1945, bringing an end to the war in the Pacific. Having witnessed so much destruction, Thompson was no longer as idealistic as she had been before the war. She continued to write her newspaper column for two years after the war and also published several books. She became deeply interested in the struggle between citizens of the new state of Israel and Arabs who had been uprooted by its creation. Thompson's pro-Arab stance angered some of her former admirers, who accused her of being anti-Semitic. She responded that she was not opposed to Jews but to the violence some Jews used against Arabs.

During the 1950s, other issues that concerned Thompson included the influence of television on young people. In particular, she was one of the first to note the amount of violence on television. She encouraged women to stand up for their rights and warned about the dangers of nuclear weapons. Thompson's last newspaper column appeared in 1958, but she continued to write her column for *Ladies Home Journal* until the end of her life. While on vacation in Lisbon, Portugal, in 1961, Thompson was alone in her hotel room when she died of a heart attack. She was buried next to her third husband, beneath a stone that reads: "Dorothy Thompson Kopf—Writer."

Sources

Books

Jakes, John, *Great Women Reporters,* Putnam (New York), 1969.

Kurth, Peter, *American Cassandra: The Life of Dorothy Thompson,* Little, Brown (Boston), 1990.

Sanders, Marion K., *Dorothy Thompson: A Legend in Her Time,* Houghton Mifflin (Boston), 1973.

Whitelaw, Nancy, *They Wrote Their Own Headlines: American Women Journalists,* M. Reynolds (Greensboro, NC), 1994.

Josip Broz Tito

Born May 7, 1892
Kumrovec, Croatia
Died May 4, 1980
Ljubljana, Yugoslavia

Politician; trade union official; factory
worker; locksmith; leader of Yugoslavia
(1945–1980)

*"Political death is the most horrible
death of all."*

(Reproduced by permission of Archive Photos, Inc.)

Josip Broz Tito was the Yugoslavian leader who successfully rallied his country against the Germans during World War II. In spite of overwhelming odds and enormous hardship, he won the hearts of his people, particularly the working class, and the respect of nations around the world. During his long tenure as government head, he resisted efforts by Russian communist dictator Joseph Stalin to invade Yugoslavia. A larger-than-life figure, Tito was able to maintain an independent style of government, called Titoism, for more than thirty years.

Embraces Communism

Josip Broz (he took the last name Tito later in life) was born the seventh of fifteen children on May 7, 1892, in the village of Kumrovec, Croatia, then part of the Austro-Hungarian Empire. In order to save money, his parents, Franjo and Marija Javersek Broz, sent him to live at the home of his maternal grandfather, where he remained until the age of eight. His formal education ended in 1904 when he was twelve. Tito's father wanted him to emigrate to the United States to find a better life, but the family could never raise the $100 required for the ship's fare. Between 1907 and 1912, Tito lived in several cities, working as a blacksmith, a locksmith, and a metal worker. He became active in trade unions, and was also exposed to the prin-

Tito (right) and his staff conduct their campaign against the Nazis from a secret mountain retreat during World War II. (Reproduced by permission of Archive Photos, Inc.)

ciples of communism. In 1913, at age twenty-one, Tito joined the Austro-Hungarian Imperial Army.

The following year, World War I (1914–1918) broke out, with the Central Powers (the Austro-Hungarian Empire, Germany, Bulgaria, and Turkey) fighting against the Allies (Great Britain, France, Russia, Italy, and the United States). Tito was immediately arrested in his homeland for antiwar activities and sent to prison. After being released in 1915, he returned to the army and was given the task of capturing prisoners and obtaining information about Allied troop movements. Within a short time, however, Tito was stabbed by a Russian soldier and spent more than a year as a prisoner in a Russian hospital. During this time he became a communist and joined the revolutionary Russian Red Army, which wanted to seize control from the Russian monarchy. In 1917 in St. Petersburg, Russia, Tito joined the Bolsheviks—a group that staged an unsuccessful coup against the government. The same group later succeeded and ruled the country as the Communist party.

After World War I ended in 1918, the country of Yugoslavia was established by joining the states of Serbia, Montenegro, Croatia, Slovenia, and other parts of the former Austro-Hungarian Empire. In 1920, after marrying a young Russian named Pelagia Belousova, Tito returned to Yugoslavia. The couple had three children in three years, but only one son, Zarko, survived. By 1923, Tito joined the Yugoslav Communist party, which had been banned by the Yugoslavian government in 1920. He was elected to a committee of trade unionists and, in 1924, was sentenced to a five-month jail term for his connection to a communist shipyard strike. Rather than serve time, Tito fled with his family to Zagreb, Yugoslavia, where he became the secretary of a metal workers union. From that time on, Tito's career revolved around politics. In 1928 he was placed on trial for procommunist trade union activities and was sentenced to five years in prison.

While Tito was incarcerated, Pelagia and Zarko returned to Russia; Pelagia and Tito were divorced in 1935. In 1937 Tito began a relationship with Herta Has, a student, and in 1941 she gave birth to his sec-

Jews Help Tito's Partisans

Yugoslavia became an independent country in 1918. At that time, according to writer Menachem Shelah, "the attitude of the [rulers] toward the Jews was benevolent, and the Jews felt secure and protected." Prior to Adolf Hitler's ascent to power in 1933, there was virtually no anti-Semitism in Yugoslavia. After the Germans occupied the country in April 1941, however, more than 60,000 of the 80,000 Yugoslavian Jews were captured and killed in Nazi concentration camps. Nevertheless, Tito's Yugoslavian Partisans worked to resist the Germans and help the Jews. In turn, the Jews played a significant role in the establishment of the Partisans' medical corps and in planning military maneuvers. Yet by the time the Partisans had gained the upper hand against the Germans in late 1942, most Yugoslavian Jews had already been exterminated. After World War II, many of the survivors relocated to Israel.

ond son, Aleksandar. Shortly thereafter, Tito left Has for another woman, Davorjanka Paunovic, who remained his secretary and companion until her death in 1946.

Works Against Russian Communists

While Tito was in prison, Peter II, the king of Yugoslavia, ordered the assassination of political opponents, including Communists. Many fled to Vienna. Tito was released from prison in 1934 and joined the political exiles in Vienna. The following year, Yugoslavian Communist party leaders rewarded his commitment to the cause by sending him to Moscow to work with the Russian Communists. Tito began undercover work for the Yugoslavian Communists, adopting a number of disguises and aliases to protect his identity—Tito was one of the names he used. In 1937 Soviet leader Joseph Stalin began to perceive the Yugoslavian Commu-

nists as enemies and issued orders for their murders. Tito was spared by Stalin, and in October 1940 became leader of the Yugoslavian Communists. By this time, World War II was raging as Germany swept across central Europe, conquering the countries in its path. On April 6, 1941, the Germans overwhelmed Yugoslavia. In response, Tito organized an armed group, popularly called the Partisans, to resist the German occupation.

By the end of 1941, Tito and his Partisan forces liberated half of the country from the Germans. In time, the Partisans succeeded in driving the Germans out of Yugoslavia. Tito became popular for his daring and his willingness to fight alongside his soldiers. Although he sometimes displayed outbursts of anger, he was compassionate toward Yugoslavian Jews. When German plans called for the destruction of the Jews, Tito told his men to help Jews who were trying to escape. He also supported Jewish efforts to establish a homeland in Israel.

Becomes Marshal of Yugoslavia

During the war, Tito's Yugoslav Communist Party (CYP) gained increasing popularity by meeting the country's food, housing, and health needs. Party membership reached 250,000 by 1943, and the Allies began supporting Tito's Partisans rather than the Yugoslavian king, Peter II. In November 1943 Tito's followers established a communist government, the National Liberation Committee, and proclaimed Tito marshal of Yugoslavia. In 1945, the CYP held an election in which all its candidates were victorious, mostly because opposing parties were prohibited. On November 29, 1945, Tito declared that the Federal Republic of Yugoslavia had officially replaced the monarchy as the legitimate government of his country. Tito gradually created a government patterned on the communist system in the Soviet Union. For instance, he used his secret police force to remove any opposition and declared a five-year plan to industrialize the country. Fearing a revolt of the peasant class, however, he never implemented plans to de-privatize agriculture. In 1946 Tito established a constitution that divided Yugoslavia into six republics: Bosnia-Herzegovina, Croatia, Macedonia, Montenegro, Serbia, and Slovenia, as well as the regions of Kosovo and Vojvodina.

Forms New Style of Government

Throughout the 1940s and 1950s, fundamental differences began to surface between Tito and

Stalin. In June 1948, fearing that Tito was too independent and did not follow "the party line" closely enough, Stalin threw Yugoslavia out of the major international association of Communist parties. Despite Tito's attempts to reconcile their differences, Stalin ordered Tito's assassination and sent Soviet troops to the border of Yugoslavia. The people of Yugoslavia, the CYP, and Western governments rallied around Tito as he moved to break up the central authority of his country's government and make it more democratic. On July 21, 1948, Yugoslavia's Fifth Party Congress unanimously supported his defiance of the Soviet Union. Moving away from communist policies, Tito established workers' councils that gave their members a voice in management decisions affecting their factories.

Tito began forming a new style of government—eventually called Titoism—that was based on a combination of communism and democracy. In 1953 he established a constitution that transferred authority from the national government to local governments, who were now permitted to run health care, education, arts, and social service programs. In time, citizens were permitted to criticize the government openly. Tito also instituted a new prison system and a legal system under which defendants were considered innocent until proven guilty. These reforms, combined with Western financial aid, helped Tito stay in power and defeat Stalin's attempts to have him overthrown. In 1952 sixty-year-old Tito married Jovanka Budisavljevic, a communist thirty-two years his junior. On January 13, 1953, the popular leader was named president of Yugoslavia, and ten years later he was granted the position for life.

While communism officially declares that all people share their resources, most high-level members of the party enjoyed special privileges. Tito and his wife lived in luxury, and he indulged his love of fine clothing and expensive cars. He spent most of his time at a lavish estate on Brijuni, an island group in the Adriatic Sea off the coast of Croatia, but also maintained handsome homes at other sites throughout the country. In his later years, Tito was visited by world figures in the fields of politics, sports, and the arts. In 1961 he published a book about his military experiences titled *Vojna djela*, which was translated into English as *Military Works*. Tito always remained a powerful force, though authority was eventually transferred to local governments. Even in the late 1970s, when he suffered from cancer and his leg was amputated, he was directly involved in governing the country. On May 4, 1980, just three days before his eighty-eighth birthday, Tito died. Hundreds of thousands of Yugoslavians wept as a carriage bore his body through the streets of Belgrade, the capital. His funeral was attended by 120 heads of state.

SOURCES

Books

Auty, Phyllis, *Tito: A Biography,* Penguin (Harmondsworth), 1974.

Djilas, Milovan, *Tito: The Story from the Inside,* translated by Vasilije Kojic and Richard Hayes, Harcourt Brace Jovanovich (New York), 1980.

MacLean, Fitzroy, *The Heretic: The Life and Times of Josip Broz-Tito,* Harper (New York), 1957.

Pavlowitch, Stevan K., *Tito: Yugoslavia's Great Dictator, A Reassessment,* Ohio State University Press (Columbus, OH), 1992.

Schiffman, Ruth, *Josip Broz Tito,* Chelsea House (New York), 1987.

Shelah, Menachem, "Yugoslavia," *Encyclopedia of the Holocaust,* edited by Israel Gutman, Macmillan (New York), 1990.

Vukcevich, Bosko S., *Tito: Architect of Yugoslav Disintegration,* Rivercross Publishing (New York), 1994.

Iva Toguri

Born July 4, 1916
Los Angeles, California, United States

Radio announcer for Radio Tokyo during World War II; tried for treason by the U.S. government

"I'm only sorry that my father never lived to see me pardoned.... 'I'm proud of you, Iva,' he used to tell me. 'You were like a tiger, you never changed your stripes, you stayed American through and through.'"

(Reproduced by permission of UPI/Corbis-Bettman)

Iva Toguri was the first woman in the United States to be tried and convicted for treason. Singled out as the infamous "Tokyo Rose" who broadcast propaganda to American troops serving in Japan during World War II, Toguri pleaded not guilty to the eight charges brought against her. Despite no written or recorded proof she had made a single treasonous broadcast, a highly publicized three-month trial resulted in a guilty verdict from an all-Caucasian jury. Toguri was sentenced to ten years in prison and given a $10,000 fine. After serving six years in a federal women's prison in West Virginia, she was released for good behavior. As new information about Toguri's trial and conviction became public and anti-Japanese sentiment began to fade, her case caught the attention of the media once again. On January 18, 1977, almost three decades after her conviction, President Gerald Ford pardoned Toguri.

A Citizen of the United States

Born July 4, 1916, in Los Angeles, California, Iva Ikuko Toguri was a nisei, a first generation child born to Japanese immigrants in America. Her father, a businessman, worked hard to provide his daughter with a good education. Raised a Methodist in a predominantly white neighborhood near Los Angeles, Toguri, unlike many nisei, spoke virtually no Japanese. At home she cared for her mother, who was paralyzed by diabetes. Toguri dreamed of becoming a doctor and, according to writer David Dyar: "listened to *The Shadow* and *Radio Orphan Annie* on the radio, joined the local Girl Scouts, played on the varsity tennis team, took piano lessons and had a crush on Jimmy Stewart." After completing high school, she attended Compton Junior College and, in 1941, graduated from UCLA with a bachelor's degree in zoology.

Toguri seemed destined for a bright future until, in 1941, news reached the family that her Aunt Shizu in Japan was seriously ill. Since Toguri's mother was too sick to undertake such a long voyage, Toguri was chosen to represent her family at her aunt's bedside. Sending her abroad was not an easy decision for her family because of the raging war in Europe and imperial Japan's control of China, Korea, and much of the South Pacific. Twenty-five-year-old Toguri set sail for Japan on July 5, 1941, with the approval of the State Department and without a U.S. passport. Her aunt soon recovered, but in December, less than five months after Toguri left home, Japan attacked Pearl Harbor forcing the United States to enter World War II officially. Toguri was one of almost 10,000 Japanese Americans who were stranded in Japan when war broke out between Japan and the United States.

Toguri was considered an enemy alien by the Japanese authorities, who demanded that she renounce her American citizenship. She steadfastly refused and requested internment with other foreign nationals, a demand that was denied because Toguri was a woman and of Japanese heritage. The *Kempeitai*, Japan's secret police, began to monitor Toguri's movements. When Toguri became overly loquacious in her pro-American sentiments, her aunt and uncle asked her to leave their home. Resources were scarce in war-time Japan, so with no money, no friends, and little command of the Japanese language, Toguri had to struggle to survive. She taught piano briefly and finally found work as a typist at the Domei News Agency. While transcribing English-language news broadcasts, she learned that her family, like hundreds of other Japanese Americans in the United States, had been forcibly interned under Executive Order 9066 and sent to the Gila River Relocation Center in Arizona. Toguri learned much later that her mother, already weak from illness, had died en route to the relocation center.

At the Domei News Agency, Toguri met Felipe d'Aquino, a Portuguese national who provided her sympathy and support. The pair would later marry. Meanwhile, the *Kempeitai*'s surveillance had turned to persistent harassment. Toguri eventually became ill from malnutrition and was hospitalized for six weeks. Upon her release, she was required to find a second job to pay back money she had borrowed from d'Aquino and her landlady to pay hospital bills. She found a second job at Radio Tokyo, typing English-language scripts written by Japanese officials for broadcast to Allied troops. At Radio Tokyo, Toguri met Major Charles Cousens, an officer who in civilian life was a famous radio personality in Sydney, Australia. Cousens, along with Allied officers Wallace Ince and Normando Reyes, had been captured by the Japanese in 1942 during fighting at Corregidor in the Philippines. Cousens and his associates were conscripted by the Japanese to produce and broadcast propaganda in English designed to demoralize Allied troops eager for news of home. Their show, *Zero Hour,* was broadcast daily. Officials at Radio Tokyo wrote propaganda that they insisted Cousens and his associates read on-air. In exchange, according to Associated Press reporter Katherine Beebe Harris, Cousens was provided with the names of prisoners of war, which were broadcast during the show in hopes the information would reach the prisoners' families.

Toguri, who risked her own safety to smuggle food and clothing to the three men, soon won Cousens's friendship and respect. When the authorities at Radio Tokyo insisted on adding a woman to the *Zero Hour* broadcasts, Cousens recommended Toguri, who joined the show in November, 1943, calling herself "Orphan Ann." She broadcast for twenty minutes each day, playing popular American songs and addressing her banter to the other "orphans" of the Pacific, the Allied soldiers with whom she identified. Toguri was only one of approximately a dozen female broadcasters (including propagandists such as Foumy "Madame Tojo" Saisho and Myrtle "Little Margie" Lipton) who became known collectively as "Tokyo Rose" among American soldiers in the Pacific, although no such specific person ever existed. Though officials at Radio Tokyo insisted that *Zero Hour* was an effective propaganda tool, Cousens and his associates, including Toguri, constantly attempted to sabotage Radio Tokyo's efforts by engaging in a subtle parody of their broadcasts. For the most part, their plan worked: Both Cousens and Ince were acquitted of treason, Cousens returning to Sydney and radio, and Ince being promoted to major in the American army.

Iva Toguri talks with reporters in September 1945. (National Archives)

After the War

In 1945 Toguri had married Felipe d'Aquino and was living with his family. She had attempted to leave Radio Tokyo but the *Kempeitai,* eager to promote the myth of "Tokyo Rose," ordered her to return. Toguri was elated when the Japanese were defeated and the war ended in August 1945. On October 17, 1945, however, she was arrested and transferred to Sugamo Prison, where she was jailed for a year. Charges were never brought against her, and finally, on October 25, 1946, she was released. She immediately applied for a passport to return to the United States, but it was delayed by a lack of proper documentation. In 1947 Toguri became pregnant, but was still weak

from her year of imprisonment. The baby died in January 1948, shortly after his birth.

In 1948 anti-Japanese sentiment in America was still strong. Although American occupation forces found no cause to prosecute Toguri, influential radio personality Walter Winchell mounted a publicity campaign to return her to the United States to stand trial. Ironically, because Toguri had never renounced her American citizenship, federal prosecutors could try her for treason. On August 28, 1948, Toguri was arrested and brought to the United States. What would become the most expensive trial in American history up to that point began in San Francisco on July 5, 1949, exactly eight years after Toguri had left home. She was charged with eight counts of treason.

No written or recorded proof existed that she had engaged in treasonous acts while working for Radio Tokyo. The court relied on the testimony of Kenkichi Oki and George Mitsushio, two Japanese American witnesses who worked with Toguri at *Zero Hour*. According to *Chicago Tribune* reporter Ronald E. Yates, the men testified that she had stated in a 1944 broadcast: "Orphans of the Pacific, you are really orphans now. How will you get home now that your ships are sunk?"

In an interview with Yates in 1976, Oki explained his testimony: "We had no choice.... The FBI and U.S. Occupation police told us we would have to testify against Iva or else they said Uncle Sam might arrange a trial for us, too." Even after hearing the testimony of Oki and Mitsushio, the all-white jury remained deadlocked until, as Cecilia Rasmussen reported in the *Los Angeles Times*, Judge Michael J. Roche reminded the jury that the trial had been "long and expensive" and ordered them to continue deliberating. The jury finally returned a guilty verdict. One juror who had resisted was jury foreman John Mann. According to *Washington Post* reporter Lou Cannon, Mann only reluctantly agreed with the rest of the jurors, saying later that he wished he "had a little more guts to stick with my vote for acquittal." Toguri was found guilty of treason on September 29, 1949. She was fined $10,000 and sentenced to ten years in prison. Her requests for appeal were denied and she was sent to a federal women's prison in Alderson, West Virginia. Her husband was forced to sign a statement in which he agreed never to enter the United States again. Toguri served six years of her sentence until her release on parole for good behavior in 1955, when she moved to Chicago and worked in a small business that her father had established in the city, taking it over after his death in 1972.

The Presidential Pardon

As early as 1954, petitions for a presidential pardon had been filed on Toguri's behalf. Over time, new information about the trial was reported in newspapers and the testimony of the two witnesses for the prosecution was discovered to be fraudulent. As the pardon movement for Toguri grew, petitions were filed again in 1968 and in 1976. A full pardon was not granted until *60 Minutes,* a popular American television news program, produced a story about Toguri's life. President Gerald Ford pardoned her on January 19, 1977. Interviewed by Yates about her ordeal, Toguri said, "I'm only sorry that my father never lived to see me pardoned.... 'I'm proud of you, Iva,' he used to tell me. 'You were like a tiger, you never changed your stripes, you stayed American through and through.'" She and her husband reluctantly divorced in the late 1970s because of her unwillingness to leave the United States.

SOURCES

Books

Christianson, Stephen, "Tokyo Rose Trial," *Great American Trials,* edited by Edward W. Knappman, Gale (Detroit), 1994, pp. 450–451.

Periodicals

Cannon, Lou, *Washington Post,* January 18, 1977.

Rasmussen, Cecilia, "L.A. Then and Now: The Painful Ordeal of Tokyo Rose," *Los Angeles Times,* May 24, 1998.

Yates, Ronald E., *Chicago Tribune,* December 8, 1991.

Other

Harris, Katherine Beebe (interview), *Washington Press Club Foundation,* Stanford, CA, October 14, 1989.

Sayonara, "Tokyo Rose" ... Hello Again, "Orphan Ann"!, http://www.dyarstraights.com/orphan_ ann/orphanan.html (August 4, 2000).

Hideki Tōjō

Born December 30, 1884
Tokyo, Japan
Died December 23, 1948
Tokyo, Japan

Japanese military leader; premier of Japan
(1941–1944)

*"Whether life is long or short, whether we
succeed or fail, is in accordance with the
will of heaven."*

(Reproduced by permission of AP/Wide World Photos)

In the years leading up to World War II, Japan aggressively began to expand its borders into nearby Asian countries, especially China. This expansion concerned leaders of other nations who envisioned Hideki Tōjō, Japanese premier and leading symbol of the country's militarism, as a despotic dictator similar to Adolf Hitler and Benito Mussolini. Although Tōjō played a major role in Japan's wartime affairs, his power and ambition were not as great as Hitler's or Mussolini's. Historians have described him as an intensely dedicated leader who misjudged the ability of the Allies to maintain and win a full-scale war.

The Kamisori

Tōjō was born in 1884 in Tokyo, Japan, into a family that had produced a long line of samurai, or warriors. His father, Eikyo Tōjō, was an army general who fought in the Sino-Japanese and Russo-Japanese Wars. In school, Tōjō was a competitive, self-confident boy nicknamed "Fighting Tōjō." After graduating from the Japanese Military Academy in 1915, he entered the army and spent a few years in Europe, first serving in Switzerland and then working as assistant military attaché in Berlin, Germany. When he returned to Japan, he took a position as an instructor in Japan's war college. During the late 1920s and early 1930s, Tōjō rose through the ranks of the military, gaining a reputa-

Doolittle Leads Revenge Attack

In the months following the December 7, 1941, surprise Japanese attack on the U.S. naval base at Pearl Harbor, Hawaii, American military commanders began planning retaliation. In 1942 they completed their strategy: Sixteen bomber planes led by Colonel Jimmy Doolittle would carry out a surprise raid on Tokyo, Japan. The bombers would be launched from the deck of the aircraft carrier *Hornet*, which sailed from San Francisco on April 2, 1942. On April 18 the aircraft carrier was spotted by a Japanese patrol boat, requiring the planes to take off immediately. They arrived at Tokyo in the middle of the day, instead of at night as they had planned. The raid began dropping bombs on Tokyo as well as Osaka, Nagoya, and Kobe.

After the attack, the planes flew toward the Chinese mainland, but the altered schedule had left the personnel at the airfield unprepared to receive them; the pilots had to either make crash landings or abandon their planes as fuel was in short supply because they had to go a greater distance. A few of the eighty-two men on the mission were killed in the raid or its aftermath. Although the raid did not have a significant effect on the outcome of the war, it boosted American spirits. It also showed the Japanese that the United States was capable of invading the tiny island nation. Doolittle received the Congressional Medal of Honor and a promotion to brigadier general.

tion as a hardworking officer and acquiring the nickname "*kamisori*" ("The Razor"). He became a member of the Control Group, which was comprised of army officers who advocated greater military presence in the government. They believed that Japan's economic and population problems could be eradicated by expansion into China and other parts of southeast Asia. The Control Group felt that Western countries, especially the United States, were hostile toward Japan and that Japan would have to defend its own interests aggressively.

By 1933, Tōjō had reached the rank of major general; in 1935 he was appointed head of military police for the Kwantung Army, the branch of the Japanese army stationed in China. Adopting a "law and order" philosophy, he strictly enforced army rules. From 1937 to 1938, he served as chief of staff of the Kwantung Army, proving his leadership abilities in combat when fighting broke out between the Chinese and the Japanese in summer 1937. The Japanese brutally attacked a number of cities and villages, engaging in a four-month battle before seizing the Chinese city of Shanghai. In addition, the Japanese launched offensives against other cities in China, including Nanking (Nanjing). Iris Chang, author of *The Rape of Nanking*, reports that in the capital city of Nanking in December 1937

Japanese soldiers murdered nearly 100,000 Chinese prisoners of war and raped, tortured, and killed hundreds of thousands of Chinese civilians.

In May 1938 Tōjō was called back to Tokyo to serve in the government of Premier Fumimaro Konoye. Tōjō advocated a strong military to improve the fledgling economy and to wage war against both China and the Soviet Union. In December 1938 he became inspector general of army aviation. By July 1940, when Tōjō was named minister of war, Japan was fighting China and had invaded Korea. The United States government protested these actions by halting the sale of U.S. goods to Japan, increasing Japan's economic hardships. Some moderate Japanese leaders wanted to withdraw troops from China and negotiate with the United States, but Tōjō opposed them. Instead, he drew up plans for further aggression, approving the Tripartite Pact (September 1940) that allied Japan with Germany and Italy in hopes of establishing a stronger position.

A Premier with a Clean Slate

When Konoye resigned in October 1941, Tōjō ascended to position of premier, while retaining his posts as head of the departments of war, education,

Tōjō on trial for war crimes in 1948. (National Archives and Records Administration)

commerce, and industry. He insisted that he begin his new job with a clean slate, meaning that he did not have to honor any earlier promises to negotiate with the United States. Although the military was now in control of the country and Tōjō was its top leader, he was still required to answer to a Supreme Command made up of civilian and military leaders, as well as the puppet leader Emperor Hirohito. On December 7, 1941, even as Japanese diplomats were in Washington, D.C., meeting with U.S. leaders, Japan launched a surprise attack on the U.S. naval base at Pearl Harbor, Hawaii. The next day, the United States declared war on Japan. Meanwhile, Tōjō broadcast a radio message to the Japanese people, warning them that they should expect a long war in order to defeat the enemy.

Tōjō, however, did not anticipate the strength of the Allied forces and their determination to win the war. Although Japanese troops achieved some success with invasions of the Philippines and Singapore, their fortunes began to decline as the war continued and they lost several important battles. Persistently pushing the war effort, Tōjō rejected the idea of a negotiated peace treaty. Under heavy pressure to leave the government, Tōjō resigned from his position as premier on July 18, 1944. He

was harshly criticized by the public, who blamed him for Japan's problems. In July 1945 U.S. troops defeated the Japanese on Saipan, part of the Marianas island chain in the South Pacific, putting American bomber planes in range of the main Japanese islands. In early August the Allies dropped atomic bombs on two Japanese cities, Hiroshima and Nagasaki, and the war soon came to an end. Shortly thereafter, the Japanese agreed to an unconditional surrender.

General Douglas MacArthur headed the occupation government of Japan to help the nation prepare for economic recovery and transition to a democratic society. MacArthur arrived in Tokyo in September 1945 and immediately called for the arrest of all Japanese thought to have committed war crimes, especially top military leaders and civilian officials. When Tōjō learned that Japanese and American officials had arrived at his home to arrest him, he shot himself in the chest—an act of seppuku (committing suicide to avoid dishonoring one's ancestors). The wound did not kill him, however—American doctors saved his life. Tōjō was held in prison until May 1946, when he stood trial before the International Military Tribunal of the Far East. During the two-year trial, Tōjō accepted responsibility for his country's actions in the war, claiming that he had acted in the interest of Japan's survival. The court found Tōjō guilty on numerous counts, including waging aggressive wars against peaceful nations; conspiring with others to make Japan the dominant force in the Pacific; and allowing atrocities to be committed by the Japanese against Allied POWs and civilians of occupied nations. He was sentenced to death and was hanged on December 23, 1948, along with six other Japanese war criminals. In one of his final statements, Tōjō wished to apologize for horrible acts committed by Japanese forces. However, he thought that the United States military forces should also apologize for the horrible acts they committed during air raids over Japan, especially dropping atomic bombs on the citizens of Hiroshima and Nagasaki.

While he was being led to the executioner, Tojo recited a poem he had written during his final hours (as quoted in Butow's *Tojo and the Coming of the War*, p. 535).

Ware yuky mo mata kono tochi ni kaeri kon
Kuni ni mukuyuru koto no taraneba.
Saraba nari koke no shita nite ware matan
Yamato Shimane ni hana kaoru toki.

The translation means:

Even though I now depart,
I shall return again to this land,
That I may repay in full
My debt to my country.
This is farewell.
I shall wait beneath the moss,
Until the flowers again are fragrant
    [until the resurgence]
In this island country of Japan.

SOURCES

Books

Butow, Robert J. C., *Tojo and the Coming of the War*, Stanford University Press (Stanford, CT), 1961.

Browne, Courtney, *Tojo: The Last Banzai*, De Capo Press (New York), 1998.

Chang, Iris, *The Rape of Nanking*, Basic Books (New York), 1997.

Hoyt, Edwin P., *Warlord*, Scarborough House (Lanham, MD), 1993.

Born May 8, 1884
Lamar, Missouri, United States
Died December 26, 1972
Kansas City, Missouri, United States

Thirty-third president of the
United States

"The buck stops here."

(Library of Congress)

Harry S Truman

Harry S Truman is remembered as an American president who had a real knowledge of and feeling for the ordinary citizens of his country. Known as an honest, hardworking man with a lot of common sense, he was serving as vice president when, in April 1945, President Franklin D. Roosevelt died in office. Truman took over the presidency at a crucial time, with World War II almost over and Americans feeling both euphoric about the Allied victory and anxious about the economy and other issues. Over the next seven years, Truman would make some difficult decisions, especially dropping two atomic bombs on Japan, and lead the United States through important changes in foreign and domestic policy.

A Missouri Boyhood

Harry S Truman (whose middle initial is unpunctuated since it does not stand for a middle name) was born in a small farming town located about 120 miles south of Kansas City, Missouri, on May 8, 1884. His father was a farmer who supplemented the family income by buying and selling horses and mules. In 1890, after the births of two more children, the family moved to the larger town of Independence. It was here, when he was six years old, that Truman first met Elizabeth "Bess" Wallace, who would one day become his wife. As a young boy, Truman contracted diphtheria and nearly died. His exceptionally poor eyesight required strong, expensive eyeglasses that prevented him from playing sports. He spent much of his time reading and became interested in American history. In 1901 Truman graduated from high school and applied to the U.S. Military Academy at West Point, New York, but was rejected due to his poor eyesight. Lacking money to pay for college, Truman went to Kansas City to work. He spent the next four years performing various clerical jobs in a newspaper's mailroom, for a railroad, and in two banks. Even though his monthly salary increased from $35 to $120, Truman was unhappy, and in 1906 he took over a family-owned farm near Grandview (about twenty miles from Independence), where he would stay for the next eleven years.

This was an important period in Truman's life. He managed 600 acres of land and performed much of the farm work himself. It was on the farm that he began his lifelong habit of rising at 5 or 5:30 in the morning, even when he had been up late the previous evening, and it was also at this time that he began courting Bess Wallace. When the United States entered World War I in April 1917, Truman's National Guard unit was sent into action as the 129th Field Artillery, attached to the 35th Division from Missouri and Kansas. Truman arrived overseas in April 1918 and was immediately promoted to captain. In July he became the commander of Battery D, which had the reputation of being full of unruly, difficult soldiers. Truman tamed them using a mixture of firmness and friendliness. Affectionately known as "Captain Harry," he led his troops in battles at St. Mihiel and Meuse Argonne in France. Years later, after he was sworn in as president, members of the battery marched on both sides of his car during the inaugural parade. After the war, Truman returned to Missouri and married Bess in June 1919. That November, he opened a men's clothing store with a friend from the military, Edward Jacobs, but the store was not successful and went bankrupt in 1922. Through another war buddy, Truman met Thomas J. Pendergast, the Democratic boss of Kansas City. Pendergast was impressed by Truman's honesty, and needing such a man on the Democratic ticket to bolster his own reputation, he persuaded Truman to run for office.

In 1923 Truman was elected eastern judge (a position like that of county commissioner, rather than a courtroom judge) for Jackson County. To make up for his lack of legal experience, Truman studied law at night for two years at the Kansas City Law School. In February 1924 the Trumans' only child, Mary Margaret, was born. That same year, Truman was voted out of office, but in 1926 he ran for the job of presiding judge and was again elected. He served two four-year terms in this office, in charge of a 60 million dollar budget for public works.

Encouraged by his political victories, Truman ran successfully for the U.S. Senate in 1934. During his first term as a senator, he was a quiet backer of President Roosevelt's New Deal and worked on transportation issues. Although an effective politician, Truman did not receive much attention from his fellow senators or from the president. Some said his old association with Pendergast, who was convicted of income tax evasion in 1938, made other Democrats want to avoid him.

It was during Truman's second term in the Senate that he was praised as an energetic and hardworking leader who stood up for ordinary Americans. His most important role was chairman of a committee to investigate military spending. The committee uncovered a great deal of wastefulness and reportedly saved the American taxpayers 15 billion dollars. This issue was especially important to Americans after Pearl Harbor was bombed and the United States entered World War II, which brought a greater need for wise spending and efficient production.

From Vice President to President in Eighty-Two Days

By 1944, Truman had proven himself a strong leader on a national level. When President Roosevelt ran for reelection in 1944, advisors recommended that he choose Truman as his running mate. The man who was then serving as vice president, Henry Wallace, was unpopular, and Democratic leaders wanted to find a vice presidential candidate who would make a good president if Roosevelt, who was ailing, should die in office. At the time of the Democratic Convention, Truman was supporting a different vice presidential candidate and had no interest in the job himself, until he overheard Roosevelt accusing him of causing a schism in the Democratic party. Truman accepted the nomination and was elected with Roosevelt later that year. Truman had served only eighty-two days as vice president when, on April 12, 1945, he was called to the White House and informed by the president's wife, Eleanor, that Roosevelt had died. Truman took the oath of office at 7:09 that

Did Truman Make The Right Decision?

Before the bomb was dropped, the true extent of its power was known only to a few scientists and leaders, and no one could guess what its long-term effects would be. Soon after he became president in April 1945, Harry S Truman had to decide whether to drop an atomic bomb on Japan. He decided that bombing Japan was the right thing to do, but since then the question has been hotly debated. Some feel that the Allies had to drop the bomb in order to end the war, while others claim it was not the only solution. After Germany surrendered in May 1945, Allied leaders had to decide how to bring the war in the Pacific to a close. Japan had no chance of winning; its cities were in ruins after months of bombing and its economy was a shambles. Yet the Japanese still refused to surrender, and Japanese leaders encouraged their people to fight to the bitter end. Japanese troops were highly disciplined and believed that surrender would bring disgrace. During the battle for the island of Okinawa, over 100,000 Japanese soldiers died, only 11,000 surrendered, and more than 100,000 civilians were killed.

Allied leaders believed that an invasion of Japan's main islands would cause many casualties on both sides. President Truman had been told that as many as 250,000 to 1 million Allied soldiers might die. During the war, Japan had gained a bad reputation not only for the surprise attack on Pearl Harbor but also for its harsh treatment of political prisoners, and there was a widespread feeling that Japan deserved to be punished. It is also known that Japan was working on its own atomic bomb and might have used it against the United States. Yet some military commanders claimed that neither dropping the bomb nor invading would be necessary, because Japan was about to collapse. Those who now condemn Truman's decision point out that the United States had spent more than 2 billion dollars on the development of the atomic bomb—money that would essentially go to waste if it were not used. Some even contend that the main reason the bombs (especially the second one) were dropped was to test their effects on human beings. Others claim that Truman wanted to keep the Soviet Union in line by demonstrating U.S. power.

evening, becoming the thirty-third president of the United States.

Truman took over the presidency at a crucial time in the nation's history; he was immediately faced with some important tasks. On May 8—his sixty-first birthday—he announced the German surrender, an occasion of great public rejoicing that became known as V-E (Victory in Europe) Day. In June he signed the charter that brought the United Nations into existence. The most awesome responsibility facing Truman, however, was the decision whether or not to end the war in Asia by dropping the atomic bomb on Japan. The U.S government had already spent more than 2 billion dollars on the bomb, which had been developed by scientists working at Los Alamos, New Mexico. If the bomb was not used, the Allies would have to invade Japan, an endeavor in which military experts predicted an estimated 250,000 to 1 million American soldiers would lose their lives. The Japanese were expected to be fierce defenders of their homeland who would fight to the death rather than accept capture or surrender.

Truman appointed an interim committee to weigh the alternatives. The committee recommended using the bomb on a major Japanese city without warning, even though many civilians would surely be killed. Truman gave the order to go ahead, and bombs were dropped on Hiroshima on August 6, 1945, and Nagasaki on August 9. The bombs killed at least 100,000 people immediately, with many more falling ill and later dying from

What the Atomic Bombs Did to Nagasaki and Hiroshima

On August 6, 1945, at 8:15 a.m., a B-29 Superfortress bomber plane called the *Enola Gay* flew over the city of Hiroshima, Japan; Major Thomas W. Ferebee released the atomic bomb nicknamed "Little Boy." Most people ignored the air raid sirens when they saw only two planes approaching. Life proceeded as usual—many people were outside on streets and children on playgrounds—until the atomic bomb exploded. Survivors later reported seeing a blinding flash and then experiencing terror and pain. Tens of thousands of people died instantly, while survivors were severely burned. People ran and stumbled amidst the rubble of the tremendous explosion, many with their skin charred or shredded away from their bodies, some missing limbs or facial features, as they searched desperately for relief, water, and missing family members. It is estimated that approximately 130,000 to 140,000 people were killed at Hiroshima, including those killed instantly (about 70,000) as well as those who died later from burns or radiation sickness.

Another 35,000 or so died three days later when another atomic bomb—this one called "Fat Man"—landed on the city of Nagasaki, following the Japanese government's refusal to surrender after the first attack. Although the Nagasaki bomb was bigger, it did not prove as deadly because the city's natural terrain protected it somewhat from the impact of the explosion. In the decades following World War II, the approximately 350,000 survivors of the atomic bombs formed a special group in Japanese society. Called *hibakusha,* they suffered not only from physical pain and disfiguring scars but also from being ridiculed and shunned by others. Studies have also shown that the radiation to which the *hibakusha* were exposed has had longlasting effects, including increased rates of cancer, liver and heart disease, and mental retardation in babies born to survivors.

radiation sickness. Whether Truman made the right choice to use the bomb has been hotly debated ever since.

"The Buck Stops Here!"

When the Japanese signed a surrender treaty in September 1945, the war was officially over. Truman now faced a new host of difficult tasks, including returning the soldiers to normal life, closing down the various war agencies, managing the transition from a wartime to a peacetime economy, and dealing with inflation. He replaced the model of a gun on his desk with one of a plow. He also placed on his desk a plaque that read, "The buck stops here!," meaning that he took full responsibility for his own decisions.

Although he was a seasoned local politician, Truman lacked experience in foreign affairs. He learned fast, though, and during his first term he began to reverse America's usual tendency to stay out of other nations' affairs. He thought the United States should take an active role in keeping the whole world safe and free—especially free from communism. Truman opposed the spread of communism through three major programs: the Truman Doctrine, which gave billions of dollars to countries threatened by communist takeover (in particular, Turkey and Greece); the European Recovery Plan (known as the Marshall Plan), which offered economic aid to help European countries recover from the devastating effects of the war; and the North Atlantic Treaty Organization (NATO), which offered military assistance to protect countries from communist threat.

On domestic issues, Truman continued to push for many of the New Deal programs that President Roosevelt had established, which Truman now called the "Fair Deal." These included federal controls on the economy, more civil rights laws, low-cost housing, a higher minimum wage, and repeal of the Taft-Hartley Act (which put tight restrictions

Truman announcing the Japanese surrender to the press on August 14, 1945. (Reproduced by permission of AP/Wide World Photos)

on labor unions). He called for more financial aid for education and access to health insurance for all Americans. Truman's ideas, though they would become popular several decades later, were proposed to an American public who, after the end of World War II, did not want to worry about social problems. The Republican-controlled Congress blocked many of Truman's plans, opposing programs and laws that increased the size of the federal government and gave it more control over business and the economy.

When it came time for the 1948 presidential election, many thought Truman had little chance of winning. He was opposed not only by Republican candidate Thomas Dewey and by the Progressive Party, led by Henry Wallace, but also by a group called the "Dixiecrats," led by South Carolina governor J. Strom Thurmond, who were against Truman's policies in favor of equal rights for African Americans (especially the 1948 Executive Order 9981 that called for integration of the armed forces). Determined to win the presidency on his own merits, Truman began a high-energy "whistlestop" campaign during which he traveled 22,000 miles and made 271 speeches. Campaigning under the slogan, "Give 'em hell Harry!" and criticizing what he called the "Do-Nothing Eightieth Congress," Truman took his message to factory workers in the cities and to farmers in the rural areas; he was also the first U.S. president to appear in Harlem, an African American community in New York City. The morning after the election, no one was more surprised that Truman had won than the *Chicago Tribune,* which had printed the headline "Dewey Defeats Truman!" In fact, Truman had beaten Dewey by 2 million votes.

The biggest foreign policy issue of Truman's second term was the Korean war (1950–1953), which began when communist North Korea (backed by the Soviet Union and China) invaded South Korea. The United Nations Security Council voted to back South Korea and as the leading member of the United Nations, the United States sent troops to fight the North Koreans. Truman did not formally declare war, choosing instead to refer to the conflict as a "police action." This left many Americans confused about what was happening in Korea and why the United States was involved. A major controversy erupted when General Douglas MacArthur, the leader of the U.S. troops in Korea, publicly disagreed with U.S. policy in the conflict. Determined to put down any signs of insubordination, Truman fired MacArthur. The Korean war ended in 1953, after Truman had left office, with a truce that left North and South Korea in an uneasy standoff.

Meanwhile, back in the United States, both the Korean war and China's fall to communism in 1949 (when Nationalists, led by Chiang Kai-Shek, were driven from the country) had raised serious concerns about the spread of communism. Republican leaders claimed that communist sympathizers had infiltrated the U.S. government; in response, Truman set up the Federal Employee Loyalty Program in 1947. He did not respond as well to charges, some of which later proved true, that parts of his own administration were corrupt.

By 1952, Truman's popularity had dropped dramatically, and he decided not to run for president again. During the last few months of his presidency, he angered labor unions as well as mill owners by trying to end a steel strike by having the government take over the mills. The Supreme Court agreed with the mill owners that a president did not have the power to take such an action. When election time came, Truman campaigned for the Democratic candidate, Illinois governor Adlai Stevenson, who was soundly beaten by very popular former general Dwight D. Eisenhower.

Truman returned to Independence, Missouri, his childhood home, to live in his nearly 100-year-old house and work on his memoirs, which were published in three volumes: *Year of Decisions,* 1955; *Years of Trial and Hope,* 1956; and *Mr. Citizen,* 1960. The Harry S Truman Library opened in Independence in 1957 and Truman worked there every day for nine years, until ill health slowed him down. About the library he said (as quoted in an article by Susanne Roschwalb and Gordon Smith in *USA Today*), "I want this to be a place where young people can come and learn what the office of the president is, what a great office it is no matter who happens to be in it at the time." In his last years, Truman spent most of his time reading histories, biographies, and books on the development of American government. He died in Kansas City at age eighty-eight and was buried on the grounds of the Truman Library.

SOURCES

Books

Daniels, Jonathan, *The Man of Independence,* University of Missouri Press (Columbia, MO), 1998.

Ferrell, Robert H., *Harry S Truman and the Modern American Presidency,* Little, Brown (Boston), 1983.

Kirkendall, Richard S., *Harry S Truman Encyclopedia,* G. K. Hall (Boston), 1989.

McCullough, David, *Truman,* Simon & Schuster (New York), 1993.

Ross, Irwin, *The Loneliest Campaign: The Truman Victory of 1948,* Greenwood Press (Westport, CT), 1968.

Periodicals

Roschwalb, Susanne A., and Gordon L. Smith, "Harry S. Truman: America's Last Great Leader?," *USA Today,* January 1995, p. 86.

The Tuskegee Airmen

African American air squadron whose success led to the eventual desegregation of the United States armed forces

"In the end, the men and women of the Tuskegee experience broke forever the myths that allowed segregation, inequity, and injustices to exist with a thin veil of legitimacy."

—GENERAL RONALD R. FOGELMAN

At the outbreak of World War II, the American armed forces were still segregated. When African Americans demanded the right to help defend their country, President Franklin D. Roosevelt established an all-black air unit, which, since it trained at the Tuskegee Army Air Field, became known as the Tuskegee Airmen. The Tuskegee Airmen not only distinguished themselves in combat during the war, but also opened new doors for African Americans in the American military and in American society.

A New Opportunity

At the beginning of the 1940s, it became apparent that the United States might enter World War II. The military, much like the nation itself, was racially segregated. Due to the belief of many white officers that African Americans were inferior, it seemed impossible that African Americans would be allowed to pilot war planes if the United States joined the war effort. Civil rights groups were outraged that African Americans were not being treated fairly in the armed forces. They put pressure on President Franklin D. Roosevelt to push for integration, or at least for African American representation in important positions. Roosevelt, who had won re-election in 1940 with the support of African American voters, responded by forcing the U.S. Army Air Corps to establish the 99th Pursuit Squadron.

Members of the 99th U.S. Pursuit Squadron, these Tuskegee Airmen were part of the first all-black unit to go into action with the United States Army Air Corps. (Reproduced by permission of AP/Wide World Photos)

This all-black air unit was to train at Alabama's famed Tuskegee Institute. Lieutenant Benjamin O. Davis, Jr., an African American West Point graduate, was appointed to lead the squadron. The 99th Pursuit Squadron was assigned to the Thirty-Third Fighter Group commanded by Colonel William M. Momyer, who was white. African Americans from all over the country applied to be part of the unit, thrilled to have an opportunity to play an important role in the military.

Earning Their Wings

Life on the base was not easy for the pilots in training, who were in a pioneering position. They trained at Tuskegee Army Air Field (TAAF) near Chehaw, Alabama. Many local white residents were not happy that African Americans were being allowed to learn how to fly fighter planes, and created a hostile environment for the trainees. The army itself was still strictly segregated, and this air field was no exception. White instructors and other personnel had separate living quarters and facilities. Many of the African Americans were upset that the unit was segregated, but Davis urged them to focus on the tasks before them: to become good fighter pilots and to prove themselves worthy of such a position.

The attitudes of the white officers and local residents began to change when First Lady Eleanor Roosevelt made a visit to the Tuskegee Institute on April 19, 1941, and went on a test flight piloted by one of the African American trainees, Charles "Chief" Anderson. This event produced some positive publicity and demonstrated that the president and first lady had confidence in the abilities of the African American trainees. This was the first public indication that this "Tuskegee Experiment" might work. On March 7, 1942, Davis and twelve of his trainees earned their wings. This made them the first African Americans to enter the U.S. Army Air Corps.

Willa Brown

African American women, as well as men, made a name for themselves as pilots during World War II. One such woman was Willa Brown, who became the first African American officer in the Civil Air Patrol (CAP)—an organization of concerned citizens that sought to help protect America's shores from the threat of enemy invasion. The CAP also provided essential services (such as search and rescue). Brown also helped train members of the 99th.

Born on January 22, 1906, in Glasgow, Kentucky, Brown grew up in Indiana, attended Indiana State Teachers College, and later earned a master's degree in business administration from Northwestern University. While she pursued her degree at Northwestern in the 1930s, Brown began taking flying lessons. In 1935 she earned a master mechanic's certificate from Chicago's Aeronautical University, and in 1938 she received her private pilot's license. Not content to simply fly airplanes, Brown branched out and became an activist, establishing and joining several associations. In 1940 she received her Civil Aeronautics Authority ground school instructor's rating, and along with her husband, Cornelius R. Coffey, founded the Coffey School of Aeronautics, where she was director for two years.

Brown gained a great deal of respect from white pilots and used her reputation and position to fight for the integration of African Americans into the U.S. Army Air Corps. She was part of a coalition that successfully petitioned the federal government to establish the program at Tuskegee, and was selected to participate in its implementation. She went on to train several members of the 99th Pursuit Squadron, some of the most distinguished African American pilots who served during World War II.

Cadets in the Tuskegee Airmen training program learn Morse Code. (Reproduced by permission of AP/Wide World Photos)

Six Tuskegee Airmen paratroopers in Italy. (Reproduced by permission of UPI/Corbis-Bettmann)

The First Mission

In November 1942 the 99th was sent to North Africa to fight the Germans. The Germans surrendered before the airmen arrived, however, and the new pilots had to wait to prove themselves. They were assigned routine duties, such as shooting at ground targets, as white pilots refused to be escorted by members of the 99th.

On June 2, 1943, the 99th Squadron went on its first operational mission, a strafing attack on the Italian island of Pantelleria. Their job was to escort and protect large bombers and to fly low and drop bombs on enemy targets. The mission was a success. During the invasion of Sicily later, Lieutenant Charles B. Hall was the first member of the 99th to shoot down an enemy plane. After this, the 99th settled into regular duties in Italy, in charge of escorting large bombers on missions to destroy enemy targets. The pilots performed admirably and earned the grudging respect of the other units. It seemed that they had secured their right to take part in operational missions. At the end of the summer, Davis was appointed to lead the 332nd Fighter Group, which was also made up

of African Americans. He was poised to lead this group to the same success as the 99th.

Their Performance Is Questioned

When he returned to the United States, Davis learned that Colonel William M. Momyer, the white officer in command of the Thirty-Third Fighter Group, was criticizing the performance of the 99th. It was clear that he was doing so on racial grounds. Momyer claimed that in his opinion, the 99th Pursuit Squadron was inferior to all the other squadrons in the group. He said that they had not shown adequate bravery or aggressiveness. Momyer's statements were clearly products of racial bias, and were not based on the actual performance of the 99th squadron. Davis was upset by these allegations, and on October 16, 1943, he appeared before the War Department's Committee on Special [Negro] Troop Policies to respond to the charges. Although he knew the main factor in Momyer's charges was race, Davis decided to focus simply on the performance of his pilots, and prove that they did everything they were supposed to do. After Davis presented his case, Army Chief of Staff

Tuskegee Pilots Protest Segregated Facilities

In March 1945, more than 160 African American pilots from the Tuskegee group training at Freeman Field, Indiana, rebelled against the segregation they faced on the base. Not allowed into the Officers Club even though they had already earned their wings, the pilots entered the club anyway and refused to leave until they were forcibly removed and arrested. They were then commanded to sign a statement agreeing to live under segregated conditions. When 101 of the men refused to sign, they violated the 64th Article of War by refusing the commands of a superior officer, and their action was officially declared a mutiny. In April the charges were dropped, but the officers were given letters of reprimand. One officer was not so lucky: Lieutenant Roger Terry was court-martialed and convicted of assault for allegedly bumping into a superior officer during the protest. In 1995 the Air Force finally began to remove the reprimands from some of the officers' records, and reversed Terry's conviction as well.

George C. Marshall ordered an operations study of the 99th unit. This study revealed that there was no significant difference between the performance of the 99th and other squadrons.

After this study vindicated the 99th Pursuit Squadron, Davis was ready to assume control of the 332nd Fighter Group. This consisted of the 100th, 301st, and 302nd squadrons in addition to the 99th. The new squadrons trained at Selfridge Army Airfield in Michigan.

An Illustrious Record

On January 3, 1944, the 332nd Fighter Group left for Italy, where the 99th was still operating. Upon arrival, Davis was upset to learn that his group was going to be assigned to routine duties rather than real combat. Once again, his group would have to wait for the opportunity to prove themselves. That opportunity came in March, when the 332nd was assigned to escort duty, accompanying and protecting heavy bombers. Over the next year, the pilots of the 332nd, known as "Red Tails" because of their red planes, proved to be dependable fighters. As the Tuskegee Airmen's reputation for courage and proficiency grew, white pilots began specifically requesting to be escorted by the "Red Tails."

By the end of the war, the Tuskegee Airmen had built a solid combat record. It was the only fighter group that did not lose an escorted bomber to enemy fire. In 1,578 combat missions, the 332nd Fighter Group destroyed 103 enemy planes in air-to-air combat. In addition, the group destroyed many more enemy craft on the ground. Sixty-six Tuskegee Airmen were killed, and thirty-two were captured.

After the War

In the end, the "Tuskegee Experiment" was a success. The distinguished record of the Tuskegee Airmen proved that African Americans were capable of flying fighter planes and serving courageously in battle. Although racial tensions persisted, and there were still those who claimed African Americans to be inferior, the Tuskegee Airmen's achievements were impossible to deny.

In 1948 President Harry S Truman signed Executive Order 9981, officially integrating the United States armed forces. From this point on, African Americans and whites would serve side by side in all branches of the military. The Tuskegee Airmen helped pave the way to make this possible.

SOURCES

Books

Francis, Charles E., and Adolph Caso, *The Tuskegee Airmen: The Men Who Changed a Nation*, Branden Pub. (Boston), 1997.

Homan, Lynn M., and Thomas Reilly, *The Tuskegee Airmen*, Arcadia (Charleston, SC), 1998.

Scott, Lawrence P., and William M. Womack, Sr., *Double V: The Civil Rights Struggle of the Tuskegee Airmen*, Michigan State University Press (East Lansing, MI), 1994.

Warren, James C., and William B. Ellis, *The Tuskegee Airmen Mutiny at Freeman Field,* Conyers Publishing Company (Conyers, GA), 1998.

Other

The Tuskegee Airmen (film), HBO Pictures, 1996.

Joachim von Ribbentrop

Born April 30, 1893
Wesel, Germany
Died October 16, 1946
Nuremberg, Germany

Diplomat; wine merchant; clerk; foreign
minister of Germany (1938–1945)

*"Even with all I know, if in this cell Hitler
should come to me and say: 'Do this!' I
would still do it."*

*(Reproduced by permission of Bilderdienst
Suddeutscher Verlag)*

F
ew of the high-level Nazis who ruled
Germany under Adolf Hitler were members of the upper class. One exception
was Joachim von Ribbentrop, a member
of the aristocratic elite who was greatly enamored
of Hitler and always gave in to his wishes. Von
Ribbentrop was the only top Nazi who had frequently socialized with Jews prior to World War II,
but by the time the Germans surrendered in 1945,
he had become deeply involved in the Nazi extermination of Jews. Von Ribbentrop was hanged for
his role in the mass murders.

Seeks High Social Status

Joachim Ribbentrop (the "von" was added
later) was born into the family of a German military officer in 1893. Von Ribbentrop's father,
Richard, was a stern parent who believed his children must fear him. His mother, Sophie, was the
daughter of a wealthy landowner. As his father was
sent on various military assignments throughout
Germany, young von Ribbentrop often moved
during his childhood. He had an older brother,
Lothar, with whom he was close, and a younger
sister, Ingeborg. In 1902 von Ribbentrop's mother
died from tuberculosis. In 1911, when von Ribbentrop was eighteen, one of his kidneys had to be
removed, possibly also due to tuberculosis. Lothar
later died of the same disease in 1918.

Von Ribbentrop poses for a photo in his office. (Reproduced by permission of DIZ Munchen GmbH)

At school, von Ribbentrop was not a good student. A lazy, fun-loving, and frequently troubled child, he began studying harder when his father promised him a violin as a reward. Once he even considered becoming a professional violinist. After finishing his education in 1910, von Ribbentrop went to Canada. Wanting to learn foreign languages so he could travel the world, he clerked for a bank and a railroad company to finance his plans. He and Lothar also started a small import-export business, funded with money left from their mother.

World War I (1914–1918) began on August 4, 1914. That very day, von Ribbentrop left Canada to return to Germany. He enlisted in the army and spent three years serving in Poland and Russia. He was wounded in 1917 and received two Iron Cross medals. In 1918, when a French-speaking officer was needed in Turkey, he was sent there to obtain supplies for the troops. In 1920, two years after Germany's surrender ended World War I, von Ribbentrop married Annelies Henkell, the daughter of a wealthy wine producer. He became the company's representative in Berlin, Germany, and

the couple moved into a lavish home in the nearby town of Dahlem. As his socially ambitious wife pushed him forward in his career, von Ribbentrop became obsessed with status. In 1925 he paid a fee to be adopted by a relative whose ancestors had been knighted, entitling him to add "von" before his last name. The prefix denoted a connection with nobility, and Joachim became known as von Ribbentrop.

Subservient to Hitler

Von Ribbentrop joined the Nazi party in May 1932. He was appointed a colonel in its Schutzstaffel, or bodyguard unit, known as the SS. Von Ribbentrop met Hitler in August of that year, when the Nazi leader was seeking someone to read him news stories in the foreign press. Von Ribbentrop was chosen because he spoke both French and English. He made his home available to Hitler, who was plotting his own appointment as chancellor. Both before and after Hitler took power in 1933, von Ribbentrop was always totally subservient to him, and proved to be useful to the Nazi leader

Martin Luther, von Ribbentrop's Betrayer

Adolf Hitler's appointed officials were constantly vying for power, a fact Joachim von Ribbentrop encountered with his henchman, Martin Luther (1895–1945). In 1936, while von Ribbentrop was ambassador to Great Britain, he appointed Martin Franz Julius Luther manager of his residence in London, England. Von Ribbentrop's wife, Annelies, had first become fond of Luther when he helped refurbish their house. As Luther showed his capacity for scheming, von Ribbentrop charged him with the task of ensuring von Ribbentrop's victory in conflicts with other Nazis. Luther received a series of appointments from von Ribbentrop that greatly increased his power. In 1940 he was assigned to formulate a plan for the elimination of European Jews. His first suggestion to von Ribbentrop was that all Jews should be deported to the French island of Madagascar. The plan was not very practical, given the number of Jews and the size of the island, but von Ribbentrop endorsed it because he wanted the prestige of coming up with the solution to Hitler's "Jewish problem."

In August 1941 Hitler informed Luther of his own "Final Solution": the planned genocide of 11 million European Jews in gas chambers and labor camps. Although von Ribbentrop knew about the plan, he did not want to be directly involved in it. He commanded that all high-level communications on the matter be sent directly to Luther's office.

A year later, fearing that his power was being challenged by the crafty Luther, von Ribbentrop ordered him to stop any more work on the "Final Solution." A fierce scene followed in which Hitler accused von Ribbentrop of dragging his feet on the issue of the Jews. Von Ribbentrop immediately reinvolved himself and told Luther to resume his efforts. Luther was crucial to von Ribbentrop for two reasons: He excelled at keeping von Ribbentrop's rivals under control, and he was happy to assume the dirty work of the "Final Solution."

Beginning in 1941, Luther became very angry with von Ribbentrop's wife. She continued to treat him as a servant, despite his rise in the Nazi power structure, and had interfered in a potentially profitable book-selling scheme. In 1943, spurred on by some young assistants, Luther launched a plan to discredit von Ribbentrop. In February SS chief Heinrich Himmler was shown a memorandum written by Luther, supposedly providing evidence that von Ribbentrop was insane. Himmler considered taking action against von Ribbentrop, but decided it would be easier to deal with a weak and thankful von Ribbentrop than with an ambitious and victorious Martin Luther. On February 10, 1943, Himmler had Luther arrested. When informed of the arrest, von Ribbentrop went to Hitler in a rage, demanding the execution of all those involved in the plot against him. Hitler decided to be lenient with the plotters. Luther was sent to a concentration camp, where he received privileged treatment and survived to the end of the war. Others were sent to fight in Poland and the Soviet Union. Hitler and von Ribbentrop both wanted to hush up the whole matter: von Ribbentrop did not want potentially embarrassing information about him spread around, and Hitler did not want information about his followers' infighting aired in public.

because of his wealthy friends and political connections. Von Ribbentrop, who took pains to figure out what Hitler wanted before approaching him on any given topic, was despised by high-ranking Nazis, many of whom felt that he had bought his office along with his name. His manner earned him the nickname "von Ribbensnob."

When Hitler became chancellor, he made von Ribbentrop his advisor on foreign affairs. Von Ribbentrop successfully negotiated an agreement between Germany and Great Britain that allowed the build-up of the German navy and led to his appointment as German ambassador to London, England, from August 1936 to January 1938. Von Ribbentrop hoped to establish an alliance between Great Britain and Germany, but his arrogant and clumsy behavior ruined any prospects of a union. In one famous incident, he greeted the king of England with the Nazi stiff-armed salute. This was considered shocking by many British citizens and was widely reported in the world press. Rejected by the British, he became hostile and announced that Germany and Great Britain could never work out their differences. Thereafter, von Ribbentrop supported Hitler in all anti-British policies.

Supports "Final Solution"

In 1938 Hitler promoted von Ribbentrop to minister of foreign affairs. Von Ribbentrop advised Hitler that Great Britain was paralyzed by confusion and would not reciprocate against any aggressive action on the part of Germany, including the invasion of Poland; this advice would prove fatal. The crowning achievement of von Ribbentrop's career took place in August 1939, with the signing of the Munich Pact between Nazi Germany and the Soviet Union. Central to the agreement was a secret clause that provided for the division of Poland between the Germans and the Soviets, which opened the way for Germany's invasion of Poland. Great Britain did not take military action when the Nazis invaded Austria and Czechoslovakia, hoping that if Germany took over these countries, Hitler would be satisfied; this was not the case. In 1939 the Nazis invaded Poland, and the British, convinced at last that Hitler would continue to march across Europe if left unchecked, declared war on Germany. As war plans replaced diplomacy, von Ribbentrop's usefulness to Hitler lessened. In 1940 he failed to persuade Italy, France, and Spain to enter the war as allies of Germany.

Although von Ribbentrop supported a continuing alliance with the Soviets, Hitler invaded the Soviet Union in 1941. Diplomats from around the world have described von Ribbentrop as incompetent, extremely haughty, domineering, and unwilling to compromise.

Von Ribbentrop had many Jewish friends before the war, so he did not initially share Hitler's anti-Semitic stance. When he realized that Hitler was determined to find a "Final Solution" to the "Jewish problem," in order to assure the total elimination of European Jews, von Ribbentrop tried to distance himself from this mass murder of human beings. He appointed a former construction and furniture worker, Martin Luther, to serve as a middleman between Hitler and himself on the Jewish question, but when Luther began to become a rival to von Ribbentrop, he abruptly threw himself behind the "Final Solution," hoping to regain some of his former importance.

Executed as War Criminal

By 1943, von Ribbentrop's shortcomings had become apparent to Hitler. He referred to his foreign minister as a "busybody" and offered him no more support. Von Ribbentrop began spending most of his time bickering with Nazi rivals, and by 1944, his name was seldom mentioned in official documents. During a 1944 argument with von Ribbentrop, the head of the Nazi air force, Hermann Göring, took a swipe at him with his walking stick. Despite such difficulties, von Ribbentrop continued to insist on his own importance as demonstrated by both his position and the "von" in his name. On April 30, 1945, certain of the Allied victory over Germany, Hitler committed suicide. The next day, von Ribbentrop was dismissed from his post as foreign minister.

On June 14, 1945, British agents arrested von Ribbentrop and transported him to Nuremberg, Germany. He was accused of helping plan the takeover of Czechoslovakia and Poland, as well as participating in the "Final Solution." He was charged with a variety of crimes against Nazi prisoners, including murder, ill-treatment, and other acts of cruelty. In the courtroom, he appeared a tired and beaten man, displaying none of his former cockiness. At various times he cried and protested his innocence. Von Ribbentrop was found guilty of all charges brought against him. He was executed by hanging on October 16, 1946, the first Nazi criminal to receive punishment.

SOURCES

Books

Bloch, Michael, *Von Ribbentrop: A Biography,* Crown (New York), 1992.

Browning, Christopher R., "Joachim von Ribbentrop," *The Encyclopedia of the Holocaust,* Israel Gutman, editor in chief, Macmillan (New York), 1990.

Dutch, Oswald, *Hitler's 12 Apostles,* Books for Libraries Press (Freeport, NY), 1969.

Fest, Joachim C., *The Face of the Third Reich: Portraits of Nazi Leadership,* translated from the German by Michael Bullock, Da Capo Press (New York), 1999.

Schwartz, Paul, *This Man von Ribbentrop: His Life and Times,* Julian Messner (New York), 1943.

Shirer, William L., *The Rise and Fall of the Third Reich: A History of Nazi Germany,* Simon & Schuster (New York), 1981.

Snyder, Louis L., editor, "Joachim von Ribbentrop," *Encyclopedia of the Third Reich,* Marlowe (New York), 1998.

Weitz, John, *Hitler's Diplomat: The Life and Times of Joachim von Ribbentrop,* Ticknor & Fields (New York), 1992.

Zentner, Christian, and Friedemann Bedürftig, "Joachim von Ribbentrop," *The Encyclopedia of the Third Reich,* translated by Amy Hackett, volume two, Da Capo Press (New York), 1997.

Raoul Gustav Wallenberg

Swedish banker Raoul Wallenberg was searching for more meaning in his life when he volunteered for a special mission: He was sent to Budapest, Hungary, by the Swedish government to save Jews from the Nazis' *Endlösung,* or "Final Solution," in which all European Jews were to be exterminated. Wallenberg approached his assignment with ferocious dedication. Bribing, threatening, and outwitting German soldiers, he rescued thousands of Jews from certain death. At the end of World War II, Soviet officials invited Wallenberg to a meeting to discuss plans for rehabilitating refugees. He was taken to a Russian prison and was never seen or heard from again.

Born August 4, 1912
  Stockholm, Sweden
Died on an unknown date
  Soviet Union

Banker; diplomat; humanitarian; saved as many as 100,000 Jews from Adolf Hitler and the Nazis

"I came to save a nation."

A Man on a Mission

Raoul Gustav Wallenberg was the only child born to Maj and Raoul Wallenberg. His father was a naval officer and member of a prominent Swedish family. Three months prior to Wallenberg's birth, Raoul senior died of cancer. Wallenberg's mother then married Fredrik von Dardel, a Swedish Health Department worker, with whom she had two more children. From a young age, Wallenberg was sensitive and solitary, and an animal lover. Color blindness forced him to abandon the idea of becoming a naval officer like his father. Instead, interested as he was in drawing and construction, he considered a career in architecture. At the urging of his grandfather, who wanted the

(USHMM Photo Archives)

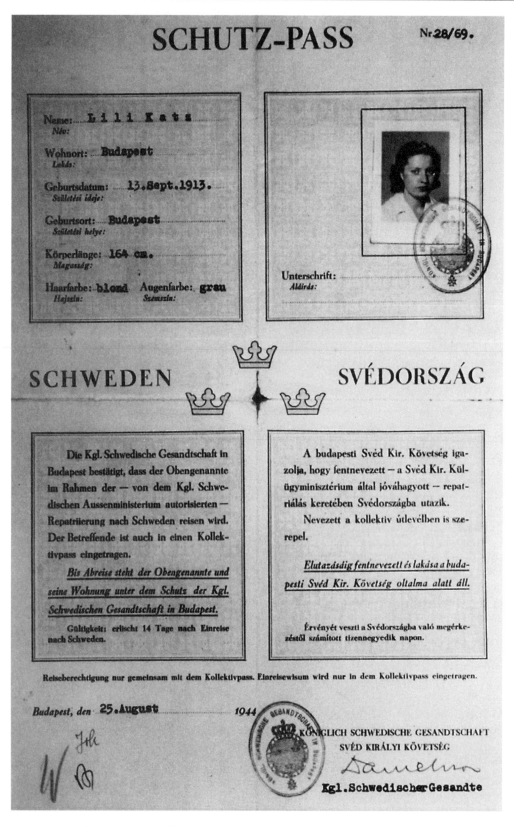

A letter of protection, bearing the initial "W" for Wallenberg, issued to Hungarian Jew Lili Katz. (Lena Kurtz Deutsch/USHMM Photo Archives)

young man to broaden his experience, Wallenberg went to the United States to attend the University of Michigan. He excelled in his studies and graduated with highest honors. During summer vacations, Wallenberg would hitchhike across America to visit various parts of the country. He wrote that these travels were an excellent opportunity to practice diplomacy, as he met many people.

Upon returning to Sweden and finding no job opportunities, Wallenberg accepted a position with a trading company in South Africa. Later, he worked as a banker in Palestine, where he met a number of Jews who had escaped from Germany; they told him about the Nazis' mistreatment of Jews. Wallenberg grew increasingly bored and restless with his bank job and returned to Stockholm in an unsuccessful attempt to find employment as an architect. He finally accepted a job with an import-export company, owned by a Hungarian Jew, which required frequent travel to Germany, Hungary, and Nazi-occupied France. Wallenberg's exposure to Europe under the Nazi regime disturbed him greatly. In 1941 Hungary had allied itself with Germany after a period of neutrality at the outset of the war. Plagued by heavy losses within two years, however, Hungary tried to make peace negotiations with the Allies. This move enraged the Germans, who took over Hungary in 1944 and immediately turned their attention to the 725,000 Jews who lived in the country.

Nazi leader Adolf Hitler dispatched Adolf Eichmann, one of the architects of the "Final Solution," to Hungary to eliminate Jews and other "undesirables." Jews in Budapest, the nation's largest city, requested help from ambassadors of neutral countries who were stationed in Hungary. The ambassadors began to issue special passes that gave Jews rights as citizens in neutral countries and therefore exempted them from Hitler's orders. Soon the Swedish ambassador was giving away so many passes that he needed extra help. Representatives of the World Jewish Congress and the U.S. government's War Refugee Board approached the Swedish government with a plan to send someone to Budapest to help the Jews escape. This person would be supplied with unlimited funds from the United States and would be able to work without filing time-consuming paperwork. Wallenberg had the necessary background and desire for such a delicate mission, and seized the opportunity. He demanded free rein, including the authority to offer bribes and payoffs to the enemy. After receiving the reluctant approval of the Swedish govern-

ment, Wallenberg departed for Budapest with other Swedes who would prepare protective passports.

"Bargaining with the Devil"

By the time Wallenberg arrived in Budapest on July 9, 1944, Eichmann had already deported more than 400,000 of Hungary's Jews to the Auschwitz-Birkenau concentration camp. Having no time to waste, Wallenberg immediately made contacts with neutral embassies and sympathetic Hungarians. He recruited spies within the Hungarian government and the Budapest police while establishing relationships with key Nazis, including Eichmann. According to writer Alan Levy: "Raoul Wallenberg had no scruples about bargaining with the devil. It was what he was being sent to Budapest to do." Wallenberg began issuing thousands of protective passports to the city's Jews. Believing that the Germans had a weakness for flashy objects, Wallenberg printed up passes in yellow and blue, complete with stamps, signatures, and Sweden's symbol of three crowns. To expedite matters, Wallenberg established a special branch of the embassy in the Jewish quarter, hiring as many as 600 people, predominantly Jewish, as staff, thus automatically granting them freedom from Nazi penalties or restrictions.

Wallenberg established thirty-one "safe houses" that were considered extensions of Swedish territory and therefore under the protection of diplomatic immunity. Camouflaged with signs reading "Swedish Library" or "Swedish Bank," the safe houses eventually sheltered approximately 15,000 Jews. Wallenberg won freedom for hundreds more on trains bound for Auschwitz by standing atop one of the cars and distributing passports to anyone who could reach them. When he ran out of passports, he distributed food and medical supplies. German soldiers who had been ordered to shoot at Wallenberg were so impressed by his courage that they deliberately aimed too high. Desperate to stop the genocide, Wallenberg threatened to charge the Nazis with war crimes after the war was over. On October 15, 1944, a representative of the Hungarian government announced on the radio that Hungary had withdrawn from the war. Later in the day, it was learned that the son of Hungarian regent Miklós Horthy had been taken hostage by the Germans and that Horthy was giving up his position. The Germans handed the country over to Ferenc Szálasi, leader of the Arrow Cross party. Members of the Arrow Cross went on a looting and killing rampage as Eichmann ordered the capture of thousands of

"Righteous Among the Nations of the World"

Yad Vashem is the Martyrs' and Heroes' Remembrance Authority in Jerusalem. Commissioned in 1953, the complex of buildings, gardens, and avenues is a memorial to the 6 million Jews murdered by the Nazis during World War II. Several hundred trees, each honoring a "Righteous Gentile," are planted along the Avenue. One of the trees is dedicated to Raoul Wallenberg. About 5,000 men and women have been designated as "Righteous Among the Nations of the World." Among them are the Swedish diplomat Per Anger, who is credited with issuing the first Swedish protective passes to Hungarian Jews; Hermann Graebe, who saved the lives of more than 300 Jews in Germany, Poland, and the Ukraine; Marion P. van Binsbergen Pritchard, who hid Jews during the Nazi occupation of Holland and was featured in the award-winning movie *The Courage to Care* (1986); and Oskar Schindler, a factory owner who saved his Jewish workers.

The Yad Vashem Holocaust Memorial in Jerusalem, Israel. The museum is devoted to preserving the memory of the Holocaust, so it will not be forgotten. (Photograph by Susan D. Rock; reproduced with permission)

Jews. Wallenberg was able to save 300 people by marching into the detainment area, handing out passes, and relocating them to the safe houses.

Wallenberg worked frantically over the next few months to save thousands. By moving from one safe house to another, he survived an assassination attempt. In November 1944 the Allies cut off the road to Auschwitz. As it became obvious that Germany was going to lose the war, the Nazis began exterminating all the prisoners. When the gas chambers were working at full capacity, Eichmann sent excess prisoners on a death march to Austria. Wallenberg stood along the route, handing out protective passes to the freezing, starving masses, comprised mainly of women and children.

Wallenberg Vanishes

When the Soviets occupied Budapest in January 1945, Wallenberg's mission was officially over. He had, however, formulated a master plan for rebuilding the city and aiding refugees, which he wanted to discuss with the Soviets before heading back to Sweden. The Soviets, suspicious of outsiders, were equally eager to talk to him—they knew about Wallenberg's contacts with the Hungarians, the Nazis, and the Americans, and they thought he was a spy. Wallenberg knew nothing of these suspicions when he was asked to report to Soviet army headquarters for questioning. After being detained for two days, he returned to Budapest in the company of several Soviet soldiers. On January 17 Wallenberg was called to another meeting at the Soviet army headquarters. Remarking to a colleague that he was not sure if he was the Soviets' guest or their prisoner, Wallenberg reported to the meeting, after which he was taken away to a Soviet prison. His fate remains unknown.

On February 6, 1957, the Soviets issued a brief memo stating that Wallenberg had been imprisoned in Moscow, the Soviet capital, until his death from a heart attack on July 17, 1947, at age thirty-four. In spite of repeated inquiries from Wallenberg's family and the Swedish government, Soviet officials stood by the statement, insisting that Wallenberg was dead and their files contained no additional information about him. In 1971 Wallenberg's mother asked famed Nazi-hunter Simon Wiesenthal for help. Wiesenthal focused worldwide attention on Wallenberg's humanitarian achievements during the Holocaust. In the mid-1990s, the U.S. Central Intelligence Agency (CIA) released secret files involving Raoul Wallenberg. The files, according to *U.S. News & World Report*, "show conclusively that Wallenberg was a valued U.S. intelligence asset." The magazine reported interviewing witnesses who said they saw Wallenberg after 1947 and possibly as late as 1989. The Russians still maintain that Wallenberg died in 1947.

SOURCES

Books

Bierman, John, *Righteous Gentile: The Story of Raoul Wallenberg, Missing Hero of the Holocaust,* Penguin Books (New York), 1995.

Larsen, Anita, *Raoul Wallenberg: Missing Diplomat,* Crestwood House (New York), 1992.

Levy, Alan, *The Wiesenthal File,* William B. Eerdmans Publishing (Grand Rapids, MI), 1994.

Linnèa, Sharon, *Raoul Wallenberg: The Man Who Stopped Death,* Jewish Publication Society (Philadelphia), 1993.

Marton, Kati, *Wallenberg,* Random House (New York), 1982.

Rittner, Carol, and Sondra Myers, editors, *The Courage to Care: Rescuers of Jews During the Holocaust,* New York University Press (New York), 1986.

Smith, Danny, *Wallenberg: Lost Hero,* Pickering (Basingstoke, Hants, UK), 1986.

Wallenberg, Raoul, *Letters and Dispatches, 1924–1944,* translated by Kjersti Board, Arcade (New York), 1995.

Werbell, Frederick E., and Thurston Clarke, *Lost Hero: The Mystery of Raoul Wallenberg,* McGraw-Hill (New York), 1982.

Periodicals

Fenyvesi, Charles, and Victoria Pope, "The Angel Was a Spy (Swedish Diplomat Raoul Wallenberg)," *U.S. News & World Report,* May 13, 1996, p. 46.

Other

Raoul Wallenberg, http://www.us-israel.org/jsource/biography/wallenberg.html (May 5, 2000).

Michiko Nishiura Weglyn

Born November 29, 1926
Stockton, California, United States
Died April 25, 1999
New York, New York, United States

Costume designer; writer; activist

"From an apolitical innocent I became a traumatized citizen. I was enraged by a democracy's flagrant disregard for elemental human rights, especially as they related to ethnicity and skin color, and by America's shocking disregard for a reverence for life which we had been taught to hold sacred."

(Courtesy of Michiko Nishiura Weglyn. Reproduced by permission)

Michiko Weglyn's first career, which she began at age twenty-one, catapulted her to fame as the first nationally prominent Japanese-American costume designer in the United States. By the 1950s, she was a regular fixture behind the scenes of such popular television programs as *The Perry Como Show, The Jackie Gleason Show,* and *The Dinah Shore Show.* Weglyn was praised for the clothing she designed for some of Hollywood's most famous celebrities, including Ginger Rogers, Betty Grable, Anne Bancroft, and Jane Powell. Her career lasted nearly two decades, and she eventually established her own manufacturing and design studio.

In 1967 Weglyn's life changed dramatically when Ramsey Clark, the U.S. Attorney General, appeared on a television show and stated that there had never been, and never would be, concentration camps in America. Having spent more than two years of her life at a Japanese American internment camp in Gila River, Arizona, Weglyn was shocked to hear those words, which she felt were a lie. Clark's statement prompted Weglyn to research and write her landmark work, *Years of Infamy: The Untold Story of America's Concentration Camps* (1976), which exposed the horror and suffering of some 120,000 Japanese Americans imprisoned in U.S. internment camps during World War II.

Farm Life

Born in Stockton, California, on November 29, 1926, Michiko Nishiura was one of two daughters of Tomojiro and Misao (Yuasa) Nishiura. The family lived in a large, dilapidated house on a 500-acre farm in Brentwood, California. While growing up, Weglyn worked on the farm for a few hours each morning before she went to school, wanting to prove to her father that she was just as valuable as the son he never had. Weglyn knew that in Japanese culture it was important to have a male heir to carry on the family name and help harvest the fields. In grade school Weglyn was shy with white children, so she found friends among Mexican American and Filipino children. She was aware of *haiseki*, or discrimination.

On December 8, 1941, the day after Japanese bombers attacked Pearl Harbor, Hawaii, pulling America into World War II, Weglyn felt ambivalent about attending school. Weglyn recalled that when she arrived, the teacher told the other students not to blame the Japanese American students. However, the general public was not as fair-minded. Weglyn's parents were concerned about public resentment, and they burned books and buried objects in the middle of the night that might show the family's connection to Japan. This included family photographs of relatives in Japan, letters, and even pieces of art. On February 19, 1942, President Franklin D. Roosevelt signed Executive Order 9066, which called for the evacuation of all persons of Japanese descent on the West Coast, two-thirds of whom were American citizens, to ten relocation camps. It was believed that imprisonment would prevent the internees from posing a threat to U.S. military efforts against Japan. Families were given six to ten days to dispose of their property and businesses. According to Weglyn, Japanese Americans followed the instructions, even though they believed it was so unfair. Neither the *Issei* (Japanese immigrants) or *Nisei* (the first generation born in America to Japanese immigrants) felt they had any say or control in the matter.

When the evacuation order reached the Nishiuras, they were in the midst of packing. Weglyn explained the situation to Harriet Shapiro in 1976:

> People wanted to buy our bicycles and automobiles for next to nothing, and the chickens for a quarter apiece. At that price Mom decided it would be better to eat as many chickens as we could before we left. To this day, when my sister and I talk about that period,

the hurried killing and eating of our pet chickens was one of the most traumatic aspects of the evacuation. Our father and mother were losing everything they had worked for, but my sister and I had little realization of that. For us it was parting with our animals: our cats, dogs, chickens, our possum, and our parrot. Most were left abandoned. I guess that's what war is like. But these are the things that are not written up in history books.

On May 12, 1942, the Nishiuras were loaded on buses that carried them to an assembly center where they found guard towers, guns, and barbed wire awaiting them. Young Weglyn was not yet sixteen years old. After several months, the family boarded another train which shuttled hundreds of families to the relocation camp in Gila River, Arizona. After two days and nights of traveling, the evacuees arrived in a barren desert that would be their home for several years.

Camp Life

The extreme heat, the unrelenting sand storms, the inedible food, the overcrowded housing, and the communal bathrooms without partitions for the toilets did not detour Weglyn from thriving in her environment. She told Shapiro that she felt a sense of relief and liberation in her new home. "Suddenly I was with my peers. I didn't have to feel inferior. I didn't have to feel small. Or to face the humiliation I had begun to feel more intensely in school. I was liked for what I was, not because of what my parents did or didn't do. I had finally gained a feeling of respect, and I was managing to do the kinds of things that had been denied me, back at home, as a person who was of Asian descent." Weglyn emerged as a true leader and achiever among her peers, becoming president of the Girl Scout troop she organized. She held a day-long Girls League Convention that brought 500 high school girls from various Arizona cities to the camp where they participated in a talent show, were given a tour of the facilities, ate together in the mess halls, and discussed timely issues. "They took back to their homes the news that we were as American as anybody else. It helped turn the feelings of distrust," Weglyn said.

In 1944 Weglyn went to Phoenix to take entrance examinations for Mount Holyoke College in Massachusetts. Prior to her exam, she stopped at a nearby drug store for a soda, but was asked to leave because she was Japanese. During the

At the Santa Anita Internment Camp in California, Japanese American men take their turn at KP duty. (Reproduced by permission of AP/Wide World Photo.)

previous two years, Weglyn had been shielded from such racism and abuse while living among only Japanese Americans at the camp. In spite of her racist reception in the outside world, Weglyn eventually traveled to the east coast and entered college. Although she does not remember the details of her arrival at Gila, she clearly remembers leaving: "I was full of the spirit of forgiveness and love and very grateful to the many dedicated fellow Americans who had made it possible for me to attend Mount Holyoke College on a full scholarship," she said to Shapiro.

In college, Weglyn discovered her aptitude for design, a subject in which her interest went all the way back to her childhood, when she had made sweaters for genetically mutant pet chickens born without feathers. At Mount Holyoke, she won a campuswide design contest for costumes, sets, and scenery for a college production. In 1945 Weglyn was forced to leave Mount Holyoke and was placed in a sanatorium for tuberculosis, which she had contracted at Gila. In 1947 she returned to school at Barnard College in New York City, but again was

forced to leave for health reasons. Weglyn later studied costume design at the Fashion Academy, also in New York City, between 1948 and 1949.

On March 5, 1950, she married Walter Matthys Weglyn, a perfume chemist who came to the United States in 1947 after having survived the Holocaust. In the 1950s, under the name Michi, Weglyn began designing theatrical costumes for ice shows, night clubs, Broadway productions, and television shows, including *The Perry Como Show,* a weekly musical variety hour. From 1964 to 1967, she was the founder and head of costume manufacturing and the design studio for Michi Associates Limited. By the time Weglyn retired from designing in the late 1960s, war was a controversial topic in the United States. The Vietnam War was raging abroad while the civil rights movement gained momentum at home. Weglyn explained in 1993 during her commencement address at California State Polytechnic University in Pomona, California:

As I look back, I would first have to credit both the Vietnam War (when the use of tech-

In California, Japanese Americans were required to report to internment camps. They also carried identification records such as this, which reveals basic information, such as height and weight, but also contains finger prints. (Reproduced by permission of AP/Wide World Photos)

nological savagery on the lives, habits, and ecosystem of a small Asian nation was shocking the entire civilized world) and the civil rights movement (when each day was filled with rage and racial violence) for the transition that took place within me. From an apolitical innocent I became a traumatized citizen. I was enraged by a democracy's flagrant disregard for elemental human rights, especially as they related to ethnicity and skin color, and by America's shocking disregard for a reverence for life which we had been taught to hold sacred. What startled me into disbelief during the heat of the antiwar and civil rights agitation was the preposterous lie spewed forth by the then-attorney general Ramsey Clark when asked on television if the protesters would be put in concentration camps. His astonished reply, that 'we have never had, do not now have, and will not ever have concentration camps here' was the catalyst. His blatant untruth convinced me that uncovering the probable lies of our long-revered wartime president Franklin Delano Roosevelt would surely lead me to the truth as to why we innocents had been consigned to prison camps.

In the FDR Library, and later at the National Archives and other repositories, Weglyn found documented proof of the U.S. government's actions. In 1976 the result of her labors, *Years of Infamy: The Untold Story of America's Concentration Camps,* was published by William Morrow and Company. With careful research and documentation, Weglyn sheds light on abuses of power in the highest reaches of a government that failed to protect the basic rights of Americans of Japanese descent. She discourages Japanese Americans from feeling guilt or shame for their heritage, wishing instead to place the burden of guilt and shame on Franklin D. Roosevelt, who signed the order establishing the camps. Her work helped release a new social activism among Japanese Americans to become more involved in promoting civil and human rights, which eventually led to the redress movement of the late 1980s and early 1990s. Both the book and Weglyn herself have been praised for changing the face of Asian-American history. Weglyn has been given much of the credit for the success of the Japanese-American redress campaign. *Rafu Shimpo* reported that in 1993 Bert Nakano, national spokesperson for the National Coalition for Redress and Reparations (NCRR), called *Years of Infamy* "the primer that people referred to in order to get familiar with the [Japanese American internment] issue."

After the publication of her book, Weglyn remained actively involved in the Asian American community. She has been named an adviser and consultant on countless projects, including the Japanese American National Museum in Los Angeles (1988–1990), the Japanese American Library in San Francisco (1987–), Loni Ding's award-winning film, *Color of Honor* (1987), the Congressional Study on the Commission on Wartime Relocation and Internment of Civilians (1981–1982), and the Smithsonian Institution's exhibit, "A More Perfect Union: The Japanese Americans and the U.S. Constitution (1975–1976)." Weglyn has received numerous honors and awards, including the Justice in Action Award from the Asian American Legal Defense and Education Fund (1987); the Anisfield-Wolf Award in Race Relations for *Years of Infamy* (1977), and the Japanese American of the Biennium Award in recognition of outstanding service from the Japanese American Citizens League (1976). In addition, Weglyn received honorary doctorates from Hunter College in 1992 and from California State Polytechnic University in 1993. Also in 1993, California State Polytechnic University established the Michi Nishiura and Walter Weglyn Endowed Chair for Multicultural Studies. In June 1994, almost five decades after health problems forced her to leave, Weglyn received an honorary doctor of letters degree from Mount Holyoke College.

SOURCES

Books

Shapiro, Harriet, "Michi," 1976.

Weglyn, Michi, *Years of Infamy: The Untold Story of America's Concentration Camps,* William Morrow (New York), 1976.

Zia, Helen, and Susan B. Gall, editors, *Notable Asian Americans,* Gale Research (New York), 1995.

Periodicals

Nakayama, Takeshi, "Nisei Author Honored by Cal Poly Pomona," *Rafu Shimpo,* June 14, 1993.

Perkins, Robert, "U.S. Infamy Recalled," *Springfield Union,* March 11, 1977.

Seko, Sachi, "Digging for Roots," *Pacific Citizen,* February 27, 1976, p. 4.

Elie Wiesel

A Holocaust survivor in his youth, Elie Wiesel later rose to prominence as an author who has brought worldwide attention to the atrocities committed by Nazis against Jews during World War II. He is known today as the "Poet of the Holocaust," having written extensively of the horrors of war. Wiesel was only fifteen years old when he and his family were deported to Birkenau, the reception center of the Auschwitz death camp, in 1944. Years later, Wiesel vividly recounted life in the camps in his autobiographical novel *Night,* which has become a classic of Holocaust literature. Now a renowned spokesperson for humanitarian causes, Wiesel has written numerous works that celebrate the Jewish faith and traditions and address the need for compassion toward fellow human beings. He received the Nobel Peace Prize in 1986 for his enduring efforts to keep the memory of the Holocaust alive so that such a tragedy would never repeat itself.

Born September 30, 1928
Sighet, Romania

Journalist; professor; social activist; concentration camp survivor; author of Holocaust literature

"Having survived by chance, I was duty-bound to give meaning to my survival."

Tranquility Shattered by Fascism

Born Eliezer Wiesel in 1928 in Sighet, a small town in Romania, he was the third of four children of Shlomo and Sarah Feig Wiesel. Shlomo was an educated man who owned a grocery store; Sarah, a high school graduate, was considered highly educated for a Jewish woman of the time. Wiesel had three sisters: Hilda, Batya, and Tzipora. His parents

(Photograph by Nancy Rica Schiff, courtesy of Archive Photos, Inc.)

An Excerpt from *Night*

Although Elie Wiesel has written several books about the Holocaust, his first autobiographical novel, *Night,* remains his most famous. In a particularly well-known passage he wrote: "Never shall I forget that night, the first night in camp, which has turned my life into one long night, seven times cursed and seven times sealed. Never shall I forget that smoke. Never shall I forget the little faces of the children, whose bodies I saw turned into wreaths of smoke beneath a silent blue sky. Never shall I forget those flames which consumed my Faith forever. Never shall I forget that nocturnal silence which deprived me, for all eternity, of the desire to live. Never shall I forget those moments which murdered my God and my soul and turned my dreams to dust. Never shall I forget these things, even if I am condemned to live as long as God Himself. Never."

stressed education, expecting him to apply himself to his studies. A serious child who preferred reading to games, he played the violin and enjoyed studying religion, particularly the Talmud and the mystical teachings of Hasidism and the Cabala. In his book *Memoirs: All Rivers Run to the Sea,* Wiesel declared: "I was hardly a model child. I complained easily. My concentration wandered. I spent too much time daydreaming with my friends instead of studying. I didn't eat enough and my parents worried constantly about how thin I was, and how pale. Lavish sums were spent dragging me from doctor to doctor, city to city to treat my migraines."

Religion was central to his family life. Wiesel wrote that he looked forward to the Sabbath because it was the only day he was able to spend with his father, who was constantly working at the shop or tending to community matters. A well-loved and sheltered child, he expected to stay in his small village forever, quietly contemplating religious texts and working in the family store. On

occasion he overheard adults talking about world events, which he assumed had little to do with him. Yet he later commented, "The local situation, on the other hand, did scare me." Increasing violence against Jews was taking place throughout Romania as the Fascist Party, an anti-Semitic group called the Iron Guard, came to power in the country. Conditions in Romania mirrored the events of World War II, which was raging across Europe.

Wiesel's homeland had been a sanctuary for Jews since they were expelled from the Ukraine in 1640. However, World War II was about to change that. Although the war had its origins in Germany, the Nazis' ultimate agenda was to take over Europe and exterminate all European Jews. The Nazis blamed the Jews for Germany's poor economy, including massive unemployment and high inflation. The Nazis decreed that Jews were not German citizens and treated them as foreigners. They took immediate measures to expel the Jews. Initially, Romania was neutral in the war, even though many Romanians sympathized with Germany. The Germans moved into Romania in 1940 under the pretense that a military presence was necessary to protect the country's oil fields from British attack.

Survives Camps, Starts New Life

In the spring of 1944, SS officer Adolf Eichmann arrived in Sighet, having received orders to exterminate an estimated 600,000 Romanian Jews in six weeks or less. Sighet's entire population of 15,000 Jews was sent to concentration camps. Fifteen-year-old Wiesel and his family were taken to Auschwitz-Birkenau, where his mother and youngest sister died. Wiesel and his father remained together through incarceration in the Buna and Buchenwald camps before his father was beaten and starved to death. Much later Wiesel wrote: "Grandma Nissel was the only one in the family, almost the only one in the whole community, who guessed it all.... She knew she would never come home. She left this wretched town in her funeral dress.... She alone was ready." For reasons he still does not understand, Wiesel survived eleven months in the camps. He was being held in Buchenwald when it was liberated in 1945. Wiesel did not learn until years after the war that two of his sisters had also survived.

Belgium was one of the few countries willing to accept Jewish refugees after the war. Having no one to return to in Sighet, Wiesel boarded a train headed for Belgium with 400 other orphans. When a change in plans diverted his train to France,

Elie Wiesel Meets President Reagan

On April 19, 1985, U.S. President Ronald Reagan presented Elie Wiesel with the Congressional Gold Medal of Achievement, which paid tribute to his contributions as chairperson of the U.S. Holocaust Memorial Council, to his work on behalf of human rights, and to his achievements as a writer. Earlier, Reagan, wishing to show friendship to Germany, had announced his intention to visit the Cemetery of Bitburg to lay a wreath in memory of German soldiers who fought in World War II. Both Jewish groups and military veterans were outraged as many Nazi storm troopers were buried there; some suggested it would be more fitting for the president to visit a concentration camp. Reagan had responded that he did not want to stir up bad memories of the Holocaust by visiting a camp. He further defended his planned visit to the cemetery by saying that many of the German soldiers that were laid to rest there were also victims of the Nazis.

When Reagan presented Wiesel with the medal, Wiesel took the opportunity to speak to the president about his upcoming visit. "That place, Mr. President, is not your place. Your place is with the victims of the SS.... For I have seen the SS at work, and I have seen their victims. They were my friends. They were my parents." After the ceremony, Reagan asked Wiesel to accompany him to the German cemetery. A stunned Wiesel refused.

French officials at the border asked any children who wanted to become French citizens to raise their hands. Wiesel neither understood nor spoke French, so he did not raise his hand. Describing the situation with other orphans, Wiesel recalled in the *Washington Post* that "[a] lot of them did. They thought they were going to get bread or something; they would reach out for anything. I didn't, so I remained stateless." Wiesel believes his inaction led to "Refused French nationality" being written on his papers. Wiesel liked France, where he lived first in an orphanage in Normandy and later in Paris. Eventually, he was reunited with his two sisters. He learned French and did whatever he could to earn a living: tutoring, directing a choir, translating. He entered a French university in 1948, supporting himself by working as a writer and reporter for various French and Jewish publications. He was unable to write about what he had seen and felt at the concentration camps. "I made a vow of silence, not to speak about it, not to write about it for ten years [after liberation]."

Breaks His Silence

The young journalist's silence came to an end in the mid-1950s when he met and interviewed the novelist François Mauriac. Upon learning of Wiesel's tragic youth, Mauriac began to cry, urging Wiesel to speak out and tell the world of his experiences. The result was *Night,* published in France as *La Nuit* in 1958. Essentially autobiographical, *Night* tells the story of a teenaged boy, plagued with guilt for having survived the camps, who is devastated by the realization that the God he had once devoutly worshiped allowed his people to be destroyed. The book became the first in a series of nonfiction books and autobiographical novels by Wiesel that deal, directly or indirectly, with the Holocaust. Today, *Night* is considered a classic of Holocaust literature.

In 1956, Wiesel was sent to New York to report on proceedings at the United Nations. Soon after he arrived, he was struck by a taxi and dragged for almost a block. One hospital refused him admittance due to his status as a refugee and because his chances for survival seemed minimal. Taken to New York Hospital, he lay in a coma for several days. He made a miraculous recovery but spent nearly a year in a wheelchair. Meanwhile, his French visa expired, and friends persuaded him to apply for U.S. citizenship. He was working for a Jewish newspaper in New York when the American edition of *Night,* which he had sold for $100, was published. In 1969, at the age of forty-one, Wiesel married Marion Rose, a fellow Holocaust survivor. In 1972, they had a son, whom they named Shlomo Elisha after Wiesel's grandfather. Wiesel wrote his novels in French, and his wife translated them into English. In 1978, he was asked by U.S. President Jimmy Carter to head the Presidential Commission on the Holocaust, later known as the U.S. Holocaust Memorial Council. The group visited former concentration camps, met with European officials to ask for records pertaining to Holocaust victims, and was responsible for the creation of the U.S. Holocaust Memorial Museum in Washington, D.C.

Starts Humanitarian Foundation

Wiesel continued his devotion to preserving the memory of Holocaust victims. In 1986, he accepted the Nobel Peace Prize for his work on behalf of victims everywhere. In his acceptance speech, Wiesel reminded audiences that we must not remain silent "when human lives are endangered, when human dignity is in jeopardy.... Wherever men or women are persecuted because of their race, religion or political views, that place must—at that moment—become the center of the universe."

Wiesel used his Nobel Prize money to found the Elie Wiesel Foundation for Humanity. The foundation's activities include sponsoring national essay contests for college students on the subject of human rights, and gathering well-known people together to discuss social issues. Wiesel continues to travel and speak out against oppression. He has written more than three dozen books, and has been the subject of at least two dozen more. His books include *Dawn, The Accident, Legends of Our Time, The Jews of Silence: A Personal Report on Soviet Jewry, A Beggar in Jerusalem, One Generation After, The Forgotten,* and *Memoir in Two Voices,* among others.

In 1995, his English-language edition of *Memoirs: All Rivers Run to the Sea* was published. It describes his childhood, his camp experiences, and his life up until his marriage. In a review of the work, Elliott Abrams noted: "In this book, as elsewhere, Wiesel offers no 'explanation' for Jewish suffering, acknowledging that 'the questions I once asked myself about God's silence remain open.'"

SOURCES

Books

Berenbaum, Michael, *Elie Wiesel: God, the Holocaust, and the Children of Israel,* Behrman House (West Orange, NJ), 1994.

Confronting the Holocaust: The Impact of Elie Wiesel, edited by Alvin H. Rosenfeld and Irving Greenberg, Indiana University Press (Bloomington, IN), 1978.

Contemporary Authors Autobiography Series, Vol. 4, Gale Research (Detroit, MI), 1986.

Contemporary Literary Criticism, Vol. 3, Vol. 5, Vol. 11, Vol. 37, Gale Research (Detroit, MI), 1975, 1976, 1979, and 1986.

Davis, Colin, *Elie Wiesel's Secretive Texts,* University Press of Florida (Gainesville, FL), 1994.

Dictionary of Literary Biography, Vol. 83, *French Novelists Since 1960,* Gale Research (Detroit, MI), 1989.

Gendler, Gail M, "Elie Wiesel: A Biographical Overview," in *Telling the Tale: A Tribute to Elie Wiesel On the Occasion of His 65th Birthday: Essays, Reflections, and Poems,* edited by Harry James Cargas, Time Being Press (St. Louis, MO), 1993.

Lazo, Caroline Evensen, *Elie Wiesel,* Macmillan (New York, NY), 1994.

Pariser, Michael, *Elie Wiesel: Bearing Witness,* Millbrook Press (Brookfield, CT), 1994.

Sibelman, Simon P., *Silence in the Novels of Elie Wiesel,* St. Martin's Press (New York, NY), 1995.

Stern, Ellen Norman, *Elie Wiesel: A Voice for Humanity,* Jewish Publication Society (Philadelphia, PA), 1996.

Stern, Ellen Norman, *Elie Wiesel: Witness for Life,* Ktav Publishing (New York, NY), 1982.

Wiesel, Elie, *Memoirs: All Rivers Run to the Sea,* Alfred A. Knopf (New York, NY), 1995.

Wiesel, Elie. *Night,* translated from the French by Stella Rodway, Hill and Wang (New York, NY), 1960.

Periodicals

Abrams, Elliott, "*Memoirs: All Rivers Run to the Sea* (book review)," *Commentary,* June 1996, p. 64.

Wiesel, Elie, "Stay Together, Always," *Newsweek,* January 16, 1995, pp. 58-59.

Simon Wiesenthal

Simon Wiesenthal survived imprisonment in thirteen concentration camps during World War II. Since that time he has devoted his life to hunting Nazi war criminals, and he has been personally responsible for bringing many to justice. Among them is SS officer Adolf Eichmann, one of the creators of the "Final Solution," who was tried and later executed in 1962. Although Wiesenthal is admired throughout the world for his dedication, he has also been denounced as a "merciless avenger." His greatest concern is that the world will forget the horrors that occurred during the Holocaust and that the "madness" will descend upon humankind again. In the late 1990s, Wiesenthal focused his energies on informing young people about the Holocaust and speaking out against neo-Nazi groups.

Childhood in Galicia

Wiesenthal was born in 1908 in Buczacz, Galicia, a poor region of the Austro-Hungarian Empire. Polish was the official language. The first of two children of Asher and Rosa Wiesenthal, he spoke Polish and Yiddish at home; his mother also spoke German. She admired German literature, which she often quoted to her children. Wiesenthal learned languages easily, eventually mastering Russian, English, and some Czech. Asher Wiesenthal was a businessman who traded food, mainly sugar. Wiesenthal's father was killed during World

Born December 31, 1908
  Buczacz, Galicia, Austria-Hungary

Architect; concentration camp survivor; Nazi hunter; activist for the remembrance of Holocaust victims

"There is no greater sin than to forget."

(Reproduced by permission of UPI/Corbis-Bettmann)

War I (1914–1918) and his widowed mother moved the family to a Jewish district in Vienna, Austria, to escape the invading Russian army. Austria, the birthplace of Adolf Hitler, was a hotbed of anti-Semitism. When the war ended, the family moved back to Buczacz, where family members endured almost constant turmoil. Although Poles, Austrians, and Ukrainians fought one another over the region, many shared a hatred of Jews.

In 1923 Wiesenthal's brother, Hillel, died in an accident. Three years later his mother married a brick maker and moved to a town called Dolina. Wiesenthal stayed behind to finish high school, living with the family of Cyla Müller, a Jewish girl he planned to marry. An accomplished artist, he decided to become an architect. But attending school in Poland was difficult for Jews. Under Polish law, only ten percent of available space at universities was allocated to Jews, and some studies, such as architecture, were completely closed. Wiesenthal went to Prague, Czechoslovakia, where he completed his studies at the Technical Institute of Prague. While there, he witnessed Hitler giving hate speeches, and he saw Jews being persecuted. After graduation, he set up a private practice, and in 1936 he married Müller. They settled into what they both believed would be a happy and prosperous life together. Eventually Wiesenthal's mother came to live with the couple.

Wiesenthal felt the Nazi shadow looming over him, as conditions for European Jews grew more and more restrictive. After Adolf Hitler and the Nazis rose to power in Germany in 1933, they passed laws stripping Jews of their rights. Anti-Jewish feelings were spreading throughout Europe. Soon, Germany planned to rid Europe of all Jews when it invaded Poland in 1939, starting World War II. Joining Germany in the conflict was the Soviet Union. Many Soviets shared Germany's anti-Semitic feelings. As the war began, the Soviets occupied Czechoslovakia and began arresting Jews, confiscating their bank accounts, and forcing them out of certain jobs.

Wiesenthal had to close his architectural firm and go to work as a factory mechanic. When the Nazis turned on the Soviet Union and invaded it and the region where the Wiesenthals lived in June 1941, Wiesenthal's mother was detained by the Nazis, along with all Jews who were either too old or too sick to work. He never saw her again and continues to be haunted by her memory. He told biographer Hella Pick: "I would give anything to have a picture of my mother." Wiesenthal and his wife were taken to a concentration camp, later being moved to a labor camp. Cyla Wiesenthal escaped in late 1942 with the help of the Polish underground, which supplied her with false identification papers. She assimilated into society by posing as a Polish Aryan named Irena Kowalska.

Wiesenthal spent the next three years being transported from one concentration camp to another. Facing certain death on several occasions, he always won last-minute reprieves from execution. He managed to escape and hide for several months in early 1944, but was captured and sent back to a camp, where he made two unsuccessful suicide attempts. Wiesenthal credits his survival to luck and continues to feel guilty that he survived while so many others perished. In January 1945, the Soviet army, which had joined the Allied forces against Germany, headed westward into German-occupied Poland. Knowing the end was near, the Nazis began to hide the evidence of their crimes by making final, desperate efforts to kill as many prisoners as possible. When the gas chambers at Auschwitz were working at full capacity, Wiesenthal was among the excess prisoners taken from there on death marches to several other camps, a step ahead of the Soviets. Many died or were killed by guards on the way. Wiesenthal's final stop was the Mauthausen camp in Austria, the last of the camps to be liberated at the end of the war. Mauthausen was known as "The Mountain of Death."

On May 5, 1945, an armored unit of the U.S. Army rolled into Mauthausen. Thirty-six-year-old Wiesenthal, one of the few inmates still alive, staggered into the courtyard and touched the white star on the first tank to enter the camp, then collapsed into the arms of an American officer. Weighing only one hundred and ten pounds, the six-foot-tall Wiesenthal was barely more than a walking skeleton. After having spent almost four years as a Nazi prisoner, he was determined to greet his liberators on his feet, not among the dead and dying in the bunkhouse. As he regained his strength, Wiesenthal was initially consumed by an overwhelming desire for violent revenge. He soon realized that efforts to destroy his enemies would make him no better than the Nazis. He believed the world needed to learn the extent of Nazi crimes. Preserving the memory of those killed in the Holocaust became more important than punishing those who had committed the atrocities.

Although still weakened by his ordeal, Wiesenthal volunteered his services to a U.S. Army war

Wiesenthal touring the Jewish Historical Museum in Amsterdam in 1987. (Reproduced by permission of Reuters/Bettmann)

crimes unit, taking statements from witnesses and gathering evidence for use in the upcoming trials of suspected Nazi criminals at Nuremberg. He had an excellent memory and was able to recall countless details about events in the camps. When the war crimes unit moved to Linz, Austria, Wiesenthal talked with hundreds of survivors as he served as head of a relief and welfare organization called the Jewish Central Committee that helped refugees track down members of their families. He recorded their names and stories for use in identifying and prosecuting Nazi criminals and to create an oral history. In the process he learned of Cyla's survival, and in late 1945 they were at last reunited. Their joy was soon overshadowed with sadness when they realized they were the sole survivors of their ninety-one family members. More than ever, Wiesenthal thought it was his responsibility as a survivor to make sure justice was done. In 1946 their only child, Paulinka, was born. "No one ever wanted a child as deliberately as we did," explained Wiesenthal to his biographer.

Searches for Eichmann

In 1947 Wiesenthal and approximately thirty volunteers established the Jewish Historical Documentation Center in Linz, near the Mauthausen camp, to assemble evidence for future trials. Interest in Nazi criminals declined as the United States and the Soviet Union became entrenched in the Cold War. The United States needed Germany's support against the Soviet Union, including the assistance of a rebuilt German army with former Nazi soldiers at its head. In 1954 a frustrated Wiesenthal closed the documentation center and went into refugee work. He sent all his files to Israel, except records on Adolf Eichmann—the man who had carried out Hitler's "Final Solution" and disappeared after the war. Wiesenthal knew that top Nazis had secured massive amounts of gold in undisclosed locations to finance their new lives abroad if Germany lost the war. He believed Eichmann was among those who had found a safe haven somewhere in the world. Although South America was a favored refuge for Nazi criminals, the United States is believed to have harbored as many as 10,000 former Nazis as well.

Throughout the 1950s, Wiesenthal's many informants passed information about Eichmann along to him. When Eichmann's wife tried to have him declared legally dead, Wiesenthal exposed the fact that her key witness was her own brother-in-law. He also produced statements from witnesses testifying that they had seen Eichmann alive after the war. In 1952 Mrs. Eichmann and her children

The Simon Wiesenthal Center

In 1977 Rabbi Marvin Hier called Simon Wiesenthal from Los Angeles to request that Wiesenthal lend his name to a proposed Holocaust center in the city. Wiesenthal was impressed that the center was the brainchild of a group of young Americans—not Holocaust survivors. They were interested in a modern institution that would be more than a building of archives and pictures that were never used.

Today, the Simon Wiesenthal Center—with offices in New York City; Paris, France; and Jerusalem, Israel—is a human rights and research institution with a membership approaching 400,000. Operating independently from Wiesenthal's Jewish Historical Documentation Center, it is involved in the search for Nazi criminals. After East and West Germany were reunited in 1990, wartime records were made available for the first time. These records sparked a new interest in the search. Recently, the center has also concentrated its efforts on learning the fate of billions of dollars in gold, property, and valuables stolen from Holocaust victims. Exhibits at the museum focus on the Holocaust and are unique in highlighting the tragic experiences of other peoples throughout history, such as the Roma (often called Gypsies). The center maintains a website (see sources).

vanished, and Wiesenthal soon learned that she had been issued a passport under her maiden name. After investigating, he learned that the school records of the Eichmann children had not been requested by any school in Germany or Austria. He believed the family had joined Eichmann in exile.

The turning point in the case came when Wiesenthal was examining some unusual stamps with a fellow collector. The man retrieved an especially beautiful stamp he had received on a letter from a friend in Argentina, a former German officer. Reading aloud to Wiesenthal from the officer's letter, the man noted that his friend had met many fellow Germans in Argentina, including that "dreadful swine Eichmann who commanded the Jews. He lives near Buenos Aires and works for a water company." Lacking funds to track Eichmann down himself, Wiesenthal immediately passed his information along to the World Jewish Congress and the Israeli government. By late 1959 it appeared that Eichmann was indeed living with his family in Argentina under an assumed name. Israeli agents confirmed his identity and kidnapped him in Buenos Aires. Tried and convicted in Israel with evidence collected and handed over, in part, by Wiesenthal, Eichmann was hanged for his crimes on May 31, 1962. Information that emerged at Eichmann's trial confirmed the horrors of the Holocaust for anyone who doubted it happened, and Wiesenthal gained a reputation as a fearless Nazi hunter. The revelations at the trial also quieted any notions that Holocaust victims had put up little or no resistance to the Nazis.

In 1961 Wiesenthal was encouraged by renewed interest in Nazi criminals following Eichmann's capture and trial. Over the objections of his wife, who wished to put the past behind them, Wiesenthal reopened the Jewish Historical Documentation Center in Vienna. He vowed to devote all of his time to the pursuit of justice. Funded by donations and the proceeds from Wiesenthal's speeches and writings, the center has continued to assemble files on suspected Nazi criminals. Among the notable criminals to be captured was Karl Silberbauer, a member of the Gestapo who arrested teenager Anne Frank who kept a diary while hiding out from the Nazis in Holland. Wiesenthal was especially pleased at Silberbauer's capture in light of rumors among school children that Anne Frank had never really existed. Another notable criminal apprehended as a result of Wiesenthal's efforts was Franz Stangl, commandant of the Treblinka concentration camp, where approximately 870,000 people died.

Wiesenthal regrets that Josef Mengele, the "Angel of Death," was not found alive. Mengele was the Nazi doctor at Auschwitz who performed inhumane experiments on hundreds of prisoners there. The Jewish Historical Documentation Center has brought more than 1,000 suspected Nazi criminals to trial. The German government's files on Nazi criminals contain at least 100,000 names, but Wiesenthal has resigned himself to the fact that most of them will never be brought to justice. Many have died of old age. Some of the more recent cases involved Nazis who are now quite elderly and in poor health.

As he grows older, Wiesenthal spends more of his time educating young people about the Holocaust and speaking out against neo-Nazi movements. According to Pick, Wiesenthal does this because he believes that "no individual must ever again allow his or her conscience to be twisted or misused by any movement, any party, or any one person.... By recalling the liberation fifty years ago, and the Nazi era, the new generations will come closer to realization of the human rights ideal." With the help of a few assistants, he continues his work at the documentation center. He receives letters from around the world containing information about the Holocaust, some addressed simply to "Wiesenthal, Austria."

SOURCES

Books

Altman, Linda Jacobs, *Simon Wiesenthal,* Lucent Books (San Diego, CA), 2000.

Cooper, Abraham, "Wiesenthal," in *Encyclopedia of World Biography: 20th Century,* edited by David Eggenberger, volume 15 supplement, J. Heraty (Palatine, IL), 1987.

Levy, Alan, *The Wiesenthal File,* Eerdmans (Grand Rapids, MI), 1994.

Pick, Hella, *Simon Wiesenthal: A Life in Search of Justice,* Northeastern University Press (Boston), 1996.

Wiesenthal, Simon, *Justice Not Vengeance,* translated by Ewald Osers, Weidenfeld and Nicolson (London), 1989.

Wiesenthal, Simon, *The Murderers Among Us: The Simon Wiesenthal Memoirs,* edited with a profile of the author by Joseph Wechsberg, McGraw-Hill (New York), 1967.

Wiesenthal, Simon, *The Sunflower,* translated from the German by H. A. Piehler, W. H. Allen (London), 1970.

Periodicals

Bonfante, Jordan, "Where Have all the Nazis Gone? (Continuing Search for War Criminals)," *Time,* August 9, 1993, p. 38.

Wiener, Jon, "The Other Holocaust Museum (Simon Wiesenthal Center Museum of Tolerance)," *Tikkun,* May–June 1995, p. 22.

Other

Simon Wiesenthal Center, http://www.wiesenthal. com (October 3, 2000).

Further Reading

The following list of resources focuses on material appropriate for high school or college students. The list is divided into two major sections: Holocaust Bibliography and World War II Bibliography. The main sections are further subdivided into more specific topics. Please note that although some titles are applicable to more than one topic, they are listed only once. Please also note that web site addresses, though verified prior to publication, are subject to change.

Holocaust Bibliography

General Histories and Overviews of the Holocaust:

Adler, David A., *We Remember the Holocaust*, Henry Holt (New York), 1995.

Altman, Linda Jacobs, *Forever Outsiders: Jews and History from Ancient Times to August 1935*, Blackbirch Press (Woodbridge, CT), 1998.

Arad, Yithak, *The Pictorial History of the Holocaust*, Macmillan (New York), 1992.

Ayer, Eleanor H., *A Firestorm Unleashed: January 1942 to June 1943*, Blackbirch Press (Woodbridge, CT), 1998.

Ayer, Eleanor H., *Inferno: July 1943 to April 1945*, Blackbirch Press (Woodbridge, CT), 1998.

Ayer, Eleanor H., and Stephen D. Chicoine, *From the Ashes: May 1945 and After*, Blackbirch Press (Woodbridge, CT), 1998.

Bachrach, Susan D., *Tell Them We Remember: The Story of the Holocaust*, Little, Brown (Boston), 1994.

Bauer, Yehuda, and Nili Keren, *A History of the Holocaust*, Franklin Watts (New York), 1982.

Chaikin, Miriam, *A Nightmare in History: The Holocaust, 1933–1945*, Clarion Books (New York), 1987.

Cornwell, John, *Hitler's Pope: The Secret History of Pius XII*, Viking (New York), 1999.

Dawidowicz, Lucy S., *The War against the Jews, 1933–1945*, Bantam Books (New York), 1986.

Epstein, Eric Joseph, and Philip Rosen, *Dictionary of the Holocaust: Biography, Geography, and Terminology*, Greenwood Press (Westport, CT), 1997.

Feingold, Henry L., *The Politics of Rescue: The Roosevelt Administration and the Holocaust, 1938–1945*, Rutgers University Press (New Brunswick, NJ), 1970.

Friedman, Saul S., *No Haven for the Oppressed: United States Policy Toward Jewish Refugees, 1933–1945*, Wayne State University Press (Detroit), 1973.

Gilbert, Martin, *Auschwitz and the Allies*, Holt, Rinehart, and Winston (New York), 1981.

Gilbert, Martin, *The Holocaust: The History of the Jews of Europe during the Second World War,* Henry Holt (New York), 1986.

Gutman, Israel, editor, *The Encyclopedia of the Holocaust,* Macmillan (New York), 1990.

Herzstein, Robert E., *The Nazis,* Time-Life Books (Alexandria, VA), 1980.

Hilberg, Raoul, *The Destruction of the European Jews,* Holmes & Meier (New York), 1985.

Lanzmann, Claude, *Shoah: The Complete Text of the Acclaimed Holocaust Film,* Da Capo Press (New York), 1995.

Levin, Nora, *The Holocaust: The Nazi Destruction of European Jewry, 1933–1945,* Schocken (New York), 1973.

Lipstadt, Deborah E., *Beyond Belief: The American Press and the Coming of the Holocaust 1933–1945,* The Free Press (New York), 1986.

Lipstadt, Deborah E., *Denying the Holocaust: The Growing Assault on Truth and Memory,* Penguin (New York), 1993.

Mauldin, Bill, *Up Front,* Henry Holt (New York), 1945.

Meltzer, Milton, *Never to Forget,* Harper and Row (New York), 1976.

Morse, Arthur D., *While Six Million Died: A Chronicle of American Apathy,* Hart (New York), 1967.

Resnick, Abraham, *The Holocaust,* Lucent Books (San Diego), 1991.

Rogasky, Barbara, *Smoke and Ashes,* Holiday House (New York), 1988.

Rossel, Seymour, *The Holocaust: The Fire That Raged,* Franklin Watts (New York), 1989.

Sherrow, Victoria, *The Blaze Engulfs: January 1939 to December 1941,* Blackbirch Press (Woodbridge, CT), 1998.

Sherrow, Victoria, *Smoke to Flame: September 1935 to December 1938,* Blackbirch Press (Woodbridge, CT), 1998.

Shoenberner, Gerhard, *The Yellow Star: The Persecution of the Jews in Europe, 1933–1945,* Bantam Books (New York), 1979.

Shulman, William L., compiler, *Voices and Visions: A Collection of Primary Sources,* Blackbirch Press (Woodbridge, CT), 1998.

Snyder, Louis L., *Encyclopedia of the Third Reich,* McGraw-Hill, 1976.

Strahinich, Helen, *The Holocaust: Understanding and Remembering,* Enslow (Springfield, NJ), 1996.

Trunk, Isaiah, *Judenrat: The Jewish Councils in Eastern Europe Under Nazi Occupation,* Macmillan (New York), 1972.

Weinberg, Jeshajahu, and Rina Elieli, *The Holocaust Museum in Washington,* Rizzoli (New York), 1995.

Wigoder, Geoffrey, editor, *The Holocaust: A Grolier Student Library,* 4 volumes, Grolier Educational (Danbury, CT), 1997.

Yahil, Leni, *The Holocaust: The Fate of European Jewry, 1932–1945,* Oxford University Press (New York), 1991.

Zentner, Christian, Friedemann Bedürftig, and Amy Hackett, editors, *Encyclopedia of the Third Reich,* Collier Macmillan (New York), 1991.

Atlases:

Gilbert, Martin, *Atlas of the Holocaust,* Macmillan (New York), 1982.

United States Holocaust Memorial Museum, *Historical Atlas of the Holocaust,* Macmillan (New York), 1996.

German History, the Early Nazi Movement, the Nazi Government, and Policy toward the Jews before the Holocaust:

Allen, William Sheridan, *The Nazi Seizure of Power: The Experience of a Single German Town, 1930–1935,* Franklin Watts (New York), 1973.

Arendt, Hannah, *The Origins of Totalitarianism,* Harcourt, Brace (New York), 1966.

Auerbacher, Inge, *I Am a Star: Child of the Holocaust,* Prentice-Hall (Paramus, NJ), 1986.

Ayer, Eleanor, *Adolf Hitler,* Lucent (San Diego), 1996.

Bauer, Yehuda, *Jews for Sale?: Nazi-Jewish Negotiations, 1933–1945,* Yale University Press (New Haven, CT), 1994.

Berman, Russell A., *Paul von Hindenburg,* Chelsea House (New York), 1987.

Bullock, Alan, *Hitler: A Study in Tyranny,* Harper and Row (New York), 1964.

Cohn, Norman, *Warrant for Genocide: The Myth of the Jewish World Conspiracy and the Protocols of* the Elders of Zion, Harper & Row Publishers (New York), 1969.

Eimerl, Sarel, *Hitler over Europe: The Road to World War II,* Little, Brown (Boston), 1972.

Friedlander, Saul, *Pius XII and the Third Reich,* Knopf (New York), 1966.

Fuller, Barbara, *Germany,* Marshall Cavendish (New York), 1996.

Gallo, Max, *The Night of the Long Knives,* Harper and Row (New York), 1972.

Goldston, Robert C., *The Life and Death of Nazi Germany,* Bobbs-Merrill (New York), 1967.

Graff, Stewart, *The Story of World War II,* E. P. Dutton (New York), 1978.

Halperin, S. William, *Germany Tried Democracy: A Political History of the Reich from 1918 to 1933,* Norton (New York), 1965.

Josephson, Judith P., *Jesse Owens: Track and Field Legend,* Enslow Press (Springfield, NJ), 1997.

Kluger, Ruth Peggy Mann, *Secret Ship,* Doubleday (New York), 1978.

Marrin, Albert, *Hitler,* Viking (New York), 1987.

Mayer, Milton Sanford, *They Thought They Were Free: The Germans, 1933-35,* University of Chicago Press (Chicago), 1966.

The New Order, Time-Life Books (Alexandria, VA), 1989.

Niemark, Anne E., *Leo Baeck and the Holocaust,* E. P. Dutton (New York), 1986.

Patterson, Charles, *Anti-Semitism: The Road to the Holocaust and Beyond,* Walker (New York), 1989.

Read, Anthony, *Kristallnacht: The Nazi Night of Terror,* Times Books/Random House (New York), 1989.

Rubinstein, William D., *The Myth of Rescue,* Routledge (New York), 1997.

Schleunes, Karl A., *The Twisted Road to Auschwitz: Nazi Policy toward German Jews, 1933–1939,* University of Illinois Press (Urbana), 1970.

Shirer, William L., *The Rise and Fall of Adolf Hitler,* Random House (New York), 1961.

Shirer, William L., *The Rise and Fall of the Third Reich,* Simon and Schuster (New York), 1960.

Snyder, Louis L., *Hitler's Elite,* Hippocrene Books (New York), 1989.

Spence, William, *Germany Then and Now,* Franklin Watts (New York), 1994.

Start, Clarissa, *God's Man: The Story of Pastor Niemoeller,* Washburn (New York), 1959.

Stein, R. Conrad, *Hitler Youth,* Children's Press (Danbury, CT), 1985.

Stewart, Gail, *Hitler's Reich,* Lucent Books (San Diego), 1994.

Thalmann, Rita, and Emmanuel Feinermann, *Crystal Night, 9–10 November, 1938,* Holocaust Library (New York), 1974.

Thomas, Gordon, and Max M. Witts, *Voyage of the Damned,* Stein and Day (New York), 1974.

Toland, John, *Adolf Hitler,* Doubleday (New York), 1976.

Wepman, Dennis, *Adolf Hitler,* Chelsea House (New York), 1989.

Zurndorfer, Hannele, *The Ninth of November,* Quartet Books (Berrien Springs, MI), 1983.

The "Final Solution":

Aly, Gotz, *Final Solution: Nazi Population Policy and the Murder of the European Jews,* Oxford University Press (New York), 1999.

Bower, Tom, *Klaus Barbie, the "Butcher of Lyons,"* Pantheon Books (New York), 1984.

Breitman, Richard, *The Architect of Genocide: Himmler and the Final Solution,* Knopf (New York), 1991.

Browning, Christopher R., *Nazi Policy, Jewish Workers, German Killers,* Cambridge University Press (New York), 2000.

Browning, Christopher R., *Ordinary Men: Reserve Police Battalion 101 and the Final Solution in Poland,* HarperPerennial (New York), 1992.

Des Pres, Terrence, *The Survivor: An Anatomy of Life in the Death Camps,* Washington Square Press (New York), 1976.

Dobroszycki, Lucjan, editor, *The Chronicle of the Lódz Ghetto, 1941–1944,* Yale University Press (New York), 1984.

Friedlander, Henry, *The Origins of Nazi Genocide: From Euthanasia to the Final Solution,* University of North Carolina Press (Chapel Hill, NC), 1995.

Friedrich, Otto, *The Kingdom of Auschwitz,* Harper Perennial (New York), 1994.

Gilbert, Martin, *Auschwitz and the Allies,* Henry Holt (New York), 1990.

Goldhagen, Daniel J., *Hitler's Willing Executioners: Ordinary Germans and the Holocaust,* Knopf (New York), 1996.

Graf, Malvina, *The Kraków Ghetto and the Plaszów Camp Remembered,* Florida State University Press (Tallahassee, FL), 1989.

Gutman, Israel, *Anatomy of the Auschwitz Death Camp,* Indiana University Press (Bloomington, IN), 1998.

Gutman, Israel, *The Jews of Warsaw, 1939–1943,* Indiana University Press (Bloomington, IN), 1982.

Hellman, Peter, *The Auschwitz Album: A Book Based upon an Album Discovered by a Concentration Camp Survivor, Lili Meier,* Random House (New York), 1981.

Höss, Rudolf, *Death Dealer: The Memoirs of the SS Kommandant at Auschwitz,* edited by Steven Paskuly, translated by Andrew Pollinger, Prometheus Books (Buffalo, NY), 1992.

Kogon, Eugen, *The Theory and Practice of Hell: The German Concentration Camps and the System behind Them,* Octagon (Los Angeles), 1973.

Leitner, Isabella, *The Big Lie: A True Story,* Scholastic (New York), 1992.

Levi, Primo, *Survival in Auschwitz,* Macmillan (New York), 1987.

Lifton, Robert Jay, *The Nazi Doctors: Medical Killing and the Psychology of Genocide,* Basic Books (New York), 1988.

Millu, Liana, *Smoke over Birkenau,* Jewish Publication Society (Philadelphia), 1991.

Nomberg-Przuytyk, Sara, *Auschwitz: True Tales from a Grotesque Land,* University of North Carolina Press (Chapel Hill, NC), 1986.

Posner, Gerald L., *Mengele: The Complete Story,* McGraw-Hill (New York), 1986.

Reitlinger, Gerald, *The SS: Alibi of a Nation, 1922–1945,* Viking (New York), 1957.

Rubinstein, William D., *The Myth of Rescue,* Routledge (New York), 1997.

Steiner, Jean Francis, *Treblinka,* Simon and Schuster (New York), 1967.

Stern, Ellen Norman, *Elie Wiesel: Witness for Life,* Ktav Publishing House (New York), 1982.

Swiebocka, Teresa, compiler and editor, *Auschwitz: A History in Photographs,* Indiana University Press (Bloomington, IN), 1993.

Whiting, Charles, *Heydrich: Henchman of Death,* Leo Cooper (S. Yorkshire, England), 1999.

Wiesel, Elie, *The Night Trilogy: Night, Dawn, The Accident,* Hill and Wang (New York), 1960.

Willenberg, Samuel, *Surviving Treblinka,* Basil Blackwell (Maldin, MA), 1989.

Wyman, David S., *The Abandonment of the Jews: America and the Holocaust, 1941–1945,* Pantheon (New York), 1984.

Zyskind, Sara, *Struggle,* Lerner (Minneapolis, MN), 1989.

Poland:

Adelson, Alan, and Robert Lapides, editors, *Lódz Ghetto: Inside a Community Under Siege,* Viking (New York), 1989.

Bernheim, Mark, *Father of the Orphans: The Story of Janusz Korczak,* E. P. Dutton (New York), 1989.

Davies, Norman, *God's Playground,* Columbia University Press (New York), 1982.

Drucker, Malka, and Michael Halperin, *Jacob's Rescue: A Holocaust Story,* Bantam Skylark (New York), 1993.

Eichengreen, Lucille, *Rumkowski and the Orphans of Lódz,* Mercury House (San Francisco, CA), 1999.

Frister, Roman, *The Cap: The Price of a Life,* translated by Hillel Halkin, Grove Press (New York), 1999.

George, Willy, *In the Warsaw Ghetto, Summer 1941,* Aperture Foundation (New York), 1993.

Heller, Celia S., *On the Edge of Destruction: Jews of Poland between the Two World Wars,* Columbia University Press (New York), 1977.

Hoffman, Eva, *Shtetl: The Life and Death of a Small Town and the World of Polish Jews,* Houghton Mifflin Company (Boston), 1998.

Hyams, Joe, *A Field of Buttercups,* Prentice-Hall (Paramus, NJ), 1968.

Kaplan, Chaim A., *Scroll of Agony: The Warsaw Diary of Chaim A. Kaplan,* Indiana University Press (Bloomington, IN), 1999.

Keller, Ulrich, editor, *The Warsaw Ghetto in Photographs,* Dover (Mineola, NY), 1984.

Klein, Gerda Weissmann, *All but My Life*, Hill & Wang Publishers (New York), 1995.

Landau, Elaine, *The Warsaw Ghetto Uprising*, Macmillan (New York), 1992.

Lewis, Mark, and Jacob Frank, *Himmler's Jewish Tailor: The Story of Holocaust Survivor Jacob Frank*, Syracuse University Press (Syracuse, NY), 2000.

Lifton, Betty Jean, *The King of Children: The Life and Death of Janusz Korczak*, St. Martin's Griffin (New York), 1997.

Lukas, Richard C., and Norman Davies, *The Forgotten Holocaust: The Poles Under German Occupation 1939–1944*, Hippocrene Books (New York), 1997.

Nelken, Halina, *And Yet, Here I Am!* University of Massachusetts Press (Amherst, MA), 1999.

Sender, Ruth Minsky, *The Cage*, Macmillan (New York), 1986.

Sender, Ruth Minsky, *To Life*, Macmillan (New York), 1988.

Spiegelman, Art, *Maus: A Survivor's Tale: And Here My Troubles Began*, Pantheon Books (New York), 1992.

Spiegelman, Art, *Maus: A Survivor's Tale: My Father Bleeds History*, Pantheon Books (New York), 1997.

Stewart, Gail B., *Life in the Warsaw Ghetto*, Lucent Books (San Diego), 1995.

Szner, Zvi, and Alexander Sened, editors, *With a Camera in the Ghetto: Mendel Grossman*, Schocken Books (New York), 1977.

Szpilman, Wladyslaw, *The Pianist*, Picador USA (New York), 1999.

Vishniac, Roman, *A Vanished World*, Farrar, Straus, and Giroux (New York), 1983.

Watt, Richard M., *Bitter Glory: Poland & Its Fate 1918–1993*, Hippocrene Books (New York), 1998.

Ziemian, Joseph, *The Cigarette Seller of Three Crosses Square*, Lerner (Minneapolis, MN), 1975.

Other Countries:

Asscher-Pinkoff, Clara, *Star Children*, Wayne State University Press (Detroit), 1986.

Bitton-Jackson, Livia, *I Have Lived a Thousand Years: Growing up in the Holocaust*, Simon and Schuster (New York), 1997.

Denes, Magda, *Castles Burning: A Child's Life in War*, W. W. Norton (New York), 1997.

Frank, Anne, *The Diary of a Young Girl: The Definitive Edition*, edited by Otto Frank and Mirjam Pressler, Doubleday (New York), 1995.

Gies, Miep, and Alison L. Gold, *Anne Frank Remembered: The Story of the Woman Who Helped to Hide the Frank Family* Simon and Schuster (New York), 1987.

Gold, Alison L., *Memories of Anne Frank: Reflections of a Childhood Friend*, Scholastic (New York), 1997.

Handler, Andrew, and Susan Meschel, editors, *Young People Speak*, Franklin Watts (New York), 1993.

Hutok, J. B., *With Blood and with Iron: The Lidice Story*, R. Hale (London), 1957.

Isaacman, Clara, *Clara's Story*, Jewish Publication Society (Philadelphia), 1984.

Klarsfeld, Serge, *The Children of Izieu: A Human Tragedy*, Abrams (New York), 1985.

Lewy, Guenter, *The Nazi Persecution of the Gypsies*, Oxford University Press (New York), 2000.

Lindwe, Willy, *The Last Seven Months of Anne Frank*, Pantheon (New York), 1991.

Marrus, Michael R., *Vichy France and the Jews*, Basic Books (New York), 1981.

Perl, Lila, and Marian Blumenthal Lazar, *Four Perfect Pebbles: A Holocaust Story*, Greenwillow Books (New York), 1996.

Rol, Ruud van der, and Rian Verhoeven, *Anne Frank: Beyond the Diary*, Viking (New York), 1993.

Roth-Hano, Renée, *Touch Wood: A Girlhood in Occupied France*, Four Winds Press (Portland, OR), 1988.

Siegal, Avanka, *Grace in the Wilderness: After the Liberation, 1945–1948*, Farrar, Straus, Giroux (New York), 1985.

Siegal, Avanka, *Upon the Head of the Goat: A Childhood in Hungary, 1939–1944*, Farrar, Straus, Giroux (New York), 1981.

Velmans, Edith, *Edith's Story*, Soho Press (New York), 1998.

Zuccotti, Susan, *The Italians and the Holocaust: Persecution, Rescue and Survival,* Basic Books (New York), 1987.

Resistance, Survival, and Rescue:

Ainszstein, Reuben, *Jewish Resistance in Nazi-Occupied Eastern Europe: With a Historical Survey of the Jew as a Fighter and Soldier in the Diaspora,* Barnes & Noble (New York), 1975.

Aliav, Ruth, *The Last Escape: The Launching of the Largest Secret Rescue Movement of All Time,* Doubleday (Garden City, NY), 1973.

Atkinson, Linda, *In Kindling Flame: The Story of Hannah Senesh,* Lee & Shepard (New York), 1985.

Ayer, Eleanor A., *The United States Holocaust Memorial Museum,* Silver Burdett Press (Parsippanny, NJ), 1995.

Bauer, Yehuda, *They Chose Life: Jewish Resistance in the Holocaust,* American Jewish Committee (New York), 1973.

Berenbaum, Michael, *The World Must Know,* Little, Brown (Boston), 1993.

Bierman, John, *Righteous Gentile: The Story of Raoul Wallenberg,* Viking (New York), 1981.

Blatt, Thomas Toivi, *From the Ashes of Sobibor: A Story of Survival,* Northwestern University Press (Evanston, IL), 1997.

Block, Gay, and Malka Drucker, *Rescuers,* Holmes and Meier (New York), 1992.

Bosanquest, Mary, *The Life and Death of Dietrich Bonhoeffer,* Harper and Row (New York), 1968.

Chevrillon, Claire, *Code Name Christiane Clouet: A Woman in the French Resistance,* Texas A & M University (College Station, TX), 1995.

Elkins, Michael, *Forged in Fury,* Ballantine Books (New York), 1971.

Flender, Harold, *Rescue in Denmark,* Simon and Schuster (New York), 1963.

Friedman, Ina R., *Flying against the Wind: The Story of a Young Woman Who Defied the Nazis,* Lodge Pole Press (Brookline, MA), 1995.

Gelman, Charles, *Do Not Go Gentle: A Memoir of Jewish Resistance in Poland, 1941–1945,* Archon Books, (North Haven, CT), 1989.

Gilbert, Martin, *The Boys: The Untold Story of 732 Young Concentration Camp Survivors,* Henry Holt & Company (New York), 1997.

Greenfield, Howard, *The Hidden Children,* Ticknor and Fields (New York), 1993.

Gutman, Israel, *Resistance: The Warsaw Ghetto Uprising,* Houghton Mifflin (Boston), 1994.

Haas, Gerda, *These I Do Remember: Fragments from the Holocaust,* Cumberland (Brooklyn, NY), 1982.

Hallie, Philip, *Lest Innocent Blood Be Shed,* Harper & Row (New York), 1980.

Healey, Tim, *Secret Armies; Resistance Groups in World War II,* Macdonald (London), 1981.

Helmreich, William B., *Against All Odds: Holocaust Survivors and the Successful Lives They Made in America,* Simon & Schuster (New York), 1992.

Hewins, Ralph, *Count Folke Bernadotte: His Life and Work,* Hutchinson (New York), 1950.

Holocaust Education—Women of Valor, http://www.interlog.com/~mighty/valor/kath_f.htm (September 12, 2000).

Jewish Partisans, http://www.ushmm.org/outreach/jpart.htm (September 12, 2000).

Keneally, Thomas, *Schindler's List,* Simon and Schuster (New York), 1982.

Kertyesz, Imre, *Fateless,* Northwestern University Press (Evanston, IL), 1992.

Kurzman, Dan, *The Bravest Battle: The Twenty-Eight Days of the Warsaw Ghetto Uprising,* Da Capo Press (New York), 1993.

Landau, Elaine, *The Warsaw Ghetto Uprising,* Macmillan (New York), 1992.

Landau, Elaine, *We Survived the Holocaust,* Franklin Watts (New York), 1991.

Laska, Vera, editor, *Women in the Resistance and in the Holocaust: The Voices of Eyewitnesses,* Greenwood Press (Westport, CT), 1983.

Linnea, Sharon, *Raoul Wallenberg: The Man Who Stopped Death,* Jewish Publication Society (Philadelphia), 1993.

Marton, Kati, *Wallenberg,* Random House (New York), 1982.

Meltzer, Milton, *Rescue: The Story of How Gentiles Saved Jews in the Holocaust,* Harper and Row (New York), 1988.

Mochizuki, Ken, *Passage to Freedom: The Sugihara Story,* Lee and Low Books (New York), 1997.

Pettit, Jayne, *A Time to Fight Back: True Stories of Wartime Resistance,* Houghton Mifflin (Boston), 1996.

Rashke, Richard, *Escape from Sobibor,* University of Illinois Press (Urbana, IL), 1995.

Rittner, Carol, *The Courage to Care,* New York University Press (New York), 1986.

Roberts, Jack L., *Oskar Schindler,* Lucent Books (San Diego), 1996.

Rosenberg, Maxine B., *Hiding to Survive: Stories of Jewish Children Rescued from the Holocaust,* Clarion (New York), 1994.

Schul, Yuri, *They Fought Back: The Story of Jewish Resistance in Nazi Europe,* Schocken Books (New York), 1967.

Stadtler, Bea, *The Holocaust: A History of Courage and Resistance,* Behrman House (West Orange, NJ), 1994.

Stein, R. Conrad, *Resistance Movements,* Children's Press (Chicago), 1982.

Sutin, Lawrence, editor, *Jack and Rochelle: A Holocaust Story of Love and Resistance,* Graywolf Press (Saint Paul, MN), 1996.

Vinke, Hermann, *The Short Life of Sophie Scholl,* Harper and Row (New York), 1984.

Vogel, Ilse-Margaret, *Bad Times, Good Friends,* Harcourt Brace Jovanovich (New York), 1992.

Weinstein, Irving, *That Denmark Might Live; The Saga of Danish Resistance in World War II,* Macrae Smith (Philadelphia), 1967.

Werner, Harold, *Fighting Back,* Columbia University Press (New York), 1994.

Wind, Renate, *Dietrich Bonhoeffer: A Spoke in the Wheel,* Eerdmans (Grand Rapids, MI), 1992.

Wood, E. Thomas, *Karski: How One Man Tried to Stop the Holocaust,* John Wiley & Sons (New York), 1994.

Wygoda, Hermann, *In the Shadow of the Swastika,* University of Illinois Press (Urbana, IL), 1998.

Zahn, Gordon, *In Solitary Witness: The Life and Death of Franz Jaggerstatter,* Holt, Rinehart, and Winston (New York), 1964.

Zassenhaus, Hiltgunt, *Walls: Resisting the Third Reich, One Woman's Story,* Beacon Press (Boston), 1974.

Zeinert, Karen, *The Warsaw Ghetto Uprising,* Millbrook Press (Brookfield, CT), 1993.

Zuccotti, Susan, *The Italians and the Holocaust: Persecution, Rescue, and Survival,* University of Nebraska Press (Lincoln, NE), 1996.

Justice:

Arendt, Hannah, *Eichmann in Jerusalem: A Report on the Banality of Evil,* Penguin (New York), 1977.

Gilbert, G. M., *Nuremberg Diary,* New American Library (New York), 1947.

Hausner, Gideon, *Justice in Jerusalem,* Harper and Row (New York), 1966.

Jackson, Robert H., *The Nürnberg Case, As Presented by Robert H. Jackson, Chief Counsel for the United States, Together with Other Documents,* Cooper Square Publishers (New York), 1971.

Landau, Elaine, *Nazi War Criminals,* Franklin Watts (New York), 1990.

Morin, Isobel V., *Days of Judgment: The World War II War Crimes Trials,* Millbrook Press (Brookfield, CT), 1995.

Noble, Iris, *Nazi Hunter: Simon Wiesenthal,* J. Messner (New York), 1979.

Persico, Joseph E., *Nuremberg: Infamy on Trial,* Viking (New York), 1994.

Ryan, Allan A., *Quiet Neighbors: Prosecuting Nazi War Criminals in America,* Harcourt Brace Jovanovich (San Diego), 1984.

Taylor, Telford, *The Anatomy of the Nuremberg Trials: A Personal Memoir,* Knopf (New York), 1992.

Wiesenthal, Simon, *Justice Not Vengeance,* translated from German by Edward Osers, Grove Weidenfeld (London), 1989.

Wiesenthal, Simon, *The Murderers Among Us: The Simon Wiesenthal Memoirs,* edited, with a profile of the author, by Joseph Wechsberg, McGraw-Hill (New York), 1967.

Displaced Persons:

Blumenson, Martin, *Liberation,* Time-Life Books (Alexandria VA), 1983.

Botting, Douglas, *The Aftermath: Europe,* Time-Life Books (Alexandria, VA), 1983.

Gilbert, Martin *The Holocaust: A History of the Jews of Europe during the Second World War,* Holt, Rinehart and Winston (New York), 1998.

Gilbert, Martin, *Israel: A History,* William Morrow (New York), 1998.

Levi, Primo, *The Reawakening,* Collier Books (New York), 1996.

Nesaule, Agate, *A Woman in Amber: Healing the Trauma of War and Exile,* Soho Press (New York), 1995.

O'Brien, Conor Cruise, *The Siege: The Saga of Israel and Zionism,* Simon and Schuster (New York), 1986.

Sykes, Christopher, *Crossroads to Israel,* Indiana University Press (Bloomington, IN), 1973.

Yahil, Leni, *The Holocaust: The Fate of European Jewry,* Oxford University Press (Oxford), 1987.

World War II Bibliography

General Sources:

Allen, Peter, *The Origins of World War II,* Bookwright Press (New York), 1992.

The Avalon Project at the Yale Law School—World War II: Documents, http://www.yale.edu/lawweb/avalon/wwii/wwii.htm (September 8, 2000).

Bradley, Omar N., *A Soldier's Story,* Holt, Rinehart & Winston (New York), 1951.

Calvocoressi, Peter, Guy Wint, and John Pritchard, *Total War: Causes and Courses of the Second World War,* Pantheon (New York), 1987.

Churchill, Winston, *The Second World War,* Houghton (New York), 1948–1954, reprinted, 1986.

Collier, Basil, *The Second World War: A Military History,* William Morrow (New York), 1967.

Eisenhower, General Dwight D., *Crusade in Europe,* Doubleday (New York), 1948.

Ethell, Jeffrey L., and Robert T. Sand, *Air Command: Fighters and Bombers of World War II,* Motorbooks International (Osceola, WI), 1998.

Fleming, Peter, *Operation Sea Lion,* Simon and Schuster (New York), 1957.

Graff, Stewart, *The Story of World War II,* E. P. Dutton (New York), 1978.

Hills, Ken, *Wars That Changed the World: World War II,* Marshall Cavendish (New York), 1988.

Keegan, John, *The Battle for History: Re-Fighting World War II,* Vintage Books (New York), 1996.

Keegan, John, *The Second World War,* Penguin (New York), 1990.

Krull, Kathleen, *V Is for Victory,* Knopf (New York), 1995.

Lawson, Don, *Great Air Battles: World War I and II,* Lothrop, Lee & Shepard (New York), 1968.

Leckie, Robert, *Delivered from Evil: The Saga of World War II,* HarperPerennial (New York), 1987.

Leckie, Robert, *The Story of World War II,* Random House (New York), 1964.

Leutze, James R., *Bargaining for Supremacy: Anglo-American Naval Collaboration, 1937–1941,* University of North Carolina Press (Chapel Hill, NC), 1977.

MacArthur, Douglas, *Reminiscences,* Da Capo Press (New York), 1985.

MacDonald, Charles B., *Company Commander,* Burford Books (Springfield, NJ), 1999.

Marrin, Albert, *The Airmen's War: World War II in the Sky,* Atheneum (New York), 1982.

Michel, Henri, *The Second World War,* translated by Douglas Parmee, Deutsch (London), 1975.

Military History: World War II (1939–1945), http://www.cfcsc.dnd.ca/links/milhist/wwii.html (September 8, 2000).

A People at War, http://www.nara.gov/exhall/people/people.html (September 8, 2000).

Reynolds, Quentin J., *Only the Stars Are Neutral,* Random House (New York), 1942.

Roskill, Stephen W., *The Navy at War, 1939–1945,* Collins (London), 1960.

Ross, Stewart, *Propaganda,* Thomson Learning (New York), 1993.

Ross, Stewart, *World Leaders,* Thomson Learning (New York), 1993.

Snyder, Louis L., *World War II,* Franklin Watts (New York), 1981.

Wilmot, Chester, *The Struggle for Europe,* Harper & Row Publishers (New York), 1952.

World War II, http://www.awesomelibrary.org/Classroom/Social_Studies/History/World_War_II.html (September 8, 2000).

Atlases:

Freeman, Michael, and Tim Mason, editors, *Atlas of Nazi Germany,* Macmillan (New York), 1987.

Young, Peter, *Atlas of the Second World War,* Berkley Windhover (New York), 1974.

Asia and the Pacific:

Alexander, Joseph H., *Utmost Savagery: The Three Days of Tarawa,* Naval Institute Press (Annapolis, MD), 1995.

Astor, Gerald, *Operation Iceberg: The Invasion and Conquest of Okinawa in World War II*, D. I. Fine (New York), 1995.

Battling Bastards of Bataan, http://home.pacbell.net/fbaldie/Battling_Bastards_of_Bataan.html (September 26, 2000).

Blassingame, Wyatt, *The U.S. Frogmen of World War II*, Random House (New York), 1964.

Bradley, James, and Ron Powers, *Flags of Our Fathers*, Bantam (New York), 2000.

Castello, Edmund L., *Midway: Battle for the Pacific*, Random House (New York), 1968.

Chang, Iris, *The Rape of Nanking: The Forgotten Holocaust of World War II*, Basic Books (New York), 1997.

Conroy, Robert, *The Battle of Bataan: America's Greatest Defeat*, Macmillan (New York), 1969.

Daws, Gavan, *Prisoners of the Japanese: POWs of World War II in the Pacific*, W. Morrow (New York), 1994.

Dull, Paul S., *A Battle History of the Japanese Navy (1941–1945)*, United States Naval Institute Press (Annapolis, MD), 1978.

Fahey, James, *Pacific War Diary: 1942–1945*, Houghton Mifflin (Boston), 1992.

Frank, Richard B., *Guadalcanal: The Definitive Account of the Landmark Battle*, Penguin (New York), 1992.

Fuchida, Mitsuo, and Masatake Okumiya, *Midway: The Battle that Doomed Japan: The Japanese Navy's Story*, Naval Institute Press (Annapolis, MD), 1992.

Gayle, Gordon D., *Bloody Beaches: The Marines at Peleliu*, U.S. Marine Corps (Washington, DC), 1996.

Grant, R. G., *Hiroshima and Nagasaki*, Raintree, Steck-Vaughn (Austin, TX), 1988.

Griffith, Samuel B., *The Battle for Guadalcanal*, University of Illinois Press (Urbana, IL), 2000.

Hallas, James H., *The Devil's Anvil: The Assault on Peleliu*, Praeger (Westport, CT), 1994.

Harris, Nathaniel, *Pearl Harbor*, Dryad Press (North Pomfret, VT), 1986.

Hirschfeld, Wolfgang, *Hirschfeld: The Story of a U-Boat NCO, 1940–1946*, as told to Geoffrey Brooks, U.S. Naval Institute (Annapolis, MD), 1996.

Hoehling, A. A., *The Lexington Goes Down: A Fighting Carrier's Last Hours in the Coral Sea*, Stackpole Books (Mechanicsburg, PA), 1993.

Hubbard, Preston John, *Apocalypse Undone: My Survival of Japanese Imprisonment during WWII*, Vanderbilt University Press (Nashville, TN), 1990.

Kessler, Lynn, editor, *Never in Doubt: Remembering Iwo Jima*, Naval Institute Press (Annapolis, MD), 1999.

Linzey, Stanford E., *God Was at Midway: The Sinking of the USS Yorktown (CV-5) and the Battles of the Coral Sea and Midway*, Black Forest Press (San Diego, CA), 1996.

Manchester, William, *American Caesar: Douglas MacArthur, 1880–1964*, Little, Brown (Boston) 1978.

Manchester, William, *Goodbye, Darkness: A Memoir of the Pacific War*, Little, Brown (Boston), 1979.

Marrin, Albert, *Victory in the Pacific*, Atheneum (New York), 1983.

Mishler, Clayton, *Sampan Sailor: A Navy Man's Adventures in WWII China*, Brassey's (Washington, DC), 1994.

Morin, Isobel V., *Days of Judgment*, Millbrook Press (Brookfield, CT), 1995.

Morison, Samuel Eliot, *History of United States Naval Operations in World War II: Coral Sea, Midway and Submarine Actions, May 1942–August 1942*, Vol. 4, Little, Brown (Boston), 1950.

Petillo, Carol Morris, *Douglas MacArthur: The Philippine Years*, Indiana University Press (Bloomington, IN), 1981.

Prange, Gordon W., Donald M. Goldstein, and Katherine V. Dillon, *At Dawn We Slept: The Untold Story of Pearl Harbor*, Viking (New York), 1991.

Prange, Gordon W., Donald M. Goldstein, and Katherine V. Dillon, *God's Samurai: Lead Pilot at Pearl Harbor*, Brassey's (Washington, DC), 1990.

Raymer, Edward C., *Descent into Darkness: Pearl Harbor, 1941: A Navy Diver's Memoir*, Presidio Press (Novato, CA), 1996.

Rice, Earle, Jr., *The Attack on Pearl Harbor*, Lucent (San Diego), 1997.

Ross, Bill D., *Iwo Jima: Legacy of Valor,* Vanguard Press (New York), 1986.

Ruhe, William J., *War in the Boats: My World War II Submarine Battles,* Brassey's (Washington, DC), 1994.

Sauvrain, Philip, *Midway,* New Discovery Books (New York), 1993.

Schaller, Michael, *Douglas MacArthur: The Far Eastern General,* Oxford University Press (New York), 1989.

Schlesinger, Arthur, Jr., and Richard H. Rovere, *The MacArthur Controversy and American Foreign Policy,* Farrar, Straus and Giroux (New York), 1965.

Shapiro, William E., *Pearl Harbor,* F. Watts (New York), 1984.

Sherrow, Victoria, *Hiroshima,* New Discovery Books (New York), 1994.

Skipper, G. C., *Battle of Leyte Gulf,* Children's Press (Chicago), 1981.

Skipper, G. C., *Submarines in the Pacific,* Children's Press (Chicago), 1980.

Sledge, Eugene B., *With the Old Breed: At Peleliu and Okinawa,* Naval Institute Press (Annapolis, MD), 1996.

Smith, Myron J., Jr., *The Battles of the Coral Sea and Midway, 1942,* Greenwood Publishing (New York), 1991.

Smith, William Ward, *Midway: Turning Point of the Pacific,* Thomas Y. Crowell Company (New York), 1966.

Smurthwaite, David, *The Pacific War Atlas: 1941–1945,* Facts on File (New York), 1995.

Spector, Ronald H., *Eagle against the Sun: The American War with Japan,* Free Press (New York), 1985.

Stafford, Edward P., *The Big E: The Story of the U.S.S. Enterprise,* Random House (New York), 1962.

Stein, R. Conrad, *The Battle of Guadalcanal,* Children's Press (Chicago), 1983.

Stein, R. Conrad, *The Battle of Okinawa,* Children's Press (Chicago), 1985.

Stein, R. Conrad, *Fall of Singapore,* Children's Press (Chicago), 1982.

Stein, R. Conrad, *Hiroshima,* Children's Press (Chicago), 1982.

Stinnett, Robert B., *Day of Deceit: The Truth about FDR and Pearl Harbor,* Free Press (New York), 2000.

Sullivan, George, *The Day Pearl Harbor Was Bombed: A Photo History of World War II,* Scholastic (New York), 1991.

Takaki, Ronald, *Hiroshima: Why America Dropped the Atomic Bomb,* Little, Brown (Boston), 1995.

Taylor, Theodore, *The Battle off Midway Island,* Avon (New York), 1981.

Thomas, Gerald W, and Roger D. Walker, editors, *Victory in World War II: The New Mexico Story,* University of New Mexico Press (Las Cruces, NM), 1994.

Tregaskis, Richard, *Guadalcanal Diary,* Modern Library (New York), 2000.

Tuleja, Thaddeus V., *Climax at Midway,* W. W. Norton (New York), 1960.

Ward, Harold, *Don't Go Island Hopping during a War!,* Harold Ward, 1999.

Webber, Bert, *Silent Siege-III: Japanese Attacks on North America in World War II: Ships Sunk, Air Raids, Bombs Dropped, Civilians Killed: Documentary,* Webb Research Group (Medford, OR), 1992.

Yahara, Hiromichi, *The Battle for Okinawa,* John Wiley and Sons (New York), 1997.

Zhigeng, Xu, *Lest We Forget: Nanjing Massacre, 1937,* Chinese Literature Press (Beijing), 1995.

Zich, Arthur, and the editors of Time-Life Books, *The Rising Sun,* Time-Life Books (Alexandria, VA), 1977.

Europe, the Atlantic, Africa, and the Soviet Union, 1939–1943:

Allen, Kenneth, *Battle of the Atlantic,* Wayland (London), 1973.

Barnett, Correlli, *The Battle of El Alamein: Decision in the Desert,* Macmillan (New York), 1964.

Blanco, Richard L., *Rommel, the Desert Warrior: The Afrika Korps in World War II,* J. Mesmer (New York), 1982.

Brook-Shepherd, Gordon, *Anschluss: The Rape of Austria,* Macmillan & Company (London), 1963.

Churchill, Winston S., *The Second World War: The Gathering Storm, Vol. 1,* Cassell (London), 1948.

Ciano, Galeazzo, conte, *The Ciano Diaries, 1939–1943,* edited by H. Gibson, Doubleday (Garden City, NY), 1946.

Collier, Basil, *The Battle of Britain,* B.T. Batsford (London), 1962.

Collier, Richard, *The Sands of Dunkirk,* E. P. Dutton (New York), 1961.

Cook, Don, *Charles de Gaulle: A Biography,* Putnam (New York), 1983.

Corti, Eugenio, *Few Returned: Twenty-Eight Days on the Russian Front, Winter 1942–1943,* University of Missouri Press (Columbia, MO), 1997.

De Gaulle, Charles, *Memoirs of Hope, 1958–62,* Simon & Schuster (New York), 1971.

Drieman, J. E., editor, *Winston Churchill: An Unbreakable Spirit,* Dillon Press (Minneapolis, MN), 1990.

FitzGibbon, Constantine, *London's Burning,* Ballantine Books (New York), 1970.

Gehl, Jürgen, *Austria, Germany, and the Anschluss, 1931–1938,* Oxford University Press (New York), 1963.

Hoobler, Dorothy, and Thomas Hoobler, *World Leaders Past and Present: Joseph Stalin,* Chelsea House (New York), 1985.

Humble, Richard, *U-Boat,* Franklin Watts (New York), 1990.

James, Robert Rhodes, editor, *Winston S. Churchill: His Complete Speeches 1897–1963,* Chelsea House (New York), 1974.

Keller, Mollie, *Winston Churchill,* F. Watts (New York), 1984.

Kronenwetter, Michael, *Cities at War: London,* New Discovery Books (New York), 1992.

Lane, Tony, *The Merchant Seamen's War,* Manchester University Press (Manchester, England), 1990.

Lewis, Jonathon, and Phillip Whitehead, *Stalin: A Time for Judgment,* Pantheon (New York), 1990.

Macintyre, Donald G. F. W., *Narvik,* W.W. Norton & Company (New York), 1960.

Manchester, William, *The Last Lion: Winston Spencer Churchill* Little, Brown (Boston), 1983–88.

Marrin, Albert, *Stalin,* Viking Kestrel (New York), 1988.

McNeal, Robert, *Stalin: Man and Ruler,* New York University Press (New York), 1988.

Medvedev, Roy, *Let History Judge: The Origins and Consequences of Stalinism,* Columbia University Press (New York), 1989.

Mellor, John, *Forgotten Heroes: The Canadians at Dieppe,* Methuen (Toronto), 1975.

Payne, Robert, *The Great Man: A Portrait of Winston Churchill,* Coward, McCann and Geoghegan (New York), 1974.

Pitt, Barrie, and the editors of Time-Life Books, *The Battle of the Atlantic,* Time-Life Books (Alexandria, VA), 1977.

Reynaud, Paul, *In the Thick of the Fight,* translated by J. D. Lambert, Simon and Schuster (New York), 1955.

Reynolds, Quentin James, *The Battle of Britain,* Random House (New York), 1953.

Rose, Norman, *Churchill: The Unruly Giant,* Free Press (New York), 1994.

Ross, Stewart, *World Leaders,* Thomson Learning (New York), 1993.

Ryan, Cornelius, *A Bridge Too Far,* Simon and Schuster (New York), 1995.

Schoenfeld, Maxwell P., *Sir Winston Churchill: His Life and Times,* second edition, R.E. Krieger (Malabar, FL), 1986.

Severance, John B., *Winston Churchill: Soldier, Statesman, Artist,* Clarion Books (New York), 1996.

Shirer, William L., *The Collapse of the Third Republic,* Simon and Schuster (New York), 1969.

Shirer, William L., *The Sinking of the Bismarck,* Random House (New York), 1962.

Simon, Yves, *The Road to Vichy, 1918–1938,* translated by James A. Corbett and George J. McMorrow, Sheed and Ward (New York), 1942.

Skipper, G. C., *The Battle of Britain,* Children's Press (Chicago), 1980.

Skipper, G. C., *Battle of Stalingrad,* Children's Press (Chicago), 1981.

Skipper, G. C., *The Battle of the Atlantic,* Children's Press (Chicago), 1981.

Skipper, G. C., *Fall of the Fox, Rommel,* Children's Press (Chicago), 1980.

Skipper, G. C., *Goering and the Luftwaffe*, Children's Press (Chicago), 1980.

Skipper, G. C., *Invasion of Sicily*, Children's Press (Chicago), 1981.

Sloan, Frank, *Bismarck!*, Franklin Watts (New York), 1991.

Snell, John L., *Illusion and Necessity*, Houghton Mifflin (Boston), 1963.

Souster, Raymond, *Jubilee of Death: The Raid on Dieppe*, Oberon Press (Ottawa, Ontario, Canada), 1984.

Stein, R. Conrad, *Dunkirk*, Children's Press (Chicago), 1982.

Stein, R. Conrad, *Invasion of Russia*, Children's Press (Chicago), 1985.

Stein, R. Conrad, *Siege of Leningrad*, Children's Press (Chicago), 1983.

Taylor, Theodore, *Battle of the Arctic Seas: The Story of Convoy PQ 17*, Crowell (New York), 1976.

Topp, Erich, *The Odyssey of a U-Boat Commander: Recollections of Erich Topp*, translated by Eric C. Rust, Praeger (Westport, CT), 1992.

Ulam, Adam, *Stalin, the Man and His Era*, Beacon Press (Boston), 1989.

Vause, Jordan, and Jurgen Oesten, *Wolf: U-Boat Commanders in World War II*, Airlife (Osceola, WI), 1997.

Warth, Robert D., *Joseph Stalin*, Twayne (New York), 1969.

Weygand, Maxime, *Recalled to Service*, William Heinemann (London), 1952.

Whitelaw, Nancy, *Joseph Stalin: From Peasant to Premier*, Dillon Press (New York), 1992.

Woodrooffe, T., *The Battle of the Atlantic*, Faber (New York), 1965.

Germany:

Allen, William Sheridan, *The Nazi Seizure of Power: The Experience of a Single German Town, 1922–1945*, Franklin Watts (New York), 1984.

Ayer, Eleanor, *Adolf Hitler*, Lucent (San Diego), 1996.

Ayer, Eleanor, *Cities at War: Berlin*, New Discovery Books (New York), 1992.

Baynes, Norman H., editor, *The Speeches of Adolf Hitler, April 1922–August 1939: An English Translation of Representative Passages*, Gordon Press (New York), 1981.

Berman, Russell A., *Paul von Hindenburg*, Chelsea House (New York), 1987.

Binion, Rudolph, *Hitler among the Germans*, Elsevier (Amsterdam), 1976.

Bracher, Karl Dietrich, *The German Dictatorship: The Origins, Structure, and Effects of National Socialism*, Praeger (New York), 1970.

Bullock, Alan, *Hitler: A Study in Tyranny*, Harper and Row (New York), 1971.

Clark, Alan, *Barbarossa: The Russian-German Conflict, 1941–1945*, William Morrow (New York), 1965.

Eimerl, Sarel, *Hitler over Europe; The Road to World War II*, Little, Brown (Boston), 1972.

Fest, Joachim C., *The Face of the Third Reich: Portraits of the Nazi Leadership*, Pantheon (New York), 1970.

Friedman, Ina R., *The Other Victims: First-Person Stories of Non-Jews Persecuted by the Nazis*, Houghton Mifflin (Boston), 1990.

Gallagher, Hugh Gregory, *By Trust Betrayed: Patients, Physicians, and the License to Kill in the Third Reich*, Holt (New York), 1990.

Gilbert, Felix, editor, *Hitler Directs His War: The Secret Records of His Daily Military Conferences*, Octagon Books (New York), 1982.

Goldston, Robert C., *The Life and Death of Nazi Germany*, Bobbs-Merrill (Indianapolis), 1967.

Gordon, Harold J., *Hitler and the Beer Hall Putsch*, Princeton University Press (Princeton, NJ), 1972.

Harris, Nathaniel, *Hitler*, Trafalgar (North Pomfret, VT), 1989.

Hauner, Milan, *Hitler: A Chronology of His Life and Time*, St. Martin's Press (New York), 1983.

Heyes, Eileen, *Adolf Hitler*, Millbrook Press (Brookfield, CT), 1993.

Hitler, Adolf, *Mein Kampf*, translated by Ralph Manheim, Houghton Mifflin (Boston), 1971.

Johnson, Eric A., *Nazi Terror: The Gestapo, Jews, and Ordinary Germans*, Basic Books (New York), 2000.

Kershaw, Ian, *The "Hitler Myth": Image and Reality in the Third Reich*, Oxford University Press (New York), 1987.

Klemperer, Victor, *I Will Bear Witness 1941–1945: A Diary of the Nazi Years*, Volume 2, Random House (New York), 1998.

Langer, Walter C., *The Mind of Adolf Hitler: The Secret Wartime Report*, Basic Books (New York), 1972.

Manvell, Roger, *SS and the Gestapo*, Ballantine Books (New York), 1969.

Massaquoi, Hans J., *Destined to Witness: Growing Up Black in Nazi Germany*, W. Morrow (New York), 1999.

Merkl, Peter H., *The Making of a Stormtrooper*, Princeton University Press (Princeton, NJ), 1980.

Nevelle, Peter, *Life in the Third Reich: World War II*, Batsford (North Pomfret, VT), 1992.

Pulzer, Peter G., *The Rise of Political Anti-Semitism in Germany and Austria: 1867–1918*, John Wiley (New York), 1964.

Rich, Norman, *Hitler's War Aims*, W. W. Norton (New York), 1973.

Seaton, Albert, *The Russo-German War, 1941–1945*, Frederick A. Praeger (New York), 1970.

Shirer, William L., *Berlin Diary*, Knopf (New York), 1941.

Shirer, William L., *Twentieth Century Journey: A Memoir of a Life and the Times*, Volume 2, *The Nightmare Years, 1930–1940*, Bantam Books (New York), 1984.

Speer, Albert, *Inside the Third Reich*, Galahad Books (New York), 1995.

Spence, William, *Germany Then and Now*, Franklin Watts (New York), 1994.

Stein, R. Conrad, *Hitler Youth*, Children's Press (Chicago), 1985.

Stern, Fritz, *Dreams and Delusions: The Drama of German History*, Yale University Press (New Haven, CT), 1999.

Steward, Gail B., *Hitler's Reich*, Lucent Books (San Diego), 1994.

Tames, Richard, *Nazi Germany*, Batsford (North Pomfret, VT), 1992.

Toland, John, *Adolf Hitler*, Anchor Books (New York), 1992.

Wepman, Dennis, *Adolf Hitler*, Chelsea House (New York), 1989.

Williamson, David, *The Third Reich*, Bookwright Press (New York), 1989.

Italy and Fascism:

Chrisp, Peter, *The Rise of Fascism*, Bookwright Press (New York), 1991.

Hartenian, Lawrence R., *Benito Mussolini*, Chelsea House (New York), 1988.

Knox, MacGregor, *Mussolini Unleashed, 1939–1941: Politics and Strategy in Fascist Italy's Last War*, Cambridge University Press (New York), 1986.

Leeds, Christopher, *Italy under Mussolini*, Putnam (New York), 1972.

Lyttle, Richard, *Il Duce: The Rise and Fall of Benito Mussolini*, Atheneum (New York), 1987.

Moseley, Ray, *Mussolini's Shadow: The Double Life of Count Galeazzo Ciano*, Yale University Press, (New Haven, CT) 2000.

Stille, Alexander, *Benevolence and Betrayal: Five Italian Jewish Families Under Fascism*, Summit Books (New York), 1991.

Wiskemann, Elizabeth, *The Rome-Berlin Axis: A History of the Relations Between Hitler and Mussolini*, Oxford University Press (London), 1949.

Japan:

Barker, Rodney, *The Hiroshima Maidens: A Story of Courage, Compassion, and Survival*, Penguin Books (New York), 1985.

Behr, Edward, *Hirohito: Beyond the Myth*, Villard Books (New York), 1989.

Black, Wallace B., and Jean F. Blashfield, *Hiroshima and the Atomic Bomb*, Crestwood House (New York), 1993.

Butow, Robert J. C., *Tojo and the Coming of the War*, Stanford University Press (Stanford, CA), 1969.

Grant, R. G., *Hiroshima and Nagasaki*, Raintree, Steck-Vaughn (Austin, TX), 1988.

Hersey, John, *Hiroshima*, Vintage Books (New York), 1989.

Hogan, Michael J., editor, *Hiroshima in History and Memory*, Cambridge University Press (New York), 1996.

Hoobler, Dorothy, and Thomas Hoobler, *Showa: The Age of Hirohito*, Walker (New York), 1990.

Maruki, Toshi, *Hiroshima No Pika,* Lothrop, Lee & Shepard (New York), 1982.

Oe, Kenzaburo, *Hiroshima Notes,* Grove Press (New York), 1996.

Sekimori, Gaynor, *Hibakusha: Survivors of Hiroshima and Nagasaki,* Kosei (Tokyo), 1986.

Selden, Kyoko, and Mark Selden, editors, *The Atomic Bomb: Voices from Hiroshima and Nagasaki,* M.E. Sharpe (Armonk, NJ), 1989.

Severns, Karen, *Hirohito,* Chelsea House (New York), 1988.

Sherrow, Victoria, *Hiroshima,* New Discovery Books (New York), 1994.

Sherwin, Martin J., *A World Destroyed: Hiroshima and the Origins of the Arms Race,* Stanford University Press (Stanford, CA), 2000.

Stein, R. Conrad, *Hiroshima,* Children's Press (Chicago), 1982.

Japanese War Crimes:

Askin, Kelly Dawn, *War Crimes Against Women: Prosecution in International War Crimes Tribunals,* Martinus Nijhoff (The Hague), 1997.

Brackman, Arnold C., *The Other Nuremberg: The Untold Story of the Tokyo War Crimes Trials,* Morrow (New York), 1987.

Ginn, John L., *Sugamo Prison, Tokyo: An Account of the Trial and Sentencing of Japanese War Criminals in 1948, by a U.S. Participant,* McFarland (Jefferson, NC), 1992.

Hosoya, Chihiro, et. al., *The Tokyo War Crimes Trial: An International Symposium,* Kodansha (Tokyo), 1986.

International Military Tribunal for the Far East, *The Tokyo Major War Crimes Trial: The Records of the International Military Tribunal for the Far East: With an Authoritative Commentary and Comprehensive Guide,* edited by R. John Pritchard, published for the Robert M.W. Kempner Collegium by Edwin Mellen Press (Lewiston, NY), 1998.

Minear, Richard H., *Victor's Justice: The Tokyo War Crimes Trial,* Princeton University Press (Princeton, NJ), 1971.

Piccigallo, Philip, *The Japanese on Trial: Allied War Crimes Operations in the East, 1945–1951,* University of Texas Press (Austin, TX), 1979.

Röling, Bernard Victor Aloysius, *The Tokyo Trial and Beyond: Reflections of a Peacemonger,* Polity Press (Cambridge, England), 1993.

Tanaka, Toshiyuki, *Hidden Horrors: Japanese War Crimes in World War II,* Westview Press (Boulder, CO), 1996.

The United States:

Ambrose, Stephen E., *Band of Brothers: E Company, 506th Regiment, 101st Airborne from Normandy to Hitler's Eagle Nest,* Simon and Schuster (New York), 1992.

Ambrose, Stephen E., *The Victors: Eisenhower and His Boys: The Men of World War II,* Simon and Schuster (New York), 1998.

Bernstein, Alison R., *American Indians and World War II: Toward a New Era in Indian Affairs,* University of Oklahoma Press (Norman, OK), 1999.

Brimner, Larry Dane, *Voices from the Camps,* Franklin Watts (New York), 1994.

Brokaw, Tom, *The Greatest Generation,* Random House (New York), 1998.

Brokaw, Tom, *The Greatest Generation Speaks: Letters and Reflections,* Random House (New York), 1999.

Burns, James M., *Roosevelt: The Soldier of Freedom,* Harvest/Harcourt (New York), 1973.

Cannon, Marian, *Dwight David Eisenhower: War Hero and President,* Franklin Watts (New York), 1990.

Cohen, Stan, *V for Victory: America's Home Front During World War II,* Pictorial Histories Publishing (Missoula, MT), 1991.

Darby, Jean, *Douglas MacArthur,* Lerner (Minneapolis, MN), 1989.

Davis, Kenneth S., *FDR: The New Deal Years, 1933–1937,* Random House (New York), 1979.

Davis, Kenneth S., *FDR: The New York Years, 1928–1933,* Random House (New York), 1979.

Devaney, John, *Franklin Delano Roosevelt, President,* Walker (New York), 1987.

Divine, Robert A., *The Reluctant Belligerent: American Entry into World War II,* John Wiley and Sons (New York), 1965.

Dolan, Edward F., *America in World War II: 1942,* Millbrook Press (Brookfield, CT), 1991.

Dolan, Edward F., *America in World War II: 1943,* Millbrook Press (Brookfield, CT), 1992.

Donovan, Robert J., *PT 109: John F. Kennedy in World War II,* McGraw-Hill (New York), 1961.

Duden, Jane, *1940s,* Crestwood (New York), 1989.

Francis, Charles E., *The Tuskegee Airmen: The Men Who Changed a Nation,* Branden Publishing (Boston), 1993.

Freedman, Russell, *Franklin Delano Roosevelt,* Franklin Watts (New York), 1983.

Fremon, David K., *Japanese American Internment in American History,* Enslow Publishers (Springfield, NJ), 1966.

Gilbo, Patrick F., *The American Red Cross: The First Century,* Harper and Row, Publishers (New York), 1981.

Goodwin, Doris Kearns, *No Ordinary Time, Franklin and Eleanor Roosevelt: The Home Front in World War II,* Simon and Schuster (New York), 1994.

Graham, Otis L., Jr., and Meghan Robinson Wander, editors, *Franklin D. Roosevelt, His Life and Times: An Encyclopedic View,* G. K. Hall (Boston), 1985.

Hacker, Jeffrey H., *Franklin D. Roosevelt,* Franklin Watts (New York), 1983.

Harris, Jacqueline L., *The Tuskegee Airmen: Black Heroes of World War II,* Dillon Press (Parsippany, NJ), 1995.

Harris, Mark Jonathan, Franklin Mitchell, and Steven Schechter, editors, *The Homefront: America during World War II,* G. P. Putnam's Sons (New York), 1984.

Holway, John B., *Red Tail Black Wings: The Men of America's Black Air Force,* Yucca Tree (Las Cruces, NM), 1997.

Homan, Lynn M., and Thomas Reilly, *Tuskegee Airmen,* Arcadia Tempus Publishing Group (Charleston, SC), 1998.

Langer, William L., and S. Everett Gleason, *The Undeclared War, 1940–1941,* P. Smith (Gloucester, MA), 1968.

Lawson, Ted W., *Thirty Seconds Over Tokyo,* Buccaneer Books, 1999.

Levine, Ellen, *A Fence Away from Freedom,* G. P. Putnam (New York), 1995.

Mauldin, Bill, *Back Home,* William Sloane Associates (New York), 1947.

Mauldin, Bill, *The Brass Ring,* W. W. Norton (New York), 1971.

McKissack, Patricia, and Frederick McKissack, *Red-Tail Angels: The Story of the Tuskegee Airmen of World War II,* Walker (New York), 1995.

Miller, Nathan, *FDR: An Intimate History,* originally published in 1983, reprinted, Madison Books/University Press of America (Lanham, MD), 1991.

Morgan, Ted, *FDR: A Biography,* Simon and Schuster (New York), 1985.

Murphy, Audie, *To Hell and Back,* Holt (New York), 1949.

O'Connor, Barbara, *The Soldiers' Voice: The Story of Ernie Pyle,* Carolrhoda Books (Minneapolis, MN), 1996.

Olesky, Walter, *Military Leaders of World War II,* Facts on File (New York), 1994.

Perkins, Frances, *The Roosevelt I Knew,* Viking (New York), 1946.

Pfeifer, Kathryn Browne, *The 761st Tank Battalion,* Henry Holt (New York), 1994.

Pyle, Ernie, *Brave Men,* Henry Holt (New York), 1944.

Rubenstein, Harry R., and William L. Bird, *Design for Victory: World War II Posters on the American Home Front,* Princeton Architectural Press (New York), 1998.

Spies, Karen Bornemann, *Franklin D. Roosevelt,* Enslow (Springfield, NJ), 1999.

Stanley, Jerry, *I Am an American: A True Story of Japanese Internment,* Crown (New York), 1994.

Stein, R. Conrad, *The Home Front,* Children's Press (Chicago), 1986.

Stein, R. Conrad, *Nisei Regiment,* Children's Press (Chicago), 1985.

Sweeney, James B., *Famous Aviators of World War II,* Franklin Watts (New York), 1987.

Uchida, Yoshika, *Desert Exile: The Uprooting of a Japanese-American Family,* University of Washington Press (Seattle), 1982.

Whitman, Sylvia, *Uncle Sam Wants You: Military Men and Women in World War II,* Lerner (Minneapolis, MN), 1993.

Whitman, Sylvia, *V Is for Victory,* Lerner (Minneapolis, MN), 1993.

Woodrow, Martin, *The World War II GI*, Franklin Watts (New York), 1986.

Wrynn, V. Dennis, *Detroit Goes to War: The American Automobile Industry in World War II*, Motorbooks International (Osceola, WI), 1993.

Women and the War:

Bowman, Constance, *Slacks and Calluses: Our Summer in a Bomber Factory,* illustrated by Clara Marie Allen, Smithsonian Institution Press (Washington, DC), 1999.

Carl, Ann B., *A Wasp Among Eagles: A Woman Military Test Pilot in World War II*, Smithsonian Institution Press (Washington, DC), 1999.

Cole, Jean Hascall, *Women Pilots of World War II*, University of Utah Press (Salt Lake City, UT), 1992.

Colijn, Helen, *Song of Survival: Women Interned*, White Cloud Press (Ashland, OR), 1995.

Colman, Penny, *Rosie the Riveter: Women Working on the Home Front in World War II*, Crown (New York), 1995.

Danner, Dorothy Still, *What a Way to Spend a War: Navy Nurse POWs in the Philippines*, Naval Institute Press (Annapolis, MD), 1995.

Fessler, Diane Burke, *No Time for Fear: Voices of American Military Nurses in World War II*, Michigan State University Press (East Lansing, MI), 1996.

Frank, Miriam, Marilyn Ziebarth, and Connie Field, *The Life and Times of Rosie the Riveter: The Story of Three Million Working Women during World War II*, Clarity Educational Productions (Emeryville, CA), 1982.

Green, Anne Bosanko, and D'Ann Campbell, *One Woman's War: Letters Home from the Women's Army Corps, 1944–1946*, Minnesota Historical Society (St. Paul, MN), 1989.

Gruhzit-Hoyt, Olga, *They Also Served: American Women in World War II*, Birch Lane Press (Secaucus, NJ), 1995.

Gunter, Helen Clifford, *Navy WAVE: Memories of World War II*, Cypress House (Fort Bragg, CA), 1994.

Hicks, George L., *The Comfort Women: Japan's Brutal Regime of Enforced Prostitution in the Second World War*, W.W. Norton & Company (New York), 1995.

Holm, Jeanne, and Judith Bellafaire, editors, *In Defense of a Nation: Servicewomen in World War II*, Vandamere Press (Arlington, VA), 1998.

Honey, Maureen, editor, *Bitter Fruit: African American Women in World War II*, University of Missouri Press (Columbia, MO), 1999.

Howard, Keith, editor, *True Stories of the Korean Comfort Women*, Cassell (London), 1995.

Jopling, Lucy Wilson, *Warrior in White*, Watercress Press (San Antonio, TX), 1990.

Kaminski, Theresa, *Prisoners in Paradise: American Women in the Wartime South Pacific*, University Press of Kansas (Lawrence, KS), 2000.

Keith, Agnes Newton, *Three Came Home*, Little, Brown (Boston, MA), 1947.

Kelsey, Marion, *Victory Harvest: Diary of a Canadian in the Women's Land Army, 1940–1944*, McGill-Queens University Press (Toronto), 1997.

Lucas, Celia, *Prisoners of Santo Tomas: A True Account of Women POWs Under Japanese Control*, Cooper (London), 1975.

Monahan, Evelyn M., and Rosemary Neidel-Greenlee, *All This Hell: U.S. Nurses Imprisoned by the Japanese*, University of Kentucky Press (Lexington, KY), 2000.

Noggle, Anne, and Dora Dougherty Strother, *For God, Country, and the Thrill of It: Women Airforce Pilots in World War II*, Texas A&M University Press (College Station, TX), 1990.

Norman, Elizabeth M., *We Band of Angels: The Untold Story of American Nurses Trapped on Bataan by the Japanese*, Random House (New York), 1999.

Nova, Lily, and Iven Lourie, editors, *Interrupted Lives: Four Women's Stories of Internment During World War II in the Philippines*, Artemis Books (Nevada City, CA), 1995.

Reynoldson, Floria, *Women and War*, Thomson Learning (New York), 1993.

Scharr, Adela Riek, *Sisters in the Sky, Volume 1: The WAFS*, Patrice Press (St. Louis, MO), 1986.

Scharr, Adela Riek, *Sisters in the Sky, Volume 2: The WASP*, Patrice Press (St. Louis, MO), 1988.

Sinott, Susan, *Doing Our Part: American Women on the Home Front during World War II*, Franklin Watts (New York), 1995.

Tomblin, Barbara Brooks, *G. I. Nightingales: The Army Nurse Corps in World War II,* University Press of Kentucky (Lexington, KY), 1996.

Treadwell, Mattie E., *United States Army in World War II: Special Studies: The Women's Army Corps,* Office of the Chief of Military History, Department of the Army (Washington, DC), 1954.

Weatherford, Doris, *American Women and World War II,* Facts on File (New York), 1992.

Weitz, Margaret Collins, *Sisters in the Resistance: How Women Fought to Free France, 1940–1945,* John Wiley and Sons (New York), 1998.

Williams, Vera S., *WACs: Women's Army Corps,* Motorbooks International Publishers, 1997.

Williams, Vera S., *Women Airforce Service Pilots of World War II,* Motorbooks International Publishers (Osceola, WI), 1994.

Wise, Nancy Baker, and Christy Wise, *A Mouthful of Rivets: Women at Work in World War II,* Jossey-Bass (San Francisco, CA), 1994.

Zeinert, Karen, *Those Incredible Women of World War II,* Millbrook Press (Brookfield, CT), 1994.

Children in the War:

Bertini, Tullio Bruno, *Trapped in Tuscany, Liberated by the Buffalo Soldiers: The True World War II Story of Tullio Bruno Bertini,* Dante University Press (Boston), 1998.

Besson, Jean-Louis, *October 45: Childhood Memories of the War,* Creative Editions (Mankato, MN), 1995.

Butterworth, Emma Macalik, *As the Waltz Was Ending,* Four Winds (New York), 1982.

Chapman, Fern Schumer, *Motherland: A Daughter's Journey to Reclaim the Past,* Viking (New York), 2000.

Cross, Robin, *Children and War,* Thomson Learning (New York), 1994.

Drucker, Olga Levy, *Kindertransport,* Henry Holt (New York), 1992.

Emmerich, Elsbeth, *My Childhood in Nazi Germany,* Bookwright Press (New York), 1991.

Foreman, Michael, *War Boy: A Country Childhood,* Arcade (New York), 1990.

Heyes, Eileen, *Children of the Swastika: The Hitler Youth,* Millbrook Press (Brookfield, CT), 1993.

Holliday, Laurel, *Children in the Holocaust and World War II,* Pocket Books (New York), 1995.

Isaacman, Clara, *Clara's Story,* Jewish Publication Society (Philadelphia), 1984.

Kuper, Jack, *Child of the Holocaust,* Berkley Books (New York), 1993.

Loy, Rosetta, *First Words: A Childhood in Fascist Italy,* Metropolitan Books/Henry Holt (New York) 2000.

Lukas, Richard C., *Did the Children Cry?: Hitler's War Against Jewish and Polish Children, 1939–1945,* Hippocrene Books (New York), 1994.

Marx, Trish, *Echoes of World War II,* Lerner (Minneapolis, MN), 1994.

Nicholson, Dorinda Makanaonalani Stagner, *Pearl Harbor Child: A Child's View of Pearl Harbor—From Attack to Peace,* Arizona Memorial Museum Association (Honolulu), 1993.

Silwowska, Wiktoria, editor, *The Last Eyewitnesses: Children of the Holocaust Speak,* Northwestern University Press (Evanston, IL), 1998.

Stalcup, Ann, *On the Home Front: Growing up in Wartime England,* Linnet Books (North Haven, CT), 1998.

Toll, Nelly S., *Behind the Secret Window: A Memoir of a Hidden Childhood During World War II,* Dial Books (New York), 1993.

Tunnell, Michael O., and George W. Chilcoat, *The Children of Topaz,* Holiday House (New York), 1996.

Ungerer, Tomi, *A Childhood under the Nazis,* Tomic (Niwot, CO), 1998.

Wassiljewa, Tatjana, *Hostage to War,* Scholastic Press (New York), 1997.

Wilkomirski, Binjamin, *Fragments: Memories of a Wartime Childhood,* Schocken Books (New York), 1997.

Wojciechowska, Maia, *Till the Break of Day,* Harcourt, Brace, Jovanovich (New York), 1972.

Events in Europe, 1944 and Later:

Alperovitz, Gar, *Atomic Diplomacy: Hiroshima and Potsdam,* Simon and Schuster (New York), 1965.

Ambrose, Stephen E., *Citizen Soldiers: The U.S. Army from the Normandy Beaches to the Bulge to the Surrender of Germany,* Simon & Schuster (New York), 1997.

Balkoski, Joseph, *Beyond the Beachhead: The 29th Infantry Division in Normandy*, Stackpole Books (Mechanicsburg, PA), 1999.

Banfield, Susan, *Charles de Gaulle*, Chelsea House (New York), 1985.

Black, Wallace B., *Battle of the Bulge*, Crestwood House (New York), 1993.

Bliven, Bruce, *The Story of D-Day: June 6, 1944*, Random House (New York), 1956.

Bourke-White, Margaret, *"Dear Fatherland, Rest Quietly": A Report on the Collapse of Hitler's "Thousand Years,"* Simon and Schuster (New York), 1946.

Collins, Larry, and Dominique Lapierre, *Is Paris Burning?*, Castle, 2000.

Conot, Robert E., *Justice at Nuremberg*, Harper (New York), 1983.

Dolan, Edward F., *The Fall of Hitler's Germany*, Franklin Watts (New York), 1988.

Evans, Richard J., *In Hitler's Shadow: West German Historians and the Attempt to Escape from the Nazi Past*, Pantheon (New York), 1989.

Feis, Herbert, *Between War and Peace: The Potsdam Conference*, Princeton University Press (Princeton, NJ), 1960.

Goldstein, Donald M., Katherine V. Dillon, and J. Michael Wenger, *Nuts! The Battle of the Bulge: The Story and Photographs*, Brassey's (Washington, DC), 1994.

Hine, Al, *D-Day: The Invasion of Europe*, American Heritage Publishing Company (New York), 1962.

Keegan, John, *Six Armies in Normandy: From D-Day to the Liberation of Paris*, Penguin (New York), 1994.

Lamb, Richard, *War in Italy 1943–1945: A Brutal Story*, Da Capo Press (New York), 1996.

MacDonald, Charles B., *The Mighty Endeavor: American Armed Forces in the European Theater in World War II*, Da Capo Press (New York), 1992.

MacDonald, Charles B., *A Time for Trumpets: The Untold Story of the Battle of the Bulge*, Bantam Books (New York), 1985.

Marrin, Albert, *Overlord: D-Day and the Invasion of Europe*, Atheneum (New York), 1982.

Morin, Isobel V., *Days of Judgment*, Millbrook Press (Brookfield, CT), 1995.

Posner, Gerald L., *Hitler's Children: Sons and Daughters of the Third Reich Talk about Their Fathers and Themselves*, Random House (New York), 1991.

Rice, Earl, *The Nuremberg Trials*, Lucent Books (San Diego), 1997.

Ryan, Cornelius, *The Last Battle*, Simon & Schuster (New York), 1966.

Ryan, Cornelius, *The Longest Day: June 6, 1944*, Simon and Schuster (New York), 1994.

Sheehan, Fred, and Martin Blumenson, *Anzio, Epic of Bravery*, University of Oklahoma Press (Norman, OK), 1994.

Skipper, G. C., *Death of Hitler*, Children's Press (Chicago), 1980.

Skipper, G. C., *Mussolini: A Dictator Dies*, Children's Press (Chicago), 1981.

Stein, R. Conrad, *World War II in Europe: America Goes to War*, Enslow Press (Hillside, NJ), 1984.

Toland, John, *The Last 100 Days*, Random House (New York), 1966.

United States Department of State, *The Conferences at Malta and Yalta, 1945*, Greenwood Press (Westport, CT), 1976.

Whitelaw, Nancy, *A Biography of General Charles de Gaulle*, Dillon Press (New York), 1991.

Secret Codes and Weapons, Spies, and Sabotage:

Aldrich, Richard J., *Intelligence and the War Against Japan: Britain, America and the Politics of Secret Service*, Cambridge University Press (New York), 2000.

Alvarez, David J., editor, *Allied and Axis Signals Intelligence in World War II*, Frank Cass (Portland, OR), 1999.

Alvarez, David J., *Secret Messages: Codebreaking and American Diplomacy, 1930–1945*, University of Kansas Press (Lawrence, KS), 2000.

Ambrose, Stephen E., and Richard H. Immerman, *Ike's Spies: Eisenhower and the Espionage Establishment*, University Press of Mississippi (Jackson, MS), 1999.

Andryszewski, Tricia, *The Amazing Life of Moe Berg: Catcher, Scholar, Spy*, Millbrook Press (Brookfield, CT), 1996.

Bixler, Margaret T., *Winds of Freedom: The Story of the Navajo Code Talkers of World War II*, Two Bytes (Darien, CT), 1992.

Breuer, William B., *MacArthur's Undercover War: Spies, Saboteurs, Guerillas, and Secret Missions,* John Wiley and Sons (New York), 1995.

Daily, Robert, *The Code Talkers,* Franklin Watts (New York), 1995.

Durrett, Deanne, *Unsung Heroes of World War II: The Story of the Navajo Code Talkers,* Facts on File (New York), 1998.

Gardner, W. J. R., *Decoding History: The Battle of the Atlantic and Ultra,* United States Naval Institute (Annapolis, MD), 2000.

Goldston, Robert C., *Sinister Touches: The Secret War Against Hitler,* Dial Press (New York), 1992.

Halter, Jon C., *Top Secret Projects of World War II,* J. Messner (New York), 1978.

Harper, Stephen, *Capturing Enigma: How HMS Petard Seized the German Naval Codes,* Sutton Publishing, 2000.

Hinsley, Francis H., *British Intelligence in the Second World War,* Cambridge University Press (New York), 1993.

Hodgson, Lynn-Philip, *Inside—Camp X,* Blake Books, 1999.

Hohne, Heinz, *Canaris: Hitler's Master Spy,* Cooper Square Press (New York), 1999.

Holmes, W. J., *Double-Edged Secrets: U.S. Naval Intelligence Operations in the Pacific During World War II,* United States Naval Institute (Annapolis, MD), 1998.

Jakub, Jay, *Spies and Saboteurs: Anglo-American Collaboration and Rivalry in Human Intelligence Collection and Special Operations,* St. Martin's Press (New York), 1999.

Johnson, David Allen, *Germany's Spies and Saboteurs,* Motorbooks International (Osceola, WI), 1998.

Jones, Catherine, *Navajo Code Talkers: Native American Heroes,* Tudor Publications (Greensboro, NC), 1997.

Kahn, David A., *Hitler's Spies: German Military Intelligence in World War II,* Da Capo Press (Cambridge, MA), 2000.

Kilzer, Louis, *Hitler's Traitor: Martin Bormann and the Defeat of the Reich,* Presidio Press (Novato, CA), 2000.

Kiyosaki, Wayne S., and Daniel K. Akaka, *A Spy in Their Midst: The World War II Struggle of a Japanese-American Hero,* Madison Books (Lanham, MD), 1995.

Lawson, Don, *The Secret World War II,* Franklin Watts (New York), 1978.

MacDonnell, Francis, *Insidious Foes: The Axis Fifth Column and the American Home Front,* Oxford University Press (New York), 1995.

Marks, Leo, *Between Silk and Cyanide: A Codemaker's War 1941–1945,* Free Press (New York), 1999.

Marrin, Albert, *The Secret Armies,* Atheneum (New York), 1985.

McIntosh, Elizabeth P., *Sisterhood of Spies: The Women of the OSS,* GK Hall (Thorndike, ME), 2000.

Moon, Tom, *This Grim and Savage Game: The OSS and the Beginning of U.S. Covert Operations in World War II,* Da Capo Press (Cambridge, MA), 2000.

Paul, Doris A., *The Navajo Code Talkers,* Dorrance (Philadelphia, PA), 1973.

Paz Salinas, Maria Emilia, *Strategy, Security, and Spies: Mexico and the U.S. as Allies in World War II,* Pennsylvania State University Press (University Park, PA), 1997.

Rogers, James T., *The Secret War: Espionage in World War II,* Facts on File (New York), 1991.

Showell, Jak P. Mallman, *Enigma U-Boats: Breaking the Code—The True Story,* Naval Institute Press (Annapolis, MD), 2000.

Stevenson, William, *A Man Called Intrepid: The Secret War,* Harcourt, Brace (New York), 1976.

Sutherland, David, *He Who Dares: Recollections of Service in the SAS, SBS, and MI5,* United States Naval Institute (Annapolis, MD), 1999.

Tarrant, V. E., *The Red Orchestra,* John Wiley and Sons (New York), 1996.

Tickell, Jerrard, *Odette: The Story of a British Agent,* Chapman & Hall (London), 1949.

Warriors: Navajo Code Talkers, photographs by Kenji Kawano, Northland (Flagstaff, AZ), 1990.

Wires, Richard, *The Cicero Spy Affair: German Access to British Secrets in World War II,* Praeger (Westport, CT), 1999.

Holocaust and World War II Fiction:

Aaron, David, *Crossing by Night,* Thorndike Press (Thorndike, ME), 1993.

Abbott, Margot, *The Last Innocent Hour: A Novel,* St. Martin's Press (New York), 1991.

Allbeury, Ted, *A Time Without Shadows,* Mysterious Press (New York), 1991.

Allington, Maynard, *The Fox in the Field: A WWII Novel of India,* Brassey's (Washington, DC), 1994.

Amis, Martin, *Time's Arrow,* Harmony Books (New York), 1991.

Appelfeld, Aharon, *The Age of Wonders,* D. R. Godine (Boston), 1981.

Appelfeld, Aharon, *Badenheim 1939,* D. R. Godine (Boston), 1980.

Appelfeld, Aharon, *For Every Sin,* Weidenfeld & Nicolson (New York), 1989.

Appelfeld, Aharon, *Immortal Bartfuss,* Weidenfeld & Nicolson (New York), 1988.

Ballard, J. G., *Empire of the Sun,* V. Gollancz (London), 1984.

Bassani, Giorgio, *The Garden of the Finzi-Continis,* MJF Books (New York), 1996.

Bassett, James, *Cmdr. Prince, USN: A Novel of the Pacific War,* Simon and Schuster (New York), 1971.

Beach, Edward, *Run Silent, Run Deep,* Holt (New York), 1955.

Begley, Louis, *Wartime Lies,* Knopf (New York), 1991.

Bellow, Saul, *The Bellarosa Connection,* Penguin (New York), 1989.

Benchley, Nathaniel, *Bright Candles: A Novel of the Danish Resistance,* Harper and Row (New York), 1974.

Benchley, Nathaniel, *A Necessary End: A Novel of World War II,* Harper and Row (New York), 1976.

Boll, Heinrich, *Billiards at Half-Past Nine,* Weidenfeld and Nicholson (London), 1961.

Booth, Martin, *Hiroshima Joe,* Penguin (New York), 1987.

Boraks-Nemetz, Lillian, *The Old Brown Suitcase: A Teenager's Story of War and Peace,* Ben-Simon Publications (Port Angeles, WA), 1994.

Borowski, Tadeusz, *This Way For the Gas, Ladies and Gentlemen,* Penguin (New York), 1976.

Boulle, Pierre, *The Bridge over the River Kwai,* translated by Xan Fielding, Gramercy Books (New York), 2000.

Boyne, Walter J., *Eagles at War,* Crown (New York), 1991.

Callison, Brian, *A Flock of Ships,* Putnam (New York), 1970.

Clavell, James, *King Rat,* Little, Brown (Boston), 1962.

Dailey, Janet, *Silver Wings, Santiago Blue,* G. K. Hall (Boston), 1984.

De Hartog, Jan, *The Captain,* Atheneum (New York), 1966.

Deighton, Len, *City of Gold,* Thorndike Press (Thorndike, ME), 1992.

Deighton, Len, *Goodbye, Mickey Mouse,* Knopf (New York), 1982.

Deighton, Len, *XPD,* Thorndike Press, Thorndike, ME, 1981.

Demetz, Hanna, *The House on Prague Street,* St. Martin's Press (New York), 1980.

Dickey, James, *To the White Sea,* Houghton Mifflin (Boston), 1993.

Drucker, Malka, and Michael Halperin, *Jacob's Rescue,* Delacorte Press, (New York), 1996.

Drury, Allen, *Toward What Bright Glory?: A Novel,* Morrow (New York), 1990.

Earl, Maureen, *Boat of Stone,* Permanent Press (Sag Harbor, NY), 1993.

Epstein, Leslie, *King of the Jews,* Coward, McCann & Geoghegan (New York), 1979.

Fink, Ida, *The Journey,* Plume (New York), 1993.

Fleming, Thomas, *Loyalties: A Novel of World War II,* HarperCollins (New York), 1994.

Follett, Ken, *Churchill's Gold,* Houghton Mifflin (Boston), 1981.

Follett, Ken, *Eye of the Needle,* G. K. Hall (Boston), 1978.

Follett, Ken, *Night over Water,* Morrow (New York), 1991.

Forester, C. S., *The Good Shepherd,* Little, Brown (Boston), 1955.

Forsyth, Frederick, *The Odessa File,* Viking (New York), 1972.

Garfield, Brian, *The Paladin: A Novel Based on Fact,* Simon and Schuster (New York), 1979.

Gifford, Thomas, *Praetorian,* Bantam (New York), 1993.

Green, Gerald, *Holocaust,* Bantam (New York), 1978.

Greene, Graham, *The Tenth Man,* Simon and Schuster (New York), 1985.

Griffin, W. E. B., *The Corps,* Putnam (New York), 1990.

Griffin, W. E. B., *Honor Bound,* Putnam (New York), 1993.

Griffin, W. E. B., *Line of Fire,* Putnam (New York), 1992.

Harel, Isser, *The House on Garibaldi Street,* Viking Press (New York), 1975.

Harris, Robert, *Enigma,* Random House (New York), 1995.

Harris, Robert, *Fatherland,* Random House (New York), 1992.

Heller, Joseph, *Catch-22,* Dell (New York), 1961.

Hersey, John, *A Bell for Adano,* Knopf (New York), 1944.

Hersey, John, *The Wall,* Knopf (New York), 1950.

Hersey, John, *War Lover,* Knopf (New York), 1959.

Higgins, Jack, *Cold Harbour,* Simon and Schuster (New York), 1990.

Higgins, Jack, *The Eagle Has Flown,* Simon and Schuster (New York), 1991.

Higgins, Jack, *The Eagle Has Landed,* Holt (New York), 1975.

Hill, Grace Livingston, *All Through the Night,* J. B. Lippincott (New York), 1945.

Hunter, Stephen, *The Master Sniper,* Morrow (New York), 1980.

Iles, Greg, *Black Cross,* Dutton (New York), 1995.

Iles, Greg, *Spandau Phoenix,* Dutton (New York), 1993.

Isaacs, Susan, *Shining Through,* G. K. Hall (Boston), 1990.

Jones, James, *From Here to Eternity,* Scribner (New York), 1951.

Jones, James *The Thin Red Line,* Scribner (New York), 1962.

Katkov, Norman, *The Judas Kiss,* Dutton (New York), 1991.

Keneally, Thomas, *Schindler's List,* Simon and Schuster (New York), 1982.

Kerr, M. E., *Gentlehands,* Harper & Row (New York), 1978.

Kis, Danilo, *Hourglass,* translated by Ralph Manheim, Farrar, Straus (New York), 1990.

Klein, Edward, *The Parachutists,* Doubleday (Garden City, NY), 1981.

Korda, Michael, *Worldly Goods,* Random House (New York), 1982.

Kosinski, Jerzy, *The Painted Bird,* Modern Library (New York), 1970.

Kuznetsov, Anatoly, *Babi Yar,* Farrar, Straus and Giroux (New York), 1970.

Lanham, Edwin, *The Clock at 8:16,* Doubleday (Garden City, NY), 1970.

Lay, Beirne, Jr., and Sy Bartlett, *Twelve O'Clock High,* Harper (New York), 1948.

Leboucher, Fernande, *Incredible Mission,* Doubleday (New York), 1969.

Levitin, Sonia, *Annie's Promise,* Atheneum (New York), 1993.

Litewka, Albert, *Warsaw: A Novel of Resistance,* Sheridan Square Press (New York), 1989.

Lowry, Lois, *Number the Stars,* Houghton Mifflin (New York), 1989.

Ludlum, Robert, *The Holcroft Covenant,* R. Marek Publishers (New York), 1978.

MacInnes, Helen, *Above Suspicion,* Little, Brown (Boston), 1941.

MacInnes, Helen, *Assignment in Brittany,* Little, Brown (Boston), 1942.

MacInnes, Helen, *While Still We Live,* Harcourt Brace (New York), 1989.

MacLean, Alistair, *Force 10 from Navarone,* Doubleday (Garden City, NY), 1968.

MacLean, Alistair, *The Guns of Navarone,* Doubleday (Garden City, NY), 1957.

MacLean, Alistair, *H.M.S. Ulysses,* Collins (London), 1955.

MacLean, Alistair, *Where Eagles Dare,* Collins (London), 1967.

Mailer, Norman, *The Naked and the Dead,* Rinehart (New York), 1948.

Marvin, Isabel R., *Bridge to Freedom,* Jewish Publication Society (Philadelphia), 1991.

Matas, Carol, *After the War,* Simon & Schuster (New York), 1996.

Matas, Carol, *Daniel's Story,* Scholastic (New York), 1993.

Matas, Carol, *Lisa's War,* Scholastic (New York), 1987.

Michener, James, *Tales of the South Pacific,* Macmillan (New York), 1947.

Monsarrat, Nicholas, *The Cruel Sea,* Burford Books (Short Hills, NJ), 2000.

Morris, M. E., *The Last Kamikaze,* Random House (New York), 1990.

Nathanson, E. M., *The Dirty Dozen,* Random House (New York), 1955.

Ondaatje, Michael, *The English Patient,* Knopf (New York), 1992.

Orlev, Uri, *The Man from the Other Side,* translated from the Hebrew by Hillel Halkin, Houghton Mifflin (New York), 1989.

Ozick, Cynthia, *The Messiah of Stockholm: A Novel,* Knopf (New York), 1987.

Ozick, Cynthia, *The Shawl,* Knopf (New York), 1989.

Piercy, Marge, *Gone to Soldiers,* Summit Books (New York), 1987.

Provost, Gary, and Gail Levine-Provost, *David and Max,* Jewish Publication Society (Philadelphia), 1988.

Reeman, Douglas, *The Destroyers,* Putnam (New York), 1974.

Remarque, Erich Maria, *Arch of Triumph,* translated by Walter Sorrell and Denver Lindley, Ballantine (New York), 1998.

Remarque, Erich Maria, *The Night in Lisbon,* Harcourt, Brace & World (New York), 1964.

Remarque, Erich Maria, *A Time to Love and a Time to Die,* Harcourt Brace (New York), 1954.

Shaw, Irvin, *Young Lions,* Random House (New York), 1948.

Silman, Roberta, *Beginning the World Again,* Viking (New York), 1990.

Singer, Isaac Bashevis, *Enemies, a Love Story,* Noonday Press (New York), 1989.

Starbird, Kaye, *The Lion in the Lei Shop,* Harcourt, Brace (New York), 1970.

Steinbeck, John, *The Moon Is Down,* Viking (New York), 1942.

Struther, Jan, *Mrs. Miniver,* Harcourt, Brace (New York), 1940.

Taylor, Theodore, *To Kill the Leopard,* Harcourt Brace (New York), 1993.

Thayer, James, *S-Day: A Memoir of the Invasion of England,* St. Martin's Press (New York), 1990.

Thomas, Harlan, *A Yank in the RAF,* Random House (New York), 1941.

Trotter, William R., *Winter Fire,* Dutton (New York), 1993.

Tuccille, Jerome, and Philip Sayetta, *The Mission: A Novel about the Flight of Rudolf Hess,* D. I. Fine (New York), 1991.

Uris, Leon, *Battle Cry,* Putnam (New York), 1953.

Uris, Leon, *Exodus,* Doubleday (Garden City, NY), 1958.

Uris, Leon, *Mila 18,* Doubleday (Garden City, NY), 1961.

Uris, Leon, *QB VII,* Doubleday (Garden City, NY), 1970.

Vonnegut, Kurt, Jr., *Mother Night,* Delacorte Press (New York), 1966.

Vonnegut, Kurt, Jr., *Slaughterhouse-Five, or, The Children's Crusade: A Duty-Dance with Death,* Dell (New York), 1968.

Vos, Ida, *Anna Is Still Here,* Houghton Mifflin (Boston), 1993.

Vos, Ida, *Hide and Seek,* translated by Terese Edelstein and Inez Smidt, Houghton Mifflin (New York), 1981.

Welt, Elly, *Berlin Wild: A Novel,* Viking (New York), 1986.

Westheimer, David, *Von Ryan's Express,* Doubleday (Garden City, NY), 1964.

Westheimer, David, *Von Ryan's Return,* Coward McCann & Geoghegan (New York), 1980.

White, Theodore, *Mountain Road,* W. Sloan (New York), 1958.

Wiesel, Elie, *The Forgotten,* Summit Books (New York), 1992.

Wiesel, Elie, *Night,* Bantam (New York), 1960.

Wiesel, Elie, *The Town Beyond the Wall: A Novel,* Schocken Books (New York), 1995.

Wilder, Billy, *Stalag 17,* University of California Press (Berkeley, CA), 1999.

Wolff, Virginia Euwer, *The Mozart Season,* Henry Holt (New York), 1991.

Wouk, Herman, *The Caine Mutiny,* Doubleday (Garden City, NY), 1951.

Wouk, Herman, *War and Remembrance,* Little, Brown (Boston), 1978.

Wouk, Herman, *The Winds of War,* Little, Brown (Boston), 1971.

Yolen, Jane, *Devil's Arithmetic,* Viking Penguin (New York), 1988.

Index

Note: This is a cumulative index for volumes 1, 2 and 3. Volumes are paginated individually. Each volume number appears in boldface italics, followed by a colon. Page numbers appearing in italic type refer to pages containing illustrations: *m* indicates a map; *c* indicates a chart; and *t* indicates a table.

O

P

S